S0-BAG-528

The Delhi Sultanate

A Political and Military History

The Delhi Sultanate was the first Islamic state to be established in India. In a broad-ranging and accessible narrative, Peter Jackson traces the history of the Sultanate from its foundation in 1210 to its demise in around 1400 following the sack of Delhi by the Central Asian conqueror, Temür (Tamerlane). During the thirteenth and fourteenth centuries, the Sultanate was the principal bastion of Islam in the subcontinent. While the book focuses on military and political affairs, tracing the Sultanate's expansion, its resistance to formidable Mongol invasions from the northwest and the administrative developments that underpinned these exploits, it also explores the Sultans' relations with their non-Muslim subjects. As a comprehensive treatment of the political history of this period, the book will make a significant contribution to the literature on medieval Indo-Muslim history. Students of Islamic and South Asian history, and those with a general interest in the region, will find it a valuable resource.

PETER JACKSON is Senior Lecturer in the Department of History at Keele University. He is editor of **The Cambridge History of Iran**, volume 6 (1986), and translator and joint editor of *The Mission of Friar William of Rubruck* (1990).

Cambridge Studies in Islamic Civilization

Editorial board
DAVID MORGAN (general editor)
VIRGINIA AKSAN MICHAEL BRETT MICHAEL COOK PETER JACKSON
TARIF KHALIDI ROY MOTTAHEDEH BASIM MUSALLAM CHASE ROBINSON

Titles in the series

STEFAN SPERL, *Mannerism in Arabic poetry: a Structural Analysis of Selected Texts, 3rd Century AH/9th Century AD–5th Century AH/11th Century AD* 0 521 354854

PAUL E. WALKER, *Early Philosophical Shiism: the Ismaili Neoplatonism of Abu Yaʿqub al-Sijistani* 0 521 441293

BOAZ SHOSHAN, *Popular Culture in Medieval Cairo* 0 521 43209X

STEPHEN FREDERIC DALE, *Indian Merchants and Eurasian Trade, 1600–1750,* 0 521 454603

AMY SINGER, *Palestinian peasants and Ottoman Officials: Rural Administration around Sixteenth-century Jerusalem,* 0 521 452384 (hardback) 0 521 476798 (paperback)

TARIF KHALIDI, *Arabic Historical Thought in the Classical Period,* 0 521 465540 (hardback) 0 521 58938X (paperback)

LOUISE MARLOW, *Hierarchy and Egalitarianism in Islamic Thought,* 0 521 564301

JANE HATHAWAY, *The Politics of Households in Ottoman Egypt: the Rise of the Qazdağlis,* 0 521 571103

THOMAS T. ALLSEN, *Commodity and Exchange in the Mongol Empire: A Cultural History of Islamic Textiles,* 0 521 583012

DINA RIZK KHOURY, *State and Provincial Society in the Ottoman Empire: Mosul, 1540–1834,* 0 521 590604

THOMAS PHILIPP AND ULRICH HAARMANN (eds.), *The Mamluks in Egyptian Politics and Society,* 0 521 591155

The Delhi Sultanate

A Political and Military History

PETER JACKSON

CAMBRIDGE
UNIVERSITY PRESS

CARL A. RUDISILL LIBRARY
LENOIR-RHYNE COLLEGE

PUBLISHED BY THE PRESS SYNDICATE OF THE UNIVERSITY OF CAMBRIDGE
The Pitt Building, Trumpington Street, Cambridge, United Kingdom

CAMBRIDGE UNIVERSITY PRESS
The Edinburgh Building, Cambridge CB2 2RU, UK http://www.cup.cam.ac.uk
40 West 20th Street, New York, NY 10011–4211, USA http://www.cup.org
10 Stamford Road, Oakleigh, Melbourne 3166, Australia
Ruiz de Alarcón 13, 28014 Madrid, Spain

© Cambridge University Press 1999

This book is in copyright. Subject to statutory exception
and to the provisions of relevant collective licensing agreements,
no reproduction of any part may take place without
the written permission of Cambridge University Press.

First published 1999
Reprinted 1999

Printed in the United Kingdom at the University Press, Cambridge

Typeset in Times 10/12pt CE

A catalogue record for this book is available from the British Library

Library of Congress Cataloguing in Publication data
Jackson, Peter
The Delhi Sultanate : a political and military history / Peter Jackson
p. cm. – (Cambridge studies in Islamic civilization)
Includes bibliographical references and index.
ISBN 0 521 40477 0
1. Delhi (Sultanate) – History. I. Series.
DS459.J27 1998
954′.56023 – dc 21 98 30080 CIP

ISBN 0 521 40477 0 hardback

DS
459
.J27
1999
June 2000
ABL5007

For Rebecca

Contents

Maps

Preface

This book is designed to be a political and military history of the 'Greater' Delhi Sultanate, which after its creation in 1210 lasted for almost two hundred years and for almost half that period functioned as the sole bastion of Muslim power in the Indian subcontinent. The era from the sack of Delhi by the Central Asian conqueror Temür (Tīmūr-*i Lang*, 'the Lame'; Westernized as 'Tamerlane') in 801/1398 down to the Mughal conquest in 932/1526, during which the Sultanate was merely one of several competing Muslim kingdoms in the north, is briefly covered in the Epilogue.

The source materials for the Delhi Sultanate – largely narrative in form and written in Persian, with the addition of descriptions of India by external observers who wrote in Arabic – are markedly less satisfactory than, for instance, either those available for the Mughal empire that followed it or those composed in the contemporary Mamlūk Sultanate of Egypt and Syria. Much of the general literature on this period of Indian history has tended to adhere, in my view, far too closely to the arrangement in the narrative sources, and accordingly the reader is all too often served up a barely digestible repast of seemingly unconnected events.

I have divided the period into two phases, with the reign of 'Alā' al-Dīn Khaljī (695–715/1296–1316) marking a watershed: his era witnessed the implementation of far-reaching administrative changes, designed in large part to meet both an escalation in Mongol attacks and a more vigorous advance in Rajasthan and the south. Each of the two sections is introduced by a chapter on the sources, and the view they purvey of the sultans; but otherwise, within each section I have tried to approach the task thematically, giving prominence to the formation of the aristocracy, to administrative control and to the perennial warfare against the Sultanate's enemies, whether independent Hindu powers or the Mongols of Afghanistan and Central Asia. In chapters 12–13 and 15 an attempt has been made to bring political and military affairs into relation with economic developments, although it has to be said that material for the economic history of the Sultanate is relatively meagre. Two chapters, focusing on the reigns of Muḥammad bin Tughluq (724–752/1324–51) and of Fīrūz Shāh (752–790/

1351–88), represent a departure from the framework I have adopted; but it seemed advisable to devote a consolidated study to each of these problematic reigns. It is hoped that chapter 14, on the sultans' relations with the subject Hindu population, fits naturally between them, given Muḥammad's favour towards Hindus and his successor's allegedly more rigorous attitudes.

This book has been some years in gestation, and in writing it I have accumulated many debts. It is a pleasure to be able at last to acknowledge an award from the Leverhulme Trust which contributed towards the cost of replacement teaching for two terms in 1990–1, and the generosity of Keele University both in meeting the balance of those costs and in granting me a research award for a further term and funding research expenses. Thanks are also due to my medievalist colleagues in the History department for closing ranks when I was on sabbatical leave. I have benefited greatly from the assistance of the inter-library loans section of Keele University Library, and from the facilities offered by the Cambridge University Library, the Oriental Room of the Bodleian Library and the Indian Institute in Oxford, the John Rylands University Library at Manchester, the India Office Library and the Oriental Students' Room of the British Library (now amalgamated), the Library of the School of Oriental and African Studies in the University of London, the Bibliothèque Nationale in Paris, and the Library of the Rijksuniversiteit Leiden. The forbearance of the Librarian of the Royal Asiatic Society towards a notoriously long-term borrower is also deeply appreciated. I am grateful to the relevant Turkish authorities for permission to consult the manuscript collections in the Süleymaniye and Nuruosmaniye Libraries and the Topkapı Sarayı Müzesi in Istanbul. Dr Renato Traini, librarian at the Biblioteca dell'Accademia Nazionale dei Lincei e Corsiniana in Rome, promptly and courteously supplied me with photocopies of the relevant folios of the manuscript Caetani 21 of al-Ṣafadī's *al-Wāfī bi'l-Wafayāt*. The Bodleian Library, the British Library and the National Archives of India have also kindly provided me with microfilms of certain manuscripts in their collections.

A number of scholars contributed towards the production of this book. Some years ago, Mr Simon Digby generously lent me a photocopy of most of the manuscript of the first recension of Baranī's *Ta'rīkh-i Fīrūz-Shāhī* in his private collection, which has proved invaluable, and more recently gave me permission to use a text in which he has collated the portion of this manuscript covering the reign of Muḥammad b. Tughluq with the relevant section of that in the Bodleian Library. In India in 1991, Dr Akbar Ali Khan Arshizade, Officiating Director of the Raza Library at Rampur, extended to my wife and myself a hospitality we still remember with warm gratitude. We had good reason, too, to value the assistance of Vikram, our driver, and Toni, our guide in the old city of Delhi. For the production of the maps I am indebted to my colleague Andrew Lawrence, of the cartographic unit in the Department of Environmental Social Sciences at Keele. At the Cambridge University Press, Marigold Acland has proved an extremely patient and good-natured editor.

It will be obvious in the following pages how much I have profited from the work of other scholars who have made the eastern Islamic world, and in particular Muslim India, very much more their field than I have myself. Dr Peter Hardy and Professor Edmund Bosworth, who jointly examined my PhD thesis in 1976, have continued to sustain me with their friendship, interest and hospitality. I have gained also from the opportunity to meet and argue about the Delhi Sultanate with Dr Khurram Qadir, of the Bahauddin Zakariya University at Multan. Naturally, I enjoy undivided credit for any errors that have crept into the book.

My greatest debt is acknowledged, inadequately, in the dedication. Despite the heavy demands of her own career, my wife has never failed to offer encouragement and moral support to an author who at times appeared to be teetering on the edge of insanity. Without her this book could not have been written.

Note on transliteration

For the transliteration of Arabic and Persian, I have used the system adopted in the *Encyclopaedia of Islam*, except that *ch* is employed instead of *č*, *j* for *dj*, and *q* for *ḳ*. For the sake of uniformity, Persian names and terms derived from Arabic are spelled as if they were Arabic: thus Muhaddith rather than Muhaddis, *dhimma* for *żimma*, *ḥaḍrat* for *ḥażrat*, and *waqf* in place of *vaqf*. The Persian *iḍāfa* has been rendered throughout as -[*y*]*i*. For Turkish and Mongol proper names and terms, I have followed the UNESCO system, as employed in J. A. Boyle, *The successors of Genghis Khan* (New York, 1971). The tentative reconstruction of a proper name is indicated by an asterisk, as in *Altunapa or *Tartaq. Precise readings, as found in manuscripts or printed texts, are reproduced in capitals, with X standing for *kh*, Γ for *gh*, Č for *ch*, Š for *sh*, Ž for *zh*, ' for *ḥamza*, and the long vowels represented by A, W and Y (a 'tooth' without diacritical points appears as a dot).

Indian names present a greater problem, and here I have undoubtedly been guilty of inconsistency. The names of those places that found their way into standard Islamic geographical lore are given in Arabic-Persian form, e.g. Qinnawj and Badā'ūn in place of Kanauj and Budaon; but otherwise a hybrid (if hopefully recognizable) form has been employed, e.g. Kōl, Chandērī, Ērach, rather than Kūl, Chandīrī, Īrach. Where a European spelling has become established, however, as with Delhi and Lahore, I have given the Persian-Arabic form (*Dillī*, *Dihlī*; *Lāhawr*) alongside it at first encounter, thereafter adhering to the form in common use.

Abbreviations

Periodicals and reference works

AEMA	*Archivum Eurasiae Medii Aevi*
AOH	*Acta Orientalia Academiae Scientiarum Hungaricae*
ARIE	*Archaeological Survey of India. Annual Report on Indian Epigraphy*
BEO	*Bulletin d'Etudes Orientales de l'Institut Français de Damas*
BI	Bibliotheca Indica
BL	British Library
BN	Bibliothèque Nationale, Paris
BSO[A]S	*Bulletin of the School of Oriental [and African] Studies, University of London*
CAJ	*Central Asiatic Journal*
CCIM	H. Nelson Wright (ed.), *Catalogue of the coins of the Indian Museum, Calcutta*
CMSD	H. Nelson Wright (ed.), *The coinage and metrology of the Sulṭāns of Dehlī*
DGUP	*District gazetteers of the United Provinces of Agra and Oudh* (Allahabad, 1903–22, 48 vols.)
ED	Sir Henry Elliot, *A history of India as told by its own historians*, ed. J. Dowson (London, 1867–77, 8 vols.)
EI	*Epigraphia Indica*
EIAPS	*Epigraphia Indica. Arabic and Persian Supplement*
EIM	*Epigraphia Indo-Moslemica*
Enc.Ir.	E. Yarshater (ed.), *Encyclopaedia Iranica* (London and Costa Mesa, California, 1982– in progress)
Enc.Isl.[2]	Ch. Pellat *et al.* (eds.), *The encyclopaedia of Islam*, new edn (Leiden, 1954– in progress)
GMS	Gibb Memorial Series
HI	*Hamdard Islamicus*
HJAS	*Harvard Journal of Asiatic Studies*

HN	M. Habib and K. A. Nizami (eds.), *The Delhi Sultanat (A.D. 1206–1526)*
HS	Hakluyt Society
IA	*Indian Antiquary*
IC	*Islamic Culture*
IESHR	*Indian Economic and Social History Review*
IG	W. S. Meyer *et al.* (eds.), *The Imperial Gazetteer of India*, new edn. (Oxford, 1907–9, 26 vols.)
IHQ	*Indian Historical Quarterly*
IHR	*Indian Historical Review*
IOL	India Office Library, London
IO[N]S	*Israel Oriental [Notes and] Studies*
Iran	*Iran. Journal of the British Institute of Persian Studies*
IS	*Islamic Studies*
IU	Islamkundliche Untersuchungen
JA	*Journal Asiatique*
JAH	*Journal of Asian History*
JAOS	*Journal of the American Oriental Society*
JAS[B]	*Journal of the Asiatic Society [of Bengal]*
JASP	*Journal of the Asiatic Society of Pakistan*
JB[O]RS	*Journal of the Bihar [and Orissa] Research Society*
JCA	*Journal of Central Asia*
JIH	*Journal of Indian History*
JIS	*Journal of Islamic Studies*
JNSI	*Journal of the Numismatic Society of India*
JPHS	*Journal of the Pakistan Historical Society*
JRAS	*Journal of the Royal Asiatic Society of Great Britain and Ireland*
JSS	*Journal of Semitic Studies*
JUPHS	*Journal of the United Provinces Historical Society*
MASI	*Memoirs of the Archaeological Survey of India*
MIM	*Medieval India: a miscellany*
MIQ	*Medieval India Quarterly*
NIA	*New Indian Antiquary*
PFEH	*Papers on Far Eastern History*
PIHC	*Proceedings of the . . . Indian History Congress* [numeral refers to the number of the session]
PL	C. A. Storey, *Persian literature: a bio-bibliographical survey* (London, 1927– in progress)
PPV	Pamiatniki Pis′mennosti Vostoka
PSMI	*Proceedings of the Seminar on Medieval Inscriptions (6–8th Feb. 1970)* (Aligarh, 1974)
PUJ	*Patna University Journal*

QGIA	Deutsches Archäologisches Institut, Kairo. Quellen zur Geschichte des islamischen Ägyptens
RCEA	Et. Combe, J. Sauvaget and G. Wiet (eds.), *Répertoire chronologique d'épigraphie arabe* (Cairo, 1931– in progress)
RRL	Rampur Raza Library
SK	Süleymaniye Kütüphanesi, Istanbul
SOAS	School of Oriental and African Studies, University of London
TMENP	G. Doerfer, *Türkische und mongolische Elemente im Neupersischen*
TSM	Topkapı Sarayı Müzesi, Istanbul
TVOIRAO	*Trudy Vostochnago Otdeleniia Imperatorskago Russkago Arkheologicheskago Obshchestva*
WZKM	*Wiener Zeitschrift für die Kunde des Morgenlandes*
ZS	*Zentralasiatische Studien*

Texts

AHG	Ulughkhānī, *Ẓafar al-Wālih*, ed. Ross, *An Arabic history of Gujarat*
AH	Fakhr-i Mudabbir, *Ādāb al-Ḥarb wa'l-Shajā'a*
Bābur-Nāma	Bābur, *Bābur-Nāma*
CN	Kūfī, *Chach-Nāma*
DA	Ghaznawī, *Dastūr al-Albāb*
DGK	Amīr Khusraw, *Dībācha-yi Ghurrat al-Kamāl*
DR	Amīr Khusraw, *Diwal Rānī-yi Khaḍir Khān*
FFS	Sultan Fīrūz Shāh Tughluq, *Futūḥāt-i Fīrūz-Shāhī*
FG	Yūsuf-i Ahl, *Farā'id-i Ghiyāthī*
FJ	Baranī, *Fatāwā-yi Jahāndārī*
FS	'Iṣāmī, *Futūḥ al-Salāṭīn*
GK	Amīr Khusraw, *Ghurrat al-Kamāl*
IA	Ibn al-Athīr, *al-Kāmil fi'l-Ta'rīkh*
IB	Ibn Baṭṭūṭa, *Tuḥfat al-Nuẓẓār*
IM	Ibn Māhrū, *Inshā-yi Māhrū*
JH	'Awfī, *Jawāmi' al-Ḥikāyāt*
JT	Rashīd al-Dīn Faḍl-Allāh, *Jāmi' al-Tawārīkh*
KF	Amīr Khusraw, *Khazā'in al-Futūḥ*
MA	al-'Umarī, *Masālik al-Abṣār*
MF	Amīr Khusraw, *Miftāḥ al-Futūḥ*
NS	Amīr Khusraw, *Nuh Sipihr*
QS	Amīr Khusraw, *Qirān al-Sa'dayn*
RI	Amīr Khusraw, *Rasā'il al-I'jāz*
SA	Fakhr-i Mudabbir, *Shajarat al-Ansāb*
SFS	Anonymous, *Sīrat-i Fīrūz-Shāhī*
Siyar	Kirmānī (Amīr Khwurd), *Siyar al-Awliyā'*

SP	Rashīd al-Dīn Faḍl-Allāh, *Shuʿab-i Panjgāna*
Tāj	Ḥasan-i Niẓāmī, *Tāj al-Maʾāthir*
TFS	Baranī, *Taʾrīkh-i Fīrūz-Shāhī*
TFS[1]	Baranī, *Taʾrīkh-i Fīrūz-Shāhī*, first recension
TJG	Juwaynī, *Taʾrīkh-i Jahān-Gushā*
TMS	Sirhindī, *Taʾrīkh-i Mubārak-Shāhī*
TN	Jūzjānī, *Ṭabaqāt-i Nāṣirī*
TS	Amīr Khusraw, *Tuḥfat al-Ṣighār*
Tughluq-Nāma	Amīr Khusraw, *Tughluq-Nāma*
WH	Amīr Khusraw, *Wasaṭ al-Ḥayāt*
Shāmī, *ZN*	Shāmī, *Ẓafar-Nāma*
Yazdī, *ZN*	Yazdī, *Ẓafar-Nāma*

PART I
The thirteenth century

CHAPTER 1

The background

Caliphs, amirs and sultans

The ghosts of two great Muslim conquerors haunted the rulers of the Delhi Sultanate. One was Maḥmūd of Ghazna (d. 421/1030), whose campaigns had extended Islamic rule into the western Panjāb. The other was the Ghurid Sultan Muʿizz al-Dīn Muḥammad b. Sām, whose more recent victories over a number of Hindu states had entrenched Muslim power in the north Gangetic plain, and whose murder in 602/1206 had first propelled Muslim India on its own separate path, distinct from that taken by the lands west of the Indus. Maḥmūd and Muʿizz al-Dīn, each in his way, typified the warlords who had been carving out principalities for themselves within the Islamic world since the ninth century. The universal Caliphate of the ʿAbbasids had steadily disintegrated, leaving them with only the titular headship of the orthodox (Sunnī) Muslim community. Some provinces had been lost to the heterodox Shīʿīs. For almost three centuries (296–567/909–1171) the ʿAbbasids were challenged by the Fatimid *Imāms* representing the Ismāʿīlī Shīʿī sect. From Egypt and Syria, these counter-caliphs deployed a network of agents and propagandists whose activities extended even as far east as Sind, the region of the middle and lower Indus valley, reduced by the caliphal general Muḥammad b. Qāsim al-Thaqafī as early as 92/711. From 344/965 the Fatimid Imam's name was mentioned in the prayers at Multān, and by the end of the century at Manṣūra.[1] But in the majority of caliphal territories power passed into the hands of semi-independent, hereditary governors. Such rulers, who initially bore no title higher than *amīr* (literally 'commander'), usually went through the formality of obtaining a patent of authority (*manshūr*), a robe (*khilʿat*) and a sonorous

1 For a good introduction to the first centuries of Muslim rule in Sind, see Yohanan Friedmann, 'A contribution to the early history of Islam in India', in M. Rosen-Ayalon (ed.), *Studies in memory of Gaston Wiet* (Jerusalem, 1977), 309–33; Derryl N. MacLean, *Religion and society in Arab Sind* (Leiden, 1989). On Ismāʿīlī activity, see S. M. Stern, 'Ismaʿīlī propaganda and Fatimid rule in Sind', *IC* 23 (1949), 298–307; ʿAbbās al-Hamdānī, *The beginnings of the Ismaʿīlī daʿwa in northern India* (Cairo, 1956).

title (*laqab*) from the ʿAbbasid Caliph, in return for inserting his name in the public Friday sermon (*khuṭba*) and on the coinage (*sikka*) and, more notionally, remitting an annual tribute.

To bolster their dubious legitimacy, the provincial amirs had to act (or pose) as champions of Sunnī Islam and its caliph against both the infidel and the heretic. These functions were exercised most successfully by rulers of Turkish origin. Most of the regional dynasts imitated the ʿAbbasid Caliphs, and buttressed their own power, by maintaining regiments of Turkish slave guards (Arabic sing. *ghulām*, *mamlūk*; Persian *banda*) from the pagan steppelands of Central Asia. Ghulam status, it must be emphasized, bore none of the degrading connotations associated with other kinds of slavery. The Turkish peoples enjoyed a particularly high reputation for martial skill and religious orthodoxy, and ghulams were highly prized by their masters, receiving both instruction in the Islamic faith and a rigorous military training.[2] Nor was such confidence misplaced: as we shall see, the forging and preservation of an independent Muslim power in India were to be in large measure the work of Turkish slave commanders and their own ghulams.

Maḥmūd's dynasty, the Ghaznawids or Yaminids (352–582/962–1186), was of Turkish stock; its effective founder, Maḥmūd's father Sebüktegin, had been a Turkish slave commander. At its greatest extent, the Ghaznawid empire embraced an area from Rayy and Iṣfahān in Persia as far as Hānsī in the eastern Panjāb. Maḥmūd himself, who conducted no less than seventeen expeditions against pagan Indian rulers and who also rooted out the Ismāʿīlīs from the cities of Multān and Manṣūra, was rewarded by the ʿAbbasid Caliph for his services to Sunnī Islam with the *laqab* of *Yamīn al-Dawla* ('Right Hand of the State').[3]

Turks did not enter the civilized lands of Islam only through the slave traffic, however. They also came in as free men, in the large-scale migrations or invasions of recently converted nomadic tribal groups from Central Asia; and one such clan, the Seljüks, who originated among the Ghuzz (Oghuz) confederacy north of the Aral Sea, created in the second half of the eleventh

[2] C. E. Bosworth, 'Barbarian incursions: the coming of the Turks into the Islamic world', in D. S. Richards (ed.), *Islamic civilisation 950–1150* (Oxford, 1973), 1–16 (especially 4–10), and repr. in Bosworth, *The medieval history of Iran, Afghanistan and Central Asia* (London, 1977). D. Ayalon, 'The European-Asiatic steppe: a major reservoir of power for the Islamic world', in *Trudy XXV mezhdunarodnogo kongressy vostokovedov, Moskva 1960* (Moscow, 1963, 5 vols.), II, 47–52; *idem*, 'Preliminary remarks on the *Mamlūk* military institution in Islam', in V. J. Parry and M. E. Yapp (eds.), *War, technology and society in the Middle East* (Oxford and London, 1975), 44–58; both repr. in Ayalon, *The Mamlūk military society* (London, 1979).

[3] C. E. Bosworth, 'The imperial policy of the early Ghaznavids', *IS* 1 (1962), part 3, 49–82, repr. in his *Medieval history*. For a brief survey of the dynasty, see B. Spuler, 'Ghaznawids', *Enc.Isl.*^{2}. The standard works are Bosworth, *The Ghaznavids. Their empire in Afghanistan and eastern Iran 994:1040*, 2nd edn (Beirut, 1973); *idem*, *The later Ghaznavids, splendour and decay: the dynasty in Afghanistan and northern India 1040–1186* (Edinburgh, 1977).

century an empire that comprised the whole of Persia, Iraq and Syria. In 344/1055 the Seljük leader entered Baghdad and took the caliph under his protection, receiving in return the new and exalted style of *Sulṭān*. The Seljüks had already defeated the Ghaznawid amir, Maḥmūd's son Mas'ūd I (431/1040); and his successors, who assumed the title of sultan as a counterblast to Seljük pretensions, were gradually driven from their lands in eastern Persia. In 511/1117 the Ghaznawid Bahrām Shāh was enthroned with the assistance of the great Seljük Sultan Sanjar, who dominated the eastern Iranian world from his base in Khurāsān. The Ghaznawids thereby became tributary to the Seljüks; even so, it was not the Seljüks who would destroy them.

Mu'izz al-Dīn's family, the Shansabanids, originated among the petty princes (*mulūk*; sing. *malik*) of Ghūr, the mountainous region east of Herat.[4] Reduced to tributary status first by Maḥmūd of Ghazna and later by the Seljüks, they found their opportunity at a time of renewed upheavals in the Iranian world. In the 1120s, by one of the same processes in the eastern Asiatic steppe that would bring conquering Mongol armies westwards in the thirteenth century, the Qara-Khitan (or -Khitai), a semi-nomadic people of probably Mongolian stock and under the leadership of a Buddhist ruling dynasty, moved into Turkestan and Transoxiana (Mā warā' al-Nahr) and established their hegemony over the Muslim rulers there. Sanjar was defeated in 536/1141, and in the middle of the century, under pressure from fresh waves of Ghuzz tribesmen dislodged from their homelands by the Qara-Khitan, his empire collapsed. The Ghuzz also wrested Ghazna from Bahrām Shāh's son and successor, Khusraw Shāh, and obliged him to fall back on Lahore (Lāhawr), the administrative centre of his Indian territories. The Shansabanids, who had for some years been embroiled in a feud with the Ghaznawids, were the ultimate beneficiaries of these developments. Already, in *c.* 544/1150, the Shansabanid prince 'Alā' al-Dīn Ḥusayn had temporarily expelled Bahrām Shāh from Ghazna and sacked the city, thereby winning the undying sobriquet of *Jahānsūz* ('World-Burner'); and he took for himself the title of sultan and the ceremonial parasol (*chatr*) affected by the Seljük sovereigns. It was Ḥusayn's nephew, Ghiyāth al-Dīn Muḥammad b. Sām (558–599/1163–1203), who expelled the Ghuzz from Ghazna in 569/1173–4 and installed there his younger brother Mu'izz al-Dīn (formerly Shihāb al-Dīn) Muḥammad.

Under Ghiyāth al-Dīn and Mu'izz al-Dīn, who throughout cooperated more or less harmoniously, the Shansabanids – or Ghurids, as we may now call them, since they had reduced to subordinate status the other maliks of

[4] A. Maricq and G. Wiet, *Le minaret de Djam. La découverte de la capitale des sultans Ghorides (XIIe-XIIIe siècles)* (Paris, 1959): 31–44 contain a historical survey of the dynasty down to *c.* 1200; more generally, see C. E. Bosworth, 'Ghūrids', *Enc.Isl.*[2]; A. D. H. Bivar, 'Ghūr', *ibid.* For what follows, see also Bosworth, *Later Ghaznavids*, 111–22; *idem*, 'The political and dynastic history of the Iranian world (A.D. 1000–1217)', in J. A. Boyle (ed.), *The Cambridge history of Iran*, V. *The Saljuq and Mongol periods* (Cambridge, 1968), 157–66, 185–92.

the region – emerged as one of the great powers of the eastern Islamic world. Their principal seat was the fortress of Fīrūzkūh, identified by André Maricq in 1957 with ruins at Jām on the middle Hari Rūd, some 200 km. east of Herat; Ghiyāth al-Dīn's authority was recognized by branches of the dynasty which ruled at Bāmiyān, Mādīn and Jurwās. His chief rivals were the rulers of Khwārazm on the lower Oxus (Amū-daryā), who belonged to a dynasty founded by a Turkish ghulam and who like the Ghurids were erstwhile subordinates of the Seljük Sultan. But the Khwārazmshāhs suffered from two disadvantages that did not afflict the Ghurids. One was the overlordship of the heathen Qara-Khitan to their rear (although their military support could on occasions prove welcome); the other was the hostility of the ʿAbbasid Caliph al-Nāṣir li-Dīni'llāh (575–622/1180–1225). Encouraged by the caliph, from whom he obtained the title *Qasīm Amīr al-Mu'minīn* ('Partner of the Commander of the Faithful'), Ghiyāth al-Dīn engaged in a duel for Khurāsān with the Khwārazmshāhs, in which, prior to his death in 599/1203, the Ghurids definitely had the better of it. Muʿizz al-Dīn, who like Ghiyāth al-Dīn bore the title of sultan, ably seconded his brother's efforts; but he also looked eastwards.

Early Muslim India

For the first few centuries after Muḥammad b. Qāsim's conquest of Sind, the frontier in India between the Islamic world – the *Dār al-Islām* ('Abode of Islam') – and pagan territory – the war-zone or *Dār al-Ḥarb* – had remained relatively static. The early Muslim governors of Sind engaged in holy war (*jihād*) against their Hindu neighbours, despatching periodic expeditions as far afield as Kashmir or Mālwa.[5] But until the first decades of the tenth century, Muslim expansion eastwards was effectively barred by the powerful Gurjara-Pratihāra dynasty, which dominated northern India from its capital at Kanauj (Qinnawj) on the Ganges. Maḥmūd of Ghazna undoubtedly benefited from the eclipse of this empire and the division of its territories among a number of warring successor-states. Many of his victories in India achieved nothing more than the acquisition of unheard-of quantities of plunder: Hindu cities were sacked, notably the great seaport of Sōmnāth in Gujarāt (416/1025–6), their temples looted and golden idols piously smashed to pieces and carried off to Ghazna to replenish Maḥmūd's treasury. But for all their swashbuckling character, one result of the Ghaznawid amir's activities was the acquisition for Islam of a new foothold in the western Panjāb.[6]

[5] For a convenient list of campaigns, see J. F. Richards, 'The Islamic frontier in the east: expansion into South Asia', *South Asia* 4 (1974), 94–8; and on early Muslim India more generally, André Wink, *Al-Hind: the making of the Indo-Islamic world*, I. *Early medieval India and the expansion of Islam, 7th-11th centuries* (Leiden, 1990), esp. chap. 4.

[6] M. Nāẓim, *The life and times of Sulṭān Maḥmūd of Ghazna* (Cambridge, 1931), chapter 8.

Following their expulsion from eastern Persia, the Ghaznawids were increasingly confined to their lands in present-day Afghanistan, Makrān and Sind and to their conquests in India. Within the subcontinent they forfeited some of Maḥmūd's gains. Hānsī, for example, was wrested from them by a coalition of Hindu princes in 435/1043; and Multān again passed into the hands of the Ismāʿīlīs.[7] But the dynasty was by no means moribund. The reigns of Ibrāhīm (451–492/1059–99) and of his son Masʿūd III (492–508/1099–1115) were characterized by the continuing prosecution of the traditional mission in India. It is in 1090 that we first encounter, in an inscription of the Gāhaḍavāla king of Kanauj, the mysterious *Turushka-danda*, a tax designed either to finance the struggle against the Muslims or to meet their demands for tribute. According to the chronicler Jūzjānī, Masʿūd III's military chamberlain (*ḥājib*) Toghategin mounted a raid which penetrated beyond the Ganges and further east than any Muslim incursion since the time of Maḥmūd. The dynasty did not abandon military exploits even in an era of decline. Bahrām Shāh is said to have conducted holy wars (*ghazūhā*) in India, and his grandson Khusraw Malik appears to have fought against Hindu powers not long before the truncated Ghaznawid Sultanate was finally overwhelmed by the Ghurids.[8]

The Ghurid conquests

We possess a number of sources for the Ghurid campaigns of conquest and for the emergence of an autonomous Muslim power in northern India. The *Ṭabaqāt-i Nāṣirī* of Minhāj al-Dīn b. Sirāj al-Dīn Jūzjānī, completed in Delhi in 658/1260, is a general history of the Islamic world in twenty-three sections (*ṭabaqāt*), of which sections 19 and 20 deal with the Ghurids and their immediate successors in India. A precious source for the mid-thirteenth-century Delhi Sultanate, it is of less value for events in India prior to 623/1226 when the author was still resident in Ghūr.[9] Of the earlier works composed in India, Ḥasan-i Niẓāmī's florid and verbose *Tāj al-Maʾāthir*, begun in 602/1205–6 but completed after 626/1229, is the nearest thing we have to a narrative of events. This work, which opens with Muʿizz al-Dīn's great victory at Tarāʾin in 588/1192, may have drawn upon the victory despatches (*fatḥ-nāmas*) of Muʿizz al-Dīn's slave general Aybeg. For

7 J. Burton-Page, 'Hānsī', *Enc.Isl.*²; Bosworth, *Later Ghaznavids*, 32–3. *AH*, 252–4.

8 Toghategin: *TN*, I, 240 (tr. 107). Bahrām Shāh: *ibid.*, I, 241 (tr. 110). Khusraw Malik: *AH*, 272; partial tr. I.M. Shafīʿ, 'Fresh light on the Ghaznavids', *IC* 12 (1938), 218. *Turushka-danda*: Bosworth, *Later Ghaznavids*, 67; but for a discussion of the possible meanings, Lallanji Gopal, *The economic life of northern India, c. A.D. 700–1200*, 2nd edn (Delhi, 1989), 48–52. See also Bosworth's comments, *Later Ghaznavids*, 61–7, 84–6, 125–6, on Ghaznawid vigour, together with the evidence accumulated in A. B. M. Habibullah, *The foundation of Muslim rule in India*, 2nd edn (Allahabad, 1961), 57–60.

9 On the author, see K. A. Nizami, *On history and historians of medieval India* (New Delhi, 1983), 71–93.

all its defects, it can claim to be the first chronicle written in the Delhi Sultanate.[10] A fairly skeletal outline from 588/1192 down to the events of 602/1206, following Muʿizz al-Dīn's murder, is to be gleaned from the prologue to Fakhr-i Mudabbir's *Shajara* (or *Baḥr*) *al-Ansāb*, composed at Lahore shortly afterwards; although it does supply dates for certain events that are not given elsewhere. Regrettably, Fakhr-i Mudabbir's later work, *Ādāb al-Ḥarb wa'l-Shajāʿa*, a military and administrative treatise presented to the first Delhi Sultan, Iltutmish, in *c.* 630/1232, does not include among its numerous anecdotes any pertaining to more recent decades.[11] Similarly, only a small proportion of the material relating to India in the *Jawāmiʿ al-Ḥikāyāt*, a large collection of historical anecdotes compiled by ʿAwfī in Delhi (*c.* 628/1230–1), dates from the post-Ghaznawid era.[12] It is fortunate that events on this distant frontier made a powerful impression in Islam's heartlands. We should be much less well informed about the Ghurid campaigns were it not for the *al-Kāmil fi'l-Ta'rīkh*, a general history by Ibn al-Athīr (d. 630/1232), who wrote in the Iraqi city of al-Mawṣil (Mosul); though where he obtained most of his information was as great a mystery to at least one contemporary as it is to us.[13]

Once installed at Ghazna, Muʿizz al-Dīn was not slow to appropriate the Ghaznawids' role as the standard-bearer of orthodox Islam in the subcontinent. As Maḥmūd had done, he made war on the Ismāʿīlīs, who had re-established themselves in Multān, and captured the city (571/1175–6); the evidence suggests that although the Sūmra princes at Daybul in the Indus delta, whom he attacked in 578/1182–3, were of Indian stock, they too may have been Ismāʿīlī sympathizers. Certainly he is praised for his warfare against the Shīʿīs.[14] But the annexation of the remaining Ghaznawid territories was undoubtedly his principal goal. A series of campaigns from 577/1181–2 onwards secured first tribute from Khusraw Malik and then, in

[10] A critical edition is very much to be desired. Unless otherwise stated, references are to IOL Persian ms. 15 (Ethé, no. 210). The standard version ends in 614/1217, although in the last century Sir Henry Elliot utilized a copy (since lost) that went down to 626/1229: abstract translated in ED, II, 240–2. For a useful summary of the main recension, see S. H. Askari, 'Taj-ul-Maasir of Hasan Nizami', *PUJ* 18 (1963), no. 3, 49–127; on the author, Nizami, *On history and historians*, 55–70.

[11] M. S. Khan, 'The life and works of Fakhr-i Mudabbir', *IC* 51 (1977), 127–40. E. Denison Ross, 'The genealogies of Fakhr-ud-dín Mubárak Sháh', in T. W. Arnold and R. A. Nicholson (eds.), *ʿAjab-Nāma: a volume of oriental studies presented to Edward G. Browne* (Cambridge, 1922), 392–413.

[12] On the author's life, see M. Niẓámu'd-dín, *Introduction to the Jawámiʿu'l-ḥikáyát*, GMS, ns, VIII (London, 1929), 3–20.

[13] D.S. Richards, 'Ibn al-Athīr and the later parts of the *Kāmil*: a study of aims and methods', in D.O. Morgan (ed.), *Medieval historical writing in the Christian and Islamic worlds* (London, 1982), 84–5.

[14] *SA*, 19–20. Habibullah, *Foundation*, 36–7. S.H. Hodivala, *Studies in Indo-Muslim history* (Bombay, 1939–57, 2 vols.), I, 141. For Daybul, see S. Qudratullah Fatimi, 'The twin ports of Daybul', in Hamida Khuhro (ed.), *Sind through the centuries* (Oxford and Karachi, 1981), 97–105; Wink, *Al-Hind*, I, 181–3.

582/1186, the capitulation of Lahore. Khusraw Malik was sent to Ghiyāth al-Dīn and later put to death in captivity.

Confronting the Ghurid ruler now were a number of major Hindu powers, for which the designation 'Rājput' (not encountered in the Muslim sources before the sixteenth century) is a well-established anachronism.[15] Chief among them was the Chāhamāna (Chawhān) kingdom of Śākambhari (Sambhar), which dominated present-day Rajasthan from its capital at Ajmēr; it included much of the territory between the Sutlej and the Yamuna, and under Pṛthvīrāja III (the 'Rāī Pithūrā' of Muslim writers) claimed paramountcy throughout India north of the Vindhya mountains. Junior branches of the dynasty ruled at Nadōl and at Jālōr, and Delhi (Dillī, Dihlī), under its Tomara princes, had been tributary to the Chawhāns since the middle of the twelfth century. Chawhān supremacy was of relatively recent date, however, having been won in the teeth of strenuous opposition from the Chaulukyas, who reigned over Gujarāt from their capital at Anhilwāra (Nahrwāla; now Patan) and still nurtured designs on southern Rajasthan. To the east, the Chawhān state bordered on the Gāhaḍavāla kingdom of Kanauj (Qinnawj; the ancient Kānyakubja), which dominated much of the modern province of Uttar Pradesh, and the Chandella kingdom of Jejākabhukti (modern Bundelkhand), centred on Kālinjar. In the 1180s the Chandellas were under pressure from both the Gāhaḍavālas and the Chawhāns, and forfeited some of their western territories to Pṛthvīrāja III. The Gāhaḍavāla kingdom, on the other hand, was also busily expanding into Bihār, where it contested the débris of the defunct Pāla empire with the Sena dynasty of western Bengal.[16] In all these states, there existed a quasi-feudal hierarchy in which the kings (*rājas*, called *rāīs* by the Muslim invaders) received military service, in return for grants of land, from subordinate chieftains, called *rānakas* (or sometimes *thakkuras*), who in turn conferred estates on their own cavalry commanders, the *rāutas* (from Skr. *rājaputras*) or *nāyakas*; these two lower levels are the *rānas* and *rāwats* respectively of the Muslim sources.[17]

15 For this term, see B. D. Chattopadhyaya, 'Origin of the Rajputs: the political, economic and social processes in early medieval Rajasthan', *IHR* 3 (1976), 59–82, repr. in his *The making of early medieval India* (Oxford and Delhi, 1994), 57–88.

16 See generally H. C. Ray, *The dynastic history of northern India* (Calcutta, 1931–5, 2 vols.), chaps. 6 (Senas), 8 (Gāhaḍavālas), 11 (Chandellas), 15 (Chaulukyas) and 16 (Chāhamānas); also Dasharatha Sharma, *Early Chauhān dynasties*, 2nd edn (Delhi, 1975); R. C. Majumdar, *Chaulukyas of Gujarat* (Bombay, 1956); Roma Niyogi, *The history of the Gāhaḍavāla dynasty* (Calcutta, 1959); A. Banerji, 'Eastern expansion of the Gāhaḍavāla kingdom', *JAS*, 4th series, 5 (1963), 105–11; N. S. Bose, *History of the Chandellas* (Calcutta, 1956); and R. K. Dikshit, *The Candellas of Jejākabhukti* (New Delhi, 1977).

17 R. S. Sharma, *Indian feudalism: c. 300–1200* (Calcutta, 1965), especially chap. 5. Pushpa Prasad (ed.), *Sanskrit inscriptions of Delhi Sultanate 1191–1526* (Delhi, 1992), 56–7 (no. II:5), 58–71 (no. II:6), 78–9 (no. II:9), 80–9 (no. II:11). For examples from Muslim sources, see *SA*, 33 (with RATGAN in error for RANGAN); *Tāj*, fols. 137a, 150a; and *inter alia* the 'celebrated *rāwats*' of *TN*, II, 65 (tr. 828).

Significant gains at the expense of these Hindu powers were deferred until after Muʿizz al-Dīn's annexation of the Ghaznawid territories, which brought him control of the more northerly routes via Peshawar (Parshāwar) and the Khyber Pass. Indeed, his earliest incursion into the Dār al-Ḥarb had ended in disaster. An attack in 574/1178–9 on the Chaulukya kingdom by way of lower Sind resulted in a heavy defeat for the Ghurid Sultan near Mount Ābū. Subsequently, at a date which is variously given as 583/1187–8 or 587/1191, he invaded the eastern Panjāb and established a garrison at Tabarhindh. But he was routed at Tarā'in by a large Hindu force under Prthvīrāja and his subordinate, Govindarāja of Delhi, and obliged to retire to Ghazna; Tabarhindh was recovered by the Hindus.[18] When Muʿizz al-Dīn returned in 588/1192, however, and again offered battle near Tarā'in, he won a crushing victory, in which Prthvīrāja was captured and Govindarāja killed. The victory at Tarā'in seems to have constituted a turning-point in two respects. Firstly, the Hindu chiefs of the eastern Panjāb undertook to pay tribute to Muʿizz al-Dīn.[19] And in the second place, it is from this moment that we can date the establishment of a permanent Muslim force in the region, at Indraprastha (Indrapat), near Delhi.[20] But direct Muslim rule was not imposed on a uniform basis. While the great Chawhān fortress of Ranthanbōr was occupied, Ajmēr was left in the possession of Prthvīrāja, now Muʿizz al-Dīn's client; and following his execution for some act of duplicity shortly afterwards, it was conferred on his son. Similarly, Delhi was granted to Govindarāja's successor as a tributary prince.[21] This pattern was to be followed many times in other regions conquered by the Muslims.

Muʿizz al-Dīn continued to move down from Ghazna into India for each cold season and to take charge of the war against the infidel. In 590/1194 it was the turn of the Gāhaḍavālas, whose king Jāyachandra (the 'Jaychand' of Muslim authors) was defeated and slain by Muʿizz al-Dīn in the vicinity of Chandawār (Chandawal, near Etāwa); the Ghurid army looted his treasury at Āsī (Asnī) and occupied Banāras (now Varanasi). In 592/1196 the sultan headed an expedition which secured the fortress of Thangīr (Tahangarh, fifteen miles south of the later city of Bhayāna) from the

[18] Habibullah, *Foundation*, 60–1. *TN*, I, 398–400 (tr. 457–64, 466), where this engagement is dated in the year preceding the second battle of Tarā'in. IA, XI, 113–14/172–3, 371–2/561–2, describes the campaign twice (cf. XI, 115/174): in the second account, he dates the episode in the latter half of 583 (ended 1 March 1188), and this is confirmed at XII, 59/91.

[19] *Ibid.*, XI, 115/174, *wa-iltazamū lahu bi'l-amwāl*. *Tāj*, fol. 50b, for the chieftains of the Delhi region specifically.

[20] *Ibid.*, fol. 51a.

[21] Habibullah, *Foundation*, 61–2. On the coinage believed at one time to reflect Prthvīrāja's client status, see now P. N. Singh, 'The so-called joint issue of Muḥammad bin Sam and Prithviraja III: a reappraisal', *JNSI* 50 (1988), 120–3; John S. Deyell, *Living without silver: the monetary history of early medieval North India* (Oxford and Delhi, 1990), 267–9. That Delhi was thus subjected in two stages may help to explain the conflicting dates given for its capture in the sources, on which see Muḥammad Aziz Aḥmad, *Political history and institutions of the early Turkish empire of Delhi (1206–1290 A.D.)* (Lahore, 1949), 129 n.1.

Chandellas, and allowed the rai of Gwāliyōr to buy him off with tribute. But otherwise Muʿizz al-Dīn appears to have played a relatively limited role in the extension of Muslim power. After the death of his brother Ghiyāth al-Dīn (599/1203), his energies were largely absorbed by developments in Khurāsān, where the Khwārazmshāh ʿAlā' al-Dīn Muḥammad b. Tekish sought to recover territories previously lost to the Ghurids. In 601/1204 Muʿizz al-Dīn invaded Khwārazm itself, only to suffer a decisive defeat by the shah's Qara-Khitan overlords at Andkhūd (now Andkhoi).[22] In these circumstances, the Ghurid Sultan seems to have relied in India increasingly on his Turkish slave lieutenants.

The Ghūrīs were a people of the hills. Traditionally they fought on foot, and Jūzjānī has left us a description of their characteristic method of warfare, which involved the use by each soldier of a protective screen called a *kārwa*, made of raw bullock-hide and filled with a dense wadding of cotton.[23] It is true that we also encounter mounted Ghūrī warriors, like the 1200 horsemen from Tūlak who briefly garrisoned Tabarhindh following Muʿizz al-Dīn's first invasion of the eastern Panjāb;[24] but they were probably in short supply, and the sultans' expansionist designs required access to larger numbers of cavalry. As the empire expanded to the west, they supplemented their forces with warriors from various parts of Khurāsān: Khurāsānīs are found under Muʿizz al-Dīn's banner, for instance, in the final thrust against the Ghaznawids and in his assault on Prthvīrāja, and later among the troops who entered Lahore with Aybeg in 602/1206.[25] In addition, Ghuzz warriors appear in the army of Ghazna in the period following Muʿizz al-Dīn's death, and the Ghurid sultans, like their Ghaznawid precursors, recruited tribal cavalry from among the Khalaj, a nomadic people in the *garmsīr* ('hot') regions of Bust and Zamīndāwar, who may have been of Turkish stock but would in time become assimilated to the neighbouring Afghans.[26] Only late authors mention the Afghans proper, who were as yet confined to the Sulaymān range (consequently known at this time as *kūh-i Afghān*, 'the Afghan mountains') and who had accompanied Ghaznawid campaigns, as serving at Tarā'in.[27]

22 W. Barthold, *Turkestan down to the Mongol invasion*, 3rd edn by C. E. Bosworth, GMS, ns, V (London, 1968), 349–51. Bosworth, 'Political and dynastic history', 164–5.

23 *TN*, I, 343 (tr. 352–3). The *kārwa* is also listed in *AH*, 423, among the equipment required to conduct a siege.

24 *TN*, I, 399 (tr. 458); and for an earlier reference to mounted Ghūrīs, see I, 355–6 (tr. 372–3).

25 IA, XI, 110/168, 113/172. *SA*, 33.

26 Ghuzz: IA, XII, 144/219. On the ethnicity of the Khalaj, see V. Minorsky, 'The Turkish dialect of the Khalaj', *BSOS* 10 (1940), 426–32, repr. in his *The Turks, Iran and the Caucasus in the middle ages* (London, 1978); C. E. Bosworth, 'Khaladj, i. History', *Enc.Isl.*^{2}; C. E. Bosworth and Sir Gerard Clauson, 'Al-Xwārazmī on the peoples of Central Asia', *JRAS* (1965), 6, 8–9, repr. in Bosworth, *Medieval history*. But for a different view, cf. Irfan Habib, 'Formation of the Sultanate ruling class of the thirteenth century', in Habib (ed.), *Medieval India 1. Researches in the history of India 1200–1750* (Oxford and Delhi, 1992), 2–3 and n.12.

27 G. Morgenstierne, 'Afghān', *Enc.Isl.*^{2}. For Afghan warriors under the Ghaznawids, see

The Ghurid dynasty grew familiar with the disadvantages of relying exclusively on such forces. The nomads were proverbially volatile. When 'Alā' al-Dīn Ḥusayn 'Jahānsūz' did battle with Sanjar in 547/1152, the issue was decided by some 6000 Khalaj, Ghuzz and other Turkish nomads in his army who went over to the Seljük Sultan. For Muʿizz al-Dīn, even the Ghūrīs did not prove invariably trustworthy. During his first Tarā'in campaign, according to Ibn al-Athīr, his Ghūrī troops left him in the lurch, for which the commanders were severely disciplined; and he continued to harbour resentment against them for some years.[28] Such considerations, as well as the numerous precedents furnished by other Muslim dynasties, may have encouraged the later Ghurids to amass bodies of Turkish ghulams. Turkish slaves appear at Ghiyāth al-Dīn's court at an early date, and Jūzjānī tells us that Muʿizz al-Dīn was especially keen to acquire them.[29] Despite insubordination on the part of one or two ghulam officers in India in the wake of the sultan's defeat at Andkhūd in 601/1204, his confidence was in large measure justified. At Andkhūd Muʿizz al-Dīn's personal slaves remained with him in the thick of the conflict, and it was one of them who at length virtually carried him from the field for the sultan's own safety.[30] Professor Irfan Habib has shown how he took care to promote his ghulams (called 'Muʿizzīs', from his own *laqab*) particularly to administrative and military office in his own territories, Ghazna and India, in contrast with the older Ghurid lands.[31]

The principal credit for the Ghurid conquests in the eastern Panjāb and beyond is given in the sources to one ghulam lieutenant, Quṭb al-Dīn Aybeg. It was Aybeg who frustrated Chawhān revanchism under Prthvīrāja's brother Harīrāja ('Hīraj'); who in 589/1193 took possession of Delhi on the pretext of its ruler's treacherous designs; and who in 593/1197 defeated the Chaulukyas at Mount Ābū, thereby avenging his master's humiliation of almost twenty years before. Within the crumbling empire of the Gāhaḍavālas, Aybeg took the fortresses of Mīrat (Meerut) in 588/1192, Kōl (near modern Aligarh) in 591/1194, Badā'ūn (Budaon) in 594/1198, and Qinnawj (Kanauj) in 595/1199. Gwāliyōr surrendered to him in 597/1200–1, and in 599/1203 he occupied Kālinjar, capital of the Chandella king Paramardīdēva (Ḥasan-i Niẓāmī's 'Parmār').[32]

During these years other elements were carrying Muslim arms even deeper into India. A Khalaj warrior named Muḥammad b. Bakhtiyār had secured a base in Awadh, from where he mounted regular plundering expeditions into the Hindu tracts of Manēr and Bihār. He grew strong

André Wink, *Al-Hind: the making of the Indo-Islamic world*, II, *The Slave Kings and the Islamic conquest, 11th-13th centuries* (Leiden, 1997), 116–18.

[28] *TN*, I, 346 (tr. 359). IA, XI, 114/173, 371–2/561–2.

[29] Ghiyāth al-Dīn: *TN*, I, 354–5, *turkān-i khāṣṣ* (tr. 371). Muʿizz al-Dīn: *ibid.*, I, 410 (tr. 497).

[30] *Ibid.*, I, 403 (tr. 476–8).

[31] I. Habib, 'Formation', 4–7. See also Wink, *Al-Hind*, II, 141.

[32] For these campaigns, see Habibullah, *Foundation*, 62–9; HN, 156–90.

enough first to take the city of Bihār and then to attack the Sena kingdom in western Bengal. In the middle of Ramaḍān 601/early May 1205 Nūdiya, the capital of king Lakśmanasena ('Lakhmaniya'), was captured and sacked, and the king himself put to flight. Muḥammad b. Bakhtiyār was murdered in *c.* 602/1206 following a disastrous campaign somewhere in Assam (Kāmrūp). Although he acknowledged the Ghurid Sultan as his master and conveyed a proportion of the plunder to Aybeg, he acted independently, without the benefit of direction – or even, as far as we can tell, reinforcements – from Ghazna.[33] These operations, the fame of which would reach the ears of Ibn al-Athīr in Iraq and would cause a later author to give the Khalaj alone the credit for the Muslim conquests, reduced for Islam a considerable tract in the Ganges basin where Muʿizz al-Dīn's forces had not penetrated.[34]

The news of Muʿizz al-Dīn's defeat at Andkhūd in 601/1204 provoked a rebellion by one of his lieutenants, who seized Multān, and a more formidable rising by the Hindu Khōkhars and the people of the Salt Range (Kūh-i Jūd); and his last years were taken up with their suppression. On his murder in 602/1206 (probably by Ismāʿīlīs from Khurāsān), his empire fell apart. He left no son, and his vast inheritance was disputed by his relatives and slaves and his enemy the Khwārazmshāh ʿAlā' al-Dīn Muḥammad, who repudiated Qara-Khitan overlordship and annexed the Ghurid territories in Khurāsān. Ghazna was occupied by the late sultan's senior ghulam, Tāj al-Dīn Yildiz; but in the years 611–12/1214–16 he and the various Ghurid princes were alike overwhelmed by the Khwārazmshāh, not long before the Khwarazmian empire was destroyed (618–20/1221–3) by the advancing Mongols of Chinggis Khan.[35] The Indian provinces meanwhile went their own way. On learning of his master's death in 602/1206, Aybeg advanced from Delhi and took up residence at Lahore, where he established himself as ruler. When Aybeg died in a polo (*chawgān*) accident in 607/1210–11, his ghulam Iltutmish was invited into Delhi from Badā'ūn by a party in the city, and set himself up as ruler in opposition to Aybeg's heir.[36] Aybeg's action marks the emergence of an independent Muslim power in India; that of Iltutmish, the creation of the Delhi Sultanate, which will be the subject of the next chapter.

[33] *Tāj*, fol. 186a-b. *TN*, I, 423–7 (tr. 551–4, 560). For the Nūdiya campaign, see Habibullah, *Foundation*, 69–74; and for the date, Parmeshwari Lal Gupta, 'On the date of the Horseman type coin of Muḥammad b. Sam', *JNSI* 38 (1976), no. 1, 81–7.

[34] IA, XI, 115/174. For the role of the 'Qalaj' in the conquest of 'Hindūstān', see Ibn Saʿīd al-Maghribī (d. 673/1274 or 685/1286), *Kitāb al-Jughrāfiyya*, ed. Ismāʿīl al-ʿArabī (Beirut, 1970), 163: on this author, see Gilles Potiron, 'Un polygraphe andalou du XIIIe siècle', *Arabica* 13 (1966), 142–67.

[35] P. Jackson, 'The fall of the Ghurid dynasty', in Carole Hillenbrand (ed.), *Festschrift for Professor Edmund Bosworth* (Edinburgh; forthcoming).

[36] Habibullah, *Foundation*, 88–92.

Reasons for the Ghurid victories

It is easier to chronicle the triumphs of the Ghurid armies in India than to account for them; and certainly no satisfactory explanation is forthcoming in the sources. For the four Muslim writers who notice these events, it is enough that God grants victory to the sultan and his forces. Any analysis of the causes of Muslim success, therefore, rests on fragmentary evidence, and our conclusions can only be speculative.

We must first discuss one hypothesis which has at times been adduced in explanation of the Muslim conquest of northern India at the turn of the twelfth century. Drawing on the observations about the caste system to be found in the work of the eleventh-century Muslim writer al-Bīrūnī, the late Professor Mohammad Habib suggested that the resistance of Hindu rulers, when confronted by the invading Ghurid armies, was undermined in two respects. First, the caste system seriously impaired the military effectiveness of the Hindu kingdoms. It restricted participation in war to the warrior caste, the *kshatriyas*, and the principle of untouchability required them, on the eve of battle, to perform numerous tasks that would otherwise naturally have fallen to those of menial rank. The second disadvantage allegedly imposed on the Hindu states by the caste system was its effect upon the cohesiveness of the subject population. Islam preaches equality. Faced with this liberating message (the argument runs), the urban masses could not but draw the contrast with the social shackles that bound them and throw in their lot with the newcomers. Habib thus concluded, in words that have attained a certain notoriety, that 'this was not a conquest so-called. This was a turnover of public opinion, a sudden one no doubt, but one which was long overdue.'[37]

Although these ideas are appealing at first sight, they do not withstand closer scrutiny. As far as military effectiveness is concerned, it has been pointed out both that Hindu armies included members of other castes, such as *vaiśyas* and *sudras*, and that al-Bīrūnī's Brahman informants may have exaggerated the effectiveness of the caste regulations.[38] Regarding the question of liberation, we need to know far more than we do about the perceptions that the lower-caste Hindu populace had of their situation and the message (if any) preached by the invading Muslim troops. At the risk of stating the obvious, it might be pointed out that a recognition of one's low social status, particularly when sanctioned by religious laws, and an urge to

[37] M. Habib, 'Introduction to Elliot and Dowson's *History of India*, vol. II', in K. A. Nizami (ed.), *Politics and society during the early medieval period. Collected works of Professor Mohammad Habib* (New Delhi, 1974, 2 vols.), I, 59–74 (72 for the quotation). See also Aziz Aḥmad, *Studies in Islamic culture in the Indian environment* (Oxford, 1964), 82.

[38] Other warriors: Prabha Dixit, 'Prof. Mohammad Habib's historical fallacies', in Devahuti (ed.), *Bias in Indian historiography* (Delhi, 1980), 205. Caste regulations: S. Digby, review of Habib's collected works, in *BSOAS* 39 (1976), 457.

improve it do not necessarily – in a society untouched by the eighteenth-century European Enlightenment – go hand in hand.[39] Nor can the liberation that the Muslim conquerors offered to those who sought to escape from the caste system be taken for granted. The evidence for widespread conversion to Islam at the turn of the twelfth century simply does not exist. That such deliverance was in fact on offer seems improbable in view of our knowledge of the early centuries of Muslim rule in Sind, which is somewhat fuller than it is for conditions in the newly conquered Indian territories of the Ghurids.

The principal source for the Arab reduction of Sind in the early eighth century is the *Chach-Nāma*, a Persian work composed in *c.* 613/1216–17 but purporting to be a translation of an earlier, Arabic history. It alleges that Muḥammad b. Qāsim, the conqueror of Sind, learned of the disabilities imposed on a local people, the Jats, in the era of the deposed Brahman dynasty. One was that the Jats were to take dogs with them whenever they went out of doors, in order that they might be recognized. Muḥammad b. Qāsim ordered that such disabilities continue in force. That they did so emerges from a passage in the *Futūḥ al-Buldān* of al-Balādhurī (d. 279/892), in which a caliphal governor of Sind in the late 830s is said to have required the Jats, when walking out of doors in future, to be accompanied by a dog. The fact that the dog is an unclean animal to both Hindu and Muslim made it easy for the Muslim conquerors to retain the *status quo* regarding a low-caste tribe. In other words, the new regime in the eighth and ninth centuries did not abrogate discriminatory regulations dating from the period of Hindu sovereignty; rather, it maintained them.[40] We have no grounds for supposing that the response of the late twelfth-century conquerors to the caste system was any different.

To turn now to other possible explanations for the Ghurid victories, military technology is one sphere in which the Muslims may have enjoyed some limited superiority. Muʿizz al-Dīn is described in one Hindu source as 'lord of the north-west, where horses abound',[41] and it is accordingly possible that he was able to field a larger cavalry force than his opponents. This question has been examined by Simon Digby for the era of the Delhi Sultanate proper,[42] and will be considered further in subsequent chapters. For the moment, two other circumstances should be pointed out. One is that Ghūr had long been renowned for its metal deposits and its manufac-

[39] A point well made by Friedmann, 'A contribution', 320–1.

[40] *CN*, 33. Balādhurī, *Futūḥ al-Buldān*, ed. M. J. De Goeje, *Liber expugnationis regionum* (Leiden, 1866), 445/ed. S. al-Munajjid (Beirut, n.d.), 544. Friedmann, 'A contribution', 331–2. See also the brief remarks in Irfan Habib, 'Economic history of the Delhi Sultanate – an essay in interpretation', *IHR* 4 (1977), 297: 'There is no evidence of any direct assault from the state or the Muslims upon the caste system; nor even of any revolt from within . . .'

[41] Har Bilas Sarda, 'The Prithviraja Vijaya', *JRAS* (1913), 279.

[42] S. Digby, *War-horse and elephant in the Delhi Sultanate: a problem of military supplies* (Oxford and Karachi, 1971).

ture of weapons and coats of mail, commodities that had at one time formed part of the tribute rendered successively to the Ghaznawids and the Seljüks.[43] It is conceivable, therefore, that Muʿizz al-Dīn drew on a more plentiful supply of armaments for his Indian campaigns than recent Ghaznawid Sultans (or, for that matter, the Delhi Sultans in the next century). The other important consideration is that Ḥasan-i Niẓāmī, in describing the campaigns of Muʿizz al-Dīn and Aybeg, refers with remarkable frequency to the Muslims' use of the crossbow (*nāwak*) and makes great play of the armour-piercing properties of the crossbow bolt.[44] It is by no means clear that the Ghurids' Hindu adversaries made such use of the crossbow.[45] This formidable weapon, which was at this very time giving Latin Christian armies a decisive advantage over their enemies in the Celtic and Slavic worlds,[46] may well have performed a parallel function for the Muslim invaders of India. But this would hardly explain the victory at Tarā'in, gained in the very locality where success had eluded Muʿizz al-Dīn not long previously.

The particular tactics that the sultan adopted in the second battle of Tarā'in may have played a significant role in his victory. An anecdote in ʿAwfī's *Jawāmiʿ al-Ḥikāyāt* suggests that Muʿizz al-Dīn exploited the proximity of the enemy's elephants to the horses, whose fear of elephants renders it difficult to coordinate bodies of both animals in the field. While campfires were lit to dupe Prthvīrāja's men into believing that the entire Ghurid army had bivouacked for the night, the sultan took a division of his troops round to attack the Chawhān rear. At daybreak he fell upon Prthvīrāja's baggage. The rear was pushed against the elephants, which got out of control, so that the Chawhān army fell into confusion and Prthvīrāja was unable even to conduct an orderly retreat.[47] On the other hand, in the short account of the battle found in Jūzjānī's *Ṭabaqāt-i Nāṣirī* and obtained from an eye-witness, Muʿizz al-Dīn divided his forces.[48] While the centre,

43 *TN*, I, 335, 346 (tr. 336, 358). See also the tenth-century *Ḥudūd al-ᶜĀlam*, tr. V. Minorsky, GMS, ns, XI, 2nd edn (London, 1970), 110. Athar Ali, 'Military technology of the Delhi Sultanate (13–14th C.)', in *PIHC* 50 *(Gorakhpur 1989)* (Delhi, 1990), 167.

44 See especially *Tāj*, fols. 81a, 146b, 201a, 229a; also *AH*, 400, 423 and *passim*. On the possible role of the *nāwak*, see Irfan Habib, 'Changes in technology in medieval India', *Studies in History* 2 (Aligarh, 1980), 26–7; and for a fourteenth-century dictionary definition of *nāwak*, see Muḥammad b. Hindū Shāh Nakhchiwānī, *Ṣaḥāḥ al-Furs*, ed. ᶜAbd al-ᶜAlī Ṭāᶜatī (Tehran, 1341 Sh./1962), 188. The term originally denoted the tubular attachment but was later extended to the weapon as a whole: Kalervo Huuri, *Zur Geschichte des mittelalterlichen Geschützwesens aus orientalischen Quellen* (Helsinki and Leipzig, 1941), 105; also the review by Cl. Cahen, in *JA* 236 (1946), 169; and Cahen, 'Un traité d'armurerie composé pour Saladin', *BEO* 12 (1947–8), 153–4.

45 The occasional reference shows that they did possess the *nāwak*: e.g. *Tāj*, fols. 40b, 130b; *AH*, 247.

46 Robert Bartlett, *The making of Europe: conquest, colonization and cultural change 950–1350* (Harmondsworth, 1993), 63–4, 73–4.

47 *JH*, BN ms. Ancien fonds persan 75, fol. 185 (abstract in ED, II, 200).

48 For what follows, see *TN*, I, 400 (tr. 467–8).

the baggage and the elephants were kept several miles in the rear, bodies of picked light-armed cavalry (*sawār-i barahna wa-jarīda*), totalling 10,000 men, were ordered to harass the enemy in every direction. These are clearly shown a few lines later to have been mounted archers; and the sultan's instructions to them – to fire from all sides, and then to retreat and maintain a distance between themselves and the enemy when the Hindu army attempted to charge – are strikingly reminiscent of the tactics of nomadic Turkish horse-archers such as the Seljüks when confronted, for instance, by crusading armies in Anatolia and Syria.[49] Professor Nizami was thereby led to assume that these were the tactics which were instrumental in winning for Islam the north Gangetic plain.[50]

Yet the fact that the victory was won in part by the techniques in which Turkish nomads excelled should not blind us to the rest of the evidence. Muʿizz al-Dīn's armies did not consist overwhelmingly of Turkish nomads. The force of ten thousand light-armed horsemen was but a fraction of a much greater army comprising, says Jūzjānī, 120,000 cavalry with horses wearing armour (*bar-gustuwān*).[51] Even if this figure is exaggerated, it seems plain that the Ghurid forces at Tarā'in were in large measure made up of heavy cavalry. It is these warriors – and not light-armed horse-archers – who are immortalized on the early Muslim coinage of Bengal as the very symbol of Muslim domination.[52] The Moroccan traveller Ibn Baṭṭūṭa, who reached the Delhi Sultanate in 734/1333, comments on the fact that heavily armoured cavalrymen still made up the Delhi Sultan's forces.[53] It is worth noticing at this juncture that Turkish slave soldiers were employed as heavy cavalry – that their value to their employers, in other words, did not lie in any attempt to replicate the tactics traditionally associated with the steppe.[54] Such heavily armoured troops would hardly have mounted the kind of attacks from which crusading armies suffered. Indeed, their performance would have been more akin to the tactics of the crusaders themselves: a heavy cavalry charge, whose shock effects on a relatively immobile opponent were renowned throughout the Near East.[55] If ʿAwfī's

[49] Walter E. Kaegi, Jr, 'The contribution of archery to the Turkish conquest of Anatolia', *Speculum* 39 (1964), 96–108. R. C. Smail, *Crusading warfare 1097–1193* (Cambridge, 1956; 2nd edn, 1995), 75–83.

[50] K. A. Nizami, *Some aspects of religion and politics in India in the thirteenth century* (Aligarh, 1961), 82; and in HN, 186.

[51] *TN*, I, 400 (tr. 465–6).

[52] *CMSD*, 6 (no. 3A), 15 (nos. 49F, 49G), 16 (nos. 49H-J), and illustrations at Pls. XXII-XXIV. See also Richard M. Eaton, *The rise of Islam and the Bengal frontier, 1204–1760* (Berkeley and Los Angeles, 1993), 33–5, and the coins there illustrated. The Hindus employed *bar-gustuwān* horsemen as well: *AH*, 272; *SA*, 27.

[53] IB, II, 374 (tr. Gibb, 479).

[54] See the observations of Cl. Cahen, 'Les changements techniques militaires dans le Proche Orient médiéval et leur importance historique', in Parry and Yapp, *War, technology and society*, 121; also Wink, *Al-Hind*, II, 89.

[55] Smail, *Crusading warfare*, 112–15. Christopher Marshall, *Warfare in the Latin East,*

story embodies authentic detail from the Tarā'in campaign, and does not simply describe a stratagem sometimes adopted by Muslim commanders against Hindu armies in the past, it may possibly echo Muʿizz al-Dīn's success in rolling the core of Pṛthvīrāja's host into a solid mass – against which the light archers mentioned by Jūzjānī would have operated to deadliest effect but which would also have presented the ideal static target for a heavy cavalry attack.

Although we have scarcely any information on numbers, it is conceivable also that Muʿizz al-Dīn owed his victories to an increase in the size of his army. The figure of 120,000 cited by Jūzjānī for the Ghurid army at Tarā'in is clearly designed to make an impact on the reader, and suggests that the sultan had raised an unusually large force for the invasion. It may already have been reported in the Near East some decades before Jūzjānī wrote, and it was to make a sufficiently powerful impression on the Mughal conqueror Bābur, three centuries later, to be included in his memoirs.[56] For the army that attacked the Gāhaḍavālas, the numbers we have are set somewhat lower, at 50,000 heavily armoured cavalry[57] – still a massive force, if the figure is reliable. Many of these troops were probably volunteers: at an earlier date, Ghaznawid armies operating on the Indian front had been swollen by thousands of men seeking to serve as holy warriors (*ghāzīs*).[58] Such immigrants would have comprised both Turks and 'Tājīks', as the non-Turkish population of the Iranian world and Transoxiana were known. The latter category would have included not merely bureaucrats and the military, but descendants of the Prophet (*sādāt*, sing. *sayyid*), holy men (*shaykhs*) and scholars (*ʿulamā'*, those well versed in the Holy Law or Qur'anic sciences), like the two learned (*dānishmand*) brothers from Farghāna, troopers under Muḥammad b. Bakhtiyār mentioned by Jūzjānī, who met one of them at Lakhnawtī in 641/1243. One source of recruitment that was certainly available to Muʿizz al-Dīn was the Khalaj. We know that they were not necessarily light cavalry: the small force with which Muḥammad b. Bakhtiyār stormed into the city of Bihār consisted of two hundred heavily armed (*bar-gustuwān*) horsemen. The bands of Khalaj tribesmen who had flocked to join him only a few years after the overthrow of Pṛthvīrāja are expressly said to

1192–1291 (Cambridge, 1992), 158–63. The Hindus do not seem to have deployed mounted shock combat troops: Wink, *Al-Hind*, II, 81.

56 *Bābur-Nāma*, 479–80. The figure is found in Ibn al-Dawādārī, *Kanz al-Durar* (*c.* 730/1329), ed. Saʿīd ʿĀshūr *et al.*, VII (Cairo, 1391/1972), 134. For the date, 590, given here Ibn al-Dawādārī cites Ibn al-Sāʿī (d. 674/1276) and Ibn Wāṣil, but it is impossible to say which of these authors, if either, transmitted the figure of 120,000. Of Ibn al-Sāʿī's *al-Jāmiʿ al-Mukhtaṣar*, only the portion covering the years 595–606/1198–1209 has survived; the work of Ibn Wāṣil cited is not *Mufarrij al-Kurūb* and must therefore be his *Ta'rīkh Ṣāliḥī* (*c.* 636/1239), found only in an Istanbul ms. which is inaccessible to me.

57 *Tāj*, fol. 119b.

58 See Bosworth, *Ghaznavids*, 114; Wink, *Al-Hind*, II, 91–2 n.57.

have come 'from the direction of Hindūstān' (i.e. the Doab and Awadh), indicating at least that they were not newcomers to India.[59]

Holy war, conquest and the infidel

In the space of little more than a decade, the Ghurid armies in India had made striking progress; the Muslims now held a string of fortresses from which they more or less dominated the north Gangetic plain. It is important, on the other hand, to recognize the limits of Muslim success. Victory did not necessarily entail the displacement of Hindu rulers. As we have seen, Prthvīrāja's son was installed as his father's successor at Ajmēr, and Govindarāja's son ruled briefly at Delhi, both as the sultan's subordinates; and following the victory over Jāyachandra Aybeg is said to have installed 'a *rāna* in every direction'.[60] The Ghurid Sultan's position was that of an over-king presiding over a number of tributary princes, the *rāīs* and *rānas* who came, in Ḥasan-i Niẓāmī's words, 'to rub the ground of the exalted court of Aybeg'.[61]

Some Muslim triumphs had been merely temporary in character. Aybeg's sack of Nahrwāla in 593/1197, for instance, though dignified by Jūzjānī as 'the conquest of Gujarāt', had not led, as far as we can tell, to any acquisition of territory. The consequences of his raid on Mālwa in 596/1200 were doubtless equally ephemeral.[62] In the eastern parts of what is now Uttar Pradesh, the Gāhaḍavāla kingdom still held out.[63] Moreover, although our sources are reluctant to inform us of Muslim reverses, it is clear that of the strongholds taken by Aybeg some certainly passed back into the hands of Hindu princes, perhaps after his death, since they had to be retaken by Iltutmish. Further east, Muḥammad b. Bakhtiyār's exploits had secured only the north-western part of Bengal, where Muslim authority now centred on the town of Gawr, renamed Lakhnawtī: eastern Bengal, the region called 'Bang' by the Muslims, remained in the hands of the Sena dynasty.[64]

Even within the areas over which the Muslims ruled more or less directly, the intensity of their control is open to question, and it is necessary to

59 *TN*, I, 423 (tr. 551–2). For this restricted meaning of 'Hindūstān', see below, p. 86.

60 *Tāj*, fol. 137a. 61 *Ibid.*, fol. 150a.

62 Gujarāt: *ibid.*, fol. 173a, and *TN*, I, 417 (tr. 516). Mālwa: *SA*, 24, and *TN*, I, 407 (tr. 491): at I, 417 (tr. 516–17), Jūzjānī refers to the conquest of Hindūstān as far east as the borders of Ujjain (Ḥabībī's edn reads ČYN in error), i.e. Mālwa.

63 Machchlishahr copper-plate inscription, dated Vikrama samvat 1253/1197: P. Prasad, *Sanskrit inscriptions*, 58–70 (no. II:6). Niyogi, *History of the Gāhaḍavāla dynasty*, 113ff.

64 *TN*, I, 426–7 (tr. 558). The name 'Bangāla' is not found prior to Baranī: Aḥmad Hasan Dani, 'Shamsuddīn Ilyās Shāh, Shāh-i Bangālah', in Hari Ram Gupta *et al.* (eds.), *Essays presented to Sir Jadunath Sarkar*, Sir Jadunath Sarkar commemoration volume, II (Hoshiarpur, 1958), 50–8.

disentangle plausibility from the hyperbole of our sources. At one extreme stand the enthusiastic claims of Fakhr-i Mudabbir:

> Infidel towns have become cities of Islam. In place of images, they worship the Most High. Idol temples have become mosques, colleges (*madrasahā*) and hospices (*khānaqāhhā*). Every year several thousand infidel men and women are being brought to Islam ...[65]

We might be more inclined to accept Ḥasan-i Niẓāmī's statements that Aybeg 'uprooted idolatry' and 'destroyed temples' at Kuhrām, and that at Mīrat, Banāras (a thousand temples here) and Kālinjar idol temples were converted into mosques.[66] Such thorough-going tactics are conceivable as far as the respective urban centres were concerned. In some cases, too, architectural remains endorse Ḥasan-i Niẓāmī's claim that the stone from demolished Hindu temples was used in the erection of mosques, as for example at Delhi and for the Arhai Din ke Jhompra mosque at Ajmēr.[67] But other assertions elicit a greater degree of scepticism: that Aybeg freed the whole region (*diyār*) of Kōl, rather than just the town, from idols and idol worship is doubtful.[68] Moreover, the treatment of Hindu temples by the eighth-century Muslim conquerors of Sind had varied with the circumstances,[69] and we might reasonably assume that this was true of the early thirteenth century also. Cities which capitulated – as for instance did Gwāliyōr in 597/1200–1 – presumably obtained a better deal for their temples than did places which had to be taken by storm. Whatever the Muslim *literati* wanted people to think, the hallmark of these years was not uncompromising iconoclasm.

The language of our sources has served to distort the character of these and later campaigns, so that they have taken on the hue of a conflict that was religiously inspired – a development in turn nurtured by more modern communalistic attitudes.[70] For Jūzjānī, Muʿizz al-Dīn is always 'the holy warrior sultan' (*sulṭān-i ghāzī*), and Muslim writers designate his forces as 'the army of Islam'. When recounting the Ghurid triumphs over the Indian infidel, Jūzjānī likens them to the victories of Muʿizz al-Dīn's contemporary Saladin over the Christian Franks of Syria and Palestine.[71] Yet it is important not to overstate the significance of holy war in the Ghurid campaigns, at least as far as the sultan's motives were concerned. Booty, to pay for the conflict with the Khwārazmshāh, was undoubtedly a major

65 *SA*, 26. 66 *Tāj*, fols. 53a, 74b, 134b, 185a.
67 *Ibid.*, fols. 48a, 114. See Robert Hillenbrand, 'Political symbolism in early Indo-Islamic mosque architecture: the case of Ajmīr', *Iran* 26 (1988), 105–17.
68 *Tāj*, fol. 138a.
69 Friedmann, 'A contribution', 328–9; *idem*, 'The temple of Multan: a note on early Muslim attitudes to idolatry', *IOS* 2 (1972), 176–82.
70 For a judicious treatment of this theme, see Carl W. Ernst, *Eternal garden. Mysticism, history, and politics at a South Asian sufi center* (Albany, New York, 1992), 18–29 *passim*.
71 *TN*, I, 290 (tr. 214).

incentive; and the distribution of find-spots for the coins minted in India by the conquerors is significant, showing that a good proportion found their way back to the homeland.[72] Muslim authors make great play of the golden artefacts from Ajmēr which formed part of the Chawhān tribute, were forwarded to Ghiyāth al-Dīn Muḥammad b. Sām and came to decorate the royal palace at Fīrūzkūh and the congregational mosque at Herat.[73] Both his successful attack on Daybul and his ill-fated Nahrwāla campaign surely represent bids by Muʿizz al-Dīn to restock his treasury by looting regions whose princes enjoyed a notoriously large income from the proceeds of commerce; and there can be little doubt that the Daybul expedition, which yielded great quantities of plunder,[74] lubricated his subsequent war efforts against the Ghaznawids. Jūzjānī would later hear from Muʿizz al-Dīn's treasurer extraordinary figures for the weight of the gems obtained in plunder from India and stored at Ghazna at the time of the sultan's death.[75]

Nor was the long-drawn conflict that marked the advance of Muslim power necessarily one that simply pitted Hindu troops against Muslims. In the final assault on his co-religionist Khusraw Malik, Muʿizz al-Dīn had cooperated with the Hindu prince of Jammū, while the Ghaznawid Sultan had in turn been allied with the infidel Khōkhars of the Panjāb.[76] We do not know at what point Muʿizz al-Dīn and his generals followed the Ghaznawid example in employing contingents of Hindu troops. Aybeg's army at the siege of Mīrat certainly included Hindu soldiers; and when he advanced on Lahore in 602/1206, the 'Hindūstān forces' (*ḥasham-i Hindūstān*) that accompanied him contained, we are told, '*rānas* and *thakurs*' – Hindu chiefs at the head of their own retinues, in the service of the Muslim warlord.[77]

For all these qualifications, however, the Delhi Sultanate was firmly rooted in a long tradition of Muslim military activity within the subcontinent, and its rulers could be excused for seeing themselves as the latest in a line of Muslim holy warriors. Pride of place among these undoubtedly went to Maḥmūd of Ghazna. It is no accident that in his *Fatāwā-yi Jahāndārī*, a mirror for princes, the mid-fourteenth-century author Baranī produced what purported to be a political testament from Maḥmūd to posterity; or that his contemporary ʿIṣāmī, modelling his epic *Futūḥ al-Salāṭīn* on Firdawsī's *Shāh-Nāma* (which had been dedicated to Maḥmūd), chose effectively to begin the work with Maḥmūd's own campaigns, and credited him with the establishment of Islam in the subcontinent; or that Shams-i Sirāj ʿAfīf, describing Sultan Fīrūz Shāh's iconoclastic activities in Jājnagar

[72] Deyell, *Living without silver*, 195, 203–6. [73] *TN*, I, 375 (tr. 404). *SA*, 22–3. *Tāj*, fol. 80b.
[74] *TN*, I, 397 (tr. 451–3). [75] *Ibid.*, I, 404 (tr. 487–8).
[76] *Ibid.*, I, 398 (tr. 454–5). Bosworth, *Later Ghaznavids*, 129–30.
[77] Mīrat: *Tāj*, fol. 74a. Lahore: *SA*, 33 (reading RANGAN for the RATGAN of the text). For Indian troops in the Ghaznawid armies, see Bosworth, *Ghaznavids*, 110; also verses attributed to the Ghurid ʿAlā' al-Dīn Ḥusayn, cited in *TN*, I, 346 (tr. 357).

(Orissa) in 762/1361, likens him to Maḥmūd.[78] Admittedly the great Ghaznawid amir was *sui generis*. 'The Almighty', wrote Jūzjānī, 'had conferred upon that ruler many superior characteristics (*ʿalāmāt*) and miraculous signs (*karāmāt*), which in their number and magnificence have not been combined since in any other sovereign.'[79] But this hardly rendered Maḥmūd any less worthy of emulation; the Delhi Sultans had no more distinguished ideological forebear.[80]

78 *FS*, 28–9, 30, 609 (tr. 66–7, 68, 907). Shams-i Sirāj ᶜAfīf, *Ta'rīkh-i Fīrūz-Shāhī*, ed. Maulavi Vilayat Hosain (Calcutta, 1888–91), 170.

79 *TN*, I, 230 (tr. 83 modified); cf. also I, 229 (tr. 77–80).

80 Nizami, *Some aspects*, 107–9, and *On history and historians*, 107–9; C. E. Bosworth, 'Mahmud of Ghazna in contemporary eyes and in later Persian literature', *Iran* 4 (1966), 89–90, repr. in his *Medieval history*. Aziz Aḥmad, *Studies*, 79.

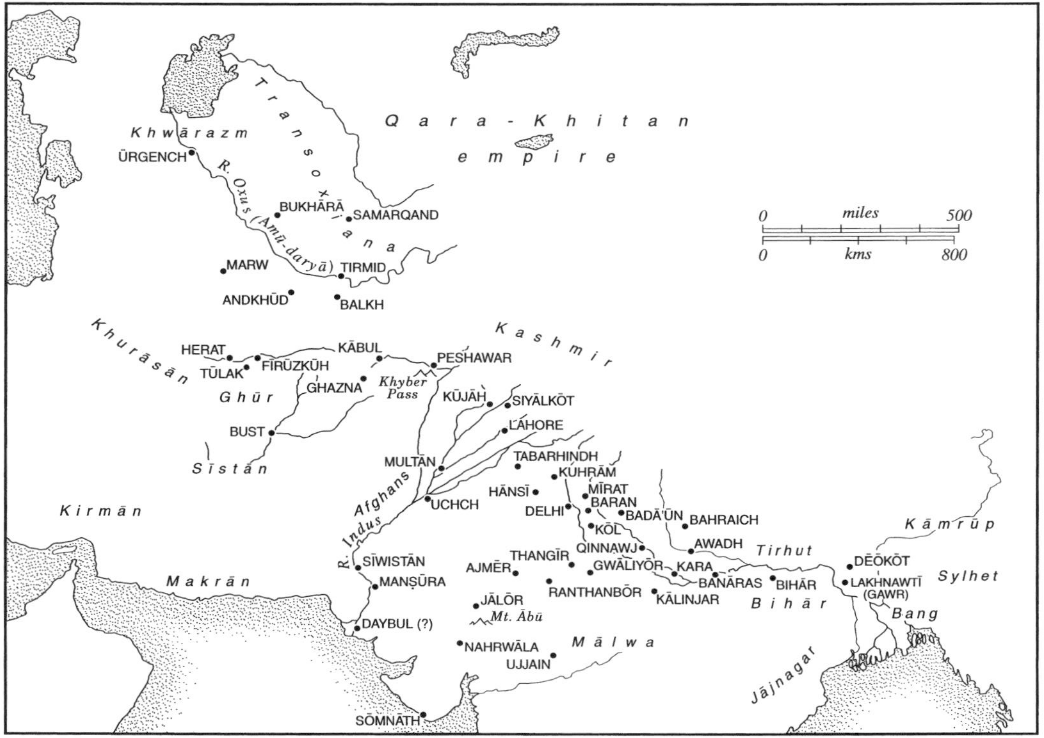

Map 1: The eastern Islamic world in 1206

CHAPTER 2

From Ghurid province to Delhi Sultanate

Ghurid government

The conquerors brought with them the institutions to which they were accustomed in the Ghurid homelands. Chief among these was the *iqṭāʿ* (frequently and misleadingly rendered as 'fief'), the transferable revenue assignment in lieu of salary for service (usually military service), which by 1200 already had a long history in the eastern Islamic territories, having been adopted by the Ghaznawids and having reached its highest expression under the Seljüks; imported into India by the Ghurids, it would form one of the characteristic institutions of the early Delhi Sultanate. Various developments had occurred in twelfth-century Persia to blur the nature of the iqtaʿ and to assimilate it to an administrative command.[1] Hence our sources, in the terminology they employ for the grants made by Muʿizz al-Dīn, are often less than helpful. Aybeg's earliest assignment, at Kuhrām, is described by Jūzjānī as iqtaʿ, whereas Fakhr-i Mudabbir speaks of it simply as the 'command' (*sipahsālārī*) there and Ḥasan-i Niẓāmī says that he was given the governorship (*ayālat*) of Kuhrām and Sāmāna.[2] Yet we are left in no doubt that the iqtaʿ was widespread in northern India by the time of the creation of the independent Delhi Sultanate. Iltutmish became iqtaʿ-holder (*muqṭaʿ*) of Baran under Aybeg; and we find iqtaʿs in Awadh before 1200 and in west Bengal following its conquest by Muḥammad b. Bakhtiyār. The term was also used of the holdings of ordinary troopers: Ibn al-Athīr refers to such men as holding iqtaʿs from Aybeg in 602/1206.[3]

1 See Claude Cahen, 'L'évolution de l'iqtaᶜ du ixᵉ au xiiiᵉ siècle', *Annales, Economies, Sociétés, Civilisations* 8 (1953), 25–52, repr. in his *Les peuples musulmans dans l'histoire médiévale* (Damascus, 1977), 231–69; *idem*, 'Iḳṭāᶜ', *Enc.Isl.*²; A. K. S. Lambton, 'Reflections on the *iqṭa*ᶜ', in G. Makdisi (ed.), *Arabic and Islamic Studies in honor of Hamilton A.R. Gibb* (Leiden, 1965), 358–76; *eadem*, *Continuity and change in medieval Persia* (London, 1988), 99–113. There is a succinct account in D.O. Morgan, *Medieval Persia 1040–1797* (London, 1988), 37–40.

2 *Tāj*, fol. 51b. *TN*, I, 417 (tr. 515).

3 IA, XII, 140/214. Bengal: *TN*, I, 422, 423, 432, 433 (tr. 549–50, 572, 574, 575). Baran: *ibid.*, I, 443, and II, 19 (tr. 604, 745).

As far as we can tell from the exiguous material in our sources, the hierarchy of Ghurid officials at Fīrūzkūh and Ghazna did not differ appreciably in its outlines from those maintained by other eastern Islamic dynasties. The *wazīr* ('minister'), as elswhere, headed the civil administration at Ghazna; we also read of the treasurer (*khāzin*) and the overseer of public morality/inspector of the markets (*muḥtasib*). The appointment of judges (*quḍḍāt*, sing. *qāḍī*) who enforced the religious law, the Sharīʿa, was also in the sultan's hands. The army had its own Sharīʿa court under its own judge (*qāḍī-yi lashgar*), though the two offices could evidently be combined.[4] It is possible to draw too sharp a line between the civil and the military. Mu'ayyad al-Mulk Sajzī, who served first Muʿizz al-Dīn and then Yildiz as wazir at Ghazna, also acted on occasions as a military commander, as would the wazirs of the early Delhi Sultans; and we find a contingent (*khayl*) of horsemen from Tūlak in Muʿizz al-Dīn's service led by its qadi, Jūzjānī's kinsman Ḍiyā' al-Dīn.[5] The distinction between 'men of the sword' and 'men of the pen' (*arbāb-i tīgh-u qalam*), to borrow the widespread term used by our sources,[6] or that between Turkish military and Persian ('Tājīk') bureaucrats, was evidently in practice sometimes rather blurred.

Most of the offices of which we read are essentially military: the commander of the sultan's guards or executioners (*sar-i jāndār*); the chief armour-bearer (*sar-i ṣilāḥdār*); the muster-master (*ʿāriḍ*), who seems to have performed the functions of a minister of war; the military chamberlain (*amīr-ḥājib*), often entrusted with command in the field; the military justiciar (*amīr-i dād*), who at Ghazna, if Ibn al-Athīr is to be believed, commanded the citadel; the intendant of the sultan's stables (*amīr-i ākhūr*), an office held by Quṭb al-Dīn Aybeg himself prior to his appointment in India; and the intendant of the hunt (*amīr-i shikār*), a position of some importance under a regime in which the chase constituted both the monarch's chief recreation and a valuable form of military exercise for the troops.[7]

Our knowledge of the administration of Muʿizz al-Dīn's conquests in northern India is patchy. Aybeg clearly had his own staff which mirrored that of the sultan at Ghazna, including a *sar-i jāndār* and an *amīr-i shikār*;[8] and there was an *ʿāriḍ* at Delhi, of whom we know only that he rejected Muḥammad b. Bakhtiyār as unfit for service and thereby unwittingly launched him on a more dazzling career.[9] At certain centres, the local

4 *Ibid.*, I, 367, 389, 405 (tr. 389, 430, 489).

5 *Ibid.*, I, 380–1, 419 (tr. 415, 534), for Mu'ayyad al-Mulk; I, 398–9, 400 (tr. 457–8, 464), for the qadi of Tūlak. On Iltutmish's wazir Junaydī, see below, p. 35.

6 *Tāj*, fols. 106b, 135b, 218a; and cf. *AH*, 138.

7 For these offices, see generally Heribert Horst, *Die Staatsverwaltung der Grosselǧūken und Ḫōrazmšāhs* (Wiesbaden, 1964), *passim*. *Amīr-i dād* at Ghazna: IA, XII, 143/217, 145/221. Aybeg as *amīr-i ākhūr*: *TN*, I, 303, 416 (tr. 248, 514). On the passion of the Ghurid Sultan Ghiyāth al-Dīn Muḥammad b. Sām for the chase, see *ibid.*, I, 364–5 (tr. 385–7).

8 *Ibid.*, I, 443 (tr. 603).

9 *Ibid.*, I, 422 (tr. 549).

military justiciar (*amīr-i dād*) seems to have enjoyed a pivotal position; perhaps, like his counterpart at Ghazna, he was in command of the citadel. Examples are the officer at Multān, treacherously killed at the onset of a rebellion in 601/1204, and ʿAlī-yi Ismāʿīl at Delhi, instigator of the coup that conferred power on Iltutmish in 607/1210–11.[10]

The emergence of an autonomous Muslim power in India

The events that followed Muʿizz al-Dīn's death represented a disjunction from previous developments. Hitherto Delhi had been merely one of the Muslims' forward bases, and Lahore had remained the capital of Muʿizz al-Dīn's Indian province just as it had been of the Ghaznawid territories in India. For Fakhr-i Mudabbir, Lahore was 'the centre of Islam in India' (*markaz-i Islām-i Hind*); while Ḥasan-i Niẓāmī, describing how the city was conferred on Iltutmish's eldest son in 614/1217, could still observe, wistfully perhaps, how Lahore had 'ever been the residence of celebrated maliks and the seat of powerful rulers'.[11] Within a few decades of Iltutmish's seizure of power at Delhi and the creation of the independent Sultanate, the steady build-up of Mongol pressure made Delhi appear a far more suitable residence for its rulers than was Lahore, a circumstance incidentally emphasized by the Mongols themselves when they took and sacked Lahore in 639/1241. But that Delhi had become the capital of Muslim India and the seat of independent monarchs was in some measure a historical accident, though our principal sources are by no means anxious to acknowledge it.

In view of his subsequent rise, it is easily forgotten that when in 588/1192 Quṭb al-Dīn Aybeg was stationed at Kuhrām he was one of Muʿizz al-Dīn's more junior slaves, in contrast, for example, with Tāj al-Dīn Yildiz, who seems to have been among the most senior and is said to have been made their commander (*sarwar*).[12] Aybeg's precise status within the Ghurid conquests is obscure. We find him appointing amirs to certain strongpoints: his own ghulams Iltutmish first to Gwāliyōr and later to Baran and Badā'ūn, and Aybeg-i Tamghāj to Tabarhindh; and other Turkish officers like Ḥasan-i Arnab to Kālinjar and Ḥusām al-Dīn Oghulbeg to Kōl.[13] The Khalaj freebooter Muḥammad b. Bakhtiyār waited upon Aybeg at Badā'ūn

[10] *Tāj*, fols. 188a, 189a. *TN*, I, 444 (tr. 605).

[11] *SA*, 30. *Tāj*, fol. 259a; see also fol. 211a, *mustaqarr-i sarīr-i salāṭīn*.

[12] *TN*, I, 411 (tr. 498); cf. also IA, XII, 141/215. A later tradition made Yildiz Muʿizz al-Dīn's adopted son: *TFS*, 550. Both names are Turkish: for *yildiz/yulduz*, 'star', see Sir Gerard Clauson, *An etymological dictionary of pre-thirteenth-century Turkish* (Oxford, 1972), 922–3; for *ay*, 'moon', and *beg*, 'prince', 'lord', Jean Sauvaget, 'Noms et surnoms de Mamelouks', *JA* 238 (1950), 31–58 (no. 37).

[13] *TN*, I, 443 (tr. 603–4). *Tāj*, fols. 138a, for Oghulbeg, and 185a, for Ḥasan-i Arnab. The second element in the latter name, usually read as 'Arnal', is clearly 'RNB in the best mss.; see also Hodivala, *Studies*, II, 53–4. Oghulbeg's name is Tu. *oghul*, 'son', 'boy' (Clauson, *Etymological dictionary*, 83–4), + *beg*, 'prince'.

and accepted from him the privilege of maintaining a band (*nawbat*) outside his residence, together with a kettle-drum and standard and a diploma that confirmed and, according to Ḥasan-i Niẓāmī, extended the territory under his control.[14] Such attentions indicate that he acknowledged Aybeg's authority as the sultan's representative.

Yet there clearly existed other commanders in India who were independent of Aybeg. It must be remembered that the sources tell us only of the operations conducted by Muʿizz al-Dīn and by Aybeg as his lieutenant, together with (in the case of Jūzjānī and Ibn al-Athīr) the activities of the Khalaj forces in Bihār and Bengal. Of other campaigns, led by other Ghurid officers, which must have taken place in these years, we learn little. Bahā' al-Dīn Toghril, a senior ghulam of the sultan, had received from Muʿizz al-Dīn in person his command at Thangīr and the task of reducing the great fortress of Gwāliyōr, so that he deeply resented the surrender of Gwāliyōr to Aybeg in 597/1200–1. His inscriptions suggest that he proclaimed himself sultan at some point following Muʿizz al-Dīn's murder.[15] We do not know in what relationship Aybeg stood to ʿIzz al-Dīn ʿAlī at Nāgawr or to Naṣīr al-Dīn Aytemür at Uchch.[16] Nor are we told whether prior to 602/1206 his writ extended to Lahore, which seems to have constituted a joint command with Multān.[17] It is indeed possible that he wielded no authority in those tracts which had formed part of the Ghaznawid state at the time of its conquest in 582/1186.

The evidence does not, in other words, sustain the belief of modern historians that Aybeg was left as the sultan's deputy in the Indian provinces in the wake of the Tarā'in victory: he is admittedly so designated by Ibn al-Athīr, but only in the context of the events following the sultan's assassination.[18] Earlier the same author describes him simply as commander of the sultan's forces in India.[19] Even on the testimony of his panegyrist Fakhr-i Mudabbir (writing soon after Aybeg's assumption of the royal dignity at Lahore), his promotion to the status of viceroy of the entire province 'from the gates of Peshawar to the furthest parts of India' had occurred only a few weeks prior to Muʿizz al-Dīn's death.[20]

14 *Tāj*, fol. 186. *TN*, I, 423–7 (tr. 551–4, 560).

15 Mehrdad and Natalie H. Shokoohy, 'The architecture of Baha' al-Din Tughrul in the region of Bayana, Rajasthan', *Muqarnas* 4 (1987), 114–32 (esp. 115); see also Mehrdad Shokoohy, *Rajasthan I* (London, 1986), 51–3; *TN*, I, 421–2 (tr. 544–7), for his earlier career. The name is Tu. *toghril*, 'bird of prey': Clauson, *Etymological dictionary*, 472; *TMENP*, III, 346–8 (no. 1345).

16 *TN*, I, 419 (tr. 531–2), for Aytemür ('YTM in Ḥabībī's edition): *ay*, 'moon', and *temür*, 'iron', see Sauvaget, 'Noms et surnoms', no. 42. The reference to ʿAlī-yi Nāgawrī is omitted in Ḥabībī's text (I, 422), but cf. his apparatus and Raverty's tr., 549.

17 IA, XII, 136/209, 137/210; and cf. *TN*, I, 398 (tr. 456). I cannot agree with I. Habib, 'Formation', 6, that Aybeg had charge of Lahore prior to 1206.

18 IA, XII, 164/248. Habibullah, *Foundation*, 63, wrongly describes Delhi as 'the capital of Muizzuddin's Indian dominion'.

19 IA, XII, 136/209, *muqaddam ʿasākiri'l-Hind*.

20 *SA*, 28.

Whatever his position when the sultan was murdered, Aybeg was able to move from Delhi to Lahore and to take up his quarters as ruler there on 18 Dhu'l-Qaʿda 602/26 June 1206. Jūzjānī at one point claims that he did so following the arrival of a diploma from the new sultan, Muʿizz al-Dīn's nephew Ghiyāth al-Dīn Maḥmūd b. Muḥammad.[21] Yet this is unlikely on chronological grounds. More probably Aybeg was encouraged to do so by a sudden access of manpower, since soon after Muʿizz al-Dīn's assassination his wazir sent back to India all those troopers currently with the late monarch's army who held iqtaʿs from Aybeg.[22] Nevertheless, in contrast with Yildiz, who at Ghazna ignored the rights of the new Ghurid sovereign, Aybeg maintained the khutba for Ghiyāth al-Dīn Maḥmūd and struck coins in his name, gestures that were rewarded in 605/1208–9 with the gift of a ceremonial parasol (*chatr*) and, allegedly, with the style of sultan.[23] He is called sultan by Ḥasan-i Niẓāmī, though no coins of his have come down to us bearing that title.[24]

Aybeg also secured recognition of his authority in Bengal after the assassination of Muḥammad b. Bakhtiyār by one of his Khalaj officers, ʿAlī-yi Mardān, in *c.* 602/1205–6. He first sent an army from Awadh under Qaymaz-i Rūmī, who defeated and killed the new Khalaj ruler, Muḥammad-i Shīrān, and installed at Dēōkōt, one of the principal Muslim-held towns, another of Muḥammad b. Bakhtiyār's Khalaj lieutenants, Ḥusām al-Dīn ʿIwaḍ. Subsequently Aybeg conferred a robe of honour on ʿAlī-yi Mardān, who had taken refuge at Lahore, and despatched him eastwards as his subordinate. On his arrival at Dēōkōt, ʿAlī-yi Mardān was received submissively by ʿIwaḍ, and established himself as ruler of the entire Muslim territory in Bengal.[25] Thus for most of his reign Aybeg was represented in the east by his own nominee, and had emerged as the paramount ruler in Muslim India.

Aybeg's most dangerous rival was Tāj al-Dīn Yildiz, with whom he engaged in a struggle for possession of Ghazna, first inciting one of Yildiz's officers to seize the place in 603/1207 and briefly occupying Ghazna in person two years later. Jūzjānī's description of this conflict as originating over Lahore suggests that Yildiz claimed to rule all Muʿizz al-Dīn's eastern territories.[26] Their rivalry seems to have kept Aybeg at Lahore during his

21 *TN*, I, 417 (tr. 521–5). 22 IA, XII, 140/214.

23 *TN*, I, 373 (Ghūr and Ghazna, erroneously included among the territories covered by the mandate in Ḥabībī's text, are omitted in BL ms., fol. 152a, and Raverty's tr. 398). IA, XII, 165/249.

24 *Tāj*, fols. 211a, 217a. P. Jackson, 'Ḳuṭb al-Dīn Aybak', *Enc.Isl.*^{2}.

25 *TN*, I, 432–3, 434 (tr. 572–6, 577–8). The name of Aybeg's general is Tu. *qaymaz*, 'he who does not turn back': Sauvaget, 'Noms et surnoms', no. 150. For Dēōkōt, at 25° 11′N., 88° 31′E., see Hodivala, *Studies*, I, 209, and II, 57.

26 *TN*, I, 417 (tr. 526); I, 412, 413–14, 417 (tr. 503, 506, 526–8), for the later struggle over Ghazna. For the earlier episode, in 603/1206–7, see IA, XII, 165–6/249–50. See generally Jackson, 'Fall of the Ghurid dynasty'.

four-year reign, either guarding against an invasion of the Panjāb or seeking yet another opportunity to take Ghazna. The dearth of evidence for military operations against independent Hindu states at this time presents a marked contrast with the era of his lieutenancy on behalf of Muʿizz al-Dīn.[27]

When Aybeg died in a polo (*chawgān*) accident in 607/1210–11, his ghulam Iltutmish was invited into Delhi from Badāʾūn by a party in the city, headed by the military justiciar (*amīr-i dād*) ʿAlī-yi Ismāʿīl, and set himself up as ruler. A certain obscurity surrounds his rival Ārām Shāh, who at one point is called Aybeg's son.[28] He seems, however, to have reacted sharply to Iltutmish's seizure of power at Delhi. His supporters included some of the Muʿizzī amirs, i.e. former officers of Muʿizz al-Dīn, who left Delhi to join the opposition to Iltutmish; the latter, on the other hand, had the backing of the Quṭbī amirs, namely the servitors of Aybeg. Ḥasan-i Niẓāmī, who ignores Ārām Shāh and for whom all this is simply a rising against his patron Iltutmish by a group of recalcitrant Turks, names as their leader the *sar-i jāndār*, *Berki. They advanced from Lahore to Delhi, where Iltutmish met and defeated them in the Bāgh-i Jūd. Ārām Shāh is alleged to have been 'martyred'; but whether he was killed in the engagement or put to death as a prisoner, we are not told.[29]

Shams al-Dīn Iltutmish[30] was at first only one of a number of Muslim rulers in the subcontinent, and his position was highly precarious, even after the overthrow of Ārām Shāh. In the following century it was remembered that he had been obliged to dispute his new kingdom with amirs who held iqtaʿs in 'Hindūstān' by grant from Muʿizz al-Dīn.[31] Jūzjānī speaks of campaigns by which Iltutmish brought under his control 'the outlying regions which were dependent on Delhi' (*aṭrāf-i mamālik-i maḍāfāt-i ḥaḍrat-i Dihlī*), singling out for particular mention Badāʾūn, Awadh, Banāras and the Siwālik; elsewhere he alludes briefly, in his list of Iltutmish's conquests, to the capture of Banāras and the flight of Qaymaz, presumably Aybeg's former officer whom we have already encountered.[32]

Further afield, Iltutmish could command no allegiance whatever. On the news of Aybeg's death, his client in Bengal, ʿAlī-yi Mardān, assumed

27 P. Hardy, 'Dihlī Sultanate', *Enc.Isl.*², III, 269a. Jackson, 'Ḳuṭb al-Dīn Aybak'.

28 Only in a chapter heading: *TN*, I, 418 (tr. 528).

29 *Ibid.*, I, 418, has simply *Ārām Shāhrā qaḍā-yi ajal dar rasīd*; but cf. BL ms., fol. 168b, *Ārām Shāhrā ... shahīd kardand* (also Raverty's tr. 530). The 'revolt' is described in *TN*, I, 444 (for the translation, which is garbled by Raverty, see I. Habib, 'Formation', 9 and n.50), and in *Tāj*, fols. 219b-224a. Modern authors have usually rendered the *sar-i jāndār*'s name as 'Turki', but the mss. read .YRKY and TYRKY. The name is possibly connected with Tu. *berk*, 'firm', 'solid': Clauson, *Etymological dictionary*, 361–2.

30 The correct form of his name has been established by Simon Digby, 'Iletmish or Iltutmish? A reconsideration of the name of the Dehli Sultan', *Iran* 8 (1970), 57–64.

31 *TFS*, 550.

32 Conquests: *TN*, I, 444–5 (tr. 607–8). Qaymaz: I, 452 (to be corrected from BL ms., fol. 179b; cf. also Raverty's tr., 627).

sovereign status, entitling himself Sultan ʿAlāʾ al-Dīn.[33] In Sind, Multān was seized by Nāṣir al-Dīn Qubacha, a former ghulam of Muʿizz al-Dīn who had been muqtaʿ of Uchch since 601/1204 and who now proclaimed his independence with the adoption of two chatrs. Lahore was disputed between Qubacha and Yildiz.[34] Iltutmish secured his position at first by acknowledging Yildiz's sovereignty, receiving in return the insignia of royal power, a chatr and a *dūrbāsh* or ceremonial baton. His earliest inscription, dated Jumādā I 608/October 1211, styles him not sultan but only king (*al-Malik al-Muʿaẓẓam*).[35] We cannot fail to be struck, again, by the relative absence of campaigns against the Hindu powers. During the first sixteen years of his reign, Iltutmish is known to have conducted only one such expedition, against the Chawhān ruler of Jālōr, which is described by Ḥasan-i Niẓāmī but is undated; it may have occurred not long after the suppression of Ārām Shāh's attempt on Delhi. That other major undertakings were deferred until the attacks on Ranthanbōr (623/1226) and Mandōr (624/1227) was clearly due to pressing concerns elsewhere.

Iltutmish's first opportunity came in 612/1215–16, when Yildiz was forced out of Ghazna by the Khwārazmshāh and fell back on the Panjāb. Having wrested Lahore from Qubacha, he then pushed into Delhi territory in an effort to make good his rights over his subordinate Iltutmish, issuing demands of the kind, says Ḥasan-i Niẓāmī, that no sovereign could demean himself to answer. Iltutmish met him on 3 Shawwāl 612/25 January 1216 on the historic battlefield of Tarāʾin, near Sāmāna: Yildiz was defeated and incarcerated in Badāʾūn, where he was later put to death.[36] But if the elimination of Yildiz conferred independence on the Delhi ruler, it did not immediately result in any significant addition to his territory. Lahore was reoccupied by Qubacha, whose empire now stretched from the Arabian Sea and the Indus delta as far north as Nandana and Peshawar. Iltutmish seized Aybeg's old capital late in 613/in the winter of 1216–17, conferring it on his eldest son Nāṣir al-Dīn Maḥmūd; but it continued to change hands thereafter, while the two rulers disputed possession of Tabarhindh, Kuhrām and Sarsatī in the eastern Panjāb.[37] And that Qubacha did not lack partisans in Delhi territory emerges from the account of Bahāʾ al-Dīn ʿAlī b. Aḥmad

[33] *Ibid.*, I, 434 (tr. 578). M. Nizamuddin, 'A rare coin of Ali Mardan Khalji – a medieval Muslim ruler of Bengal', *JNSI* 49 (1987), 50–5.

[34] *TN*, I, 418, 419 (tr. 530, 532); for Yildiz at Lahore, see I, 444 (tr. 607). Qubacha's appointment to Uchch dated from the death of its muqtaʿ, Aytemür, in battle at Andkhūd. His name is a derivative of Tu. *quba*, 'pale', 'pale yellow': Clauson, *Etymological dictionary*, 581.

[35] M. M. Shuʿaib, 'Inscriptions from Palwal', *EIM* (1911–12), 2–3; *RCEA*, X (Cairo, 1939), 72–3 (no. 3703). *TN*, I, 444 (tr. 607).

[36] IA, XII, 203/311–12. *TN*, I, 413, 445 (tr. 505, 608). *Tāj*, fols. 238b-247b, with the precise date.

[37] *TN*, I, 419, 444 (tr. 534, 607). *Tāj*, fols. 253a–259b, for Iltutmish's first occupation of Lahore. But at the advent of the Khwarazmians (below), it was held by Qubacha's son. Nandana: Nasawī, *Sīrat al-Sulṭān Jalāl al-Dīn*, ed. O. Houdas (Paris, 1891), 86, and tr.

Jāmajī in ʿAwfī's biographical dictionary *Lubāb al-Albāb*. Jāmajī, whom Iltutmish had put in command of Bahraich, declared for Qubacha and in 617/1220 sent to Uchch offering his submission. Writing at this very moment, ʿAwfī is unaware of the sequel (as, regrettably, are we), though he expresses the hope that his master Qubacha will soon acquire dominion over the whole of Hindūstān.[38] The episode suggests that Qubacha may have constituted a formidable threat to the Delhi ruler on the eve of the Khwarazmian invasion.

As usurpers, Aybeg and Iltutmish stood in need of legitimation, and obtained it, on one level, from their panegyrists. The sources for this era, with the exception of Ibn al-Athīr, all emanate from within India. They also date from the period following Muʿizz al-Dīn's death, and their accounts read as though there were a continuity between their new masters and the Ghurid dynasty. Thus Fakhr-i Mudabbir – writing, it will be recalled, at Aybeg's court soon after 602/1206 – has Aybeg taking over at Lahore in that year by virtue of his status as Muʿizz al-Dīn's deputy (*qā'im-i maqām-u walī-ʿahd*) throughout his Indian dominions.[39] Jūzjānī, who composed his *Ṭabaqāt-i Nāṣirī* in Delhi when the Sultanate had been in existence for five decades, clearly sought to gloss over Iltutmish's struggles with other former Ghurid lieutenants and to portray him and his dynasty likewise as Muʿizz al-Dīn's true successors in India. Hence in the introduction to his section on the Ghurids, the current sultan of Delhi, Nāṣir al-Dīn Maḥmūd Shāh b. Iltutmish, becomes 'the heir to that sovereignty and duly appointed successor (*qā'im-i ma'mūr*) to that kingdom'.[40] That this is not intended merely as a figure of speech is clear from what Jūzjānī says later. Approached by a courtier, who lamented the sultan's lack of sons to inherit his dominions, Muʿizz al-Dīn replied:

> 'Let other sultans have one son or two. I have several thousand sons – Turkish slaves – whose inheritance will be my kingdom: after me, they will maintain the khutba in [my] empire in my name.' And it transpired as that *ghāzī* monarch pronounced. Since his time, right down until these lines are being written, they have preserved the whole empire of Hindūstān and are still preserving it . . .[41]

Although some modern commentators have adopted this perspective on

Z. M. Buniiatov, *Zhizneopisanie Sultana Dzhalal ad-Dina Mankburny* (Baku, 1973), 131. Peshawar: *TJG*, I, 61 (tr. Boyle, 328).

38 ʿAwfī, *Lubāb al-Albāb*, ed. E. G. Browne and M. M. Qazwīnī (Leiden and London, 1903–6, 2 vols.), I, 115. The summary of Jāmajī's career in Niẓāmu'd-dín, *Introduction*, 13–14, is inaccurate.

39 *SA*, 28; cf. also 33, *īn walī-ʿahdī*.

40 *TN*, I, 323 (tr. 310 modified). Peter Hardy, 'Force and violence in Indo-Persian writing on history and government in medieval South Asia', in Milton Israel and N. K. Wagle (eds.), *Islamic society and culture. Essays in honour of Professor Aziz Aḥmad* (Delhi, 1983), 180–1.

41 *TN*, I, 410–11 (tr. 497–8 modified); cf. I, 415 (tr. 508–12), where the Muʿizzī sultans, i.e. Aybeg and Yildiz and their contemporaries, are described as the late sovereign's heirs, and I, 393 (tr. 438), where Muʿizz al-Dīn is said to have entrusted (*sipurd*) Ghazna to Yildiz.

events,[42] it is in fact highly dubious and smacks of *ex post facto* justification: in Islamic law it was the master who inherited from the slave and not *vice versa*.[43] But evidently the sovereignty of the early Delhi Sultans, in the eyes of certain of the Muslim intelligentsia, required the sanction of Muʿizz al-Dīn.

The Khwarazmian and Mongol invasions

In Iltutmish's early years, there was no guarantee that the former territories of the Ghurids in Sind and the Panjāb would not share the fate of the regions beyond the Indus and be absorbed into the Khwarazmian empire. Following his seizure of Ghazna, the Khwārazmshāh 'Alā' al-Dīn Muḥammad created for his son Jalāl al-Dīn *Mingbarnī a large appanage that stretched as far as the Indus. At some point his forces wrested Peshawar from Qubacha.[44] A casual observer might have been forgiven for supposing that the Ghurids' erstwhile lieutenants were similarly destined for political oblivion. It was fortunate for the fledgeling Delhi Sultanate, as indeed for the other powers which had inherited the Ghurid mantle in northern India, that when the Khwarazmians appeared in force in the Panjāb they came not as conquerors supported by the resources of an extensive Central Asian empire, but as fugitives. At the height of his power, the Khwārazmshāh clashed with his new and formidable neighbours, the Mongols led by Chinggis Khan, whose great westward campaign of 615–622/1218–1225 destroyed the Khwarazmian polity and devastated eastern Persia. Muḥammad died in misery on the coast of the Caspian Sea in 618/1221.[45] At an early stage in this crisis, it seems, India was being advocated as a refuge for the dynasty, possibly because its rulers were deemed inadequate to resist.[46] Some of the Khwārazmshāh's advisers urged him to make a stand at Ghazna and to retreat into India if this failed; their counsel was rejected.[47] In the event, it was the shah's son and effective successor, Jalāl al-Dīn, who entered India following a crushing defeat by Chinggis Khan on the banks of the Indus in Rajab 618/November 1221 and began a career of aggression in northern India that was to last for almost three years.

[42] Aziz Aḥmad, *Political history*, 99; see also 6, 84, 97, 118, 146, 149 (though at 13 he is prepared to consider the possibility that Muʿizz al-Dīn's dominions were misappropriated).

[43] Patricia Crone, *Roman, provincial and Islamic law* (Cambridge, 1987), 36–8. P. G. Forand, 'The relation of the slave and the client to the master or patron in medieval Islam', *International Journal of Middle East Studies* 2 (1971), 61.

[44] P. Jackson, 'Jalāl al-Dīn, the Mongols and the Khwarazmian conquest of the Panjāb and Sind', *Iran* 28 (1990), 48; the form ('Mingīrinī') adopted there for the prince's name must now be discarded on the basis of numismatic evidence (unpublished paper by Mr William Spengler).

[45] Barthold, *Turkestan*, 393–439, 446 ff. J. A. Boyle, 'Dynastic and political history of the Īl-khāns', in Boyle (ed.), *Cambridge history of Iran*, V, 303–17.

[46] See, for instance, the advice later given to Jalāl al-Dīn in India by one of his lieutenants, as reported by Nasawī, 91 (tr. Buniiatov, 136).

[47] *TJG*, II, 106 (tr. Boyle, 376).

Jūzjānī, regrettably, says very little about the Khwarazmian invasion of the Panjāb, perhaps because the episode reflected no credit on Iltutmish, who failed to collaborate with a fellow-Muslim against the pagan Mongols. Ibn al-Athīr's information on India, too, seems suddenly to dry up after the downfall of Yildiz. Jalāl al-Dīn's exile in the Panjāb and Sind is dismissed in a couple of lines; he is lost to sight until his emergence from the Makrān desert in 620/1223.[48] We are therefore fortunate that the prince's biographer Nasawī, writing in 639/1242, and the later writer Juwaynī, whose history of the Mongols dates from *c.* 658/1260, supply numerous (if sometimes conflicting) details which enable us tentatively to reconstruct events.[49] Jalāl al-Dīn was soon reinforced by fresh refugees from Persia and made war upon Qubacha, who was defeated near Uchch and obliged to become tributary to the Khwarazmians: his son, who had rebelled against him at Lahore, likewise yielded and became Jalāl al-Dīn's lieutenant there. Subsequently, when Qubacha refused to assist him against the pursuing Mongols, Jalāl al-Dīn ravaged the neighbourhood of Uchch before moving south into the lower Indus region. Here he received the submission of Sīwistān (now Sehvan), occupied Daybul, and despatched a plundering expedition to Nahrwāla in Gujarāt. At this juncture he heard reports of the eagerness with which the subjects of his surviving brother in Persia desired his return, and chose to make his way to western Persia by way of the Makrān desert late in 620/1223, in the hope of rebuilding his father's empire. He was eventually killed in Azerbaijan while in flight, again, from the Mongols in 628/1231.

The Delhi Sultan was inevitably drawn into the conflicts between his neighbours and the Khwarazmians. When Jalāl al-Dīn at some stage advanced to within a few days' journey of Delhi, requesting asylum and proposing an alliance against the Mongols, Iltutmish – not unnaturally reluctant to jeopardize his new-found autonomy by installing the Khwārazmshāh close at hand – had the envoy murdered and returned an evasive answer. Iltutmish then sent troops to aid Qubacha prior to the battle near Uchch, and subsequently moved against Jalāl al-Dīn in person: on this occasion the vanguards clashed but the two sovereigns exchanged friendly messages and withdrew. Whether Iltutmish, at least, was sincere is open to doubt. One of the reasons underlying the Khwārazmshāh's departure from India, according to Nasawī, was the news that a coalition had been formed against him by Iltutmish, Qubacha and a number of Hindu chiefs (*rāyāt wa-takākirāt*, 'rais and thakurs'), who had occupied the banks of the Jajnēr river (presumably the Sutlej) in order to cut off his retreat.

The Mongols who pursued the Khwārazmshāh into India do not appear

48 IA, XII, 276/425–6.

49 For what follows, see Jackson, 'Jalāl al-Dīn', which also discusses the sources, including the large anonymous fragment (hitherto little used), Bodleian ms. Th. Hyde 31. Brief biography of Jalāl al-Dīn in J. A. Boyle, 'Djalāl al-Dīn Kh^{w}ārazm-Shāh', *Enc.Isl.*^{2}.

to have encroached upon Iltutmish's territory.[50] Chinggis Khan, who briefly contemplated returning to Mongolia by way of a more direct route through the Himalayan foothills, sent envoys to the sultan asking his permission to move through his dominions. We are not told the fate of this embassy – simply that Chinggis Khan abandoned his intention in the face of unfavourable auguries. Juwaynī, however, alleges that he advanced several stages before turning back because there was no way through, and only then withdrew through Peshawar.[51] His general Dörbei sacked Nandana, currently held by one of Jalāl al-Dīn's lieutenants, and in the late winter of 621/1224 laid siege to Multān, where a spirited defence was conducted by Qubacha himself. But after an investment which according to Jūzjānī lasted for forty days (or three months if we accept the testimony of another source), he abandoned the attempt in view of the onset of the hot weather. As they retreated, the Mongols ravaged the regions of Multān and Lahore. Almost another two decades were to elapse before they entered the territory of the Delhi Sultanate.

Jalāl al-Dīn's departure from India did not mean the end of the Khwarazmian occupation. His lieutenant, Jahān-Pahlawān Özbeg-bei, was entrusted with the Khwārazmshāh's Indian conquests, while those parts of Ghūr and Ghazna which had not so far been ravaged by the Mongols were conferred upon Sayf al-Dīn Ḥasan Qarluq, surnamed Wafā Malik.[52] But as Mongol pressure was maintained by the forces left behind by Chinggis Khan, so the residue of Khwarazmian dominion west of the Indus began to crumble. Ghūr seems finally to have been overrun in 623/1226, and in that same year Qubacha was called upon to repulse a band of Khalaj tribesmen previously in the Khwārazmshāh's service – and presumably, therefore, under the nominal authority of Ḥasan Qarluq – who had entrenched themselves in lower Sind.[53]

Iltutmish's conquest of Muslim India

Qubacha's empire in the Indus valley had in all probability been gravely weakened already prior to this intrusion, for it had borne the brunt both of Jalāl al-Dīn's attacks and of the Mongol devastation. In the event, however, it was to receive the coup de grâce not from the north-west but from Delhi.

[50] Mongol operations in India in 618–621/1222–4 are surveyed in Jackson, 'Jalāl al-Dīn', 47–8, 50; see also Paul Ratchnevsky, *Genghis Khan: his life and legacy*, tr. T. N. Haining (Oxford, 1991), 134. For the general's name (Raverty's 'Tūrtī'), see J. A. Boyle, 'The Mongol commanders in Afghanistan and India according to the *Ṭabaqāt-i Nāṣirī* of Jūzjānī', *IS* 2 (1963), 238–9.

[51] *TN*, II, 126–7, 146 (tr. 1045–7, 1081–4). *TJG*, I, 109–10 (tr. Boyle, 137–9).

[52] Nasawī, 92 (tr. Buniiatov, 136). Sayfī, *Ta'rīkh-Nāma-yi Harāt* (*c*.1322), ed. M. Z. as-Siddíquí (Calcutta, 1944), 198, says that the rule of 'Malik Wafā' was later remembered in the Mastung region.

[53] *TN*, I, 420 (tr. 539–41).

Both Ḥasan-i Niẓāmī, speaking in the context of the Delhi forces' campaign against Lahore in 613/1216–17, and ʿAwfī, introducing Qubacha's overthrow twelve years later, allude to 'undertakings', 'promises' and 'treaties' of which Qubacha was unmindful.[54] This suggests that the alliance with Iltutmish had its price. It is possible that in order to secure assistance from Delhi against the Khwarazmians – and perhaps also against Yildiz earlier – Qubacha had either made some gesture in recognition of Iltutmish's sovereignty or had promised to surrender territory to Delhi, and that his failure to abide by his obligations served as a *casus belli*. There may well be some connection with a campaign by Iltutmish's forces to which Jūzjānī refers obscurely, some years before the final conquest of Sind and resulting, apparently, in the capture of Qubacha and the occupation of the district of Ganjrūt (or Wanjrūt) in the Multān province.[55]

Whatever the case, Qubacha had by 625/1228 finally lost the disputed regions of Tabarhindh, Kuhrām and Sarsatī, which are found at that date in the hands of officers appointed by his rival. Lahore had also been wrested from him, since Iltutmish's muqtaʿ there, Naṣīr al-Din Aytemür al-Bahā'ī, now presided over the surrender of Multān.[56] Another army appeared before Uchch, where it was soon joined by Iltutmish in person: the city capitulated at the end of Jumādā I 625/early in May 1228. Qubacha had meanwhile fled to the island stronghold of Bhakkar, pursued by a force under Iltutmish's wazir, Niẓām al-Mulk Junaydī, and on the night of 19 Jumādā II/26 May threw himself into the Indus to avoid being taken alive. From Daybul Iltutmish received the submission of its prince, Chanīsar, with the result that his sovereignty was acknowledged as far as the Arabian Sea.[57]

The conquest of Sind left Iltutmish free to move against Jalāl al-Dīn's

54 *Tāj*, fol. 251b. *JH*, I, 10, and BL ms. Or. 2676, fol. 232a.

55 *TN*, II, 4 (tr. 723), with the impossible year 628 – perhaps an error for 618 or, given the similarity of *thamān[in]* and *thalāth* in the Arabic script, for 623. The printed text has WNJRWT, and Raverty identified the place with Bijnoot (Vijnot), on the fringes of the Bikaner desert and well to the south of Uchch; but BL ms., fol. 197a, and IOL ms. 3745, fol. 268b, have KNJRWT. Ganjrūt is mentioned in the fourteenth century as a township (*qaṣaba*) in the Multān province: *IM*, 77, 93. For a brief allusion to Qubacha's defeat and capture (clearly, therefore, not the campaign of 625/1228), see *TN*, I, 452, and BL ms., fol. 180a. According to a doubtless anachronistic reference by Nasawī, 90 (tr. Buniiatov, 134), Sinān al-Dīn Chanīsar, the Sūmra ruler of Daybul, was already subordinate to Iltutmish at the time of its seizure by Jalāl al-Dīn's forces; for his name, see Hodivala, *Studies*, I, 214–15.

56 *TN*, I, 446, and II, 4, 7, 9 (tr. 613, 723, 728, 731). For Aytemür, cf. the spelling 'YTMR in *JH*, I, 13; also p. 27, n.16 above.

57 For the attack on Qubacha, see Habibullah, *Foundation*, 95–6. The year 624 given at one point by Jūzjānī for these events is an error for 625, as is clear from the context and from *JH*: see Hodivala, *Studies*, I, 205–6. *Tāj* (in ED, II, 242), which dates them in 624, is therefore wrong. Jūzjānī's month for the fall of Uchch varies between Jumādā I and Jumādā II, but I have adopted 27 Jumādā I/4 May 1228, since Iltutmish arrived outside the city on 1 Rabīʿ I and the siege lasted 2 months and 27 days: *TN*, I, 420, 446 (tr. 544, 612); *JH*, I, 10. ʿAwfī, *ibid.*, 10–22, gives a more detailed account of the campaign. For Chanīsar, see above, n.55.

legatees in the north-west. In 627/1229–30 the Delhi forces fell upon Özbeg-bei, who fled to his master in Iraq; whereupon Ḥasan Qarluq, among other local commanders, submitted to the sultan.[58] The territory controlled by these rulers is not known precisely. Numismatic evidence shows that Özbeg-bei ruled for a time in Binbān, where he was succeeded by Qarluq. His principality must also have included Nandana, Kūjāh (Gujrat), Sōdra and Siyālkōt, all lying in a tract where Jalāl al-Dīn is known to have operated and listed by Jūzjānī among Iltutmish's conquests.[59] Qarluq is later found in control of Ghazna, Binbān and Kurramān. Nasawī describes the Delhi Sultan, on the eve of his attack on Özbeg-bei, as master of the territory 'up to the neighbourhood of the gates of Kashmīr',[60] suggesting that his frontier already stood on the Jhēlam. Iltutmish's last, abortive campaign, from which he returned a dying man in 633/1235–6, was directed towards Binbān, and may well have been intended to dislodge Qarluq, who had recently submitted to the Mongols (see below, p. 105).[61]

While Iltutmish showed himself so attentive to his western frontier, he did not forget Bengal. Here the bloodthirsty reign of ʿAlī-yi Mardān, who had exhibited growing signs of insanity, ended with his murder in *c.* 609/1212–13. His successor, the more humane Ḥusām al-Dīn ʿIwaḍ, who assumed the style of Sultan Ghiyāth al-Dīn, lost Bihār to the Delhi forces.[62] Some confusion exists regarding the history of the Lakhnawtī polity during these years, since from 616/1219 onwards we encounter a sultan named Muʿizz al-Dīn ʿAlī-yi ʿIwaḍ, who was evidently Ghiyāth al-Dīn's son and who was ruling either jointly with his father or in succession to him.[63] He is unfortunately not mentioned by Jūzjānī, who did not enter India, however, until a few years later and hence is hardly a contemporary witness. According to that author, it was Ghiyāth al-Dīn who in 622/1225 fended off an invasion of Bengal by Iltutmish in person with an offer of tribute and the recognition of his suzerainty. But shortly afterwards he reneged upon the agreement and once more occupied Bihār. Iltutmish's eldest son and heir,

58 Nasawī, 92, 217 (tr. Buniiatov, 136, 267). For what follows, see Jackson, 'Jalāl al-Dīn', 51.

59 *TN*, I, 452, to be corrected from BL ms., fol. 180a (KWJRAT), and IOL ms., fol. 243a (KJRAT): the two mss. have respectively MWDWDH and MWDDH, clearly errors for SWDRH (cf. also Raverty's tr. 627). The Mongol occupation of Nandana had, of course, been shortlived.

60 Nasawī, 217, *ilā mā yalī darb Kashmīr* (tr. Buniiatov, 267).

61 *TN*, I, 449 (tr. 623); and cf. also I, 454–5 (tr. 631). On Ḥasan Qarluq's rule in Ghazna, Kurramān and Binbān, see *ibid.*, II, 162 (tr. 1128–9); I. H. Siddiqui, 'The Qarlūgh kingdom in north-western India during the thirteenth century', *IC* 54 (1980), 75–91.

62 *TN*, I, 434–5, 437–8 (tr. 578–80, 590–1).

63 A Sanskrit epigraph of Vikrama samvat 1277, Jyāstha ba. 15, Thursday (13 June 1219), from the Gayā district of Bihār, refers to a Sultan 'Mōjadīna': *ARIE* (1962–3), 24, 80 (no. 261). For an inscription of ʿAlī Shīr-i ʿIwaḍ dated 618/1221, see Z. A. Desai, 'An early thirteenth century inscription from West Bengal', *EIAPS* (1975), 6–12. That they refer to the same person is clear from coins of 620–1/1223–4 in the name of Muʿizz al-Dīn ʿAlī-yi ʿIwaḍ: *CCIM*, II, 145–6 (nos. 3, 5). Nicholas W. Lowick, 'The Horseman type of Bengal and the question of commemorative issues', *JNSI* 35 (1973), 205–8, correctly argued for the name ʿAlī here, though he wrongly assumed it represented ʿAlī-yi Mardān.

Nāṣir al-Dīn Maḥmūd, who had at one time governed Lahore, as we have seen, and who now held the iqtaʿ of Awadh, thereupon led an army into Bengal. Taking advantage of ʿIwaḍ's absence on a plundering campaign in Kāmrūp (Assam), he was able in 624/1227 to seize Lakhnawtī and then defeated and executed ʿIwaḍ on his return. Iltutmish despatched a chatr to his son, who acted as the sultan's viceroy for less than two years, dying in the first months of 626/the winter of 1228–9. Authority in the province was then usurped by Ikhtiyār al-Dīn Dawlat Shāh, also known as Bilge Malik, apparently a former officer of the Delhi Sultan, until Iltutmish invaded Bengal and overthrew him in 628/1230–1.[64] For the next twelve years, at least, those regions of Bengal in Muslim hands were to remain subject to Delhi.

With the reoccupation of Lakhnawtī, the Delhi Sultan became the only Muslim sovereign in India. His conquests enabled him to launch a new coinage, based on the pure silver *tanga*, which would in time replace the *dihlīwāls*, imitations of the billon coins formerly minted by Hindu rulers at Delhi.[65] Prior to this, moreover, he had achieved an objective by which the majority of Muslim rulers set great store: recognition from the ʿAbbasid Caliph at Baghdad. It is now accepted that Iltutmish was the only Indian Muslim ruler who received such recognition and that the titles borne by the Lakhnawtī rulers were assumed unilaterally: indeed, ʿIwaḍ's assumption of the style *Nāṣir Amīr al-Mu'minīn* ('Auxiliary of the Commander of the Faithful') may have been one incentive for Iltutmish to take the title himself.[66] Who initiated the negotiations between Delhi and Baghdad, and at what point, is uncertain; but such information as we have suggests that it may have been the caliph. We saw how al-Nāṣir endeavoured to incite the Ghurid Sultans against his enemy the Khwārazmshāh (p. 6); and two decades or so later Iltutmish, among others, might have seemed similarly worth cultivating as a possible rival on the Khwārazmshāh's southern flank.

For glimpses of the earliest diplomatic contacts with the 'king of India' we are indebted to Arabic chroniclers writing in the west. The caliph sent out as his ambassador in 617/1220–1 the shaykh Raḍī' al-Dīn Abu'l-Faḍā'il al-Ḥasan b. Muḥammad al-Ṣaghānī (d. 650/1252–3), who returned to Baghdad only in 624/1227, during the reign of al-Nāṣir's son al-Mustanṣir

64 On his coins he is called ʿAlā' al-Dunyā wa'l-Dīn Dawlat Shāh b. Mawdūd: *CMSD*, 21 (no. 53A). The Berlin ms. of *TN*, fol. 99b, confirms that Dawlat Shāh and Bilge Malik were identical. Fullest reference to the campaign of 628/1230–1 in *JH*, BL ms. Or. 2676, fol. 260. For events in Bengal, see Habibullah, *Foundation*, 97–100, who was, however, unaware of the evidence cited in the previous note.

65 Simon Digby, 'The currency system', in T. Raychaudhuri and I. Habib (eds.), *The Cambridge economic history of India*, I (Cambridge, 1982), 95–6; Deyell, *Living without silver*, 179–80, 199–203, 213–19.

66 A. H. Dani, 'Did Ghiyāth-al-Dīn ʿIwaḍ Khaljī of Bengal receive investiture from the Khalifah?', *JPHS* 3 (1955), 105–17; Roma Niyogi, 'A unique coin from Bengal and a review of ʿIwaḍ's career', *JNSI* 40 (1978–9), 42–52.

(623–640/1226–1242). The new caliph sent him back to Delhi, and it is this latter mission which is noticed by Jūzjānī, who in his brief survey of the ʿAbbasids refers to the despatch of a mandate (*ʿahd*) and a banner (*liwāʾ*) to Iltutmish in 625/1228, the very year of his own arrival at court, and says that he was present at the celebratory banquet. Elsewhere he gives a fuller description of the embassy, which arrived in Rabīʿ I 626/February 1229 and brought Iltutmish robes of honour and a diploma confirming his authority over all the territories he had conquered.[67] Al-Mustanṣir also bestowed on the sultan – we must presume – the titles *Yamīn Khalīfat Allāh* ('Right Hand of God's Deputy') and *Nāṣir Amīr al-Muʾminīn* under which he is exalted by a number of writers.[68] For ʿAwfī, he had become *Khalīfa-yi Amīr al-Muʾminīn* ('Deputy of the Commander of the Faithful').[69] The usurper Iltutmish had thus attained respectability as one of the family of orthodox Muslim princes whose rule enjoyed the highest possible sanction. That he was no more impervious to such honours than the Ghurids had been is clear from his assumption in 630/1233, following the capture of Gwāliyōr, of the quintuple *nawbat*, one of the attributes of full sovereign authority.[70]

Reasons for Iltutmish's triumph

Our survey of events has brought us to a point where the newly created Delhi Sultanate embraced a larger territory than at any time prior to the last decade of the thirteenth century. There was nothing inevitable about this process. Much of it was the result of fortuitous circumstances over which Iltutmish had no control. The Sultanate's survival was by no means guaranteed. Had it not been for the Mongols, Delhi, Sind and the Panjāb might have been swallowed up in the empire of the Khwārazmshāh Muḥammad. When he destroyed that empire, Chinggis Khan inadvertently ensured that Muslim India would go its own way. In establishing his own principality as the sole protagonist of Islam in the subcontinent, Iltutmish followed, perhaps, a deliberate policy. Allowing his neighbours to weaken one another and intervening – as he did on Qubacha's behalf against Jalāl al-Dīn – only when it was absolutely necessary, he was then able to eliminate these competitors one by one.

67 *TN*, I, 129 (section abridged in Raverty's tr.), 447, 454 (tr. 616, 629). *Tāj*, in ED, II, 243. *JH*, BL ms. Or. 4392, fol. 128a. For the role of Ṣaghānī, who is not named in the Indian sources, see al-Ṣafadī, *al-Wāfī bi'l-Wafayāt*, ed. H. Ritter *et al.* (Damascus, 1931–), XII, 241; *al-Ḥawādith al-Jāmiʿa* (early fourteenth century; wrongly attributed to Ibn al-Fuwaṭī), ed. Muṣṭafā Jawād (Baghdad, 1351/1932), 262.

68 *TN*, I, 440, 450 (tr. 597, 624). *Tāj*, fol. 217b. *JH*, I, 5. Jājarmī, preface to his tr. of Ghazālī's *Iḥyāʾ ʿUlūmi'l-Dīn*, BL ms. Or. 8194, fol. 3a (with *Muʿīn* for *Yamīn*). Anonymous tr. of Rāzī's *Sirr al-Makhtūma*, BN ms. Suppl. persan 384, fol. 2a.

69 *JH*, BL ms. Or. 2676, fols. 68a, 247b.

70 *TN*, I, 449 (tr. 620–1). Significantly, the Ghurid Sultan Ghiyāth al-Dīn Muḥammad b. Sām had likewise assumed the quintuple *nawbat* after the arrival of honorary robes from the caliph: *ibid.*, I, 361 (tr. 383). For the *nawbat*, see Hodivala, *Studies*, I, 216–17.

This does not, of course, tell us what enabled Iltutmish to defeat his various rivals. The answer can only be tentative, and must be based in large measure on developments on the Sultanate's western frontier, where the information at our disposal, if not plentiful, is at least fuller than that pertaining to Bengal. In 612/1215, if we are to believe Ibn al-Athīr, Qubacha had encountered Yildiz's invading army with 15,000 men; against Jalāl al-Dīn seven years later he mustered a force that was certainly no greater than 20,000 and may well have been half that size.[71] These numbers stand in sharp contrast with the (doubtless exaggerated) figure of 130,000 for the army which Iltutmish is said to have raised for his own campaign against the Khwarazmians.[72] Such statistics are notoriously hazardous guides to the size of medieval armies, and perhaps they are in the last analysis unusable. Yet we cannot discount the possibility that the Delhi ruler presided over a significantly larger military establishment than did his neighbour and rival, who had been obliged to disburse considerable quantities of treasure during the Mongol siege of Multān.[73] It is hardly coincidental that Iltutmish embarked on the reduction of Qubacha in the immediate wake of three highly successful campaigns: that of 622/1225 against ʿIwaḍ in Bengal, yielding the substantial sum of eighty *laks* (8,000,000) of silver (presumably *dirhams*) in tribute,[74] and the expeditions of 623–4/1226–7 which resulted in the capture of the Hindu fortresses of Ranthanbōr and Mandōr. The specie obtained by such victories would surely have enhanced Iltutmish's capacity to recruit more formidable armies.

Of the fact that a ready pool of military support lay to hand for the ruler whose resources enabled him to pay for it, there can be little doubt. We have seen how prior to this, in the era of Muʿizz al-Dīn, soldiers of fortune such as Muḥammad b. Bakhtiyār hired themselves out to the highest bidder and launched initiatives of their own. Although Fakhr-i Mudabbir undoubtedly exaggerates the enhancement in their material prosperity awaiting those who migrated to Muslim India,[75] it is likely that the region was coming to be seen as some sort of El Dorado. The irruption of the Mongols into the eastern Islamic lands after 617/1220 must have considerably increased the number of adventurers – both Turks and 'Tājīks' – eager for whatever enterprise was on offer. We may imagine a veritable reservoir of unattached warriors and officials in north-western India in the 1220s. Many of 'the chief men of Khurāsān, Ghūr and Ghazna' secured a refuge in the first instance at the court of Qubacha, according to Jūzjānī, who himself arrived at Uchch in 624/1227 and was made *qāḍī-yi lashgar* to Qubacha's

[71] IA, XII, 203/311, for the battle with Yildiz. Nasawī, 88 (tr. Buniiatov, 133), for the Khwarazmians, with 10,000; *TJG*, II, 146 (tr. Boyle, 414), has 20,000, but this perhaps includes the reinforcements sent by Iltutmish (above, p. 33).
[72] Nasawī, 90 (tr. Buniiatov, 134): 30,000 horse and 100,000 foot.
[73] *TN*, I, 420 (tr. 537–8). [74] *Ibid.*, I, 438, 445 (tr. 593, 610). [75] *SA*, 20.

son.[76] In the previous year the maliks of Ghūr had finally abandoned their homeland to the Mongols and fled to join Qubacha.[77] But others among these distinguished *condottieri* made for Delhi: they included one of the few surviving members of the Ghurid dynasty, Nāṣir al-Dīn Abū Bakr b. Sūrī, who became one of Iltutmish's maliks and died at Delhi in 620/1223.[78]

There were also not a few whose loyalties shifted. It was a time for highly volatile allegiances. In the course of Jalāl al-Dīn's negotiations with Iltutmish, two of his envoys, weary of the hardships they had been required to undergo, deserted their master and entered the service of the Delhi Sultan.[79] Qubacha in particular seems often to have been the victim of such transfers. Early in the confrontation with Jalāl al-Dīn, two important maliks – Nuṣrat al-Dīn Muḥammad b. Ḥusayn b. Kharmīl and Tāj al-Dīn Yinaltegin (the future ruler of Sīstān) – left him for the Khwarazmians.[80] What became of the maliks of Ghūr who flocked to Qubacha's court in 623/1226, we are not told; but Quṭb al-Dīn Ḥasan b. ʿAlī, who may have been one of their number,[81] is subsequently found at Iltutmish's court. Even Qubacha's wazir, ʿAyn al-Mulk Ḥusayn al-Ashʿarī, was within a short time appointed to a similar position at the court of Iltutmish's son Rukn al-Dīn Fīrūz, then muqtaʿ of Badā'ūn.[82]

It may well be that in time the Delhi Sultan appeared to offer better prospects to adventurers, whether military men or those of a more scholarly persuasion, than did his neighbours. Not the least attractive features of the Sultanate to immigrants would have been its geographical location, making possible lucrative raids into Hindu territory, like those on Ranthanbōr and Mandōr, which provided booty for the mercenary, and its need of experienced officials, which afforded employment for the savant. Jūzjānī doubtless made some such calculation when he quitted Uchch in Ṣafar 625/January 1228 to join the Delhi forces under Kezlik Khān outside the walls three months before the citadel surrendered, and took care to wait upon Iltutmish on the very day of his arrival with the

76 *TN*, I, 420 (tr. 541–2), with the month Jumādā I/May for his arrival, whereas at I, 446 (tr. 611–12), he gives Rajab/June-July; for his emigration from Ghūr, see also II, 184–5 (tr. 1203–4). On the distinguished immigrants from Khurāsān, see I, 419 (tr. 534).

77 *Ibid.*, I, 420 (tr. 539–41): a year and a half after the Mongol investment of Multān, i.e. early in 623/1226.

78 *Ibid.*, I, 340 (tr. 345); he is listed among Iltutmish's maliks at I, 451 (tr. 626). He belonged to the branch that ruled the petty principality of Mādīn.

79 Nasawī, 91 (tr. Buniiatov, 135).

80 Nuṣrat al-Dīn: *ibid.*, 88, 140, 141 (tr. Buniiatov, 132, 186, 188). Yinaltegin: *TN*, I, 284 (tr. 200); and for his subsequent career, C. E. Bosworth, *The history of the Saffarids of Sistan and the maliks of Nimruz (247/861 to 949/1542–3)* (Costa Mesa, California, 1994), 407–10.

81 *TN*, II, 135, 140–1 (tr. 1061, 1070–1): Quṭb al-Dīn set out for 'Hindūstān' in 620/1223 along with other maliks, though his companions were allegedly all slain by the Mongols en route. For the 'Ḥusayn' of the printed text, BL ms. reads 'Ḥasan' throughout (fols. 183a, 185b, 193a, 220a, 240).

82 *TN*, I, 454 (tr. 631).

main army soon afterwards.[83] ʿAwfī too seems to have been ready enough to abandon his benefactor Qubacha. A scholar who himself reached Delhi in 620/1223 speaks of the flight from the Mongols to Iltutmish's court of 'Muslims of Khurāsān, of Transoxiana (Mā warā' al-Nahr), of Ghūr, of Ghazna, nay all the Muslims of the east (*bal kāffa-yi musulmānān-i mashriq*)'.[84] In this context, Jūzjānī's encomium on the sultan – that he was ever generous in his gifts to landowners (*dahāqīn*) and strangers from great cities (*ghurabā-yi amṣār*), and that he made his capital a haven for those escaping from the Mongol deluge[85] – is not without significance. And his verdict is echoed by authors of the following century, notably ʿIṣāmī, who speaks of the arrival of 'sayyids from the Arab lands and 'ulama' from Bukhārā'.[86] Iltutmish is the only Delhi monarch, other than Muḥammad b. Tughluq in the fourteenth century, who is known to have sought deliberately to attract immigrant notables in this fashion. It is an intriguing possibility that he benefited from widespread desertions by many of those who had only recently obtained asylum in Sind and who judged that Qubacha was not the power most likely to guarantee their future security or, indeed, prosperity.

The immigrant nobility under Iltutmish

At the end of his chapter on Iltutmish, Jūzjānī furnishes a list of his nobles, including Ghūrīs, Turks and 'Tājīks'. The great majority are merely names to us; they are mentioned neither elsewhere in the *Ṭabaqāt-i Nāṣirī* nor in any other source. Some, however, are met with in the body of the chapter, and others, who were the sultan's own ghulams, are also accorded biographies in *ṭabaqa* 22: to these we shall return shortly. A few correspond to amirs specified by Ḥasan-i Niẓāmī as having supported Iltutmish in the fight against Ārām Shāh's party or having not long afterwards accompanied him on his Jālōr campaign: ʿIzz al-Dīn Bakhtiyār, commemorated in one of the very earliest epitaphs so far discovered in the Sultanate's territories; Naṣīr al-Dīn Mardān Shāh; and Iftikhār al-Dīn Muḥammad-i ʿUmar, described by Jūzjānī as the chief amir (*malik al-umarā'*) and commander at Kara.[87] We can even detect a certain continuity with the era of the Ghurid conquests. Rukn al-Dīn Ḥamza, named by both authors as one of

83 *Ibid.*, I, 447, and II, 3 (tr. 615, 722–3). For Kezlik Khān's title (Tu. *kezlik*, 'small knife'), see Clauson, *Etymological dictionary*, 760; *TMENP*, IV, 3–4 (no. 1714).

84 Jājarmī, BL ms. Or. 8194, fol. 3b. See also the Persian translation of Bīrūnī's *al-Ṣaydana fi'l-Ṭibb*, BL ms. Or. 5849, fol. 4a; Nazir Aḥmad, 'Bérúní's Kitáb-aṣ-Ṣaydana and its Persian translation', *Indo-Iranica* 14, part 3 (1961), 17.

85 *TN*, I, 440–1 (tr. 598–9).

86 *FS*, 114–15 (tr. 226–7). *TFS*, 27.

87 *Tāj*, fols. 221b, 229a. Jūzjānī's list of maliks is at *TN*, I, 452 (reading KWH for KRH, but cf. Raverty's tr., 627). For ʿIzz al-Dīn Bakhtiyār (d. 616/1219), see Iqtidar Husain Siddiqi, 'Historical information in the thirteenth century collections of Persian poems', *Studies in Islam* 19 (1982), 57–8.

Iltutmish's amirs, is possibly identical with the homonymous figure active in Muʿizz al-Dīn's service and employed on an embassy to Prthvīrāja III in 587/1191.[88] It is more certain that both ʿIzz al-Dīn ʿAlī, at one time muqtaʿ of Nāgawr, and Ḥusām al-Dīn Oghulbeg in Awadh had held office since Muʿizz al-Dīn's reign.[89]

What became of most of the old nobility is obscure. As we have seen, Quṭbī amīrs had supported Iltutmish at the outset, and Jūzjānī's list includes two amirs with the sobriquet 'Quṭbī', presumably former ghulams of Aybeg. But the Muʿizzī amirs had rallied to Ārām Shāh, which is why the Muʿizzīs mentioned by Fakhr-i Mudabbir as among Aybeg's entourage at Lahore in 602/1206 are lost to sight thereafter.[90] It is accordingly possible that Iltutmish was obliged to constitute in effect a new class of high-ranking officers. Immigrant notables would in time have furnished him with the means of doing so. Some were Turkish grandees of free status. Ḥasan-i Niẓāmī indicates that in meeting *Berki's attack Iltutmish benefited from the support of Sayf al-Dīn Fīrūz, who is to be identified with a cousin of Yinaltegin called by Jūzjānī Fīrūz-i Iltutmish and Fīrūz b. Sālār, and who was apparently a warlord originating from the Qangli confederacy in the steppes north of Khwārazm.[91] ʿAlā' al-Dīn Jānī, bombastically described by Jūzjānī as a 'prince of Turkistān', received Lakhnawtī as his iqtaʿ following Iltutmish's victorious campaign of 628/1230–1 and is subsequently found at Lahore.[92] The Ghūrī malik Quṭb al-Dīn Ḥasan became comptroller of Iltutmish's household (*wakīl-i dar*); and ʿIzz al-Dīn Muḥammad Sālārī, who was also probably a Ghūrī, served as *bārbeg* (i.e. *amīr-ḥājib*).[93] We have seen how bureaucrats as well as soldiers sought asylum in India from the Mongol onslaught, and among those in office at Iltutmish's death are men with *cognomina* from Khurāsān like Shafūrqānī and Ṭāyaqānī;[94] though whether they were first-generation immigrants is unknown. A similar

[88] Rukn al-Dīn does not appear in the list of maliks as given in Ḥabībī's text of *TN*, but cf. IOL ms., fol. 242b, and Raverty's tr., 626. *Tāj*, fols. 77b–78a, 229a; for the embassy to Prthvīrāja, see fol. 38a.

[89] For ʿAlī and Oghulbeg in Muʿizz al-Dīn's reign, see *TN*, I, 422–3 (tr. 549), and pp. 26–7 above. For ʿAlī among Iltutmish's maliks, *TN*, I, 452; and for Oghulbeg, *ibid.*, I, 451 note, and cf. BL ms., fol. 179a (tr. 627); also *JH*, BL ms. Or. 2676, fols. 263b-264a (Niẓámu'd-dín, *Introduction*, no. 1729). By 620/1223 Nāgawr was held by the otherwise unknown Karīm al-Dīn Ḥamza: *TN*, I, 284 (tr. 200; but BL ms., fol. 179b, reads Najīb al-Dīn).

[90] *SA*, 25, 73. They are the *sipahsālārs* Ḥusām al-Dawla wa'l-Dīn Aḥmad (-i ?) ʿAlī Shāh, Mubāriz al-Dawla wa'l-Dīn Toghriltegin ʿAlī (-yi ?) Ḥasan, and Asad al-Dawla wa'l-Dīn ʿAlī (-yi ?) Muḥammad Abu'l-Ḥasan. The last two are both entitled *ulugh* ('great') *dādbeg* (i.e. *amīr-i dād*).

[91] *Tāj*, fol. 221b. For Fīrūz, see also *TN*, I, 284, 299 (text reads 'Nīmrūz' in error), 452 (tr. 199, 235, 625). His father's sister was the wife of the Khwārazmshāh Il-Arslan and hence grandmother to the Ghurid Sultans' enemy ʿAlā' al-Dīn Muḥammad. Nasawī, 36 (tr. Buniiatov, 81), confirms the relationship. *TN*, I, 298 (tr. 235), gives a garbled account of this family.

[92] *Ibid.*, I, 448, 452, 455, and II, 9 (tr. 618, 626, 634, 731–2).

[93] *TFS*, 39. For Sālārī, see *TN*, I, 446 (tr. 613), and *JH*, I, 12; also Habib, 'Formation', 13.

[94] *TN*, I, 456, and II, 30 (with SRQANY in error; cf. tr. 635, 761).

obscurity shrouds the antecedents of Iltutmish's wazir, Mu'ayyad al-Mulk (later Niẓām al-Mulk) Qiwām al-Dawla wa'l-Dīn Muḥammad b. Fakhr al-Mulk Sharaf Abī Saʿd Junaydī, and the sultan's *ʿāriḍ*, ʿImād al-Mulk Sharaf al-Dawla wa'l-Dīn Abū Bakr, of whom we learn only that he was of illustrious lineage and was not a Turk.[95] But whatever their origins or talents, no Muslim ruler would have felt easy in relying exclusively on adherents of free status. Like Muʿizz al-Dīn, Iltutmish took care to build up a corps of Turkish slaves (Persian *bandagān*; sing. *banda*), known as the 'Shamsīs', whose loyalty was focused on him alone. Under his successors, they would come to play a more prominent role in the government of the Sultanate.

95 For the wazir's full name and style, see *JH*, BL ms. Or. 4392, fol. 128a (cf. also ms. Or. 2676, fol. 68a); Jājarmī, BL ms. Or. 8194, fol. 3a. Baranī later heard that Junaydī was of plebeian origin, the grandson of a weaver (*jūlāha*): *TFS*, 39. ʿImād al-Mulk: *JH*, BL ms. Or. 2676, fols. 263b-264a.

CHAPTER 3

Sultans and sources

Shams al-Dīn Iltutmish died on 20 Shaʿbān 633/29 April 1236. In contrast with Aybeg, he founded a dynasty, which ruled until Iltutmish's own slave Balaban,[1] hitherto viceroy (*nā'ib*) to Nāṣir al-Dīn Maḥmūd Shāh b. Iltutmish, usurped the throne in 664/1266 and reigned as Sultan Ghiyāth al-Dīn. Balaban's dynasty too was shortlived. After the brief reigns of his grandson Muʿizz al-Dīn Kayqubād and the latter's infant son Shams al-Dīn Kayūmarth, its life was snuffed out in 689/1290 by the Khalaj officer Jalāl al-Dīn Fīrūz, the first of the Khaljī Sultans. Designations like 'Slave kings' and 'Slave dynasty', traditionally applied to the thirteenth-century Delhi Sultans, are misnomers. Only Iltutmish and Balaban were ghulams; the majority of the rulers, their respective descendants, had at no time been slaves. In this book, therefore, the two dynasties will be termed 'Shamsids' and 'Ghiyathids' in the interests of greater accuracy.

Jūzjānī and the Shamsids

The historian of the thirteenth-century Delhi Sultanate is not embarrassed by a wealth of literary sources. With the exception of the accounts of the Khwarazmian and Mongol operations in India given by Juwaynī and Nasawī, no external source has survived from the period between Ibn al-Athīr and the end of the thirteenth century which refers to contemporary events in the subcontinent. One reason may well be the lack of contact with the Caliphate. That the reigns of Iltutmish's first two successors were noticed in the lost work of the Baghdad historian Ibn al-Sāʿī (d. 674/1276), we learn from a citation by a mid-fourteenth-century chronicler writing in Mamlūk Syria.[2] Ibn al-Sāʿī had presumably derived his information from the caliphal envoy Ṣaghānī, who left India for Baghdad in 637/1239 after a

[1] For *balaban*, 'sparrow-hawk', see Sauvaget, 'Noms et surnoms', no. 61.

[2] (al-Mufaḍḍal) Ibn Abi'l-Faḍā'il (*c.* 1350), *al-Nahj al-Sadīd*, partial edn and tr. Samira Kortantamer, *Ägypten und Syrien zwischen 1317 und 1341*, IU 23 (Freiburg i. Br., 1973), Ar. text 28–9 (German tr. 107). There is a virtually identical passage in the fourteenth-century Baghdad chronicle *al-Ḥawādith al-Jāmiʿa*, 104. On Ibn al-Sāʿī, see above, p. 18, n.56.

stay of eleven years.[3] Whether the last ʿAbbasid Caliphs exchanged embassies with Iltutmish's successors, we are not told. The Delhi monarchs continued to employ the style 'Auxiliary of the Commander of the Faithful' (*Nāṣir Amīr al-Mu'minīn*) on their coins down to the extinction of the Baghdad Caliphate by the Mongols in 656/1258 and even beyond.[4] But it is unlikely that this rested on official conferment: had his patron Nāṣir al-Dīn Maḥmūd Shāh, at least, received confirmation of his title from Baghdad, Jūzjānī would assuredly have told us. It is a measure of the Sultanate's isolation during this period that chroniclers in Mamlūk Egypt, who periodically listed contemporary foreign rulers at the head of an annal, named the Delhi Sultan correctly only once (in 662/1264) in the course of the period from 635/1237 onwards.[5] Not until 700/1300–1, after the invasion of Gujarāt by the forces of ʿAlā' al-Dīn Khaljī had opened up a new channel of communication with the Mamlūk empire, did its chroniclers again include the sultan's name at regular intervals in lists of contemporary sovereigns.[6]

Although a number of references to major figures and historical events can be gleaned from the works of Persian poets such as Sirājī and ʿAmīd Sunnāmī, who graced the sultan's court or those of his Muslim neighbours in India around the middle of the century,[7] for the era of Iltutmish's progeny down to 658/1260 we are overwhelmingly dependent on a single narrative source, the final three sections of Jūzjānī's *Ṭabaqāt-i Nāṣirī*. Of all the historians of the Sultanate, Jūzjānī had the best vantage-point from which to observe events, since he occupied on three occasions one of the highest civil offices, that of grand qadi (*qāḍī al-quḍḍāt*) of the empire. Yet though comparatively rich in data for this period, the *Ṭabaqāt* is not an easy work to use. Some events are recounted in such opaque terms that their significance is almost completely lost. The arrangement of the material is also extraordinarily confused: the same episode may be described twice at different points – both under the relevant reign in tabaqa 21 and in one or more of the biographies of Shamsī slaves that make up tabaqa 22 – but with varying and indeed conflicting details. It is as if the chronicler's aim was to camouflage rather than to illuminate events. This is all the more regrettable given the absence of any alternative sources. Jūzjānī's work was quarried by

[3] al-Ṣafadī, *Wāfī*, XII, 241.

[4] The caliph's name was first omitted on the coins of the Khaljī Sultan Rukn al-Dīn Ibrāhīm (695/1296): Edward Thomas, *Chronicles of the Pathan kings of Delhi* (Delhi, 1871), 255.

[5] Ibn al-Dawādārī, VIII, 102. Ibn Abi'l-Faḍā'il, *al-Nahj al-Sadīd*, partial edn and tr. E. Blochet, 'Moufazzal Ibn Abil-Fazaïl. Histoire des Sultans Mamlouks', *Patrologia Orientalis* 12–20 (1919–29), 123.

[6] Al-Yūnīnī (d. 726/1326), *al-Dhayl ʿalā' Mir'āti'l-Zamān*, TSM ms. III Ahmet 2907/e.3, fols. 196a (700; with incorrect name), 210b (701); III Ahmet 2907/e.4, fols. 25b, 36a, 43b, 157b, 179a, 212b (with varying degrees of inaccuracy). Ibn Abi'l-Faḍā'il, ed. Blochet, 534–5, 556, also begins naming the Delhi Sultan (incorrectly) in 700.

[7] Siddiqi, 'Historical information'. *TFS*, 113, mentions Khwāja Shams-i Muʿīn, who wrote 'volumes' (*mujalladāt*) in praise of Quṭb al-Dīn Ḥasan Ghūrī, but his work has not survived.

all the later authors who cover these years, and it is only rarely that one of them – ʿIṣāmī, for instance, or the fifteenth-century chronicler Sirhindī – supplies any additional information, its provenance and reliability alike far from certain.

This tendency towards obfuscation is illustrated by Jūzjānī's treatment of the succession to Iltutmish. The sultan's eldest son, Nāṣir al-Dīn Maḥmūd Shāh, who died in Lakhnawtī in 626/1229, had been widely expected to succeed him. Following the Gwāliyōr expedition in 630/1233, Rukn al-Dīn Fīrūz Shāh, as the next son, had been appointed muqtaʿ of Lahore, a position once occupied by Nāṣir al-Dīn Maḥmūd. Fīrūz Shāh accompanied Iltutmish back to Delhi not long before the sultan's death, as if he was being groomed for the throne, and Jūzjānī confirms that the eyes of the people were on the prince.[8] A work composed in Iltutmish's last years appears to corroborate this, since it is dedicated to the sultan and Fīrūz Shāh jointly, as if the latter were heir-apparent.[9] Fīrūz Shāh duly ascended the throne within a few days of his father's death. But Jūzjānī at one point alleges that in the wake of the Gwāliyōr expedition Iltutmish had marked out for the succession his eldest daughter Raḍiyya, who may thus have been his firstborn child and whose mother was his chief wife, and had caused a diploma to be drawn up in her favour. When certain officials objected, he allegedly predicted that none of his sons would be found fit to rule.[10] It is noteworthy, however, that Jūzjānī was at Gwāliyōr at this time and did not return to Delhi until 635/1238 (i.e. during Raḍiyya's reign):[11] he could not have been present, and he does not in fact claim to have seen the diploma. In these circumstances, the story may well be apocryphal and have been circulated by those who enthroned her: according to the fourteenth-century Moroccan visitor Ibn Baṭṭūṭa, her tomb had become an object of pilgrimage,[12] and it is noteworthy that, as we shall see (pp. 69–70), Balaban himself was indebted to her for his first promotion to office. Subsequently, in view of its disparagement of Iltutmish's sons (including, of course, the reigning sultan Nāṣir al-Dīn Maḥmūd Shāh),[13] the tale could have acquired a new significance at the time Jūzjānī was writing, when the displacement of the Shamsid dynasty was perhaps already on the horizon.

Jūzjānī's own views of Iltutmish's first four successors can be gleaned from the *Ṭabaqāt*. Fīrūz Shāh (633–634/1236) was a pleasure-loving youth who left the reins of government to his mother, the energetic and vindictive Shāh Terken. His brief reign was dominated by a revolt on the part of a

[8] *TN*, I, 454–5 (tr. 630, 631).

[9] Anonymous, tr. of Rāzī's *Sirr al-Makhtūma*, BN ms. Suppl. persan 384, fol. 2a.

[10] *TN*, I, 458 (tr. 638–9). Nizami (in HN, 230–1) believes that Iltutmish originally designated Raḍiyya, but then changed his mind and groomed Fīrūz Shāh instead.

[11] *TN*, I, 448–9, 460 (tr. 620, 643–4).

[12] IB, III, 169 (tr. Gibb, 632).

[13] As Nizami points out, in HN, 230–1 n.84; cf. also his *On history and historians*, 84. It is unfortunate that elsewhere (HN, 253, 256) Nizami's insight is impaired by his acceptance of ʿIṣāmī's testimony that Maḥmūd Shāh was not Iltutmish's son but his grandson.

group among Iltutmish's senior amirs, including the wazir Junaydī, who may have supported Fīrūz Shāh's brother Ghiyāth al-Dīn Muḥammad as a candidate for the throne.[14] The rebellion was eventually put down by Raḍiyya, who had been enthroned in his place. We are clearly intended to draw a contrast both with Fīrūz Shāh's elder brother, the 'wise and prudent' (*farzāna-u ʿāqil-u bikhrad*) Nāṣir al-Dīn Maḥmūd Shāh, whose premature death can be seen as a heavy blow to the Sultanate,[15] and with his successor. Raḍiyya (634–7/1236–1240) is credited with all the attributes of a successful ruler except one, namely that she was not a man; she is the only Shamsid sultan whom Jūzjānī describes as a war leader (*lashgarkash*).[16] Tradition makes much of Raḍiyya's adoption of masculine garb and her public appearances riding on an elephant.[17] But whatever the 'ulama' thought of this, it is clear that Raḍiyya's backers had intended her to be a figurehead and that her offence lay in her growing self-assertiveness. Initially her coinage, on which her father's name was associated with her own, had testified to her insecurity; but in *c.* 635/1237–8 Iltutmish's name was dropped.[18] Deposed in favour of her brother Bahrām Shāh, she was imprisoned in Tabarhindh and killed in 638/1240 in a vain bid to recover the throne.

Of Muʿizz al-Dīn Bahrām Shāh (637–9/1240–2) we are told that he was a courageous sovereign who had a penchant, however, for shedding blood.[19] He was overthrown when many of his commanders mutinied and stormed Delhi. Bahrām Shāh had become highly unpopular with the 'ulama', one of whose number he had executed and who participated in an abortive conspiracy to dethrone him; the *shaykh al-islām*, whom he sent out to negotiate with the rebel amirs, went over to the enemy.[20] In these circumstances, Jūzjānī's partiality for the sultan is difficult to understand; but the reason may be nothing more complex than that he owed to Bahrām Shāh his first appointment as grand qadi.[21] The events culminating in Bahrām Shāh's overthrow appear to have sickened him, since he resigned his office and left Delhi for Lakhnawtī, where he remained for over two years. He was thus absent during the early years of Fīrūz Shāh's son ʿAlāʾ al-Dīn Masʿūd Shāh (639–44/1242–6), who, we are blandly assured, was generous, right-thinking and endowed with every laudable quality. But the new sultan in turn fell under evil influences and took to executing his maliks and amirs,[22] so that his uncle, Iltutmish's youngest son Nāṣir al-Dīn Maḥmūd Shāh, was secretly invited to supplant him.

Of the various changes of sovereign noticed in the *Ṭabaqāt*, this particular

[14] Siddiqi, 'Historical information', 56–7. [15] *TN*, I, 453, 454 (tr. 628, 630).
[16] *Ibid.*, I, 457 (tr. 637–8). [17] *Ibid.*, I, 460 (tr. 643). IB, III, 167 (tr. Gibb, 631).
[18] *CMSD*, 40 (nos 161, 161A): apparently coins struck in Lakhnawtī, however, bore Raḍiyya's name alone throughout, *ibid.*, 41 (nos 161B-D).
[19] *TN*, I, 462 (tr. 649). [20] *Ibid.*, I, 464, 466, 467 (tr. 652, 657, 658–9).
[21] *Ibid.*, I, 466 (tr. 657–8). [22] *Ibid.*, I, 468, 471 (tr. 660, 668–9).

coup is the most obscure – not surprisingly, perhaps, since the monarch who now ascended the throne is the one to whom Jūzjānī dedicates his history. Maḥmūd Shāh (644–664/1246–1266) is the most shadowy of all the thirteenth-century sultans.[23] The era appears to be dominated by Jūzjānī's patron, Bahā' al-Dīn Balaban-i Khwurd ('the Lesser'), entitled Ulugh Khān, the future sultan. Balaban, whose daughter the sultan married and who acted as viceroy (na'ib), with a brief interval of about one year, from 647/1249 until Maḥmūd Shāh's death, seems to play Earl Godwin to Maḥmūd Shāh's Edward the Confessor. Jūzjānī says that the sultan possessed 'the qualities of saints and the characteristics of prophets' (*awṣāf-i awliyā' wa-akhlāq-i anbiyā'*), and includes among his many virtues piety, faith, asceticism and continence (*taqwā-u diyānat-u zahādat-u ṣiyānat*).[24] Professor Nizami has suggested that Jūzjānī constructed this picture in order to justify Balaban's dominance.[25] Maḥmūd Shāh's image was undoubtedly persistent. Tales circulated in the following century that he had found an outlet for both his energies and his piety in calligraphy: he copied Qur'āns and purchased his food with the proceeds.[26] His austere lifestyle even attracts comment from a later chronicler writing outside India.[27] It is accordingly difficult to avoid the impression of a monarch who was somewhat detached from his own court. Factions jostle for power at the centre and for the most desirable iqtaʿs; leading grandees are ruthlessly cut down or sent into exile in the provinces; behind a façade of military expeditions and conspiratorial intrigues the figure of Balaban, as the sultan's deputy, is never far away. But what Nāṣir al-Dīn Maḥmūd Shāh thought of all this – whether, for instance, he welcomed or deplored either Balaban's fall from power in 651/1253 or his reinstatement in the following year – we cannot discern.

Jūzjānī wrote only a few years prior to Balaban's accession. It is Balaban who receives by far the longest biography of the twenty-five Shamsī ghulams, and Jūzjānī's expressions of gratitude to him for gifts and pensions recur frequently in the book.[28] Even if we accept the tradition attributed to Balaban, and found in the hagiographical *Sarūr al Ṣudūr*, that Jūzjānī the qadi did not fear him,[29] Jūzjānī the chronicler seems, nevertheless, to have felt inhibited from revealing circumstances which cast his benefactor in a poor light. Nor is he able or willing to do full justice to Balaban's enemies: although Küshlü Khān ('Izz al-Dīn Balaban) is the subject of a biography in tabaqa 22 and is praised for his favour towards the 'ulama' and ascetics,[30]

[23] For a survey of the reign, see Mohibbul Ḥasan, 'Maḥmūd I, Nāṣir al-Dīn', *Enc.Isl.*².
[24] *TN*, I, 477 (tr. 674). [25] Nizami, *On history and historians*, 82–3.
[26] *TFS*, 26. *FS*, 156 (tr. 280–2). IB, III, 169 (tr. Gibb, 632). *DR*, 50, describes Maḥmūd Shāh as 'immersed in the affairs of God'.
[27] Ibn Abi'l-Faḍā'il, ed. Kortantamer, Ar. text 29 (German tr. 107).
[28] *TN*, I, 481, and II, 2, 52–3, 61, 62, 69 (tr. 681, 720, 808, 821–2, 823, 835).
[29] Cited in Nizami, *On history and historians*, 93. [30] *TN*, II, 36 (tr. 775–6).

the na'ib's other great rival, Qutlugh Khān, is accorded no such distinction and is referred to only in passing. At this time, moreover, the proximity of the pagan Mongols both threatened the integrity of the Sultanate and afforded an incentive to refractory grandees to defy the Delhi government. Balaban was restored to power in 652/1254 as a result of manoeuvres in which certain of his confederates were in league with the Mongols. But Jūzjānī's own account is noticeably coy on the subject, and were it not for the details on India furnished by authors, like Waṣṣāf and Rashīd al-Dīn, writing in the dominions of the Mongol Ilkhan in Persia, we should have little idea of the complexity of these events.

Sources after 658/1260

After 658/1260 Jūzjānī's voice falls silent, and we enter upon an era for which genuinely primary source material is extremely meagre. To write a connected account of the reigns of Balaban (664–85/1266–87), of his grandson Muʿizz al-Dīn Kayqubād (685–9/1287–90) or of Jalāl al-Dīn Fīrūz Shāh Khaljī (689–95/1290–6) is even more difficult than for the fourteenth-century sultans, since there are no contemporary narrative sources.[31] In large measure we are dependent either on authors who cover a considerable period but who wrote in the middle of the fourteenth century, or on those who composed shorter works to commemorate specific events. The exception is a historical tradition that was current in Persia by the end of the century. This, the earliest survey of the period down to ʿAlā' al-Dīn Khaljī's reign which has survived, is found in the brief history of the Sultanate which Waṣṣāf inserted in his *Tajziyat al-Amṣār* (designed as a sequel to Juwaynī's work) in or just before 702/1303 and presented to the Ilkhan Ghazan. This part of Waṣṣāf's work was copied within the next year or so into the Indian section of the great historical encyclopaedia, *Jāmiʿ al-Tawārīkh*, of the Ilkhanid wazir Rashīd al-Dīn Faḍl-Allāh al-Hamadānī.[32] Rashīd al-Dīn added the odd detail of his own; though his statement that Uchch and Multān are governed by the sultan's son indicates that some of his information dated from the reign of Jalāl al-Dīn Khaljī or perhaps even that of Balaban.[33]

It was under Balaban that the celebrated poet Yamīn al-Dīn Abu'l-Ḥasan, better known as Amīr Khusraw Dihlawī (b. 651/1253; d. 725/1325),

[31] For these reigns, see HN, 277–325; Habibullah, *Foundation*, chaps. 7–8; K. S. Lal, *History of the Khaljis A.D. 1290–1320*, 3rd edn (Delhi, 1980), chap. 2.

[32] For the date at which this section of his work was presented to the Ilkhan, see Waṣṣāf, *Tajziyat al-Amṣār wa-Tazjiyat al-Aʿṣār*, lithograph edn (Bombay, 1269/1853), 405. Rashīd al-Dīn's Indian chapters were composed over the years 702–3/1302–4: see *JT*, ed. Karl Jahn, *Die Indiengeschichte des Rašīd ad-Dīn* (Vienna, 1980), introduction, 9.

[33] *Ibid.*, Pers. text Taf. 13, Ar. text Taf. 51 (German tr. 36). Rashīd al-Dīn also states that Bengal is under the rule of a cousin of the Delhi Sultan who has repudiated his authority: Pers. text Taf. 15–16, Ar. text Taf. 52 (tr. 39).

who was the son of one of Iltutmish's ghulam troopers, began work on his first *dīwāns*, *Tuḥfat al-Ṣighār* (*c.* 671/1272–3) and *Wasaṭ al-Ḥayāt* (although this was not completed perhaps until *c.* 690/1291). These and his third *dīwān*, *Ghurrat al-Kamāl* (693/1294) occasionally allude to contemporary events, and the preface (*dībācha*) to the last-named work contains a valuable autobiographical sketch. During the reigns of Kayqubād and Jalāl al-Dīn Khaljī, Khusraw composed his earliest epic narrative poems (*mathnawīs*), respectively *Qirān al-Saʿdayn*, centred on the reconciliation between Kayqubād and his father Bughra Khān in 686/1287, and *Miftāḥ al-Futūḥ*, commemorating the victories of Jalāl al-Dīn in 690/1291. Khusraw's principal defect – excessive adulation of the reigning sultan – is amply illustrated in the opening of his one prose work, the *Ta'rīkh-i ʿAlā'ī* or *Khazā'in al-Futūḥ* (711/1311–12), where a bland account of the accession of Jalāl al-Dīn's nephew ʿAlā' al-Dīn Khaljī in 695/1296 omits all mention of the old sultan's murder. In the short but occasionally useful sketch of the Sultanate's history from Iltutmish onwards, with which he prefaces his *Diwal Rānī* or *ʿAshīqa* (centred on the love between ʿAlā' al-Dīn's son Khiḍr Khān and a Hindu princess), he could afford to be more forthright, since by the time he completed the poem, in 720/1320, ʿAlā' al-Dīn and his sons were all dead.[34]

These works apart, we are thrown back on the *Ta'rīkh-i Fīrūz-Shāhī* of Ḍiyā'-yi Baranī[35] (completed in 758/1357) and the epic *Futūḥ al-Salāṭīn* of ʿIṣāmī (750/1349), together with the baldly annalistic *Ta'rīkh-i Mubārak-Shāhī* of Yaḥyā b. Aḥmad Sirhindī, who wrote as late as 838/1434. The sources available to ʿIṣāmī and Sirhindī are unknown; the latter may possibly have used the now lost continuation (*mulḥaqāt*) of the *Ṭabaqāt-i Nāṣirī*, attributed by the seventeenth-century compilator Firishta to ʿAyn al-Dīn Bījāpūrī (d. 795/1393), who like ʿIṣāmī was a subject of the breakaway Deccan Sultanate.[36] About Baranī's sources we are better informed. He claims for the period prior to Jalāl al-Dīn Khaljī's accession that he is relying on hearsay from his father and uncle, who were officers in the service of the first two Khaljī sovereigns, and his maternal grandfather, Ḥusām al-Dīn, who had been comptroller of the household (*wakīl-i dar*) of Balaban's *bārbeg* (*amīr-ḥājib*) and whom that sultan subsequently appointed as governor (*shiḥna*) of Lakhnawtī.[37] Sometimes he attributes his informa-

[34] On these works, see M. Wahid Mirza, *The life and works of Amir Khusrau* (Calcutta, 1935).

[35] He is called Ḍiyā' al-Dīn Baranī by later authors: Irfan Habib, 'Baranī's theory of the history of the Delhi Sultanate', *IHR* 7 (1980–1), 99 n.1; Muḥammad Bihāmadkhānī, *Ta'rīkh-i Muḥammadī* (fifteenth century), BL ms. Or. 137, fol. 409b.

[36] Firishta, *Gulshan-i Ibrāhīmī*, lithograph edn (Bombay, 1247/1831–2, 2 vols.), I, 5, 131, 165. On Bījāpūrī, see A. T. M. ᶜAbd al-Jabbār, *Mahbūb dhi'l-Manan Tadhkhira Awliyā' Dakkān* (Hyderabad, Deccan, 1332/1914), 538–41, who claimed to have possessed a ms. of the *Mulḥaqāt* which was subsequently lost.

[37] Ḥusām al-Dīn: *TFS*, 32, 41, 61, 119; and see also 87. Baranī's father and uncle: *ibid.*, 25, 39, 60, 127.

tion to Amīr Khusraw and to the latter's friend and fellow-poet Amīr Ḥasan Dihlawī, with both of whom he claims to have been on close terms.[38] Occasionally he also cites other informants, including otherwise unknown notables who had served Balaban.[39] But the assertion of this seventy-four-year-old author that from the reign of Jalāl al-Dīn Khaljī onwards he is reliant on what he himself had witnessed (he would have been six at Jalāl al-Dīn's accession and twelve when the sultan died) hardly inspires confidence.[40] He possibly drew some of his information from the boon-companions (*nudamā'*) of Jalāl al-Dīn, including Amīr Arslan *Kalāhī, whom he describes as expert in history and in the practices of kings (*ādāb-i mulūk*);[41] but this is by no means certain. In the circumstances, it is reassuring that Baranī and ʿIṣāmī, who wrote independently of each other, frequently agree in their outline of events, so that they may at least have drawn on a common folk memory. Shades of similar traditions also appear in the brief history of Delhi which Ibn Baṭṭūṭa incorporated in his travelogue.

If Jūzjānī has a tendency to bemuse the reader through a wealth of sometimes contradictory detail, the problems attached to Baranī's work are of a different order. Although the *Ta'rīkh-i Fīrūz-Shāhī* was intended as a sequel to Jūzjānī's *Ṭabaqāt*,[42] it is in some respects inferior to it, containing as it does relatively few dates (and some of those inaccurate) and at times describing events in a vague and impressionistic fashion. The author himself calls his work an epitome (*ījāz-u ikhtiṣār*) and denies aiming at completeness.[43] On the other hand, he attempts what none of our other sources remotely approaches, namely an explanation of events and policies, which in itself has raised acute problems of interpretation.[44]

With regard to Balaban's reign, for example, the reader is struck by a laudable attention to analysis and characterization. The former ghulam of Iltutmish who now supplanted his master's dynasty is portrayed by Baranī as a grim ruler who was determined to be more than merely *primus inter pares*.[45] He consciously sought to distance the sovereign behind a screen of increased pomp and ceremony, employed a network of spies and informers to monitor the activities of his amirs, and destroyed a number of his former colleagues among the aristocracy. This stickler for etiquette would not even allow his private attendants to see him without his jacket (*yaktā*).[46] Himself a parvenu, Balaban is said to have refused to promote men of low origins

38 *Ibid.*, 67, 68, 113, 183, 360.

39 Khwāja Tāj al-Dīn Makrānī: *ibid.*, 36. Khwāja Dhakī, a nephew of Balaban's wazir Baṣrī: *ibid.*, 114. Qadi Sharaf al-Dīn *Barmās (?): *ibid.*, 168 (printed text has SRPA'YN, but cf. BL ms., fol. 90b).

40 *Ibid.*, 175. For Baranī's age when writing, see *ibid.*, 573.

41 *Ibid.*, 199. 42 *Ibid.*, 20–1. 43 *Ibid.*, 361.

44 See, for instance, P. Hardy, *Historians of medieval India* (London, 1960), chap. 2; Harbans Mukhia, *Historians and historiography during the reign of Akbar* (New Delhi, 1976), 3–5, 10–11, 19–26; I. Habib, 'Baranī's theory'.

45 *TFS*, 30, 34–5. 46 *Ibid.*, 33, 34–5, 40.

and constantly to have stressed the need to restrict the ranks of the aristocracy to those of noble birth. The impression of an intimate portrait that is all too seldom found in medieval chronicles is reinforced by a number of speeches reportedly made by the sultan in conversation with his maliks or his sons. We might feel ourselves to be holding the keys to a veritable treasure-house of Balaban's own policies and political theory, and this is reflected in modern historiography. Indeed, Balaban has been hailed as 'perhaps the only sultan of Delhi who is reported to have discussed at length his views about kingship'.[47] There are grounds, however, for approaching such reported speech with considerable reserve. Dr Peter Hardy has demonstrated that the views expressed in these sections are those of Baranī himself and are to be found also, but more conspicuously, in his *Fatāwā-yi Jahāndārī* (written some time in the 1350s), a handbook of advice for sultans set squarely in the Persian *Fürstenspiegel* tradition.[48]

The Ghiyathid era

The circumstances surrounding Nāṣir al-Dīn Maḥmūd Shāh's fate in 664/1266[49] are especially problematic. The earliest report that Balaban murdered Maḥmūd Shāh occurs, in fact, in Waṣṣāf's history of India; Ibn Baṭṭūṭa heard a similar story three or four decades later, and it is found also in 'Iṣāmī's *Futūḥ al-Salāṭīn*.[50] On the other hand, Baranī makes no reference to foul play, and Sirhindī expressly claims that Maḥmūd Shāh died a natural death.[51] It may well be, therefore, that Balaban has been unjustly maligned; although it must be said that none of these sources – whether or not it charges Balaban with regicide – tells us what became of the sons Maḥmūd Shāh is known to have fathered. The prince whose birth to Balaban's daughter in 657/1259 is greeted in such effusive terms by Jūzjānī would surely have been regarded as the future sultan.[52] It is possible that the na'ib

[47] Nizami, *Some aspects*, 280. For similar views, see Sir Wolseley Haig, in *The Cambridge history of India*, III, *Turks and Afghans* (Cambridge, 1928), 74–5; Habibullah, *Foundation*, 162–3, 179; Aziz Aḥmad, *Political history*, 259–63, 267–71.

[48] P. Hardy, 'The *oratio recta* of Baranī's *Ta'rīkh-i Fīrūz Shāhī* – fact or fiction?', *BSOAS* 20 (1957), 315–21.

[49] The date 11 Jumādā I 664/18 February 1266 is given in *TMS*, 39, and supported by Maḥmūd Shāh's coins, which go down to 664. But it should be noted that Sirhindī gives the duration of the reign as 19 years, 3 months and 16 days: this would place the sultan's death in 663/1265. In any event, the years 662 and 665 supplied respectively by *TFS*, 25, and by *FS*, 163, 164 (tr. 290, 291), are wrong.

[50] Waṣṣāf, 310; *JT*, ed. Jahn, *Indiengeschichte*, Pers. text Taf. 22, Ar. text Taf. 57 (German tr. 48). *FS*, 163 (tr. 289–90). IB, III, 170, 174 (tr. Gibb, 632, 635).

[51] *TMS*, 39. For two opposing views on Maḥmūd Shāh's death, see Habibullah, *Foundation*, 161, who argues that murder is improbable, given Balaban's position and his previous relations with the sultan; and K. A. Nizami, 'Balaban the regicide', in his *Studies in medieval Indian history* (Aligarh, 1956), 48–62, and in HN, 274–5.

[52] *TN*, I, 496 (tr. 714). As he is not named, we do not know which of the four sons listed at I, 475 (tr. 672), was Balaban's grandson. Raverty's insertion of 'the late' after each name is not justified on the evidence of the best mss.

was satisfied with the prospect of his grandson's succession but that the boy died in infancy, precipitating a crisis which was resolved by the elimination of Maḥmūd Shāh and his issue by other unions. We can only speculate.

In contrast with Iltutmish, Balaban was blest with two able adult sons: Muḥammad, who held Sind until his untimely death in battle with the Mongols in 683/1285 (and hence was known as *Khān-i Shahīd*, 'the Martyr Prince'); and Maḥmūd, entitled Bughra Khān, who was appointed governor of Lakhnawtī. But like his old master he lost a promising heir and was followed by a frivolous youth. On the old sultan's death in 685/1287, a party headed by the influential castellan (*kōtwāl*) of Delhi, Fakhr al-Dīn, who had been on bad terms with the 'Martyr Prince', ignored the claims both of Muḥammad's son Kaykhusraw and of Bughra Khān in the east, and enthroned the latter's hedonistic son Kayqubād. Their opponents, such as the wazir Baṣrī, suffered dismissal and exile.[53] Kaykhusraw was subsequently murdered; Bughra Khān, who assumed the style of Sultan Nāṣir al-Dīn and advanced westwards to challenge Kayqubād, was reconciled with his son at a meeting on the banks of the river Sarju (the episode commemorated in Khusraw's *Qirān al-Saʿdayn*). Accepting the fait accompli, he restricted his ambitions to Bengal, which remained an independent sultanate until 724/1324.

The young sultan, who moved his residence to Kīlōkhrī, a few miles away, celebrated his freedom from the restraint of his grandfather's reign by giving himself up to pleasure and leaving the affairs of state to the powerful *dādbeg* (*amīr-i dād*) Niẓām al-Dīn. An able but unscrupulous man, Niẓām al-Dīn profited from Kayqubād's unconcern about the affairs of state to bring down the wazir and the great nobles of the previous reign, and then induced the sultan to sanction the murder of his cousin Kaykhusraw, who had made the elementary mistake of seeking Mongol assistance. Eventually Kayqubād tired of the *dādbeg* and had him poisoned.[54] Niẓām al-Dīn's role is a difficult one to assess; it is noteworthy that Sirhindī's account mentions him only in passing and makes no allusion to his paramountcy. But for Baranī the execution or exile of the chief men of Balaban's reign, followed by the sultan's illness and deposition in favour of his son Kayūmarth, undermined the regime: there was rivalry among the maliks, with none strong enough to triumph. The Khalaj amir Jalāl al-Dīn rallied his followers, seized control of Kayūmarth and became na'ib; after a short interval he set aside the infant sultan and occupied the throne himself in Rabīʿ II 689/April–May 1290. The helpless

53 *TFS*, 122 (and cf. 107). *TMS*, 52. *FS*, 184–6, 196 (tr. 315–16, 328). An echo of Fakhr al-Dīn's role is found in the slightly garbled tale picked up by IB, III, 175–6 (tr. Gibb, 635–6), where he is referred to correctly as *malik al-umarāʾ* but also, in error, as na'ib.

54 *TFS*, 170. The account in *FS*, 198–200 (tr. 330–2), where Niẓām al-Dīn is made to drink poison he had prepared for Kayqubād, reads like the stuff of romance. For Kaykhusraw, see *ibid.*, 196–8 (tr. 328–30).

Kayqubād had not long survived his deposition, dying on 19 Muḥarram 689/1 February 1290. In Sirhindī's version, he simply perishes of starvation and neglect; according to another tradition, however, Kayqubād was murdered on Jalāl al-Dīn's orders by an officer whose father he had executed. In the *Ta'rīkh-i Fīrūz-Shāhī* events move inexorably towards the overthrow of the Ghiyathids and the transfer of power to the Khaljīs. Thus Bughra Khān, after the reconciliation, is said to have told his attendants that he would never see his son again and to have prophesied the imminent downfall of Balaban's dynasty.[55]

Given these forebodings, the portrayal of Jalāl al-Dīn Fīrūz Shāh Khaljī (689–95/1290–6) comes as something of a surprise – indeed, an anti-climax. In Baranī's view, kings had to balance the opposing qualities of benevolence and severity that are necessary if kingship is truly to be a lieutenancy (*khilāfat*, *niyābat*) on behalf of God.[56] It is clear that, for him, Jalāl al-Dīn did not embody this balance. This seasoned warrior, who prior to his accession had spent many years fighting the Mongols on the western frontiers of the Sultanate, is written off as a pious, mild and merciful ruler who shrank from conflict that would cost the lives of Muslim soldiers and was reluctant to shed the blood of his opponents; even *thags* ('thugs') captured in Delhi were shipped off down the Ganges towards Lakhnawtī.[57] The sultan pardoned alike Balaban's nephew, Malik Chhajjū, who rose in revolt against him in 689/1290, and a group of nobles who had engaged in a half-hearted plot against him slightly later.[58] In the speeches put into the conspirators' mouths by Baranī, they are made to criticize Jalāl al-Dīn as unworthy of the sovereignty; it is not unlikely that his clemency towards Chhajjū's adherents outraged those who had severed their ties with the old dynasty. But Jalāl al-Dīn reacted differently towards the dervish Sīdī Muwallih, whose hospice (*khānaqāh*) had become the centre of another aristocratic conspiracy and whose death at the sultan's instigation is seen by both Baranī and 'Iṣāmī as presaging the collapse of the regime.[59] If Jalāl al-Dīn's downfall, however, was divine retribution for his treatment of a Muslim holy man, it came about more immediately because of his childlike trust in, and indulgence towards, his scheming nephew 'Alā' al-Dīn, who murdered him at a meeting on the banks of the Ganges on 16 Ramaḍān 695/18 July 1296 and seized the throne. Yet the old sultan was not altogether negligible. On Baranī's own testimony, Jalāl al-Dīn headed expeditions against the Hindu kingdoms of Rajasthan, and halted an

55 *TFS*, 150, 156.

56 For a summary of Baranī's views, see Peter Hardy, 'Didactic historical writing in Indian Islam: Żiyā al-Dīn Baranī's treatment of the reign of Sultan Muḥammad Tughluq (1324–1351)', in Yohanan Friedmann (ed.), *Islam in Asia*, I, *South Asia* (Jerusalem, 1984), 41–4.

57 *TFS*, 186, 213; 189 for the *thags*, on whom see Hodivala, *Studies*, I, 266–7.

58 *TFS*, 190–2. *TMS*, 64–5.

59 *TFS*, 208, 212. *FS*, 217 (tr. 382).

invasion by a Mongol prince who withdrew without a battle. Khusraw's *Miftāḥ al-Futūḥ*, written only twelve months into the reign, reveals that even within that time Jalāl al-Dīn also campaigned in the sub-Himalaya against both the Mongols and the Hindus, in addition to suppressing a major insurrection by adherents of the Ghiyathid dynasty. He conveys the impression of remarkable energy on the part of the sultan.

It is worth comparing Baranī's view of Jalāl al-Dīn with his perspective on Balaban. During the first few years of his reign, Balaban led an expedition to Lahore and the Salt Range (Kūh-i Jūd) and engaged in campaigns against both the turbulent Mēōs (Mīwāt) in the vicinity of the capital and the unsubdued infidels of Katēhr, east of Badā'ūn. Thereafter, apart from his long march to Bengal to crush its rebellious governor, Toghril, he does not seem to have taken the field in person. It is noteworthy that the task of repelling the Mongols was left to his sons and other lieutenants. There are hints that such apparent sluggishness underlay the widespread desertions to Toghril not only in Bengal but even from Delhi following the early defeat of Balaban's generals.[60] Baranī evidently sees it as his duty to explain Balaban's failure to prosecute the war against the infidel, and he does so by staging an exchange between the sultan and some of his fellow Shamsīs. Urged to undertake plundering campaigns far afield in Hindu territory in the manner of Aybeg and Iltutmish, Balaban is made to justify his policy: caution was vital because the Mongols were now launching annual raids on India and it was no longer possible, as it had been in bygone days, to leave the capital and embark on distant enterprises.[61] At first sight, this might appear to furnish a persuasive rationale for the sultan's relatively unadventurous policy after *c.* 1270; but whether we can in fact take it as a reflection of Balaban's own views is open to serious doubt (see below, p. 253). Thus the contrast between Balaban, the 'strong' ruler whose energies were somewhat muted, and Jalāl al-Dīn, the weakling who was nevertheless strikingly active, presents us with something of a paradox.

Kingship, stability and hereditary succession

The period of sixty-two lunar years that separates the death of Iltutmish on 20 Sha'bān 633/29 April 1236 from the accession of 'Alā' al-Dīn Muḥammad Shāh Khaljī in 695/1296 witnessed the reigns of ten sultans. Those of Iltutmish's immediate successors – Fīrūz Shāh (633–4/1236), Raḍiyya (634–7/1236–40), Bahrām Shāh (637–9/1240–2) and Mas'ūd Shāh (639–44/1242–6) – were particularly ephemeral; Kayqubād (685–9/1287–90), the latter's son Kayūmarth (689/1290), Jalāl al-Dīn Khaljī (689–95/1290–6) and his son Rukn al-Dīn Ibrāhīm (695/1296) each alike enjoyed authority

[60] *TFS*, 83, 84. [61] *Ibid.*, 50–1.

for only a brief period. The longest reign is that of Balaban himself (664–85/1266–87), closely followed by that of the last Shamsid, Nāṣir al-Dīn Maḥmūd Shāh (644–64/1246–66): when these are subtracted from the total, the average reign occupies less than three lunar years. Of the ten sovereigns, only Balaban is known with certainty to have died a natural death. His predecessor's fate is obscure (above, p. 52), but the others died violently, in all cases but one at the instigation, or at least following the accession, of the ruler who replaced them; the exception, Raḍiyya, at the hands of Hindus in the wake of a failed bid to oust her successor.

There does not appear to have been an accepted rule of succession, and the role played by designation was extremely limited: in fact, with the possible exception of the founder of the Sultanate (above, p. 46), no sultan prior to Ghiyāth al-Dīn Tughluq Shāh (d. 724/1324) was succeeded by his designated heir. As far as we can tell, none of the Shamsids was given the opportunity to nominate a successor: it is not even known whether Raḍiyya, Bahrām Shāh or Masʿūd Shāh left any issue or whether Maḥmūd Shāh was survived by any of his sons. Nor were Balaban's preparations for the succession attended by better fortune than those of his Shamsid predecessors, since Kayqubād, as we have seen, was not his heir. Kayqubād and his child were within a few years supplanted by Jalāl al-Dīn, whose own sons were disinherited in 695/1296 by his nephew and murderer, ʿAlā' al-Dīn.

For much of the thirteenth century, therefore, the history of the Sultanate hardly seems to be characterized by the essentials of stable government and might not suggest that the hereditary principle carried much weight. But if the succession failed to observe any logical pattern, it cannot be said, even so, that heredity was immaterial. On the contrary: connections both with the present and with past ruling dynasties seem to have been of some moment. The attempt by Iltutmish's ghulam ʿIzz al-Dīn Balaban (later Küshlü Khān) to have himself proclaimed sultan following Bahrām Shāh's overthrow in 639/1242 was thwarted by the prompt action of a group of his colleagues, who gathered solemnly at their master's tomb and ensured that the throne stayed within Iltutmish's family: ʿIzz al-Dīn had to acquiesce, and the choice fell on ʿAlā' al-Dīn Masʿūd Shāh.[62] It might well be asked how, if loyalty to Iltutmish's dynasty was so strong, Ulugh Khān Balaban was able to justify his displacement of Iltutmish's heirs. To this we can return no sure answer. What Balaban did in 664/1266 was essentially what ʿIzz al-Dīn had attempted to do, but he had undoubtedly spent a longer time entrenching himself at the centre. There are grounds for believing that Balaban was married to a daughter of Iltutmish (below). He had, moreover, a claim which was denied to ʿIzz al-Dīn. It was thought – or Jūzjānī, writing in 658/1260, wanted it to be thought – that Balaban sprang from the ruling

[62] *TN*, II, 36 (tr. 780).

line of khans of Iltutmish's own clan, the Ölberli (p. 63 below).[63] This conceivably formed part of the propaganda deployed in Balaban's interest when the time came to supplant the Shamsids only a few years later.

Yet the legitimizing properties of Shamsid blood did not fade even under subsequent dynasties. Amīr Khusraw makes Muʿizz al-Dīn Kayqubād boast to his father of his descent not only from Sultan Balaban but from Iltutmish and from Nāṣir al-Dīn Maḥmūd Shāh (whose daughter was his mother).[64] The sultans were naturally unwilling to tolerate the forging of such links by others. One reason why Jalāl al-Dīn Khaljī reacted so harshly to the conspiracy to enthrone the dervish Sīdī Muwallih may have been that the latter's supporters planned to marry him to a daughter of 'Sultan Nāṣir al-Dīn' (whether the Shamsid Maḥmūd Shāh or the Ghiyathid Bughra Khān is not made clear).[65] And when, a few years later, during the absence of ʿAlā' al-Dīn Khaljī on campaign at Ranthanbōr (700/1301), a party in Delhi seized their opportunity to revolt and instal a dervish as sultan, Baranī considers it worthy of notice that this cipher was Iltutmish's maternal grandson.[66] One of ʿAlā' al-Dīn Khaljī's concerns when he forbade his maliks to form relationships (*qarābathā*) without his consent was surely to prevent them cementing unions with older royal lines.[67]

What, at a juridical level, constituted a sultan's title to rule? Sources for the thirteenth century give some prominence to the inauguration of a new reign by a pledge of allegiance (*bayʿat*).[68] This is first mentioned in 634/1236, when according to Jūzjānī the Turkish amirs who abandoned Fīrūz Shāh entered the capital and performed the *bayʿat* to Raḍiyya. On her deposition in 637/1240 the maliks and amirs made a 'general act of allegiance' (*bayʿat-i ʿāmm*) to Bahrām Shāh and to the newly created viceroy (na'ib) Aytegin in the royal quarter (*dawlatkhāna*) in Delhi. Jūzjānī, whose phrasing suggests that he may himself have participated in the ceremony, says that it was attended by 'the maliks, amirs, 'ulama', sadrs and the leading figures both in the military and the capital (*akābir-i lashgar-u ḥaḍrat*)'. On the news that Lahore had fallen to the Mongols in 639/1241, Bahrām Shāh took the precaution of having the *bayʿat* repeated by 'the

[63] *Ibid.*, II, 43, 45, 47–8 (tr. 791, 796, 799–800), and Jūzjānī's verses in praise of Balaban, calling him 'khan of the Ilbarī and king (*shāh*) of the Yemek', at II, 220–1 (tr. 1295); cf. the information about Iltutmish's father at I, 441 (tr. 599). P. B. Golden, 'Cumanica II. The Ölberli (Ölperli): the fortunes and misfortunes of an Inner Asian nomadic clan', *AEMA* 6 (1986 [1988]), 27–8. On the Yemek or Kimek, a Turkish people who had presided over a loose confederacy of tribes in the Irtysh region until its disintegration in the eleventh century under pressure from the Qipchaq, see *Ḥudūd al-ʿĀlam*, tr. Minorsky, 99–100 and notes at 304–10; P. Pelliot and L. Hambis, *Histoire des campagnes de Gengis Khan. Cheng-wou Ts'in-tcheng-lou* (Leiden, 1951, vol. I only), 95–6; Golden, 'The peoples of the south Russian steppe', in D. Sinor (ed.), *The Cambridge history of early Inner Asia* (Cambridge, 1990), 277–80. Nizami (HN, 251–2 n.40) is (no doubt rightly) dismissive of the story of Balaban's royal ancestry.

[64] *QS*, 22, 118. HN, 307. [65] *TFS*, 210–11. [66] *Ibid.*, 279.

[67] *Ibid.*, 286. [68] E. Tyan, 'Bayʿa', *Enc.Isl.*²

people of the city' (*khalq-i shahr*). The oath must therefore have been taken by the leading Muslim citizens of Delhi, who, as we shall see, were still being termed *khalq* ('the people' *par excellence*) by Baranī, over a century later. This widening of the circle of persons from whom the pledge was required set a precedent for the following reign, for at the accession of 'Alā' al-Dīn Mas'ūd Shāh, the amirs, we are told, 'administered to the people a public act of homage' (*khalqrā bay'at-i 'āmm dādand*).[69]

Jūzjānī provides the fullest description of the *bay'at* in connection with the accession of Nāṣir al-Dīn Maḥmūd Shāh in 644/1246, and shows that there were in fact two ceremonies, involving respectively the grandees and the citizens of Delhi:

> The maliks, amirs, sadrs, grandees (*kubrā'*), sayyids (*sādāt*) and 'ulama' hastened to the exalted court and attained the kissing of the blessed hand of that emperor (*shahanshāh*) ... Each, as befitted his status (*ḥāl*), offered congratulations on his accession. And on Tuesday the 25th [of Muḥarram] he held a general audience in the hall of the Kushk-i Fīrūzī in the fort (*qaṣr*) of the Dawlatkhāna; and they administered to all the people (*khalq*) a general oath of allegiance (*bay'at-i 'āmm*) to [recognize] the sovereignty and to obey the edicts of that ... monarch.[70]

Although we have less information about the *bay'at* given to Maḥmūd Shāh's successors, it appears to have followed a similar pattern, for Ibn Baṭṭūṭa was told that the oath to Kayqubād was taken first of all by the Malik al-Umarā' (the kotwal Fakhr al-Dīn), then by the amirs and principal officers, and the next morning by 'the rest of the people' (i.e. of Delhi).[71] From Balaban's reign, at least, a new sultan was expected to order the release of prisoners, a practice still observed at the time of Quṭb al-Dīn Mubārak Shāh's accession in 716/1316.[72]

The extension of the *bay'at* reflects the growing importance of the leading Muslim citizens of old Delhi, who had played some part in the accession of Raḍiyya and who must have given Bahrām Shāh considerable support to enable him to withstand a siege in the capital for almost three months in 639/1242.[73] Nor did their capacity to influence events cease when Kayqubād transferred his residence to Kīlōkhrī, a few miles closer to the Yamuna and referred to as 'the new town' (*shahr-i naw*) in 658/1260.[74] In 689/1290 their attachment to the Ghiyathid dynasty and hostility to the new regime would prevent Jalāl al-Dīn Khaljī from installing himself in Delhi

69 *TN*, I, 456, 463, 466, 468, and II, 23 (tr. 636, 649, 656, 661, 750–1).
70 *Ibid.*, I, 477 (tr. 675–6 modified).
71 IB, III, 176–7 (tr. Gibb, 636). *TMS*, 39–40, 53. For the *bay'at* to Jalāl al-Dīn at Kīlōkhrī, see *TFS*, 181.
72 Amīr Ḥasan Dihlawī, *'Ishq-Nāma* (700/1301), tr. M. I. Borah, 'A short account of an unpublished romantic maṣnavī of Amir Ḥasan Dihlavī', *NIA* 2 (1939–40), 260. *TFS*, 339, 382. *FS*, 354 (tr. 551–2).
73 *TN*, I, 456, 467 (tr. 635–6, 659). IB, III, 166–7 (tr. Gibb, 631). HN, 241–2.
74 For Kīlōkhrī, see *TN*, II, 83 (tr. 856–7); the earliest mention is at I, 456 (tr. 634, 636).

for some time.[75] At times, too, they would fall foul of their sultan. Following an abortive revolt in 700/1301, ʿAlāʾ al-Dīn Khaljī conceived an aversion for the notables of Delhi. Many sadrs were banished, and the sultan would not enter the city but took up residence instead in the suburbs (*ʿimrānāt*); it may have been partly for this reason that he afterwards fortified Sīrī and made it his headquarters.[76] Later there are reports of antipathy between the people of Delhi and Muḥammad b. Tughluq (p. 165 below).

The historians of the Delhi Sultanate still await as yet the techniques of literary analysis adopted by Marilyn Robinson Waldman in her monograph on the Ghaznawid chronicler Bayhaqī.[77] But it has been pointed out that they move on a different plane from those who now use their writings. They (and perhaps Baranī in particular) sought to reflect an ideal temporal order, in which the world is governed jointly by pious scholars and pious sultans, and one in which change is intelligible in terms not of the human actions the historians themselves narrate, but of divine providence.[78] Certainly the verdicts of a Jūzjānī or a Baranī may reveal as much about what was expected of a ruler as about real personalities. It was necessary to dispense justice to one's subjects and to supervise the affairs of state in person; to endow charitable Islamic foundations and to treat with respect the ʿulamaʾ and other members of the religious class, virtues for which even the tyrannical Shāh Terken is praised[79] and in which Bahrām Shāh was notably deficient. Nor was mildness necessarily a virtue in a sultan. Rukn al-Dīn Fīrūz Shāh's clemency and humanity (*ḥilm-u muruwwa*) attract favourable comment, but his reluctance to injure another human being is expressly presented as the cause of his downfall; and Masʿūd Shāh's merciful treatment of his uncles, whom he released from confinement, ultimately provided the amirs with a serviceable alternative to his rule.[80] The monarch had to know when to act harshly and when to show mercy, thus avoiding the extremes of either Balaban or Jalāl al-Dīn. A sultan's addiction to pleasure is frequently depicted as conducive to chaos, and an antipathy towards luxury, pomp and display, as evinced by Bahrām Shāh, was

75 *TFS*, 172, 173.
76 *Ibid.*, 283. *FS*, 277 (tr. 453), confirms his resentment. For ᶜAlāʾ al-Dīn and Sīrī, see Lal, *History of the Khaljis*, 326.
77 M. W. Waldman, *Towards a theory of historical narrative: a case-study of Perso-Islamicate historiography* (Columbus, Ohio, 1980) (cf. also E. A. Poliakova, 'The development of a literary canon in medieval Persian chronicles: the triumph of etiquette', *Iranian Studies* 17 (1984), 237–56). But see Peter Hardy, 'Approaches to pre-modern Indo-Muslim historical writing: some reconsiderations in 1990–1', in Peter Robb (ed.), *Society and ideology. Essays in South Asian history presented to Professor K. A. Ballhatchet* (Oxford and Delhi, 1993), 49–71.
78 Peter Hardy, 'The Muslim historians of the Delhi Sultanate: is what they say really what they mean?', *JASP* 9 (1964), part 1, 59–63; also his 'Force and violence', esp. 196–204.
79 *TN*, I, 454 (tr. 630–1).
80 *Ibid.*, I, 454, 457, 470 (tr. 630, 637, 664–5).

praiseworthy.[81] So was generosity, provided that it was directed towards those who mattered (and not to lowborn favourites, as was the munificence of Fīrūz Shāh, Masʿūd Shāh and Kayqubād). We might also observe, perhaps, that it was vital to cherish the maliks and amirs, including those inherited from one's predecessor: the Shamsid era and the reign of Kayqubād both furnished cautionary tales about the fate of sultans who disregarded this last precept.

[81] *Ibid.*, I, 462 (tr. 649).

CHAPTER 4

Turks, Tājīks and Khalaj[1]

Turks and military slavery

Tabaqa 22 of Jūzjānī's work comprises biographies of twenty-five Shamsī ghulams. Although the chronicler does not specify slave status in every case, his usage of the word 'Turk' suggests that for him it had come to denote simply a Turkish slave (see appendix I). Already, during Iltutmish's reign, a few of these amirs had been granted Turkish titles that included the element *khān* – not borne, it should be noted, by Ghūrī or Tājīk notables and thus representing an innovation.[2] But a significant proportion of the twenty-five attained high office only some time after their master's death. The future Sultan Balaban, as Jūzjānī's own patron and viceroy (na'ib) to the reigning monarch, receives the longest biography. The list of ghulams represented by the biographies is also, of course, far from exhaustive; both here and elsewhere in the *Ṭabaqāt* other slaves of Iltutmish, who are not accorded biographies of their own, are brought to our notice.

The pronounced slant of tabaqa 22 towards Turkish slave officers serves to obscure an important fact. At no point did Turkish ghulams enjoy the monopoly of rank and office that they seem to have exercised in Mamlūk Egypt. One important difference was the opportunities for advancement available to the offspring of ghulams in the Delhi Sultanate. This was not the case in Egypt, where the sons of mamluks – the *awlād al-nās* – were deliberately excluded from the highest positions in the state.[3] In India Turkish ghulams also had to share power with other, non-servile groups. These included not only free Turkish nobles, Khalaj, Ghūrīs, Tājīks and (from Balaban's reign) Mongols, but also other slave elements, both black

[1] This chapter is a greatly expanded version of my 'The *Mamlūk* institution in early Muslim India', *JRAS* (1990), 340–58.
[2] I. Habib, 'Formation', 11 and n.62.
[3] D. Ayalon, 'Studies on the structure of the Mamluk army – II', *BSOAS* 15 (1953), 456–8, repr. in his *Studies on the Mamlūks of Egypt (1250–1517)* (London, 1977); see also his 'Awlād al-nās', *Enc.Isl.*[2].

African (*Ḥabashī*, literally 'Abyssinian')[4] and Indian. Although Jūzjānī mentions Hindu infantrymen, *pāīks*,[5] as serving in Muslim campaigns, it is not until Balaban's reign that we read of them forming a royal guard; and they came to play a more prominent role only in the Khaljī era. Afghan troops, lastly, were part of the military establishment of the thirteenth-century Sultanate, though appearing only fitfully in the sources.[6]

It is impossible to document the training of the Sultanate's Turkish slaves, as has been done for Mamlūk Egypt, or to compose a survey of the slave contingents, of the kind that Professor Edmund Bosworth has produced for the Ghaznawids.[7] As we might guess even without Jūzjānī's occasional references, the accomplishments especially valued were equestrian skills and marksmanship.[8] But other skills were not unknown, for Aybeg had received instruction from his first master in reciting the Qur'ān and was accordingly known as *Qur'ān-khwān*.[9] The sources do not usually tell us at what point a slave was manumitted. Jūzjānī alleges that on Muʿizz al-Dīn's death both Aybeg and Yildiz requested manumission from the new sultan of Ghūr. According to the same author Iltutmish had even prior to this been freed by Aybeg on Muʿizz al-Dīn's express instructions, and Ibn Baṭṭūṭa later heard a story that he showed his deed of manumission to the jurists of Delhi when he became sultan.[10] We learn from Baranī alone that Balaban had been freed at some point prior to his accession.[11] Slaves of the reigning sultan bore the designation 'Sulṭānī'.[12] Whether or not there was a recognizable *cursus honorum* is unclear.

The information we are given concerning the twenty-five Shamsī slaves reveals diverse ethnic and geographical origins. Only one was apparently an Indian – Hindū Khān, who may have ranked as the major-domo in overall charge of the sultan's ghulams, since Jūzjānī says that he bore the style of *mihtar-i mubārak* and that he stood in the relation of a father to his fellow-Shamsīs.[13] The Turkish ghulams included Rūmīs (presumably Greeks or Slavs from Byzantine territory)[14] and 'Khitā'īs' (Khitan from northern

[4] C. F. Beckingham, 'Ḥabash, Ḥabasha, iii', *Enc.Isl.*².

[5] Sir Henry Yule and A. C. Burnell, *Hobson-Jobson: a glossary of colloquial Anglo-Indian words and phrases*, new edn W. Crooke (London, 1903), 748–9, 'pyke, paik'.

[6] *TN*, II, 80 (tr. 852). *TS*, IOL Persian ms. 412, fol. 52 (extracts tr. in Mirza, *Life and works*, 51–2). *QS*, 47. *TFS*, 58.

[7] Hassanein Rabie, 'The training of the Mamlūk Fāris', in Parry and Yapp, *War, technology and society*, 153–63. C. E. Bosworth, 'Ghaznevid military organization', *Der Islam* 36 (1960), 40–50; also *idem*, *Ghaznavids*, 101–6.

[8] *TN*, I, 416 (tr. 513), for Aybeg; I, 443 (tr. 604–5), on the exploits of Iltutmish in battle with the Khōkhars; II, 27 (tr. 756), for *Kirit Khān.

[9] *SA*, 21. [10] *TN*, I, 373, 444 (tr. 398, 605). IB, III, 164 (tr. Gibb, 629–30).

[11] *TFS*, 25, *āzād shuda* (and *pace* Nizami, in HN, 281).

[12] HN, 224. Aziz Aḥmad, 'The early Turkish nucleus in India', *Turcica* 9 (1977), 101, 102, wrongly assumes that the suffix denotes immigrants of free status.

[13] *TN*, II, 18–19 (tr. 744–6). For the position of *mihtar-i sarāī* at the Ghaznawid court, see Bosworth, *Ghaznavids*, 104.

[14] ʿIzz al-Dīn Kabīr Khān Ayaz (*ayaz*, 'clear', 'cloudless': Sauvaget, 'Noms et surnoms', no.

China), whose ethnic background may or may not distinguish them from the Qarakhitā'īs (i.e. Qara-Khitan).[15] Several of the Shamsīs belonged to the Qipchaq, the group of tribes which occupied the steppes north of the Black Sea and the Caspian.[16] And particular mention should be made, lastly, of those who belonged to Iltutmish's own people, the Ölberli, a subgroup of the Qipchaq (or possibly of the Qangli, who were closely related to them): they included Bahā' al-Dīn Balaban, the future sultan, known as Balaban-i Khwurd ('the Lesser').[17]

Although the Shamsīs included a few former ghulams of other rulers,[18] most were obtained direct from slave traders: Ibn Baṭṭūṭa heard much later that Iltutmish as sultan sent merchants to Samarqand, Bukhārā and Tirmid to buy Turkish slaves on his behalf.[19] The date of purchase ranged over a considerable period, beginning when Iltutmish was muqta' of Baran.[20] The avenues varied by which Turkish youths destined for Egypt and Syria came into the hands of slave traders,[21] and the same must be true of Muslim India. Iltutmish himself had allegedly been sold into slavery by his envious brothers, which enabled Jūzjānī to liken him to the Patriarch Yūsuf (Qur'ān, *sūra* 12:7–20).[22] Of Sayf al-Dīn Aybeg (later *dādbeg*), it is said that he was enslaved 'through the perversity of kindred'. Two others were

36), Badr al-Dīn Sonqur (*sonqur*, 'gerfalcon': *ibid.*, no. 22), and another Badr al-Dīn Sonqur who would later obtain the title Nuṣrat Khān: *TN*, II, 5, 24, 42 (tr. 724, 752, 787).

15 Khitā'īs: Sayf al-Dīn Aybeg, nicknamed *Yaghantut* ('seize elephant[s]'), and Sayf al-Dīn Ikit Khān Aybeg-i Khitā'ī, *ibid.*, II, 9, 28 (tr. 731, 757). Qarākhitā'īs: ᶜIzz al-Dīn Toghril Toghan Khān (*toghan*, 'falcon': Sauvaget, no. 140), Ikhtiyār al-Dīn Aytegin Qaraqush Khān (*aytegin*, 'moon-prince': *ibid.*, no. 41; *qaraqush*, 'eagle': Clauson, *Etymological dictionary*, 670) and another Ikhtiyār al-Dīn Aytegin (later the first ghulam to hold the office of na'ib): *TN*, II, 13, 19, 22 (tr. 736, 746, 749). For the title Ikit Khān, see below, p. 73, n.76.

16 Qamar al-Dīn Qiran Temür Khān (*qiran*, 'one who slaughters': Sauvaget, 'Noms et surnoms', no. 182); Tāj al-Dīn Sanjar (*sanjar*, 'one who pierces': *ibid.*, no. 107), nicknamed *qabaqulaq* ('of the protruding ears': see Clauson, *Etymological dictionary*, 580–1, 621, and Jackson, '*Mamlūk* institution', 342 n.7); Tāj al-Dīn Sanjar *Kirit Khān; Ikhtiyār al-Dīn Yüzbeg Toghril Khān; ᶜIzz al-Dīn Balaban (later to be styled Küshlü Khān); and Sayf al-Dīn Aybeg Shamsī-yi ᶜAjamī: *TN*, II, 17, 25, 27, 30, 36, 40 (tr. 742, 754, 756, 761, 775, 788–9).

17 To distinguish him from ᶜIzz al-Dīn Balaban (see preceding note, and below). The others were his brother Sayf al-Dīn Aybeg (later entitled Kishli Khān); and their cousin Nuṣrat al-Dīn Sanjar (Shīr Khān): Raverty read Shīr Khān's personal name as Sonqur, but BL ms., fol. 211a, and IOL ms., fol. 291b, read SNJR. For the ascription of Iltutmish and these ghulams to the Ölberli ('LBRY in Ḥabībī's edition), see *TN*, I, 440, 441, and II, 43, 45, 47 (tr. 598, 599, 791, 796, 800); also Golden, 'Cumanica II. The Ölberli'. On the Qipchaq–Qangli relationship, see Pelliot and Hambis, *Histoire des campagnes*, 95–116; *Ḥudūd al-ᶜĀlam*, tr. Minorsky, 304–10; C. E. Bosworth, 'Ḳanghlī', *Enc.Isl.*^{2}.

18 ᶜIzz al-Dīn Kabīr Khān Ayaz, bought from the family of Yildiz's *amīr-i shikār*; Naṣīr al-Dīn Aytemür al-Bahā'ī, so called because he had belonged to Bahā' al-Dīn Toghril; and Nuṣrat al-Dīn *Tāīsī, the one-time slave of Muᶜizz al-Dīn himself: *TN*, II, 5, 7, 10 (tr. 724–5, 727, 732). The meaning of Tāīsī's name, given consistently as TAYSY in BL ms. (fols. 182b, 199b, 200b, 202a, 218a), is unknown.

19 IB, III, 171 (tr. Gibb, 633).

20 *TN*, II, 4 (tr. 723).

21 D. Ayalon, 'Mamlūk', *Enc.Isl.*^{2}, VI, 314.

22 *TN*, I, 441 (tr. 599–600); and cf. the remarks about Yūsuf (Joseph) at I, 439 (tr. 596–7).

rumoured to be of Muslim parentage and thus unlawfully enslaved.[23] Kishli Khān is said to have been enslaved when young, having fallen into Mongol hands.[24] From the 1220s the westward advance of the Mongols gave rise to a sharp increase in the supply of Turkish slaves, particularly from the Caspian and Pontic steppes. Unscrupulous rulers seized on those who sought asylum with them, like the Turkish chieftain in the Crimea who in 640/1242–3 sold the future Mamlūk Sultan Baybars into slavery;[25] desperate fugitives exchanged their own offspring for the necessities of life; and the conquerors themselves converted human booty into more liquid assets by unloading their able-bodied captives onto the market. Iltutmish may also have profited from internal convulsions among the stricken Ölberli.[26]

The attractions of an élite corps of military slaves who possessed no local ties and whose sole loyalty was to the master who had bought, nurtured and trained (and sometimes manumitted) them are obvious. A number of authors, including the *littérateurs* Jāḥiẓ in the ninth century and Ibn Ḥassūl in the eleventh, and the Seljükid wazir Niẓām al-Mulk (d. 485/1092), had sung the praises of Turkish ghulams.[27] At the beginning of the thirteenth century Fakhr-i Mudabbir (admittedly writing for a monarch who was himself a ghulam) was the latest in a long line of authors to do so. There is no kind of infidel people, he says,

> which is brought over to Islam and does not look with longing at home, mother, father, and kindred: for a time they are bound to adopt Islam, but in most cases they apostatize and relapse into paganism. The exception is the Turkish race, who, when they are brought over to Islam, fix their hearts in Islam so firmly that they no longer remember home or region or kinsfolk ... The Turk is like a pearl that lies in the oyster in the sea. For as long as it is in its habitat, it is devoid of power and worth;

[23] Sayf al-Dīn: phrase omitted in Ḥabībī's edition, *ibid.*, II, 41, but cf. BL ms., fol. 211a, *ba-ᶜinād-i aqribā'* (also Raverty's tr., 790). Muslim parentage: *TN*, II, 24, 33–4 (tr. 752, 766).

[24] *Ibid.*, II, 45 (tr. 796).

[25] Peter Thorau, *The lion of Egypt: Sultan Baybars I and the Near East in the thirteenth century*, tr. P. M. Holt (London, 1992), 28. Al-Yūnīnī, *al-Dhayl ᶜalā' Mir'āti'l-Zamān* (Hyderabad, AP, 1374–81/1954–61, 4 vols.), III, 240.

[26] *TN*, II, 45 (tr. 796). Golden, 'Cumanica II. The Ölberli', 28; and Thomas T. Allsen, 'Prelude to the Western campaigns: Mongol military operations in the Volga-Ural region, 1217–1237', *AEMA* 3 (1983), 5–24 (esp. 16).

[27] C. T. Harley Walker, 'Jāḥiẓ of Basra to al-Fatḥ ibn Khāqān on the "Exploits of the Turks and the army of the Khalifate in general"', *JRAS* (1915), 631–97 (esp. 662 ff., 682, 685). Ibn Ḥassūl, *Risāla*, ed. Abbās Azzawi and tr. Şerefeddin Yaltkaya, 'İbni Hassul'ün Türkler hakkında bir eseri', *Belleten* 4 (1940), Ar. text 40–3, Tu. tr. 259–61 (I owe this reference to the kindness of Dr Carole Hillenbrand). Extracts from this last passage are translated in D. Ayalon, 'The Mamlūks of the Seljuks: Islam's military might at the crossroads', *JRAS*, 3rd series, 6 (1996), 314–15. See further *ibid.*, 316–19; and for further references, *idem*, 'Aspects of the Mamlūk phenomenon, I. The importance of the Mamlūk institution', *Der Islam* 53 (1976), 212–16, repr. in his *Mamlūk military society*; André Wink, 'India and Central Asia: the coming of the Turks in the eleventh century', in A. W. Van den Hoek *et al.* (eds.), *Ritual, state and history in South Asia. Essays in honour of J. C. Heesterman* (Leiden, 1992), 764–5.

but when it emerges from the oyster and from the sea, it acquires value and becomes precious, decorating the crown of kings and adorning the neck and ears of brides.[28]

This is not to say, however, that contemporaries were oblivious of the Turk's limitations. In one of 'Awfī's anecdotes Iltutmish deliberately chooses a Tājīk to investigate an officer's financial interests, a delicate task for which, we are told, the 'impetuosity' (*taḥawwur*) of a Turk would have disqualified him.[29] And it is a moot question how deeply Islam was ingrained in these first-generation converts. If Turkish slaves may have enjoyed the benefits of being reared as orthodox Muslims, their origins lay, nevertheless, in the pagan steppelands of Central and Western Asia. This is not the place to examine the question of pagan survivals within Muslim Turkish societies.[30] But Raḍiyya's enthronement may be symptomatic. Although the accession of a female monarch (as opposed to a regent) was without precedent in the Islamic world, the list of Qara-Khitan sovereigns in the twelfth century furnishes two examples. Some of Iltutmish's ghulams belonged, as we saw, to the Khitan or the Qara-Khitan, and in general women in the eastern steppe enjoyed greater freedom.[31] It may well be that in raising up their master's daughter Turkish officers were strongly influenced by their pagan background.

The problem of the Chihilgānīs

Although Baranī's *Ta'rīkh-i Fīrūz-Shāhī* opens with Sultan Balaban's accession, he prefaces his account of the reign with some remarks about Balaban's predecessors. They are very brief, but they do at least endeavour to make sense of the Shamsid era. In Iltutmish's time, he says,

illustrious maliks and amirs ... and many wazirs and notables (*ma'ārif*) came to the court of Sultan Shams al-Dīn [Iltutmish] from fear of the slaughter and terror of the accursed Mongol Chingīz Khan ... But after the death of Sultan Shams al-Dīn his Turkish *chihilgānī* slaves grew powerful. The sons of Sultan Shams al-Dīn ... were unable to fulfil the duties of kingship ... and as a consequence of the ascendancy of the Turkish Shamsī slaves all those great men of high birth ... were destroyed on every pretext during the reigns of Sultan Shams al-Dīn's sons, who had no notion of the world or about rulership. And following the elimination of those grandees and commanders, the Shamsī slaves rose and became khans. Every one of them attained

[28] *SA*, 35–7. [29] *JH*, BL ms. Or. 2676, fol. 263b.

[30] J. P. Roux, 'Recherche des survivances pré-islamiques dans les textes turcs musulmans: le *Bābar-Nāme*', *JA* 256 (1968), 247–61, and 'Recherche des survivances pré-islamiques dans les textes turcs musulmans: le *Kitab-i Dede Qorqut*', *JA* 264 (1976), 35–55.

[31] The point is made by Habibullah, 'Sultānah Rāziah [*sic*]', *IHQ* 16 (1940), 752, though his other examples comprise female regents. See further my 'Sulṭān Raḍiyya bint Iltutmish', in Gavin R. G. Hambly (ed.), *Women in the medieval Islamic world: power, patronage, piety* (New York, 1998), 181–97. On the Qara-Khitan, see Karl A. Wittfogel and Fêng Chia-shêng, *History of Chinese society: Liao 907–1125* (Philadelphia, 1949), 643, 644, 646; also the remarks about the Liao rulers of China *ibid.*, 199–202. Jūzjānī was aware of only one female Qara-Khitan monarch: *TN*, II, 95–6 (tr. 911).

new riches, palaces, pomp and magnificence ... Because the Shamsī slaves were of one master (*khwājatāsh būda*), and all forty became great at one time, one did not bow before another or obey him, and they demanded equality in iqtaʿs, troops, high rank and honour ... As a result of the inexperience of Iltutmish's sons and the supremacy of the Shamsī slaves, the monarchy had forfeited all majesty.[32]

Who were the Chihilgānīs? This question was investigated in a stimulating article by Professor Gavin Hambly, who reached no definite conclusion as to the origin or meaning of a term not used by Jūzjānī or, in fact, in any Indian source other than Baranī's work.[33] It is true that at one point above Baranī employs instead the term 'forty' (*chihil*), which led the sixteenth-century compilators Harawī and Firishta to assume that Iltutmish had forty slaves: this in turn induced modern historians to speak of a 'college' of forty.[34] Yet the concept is of dubious value. On every other occasion Baranī has recourse to the distributive numeral, which strongly suggests that the Chihilgānīs were so termed because each commanded a corps of forty ghulams. It is worth noting that in contemporary Egypt there were amirs commanding units of forty royal mamluks; we should perhaps conclude that the Chihilgānīs formed a parallel group of commanders within the ranks of Iltutmish's Shamsī slaves.[35] As Hambly observes, Baranī ascribes only three amirs by name to the ranks of the Chihilgānīs;[36] it is worth noting that they are all relatively junior ghulams of Iltutmish.

The rise of the Shamsī ghulams

The bloody conflict outlined by Baranī is nowhere mentioned explicitly by Jūzjānī, writing when the hegemony of the Shamsī ghulams was at its zenith; but its onset is clearly visible in his account of the turbulent era of Iltutmish's heirs. In all likelihood Fīrūz Shāh, who according to ʿIṣāmī failed to accord his father's Turkish slaves sufficient attention,[37] relied excessively upon a number of Tājīk bureaucrats whom the Turkish slaves

[32] *TFS*, 27–8; for a fuller translation of the passage, see I. Habib, 'Formation', 15–16. There is a brief reference to this phase of the Sultanate's history at *TFS*, 550.

[33] Gavin R. G. Hambly, 'Who were the Chihilgānī, the forty slaves of Sultan Shams al-Dīn Iltutmish of Delhi?', *Iran* 10 (1972), 57–62. For an alternative view, see Khurram Qadir, 'The amiran-i-chihalgan of northern India', *JCA* 4, no. 2 (1981), 59–146.

[34] Niẓām al-Dīn Aḥmad Harawī, *Ṭabaqāt-i Akbarī*, ed. B. De (Calcutta, 1931–5, 3 vols.), I, 78 (tr. 93), and Firishta, I, 130. Both were possibly influenced by ʿIṣāmī's story that Iltutmish was offered forty slaves and bought them all except Balaban, the future sultan: *FS*, 122 (tr. 238). For the 'college', see Haig in *Cambridge history of India*, III, 61–2; Habibullah, *Foundation*, 346; Nizami, *Some aspects*, 127 n.7, and in HN, 232–4. I. Habib, 'Formation', 16, takes 'forty' in a less literal sense.

[35] Ayalon, 'Studies on the structure of the Mamluk army – II', 469–70.

[36] Ulugh Khān Balaban, his cousin Shīr Khān, and Temür Khān (later muqtaʿ of Sāmāna and Sunnām after Shīr Khān's death: below, p. 77): *TFS*, 25, 65; Hambly, 'Who were the Chihilgānī?', 61.

[37] *FS*, 130 (tr. 248, but n.1 *ibid.* is misleading, since it cites as examples nobles who were not slaves).

massacred at Tarā'in in the course of the sultan's campaign against the rebel Kabīr Khān and his allies. Raḍiyya, by contrast, was vigorously supported by her father's Turkish ghulams (*umarā-yi turk ki bandagān-i Shamsī būdand*).[38] But she soon began to construct a power-base of her own. When the Turk Sayf al-Dīn Aybeg-i *Tutuq, whom she had appointed as her deputy in command of the army (*nā'ib-i lashgar*) with the style of Qutlugh Khān, died in 635/1237, his office passed not to a Turk but to the Ghūrī amir Quṭb al-Dīn Ḥasan b. ʿAlī.[39] She was deposed because in promoting an African (Ḥabashī) slave, Jamāl al-Dīn Yāqūt, to the rank of intendant of the stable (*amīr-i ākhūr*) she had alienated the 'Turkish maliks and amirs who were Iltutmish's slaves' and in particular the *amīr-ḥājib*, Ikhtiyār al-Dīn Aytegin.[40] A rising by Kabīr Khān at Lahore in 636/1239 failed, but in the next year Aytegin and his ally *Altunapa, the governor of Tabarhindh, contrived a mutiny while the sultan was on campaign, and Yāqūt was executed; Raḍiyya was incarcerated at Tabarhindh under the supervision of *Altunapa.[41]

With the enthronement of Muʿizz al-Dīn Bahrām Shāh (637–9/1240–2), the Turkish amirs took further steps to concentrate power in their own hands, with the formal institution of the office of na'ib (viceroy), which was conferred on the *amīr-ḥājib* Aytegin; it is significant that their oath of allegiance (*bayʿat*) to the new sovereign was conditional upon Aytegin's appointment.[42] But when Aytegin usurped certain imperial prerogatives, Bahrām Shāh grew resentful of his tutelage and had him murdered in Muḥarram 638/July 1240; the office of na'ib lapsed.[43] For a short time the direction of affairs was in the hands of another Shamsī, the new *amīr-ḥājib* Badr al-Dīn Sonqur-i Rūmī. Sonqur rendered the sultan valuable service in the campaign against *Altunapa, who had reacted to the elimination of his ally Aytegin by marrying Raḍiyya and marching on Delhi to restore her to the throne.[44] The principal role, however, was passing to Junaydī's successor as wazir, Niẓām al-Mulk Muhadhdhab al-Dīn, who fell out with Sonqur and poisoned the sultan's mind against him. When Sonqur hatched

38 *TN*, II, 36 (tr. 779); at I, 458 (tr. 640), they are called simply *umarā-yi turk*.

39 *Ibid.*, I, 459 (tr. 641–2). Sayf al-Dīn's sobriquet, given as BHTW in Ḥabībī's text and as 'Bihaq' by Raverty, appears as TTQ in BL ms., fols. 182b, 183a. This looks like the Tu. title *tutuq/totaq*, on which see Denis Sinor, 'The Turkish title *tutuq* rehabilitated', in *Turcica et Orientalia. Studies in honor of Gunnar Jarring* (Istanbul, 1988), 145–8; alternatively it could be a nickname, *tutuq*, 'tongue-tied' (Clauson, *Etymological dictionary*, 453), or 'lip' (Sauvaget, 'Noms et surnoms', no. 124). For his epitaph, from Abūhar, see *ARIE* (1970–1), 18–19, 119 (no. 4).

40 HN, 240, 243. *TN*, II, 21, 22–3 (tr. 748, 750); BL ms., fol. 183a, gives Yāqūt the title 'chief amir' (*amīr al-umarā'*), a phrase omitted in the printed text of *TN* (I, 460).

41 See generally Habibullah, *Foundation*, 119–21. *Altunapa's name is spelled 'LTWNYH in the printed text (Raverty's 'Altūnīah'), but I suspect that *yā'* is an error for *pā'* or *bā'* and that we have here Tu. *altun*, 'golden', + *aba*/*apa*, 'ancestor', or *oba*, 'clan', 'tribe', found among the Qipchaq/Polovtsy: *Pol'noe sobranie russkikh letopisei*, I. *Lavrent'evskaia letopis'*, 2nd edn (Leningrad, 1926–8), col. 278; Clauson, 5–6, 131.

42 *TN*, I, 463 (tr. 649).

43 Habibullah, *Foundation*, 121–2.

44 *TN*, II, 24 (tr. 753).

a conspiracy to replace Bahrām Shāh with one of his brothers, the wazir reported it and Sonqur was banished from court to his iqtaʿ of Badā'ūn in Ṣafar 639/August 1241. Returning without permission three months later, he was imprisoned and put to death.[45]

Bahrām Shāh in turn was overthrown in 639/1242 when, under the influence of one of his courtiers, Fakhr al-Dīn Mubārak Shāh Farrukhī, he contemplated the wholesale removal of the Turkish slave officers.[46] In Jumādā I 640/October 1242 the Turkish commanders attacked and killed the wazir Muhadhdhab al-Dīn, who had played them off against Bahrām Shāh and who now sought to concentrate power in his own hands and to exclude the Turkish amirs from all state business; he seems to have been the last wazir with military inclinations for almost a century. The fact that the ringleaders were not punished but were in fact rewarded suggests that the new sultan, Masʿūd Shāh, was behind them.[47] Like his two predecessors, however, Masʿūd Shāh tried to cut the Turkish amirs down to size. Although Jūzjānī does not define the 'nobodies' (*nākasān*) who had wielded influence at court during the final months of his regime, a later account suggests that he relied on black African slaves.[48]

Thus far, then, Jūzjānī and other authors do provide corroborating evidence for Baranī's analysis. There are grounds, nevertheless, for regarding that analysis as deficient in two respects. At no time, firstly, did a party comprising Turkish ghulams exclude free elements, whether Turks or not. Opposition to Rukn al-Dīn Fīrūz Shāh (and then initially to Raḍiyya) brought together the Turkish ghulam Kabīr Khān, the free Turkish noble ʿAlā' al-Dīn Jānī, the Ghūrī amir Sālārī, and the presumably Tājīk Junaydī.[49] Several Tājīk officials were implicated in Badr al-Dīn Sonqur's plot to remove Bahrām Shāh: among them were the chief qadi, Jalāl al-Dīn Kāsānī, who was deposed and banished from Delhi, and the accountant-general (*mushrif-i mamālik*) Tāj al-Dīn Mūsawī, who was executed with Sonqur in 639/1241.[50] Prior to his execution, Sonqur vainly sought the protection of the Ghūrī amir Quṭb al-Dīn Ḥasan.[51] Jūzjānī assures us that Ghūrī and Tājīk as well as Turkish maliks were affronted at the position of Yāqūt in Raḍiyya's counsels; and of Bahrām Shāh we learn, again, that he

[45] Habibullah, *Foundation*, 122–3.

[46] *TN*, I, 466–7, and II, 20, 30 (tr. 658–9, 747, 761–2).

[47] *Ibid.*, I, 469, and II, 27, 42 (tr. 662, 757, 787). Tāj al-Dīn Sanjar *Kirit Khān was promoted to the rank of intendant of the imperial elephants (*shiḥna-yi pīl*) and subsequently to that of *sar-i jāndār*, while Badr al-Dīn Sonqur Ṣūfī-yi Rūmī (the future Nuṣrat Khān, not to be confused with his namesake above) took over the dead wazir's territory of Kōl.

[48] *Ibid.*, I, 471 (tr. 668–9). *FS*, 144. *TMS*, 34.

[49] *TN*, I, 455–6, 458 (tr. 633–4, 639). It is noteworthy that Kabīr Khān and Jānī had suffered a lapse from favour during Iltutmish's latter years and that Sālārī, who had served the late sultan as *amīr-ḥājib*, is not so described under the new reign. Jānī and Kabīr Khān: *ibid.*, II, 6, 9 (tr. 726, 731–2). Sālārī: Habib, 'Formation', 13; also *JH*, I, 12.

[50] *TN*, I, 464–5 (tr. 652–3, 654).

[51] *Ibid.*, II, 25 (tr. 753).

aroused the fears of Ghūrī as well as Turkish amirs.[52] The rejection of ʿIzz al-Dīn Balaban and the choice of Masʿūd Shāh similarly demonstrate an alliance of different elements. The notion of the sovereignty passing to one of Iltutmish's Turkish ghulams perhaps found little favour with the Ghūrīs, while the other Shamsīs for their part were unwilling to jettison the family of their old master. It has been rightly pointed out that the structure of power that emerged in 639/1242 bears the marks of a compromise among the various groups within the élite.[53] The office of na'ib was revived and conferred on Quṭb al-Dīn Ḥasan; a senior Shamsī, Qaraqush Khān, was made *amīr-ḥājib*; and Tāj al-Dīn Sanjar-i Qabaqulaq, one of the three amirs said to have checked ʿIzz al-Dīn Balaban's pretensions, received the iqtaʿ of Badā'ūn.[54] Collaboration between Turk and non-Turk was evidently not beyond the bounds of possibility. It appears, however, that what made the internal crisis in the Sultanate so protracted, and so dangerous, was a split among the Shamsīs themselves.

The second defect of Baranī's analysis is that it treats the Shamsīs as a monolithic group. Historians of the parallel Mamlūk military slave institution in Egypt and the Near East are accustomed to speaking of *khushdāshiyya*, the sense of comradeship and unity of interest that bound together the slaves of the same master. Such sentiments, however, often failed to outlive the master himself, and to pay too much attention to *khushdāshiyya* is to court the risk of over-simplification.[55] It is surely possible – though the sources do not reveal it – that individuals among Iltutmish's élite corps of ghulams were conscious of closer links with colleagues from the same tribal background. What is still more likely is that there was initially a stronger sense of solidarity among the junior ghulams, who would have been a distinct group with interests of their own.

We should note how many of the Turkish slaves who were instrumental in Fīrūz Shāh's downfall and Raḍiyya's accession seem to have been junior ghulams still employed in the imperial household. A group described by Jūzjānī as 'the Turks of the court' (or 'the capital') had manifested their disenchantment with Fīrūz Shāh at an early stage by leaving Delhi for 'Hindūstān', conceivably in order to join his brother in Awadh. But they were intercepted; among them was Balaban 'the Lesser', who suffered a brief spell of imprisonment.[56] It was 'the Turkish amirs and personal slaves who were serving in the centre' (*umarā-yi turk-u bandagān-i khāṣṣ ki dar khidmat-i qalb būdand*) who had mutinied at Tarā'in; and these same officers, called now 'the centre [consisting] of Turkish amirs' (*qalb-i umarā-*

[52] *Ibid.*, II, 22–3, 164 (tr. 750, 1133). [53] Habibullah, *Foundation*, 24.

[54] *TN*, I, 468 (tr. 661–2); cf. also II, 20, 26, 36–7 (tr. 747, 755, 780).

[55] D. Ayalon, 'L'esclavage du mamelouk', *IONS* 1 (1951), 29–31, 34–7, repr. in his *Mamlūk military society*; cf. also the remarks of Robert Irwin, *The Middle East in the middle ages: the early Mamluk Sultanate 1250–1382* (London and Sydney, 1986), 65, 88–90.

[56] *TN*, II, 48–9, 51 (tr. 802, 805).

yi turk), who deserted Fīrūz Shāh at Kīlōkhrī and recognized Raḍiyya.[57] In all probability Iltutmish had purchased many of them at a relatively recent date. ʿIzz al-Dīn Balaban (Küshlü Khān), for example, one of the two men named as the ringleaders at Tarā'in, had been acquired during the siege of Mandōr (i.e. in 624/1227); by the time of Iltutmish's death he had become muqtaʿ of Baran.[58] But the *émeute* surely involved many others who now received important offices at court or their first iqtaʿs as a reward for bringing Raḍiyya to the throne. *Altunapa, to whom she transferred Baran, had been Iltutmish's chief canopy-bearer (*sar-i chatrdār*).[59] Bahā' al-Dīn Balaban 'the Lesser', purchased by Iltutmish only in 630/1232–3, was at his master's death merely a falconer (*khāsadār*); Raḍiyya promoted him to *amīr-i shikār*.[60] Of his brother Sayf al-Dīn Aybeg (the future Kishli Khān), purchased in the course of an embassy from Iltutmish to Egypt and Baghdad which can be reliably dated to 629/1231–2, we are told that until Raḍiyya's accession he had simply served in the sultan's private household (*khidmat-i dargāh-i khāṣṣ mīkard*); but he now became deputy commander of the guard (*nā'ib-i sar-i jāndār*). Tāj al-Dīn Sanjar (later Arslan Khān), obtained from the same source and probably around the same time, was like Balaban a falconer; but Raḍiyya made him cupbearer (*chāshnīgīr*) and subsequently allotted him the iqtaʿ of Balārām.[61] The status and aspirations of such ghulams would have set them not only against outsiders – including free Turkish grandees – but even, on occasions, against Iltutmish's more senior slaves like Kabīr Khān, who had long ago attained high rank in the state apparatus and received an iqtaʿ. The history of Iltutmish's successors is in large measure the story of the rise of his junior slaves to positions of power and of the tensions among them that threatened to tear the infant Delhi state asunder.

Balaban and his rivals

Balaban 'the Lesser', who under Bahrām Shāh had been promoted from *amīr-i shikār* to *amīr-i ākhūr*, had distinguished himself in the siege of Delhi in 639/1242, for which he received the iqtaʿ of Hānsī. Since he is known to have enjoyed the patronage of the late *amīr-ḥājib* Badr al-Dīn Sonqur, who

57 *Ibid.*, I, 456 (tr. 634–5, 636).

58 *Ibid.*, II, 36 (tr. 777–9 garbled). *Küshlü[k]* means 'strong', 'powerful': *TMENP*, III, 639 (no. 1676).

59 *TN*, II, 21 (tr. 748).

60 *Ibid.*, II, 48, 51 (tr. 802, 806); for the date of purchase, II, 48 (tr. 801). The meaning of *khāsadār* was established by Hodivala, *Studies*, II, 67–8.

61 Kishli Khān: *TN*, II, 45, 46 (tr. 796–8). Arslan Khān: *ibid.*, II, 33, 34 (tr. 766 and n. 3, 767); for *arslan*, 'lion', see Sauvaget, 'Noms et surnoms', no. 4. Embassy from Delhi to Egypt in 629/1231–2: Ibn al-Dawādārī, VII, 305. *Kishli*, which may mean 'humanity' (Clauson, *Etymological dictionary*, 754), is found in the title of a Khwarazmian amir earlier in the century: *TJG*, I, 80 (tr. 103, mistakenly equating it with *küshlü*).

had secured for him his first iqtaʿ at Rēwārī, he doubtless participated in the revolt against Bahrām Shāh from a desire to avenge his old friend. The same circumstance may have led him to share also in the attack on Sonqur's enemy Muhadhdhab al-Dīn, since Jūzjānī's phrasing suggests a link between the wazir's death and Balaban's promotion to *amīr-ḥājib*.[62] This was at the expense of Qaraqush Khān, who was dismissed to his iqtaʿ of Bhayāna. It is difficult to know what to make of his subsequent transfer from Bhayāna to Kara or the bald statement at the end of his biography that in 644/1246, following the overthrow of Masʿūd Shāh, he was killed in that region.[63] All this might indicate that he was a rival of Balaban, who had possibly engineered his demotion; but we cannot be sure. At any rate, Balaban was almost certainly instrumental in Masʿūd Shāh's removal and the enthronement of Maḥmūd Shāh (644–64/1246–66), events related by Jūzjānī in highly anodyne terms.

In 647/1249 Balaban became na'ib and was granted the style of Ulugh Khān, and the sultan married his daughter. His allies among the nobility were also favoured. The new viceroy transmitted his office of *amīr-ḥājib* to his brother Sayf al-Dīn Aybeg, now styled Kishli Khān, and a number of other supporters were promoted: the Shamsī Tāj al-Dīn *Teniz Khān, who is invariably described as a faithful henchman of Balaban, became deputy *amīr-ḥājib*; Balaban's own slave, Ikhtiyār al-Dīn Aytegin-i *mūī-yi darāz* ('the long-haired'), hitherto deputy to the *amīr-i ākhūr*, moved up to succeed Kishli Khān in that office.[64] The wazir Ṣadr al-Mulk Najm al-Dīn Abū Bakr, who had succeeded Muhadhdhab al-Dīn around the time of Balaban's own appointment as *amīr-ḥājib*, appears to have been another ally.[65]

From about this juncture we begin to discern the dim outline of an opposition group, also led by Shamsīs. Already, we are told, Balaban's promotion to the dignity of *amīr-ḥājib* had been resented by other maliks.[66] The new na'ib and his allies proceeded to make a concerted attack on ʿIzz al-Dīn Balaban, who in 639/1242 had been consoled with the style of Küshlü Khān and an extensive but distant iqtaʿ of Nāgawr and had since 643/1246 held the additional grant of Multān. Dissatisfied with this, he obtained from Maḥmūd Shāh Uchch as well, on condition that he relinquish Nāgawr; but he failed to honour his part of the bargain. Multān, which Küshlü Khān lost to Ḥasan Qarluq's forces, was subsequently occupied by Ulugh Khān Balaban's cousin Shīr Khān, from whom Küshlü

62 *TN*, I, 469, and II, 51–2 (tr. 663–4, 806–7); but cf. II, 53 (tr. 809), where Balaban's appointment alone is mentioned and is dated in 642/1244–5.

63 *Ibid.*, II, 20 (tr. 747).

64 *Ibid.*, II, 59–60 (tr. 820–1); cf. also II, 29, 46 (tr. 759, 798). *Teniz Khān's title figures in Ḥabībī's text as TR; Raverty reads 'Tīz', and in BL ms., fol. 206, while there is no dot above the middle 'tooth', the final letter is clearly Z. For Tu. *teniz/deniz*, 'sea', 'ocean', see Clauson, *Etymological dictionary*, 527; *TMENP*, III, 205–7 (no. 1192). That Aytegin-i Mūī-yi Darāz was Balaban's slave we know from *TFS*, 83.

65 *TN*, I, 469 (tr. 663–4). Habibullah, *Foundation*, 126.

66 *TN*, II, 52 (tr. 807).

Khān vainly endeavoured to take it. After a campaign headed by Ulugh Khān and the sultan ousted him from Nāgawr, which was conferred on the na'ib's brother Kishli Khān, Küshlü Khān retired to Uchch, where he was taken prisoner by Shīr Khān and released only after ordering the garrison to surrender. Küshlü Khān, who had thus been deprived of all his iqtaʿs in favour of the viceroy's supporters and kinsmen, was compensated with Badā'ūn early in 649/1251.[67]

Küshlü Khān had his revenge during a campaign to the north-west in 650–1/1252–3, when Ulugh Khān Balaban was dismissed first to Hānsī and then, deprived of Hānsī in favour of an infant son of the sultan, to Nāgawr. He was replaced as na'ib by Quṭb al-Dīn Ḥasan, and in a general reshuffle of appointments his friends and family were demoted. Kishli Khān, *Teniz Khān and the wazir Ṣadr al-Mulk were all removed from office; Jūzjānī for the second time forfeited his post of chief qadi; and Shīr Khān, whose extensive iqtaʿs comprised Uchch, Multān and Tabarhindh, was dislodged by the sultan's forces and retired into Mongol territory. Küshlü Khān and his allies, who included the shadowy Qutlugh Khān and the Indian ʿImād al-Dīn Rayhān, shared out offices and iqtaʿs among themselves: Rayhān became *wakīl-i dar*, and Küshlü Khān recovered his old iqtaʿs in Sind.[68]

Jūzjānī tells us frustratingly little about Ulugh Khān Balaban's enemies. Although he devotes a fair-sized biography to Küshlü Khān, no such compliment is paid to Qutlugh Khān, who was sufficiently important to marry the sultan's mother.[69] To label the opposition to Balaban as an 'anti-Turkish' faction[70] is to be misled by Jūzjānī's polemic contrasting 'Turks' and 'Hindus'. By his own admission they included Küshlü Khān and Qutlugh Khān as well as lesser figures like the latter's son-in-law ʿIzz al-Dīn Balaban-i Yüzbegī; and he specifically mentions Turks who were allied with Rayhān out of hostility to Ulugh Khān.[71] Jūzjānī writes bitingly of Rayhān

[67] *Ibid.*, II, 37–8 (tr. 780–4); see also I, 484–5, and II, 44, 46, 61–2 (tr. 689–90, 792, 798, 822–3).

[68] Shīr Khān: *ibid.*, I, 487 (but reading *az maṣāff-i kunār-i āb-i Sindh* for the *az maṣāff-i kuffār-i āb-i Sindh* of the text), and II, 34 (tr. 695–6, 767); see also II, 38 (tr. 784) and 44 (to be corrected from IOL ms., fol. 291a; Raverty's tr., 792, garbled). *FS*, 146–9 (tr. 269–74), seems to have a distorted account of this campaign, allegedly against the Mongols and dated 656. The year, which Habibullah (*Foundation*, 136) puts even later, is impossible, since Quṭb al-Dīn Ḥasan (d. 653/1255) is listed among the commanders and Balaban-i Zar (i.e. Küshlü Khān) is left at Uchch and Multān on the sultan's return. For Shīr Khān's flight to the Mongols, see p. 111 below; for the rest, Habibullah, *Foundation*, 126; he had wrongly assumed (*ibid.*, 125) that Quṭb al-Dīn had not survived ʿAlā' al-Dīn Masʿūd Shāh.

[69] *TN*, I, 489 (tr. 701); cf. also I, 493, and II, 39 (tr. 710, 785). S. B. P. Nigam, *Nobility under the Sultans of Delhi A.D. 1206–1398* (Delhi, 1968), 40, believes that the marriage, which he dates at the onset of 1255, alienated the sultan; but we have no evidence as to when it took place.

[70] Habibullah, *Foundation*, 126, 132, 195. Nizami, *Some aspects*, 141, and in HN, 262. Cf. also P. Saran, 'Politics and personalities in the reign of Nasir-ud-Din Mahmud the slave [*sic*]', in his *Studies in medieval Indian history* (Delhi, 1952), 228.

[71] *TN*, II, 68 (tr. 833); cf. II, 70 (tr. 836), for 'Turks' and 'Hindus', but also a reference to

as a baseborn Indian eunuch (*majbūb-u nāqiṣ-u az qabā'il-i Hind*); this suggests, incidentally, that he was of slave status and renders it unlikely that he belonged to what could properly be termed an emerging Indian Muslim noble class. Rayhān's candidate for the office of chief qadi, Shams al-Dīn, hailed from Bahraich, and the iqtaᶜ of Bahraich is later said to have been restored (*rujūᶜ shuda*) to Rayhān on his dismissal from court in 653/1255.[72] Since Bahraich had been Maḥmūd Shāh's iqtaᶜ prior to his accession, there is a strong possibility that Ulugh Khān's enemies drew support from the sultan's own power-base and that Rayhān was the sultan's own slave; Maḥmūd Shāh himself, as well as his mother and her husband, was doubtless behind them.

Balaban and his followers regained power by dint of allying with the sultan's renegade brother Jalāl al-Dīn Masᶜūd, who six years previously had fled from his iqtaᶜs by way of Santūr to take refuge with the Mongols.[73] Jūzjānī is reticent concerning his subsequent activities, and we are dependent instead on the history of India presented by Waṣṣāf and Rashīd al-Dīn, writing in Mongol Persia.[74] According to their version of events, Jalāl al-Dīn had grown apprehensive of the hostility of a number of Iltutmish's old slaves. Although the Iranian tradition does not offer a wholly reliable guide to the history of the Sultanate and various details are incorrect,[75] these slaves can, with one exception (Qutlugh Khān), be identified with persons named by Jūzjānī as allies of Ulugh Khān Balaban.[76] Jalāl al-Dīn Masᶜūd's return with a Mongol army, and the creation of a client state for him around Lahore and the north-western Panjāb, will be dealt with later

Rayhān's association with Qutlugh Khān. For Yüzbegī, see *ibid.*, I, 487 and II, 64 (tr. 695, 827).

72 *Ibid.*, II, 66 (tr. 829), for a brief notice of Rayhān; I, 487, and II, 64 (tr. 694, 827), for Shams al-Dīn; II, 69, for Rayhān and Bahraich. Nigam, *Nobility*, 39 n.37, also links Rayhān with Bahraich.

73 *TN*, I, 482 (tr. 683–4). For Santūr, see Hodivala, *Studies*, I, 229.

74 Waṣṣāf, 310; *JT*, ed. Jahn, *Indiengeschichte*, Ar. text Taf. 57, Pers. text Taf. 21–22 (German tr. 47–8); Qāshānī (*c.* 1318), *Ta'rīkh-i Uljāītū Sulṭān*, ed. Mahin Hambly (Tehran, 1348 Sh./1969), 184–5.

75 The late date given for the prince's flight, 651/1253–4, is probably that of his reappearance in India with a Mongol army. Another error is that Jalāl al-Dīn is said to have been an earlier sultan, deposed by Ulugh Khān in favour of Raḍiyya. Qutlugh Khān is listed among Ulugh Khān's confederates. If this is not an error, then the two men may have become enemies only after Jalāl al-Dīn's departure; Waṣṣāf's account does in fact claim that Qutlugh Khān subsequently grew fearful of Ulugh Khān.

76 See Hodivala, *Studies*, II, 78. 'Sungur Khān' is very probably Shīr Khān Sanjar. Aybeg-i Khitā'ī, muqtaᶜ of Baran, bore the style of *Ikit Khān: Raverty gives his style as 'Ban' or 'Bat' Khān, but cf. BL ms., fols. 192b, 194a, and IOL ms., fols. 262a, 263b (also Ḥabībī's apparatus, I, 488, 491). Sayf al-Dīn Aybeg-i Shamsī ᶜAjamī, whom Jūzjānī entitles 'Erkli Dādbeg' (Tu. *erkli*, 'having authority', 'one's own master': Clauson, *Etymological dictionary*, 224), had held the office of *amīr-i dād* since 640/1242–3. 'Yūzbak' is Ikhtiyār al-Dīn Yüzbeg Toghril Khān (*yüzbeg*, 'commander of a hundred': *ibid.*, 983), who had apparently replaced Jalāl al-Dīn himself as muqtaᶜ of Qinnawj and who was also surely a member of the na'ib's affinity, since just prior to the Qinnawj grant Balaban had been instrumental in his restoration to the sultan's favour.

(p. 111). When in 652/1254 he advanced east from Lahore, he was joined by a number of amirs, headed by Ulugh Khān, who had lost out in the power struggle of the previous year.[77] Inconclusive manoeuvres by the rebels and the sultan's army were followed by a compromise of which Rayhān was the immediate victim: he was relieved of his office and dismissed to his new iqta' of Badā'ūn.[78] It seems that he was discarded by the sultan and by certain of those who had earlier profited from Ulugh Khān's removal. One of them was surely Arslan Khān, who had supplanted Shīr Khān at Tabarhindh but who now appears among Jalāl al-Dīn Mas'ūd's followers. Another was Qutlugh Khān's son-in-law, 'Izz al-Dīn Balaban-i Yüzbegī, who negotiated with Jalāl al-Dīn Mas'ūd and Ulugh Khān on the sultan's behalf and who narrowly escaped assassination by Rayhān's agents: he is found enjoying the court's favour henceforward.[79] Jalāl al-Dīn Mas'ūd, on the other hand, had reaped less from the settlement than he might have anticipated. Along with his confederates, he was reconciled with Maḥmūd Shāh; but we read only that Lahore was recognized as his iqta', and he seems to have withdrawn there and ceased to play any role in events at the centre. At any rate, there is no mention of him as accompanying the imperial army when Ulugh Khān Balaban and the sultan re-entered Delhi in Dhu'l-Ḥijja 652/ January 1255.[80]

Ulugh Khān Balaban was swift to reimpose his dominance at court. In Rabī' II 653/June 1255 the na'ib Quṭb al-Dīn Ḥasan, who appears to have attempted to mediate in the preceding struggle, was arrested and executed, allegedly for some remark which had offended the sultan. Ulugh Khān was restored to the viceroyalty, while the dead man's iqta' of Mīrat was transferred to Kishli Khān, once more *amīr-ḥājib*.[81] Ulugh Khān had also wasted little time in moving against the opposition group. At the very beginning of 653/1255, Qutlugh Khān and the sultan's mother were dismissed from court and ordered to take up residence in Qutlugh Khān's new iqta' of Awadh. Around the same time Rayhān was deprived of Badā'ūn in favour of Ulugh Khān's adherent *Teniz Khān and transferred to the more distant Bahraich, where in Rajab 653/August 1255 he was killed by Tāj al-Dīn Sīwistānī.[82] Qutlugh Khān maintained the struggle for some time in Awadh, before joining forces with Küshlü Khān from Sind in 655/ 1257; attempting to manufacture a coup in Delhi which was frustrated by

[77] Including Kishli Khān from Kara and Aybeg-i Khitā'ī from Sunnām and Manṣūrpūr. The unnamed amir from Awadh, *TN*, II, 66 (tr. 830), is probably Yüzbeg Toghril Khān, who received that territory after being removed from Qinnawj for insubordination by Quṭb al-Dīn Ḥasan b. 'Alī: *ibid.*, II, 31 (tr. 762), where no dates are given, but this seems the most plausible reconstruction of events.

[78] *Ibid.*, I, 488–9, and II, 66–8 (tr. 699–700, 830–4).

[79] *Ibid.*, II, 68, 78 (tr. 832, 833, 849). Balaban-i Yüzbegī may have continued to bask in the court's favour as late as 656/1258 (below, p. 92).

[80] *TN*, I, 489, and II, 68–9 (tr. 700, 834).

[81] *Ibid.*, I, 489, and II, 46 (tr. 702, 798–9).

[82] *Ibid.*, I, 489, 490, and II, 69, 70 (tr. 701, 702–3, 834, 835–6).

Ulugh Khān's adherents, the allies briefly besieged the capital but were obliged to retreat following the na'ib's arrival with his army.[83] Nothing more is heard of Qutlugh Khān, who may have left India to seek shelter with the Mongols.[84] Küshlü Khān, for his part, retired to Sind: according to Jūzjānī, his forces were heavily depleted, since most of the contingents from Uchch and Multān deserted him and many took service with Ulugh Khān and the court.[85] As far as we can tell from Jūzjānī's account of the next few years, Ulugh Khān Balaban's opponents were excluded from any share of power at the centre; he held the viceroyalty unchallenged until his usurpation of the throne itself some ten years later.

In his analysis of the period preceding Balaban's accession as sultan, Dr Nigam sees the pattern as the elimination of rival elements such as Africans or Tājīks, which left the Turks unchallenged, followed by a phase in which rival Turkish factions struggled for power but in a more restrained fashion, involving bloodless changes of regime and compromises.[86] Whether the conflicts of the 1250s were in fact more restrained, on one level, is highly questionable. Admittedly there was no repetition of the massacre of 634/1236, which has the appearance of small-scale genocide; but we still see the political murders of individuals like Quṭb al-Dīn Ḥasan. The virulence of the struggle surprised not only contemporary observers but even the protagonists. When Küshlü Khān was obliged in 648/1250 to go to relieve Uchch, which was under attack from Shīr Khān, he pinned his hopes, we are told, on the fact that they were both 'of one house and one threshold'.[87] In other words, since the two amirs had been slaves of Iltutmish, he anticipated that they would be able to reach some amicable arrangement. He was to be disappointed: Shīr Khān placed him in custody and released him only when the city had been taken. 'Never could there be a more amazing case than this', exclaims Jūzjānī, describing how Balaban's forces and those of Küshlü Khān and Qutlugh Khān confronted each other in 655/1257; 'for they were all alike of one purse and messmates of one dish, between whom the accursed Satan had brought forth such discord.'[88] There are grounds for suggesting, in fact, that the situation in the 1250s was not less but more dangerous because it could not be resolved merely by the mass disposal of a group of Tājīk bureaucrats. Rather, it involved a contest between two more nearly equal parties, who engaged in full-blown civil war. Both groups, moreover, were prepared to seek the assistance of the pagan Mongols. Ulugh Khān Balaban and his confederates regained power by

[83] *Ibid.*, I, 490–1, 492–4, and II, 39, 69–75 (tr. 703–6, 707–10, 784–6, 835, 836–44).

[84] *JT*, ed. Jahn, *Indiengeschichte*, Ar. text, Taf. 57, alone specifies that Qutlugh Khān made for Möngke's court; the Persian text (Taf. 22), like Waṣṣāf, 310, and Qāshānī, 184–5, says merely that he set out in Jalāl al-Dīn's wake (tr. 48 has misleadingly 'schlossen sich Ǧalāl ad-Dīn an'). He was allegedly accompanied by 'Sungur Khān' (i.e. Shīr Khān): this is unlikely, though Shīr Khān too is known to have fled to the Mongols.

[85] *TN*, I, 493, and II, 39 (tr. 710, 786). [86] Nigam, *Nobility*, 37–8.

[87] *TN*, II, 38 (tr. 783). [88] *Ibid.*, II, 73 (Raverty's tr. 841 modified).

allying with a Mongol satellite; and Küshlü Khān, as we shall see, reacted to his defeat by turning Sind into a Mongol encampment.

The Ghiyathid aristocracy

We have, unfortunately, minimal information on Balaban's assumption of the Sultanate when Maḥmūd Shāh died; as we saw (p. 52), even the manner of the late sultan's death and the fate of his offspring are unclear. It is likely, though by no means certain, that the Shamsid regime was terminated by the use of open force. Nāṣir al-Dīn Maḥmūd Shāh is the only Shamsid monarch apart from Fīrūz Shāh known to have had his own establishment prior to his accession, so that he was accompanied to Delhi from Bahraich by 'great numbers of horsemen and paiks' (*mabālighī-yi mard-i pāīk-u suwār*).[89] His possession of independent resources of manpower may be one reason why he retained the throne for longer than the brief interval vouchsafed to other members of his dynasty, especially if he was behind the opposition to Ulugh Khān.

Ulugh Khān Balaban's long career prior to his enthronement, particularly as muqtaʿ of Hānsī since 639/1242, had furnished him with the means to acquire a force of personal retainers (*ḥashamhā-yi khāṣṣ*).[90] It doubtless included the equipage of a thousand paik slaves that accompanied him on his hunting expeditions as sultan and is described as being 'of long standing' (*qadīm*).[91] Before he became sultan, he also possessed Turkish ghulams of his own. We meet them already in the pages of the *Ṭabaqāt-i Nāṣirī*: important and influential officers like Aytegin-i Mūī-yi Darāz and the *sipahsālār* Qarachomaq, who represented Ulugh Khān in the negotiations of 652/1254 with the sultan.[92] Their tribal origins are unknown. Presumably they were purchased after the final Mongol assault on the Qipchaq in 1239–40, when his own fellow-tribesmen, the Ölberli, were finally scattered and many fled across the Black Sea into Anatolia;[93] like the Egyptian Sultan al-Ṣāliḥ Ayyūb, Balaban could have profited from a glut on the market in Turkish youths.

It must also be borne in mind that his long tenure of the viceroyalty since 647/1249, with only a brief interruption, enabled Ulugh Khān Balaban to manoeuvre his own supporters and friends into strategic positions. His brother Kishli Khān was succeeded as *amīr-ḥājib* on his death in 657/1259 by his son ʿAlā' al-Dīn Muḥammad, who retained the office well into

[89] *Ibid.*, I, 479 (Raverty's tr. 677 unaccountably renders *mard* as 'domestics').
[90] *Ibid.*, II, 72, 74 (tr. 839, 841). [91] *TFS*, 55.
[92] *TN*, II, 67 (tr. 831–2). His name is Tu. *qara*, 'black', + *chomaq*, 'mace' (Clauson, *Etymological dictionary*, 422–3; cf. Sauvaget, 'Noms et surnoms', no. 93). For Aytegin, see above, p. 71.
[93] al-Yūnīnī, III, 240. Irwin, *Middle East*, 17–18, calling them 'Barali'.

Balaban's reign.[94] It is possible (though by no means guaranteed) that those who emerge as supporters of Balaban in earlier crises backed his seizure of the throne. Nuṣrat Khān Badr al-Dīn Sonqur, for example, who had moved swiftly to Delhi's assistance in 655/1257 when it was besieged by the na'ib's enemies, is known to have remained a muqtaʿ until at least 669/1271.[95] In the preface to his *Ghurrat al-Kamāl*, moreover, Amīr Khusraw contrives a word-play alluding to his maternal grandfather, the *ʿāriḍ* ʿImād al-Mulk (d. *c.* 671/1272–3), as 'sultan-maker'; and we know from the same author that ʿImād al-Mulk's own establishment had a complement of 200 Turkish and 2000 Hindu slaves and 1000 horsemen.[96] Possibly ʿImād al-Mulk – a Shamsī according to Baranī – was instrumental in Ulugh Khān Balaban's usurpation of the throne: certainly the *ʿāriḍ*'s department had been active in the defence of Delhi on Balaban's behalf in 655/1257.[97]

A later tradition claims that Balaban, as sultan, abolished the office of na'ib, although it is known to have been revived before his death.[98] Baranī says that in his aim of destroying his former colleagues (*khwājatāshān*), the great Shamsī maliks, he had a number poisoned, so that his cousin Shīr Khān, who held the iqtaʿs of Lahore, Sunnām and Dēōpālpūr, would not come to court either during Maḥmūd Shāh's reign or in Balaban's, for fear of meeting the same fate; eventually, however, in *c.* 668/1269–70, Balaban had him poisoned also. Those Shamsīs who survived did so only by virtue of the sultan's own favour.[99] Baranī names two of them, Temür Khān and ʿĀdil Khān. Temür Khān appears as Temür Khān Sonqur-i ʿAjamī, malik of Kuhrām, in Jūzjānī's list of Maḥmūd Shāh's nobles: after Shīr Khān's death, Balaban granted him the iqtaʿs of Sunnām and Sāmāna. ʿĀdil Khān is surnamed Shamsī-yi ʿAjamī, which suggests his identity with the *amīr-i dād* Sayf al-Dīn Aybeg (above, n.76).[100] Of the ultimate fate of these

94 *TN*, I, 495 (tr. 713). *TFS*, 35, 36–7, 113–14.

95 *TN*, II, 42 (tr. 787–8). G. Yazdani, 'Inscription of Sulṭān Balban from Bhayana, Bharatpur State', *EIM* (1937–8), 5–6 (though identifying him in error with the Nuṣrat Khān of ʿAlā' al-Dīn Khaljī's reign).

96 *DGK*, IOL Persian ms. 51 (Ethé 1186), fol. 34b, *agar nishān-i sulṭānī nadāsht sulṭān-nishānī dāsht* (loosely translatable as 'If he was not [himself] the sultan, he [nevertheless] made the sultan'). The phrase is mangled in the printed edition by Sayyid Wazīr al-Ḥasan ʿĀbidī (Lahore, 1975), 67, which also gives in error a figure of 100,000 for the Hindu slaves and omits the Turks.

97 *TN*, I, 493 (tr. 709). For a sketch of ʿImād al-Mulk's career, see *TFS*, 114. He is possibly identical with Iftikhār al-Mulk Sharaf al-Dīn Muḥammad Rashīdī, who is said to have occupied the *dīwān-i ʿarḍ-i mamālik* when Balaban was na'ib: *DA*, RRL Persian ms. 1231, fol. 56b, and tr. Sh. Abdur Rashid, 'Dastur-ul-Albab fi ʿIlm-il-Hisab', *MIQ* 1 (1950), 93. That ʿImād al-Mulk's name was Muḥammad is clear from *TS*, IOL Persian ms. 412, fol. 36b, where his son is addressed as 'Maḥmūd-i Muḥammad'. The assumption that he was of Indian extraction is not warranted by the sources.

98 *DA*, fol. 56b (tr. Rashid, 93). But see *TMS*, 51, 52, for the na'ib Köchü.

99 *TFS*, 47–8, 65; and a brief reference at 550.

100 *Ibid.*, 36, 50, 65, 83. Temür Khān in Maḥmūd Shāh's reign: *TN*, I, 476, and BL ms., fol. 188b (tr. 673). For an inscription of Aybeg-i Shamsī-yi ʿAjamī's son Muḥammad at Farrukhnagar in Gurgā'ūn, dated 674/1276, see G. Yazdani, 'The Inscriptions of the Turk

grandees, however, we are not informed. That Balaban's purge was by no means complete is evident from Baranī's comment on the number of sons of Shamsī ghulams who held office in the Ghiyathid era.[101]

By modern historians Balaban has been charged with sapping the roots of Turkish power in India.[102] But his purpose, of course, in bringing down a number of his former colleagues was to promote his own slaves. Toghril, who usurped control of the distant province of Lakhnawtī and was overthrown in *c.* 680/1281–2, is the most notorious of them. Balaban's favourite ghulam, according to Baranī, was Ikhtiyār al-Dīn Begbars, who became *amīr-ḥājib/bārbeg*, possibly in succession to ʿAlā' al-Dīn Muḥammad b. Kishli Khān, accompanied the sultan on his Bengal campaign and was given the job of hunting down Toghril when the revolt collapsed.[103] Others of whom we are told incurred the sultan's displeasure and forfeited their high offices and even in some cases their lives, as did Malik *Buqubuq (see p. 101) and Aytegin-i Mūī-yi Darāz (Amīn Khān), muqtaʿ of Awadh, hanged in *c.* 678/1279–80 for his failure to suppress Toghril's revolt. The sons of Balaban's slaves, referred to as his *mawlāzādagān* ('sons of freedmen'), also played a significant role in the affairs of state. An example is the *sar-i jāndār* Ikhtiyār al-Dīn ʿAlī b. Aybeg, popularly known as Hātim Khān, who was granted Amrōha as his iqtaʿ early in Balaban's reign and under Kayqubād received Awadh and the style of Khān Jahān; the poet Amīr Khusraw was for some years in his service.[104] In the reign of Balaban's successor there was still a recognizable and self-conscious group of 'Ghiyāthīs', former ghulams of the old sultan or their offspring, like Ikhtiyār al-Dīn Alp Ghāzī who opposed the newly established Khaljī regime in 689/1290.[105]

Although Balaban, therefore, changed many of the personnel, ghulam status and ancestry persisted as qualifications for high office. Yet in the course of his reign the ruling class was certainly broadened. No more than his Shamsid predecessors did Balaban preside over an élite that was exclusively of Turkish origin and composed only of his close kin or his slaves and their progeny. Baranī depicts him as virulently hostile to the

Sulṭāns of Delhi', *EIM* (1913–14), 26–7; *RCEA*, XII, 206–7 (no. 4711). In addition, Balaban's old ally Nuṣrat Khān was still in command at Bhayāna in 669/1271 (above).

101 *TFS*, 66. Tāj al-Dīn, the son of Qutlugh Khān-i Shamsī, is named as one of the 'amirs of Hindūstān' sent against the rebel Toghril: *ibid.*, 83. His father is probably the Qutlugh Khān who died in 635/1237 (above, p. 67).

102 E.g. by Saran, 'Politics and personalities', 242–3; Nigam, *Nobility*, 42, saying that Balaban 'sought to destroy the Turkish nobility'; Nizami, *Some aspects*, 143, and in HN, 285–6.

103 *TFS*, 61, for his closeness to Balaban; and see also 24, 81, 88. His name, usually transliterated 'Bektars', shows clearly in BL ms., fols. 32a, 47a, as BYKBRS; for the same form in contemporary Egypt, see al-Ṣafadī, *Wāfī*, X, 187–8.

104 *TFS*, 36, 118–19; and for Awadh, *QS*, 221; *RI*, V, 55. *Mawlāzāda* is explained in Hodivala, *Studies*, I, 342. On Khusraw, see Mirza, *Life and works*, 66, 69, 70–3.

105 *TMS*, 63: on him, see n.128 below. For another example of an amir with this sobriquet, 'Qutlugh Sulṭānī Ghiyāthī', see Yazdani, 'Inscriptions of the Turk Sulṭāns', 31–2.

promotion of the lowborn and as refusing to appoint a certain Kamāl-i Mahyār to the post of revenue-intendant (*khwāja*) at Amrōha. We might be less inclined to accept this testimony at face value and to dismiss it as Baranī's personal view mediated through the sultan, were not a slightly fuller version of the story found in a fifteenth-century source. But Balaban's objection was clearly based on the fact that Kamāl-i Mahyār was the son of a Hindu slave.[106] His own career having been temporarily blighted by the Indian ghulam Rayhān, the sultan could well have conceived an aversion for persons of the same background. It is noteworthy that Balaban's antipathy did not extend to Indians – whether converts or not – of noble extraction. We are told that his servitors included a certain 'Hatyā Pāīk', presumably a Hindu aristocrat, who received the high stipend of 100,000 *jītals* (i.e. approximately 2000 *tangas*).[107] In the wake of his campaign against the people of the Salt Range (Kūh-i Jūd) in *c.* 665/1266–7, Balaban brought back with him to Delhi the two sons of their raja, who adopted Islam. The appearance of both these princes, ʿAlī Shāh Kūhijūdī and ʿIzz al-Dīn Khurram, together with the despised Kamāl-i Mahyār, among the maliks of Balaban's grandson Kayqubād may be taken to signal the rise of an Indian Muslim aristocracy even prior to the Khaljī era, with which it is traditionally associated.[108]

The nobility still included Tājīks, of whom the most prominent in Balaban's latter years was the kotwal of Delhi, Fakhr al-Dīn, entitled 'Chief Amir' (*Malik al-Umarā'*). Baranī, who claims that Fakhr al-Dīn and his father had occupied this post between them for eighty years, thereby allows us to identify the father as Jamāl al-Dīn Nīshāpūrī, described as *ulugh kōtwālbeg* in 655/1257 when Delhi was under attack by Balaban's enemies: Nīshāpūrī origins would explain the grandiloquent title *Khān-i Khurāsān* which Fakhr al-Dīn acquired under Kayqubād.[109] His nephew and son-in-law, Niẓām al-Dīn, who became Kayqubād's *dādbeg* and who is described as a survivor 'from among the illustrious Shamsī and Balabanī maliks', is a mysterious figure and seems to emerge out of thin air, unless he is to be identified with Niẓām al-Dīn Būzghāla, Balaban's *wakīl-i dar*.[110] During Balaban's reign, too, Muslim notables continued to arrive from the many territories occupied by the Mongols.[111] One especially distinguished immigrant was the deposed sultan of Kirmān, Ḥajjāj, who remained for ten years

[106] *TFS*, 36–7. Sayyid Ashraf Jahāngīr Simnānī, *Maktūbāt-i Ashrafī*, BL ms. Or. 267, fol. 66b.
[107] *TFS*, 210.
[108] *TMS*, 40, 54. See *TFS*, 126, for all three among Kayqubād's nobles. I. H. Siddiqui, 'Social mobility in the Delhi Sultanate', in I. Habib (ed.), *Medieval India 1*, 24.
[109] Jamāl al-Dīn: *TN*, I, 493 (tr. 709). Fakhr al-Dīn: *TFS*, 117–18, 126 (to be corrected from BL ms., fol. 67b); his career is outlined by B. S. Mathur, 'Malik-ul-Umara Fakhruddin – the kotwal of Delhi', *IC* 39 (1965), 205–8.
[110] *TFS*, 131, 168; cf. also 24, 36, 37, 191. *Buzghāla* means 'kid' in Persian: see the word-play in *TS*, IOL Persian ms. 412, fol. 40a.
[111] Firishta, I, 131, citing ᶜAyn al-Dīn Bījāpūrī.

and left for his homeland only after the accession of Jalāl al-Dīn Khaljī, but died en route at Bhakkar towards the end of 690/1291.[112]

It appears that Balaban may have consciously built up the power of Khalaj amirs and profited from the influx of Mongol notables following the upheavals in Mongol territory after *c.* 1260 (below, pp. 108–10, 115–16). His brother Kishli Khān, as *amīr-ḥājib* in the 1250s, is said to have been on good terms with the Khalaj amirs, among others, while at a later date Khalaj officers served in Sind under Balaban's son Muḥammad, the 'Martyr Prince'.[113] Amīr Jamāl Khaljī, whom Balaban created *nā'ib-i dādbeg*, was probably his *ḥājib* Jamāl al-Dīn ʿAlī, employed as his envoy to the Mongols in 658/1260.[114] If we can trust Waṣṣāf, the future sovereign Jalāl al-Dīn Khaljī was a refugee from Mongol territory in the 1260s who had held command (*amārat*) of the Khalaj on behalf of the ruler of Binbān;[115] if he is the person referred to by Jūzjānī as 'the Mongol "resident" (*shiḥna*) in Binbān, who was the son of the amir Yughrush', Jalāl al-Dīn himself may have accompanied the Mongol embassy to Delhi in 658/1260.[116] Baranī, who lists him and his brother Shihāb al-Dīn Masʿūd among Balaban's maliks, has Jalāl al-Dīn later recalling with emotion Balaban's enthronement.[117]

Mongol immigrants, by contrast, were a new element in the politics of the Sultanate. In much the same way as Mongol commanders and their followers, worsted in some conflict with their confrères, began to seek asylum in the dominions of the Mamlūk Sultans of Egypt and Syria after 660/1262,[118] so Mongol notables fled into the territories of the sultan of Delhi. According to a fourteenth-century author, a whole quarter of the capital was named 'Chingīzī' after them in Balaban's era. If not already Muslims, they at any rate embraced Islam after their arrival and, like their

112 Nāṣir al-Dīn Kirmānī, *Simṭ al-ʿUlā' li'l-Ḥaḍrati'l-ʿUlyā'* (*c.*1315), ed. ʿAbbās Iqbāl (Tehran, 1328 Sh./1949), 49. Anonymous, *Ta'rīkh-i Sīstān*, ed. Malik al-Shuʿarā Bahār (Tehran, 1314 Sh./1935), 405, and tr. L. P. Smirnova (Moscow, 1974), 376. Ḥamd-Allāh Mustawfī Qazwīnī, *Ta'rīkh-i Guzīda*, ed. ʿAbd al-Ḥusayn Nawā'ī (Tehran, 1339 Sh./1960), 532 (but with the wrong year, 669, for his flight). Rashīd al-Dīn says that Ḥajjāj remained in India for almost fifteen years: *JT*, II, ed. E. Blochet, GMS, XVIII (Leiden and London, 1911), 552, and tr. J. A. Boyle, *The successors of Genghis Khan* (London and New York, 1971), 305/tr. Iu. P. Verkhovskii, *Sbornik letopisei*, II (Moscow and Leningrad, 1960), 198. Brief references in Waṣṣāf, 291, and in Shabānkāra'ī (738/1337), *Majmaʿ al-Ansāb*, ed. Mīr Hāshim Muḥaddith (Tehran, 1363 Sh./1984), 199. That the Kirmān ruler left Sīstān on the news of the Ilkhan Abaqa's advance into Khurāsān places his departure in 678/1279: see *JT*, III, ed. A. A. Alizade and tr. A. K. Arends (Baku, 1957), text 152–3, tr. 94, and for the date, Jean Aubin, 'L'ethnogénèse des Qaraunas', *Turcica* 1 (1969), 85 n.4.

113 *TN*, II, 46 (tr. 798). *TMS*, 47.

114 *TFS*, 24. *TN*, II, 86 (tr. 860).

115 Waṣṣāf, 311; *JT*, ed. Jahn, *Indiengeschichte*, Ar. text Taf. 57 (Pers. text Taf. 23 corrupt; cf. German tr. 48–9); Qāshānī, 185.

116 *TN*, II, 88 (tr. 862). *TMS*, 56, 61, calls his father Yughrush (BΓRŠ in the mss.).

117 *TFS*, 24, 178. For Shihāb al-Dīn, see also *ibid.*, 186; *DR*, 54; Ibn Abi'l-Faḍā'il, ed. Kortantamer, Ar. text 29 (German tr. 108).

118 D. Ayalon, 'The Wafidiya in the Mamluk kingdom', *IC* 25 (1951), 81–104, repr. in his *Studies*.

successors who entered the Sultanate in the time of ʿAlā' al-Dīn Khaljī, are designated as 'neo-Muslims' by Baranī.[119] Maliks with unmistakably Mongol names among the nobles of Balaban and his successor include Bayanchar; Ulaghchi, the son of Turghai, Balaban's 'chief armour-bearer of the left hand' (*sar-i ṣilāḥdār-i maysara*); Turumtai, one of the commanders who failed to suppress the Bengal revolt; and Ja'urchi, Kayqubād's *sar-i jāndār*.[120]

These neo-Muslim amirs seem initially to have formed part of the coalition that secured the throne for Kayqubād and to have shared power with Niẓām al-Dīn, since they are described as enjoying office and favour (*shughldār-u muqarrab*). But having disposed of other competitors, such as the wazir, Niẓām al-Dīn turned against them also. The Mongol amirs, including his former allies Kerei and the *sar-i jāndār* Ja'urchi, were rounded up and most of them executed, although Ja'urchi and Mughaltai were merely exiled.[121] Many of Balaban's *mawlāzādas* who were related to them by marriage were also eliminated, notably Malik Shāhik, entitled Azhdar Khān, who was *amīr-ḥājib* and muqtaʿ of Multān, and Malik *Turki, the *ʿāriḍ*.[122] It looks very much as if Niẓām al-Dīn, rather than Balaban, did most to undermine the Turkish ghulams during the few years prior to the seizure of power by the Khaljīs.

Even after Niẓām al-Dīn's removal, however, Mongol amirs were still at large. ʿIṣāmī may be correct in naming those who later murdered Kayqubād as the sons of *Turki, i.e. Kayqubād's *ʿāriḍ* who had perished during Niẓām al-Dīn's ascendancy. That the ex-sultan is said to have been wrapped in his bedclothes and kicked to death recalls pagan Mongol practice, which did not permit royal blood to be spilled on the ground.[123] And members of Balaban's slave establishment who had weathered the purge were able to assume power: it was 'Balaban's slaves among the maliks, amirs, nobles and military commanders' who despaired of the ailing Kayqubād early in 689/1290 and endeavoured to rule through his infant son Kayūmarth.[124] Again we see a coalition of different elements, since this group, headed by Aytemür *Kachhan and Aytemür Surkha, who on Niẓām al-Dīn's downfall

119 Firishta, I, 131, citing Bījāpūrī's *mulḥaqāt* to *TN*. *TFS*, 133.

120 Bayanchar's name is garbled as NAHJN in *TFS*, 126, and as 'HḤN *ibid.*, 183 (for the correct form BAYNJR, see BL ms., fols. 67b, 99a). Ja'urchi: *TMS*, 53, and *FS*, 184–8 (tr. 315–19). Turumtai: *FS*, 165–6 (tr. 292–3). Turghai and Ulaghchi: *TFS*, 24, 126, 183. The father's name is actually Tu. *turghai*, 'lark', 'sparrow': Sauvaget, 'Noms et surnoms', no. 128; Clauson, *Etymological dictionary*, 541. For Mo. *ulaghchi*, 'officer of the postal relay-system', see Paul Pelliot, *Notes sur l'histoire de la Horde d'Or* (Paris, 1950), 34–5; for Bayanchar (Mo. *bayan*, 'rich', + suffix *char*), *ibid.*, 52, 89; and for Mo. *turumtai*, 'male hawk', see F.D. Lessing, *A Mongolian–English dictionary* (Berkeley and Los Angeles, 1960), 827.

121 *TFS*, 133–4. *TMS*, 53. *FS*, 186–8 (tr. 317–19).

122 *TFS*, 134. *TMS*, 55–6.

123 *TFS*, 173. Cf. J. A. Boyle, 'The death of the last ʿAbbasid Caliph: a contemporary Muslim account', *JSS* 6 (1961), 150, repr. in his *The Mongol world-empire* (London, 1977).

124 *TFS*, 171.

had become respectively *bārbeg* (*amīr-ḥājib*) and *wakīl-i dar*, allowed the Khalaj Jalāl al-Dīn to be summoned from his iqtaʿ of Sāmāna and given the office of *ʿāriḍ* and the iqtaʿ of Baran, with the style of Shāyista Khān.[125] But the two Aytemürs sought to destroy Jalāl al-Dīn. Aytemür *Kachhan fell in the struggle, while Surkha was killed in a vain bid to secure Kayūmarth.[126]

Jalāl al-Dīn's rise to power appears to have been the product of a compromise. As Baranī admits, a number of Turkish maliks and amirs had thrown in their lot with him,[127] and there had been negotiations with the Ghiyāthī party, headed by Balaban's nephew Malik Chhajjū; though why Chhajjū refused Jalāl al-Dīn's offer of the dignity of na'ib and opted to retire to the iqtaʿ of Kara is not explained. Jalāl al-Dīn's own enthronement in 689/1290 was the signal for Chhajjū to revolt in Awadh at the head of Balaban's Turkish slaves and their families and certain of the 'neo-Muslim' Mongol amirs. Chhajjū and many of his supporters were captured; Jalāl al-Dīn is said to have treated them leniently, though they forfeited their iqtaʿs and offices and Chhajjū himself, who was sent to Multān, is not heard of again.[128]

The 'Khaljī Revolution'

Jalāl al-Dīn's accession marked a break with the past in a way in which Balaban's usurpation had not. Early Muslim geographers and historians had regarded the Khalaj as a Turkish people;[129] but accounts of the transfer of power from the Ghiyathids to the Khaljīs indicate that in late-thirteenth-century Delhi they were regarded as a race quite distinct from the Turks.[130] This may well be due to the particular sense acquired by the word 'Turk', which in large measure had come to mean a Turkish ghulam (appendix I).

125 *TMS*, 55–6. For the title Shāyista Khān, see *TFS*, 126, 170 (SYAST; but cf. BL ms., fol. 91b).

126 I have largely preferred the circumstantial account in *TMS*, 56–61, to that of *TFS*, 172–3, where these events appear to be conflated to form a single episode, with *Kachchan's death closely followed by Surkha's. The version in *FS*, 203–9 (tr. 365–72), seems to belong to the same tradition as Sirhindī's. On one point Sirhindī is definitely in error. He calls the child sultan Kaykā'ūs (actually the name of Bughra Khān's younger son and successor at Lakhnawtī), but Baranī's Kayūmarth is corroborated by *QS*, 137, 142 etc., and by Ibn Abi'l-Faḍā'il, ed. Kortantamer, Ar. text 29 (German tr. 108).

127 *TFS*, 172.

128 The rebels included Balaban's *mawlāzāda* Amīr ᶜAlī Hātim Khān, *sar-i jāndār* and muqtaᶜ of Awadh; two other former Ghiyāthī commanders, Azhdar Khān's son Ikhtiyār al-Dīn Alp Ghāzī, muqtaᶜ of Kasrak (who was killed), and Malik Bahādur; and the 'neo-Muslim' amirs Bayanchar and Ulaghchi. HN, 313–15. The sources are *TMS*, 62–4; *TFS*, 181–4; and (the most detailed) *MF*, 7–22. For Alp Ghāzī as one of Kayqubād's maliks, see *TFS*, 126 (omitting 'LP; but cf. BL ms., fol. 68a). His parentage is given in *GK*, IOL Persian ms. 412, fol. 284a ('ZDR JAN in error for 'ŽDR XAN); cf. also *WH*, *ibid.*, fols. 114b, 143a (*pūr-i Azhdar Malik*).

129 References are conveniently collected in Aziz Aḥmad, 'Early Turkish nucleus', 103–5. See also Shabānkāra'ī, 87, who calls Jalāl al-Dīn 'likewise a Turk from among the Türkmen Khalaj' (*ham turkī būd az tarākima-yi khalaj*).

130 *TFS*, 171–2; cf. also 150, *az aṣl-u qawm-i dīgar*.

The transfer of power to Jalāl al-Dīn was greatly resented by the notables of Delhi, members of the great households (*khaylkhānahā*), many of whom may have been Turkish ghulams or their offspring and had been ensconced in the capital since at least Balaban's day.[131]

Whether the change of dynasty had profound implications for the composition of the aristocracy, however, by diluting the Turkishness of the governing class, is another question. Nobles of Turkish slave ancestry may indeed have been the principal casualties of the Khaljī seizure of power. Baranī portrays the sons of Balaban's maliks during Jalāl al-Dīn's reign as a pool of dispossessed nobles, alert for opportunities to undermine the new regime. For a time it seems that various grandees from Balaban's era who had lost their offices and stipends attached themselves to the new sultan's eldest son, Maḥmūd, entitled Khān-i Khānān; but on his premature death in *c.* 691/1292 they engaged in a conspiracy to replace Jalāl al-Dīn with the dervish Sīdī Muwallih and to redistribute court offices and iqtaʿs among the sons of Balaban's khans and maliks. By no means all of them were Turks: they included the former grand qadi Kāsānī, *Hatyā Pāīk and the kotwal *Birinjīn.[132] Although the charges could not be proven, two of the accused nobles were executed and the rest despoiled of their property and banished to outlying regions.[133] The conspiracy seems to have been divulged to the sultan by a Mongol amir named Alughu, who had joined his court in 691/1292.[134]

As we might expect, the new sultan took care to promote fellow-Khalaj tribesmen, particularly members of his somewhat large family, which comprised at the very least three sons; a brother, Malik Khāmush, who became *ʿāriḍ*; an uncle; and four nephews, one of whom was ʿAlāʾ al-Dīn Muḥammad (the future sultan), the offspring of Jalāl al-Dīn's deceased elder brother, Shihāb al-Dīn Masʿūd. Other newly promoted Khalaj amirs include the sultan's kinsman Aḥmad-i Chap (at one time chamberlain to Aytemür Surkha, and so called from the clipped pronunciation of *ḥājib* by the Khalaj), who became *sar-i jāndār-i maymana*, and probably Malik ʿIwaḍ, who bore a name common among the Khalaj.[135]

Yet Sirhindī, who asserts that the majority of posts went to the new sultan's kinsfolk,[136] overstates the case. An examination of the nobles listed

131 *Ibid.*, 172, 173.

132 For the kotwal's name, which appears as BRNJTN in *TFS*, see BL ms., fol. 113b (BRNJYN). Birinjīn had presumably succeeded Fakhr al-Dīn, whose death during Jalāl al-Dīn's reign is mentioned only by late sources: *AHG*, II, 782; Firishta, I, 161. For Khān-i Khānān's personal name, see *GK*, cited in Mirza, *Life and works*, 83 and n.3.

133 *TFS*, 210–11. For differing interpretations of this episode, see Hodivala, *Studies*, I, 267–8, and Simon Digby, 'Qalandars and related groups', in Friedmann, *Islam in Asia*, I, 67–8.

134 *TMS*, 65; for his arrival, see *TFS*, 218–19.

135 *TMS*, 62. Jalāl al-Dīn's relatives are listed in *FS*, 226–7 (tr. 392–3). On Aḥmad-i Chap, see Hodivala, *Studies*, I, 266.

136 *TMS*, 62.

by both Baranī and Sirhindī in their accounts of Jalāl al-Dīn's reign reveals that a large proportion had been prominent under the Ghiyathids and did not belong to the Khalaj. The most obvious instances are Khwāja Khaṭīr al-Dīn, who had been disgraced by Niẓām al-Dīn but who was now restored as wazir, and the kotwal Fakhr al-Dīn, who was confirmed in office.[137] Malik Fakhr al-Dīn Kūchī and his brother Malik Tāj al-Dīn possibly belonged to a family which had produced amirs in Iltutmish's day; under Jalāl al-Dīn they are found acting respectively as *dādbeg* and as muqtaʿ of Awadh.[138] Other examples of nobles who had served the Ghiyathids are the Indian converts Malik ʿAyn al-Dīn ʿAlī Shāh Kūhijūdī and his brother Malik Ikhtiyār al-Dīn Khurram, of whom the latter was now promoted to *wakīl-i dar*.[139] Such examples could be multiplied.[140] We even find Ikhtiyār al-Dīn-i Hindū Khān-i Ghiyāthī – from his cognomen (*nisba*) evidently the son of one of Balaban's slaves – as *nā'ib-i wakīl-i dar* under the new sultan.[141] Although some of these men would later be implicated in a half-hearted conspiracy against Jalāl al-Dīn,[142] it is noteworthy that none of them is said to have supported Chhajjū's revolt and that the Kūhijūdī brothers and Tāj al-Dīn Kūchī fought under the Khaljī banners on that occasion.[143]

The opening years of the Khaljī dynasty exhibit a striking continuity with the preceding era; and the ruling élite following Jalāl al-Dīn's accession bears the stamp of compromise that we noticed in connection with earlier changes of regime. By contrast, the impression given is that a dramatic shift in the composition of the ruling class – the real 'Khaljī revolution' – came

137 *TFS*, 174, 177.

138 For Tāj al-Dīn and Fakhr al-Dīn, see also *ibid.*, 203; *MF*, 14. Their father may have been Balaban's *dādbeg*, Malik Naṣīr al-Dīn Kūchī: *TFS*, 24 (though *FS* gives this as the name of Fakhr al-Dīn's brother). For earlier Kūchī maliks, *TN*, I, 456, 458, 459, and II, 6, 13 (tr. 633–4, 639, 640, 726, 735).

139 *TMS*, 84 (KHJWRY in error). *MF*, 27, 33–4. *TFS*, 174 ('XBAR for 'XTYAR, to be corrected from BL ms., fol. 93b), 177, 195, 233.

140 Malik Ikhtiyār al-Dīn Begtüt, *nā'ib-i amīr-ḥājib* under both Kayūmarth and Jalāl al-Dīn: *TMS*, 60, and *TFS*, 126 (SKNT, to be corrected from BL ms., fol. 68a); and for the name, L. Rásonyi, 'Les noms de personnes impératifs chez les peuples turcs', *AOH* 15 (1962), 241–2. Malik Mughaltai, previously exiled by Niẓām al-Dīn: *TMS*, 64–5. Malik Naṣīr al-Dīn Rāna, who retained his office of *shiḥna-yi pīl* from Balaban's reign through to that of ʿAlā' al-Dīn Khaljī: *TMS*, 58. Malik Nuṣrat-i Ṣabāḥ, whose father had likewise been a malik and who now became chief inkwell-holder (*sar-i dawātdār*): *TFS*, 174 (JNAḤ for ṢBAḤ, to be corrected from BL ms., fol. 93b), 198, 204; *FS*, 227 (tr. 393); *MF*, 14. Others mentioned in *MF* include Malik ʿAyn al-Dīn *Hiranmār, who became Jalāl al-Dīn's *amīr-i shikār*; Malik Maḥmūd, Jalāl al-Dīn's *sar-i jāndār*; Malik *Kīkī, who governed Kōl for the new sultan.

141 *TMS*, 62, 69.

142 *Hiranmār forfeited his office of *sar-i jāndār* and Tāj al-Dīn seems to have been deprived of Awadh, but Mughaltai and Mubārak were merely banished to their iqtaʿs for one year: *TFS*, 190–2; *TMS*, 64–5.

143 Except where other references have been given, the reconstruction in this paragraph is based on *TFS*, 126, 174, 177; *TMS*, 54, 62; and *MF*, 14, 28. Nigam, *Nobility*, 53 and Appendix C, reaches conclusions broadly similar to mine, though relying on the corrupt readings in the printed text of *TFS*.

with ʿAlāʾ al-Dīn. Initially the new sovereign was careful to reward those Jalālī grandees who had deserted his cousins. But once ʿAlāʾ al-Dīn's henchmen had secured the surrender of Multān in Muḥarram 696/ November 1296 and Jalāl al-Dīn's sons and their supporters had been blinded, the regime was strong enough to move against the Jalālī amirs. In the second year of the reign (late 696–late 697/1297–8), the great majority of them, including Hiranmār (now Amīn Khān), who had briefly held Multān, and Abachi (Arslan Khān), were arrested and imprisoned, blinded or executed; their wealth, iqtaʿs and offices were confiscated, and their military contingents transferred to ʿAlāʾ al-Dīn's own *clientela.* According to Baranī, only three, who had not betrayed Jalāl al-Dīn's sons or accepted gifts from the new regime, were spared.[144] Even this did not end the purge of the old nobility. The Malik al-Umarāʾ Fakhr al-Dīn, kotwal of Delhi, had probably died during Jalāl al-Dīn's reign; but his sons were rounded up and executed in 700/1301 on suspicion of complicity with a rising in Delhi led by their freedman Ḥājjī Mawlā.[145] Baranī exaggerates when he claims that in his own day no descendants of Balaban's nobles survived (see below, pp. 189–90);[146] but there can be little doubt that their almost total disappearance dates from the reign of ʿAlāʾ al-Dīn.

[144] *TFS*, 242, 247–8, 249–51. *TMS*, 71–2.
[145] *TFS*, 282. For Fakhr al-Dīn's death, see above, n.132.
[146] *TFS*, 48; cf. also HN, 302.

CHAPTER 5

The centre and the provinces

The terminology applied to the sultan's dominions was frequently unspecific. Jūzjānī writes of 'the empire of Delhi' (*mamālik-i Dihlī*) and Baranī of 'the provinces of the Delhi empire' (*bilād-i mamālik-i Dihlī*).[1] Ibn Baṭṭūṭa speaks of Muḥammad b. Tughluq's empire as 'Hind and Sind',[2] distinguishing the territory that had been won for Islam in the eighth century from the rest of the subcontinent. A Muslim geographer of an earlier generation distinguishes 'Hindūstān', the conquests of the Ghurids and their *epigoni*, from the wider Indian world, which he terms 'Hind'.[3] This usage echoes that of writers within India. Jūzjānī sometimes calls the Sultanate, like the Ghaznawid and Ghurid conquests before it, 'the territories (*mamālik*) of Hindūstān';[4] and we read accordingly of rulers obtaining the 'throne' (*takht*), or 'the kingdom' (*mulk*), of Hindūstān.[5] But in the thirteenth and fourteenth centuries, confusingly, 'Hindustān' also had a narrower significance for Muslim authors within the subcontinent. It denoted the Doab – the mesopotamia (*miyān-i dū āb*) between the Yamuna and the Ganges – along with the other partially subjugated regions to the east and south-east. People flee from Delhi 'to Hindūstān';[6] we hear of 'the iqtaʿs in the direction of Hindūstān' (*simṭ-i Hindūstān*)[7] and of the amirs and troops of Hindūstān, clearly in this restricted sense of the regions of the Doab, Awadh and Kara.[8] Such latitude in the use of geographical terms can

1 *TN*, II, 39 (tr. 785). *TFS*, 468.

2 IB, III, 94, 161, 215, 248 (tr. Gibb, 593, 628, 657, 674); see also al-Ṣafadī, *Wāfī*, III, 172.

3 Ibn Saʿīd al-Maghribī, *Kitāb al-Jughrāfiyya*, 134, 163.

4 *TN*, I, 6, 398, and II, 88, 90 (tr. xxxii, 455, 863, 874–9); cf. also I, 418 (tr. 530), where the term is used of the whole of Muslim-ruled territory in the subcontinent, including Sind; also II, 9, 32, *mamlikat-i Hindūstān* (tr. 731, 764).

5 *Ibid.*, II, 162, 169 (tr. 1129, 1153). *TFS*, 249. *FS*, 604, 605 (tr. 898, 899).

6 *TN*, II, 49 (tr. 802).

7 *Ibid.*, II, 66 (tr. 830): they comprised 'Kara and Mānikpūr, Awadh and Tirhut as far as Badā'ūn'. *TFS*, 272, 300. *TMS*, 63.

8 *TN*, I, 453, and II, 15, 29, 66 (tr. 629, 739, 759, 760, 830). The person in command was usually the muqtaʿ of Awadh. *Ibid.*, II, 72 (tr. 839), 'Hindūstān' clearly denotes Awadh, as distinct from the hill-state of Santūr; but cf. II, 58–9 (tr. 818), where it also implicitly includes the Chawhān kingdom of Ranthanbōr. *TFS*, 57, 141, 181, 182, 257, 300, 301, 328.

give rise to confusion. Baranī strikes perhaps the most incongruous note of all when he describes Sultan Balaban's vanquished 'Hindūstānī' troops (from Awadh) being despoiled by 'Hindus'.[9]

Even in the thirteenth century the Sultanate technically embraced a vast area and comprised several regions which could be termed kingdoms in their own right. Lahore, as 'the residence of Khusraw Malik'[10] (the last Ghaznawid sultan) and successively the appanage of Iltutmish's two elder sons (pp. 30, 46 above), was one. Another was Lakhnawtī, wrested by Iltutmish with such difficulty from its Khalaj rulers and extensive enough to be termed a 'clime' (*iqlīm*).[11] Both Jūzjānī and Baranī speak of the 'throne' (*takht*) or 'kingship' (*mulk*) and the 'insignia of rulership' (*pādishāhī*) being conferred on those sent to govern Lakhnawtī – whether Balaban's son in *c.* 680/1281 or great amirs like ʿAlā' al-Dīn Jānī and (later) his son Qilich Khān Masʿūd.[12] Viceroys of this eminence received certain quasi-imperial privileges such as the right to the durbash, or baton, and the chatr or ceremonial parasol: thus Iltutmish sent his son Nāṣir al-Dīn Maḥmūd in Bengal a red chatr in 626/1229, and Balaban conferred a chatr and a durbash on one son, Bughra Khān, at Lakhnawtī, and a chatr on the other, Muḥammad, at Multān, later transferring this emblem of authority to Muḥammad's son Kaykhusraw when his father died.[13] By this time Multān had replaced Lahore as the territory allotted to the heir-apparent, though whether Jalāl al-Dīn Khaljī, in conferring the city on his son Erkli Khān, granted him the customary insignia we are not told. The policy seems to have continued into the fourteenth century, when ʿAlā' al-Dīn Khaljī bestowed similar insignia – a red chatr, a robe of honour, and two standards – on his eldest son Khiḍr Khān at Chitōr in 703/1303, in much the same way as he conferred a chatr on the submissive Yadava king of Dēōgīr in 706/1307.[14]

The Delhi Sultanate could not, perhaps, be clearly defined in spatial terms. During the thirteenth century it should be seen as a collection of sub-kingdoms,[15] some ruled by Hindu potentates who periodically rendered tribute, others by princes of the sultan's dynasty or by Muslim amirs and muqtaʿs.[16] What ultimately determined the extent of the monarch's rule was recognition by the provincial governors, particularly those of outlying regions. Jūzjānī's claim that at Raḍiyya's accession 'all the maliks and amirs from the territory of Lakhnawtī as far as Dīwal (Daybul) and Damrīla

[9] *Ibid.*, 84. [10] *TN*, I, 454 (tr. 631). [11] E.g. *TFS*, 82, 93.

[12] *Ibid.*, 82, 92. *TN*, I, 448, and II, 13, 31, 35, 78.

[13] *Ibid.*, I, 454 (tr. 630). *TFS*, 66, 92, 110; for Bughra Khān, see also *DGK*, 69.

[14] Yadava king: *KF*, 63–4; *TFS*, 326. Khiḍr Khān: *DR*, 67; *TFS*, 367; *TMS*, 77.

[15] A point made by Peter Hardy, 'The growth of authority over a conquered political elite: the early Delhi Sultanate as a possible case study', in John S. Richards (ed.), *Kingship and authority in South Asia* (Madison, Wisconsin, 1978), 203–4.

[16] This is implicit in the views which Baranī puts into Balaban's mouth: *TFS*, 93.

manifested submission',[17] is (whether true or not) a more idiomatic statement concerning a sultan's authority than any amount of grandiloquence about the throne of 'the whole of the empire of Hindūstān'.

Disintegration and recovery

During the thirteenth century the empire created by Iltutmish fluctuated considerably in extent, as the conflicts within the ranks of the aristocracy, particularly the struggle between Ulugh Khān Balaban and his enemies in the 1250s, were often played out also in the provinces. That we know less about developments in territories at a distance from Delhi reflects in some measure the nature of the source material. The regional histories spawned from the fifteenth century onwards by the successor states fail to supplement Jūzjānī's testimony for the thirteenth, and apart from the period of his exile in Lakhnawtī (640–3/1242–6) Jūzjānī's perspective is always that of the centre and the court. Nevertheless, his tabaqa 22 – on the Shamsī maliks – does furnish a good deal of data on the iqtaʿs.

Following Iltutmish's death in 633/1236, Jūzjānī tells us, respect for 'the kingdom of Hindūstān' suffered a sharp decline, so that rivals sprang up on all sides and desired to appropriate its territories.[18] Many of these unspecified enemies would have been Hindu princes, while in Sind the most formidable adversary confronting Iltutmish's successors was initially the former Khwarazmian lieutenant Ḥasan Qarluq. But the sultan's own officers also profited from the situation at the centre. Jūzjānī's cryptic remark that the Shamsī slave Sayf al-Dīn Aybeg, muqtaʿ of Uchch, 'grew powerful' on Iltutmish's death might suggest that he briefly asserted his independence of Delhi before he was killed in a riding accident.[19] Sind is expressly included among the territories that submitted to Raḍiyya, and the next officer in charge of Uchch of whom we are told was her appointee, Hindū Khān, who was removed after her deposition.[20] The Mongol invasion of the Sultanate early in 639/1241–2 furnished new opportunities for self-aggrandisement. At Lahore Qaraqush Khān Ikhtiyār al-Dīn Aytegin, who had been installed there by Raḍiyya after the suppression of Kabīr Khān's revolt in 637/1239–40 (p. 67 above), had supported her attempt to regain the throne in the following year,[21] and so was at this time technically in rebellion against Bahrām Shāh. An army sent from Delhi turned back to besiege the capital and overthrow the sultan; but its purpose – not to relieve Lahore, we are told, but merely to guard the frontier[22] –

17 *TN*, I, 459, omitting Damrīla; but cf. BL ms., fol. 182b (also Raverty's tr., 641).
18 *Ibid.*, II, 9 (tr. 730–1).
19 *Ibid.*, II, 8–9 (tr. 730–1): the phrase *qūī-yi ḥāl gashta* is omitted in the printed text, but is found in BL ms., fol. 199a.
20 *TN*, I, 459 (tr. 641); II, 19 (tr. 746), for Hindū Khān.
21 *Ibid.*, I, 462 (tr. 647).
22 *Ibid.*, I, 466 (tr. 657).

reflects the fact that under Qaraqush Khān the city was now regarded as lying outside the sultan's dominions. In Multān Kabīr Khān Ayaz had proclaimed his independence with the adoption of a chatr, and occupied Uchch.[23] At this critical juncture, therefore, neither Lahore nor Sind formed part of the Sultanate.

Kabīr Khān Ayaz and his son Tāj al-Dīn Abū Bakr in turn defended their principality against Ḥasan Qarluq. The rule of this shortlived dynasty, for which Professor Nizami coined the appropriate name of 'Ayāzī', ended with Abū Bakr's death in the early 1240s, when Ḥasan Qarluq finally obtained Multān.[24] Although Sind was recovered by the sultan's forces in the wake of the Mongol invasion of 643/1245,[25] the risk of secession grew with the onset of the conflicts of Nāṣir al-Dīn Maḥmūd Shāh's reign. Sind effectively ceased to form part of the Sultanate shortly afterwards, when Küshlü Khān, thwarted in his joint bid with Qutlugh Khān to seize Delhi (pp. 74–5 above), appealed to the Mongols. Jūzjānī, writing when the Mongols had dismantled Multān's fortifications, betrays by his phrasing that Sind now lay outside 'the borders of the empire of Delhi' (*sarḥaddhā-yi mamālik-i Dihlī*).[26]

Lahore is described as ruined (*kharāb*) in the wake of the Mongol sack in Jumādā II 639/December 1241,[27] although the city seems to have been held for a couple of years by Ikhtiyār al-Dīn Yüzbeg (Toghril Khān).[28] Thereafter Jūzjānī makes little mention of Lahore,[29] which like the regions lying beyond it, in the far north-west, had apparently come to form part of the Mongol dominions. From *c.* 651/1253 we find the renegade prince Jalāl al-Dīn Mas'ūd b. Iltutmish at Lahore as a Mongol client (p. 111 below). He maintained himself there only for a short time, being dislodged by Shīr Khān on the latter's return from the Mongol court.[30] Although he once more became an ally of the Delhi government, Shīr Khān soon began to evince designs on his old iqta' of Tabarhindh, which was currently held by Arslan Khān, and engaged in conflict with him too. At this point the court interposed, winning Shīr Khān over with the grant of Tabarhindh and 'the whole of the territory and iqta's which he had previously held', including presumably Lahore. Yet the place was doubtless impossible to hold, and Shīr Khān seemingly abandoned it. When in 657/1259 the sultan obliged

23 *Ibid.*, II, 6 (tr. 727).
24 At Uchch Hindū Khān's officials, however, remained in place: for this and Ḥasan Qarluq's seizure of the city, *ibid.*, II, 169–70 (tr. 1153). 'Ayāzī dynasty': HN, 249, 255, 260. On Abū Bakr, see Siddiqi, 'Historical information', 64.
25 *TN*, II, 28, 37 (tr. 758, 781).
26 *Ibid.*, II, 39 (tr. 785); and cf. also II, 86 (tr. 860).
27 *Ibid.*, II, 169 (tr. 1153). For the date, see below, p. 105 and n.12.
28 *TN*, II, 30 (tr. 762).
29 *Ibid.*, II, 43, has Lahore being granted to Shīr Khān along with Tabarhindh in 643/1245, but cf. BL ms., fol. 211 (also Raverty's tr., 793), where Lahore is omitted.
30 *TN*, II, 44 (tr. 793).

him to exchange his extensive assignment with Nuṣrat Khān, the muqtaʿ of Bhayāna, there is no mention of Lahore among the latter's new holdings.[31]

To the east, Awadh could be characterized as another problematic region in the 1250s. Qutlugh Khān, who was sent there after his removal from court in 653/1255, encroached on the territory of Badā'ūn, and defeated a force under its muqtaʿ *Teniz Khān, reinforced by troops from Delhi under Begtemür Or Khān-i Ruknī; Or Khān was killed.[32] In 654/1256 Awadh was entrusted to Arslan Khān, who had been a prominent supporter of Ulugh Khān Balaban two years before; and the new muqtaʿ performed sterling service by obstructing Qutlugh Khān's efforts to occupy Kara. But then, says Jūzjānī, Arslan Khān's attitude towards the government underwent a change and he grew rebellious. When preparations were under way at Delhi early in 656/1258 for a campaign to drive the Mongols from Sind, Arslan Khān and Qilich Khān Jalāl al-Dīn Masʿūd, the son of ʿAlā' al-Dīn Jānī and muqtaʿ of Kara, neglected to bring their contingents. Ulugh Khān Balaban marched on Kara, and the two recalcitrant amirs were brought to heel.[33] Qilich Khān received a patent for Lakhnawtī; Arslan Khān was transferred to Kara, although as we shall see his new iqtaʿ was not of a size to contain his ambitions.

Beyond Awadh, tenuous links bound Delhi to the distant Muslim-held territories in Bengal. In the fourteenth century this region would be known as the 'lowlands' (*furū-dast*),[34] to distinguish it from the 'upper country' (*bālā-dast*), which vaguely embraced the north-west and the lands beyond the Indus towards Transoxiana. ʿAfīf, a westerner of course, makes the 'lowlanders' (*furūdastān*) confess to being no match for those from the uplands (*bālādastān*).[35] Yet to conquer and hold Bengal – 'a land for foot-soldiers' (*zamīn-i rijāla*), as the Tughluqid Sultan Fīrūz Shāh would describe it in 1354[36] – was no easy task. It was proverbially wealthy – 'a Hell full of dainties' (*dūzakh ast pur-i niʿmat*), to quote Ibn Baṭṭūṭa.[37] None of the amirs of Hindūstān, says Baranī, could rival in terms of men, elephants or treasure whoever controlled Bengal; and the conduct of many of its governors during the thirteenth century fully vindicated the nickname 'Bulghākpūr' ('city of insurrection') which he says men gave to Lakhnawtī.[38]

After Iltutmish's death, the sultans had to recognize the autonomy of

[31] *Ibid.*, II, 42–3 (tr. 788); for the exchange, see also II, 44 (tr. 794).
[32] *Ibid.*, I, 490, and II, 29 (tr. 703, 759–60).
[33] *Ibid.*, II, 34–5, 77–8 (tr. 768–9, 847–8). For Qilich Khān, who has frequently been confused with other grandees, see appendix II.
[34] *TFS*, 189. *SFS*, 33, 48. Bihāmadkhānī, fol. 421b, uses the term more broadly, for the regions east of the Yamuna.
[35] ᶜAfīf, 153; for the sense, see Hodivala, *Studies*, II, 127.
[36] ᶜAfīf, 119. On this phrase, see Hodivala, *Studies*, I, 312–13, who translates it as 'a land of foot-soldiers': in view of the phrase that follows regarding the difficulty of life among the islands, I suspect that the sultan meant, rather, 'a land [fit only] for foot-soldiers', i.e. that the heavily armoured horsemen of the Delhi Sultanate were ineffective here.
[37] IB, IV, 210 (tr. Gibb and Beckingham, 867). [38] *TFS*, 82.

their representatives at Lakhnawtī while receiving little in return. Since 631/1233–4 the muqtaʿ of both Bihār and Lakhnawtī had been the Shamsī slave ʿIzz al-Dīn Toghril Toghan Khān. The geographical location of his iqtaʿ conferred on Toghan Khān a good deal of independence, and once Iltutmish was dead he engaged with impunity, it seems, in warfare against the muqtaʿ of Lakhnōr (the region on the west bank of the Ganges), slaying him and appropriating part of his territory. Both Raḍiyya and Bahrām Shāh nevertheless legitimized Toghan Khān's irregular actions by sending him a red chatr and standards; and after the accession of Masʿūd Shāh, Toghan Khān dropped all pretence of loyalty to the Delhi court. An inscription from Bihār dated 640/1242 accords him a variety of grandiose titles and makes no reference to the sultan. In this same year he advanced into the Kara-Mānikpūr region in an abortive attempt to occupy Awadh.[39]

Following a disastrous campaign against the Hindu kingdom of Jājnagar (Orissa) late in 641/early in 1244, however, Toghan Khān asked the sultan for reinforcements. Masʿūd Shāh thereupon despatched to Lakhnawtī not merely a red chatr and a standard but a robe of honour and an ornate tent. But these attentions were apparently designed simply to throw Toghan Khān off guard. We learn elsewhere that Tāj al-Dīn Sanjar *Kirit Khān died from an arrow-wound outside the city of Bihār in an obscure conflict soon after 640/1242,[40] which – unless the place had been lost by the Muslims and the enemy was a Hindu king – suggests that the government may already have been attempting to retrieve Bihār. Now, on Toghan Khān's appeal for help, orders were issued to the muqtaʿ of Awadh, Temür Khān, and other commanders to move into Bengal. When this supposedly relieving force reached Lakhnawtī, it engaged in hostilities not with the Hindus, who had withdrawn, but with Toghan Khān. Compelled to come to terms, he surrendered the province to Temür Khān and accompanied the other amirs back to Delhi. At this juncture Masʿūd Shāh's government indulged in another attempt to play the two enemies off against each other, granting Toghan Khān in 643/1245 Temür Khān's iqtaʿ of Awadh. Temür Khān's reaction to the seizure of Awadh from his officers is not described; but he remained in control of Lakhnawtī until both men died, on the same day in Shawwāl 644/March 1247, during the reign of Nāṣir al-Dīn Maḥmūd Shāh.

The history of Lakhnawtī over the next few years is obscure. An inscription of 647/1249 commemorates as the current muqtaʿ Jalāl al-Dīn Masʿūd (the later Qilich Khān), son of ʿAlāʾ al-Dīn Jānī.[41] But he is not mentioned at this stage by Jūzjānī, who next names Ikhtiyār al-Dīn Yüzbeg

39 It was on the borders of Kara that Jūzjānī waited on him before accompanying him back to Lakhnawtī: *TN*, I, 469 (tr. 662–3). For Toghan Khān's career, see *ibid.*, II, 13–17 (tr. 736–42). Yazdani, 'Inscriptions of the Turk Sulṭāns', 16–17; *RCEA*, XI, 143 (no. 4215).
40 *TN*, II, 27–8 (tr. 757).
41 Yazdani, 'Inscriptions of the Turk Sulṭāns', 19–22; *RCEA*, XI, 211 (no. 4320).

Toghril Khān in command of the province. The career of this compulsive rebel epitomizes the problems posed for the government by over-mighty subjects. On the accession of Masʿūd Shāh, Yüzbeg had been entrusted with Tabarhindh. Then – most probably at the time of that monarch's expedition to Uchch in 643/1245–6 – he was transferred to Lahore, where he first engaged in conflict with an otherwise unknown malik and then defied the sultan's authority. As we have noted, Ulugh Khān Balaban secured for him both a pardon and a new iqtaʿ at Qinnawj, where he seems to have again proved refractory, probably in support of Balaban. Reduced to obedience by an expedition under Quṭb al-Dīn Ḥasan b. ʿAlī, he was brought back to court and subsequently assigned Awadh. It is likely that he supported Ulugh Khān Balaban's return to power in 652/1254. From this date, however, Yüzbeg Toghril Khān is found in command at Lakhnawtī. Here a major victory over the raja of Jājnagar, who had successfully resisted Toghan Khān's aggression over ten years previously, encouraged him to assert his independence of Delhi; he assumed three chatrs and had coins struck and the khutba read in his own name as Sultan Mughīth al-Dīn. He died a few years later, in the course of a disastrous invasion of neighbouring Kāmrūp (Assam).[42]

Yüzbeg Toghril Khān's death seems to have occurred before Ṣafar 655/February–March 1257, when coins were again being struck at Lakhnawtī in the name of Nāṣir al-Dīn Maḥmūd Shāh.[43] At the end of 656/1258 Lakhnawtī was conferred once more on Qilich Khān Jalāl al-Dīn Masʿūd-i Jānī, who had recently been guilty of insubordination along with Arslan Khān. But only a few months later, in Jumādā II 657/June 1259, Ulugh Khān Balaban persuaded the sultan to recognize as muqtaʿ ʿIzz al-Dīn Balaban-i Yüzbegī, whom we have already encountered as the son-in-law of the rebel Qutlugh Khān and who had just secured the court's favour by sending impressive gifts to Delhi.[44] In the event, however, Balaban-i Yüzbegī lost the province not to Qilich Khān (who is not heard of again) but to the latter's confederate. Acting without sanction from Delhi and giving out even to his own sons and troops that he was engaged in a plundering expedition into infidel Mālwa, Arslan Khān left Kara and marched swiftly on Lakhnawtī. The city was taken and sacked, and Balaban-i Yüzbegī, who returned from operations in eastern Bengal (Bang) to offer battle to the invaders, was captured and put to death. This was the state of affairs in the east when Jūzjānī stopped writing in 658/1260.[45]

[42] *TN*, II, 30–3 (tr. 762–6), for Toghril Khān's biography. His career is conveniently summarized by Habibullah, *Foundation*, 129–30. For his coins, see now Roma Niyogi, 'A new coin of Mughisu-d-Din Yūzbak of Bengal', *JNSI* 40 (1978–9), 136–8.

[43] *CMSD*, 55 (no. 225C).

[44] *TN*, I, 495, and II, 35, 78 (tr. 712, 770, 848–9).

[45] *Ibid.*, II, 35 (tr. 769–72). Laiq Aḥmad, 'Kara, a medieval Indian city', *IC* 55 (1981), 85, confuses the events of these years and assumes that Arslan Khān's sack of Lakhnawtī preceded the recalcitrance mentioned above.

Baranī's testimony may indicate that Arslan Khān remained defiant in Lakhnawtī until his death, since the despatch of elephants from Bengal to Delhi upon Balaban's accession in 664/1266 by his son and successor, Tatar Khān Muḥammad, was viewed as something out of the ordinary.[46]

Events in these outlying regions highlight the restrictions on the power of the sovereign. Amirs frequently revolted; in distant Bengal, at least, they might do so with impunity for some years. In order to assert itself, the government on more than one occasion resorted to acts of duplicity. The sultan might confer a rebel's territory on a rival only to make use of the dispossessed amir as a counterweight to the now over-powerful commander who had taken his place, as seems to have transpired in 642/1244 first in the removal of Toghan Khān from Lakhnawtī and then in his despatch to Awadh. Sometimes the court made virtually simultaneous grants of the same iqtaʿ to two different nobles and left them to fight it out. This occurred in 653/1255, when the conferment of Bahraich on Tāj al-Dīn Sanjar Sīwistānī followed suspiciously close on the heels of its allocation to ʿImād al-Dīn Rayhān (p. 74). It may have been the policy regarding Lakhnawtī in 656/1258, when the regime's contradictory actions defy interpretation. Perhaps the court had briefly envisaged the removal of Balaban-i Yüzbegī, as a surviving connection of Qutlugh Khān. But it is equally possible that the reconciliation between Qilich Khān and the regime at Delhi was merely superficial and that the grant of Lakhnawtī represented an attempt to double-cross him.

In the latter part of Maḥmūd Shāh's reign the Delhi empire had contracted to the point where it embraced an area hardly larger than that ruled at his accession by Iltutmish. When Jūzjānī wrote, it might well have appeared to be in a state of disintegration. Why it did not disintegrate, we shall probably never fully understand. As regards the western provinces, a partial explanation is surely furnished by divisions within the Mongol ranks (see below, pp. 108–10, 115–16). But such information as we have concerning the Sultanate's internal history furnishes no answer. Between Jūzjānī's completion of his *Ṭabaqāt* in 658/1260 and the commencement of Baranī's history with the accession of Balaban stands a hiatus of six years that may well have been crucial for the Sultanate's survival.

To say that the government's authority over its distant provinces was restored during Balaban's own reign is to beg a large question, for the treatment of events by Baranī, ʿIṣāmī and Sirhindī is far less detailed than Jūzjānī's handling of the vicissitudes of Maḥmūd Shāh's era; it cannot be emphasized sufficiently that we know more about Balaban as khan and na'ib than we do of his time as sultan. Nevertheless, there can be no doubt that under Balaban some kind of *rassemblement* occurred of the territories

[46] *TFS*, 53; see also 66, where he is called Muḥammad and described as '*pādishāh* of Lakhnawtī'.

that had at one time acknowledged Iltutmish. He is known to have led an army to Lahore within a few years of his accession and to have restored and repopulated the city,[47] so that it can once more be deemed to have formed part of the Sultanate; though it is surely significant that we find no reference to its being granted as iqtaʿ again before the fourteenth century. Sind was also recovered. At some point towards the end of Maḥmūd Shāh's reign, Küshlü Khān lost control of the province, in obscure circumstances. In a problematic passage, ʿIṣāmī says that Ulugh Khān Balaban profited from Küshlü Khān's absence to seize Multān.[48] His disappearance may be connected with the advent of the Negüderi Mongols, which will be examined later (see pp. 115–16). At any rate Balaban was able to instal as viceroy in Sind his own elder son Muḥammad (Khān-i Shahīd),[49] who governed until his untimely death in battle with the Mongols at the very end of 683/in March 1285.

Lakhnawtī appears to have been regained with comparative ease, since Tatar Khān died in, or soon after, 665/1266–7[50] and Balaban despatched his own representatives to the province. The sources differ, Baranī and ʿIṣāmī alleging that the sultan's ghulam Toghril was sent out to Lakhnawtī as governor (*wālī*), while Sirhindī has Balaban appointing Amīn Khān (i.e. Aytegin-i Mūī-yi Darāz; see p. 78) to the post, with Toghril as his deputy (na'ib).[51] In any event, the province proved no less turbulent for Balaban than for his Shamsid predecessors. Toghril rebelled in *c.* 678/1279–80, and – in a gesture strikingly remininscent of Yüzbeg a generation earlier – assumed the style of Sultan Mughīth al-Dīn. He defied two successive campaigns by the sultan's lieutenants before he was overwhelmed by an army under Balaban in person, probably in 680/1281–2.[52]

Balaban then entrusted Lakhnawtī to his younger son, Bughra Khān Maḥmūd, who proclaimed his own sovereignty after the old sultan's death in 685/1287, when he found his expectations of the throne cheated by his son Kayqubād, and briefly occupied Awadh.[53] The status of Lakhnawtī after father and son were reconciled in 686/1287 is therefore unclear; but

47 *Ibid.*, 61. *TMS*, 40. Cf. also *FS*, 164 (tr. 291).
48 *Ibid.*, 154–5 (tr. 278–80).
49 *TFS*, 66, dating this after the death of Shīr Khān, which at 64–5 is said to have occurred 'four or five years' into the reign.
50 For an inscription of Tatar Khān dated 665/1266–7, see Yazdani, 'Inscriptions of the Turk Sulṭāns', 23–5; *RCEA*, XII, 121–2 (no. 4854).
51 *TFS*, 81. *FS*, 165 (tr. 292). *TMS*, 40.
52 *TFS*, 81, 83–92; at 81, Baranī places Toghril's revolt 'fifteen or sixteen years' after Balaban's accession, i.e. in 677–8/1278–80 if we start from his incorrect year 662 for the sultan's enthronement. This can be reconciled with the report on Balaban's campaign against Jājnagar (Orissa) found in *RI*, V, 5–13, and dated 5 Shawwāl 680/17 January 1282 (*ibid.*, 13). Firishta, I, 138, also dates the revolt precisely to 678, though on what authority is unclear. *FS*, 164 (tr. 291), puts the rising a mere eight years after Balaban's accession, and later, 168 (tr. 296), supplies the impossible year 670.
53 *QS*, 36, 44–6.

following the transfer of power in Delhi to Jalāl al-Dīn Khaljī in 689/1290 Bughra Khān and his successors certainly acted as independent monarchs. Epigraphical evidence shows that their authority extended also over the Muslim territory in southern Bihār.[54] This branch of the Ghiyathid dynasty was shortlived. Bughra Khān's young son and successor, Rukn al-Dīn Kaykā'ūs, who died around the turn of the century, was followed first by an obscure ruler named Shams al-Dīn Dawlat Shāh and then by Shams al-Dīn Fīrūz Shāh, who is probably identical with Kaykā'ūs's amir Fīrūz-i Aytegin and who founded a new dynasty.[55] At some point ʿAlā' al-Dīn Khaljī may have attacked Bengal;[56] but it was only with the outbreak of a struggle among Fīrūz Shāh's sons, leading to the intervention of Ghiyāth al-Dīn Tughluq Shāh in 724/1324, that the region again became a province of the Delhi Sultanate (see below, pp. 200–1).

The iqtaʿ and provincial government

At the heart of the thirteenth-century Sultanate lay the *khāliṣa* or 'reserved' lands – what might be called the 'royal demesne' – from which the sultan's own officials collected revenue directly and which provided his most immediate resources. Regarding the full extent of the khalisa we have no information, although it is usually taken to have included the environs (*ḥawālī*) of Delhi.[57] Other territories were granted out as iqtaʿ. The term 'iqtaʿ' applied not only to the large assignments enjoyed by great amirs but also to the smaller ones established by Iltutmish in the Doab, according to Baranī, who tells us that each grantee (*iqṭāʿdār*) was expected to raise from one to three horsemen.[58] It is possible that Amīr Khusraw's father, Sayf-i Shamsī (d. *c.* 659/1261), held such an iqtaʿ.[59] Early in his reign Sultan Balaban sought to resume many of these small iqtaʿs into the khalisa, on the grounds that the grantees were now too old to serve or had died and had transmitted their holdings to heirs who performed no service; in the event, says Baranī, he was dissuaded by the kotwal Fakhr al-Dīn.[60] Although the chronicler does not say so, the episode was doubtless a measure of

[54] A. A. Kadiri, 'Inscriptions of the Sultans of Bengal from Bihar', *EIAPS* (1961), 35–6; Q. Aḥmad, *Corpus of Arabic and Persian inscriptions of Bihar (AH 640–1200)* (Patna, 1973), 9–10 (no. 3).

[55] On Dawlat Shāh, see John S. Deyell, 'A reassessment of the new coin of Daulat Shah of Bengal', *JNSI* 41 (1979), 82–90. For Fīrūz Shāh's line, see Abdul Majed Khan, 'The historicity of Ibn Batuta re Shamsuddin Firuz Shah, the so-called Balbani king of Bengal', *IHQ* 18 (1942), 65–70; R. C. Majumdar, *History of mediaeval Bengal* (Calcutta, 1973), 18.

[56] According to the anonymous translator of *Baḥr al-Ḥayāt*, IOL Persian ms. 432 (Ethé, no. 2002). *TFS*, 227–9, 254, speaks only of his designs on Bengal. An ode in *GK* (tr. in ED, III, 543) refers to a campaign in Bihār and the seizure of Bengal elephants from Lakhnawtī.

[57] On the *khāliṣa*, see W. H. Moreland, *The agrarian system of Moslem India* (Cambridge, 1929), 29 and n.1; more generally, A. K. S. Lambton, 'Khāliṣa', *Enc.Isl.*²

[58] *TFS*, 62. [59] On him, see *DGK*, 66, 67: he died when Khusraw was seven.

[60] *TFS*, 60, 61–4.

Balaban's need for fresh resources with which to reward his own retinue who had supported his accession.

Our information about the conferment of iqtaʿs is of course more plentiful for the larger kind; and it is also far greater where Shamsī ghulams are concerned than it is for nobles of free status, about whom we know very little. Some regions appear regularly as iqtaʿs in Jūzjānī's *Ṭabaqāt*. Iltutmish had at one time held 'the iqtaʿ of the town (*qaṣaba*) of Baran with its dependencies (*maḍāfāt*)', for example, and Baran was frequently granted out as iqtaʿ during his reign and those of his Shamsid successors.[61] It is unclear whether certain major offices automatically carried with them the grant of particular localities. Certainly, a close link can be detected between the office of wazir and the town of Kōl; though this ceased with the overthrow of Muhadhdhab al-Dīn in 640/1242.[62] In the biography of Aybeg-i Shamsī-yi ʿAjamī we read of 'the iqtaʿs of the *amīr-i dād*', and Jūzjānī's phrasing suggests at least that in his capacity of *dādbeg* of the empire that amir received the iqtaʿ of Palwal and Kāma.[63] By Kayqubād's reign, there seems to be a clear connection between the office of *ʿāriḍ* and the iqtaʿ of Baran.[64]

There are indications that a few major strongholds were 'reserved' (*maḥrūsa*) as part of the sultan's khalisa and were consequently not granted as iqtaʿ. The place most consistently referred to as *maḥrūsa* is Gwāliyōr following its recapture in 630/1232–3.[65] On that occasion Iltutmish appointed an *amīr-i dād* and a castellan (*kōtwāl*).[66] Subsequently, when its troops were placed under the authority of the muqtaʿ of Bhayāna and Sulṭānkōt, he was instructed to make Gwāliyōr his headquarters and is said to have held the intendancy (*shiḥnagī*) of that territory (*wilāyat*).[67] Certain other important towns are referred to as *maḥrūsa*, but their status appears to have varied. The city of Bihār, for instance, is once termed *maḥrūsa*, but it is also spoken of as an iqtaʿ.[68] Tabarhindh is more often described as *maḥrūsa*,[69] and accordingly we find Qaraqush Khān appointed as 'intendant (*shiḥna*) of the private domain (*khāliṣāt*) of Tabarhindh'.[70] On one or two other occasions the relationship between the city and its commander is unclear: *Kezlik Khān is described as the 'malik' of Tabarhindh and Arslan Khān is said to have been entrusted with the *maḥrūsa* of Tabarhindh.[71] Similarly, although Jūzjānī applies the term *maḥrūsa* to Uchch when

61 *TN*, I, 443, and II, 8, 21, 25, 27, 29 (tr. 604, 730, 748, 754, 757 [with Badā'ūn in error], 759).

62 Z. A. Desai, 'Inscriptions of the Mamlūk Sulṭāns of Delhi', *EIAPS* (1966), 8–11; *TN*, I, 456, 469 (tr. 634, 662). For grantees among the military aristocracy later in the thirteenth century, see *ibid*., II, 42 (tr. 787); *RCEA*, XI, 258–9 (no. 4394); *TFS*, 66, 88, 113.

63 *TN*, II, 41 (tr. 790–1).

64 *TFS*, 134, 170.

65 *TN*, I, 460, and II, 19, 24, 25, 78, 214.

66 *Ibid*., I, 448 (tr. 620 renders *kōtwāl* as 'seneschal').

67 *Ibid*., II, 10–11 (tr. 732).

68 *Ibid*., II, 9, 28 (tr. 731; and cf. also 757).

69 *Ibid*., II, 4, 34, 38, 43, 44 (tr. 723, 767, 784, 792).

70 *Ibid*., II, 20 (tr. 746).

71 *Ibid*., I, 446 (tr. 613), for *Kezlik Khān; II, 34 (tr. 767), for Arslan Khān.

describing its conquest by Iltutmish in 625/1228 and its conferment on *Kezlik Khān, we read that in 629/1231–2 'the city and iqtaʿ of Uchch' were granted to Sayf al-Dīn Aybeg.[72] One is tempted to infer from this wording that the fortified city itself formed no part of an iqtaʿ grant and that whatever authority the muqtaʿ wielded here rested on a different basis. But this is clearly not the case with Tabarhindh at those times when it figures unequivocally as an iqtaʿ. Ikhtiyār al-Dīn *Altunapa is described as its muqtaʿ under Raḍiyya (at a period when it is nevertheless designated as *maḥrūsa*);[73] ʿAlā' al-Dīn Masʿūd Shāh granted the city as iqtaʿ to Ikhtiyār al-Dīn Yüzbeg (Toghril Khān);[74] and later in the reign of the same sultan we read that 'the fortress of Tabarhindh was assigned to Shīr Khān as iqtaʿ and the whole of the dependencies (*maḍāfāt*) of the *maḥrūsa* of Tabarhindh were bestowed upon him'.[75] Such terminology precludes any possibility that the iqtaʿ grant extended only to the hinterland and did not apply to the stronghold itself.

In some cases the terms in which a grant is couched vary between one recipient and another; and we even find the same grant described in different language at two different points in the *Ṭabaqāt*. Kabīr Khān is said to have been granted 'the city and fortress of Multān, its townships (*qaṣabāt*) and its districts near and far (*aṭrāf-u ḥawālī*)', and appointed to the governorship (*ayālat*); elsewhere he is duly termed *wālī* of Multān.[76] Later, however, when held by Qaraqush Khān and a second time by Kabīr Khān himself, Multān is called an iqtaʿ.[77] 'The territory (*wilāyat*) of Awadh and its dependencies (*maḍāfāt*)' were allotted to Temür Khān by Raḍiyya, and Qutlugh Khān received the 'government' (*ayālat*) of Awadh in 653/1255;[78] but elsewhere these officers are referred to as muqtaʿs of Awadh, which on other occasions also is expressly said to have constituted an iqtaʿ.[79] In rare cases, we gain the impression that the muqtaʿ held the specific rank of *amīr-i dād* in the town entrusted to him, as did Aybeg-i Shamsī-yi ʿAjamī in Kasrak and subsequently in Baran.[80] Even in the case of those provinces with more prestigious connotations, like Lahore, the status of the grant probably varied with that of the grantee. Within a few years, in the hands of amirs rather than a prince of the blood, Lahore, though still at one point designated as a *mamlikat*, was being assigned as iqtaʿ.[81]

Vague and contradictory terminology prevents us from imposing neat categories on thirteenth-century arrangements. We clearly cannot expect consistency from our sources, and perhaps in any case the distinction between gubernatorial status (*ayālat*) and that of muqtaʿ is of no practical significance. Although the iqtaʿ was in origin a revenue assignment, the

72 *Ibid.*, II, 3, 8 (cf. Raverty's tr., 724, 730).
73 *Ibid.*, I, 460; cf. I, 462 (twice).
74 *Ibid.*, II, 30.
75 *Ibid.*, II, 43.
76 *Ibid.*, I, 455–6, and II, 5.
77 *Ibid.*, II, 20, 163.
78 *Ibid.*, II, 17, 69.
79 *Ibid.*, I, 458, 489, and II, 16, 17, 27.
80 *Ibid.*, II, 42 (tr. 791).
81 *Ibid.*, I, 455, 459, 460, 465, and II, 7, 30, 163; also II, 6, for the *mamlikat* of Lahore.

muqtaʿ was not some remote pensionary or military aide at court who had no connection with the territory in his grant, but an officer who incurred genuine administrative responsibilities. Earlier in the century Ḥasan-i Niẓāmī had inserted in his *Tāj al-Maʾāthir* the instructions purportedly given to the unnamed amir who had received the *ayālat* of the newly conquered fortress of Banāras. He was to care for the interests of both the men of the sword and the men of the pen, to protect them from the infidel, to oversee the labours of the peasants (*raʿāyā*), to ensure the security of the fortresses, and to discharge the requirements of charity and good works. The injunctions said to have been issued to Ḥusām al-Dīn Oghulbeg at Kōl a year or so later are not dissimilar. His duties include not only the waging of *jihād*, the guarding of highways and the encouragement of trade, but also honour and preferment to members of the 'religious class' and the administration of justice without distinction between those of good birth and the common people.[82]

Some muqtaʿs, if our sources can be trusted, attained these high standards. The Bhayāna region owed its flourishing condition to the efforts of Bahāʾ al-Dīn Toghril, Muʿizz al-Dīn's ghulam commander who had become its first muqtaʿ in 592/1196.[83] 'Whatever district (*nāḥiyat*) or iqtaʿ or territory (*wilāyat*) was placed under his control', says Jūzjānī of Aybeg-i Shamsī-yi ʿAjamī, 'has flourished, and the generality of the subjects (*ʿāmma-yi raʿāyā*) have been content.'[84] The same author assures us that when the two uncles of ʿAlāʾ al-Dīn Masʿūd Shāh (one of them the future sultan Maḥmūd Shāh) went to their newly conferred grants, they busied themselves not only with the holy war but also with improving the conditions of the peasantry.[85] Of *Kezlik Khān (d. 629/1231–2) at Uchch, it is said that he strove for the security and repose of the peasants and performed good works and acts of charity.[86] Balaban is praised by Baranī for bringing prosperity to every territory conferred on him as malik or as khan; and Jūzjānī says that when he first arrived at Hānsī he 'gave his attention to cultivation (*ʿimārat*), and the people derived contentment from the monuments of his justice and the rays of his generosity'.[87] So too another future sultan, Jalāl al-Dīn Khaljī, allegedly caused his assignment of Pāyal to flourish.[88] None of this necessarily testifies, of course, to an enlightened outlook on the part of the muqtaʿ. He had a vested interest in the material condition of the tract of which he enjoyed the revenues; and possibly in any case such eulogies, like the instructions cited by Ḥasan-i Niẓāmī or the exhortations later ascribed to Sultan Ghiyāth al-Dīn Tughluq,[89] tell us at least as much about what was expected of the muqtaʿ as about what was

82 *Tāj*, fols. 135b–136a, for Banāras; fols. 138a–141a for Kōl.
83 *TN*, I, 421 (tr. 545, 547).
84 *Ibid.*, II, 41 (tr. 789–90 modified).
85 *Ibid.*, I, 470 (tr. 665).
86 *Ibid.*, II, 5 (tr. 724).
87 *TFS*, 45. *TN*, II, 52 (tr. 807 modified).
88 *FS*, 201 (tr. 364).
89 *TFS*, 430.

actually accomplished. Hardy's reminder that the thirteenth-century muqtaʿ was one 'commissioned by the sultan to take charge not of a local territorial unit but of a local situation'[90] is surely salutary. The task of the grantee may have consisted primarily in receiving the tribute from the more compliant Hindu chiefs at some strongpoint and using it as a base for military operations to extract further tribute and plunder from their less accommodating peers.[91] In a large number of cases, Jūzjānī can find little more to say of an amir's activities within a particular iqtaʿ than that he chastised Hindu 'recalcitrants' (*mutamarridān*) and 'rebels' (*mufsidān*), and destroyed their lairs (*mawāsāt*).[92] Few are credited with founding mosques and implanting Islamic institutions.[93]

It is possible that in the latter half of the thirteenth century the relative wealth and importance of an iqtaʿ may have been expressed in terms of the number of horsemen the grantee maintained. Thus Baranī tells us that Balaban's slave Malik *Buqubuq, muqtaʿ of Badā'ūn, had 4,000 horsemen in his service (*chākir*), and that Malik Nuṣrat-i Ṣabāḥ, muqtaʿ of Gānūrī and Chawpāla (now Moradabad) in the reign of Jalāl al-Dīn Khaljī, had 700 horsemen.[94] These figures appear modest alongside the capacity of Shīr Khān, who a generation earlier had held Sunnām, Lahore, Dēōpālpūr and 'the iqtaʿs in the path of the Mongol advance', to raise 'several thousands',[95] or the army assembled by Tāj al-Dīn Sanjar-i Qabaqulaq at Badā'ūn in 640/1242, which numbered 'eight thousand horse and numerous infantry and paiks' and incurred the jealousy of unnamed rivals.[96]

It is to be assumed – though we have little information on the fiscal aspects of the iqtaʿ – that in this period local revenues outside the khalisa were delivered to the muqtaʿ's appointees rather than to the central government in Delhi. Within his territory the muqtaʿ in turn distributed iqtaʿ grants with a view not only to recruiting warriors but also to enlisting the administrative capacities of the learned. Among the kindnesses Jūzjānī received at the hands of Tāj al-Dīn Sanjar-i Qabaqulaq when he visited Badā'ūn in 640/1242 was the bestowal of an iqtaʿ; though 'destiny and fortune' beckoned the chronicler on towards Lakhnawtī.[97] There seems no reason to doubt that in the Shamsid era the system functioned much as it did later in the century, under Balaban and Jalāl al-Dīn Khaljī. The muqtaʿ retained so much of the revenue (*kharāj*) from his grant as he required to pay and fit out his troops, or for other administrative purposes, and

90 Hardy, 'Growth of authority', 203.
91 I. Habib, 'Economic history of the Delhi Sultanate', 295.
92 *TN*, II, 7–8, 17, 27, 42, 47, 52 (tr. 728, 743, 757, 787, 799, 809). For the *mawās*, see p. 125 below.
93 *TN*, II, 26 (tr. 755).
94 *TFS*, 40, for *Buqubuq, and 204 (reading corrected from BL ms., fol. 110b), for Nuṣrat-i Ṣabāḥ.
95 *Ibid.*, 65.
96 *TN*, II, 26 (tr. 755).
97 *Ibid.* (tr. 756).

remitted the surplus (*fawāḍil*) to the capital.[98] Baranī indicates that by Balaban's era the sultan nominated an accountant (*khwāja*) to operate within the province alongside the muqtaʿ, reflecting the government's concern to ascertain the extent of the revenue available.[99] Balaban also planted informers (*barīdān*) in the iqtaʿs to report on the activities of his amirs and their families.[100] Baranī tells us that Balaban's son Muḥammad personally conveyed the surplus revenue from Sind to his father's court every year and that he brought three years' revenue following the sultan's return from Bengal.[101] We have no information regarding the proportion of the surplus. In exceptional circumstances, as for particularly demanding military operations, the muqtaʿ was permitted to keep the surplus also. So it was that in *c.* 694/1295 the future sultan ʿAlāʾ al-Dīn was allowed to retain the surplus revenue from his iqtaʿs of Kara and Awadh on the pretext of heading an expedition to Chandērī;[102] though in the event he made for Dēōgīr and won the booty that enabled him to overthrow his uncle the sultan.

What proportion of his time the muqtaʿ was expected or able to spend in his territory is unclear. By the 1290s we begin to hear of a deputy (*nāʾib*) in some iqtaʿs. Baranī's father became both na'ib and khwāja of Baran at ʿAlāʾ al-Dīn's accession.[103] His responsibilities, presumably, included the supervision of revenue collection and the fitting out of troops. A muqtaʿ with major administrative commitments in Delhi was evidently not expected to see to these matters in person. Jūzjānī, describing how Ulugh Khān Balaban in 653/1255 had to go to Hānsī to oversee the mustering of contingents from the Siwālik region (Hānsī, Sarsatī, Jind and Barwāla), which had been subject to delay, appears to suggest that this was unusual.[104]

Those who fell foul of the government could suffer banishment to their iqtaʿs, a fate met with relatively frequently in the pages of the *Ṭabaqāt-i Nāṣirī*. To draw examples from the power struggle of the 1250s, Ulugh Khān Balaban, when he forfeited the office of na'ib in 651/1253, was ordered to retire to Hānsī; in 653/1255 his enemies Rayhān and Qutlugh Khān were dismissed respectively to Badāʾūn and to Awadh; and in 655/1257 any of their confederates among the religious aristocracy of Delhi who held an iqtaʿ in the vicinity (*ḥawālī*) of the capital were ordered to take up residence there.[105] Almost four decades later, certain of the amirs accused of conspiring against Sultan Jalāl al-Dīn Khaljī were punished by being sent to their iqtaʿs for one year, a penalty which Baranī evidently intended his

98 *TFS*, 164, 220–1. I. Habib, 'Agrarian economy', in Raychaudhuri and Habib, 69, more cautiously, suggests that the despatch of the surplus from the iqtaᶜs was being demanded 'well before the fall of Balban's dynasty'.

99 *TFS*, 36–7 (in the iqtaᶜ of Amrōha); and see I. Habib, 'Agrarian economy', 69–70.

100 *TFS*, 40, 44–5. 101 *Ibid.*, 69, 108–9. 102 *Ibid.*, 220–1.

103 *Ibid.*, 248. 104 *TN*, II, 70–1 (tr. 837); see also I, 490 (tr. 703).

105 *Ibid.*, I, 486, 489, 492 (tr. 693, 700, 701, 708); also II, 64, 69 (tr. 826, 834).

readers to view as excessively lenient.[106] Badā'ūn often figures as the destination of those who lapsed from favour at court, as it was for Badr al-Dīn Sonqur in 638/1241, for Küshlü Khān in 649/1251 and for Rayhān three years later (in each case, as its newly appointed muqtaʿ), and for the deposed qadi ʿImād al-Dīn Shafūrqānī in 646/1248.[107] The fate of Qadi Jalāl Kāsānī, who was implicated in the Sīdī Muwallih affair, was to be sent off to Badā'ūn as qadi.[108] Under Sultan Balaban the penalties were harsher. His slave Malik *Buqubuq, *sar-i jāndār* and muqtaʿ of Badā'ūn, was executed for slaying a chamberlain (*farrāsh*), and the *qorabeg* Haybat Khān, who held the iqtaʿ of Awadh, narrowly escaped the same sentence for likewise killing a man.[109] But perhaps these were the exceptions.

Evidence from the period of Ulugh Khān's ascendancy as na'ib, from 653/1255 onwards, suggests that certain grants and offices were becoming hereditary, especially those held by the religious aristocracy, who tended to enjoy incomes exempt from any kind of service and known as *inʿāmāt*. Jūzjānī received grants in this category from Ulugh Khān Balaban, namely a village in the Hānsī region, of which he took possession in 647/1249–50, and another village (in an unspecified location), together with a pension in cash, on the completion of his *Ṭabaqāt*.[110] When the *Shaykh al-Islām* Jamāl al-Dīn Bisṭāmī and the qadi Kabīr al-Din died in 657/1259, their offices (*manāṣib*) were conferred on their sons; and in like fashion the *inʿāmāt* of the imam Ḥamīd al-Dīn of Mārīgala, who died a few months later, passed to his children. It comes as a greater surprise to find this trend affecting military and administrative office. Kishli Khān was succeeded as *amīr-ḥājib* in this same year by his son ʿAlā' al-Dīn Muḥammad, and in Balaban's reign the *ʿāriḍ* was followed by his son.[111] In the early Khaljī era Tāj al-Dīn ʿIrāqī transmitted his office of *amīr-i dād-i lashgar* to his son Kabīr al-Dīn.[112] Apropos of iqtaʿs, however, the hereditary principle carried less weight. We know of no muqtaʿ whose grant passed on his death to a relative; but Jūzjānī reveals that Arslan Khān was deemed to merit the iqtaʿ of Bhayāna on the grounds that he had married the daughter of Bahā' al-Dīn Toghril, its first muqtaʿ.[113] In the reign of Nāṣir al-Dīn Maḥmūd Shāh, Qilich Khān Jalāl al-Dīn Masʿūd, ʿAlā' al-Dīn Jānī's son (see appendix II), was twice granted Lakhnawtī, which his father had briefly

106 *TFS*, 192.

107 Sonqur: *TN*, I, 465, and II, 25 (tr. 654, 753). Others: *ibid.*, I, 482, 485, 489, and II, 68 (tr. 685, 690, 700, 833).

108 *TFS*, 211. 109 *Ibid.*, 40–1, 84.

110 *TN*, I, 481, 484, and II, 61, 220 (tr. 681, 687, 821–2, 1294–5).

111 *Ibid.*, I, 495 (tr. 713); for ʿAlā' al-Dīn as *amīr-ḥājib* under Balaban, see also *TFS*, 24, 35, 36, 113. *TS*, IOL Persian ms. 412, fol. 36b.

112 *TFS*, 361.

113 *TN*, II, 34 (tr. 767). It is also possible (though Jūzjānī makes no explicit link here) that Temür Khān's claim to Lakhnawtī, when he wrested it from Toghan Khān in 642/1244, derived from his marriage to a daughter of its former muqtaʿ, Sayf al-Dīn Aybeg-i Yaghantut: *ibid.*, II, 18 (tr. 744).

CARL A. RUDISILL LIBRARY
LENOIR-RHYNE COLLEGE

held in iqtaʿ under Iltutmish.[114] There is perhaps meagre evidence that the hereditary principle was not totally irrelevant in the allocation of major iqtaʿs in the thirteenth century, several decades before the Tughluqid Sultan Fīrūz Shāh made it the chief criterion.

[114] *Ibid.*, II, 78 (tr. 848–9); *RCEA*, XI, 211 (no. 4320). For Jānī, see *TN*, I, 448, and II, 9 (tr. 618, 731–2).

CHAPTER 6

The Mongol threat

The Mongol world-empire

When Chinggis Khan died in 1227, without having returned to western Asia, his empire extended from the steppes of present-day Mongolia to north-eastern Persia and the Hindu Kush. It was not until the election of his son and successor, Ögödei, as great khan (*qaghan/qa'an*), at an assembly (*quriltai*) in Mongolia in 1229, that the Mongols again paid any attention to the Indian borderlands, and only in 639/1241 that they first entered the territory of the Delhi Sultan, thus inaugurating a long period of hostilities with the Sultanate which lasted beyond the sack of Delhi by the Central Asian conqueror Temür in 801/1398. These conflicts are less fully covered than Chinggis Khan's own invasion of India. The principal sources for Mongol activities in eastern Persia and Central Asia – Juwaynī's *Ta'rīkh-i Jahān-Gushā* (658/1260), Rashīd al-Dīn's *Jāmiʿ al-Tawārīkh* (*c.* 703/1303–4) and Waṣṣāf's *Tajziyat al-Amṣār* – devote comparatively little attention to Mongol relations with the subcontinent. As we have seen, Waṣṣāf's work includes also a brief history of the Delhi Sultanate down to the early years of ʿAlā' al-Dīn Khaljī, which was in turn utilized by Rashīd al-Dīn and by Qāshānī (*c.* 718/1318). Details of a few Mongol campaigns in India can also be gleaned from the history of Herat (*Ta'rīkh-Nāma-yi Harāt*) by Sayfī (*c.* 722/1322). But these Iranian historical traditions only partially fill in the gaps left by Indo-Muslim chroniclers like Jūzjānī and Baranī, who report Mongol invasions but conversely display virtually no interest in conditions within the Mongols' own territories.

By Ögödei's death the Mongols had adopted an ideology of world conquest, according to which the whole earth was already granted to them by the eternal sky-god (Tenggeri). Other rulers had a clear duty to recognize their place within this world-empire, to submit in person to the qaghan, to put their troops at his disposal, to accept a Mongol resident (*shiḥna*) and to dismantle their fortifications. Any restraint the Mongols manifested in making good their title to the whole world sprang only from tactical considerations. It was sometimes necessary to make a truce with one ruler in order to concentrate on another enemy elsewhere. But in the Mongols' vocabulary, 'peace' and 'submission' were the same word (Tu. *īl/el*): the qaghan had no allies, only subjects.[1]

As we saw (p. 34), the Mongols' principal attacks in 620–1/1223–4 were directed against Nandana and the Lahore region, then under Khwarazmian domination, and Multān, which belonged to Qubacha. Professor Habibullah suggested that Chinggis Khan refrained from further operations in India out of regard for the Delhi Sultan's neutrality, as demonstrated in his failure to assist Jalāl al-Dīn. The Mongol conqueror is further credited with 'moderation' and a 'scrupulous observance of international practice'.[2] If so, Chinggis Khan's policy towards India in 1223 affords a unique instance of this spirit. There is, in any case, no reason why he should have regarded India as an immediate objective, on a par with the empire of the Khwārazmshāh. At this time, Khwārazm, Transoxiana and the Ghazna region had yet to be pacified, and while he was based south of the Hindu Kush divisions of his army were engaged in vital campaigns to suppress revolts in Khurāsān. Even the troops that Ögödei later sent to this region were designated in the so-called 'Secret history of the Mongols' merely as a reserve force (Mo. *gejige*) for the main army operating in Persia under Chormaghun.[3]

It is possible that Iltutmish made some gesture of submission of which Jūzjānī does not tell us. Ninety years later, in 710/1310–11, in an embassy to Sultan 'Alā' al-Dīn Khaljī, the Ilkhan Öljeitü reminded him how his predecessors had, 'both in the time of Chinggis Khan and in the time of ... Ögödei Qa'an, breathed the breath of conciliation and obedience and through the words of envoys had laid the countenance of loyalty on the face of the earth'.[4] This may, of course, amount to no more than diplomatic swagger. The arrival of 'the ruler of In-tu (Hind)' at Ögödei's court, reported under the year 1229 in the Chinese dynastic history of the Mongol period, the *Yüan Shih*,[5] perhaps refers to some Hindu prince or to Ḥasan Qarluq, the ruler of Binbān. Yet we know that Iltutmish did receive embassies from the Mongols, since Jūzjānī assures us that he never

[1] Eric Voegelin, 'The Mongol orders of submission to European powers, 1245–1255', *Byzantion* 15 (1940–1), 378–413. Klaus Sagaster, 'Herrschaftsideologie und Friedensgedanke bei den frühen Mongolen', *CAJ* 17 (1973), 223–42. Igor de Rachewiltz, 'Some remarks on the ideological foundations of Chingis Khan's empire', *PFEH* 7 (1973), 21–36. David Morgan, 'The Mongols and the eastern Mediterranean', in B. Arbel *et al.* (eds.), *Latins and Greeks in the eastern Mediterranean after 1204* (London, 1989 = *Mediterranean Historical Review* 4, no. 1), 200, suggests that this ideology postdated rather than preceded the burst of expansion under Chinggis Khan.

[2] Habibullah, *Foundation*, 206.

[3] *Mangghol un niuca tobca'an*, para. 270, ed. (in transcription) L. Ligeti, *Histoire secrète des Mongols* (Budapest, 1971), 243; tr. F. W. Cleaves (Cambridge, Mass., 1984), 210; tr. Igor de Rachewiltz, in *PFEH* 31 (March 1985), 26 and n. at 58.

[4] Waṣṣāf, 528.

[5] Waltraut Abramowski, 'Die chinesischen Annalen von Ögödei und Güyük', *ZS* 10 (1976), 125.

killed their envoys but simply sent them off under guard in some fashion (*ba-ṭarīqī*).[6]

The first Mongol encroachments

The reign of Ögödei (626–39/1229–41) witnessed a steady build-up of pressure beyond the frontier of the Sultanate. After the first quriltai, troops under Dayir Noyan advanced from Herat into Sīstān and overthrew its ruler, Yinaltegin (632/1235).[7] It was probably the Mongol forces in Ṭukhāristān, Qunduz and Ṭāliqān, as also, it seems, those in Ghazna, together totalling two *tümens* (20,000), under the command of Mönggedü (Mengütei),[8] which soon afterwards moved into Kābul, Ghazna and Zābulistān and obliged Ḥasan Qarluq to accept a Mongol resident (*shiḥna*).[9] At a second quriltai in 632/1235, further Mongol troops under *Oqotur were ordered to advance on India, and Kashmir was ravaged in the course of a campaign lasting six months.[10] In 636/1238–9 Qarluq, who had become tributary to the Mongols, was suddenly attacked by the generals (*noyans*) Anban and Negüder and expelled from his territories of Ghazna, Kurramān and Binbān. He fell back on the Sultanate, launching an attack on Uchch which was repulsed by its muqtaʿ, Sayf al-Dīn Aybeg.[11]

The Mongols' campaign against Ḥasan Qarluq brought them to the frontiers of the Delhi Sultanate, and they now occupied the territories which had served as the springboard for the Ghurid invasions of India two generations earlier. In 639/1241 an army under the joint leadership of Dayir and Mönggedü invested Lahore. The muqtaʿ, Qaraqush Khān, fled, and although Dayir was killed in the fighting the city fell on 16 Jumādā II/22 December 1241:[12] the reaction from Delhi, where Bahrām Shāh was highly

[6] *TN*, II, 214 (tr. 1284).

[7] Bosworth, *History of the Saffarids*, 409–10. For Dayir, see Boyle, 'Mongol commanders', 240; Aubin, 'L'ethnogénèse', 70–1.

[8] *TN*, II, 153, 169 (tr. 1109, 1152). *JT*, I, part 1, ed. A. A. Romaskevich *et al.* (Moscow, 1965), 188, and tr. A. A. Khetagurov, *Sbornik letopisei*, I, part 1 (Moscow and Leningrad, 1952), 109 (where the subject of the sentence is wrongly taken to be Möngke), similarly describes the camping-grounds of this army as 'Qunduz-i Baghlān and the confines (*ḥudūd*) of Badakhshān'. For the form of Mönggedü's name, see Boyle, 'Mongol commanders', 242 and n.67. On the *tümen*, a unit of (sometimes notionally) 10,000, see D. O. Morgan, *The Mongols* (Oxford, 1986), 89.

[9] *TN*, II, 159 (tr. 1119).

[10] *JT*, II, 42 = II, part 1, ed. A. A. Alizade (Moscow, 1980), 120 (tr. Boyle, 55/tr. Verkhovskii, 36). *JT*, ed. Jahn, *Indiengeschichte*, Ar. text Taf. 61 (German tr. 56); there is a lacuna in the TSM ms. here. The BL Persian ms. Add. 7628, fol. 391a, says that the Mongols stayed six months and that the raja of Kashmir returned after seven *years*. This error misled Jahn, 'A note on Kashmir and the Mongols', *CAJ* 2 (1956), 177; his date for the invasion (*ibid.*, 179) is also wrong.

[11] *TN*, II, 8–9, 162 (tr. 730, 1128–9).

[12] *Ibid.*, II, 163–5 (tr. 1133–6); II, 166 (tr. 1142), for the date, which is given as Jumādā I at I, 465–6 (tr. 655); for the joint command, see II, 6 (the meaning of *dar muwāfaqat* is obscured in Raverty's tr., 727). Raverty (1135 n.5) rejects Jūzjānī's testimony on the grounds that

unpopular with the military, was ineffectual. In 643/1245–6 a campaign by Mönggedü dislodged from Multān Ḥasan Qarluq, who had recently seized the city, and forced him to flee by boat down the Indus towards Sīwistān and Daybul; the Mongols then invested Uchch for a time, before an expedition by Sultan ʿAlāʾ al-Dīn Masʿūd Shāh obliged them to retreat. Uchch and Multān were pacified by a detachment under Aybeg-i Khitāʾī, the *sar-i jāndār* and muqtaʿ of Baran.[13]

Jūzjānī gives prominence in his account of this campaign to the role of the future sultan Balaban in securing Mönggedü's withdrawal, and proudly describes how the Delhi forces went over to the offensive in the winter of 644/1246–7, early in the reign of Nāṣir al-Dīn Maḥmūd Shāh, when Balaban advanced as far as the Indus, greatly intimidating the Mongol frontier patrols. But the chronicler's statement that the Mongols were thereby deflected from invading in this year betrays the fact that their inroads had become an annual event.[14] In any case, they soon sought to take advantage of the fighting around Multān between Küshlü Khān and his rival Shīr Khān (see pp. 71–2), for Jūzjanī records the despatch of a great number of Mongol prisoners to court in 648/1250–1 by *Kürbüz, Shīr Khān's deputy at Multān.[15]

Tensions within the Mongol empire

Mongol operations on the Sultanate's western frontier since 639/1241 had proved less than impressive. Why, we cannot be certain. Dayir's death would account only for the immediate withdrawal from Lahore. The notions that the climate made India an unattractive goal and that the Panjāb was ecologically unsuited to the Mongols' own brand of pastoral nomadism must be discarded. It is true that the heat had compelled Dörbei to withdraw from Multān in 621/1224;[16] but this would hardly explain the failure of the Mongols to establish themselves in the Panjāb. Not only were they accustomed to climatic extremes in their original habitat, but in the fourteenth century we find them wintering in India on a regular basis, which suggests that they found adequate pasturage for their livestock. The aims of the Mongol invasions of India will be discussed more fully in chapter 11.

More important in the longer term were the tensions within the imperial dynasty. Firstly, the lines between the qaghan's sphere of authority and those of his more important kinsfolk were increasingly blurred. On the one hand, Chinggis Khan had allotted to each of his relatives a specific

Dayir is mentioned as still alive in Möngke's reign (1251–9). But this is a misunderstanding based on the vagueness of Rashīd al-Dīn: see *JT*, III, 21–2 (tr. Arends, 22).

13 *TN*, I, 471, and II, 28, 54–6, 170–1 (tr. 667–8, 758, 809–13, 1153–6).

14 *Ibid.*, I, 479–80, and II, 56–7 (tr. 677–9, 814–16).

15 *Ibid.*, I, 484 (tr. 688); for the appointment of *Kürbüz to Multān, see II, 38, 44 (tr. 782, 792).

16 *TJG*, I, 112 (tr. Boyle, 142).

pasturage together with a certain number of nomadic subjects – the complex termed in Mongolian *ulus*. Juwaynī describes the largest of such units, those granted to the conqueror's four sons, Jochi, Ögödei, Chaghadai and Tolui, as radiating out from the homeland in Mongolia in a westerly direction according to seniority. As the eldest, Jochi was entrusted with the westernmost territory 'as far as the hooves of Mongol horses had trodden';[17] and when he died, shortly before Chinggis Khan, his son Batu became the real founder of the Mongol power in the Pontic and Caspian steppes, known to historians as the Golden Horde.

On the other hand, the Mongol conquests were regarded as the joint possession of the entire imperial family. The sedentary regions appear from Ögödei's reign onwards to have been run by 'satellite administrations' comprising representatives of both the qaghan and neighbouring princes.[18] The principle of joint rule found expression also in the *tama* system, which was elucidated by the late Jean Aubin. The forces sent to each newly conquered territory included contingents furnished by each branch of the imperial family, so that the interests of one prince could not be furthered without the consent of relatives whose forces were operating alongside his own. Thus in the Indian borderlands in the 1230s the families of Chinggis Khan's four sons were each represented by a commander.[19]

We should note, secondly, the absence of recognizable rules for the succession to the qaghanate. A prince designated by the previous monarch was often ignored in favour of a more competent or senior member of the dynasty, a system for which the late Professor Joseph Fletcher borrowed from the Celtic world the label 'tanistry'.[20] Thus during the five-year interregnum that separated the death of the qaghan Ögödei in Mongolia in December 1241 from the election of his son Güyüg (644–6/1246–8), rumours reached Delhi of bitter conflicts among the princes, including the sons of Chinggis Khan's younger brother Temüge.[21] Güyüg's early death, which averted a fratricidal war with his cousin Batu in Central Asia, was followed by another interval of three years, after which Batu and his party elbowed aside Güyüg's offspring and secured the imperial dignity for Tolui's son Möngke (1251–9). Opposition from the two middle branches of the dynasty was ruthlessly crushed; in a major redistribution of resources, the majority of the Ögödeyid and Chaghadayid princes were deprived of their pasturelands and were put to death or exiled.[22]

To rally support behind the new regime, campaigns were instituted on

[17] *Ibid.*, I, 31 (tr. Boyle, 42).
[18] Paul D. Buell, 'Sino-Khitan administration in Mongol Bukhara', *JAH* 13 (1979), 141–7.
[19] Sayfī, 174. For the *tama* system, see Aubin, 'L'ethnogénèse', 74–5.
[20] J. Fletcher, 'The Mongols: ecological and social perspectives', *HJAS* 46 (1986), 17, 24–8.
[21] *TN*, II, 166–7 (tr. 1143–4). See P. Jackson, 'The dissolution of the Mongol empire', *CAJ* 22 (1978), 197–9.
[22] *Ibid.*, 200–8.

fronts as far distant as China and Western Asia.[23] In 1252–3 Sali Noyan was sent to the Indian borderlands at the head of fresh troops, and was given authority over all the forces commanded in the past by Dayir and by *Oqotur. Sali was himself subordinated to Möngke's brother Hülegü,[24] who in 653/1255 was to march westwards at the head of a great army and would crush both the Ismāʿīlī Assassins in northern Persia (654/1256) and the ʿAbbasid Caliphate at Baghdad (656/1258). In accordance with the *tama* system, the qaghan's forces were accompanied by contingents representing other princes of the imperial dynasty, among which the troops supplied by the Jochids predominated.[25]

The distant location of the Jochid ulus gave its princes a good deal of practical independence from the qaghan. Batu's power extended well beyond the confines of what would later be Horde territory: Jūzjānī testifies to his authority throughout those parts of Persia occupied by the Mongols, and Sayfī furnishes more specific evidence, showing how Batu intervened in the affairs of Herat in the 1240s.[26] According to reports which reached Egypt ten years or so later, the Golden Horde was entitled to anything from a third to two-fifths of the spoils from Persia.[27] But although Hülegü's presence in Western Asia might have been seen as a challenge to the Jochids' position there, friction arose only after the death of Möngke in 1259 and the outbreak of a struggle in the following spring between his brothers Qubilai and Arigh Böke in the Far East.

Even as he ceased writing, Jūzjānī had heard the first rumours of tension between Hülegü and his cousin Berke, Batu's brother and now ruler of the Golden Horde. The reason given – the outrage felt by Berke, who had been reared as a Muslim, at the fate of the ʿAbbasid Caliph – is also found in sources from the Mamlūk empire.[28] In fact, however, conflict between Berke and Hülegü was deferred for some three years following the sack of Baghdad, and authors writing further west, who were better placed to observe events, attribute the clash to two quite different causes. One is that Hülegü deprived the Golden Horde of its customary share of the spoils from Persia. The other reason furnished in the sources for the enmity between Hülegü and Berke is that they supported rival candidates in the

[23] T. T. Allsen, *Mongol imperialism: the policies of the Grand Qan Möngke in China, Russia, and the Islamic lands, 1251–1259* (Berkeley and Los Angeles, 1987), 1–5.

[24] *JT*, I, part 1, 188 (tr. Khetagurov, 110); *JT*, III, 21–2 (tr. Arends, 21). Aubin, 'L'ethnogénèse', 73, 79. Sali's despatch to India is dated in July 1253 by the *Yüan Shih*: Waltraut Abramowski, 'Die chinesischen Annalen des Möngke', *ZS* 13 (1979), 22.

[25] Jackson, 'Dissolution', 220–1.

[26] *TN*, II, 176 (to be corrected from BL ms., fol. 155b; cf. Raverty's tr., 1172). Sayfī, 122–8, 136–9. For Batu, see Jackson, 'Dissolution', 212–13, 218.

[27] D. Ayalon, 'The Great *Yāsa* of Chingiz Khān: a re-examination', part B, *Studia Islamica* 34 (1971), 174, repr. in his *Outsiders in the lands of Islam* (London, 1988). Jackson, 'Dissolution', 220–1.

[28] *TN*, II, 198 (tr. 1257). al-Yūnīnī, II, 365. al-Ṣafadī, *Wāfī*, X, 118.

succession dispute: Berke acknowledged Arigh Böke, whereas Hülegü favoured Qubilai.[29]

Hülegü's precise status at the time of Möngke's death is problematic. When describing the terms of his commission, the Ilkhanid chronicler Rashīd al-Dīn uses highly guarded language. According to his version of events, Möngke privately intended his brother to remain in Persia and transmit it to his descendants (the so-called 'Ilkhans'), but he made a show of ordering him to return to Mongolia once the conquest was completed.[30] This reads suspiciously like an attempt to justify the position of the Ilkhans retrospectively. It must be emphasized that we have no other evidence for any such purpose on Möngke's part, and sources composed within the Mamlūk empire assert, on the contrary, that at some point after the fall of Baghdad Hülegü rebelled and established himself as the ruler of the province.[31] Even the actual title (*īl* < *el*, 'subordinate', *khan*) taken by Hülegü and his line is not attested prior to 658/1260.[32] He appears to have profited from the outbreak of conflict in the Far East to convert his position from that of commander-in-chief in Persia to that of ruler of an ulus on a par with his kinsmen, receiving from Qubilai the legitimation he so needed. The Jochid princes and generals in his army were arrested and executed or imprisoned, and most of their troops slaughtered; and he was then free to encroach on the territories south of the Caucasus that the Jochids regarded as their own. As a consequence, war broke out in 1261.[33]

The events following Möngke's death marked the dissolution of the Mongol empire. Even after Arigh Böke's submission in 1264, Qubilai, who reigned from the new capital of Khanbaligh (Ta-tu) in northern China, could count on the allegiance only of Hülegü and his descendants, the Ilkhans of Persia, so that it is possible to speak of a 'Toluid axis' comprising these two geographically remote powers. From *c.* 1270, moreover, he was confronted with a coalition of enemies in Transoxiana and Turkestan. Here the Chaghadayid prince Alughu, who had defected to Qubilai from Arigh

[29] John W. Dardess, 'From Mongol empire to Yüan dynasty: changing forms of imperial rule in Mongolia and Central Asia', *Monumenta Serica* 30 (1972–3), 128–31. P. Jackson, 'The accession of Qubilai Qa'an: a re-examination', *Journal of the Anglo-Mongolian Society* 2 (1975), 1–10. *Idem*, 'Dissolution', 226–7. Morris Rossabi, *Khubilai Khan: his life and times* (Berkeley and Los Angeles, 1988), 46–62.

[30] *JT*, III, 24 (tr. Arends, 22).

[31] *MA*, ed. and tr. Klaus Lech, *Das mongolische Weltreich* (Wiesbaden, 1968), Ar. text 2 (German tr. 91).

[32] Reuven Amitai-Preiss, 'Evidence for the early use of the title *il-khān* among the Mongols', *JRAS*, 3rd series, 1 (1991), 353–61. Thomas T. Allsen, 'Changing forms of legitimation in Mongol Iran', in G. Seaman and D. Marks (eds.), *Rulers from the steppe: state formation on the Eurasian periphery* (Los Angeles, 1991), 227.

[33] For a more detailed investigation of the origins of this conflict, see Jackson, 'Dissolution', 226–35; also *idem*, 'From *ulus* to khanate: the making of the Mongol states, *c.* 1220–1290', in R. Amitai-Preiss and D. O. Morgan (eds.), *The Mongol empire and its legacy* (forthcoming).

Böke, had nevertheless profited from the civil war to re-establish Chaghadai's ulus on quite new foundations, appropriating for himself the revenues of the neighbouring sedentary regions which should have gone to the qaghan; Baraq, whom Qubilai despatched west to rule Chaghadai's ulus after Alughu's death, soon defied him. But the most dangerous enemy confronting Qubilai in this region was Qaidu, a grandson of Ögödei, who was recognized as their khan by a number of Chaghadayid and Ögödeyid princes and noyans in 670/1271 when Baraq died.[34] Qaidu's empire was an extensive one. He took over the fiscal administration of the sedentary regions of Central Asia, whose officials were now his appointees, and he is found nominating the rulers of Chaghadai's ulus, who seem to have acted as his subordinates. He and his allies remained hostile to the regime at Khanbaligh until his death in 1303; and the Mongol world did not acknowledge a single qaghan again until 1304 (below, p. 220).[35]

The disintegration of their empire into a number of rival khanates seriously impaired the Mongols' capacity to prosecute expansionist campaigns on any front, whether in China, in eastern Europe, in Syria or in India. The Ilkhans were required to keep vigilant watch for an invasion of Transcaucasia by the forces of the Golden Horde. Periodic attacks by the Chaghadayid Mongols, and particularly that of 668/1270, effectively turned Khurāsān at times into a no-man's land.[36] The Ilkhans retaliated in 671/1272–3 by sacking Bukhārā.[37] The abandonment of the old claim to world-rulership is most starkly demonstrated in the new-found readiness of Mongol princes to ally with outside powers against their own kinsfolk. The Ilkhans were confronted from 662/1263–4 by an understanding between their northern neighbours, the Golden Horde, and the Mamlūk regime in Egypt and Syria. Their own efforts to counteract this by negotiating for joint action with the Mamlūks' enemies in Catholic Europe were unavailing.[38]

[34] Jamāl al-Qarshī, *Mulḥaqāt al-Ṣurāḥ*, ed. in V. V. Bartol'd, *Turkestan v epokhu mongol'skogo nashestviia* (St. Petersburg, 1898–1900, 2 vols.), I (texts), 138. Waṣṣāf, 76. *JT*, II, 192 (tr. Boyle, 153/tr. Verkhovskii, 100), and III, 138 (tr. Arends, 87).

[35] The fullest survey of Qaidu and his empire is to be found in Michal Biran, *Qaidu and the rise of the independent Mongol state in Central Asia* (Richmond, Surrey, 1997). Briefer accounts in W. Barthold, *Four studies on the history of Central Asia* (Leiden, 1956–62, 4 parts in 3 vols.), I, 124–9; Pelliot, *Notes on Marco Polo* (Paris, 1959–73, 3 vols.), I, 124–9; J. A. Boyle, 'Ḳaydu', *Enc.Isl.*^{2}; more generally, Dardess, 130–1.

[36] *JT*, III, 148 (tr. Arends, 92).

[37] Berthold Spuler, *Die Mongolen in Iran*, 4th edn. (Leiden, 1985), 63.

[38] S. Zakhirov, *Diplomaticheskie otnosheniia Zolotoi Ordy s Egiptom* (Moscow, 1966). Reuven Amitai-Preiss, *Mongols and Mamluks: the Mamluk–Īlkhānid war, 1260–1281* (Cambridge, 1995), 78–86, 94–105. J. A. Boyle, 'The Ilkhans of Persia and the princes of Europe', *CAJ* 20 (1976), 25–40. Morgan, *Mongols*, 183–6. For a more detailed survey of the halting of the Mongol advance in 1260–2, see Jackson, 'Dissolution', 236–43.

The Sultanate's 'Mongol crisis'

The build-up of Mongol power in Persia had been all the more menacing in view of the fact that the Mongols were being drawn into the internal affairs of the Delhi Sultanate following the flight into Mongol territory in 646/1248 of Maḥmūd Shāh's brother Jalāl al-Dīn Masʿūd. The sources composed in Persia state that Möngke ordered Sali Noyan to assist him to recover 'his ancestral realm'. Successive attacks by Sali on Multān and Lahore, which are described by Sayfī and in which the governor of Multān bought off the invaders, seem to have formed part of this effort. Regarding the fate of Lahore we are told nothing, since Sayfī breaks off at this juncture to describe the fortunes of Shams al-Dīn Muḥammad Kart, the client malik of Herat, who had accompanied Sali's forces but now withdrew and returned home. The expedition of Maḥmūd Shāh's forces towards Sind by way of Lahore in 650/1252, in which Ulugh Khān Balaban fell from favour (see p. 72), must have been a response to this inroad.[39] As a result, the Mongols were unable to penetrate further than Jajnēr and fell back, but the prince was installed as client ruler of Lahore, Kūjāh and Sōdra, which were subject (*īl*) to them.[40]

Jalāl al-Dīn Masʿūd's authority in these regions did not last long after his participation in the campaign which restored Ulugh Khān Balaban to power in 652/1254. At some point soon afterwards, he was joined by Balaban's cousin Shīr Khān, who had also taken refuge in Mongol territory and returned in the wake of the na'ib's reinstatement. The two men fell out, and Jalāl al-Dīn, who retired and left his dependants and troops in the hands of his rival, probably died within the next few years. When Shīr Khān engaged in conflict with Arslan Khān, the muqtaʿ of Tabarhindh, the Delhi government intervened and granted him, in return for his allegiance, not only Tabarhindh but 'the whole of the territory and iqtaʿs which he had previously held': this formula must have been designed to embrace Lahore, Uchch and Multān.[41]

[39] *TN*, I, 486 (to be corrected from BL ms., fol. 192a; cf. Raverty's tr., 692). Sayfī, 157–9 (*sub anno* 644). Habibullah (*Foundation*, 215) was thereby led to connect the invasion with Balaban's campaign in the Salt Range. But Sayfī's chronology is unreliable for this period (see Aubin, 'L'ethnogénèse', 72–3), and the year is too early for either Sali or Shams al-Dīn Kart to be in the Indian borderlands. That Sayfī mentions the *ʿīd-i Qurbān* (10 Dhu'l-Ḥijja) as falling during the siege of Multān (158) is an argument in favour of locating this expedition in 650, where it harmonizes with the time of year specified by Jūzjānī. The governor of Lahore, whom Sayfī names as KRT Khan (Kirit Khān?), cannot be identified. We should, perhaps, have expected Toghril Khān (Yüzbeg): see above, p. 92.

[40] Waṣṣāf, 310; *JT*, ed. Jahn, *Indiengeschichte*, Ar. text Taf. 57, Pers. text Taf. 22 (tr. 48 reads 'Ḥaibar' for the *ḤḤ*NYR of the mss.); Qāshānī, 185. For this episode, see Karl Jahn, 'Zum Problem der mongolischen Eroberungen in Indien (13.-14. Jahrhundert)', in *Akten des XXIV. internationalen Orientalisten-Kongresses München . . . 1957* (Wiesbaden, 1959), 618.

[41] *TN*, II, 44 (tr. 793). This settlement must have occurred prior to 654/1256, when we find Arslan Khān in Awadh. That Jalāl al-Dīn Masʿūd was dead by 658/1260 is indicated by the

Mongol interests in the Lahore region had already suffered a setback, it is fair to assume, as a result of Jalāl al-Dīn Masʿūd's reconciliation with Maḥmūd Shāh.[42] Now he had been supplanted by Shīr Khān, who was subject to the sultan and, encouraged by Delhi, harboured designs on Sind. This region too had recently become a Mongol protectorate. Following his triumphant return to Uchch and Multān in 651/1254 Küshlü Khān had used the good offices of Shams al-Dīn Muḥammad Kart of Herat to offer his submission and had accepted a Mongol *shiḥna*. When he and his confederates failed to take Delhi in 655/1257 (see pp. 74–5), Küshlü Khān turned to his Mongol overlords. His appeal to Hülegü for assistance – made, according to Jūzjānī, in person – elicited an immediate response. In the winter of 655/1257–8 Sali Noyan entered Sind in strength and dismantled the fortifications of Multān; his forces may also have invested the island fortress of Bhakkar on the Indus.[43] Although the sultan's army moved out of Delhi, its stance appears to have been purely defensive. The government was evidently concerned not to provoke the Mongols. In Ṣafar 657/February 1259 Shīr Khān was transferred to an extensive assignment centred on Bhayāna and hitherto held by Nuṣrat Khān, who now replaced him at Tabarhindh, and Jūzjānī expressly ascribes the exchange to the need to avert conflict on the frontier, presumably with Küshlü Khān.[44] The impression of a propitiatory attitude is heightened by the continued failure of the Delhi forces to take action against the Mongols during these months, while the enemy assailed the sultan's territory.

When Jūzjānī wrote, the Mongols had overwhelmed 'the whole of the land of Tūrān and the east'. Everywhere 'from the borders of China, Turkistān, Mā warā' al-Nahr, Ṭukhāristān, Zāwul[istān], Ghūr, Kābul, Ghaznayn, Iraq, Ṭabaristān, Arrān, Ādharbāījān, the Jazīra, Anbār, Sīstān, Makrān, Kirmān, Fārs, Khūzistān, Diyārbakr, and Mawṣil, as far as the limits of Rūm and Syria', Muslim rulers had been swept away.[45] During the previous two decades, the territories that owed allegiance to the Delhi Sultan had shrunk dramatically under the impact of the Mongol advance. Iltutmish's operations against the Khwārazmshāh's lieutenants, which we noticed earlier (p. 36), had brought under his control a number of important

formula *ʿalayhi'l-raḥmatu* in Jūzjānī's list of Iltutmish's offspring in BL ms., fol. 179b, and IOL ms., fol. 242b.

42 *TN*, I, 489 (tr. 700), says that Lahore was recognized as his iqtaʿ.

43 *Ibid.*, I, 494, and (with *lashgarhā* in error for *kungurhā*) II, 76 (tr. 711, 844); for Küshlü's submission, see II, 38–40 (tr. 784, 786). Bhakkar: Sayfī, 250–7 (*sub anno* 657). Küshlü Khān's dealings with the Mongols are perhaps linked with the embassy from 'a sultan of India' which accompanied a Western European missionary on the early stages of his journey from Möngke's court in July–August 1254 (although this could equally refer to Shīr Khān): William of Rubruck, 'Itinerarium', xxxvi, 3, in A. Van den Wyngaert (ed.), *Sinica Franciscana*, I. *Itinera et relationes Fratrum Minorum saeculi XIII et XIV* (Quaracchi-Firenze, 1929), 306; tr. P. Jackson and D. O. Morgan, *The mission of Friar William of Rubruck*, HS, 2nd series, 173 (Cambridge, 1990), 247 and n.2.

44 *TN*, II, 44 (tr. 794).

45 *Ibid.*, II, 90–1 (tr. 870–1, 879–85).

strongholds between the Jhēlam and the Rāvī. Jūzjānī lists among his conquests Kūjāh (the modern Gujrat), Nandana, Sōdra and Siyālkōt; Kūjāh and Nandana are described as border regions (*sarḥadd*).[46] But in Raḍiyya's reign the Mongols already held the tracts beyond the Chenāb, which is doubtless why the rebel Kabīr Khān, when pursued north by Raḍiyya's forces in 637/1239, was unable to retreat further than 'the confines of Sōdra'.[47] By the time the renegade prince Jalāl al-Dīn Masʿūd returned with Mongol aid in *c.* 650/1252, Lahore, Kūjāh and Sōdra, as we saw, were all subject to them, and Jajnēr is described as border territory.[48] Even Jalāl al-Dīn's defection proved only a temporary setback, since Jūzjānī's phrasing betrays the fact that as a result of Sali Noyan's campaigns Sind lay outside the dominions of his sovereign Nāṣir al-Dīn Maḥmūd Shāh.[49] The Mongols, who through their satellites controlled Binbān, the Salt Range and the middle and upper Indus valley, now threatened the heartlands of the Delhi Sultanate. Describing the events of the late 1250s, Jūzjānī twice refers to Tabarhindh as 'the frontier'.[50] It is the 'frontier of Islamic territory, such as the province of Sind, Lahore, and the direction (*ṭaraf*) of the river Bēāh' that the Mongols were attacking by 656/1258; when Nuṣrat Khān exchanged iqtaʿs with Shīr Khān in the following year, he received 'the frontiers (*sarḥaddhā*) as far as the River Bēāh fords'; and a few years into Balaban's reign the Mongols were crossing the Bēāh.[51]

In these circumstances, the tradition (*ḥadīth*) that the Mongol tide would begin to ebb once it reached Lahore[52] provided cold comfort. By 1260 their dominion showed no sign of contraction. Moreover, the advent of the Mongols was believed to herald the end of time. ʿAwfī saw them as the harbingers of Gog and Magog.[53] And had not several authors transmitted the Prophet's statement that the first sign of the end of time would be the irruption of the 'Turks'?[54] Jūzjānī's reiterated prayer that the sovereignty of Nāṣir al-Dīn Maḥmūd Shāh would endure until the Day of Resurrection (*tā qiyām-i qiyāmat*)[55] is perhaps more than merely sycophantic hyperbole. For Muslims of his generation, the last things were not far off.[56] When relating the Mongol occupation of Uchch and Multān in 655/1257–8, the chronicler permits his anxiety at one point to seep through the skein of his otherwise matter-of-fact account of these events.[57]

[46] *Ibid.*, II, 22, where Iltutmish grants both places as iqtaᶜ (KWJAT, to be corrected from BL ms., fol. 204a, which has KWJAH; also tr. 750).
[47] *Ibid.*, II, 6 (tr. 726–7).
[48] Waṣṣāf, 310; *JT*, ed. Jahn, *Indiengeschichte*, Ar. text Taf. 57, Pers. text Taf. 22 (and see n.40 above); Qāshānī, 185.
[49] *TN*, II, 86 (tr. 860).
[50] *Ibid.*, II, 44 (tr. 793, 794).
[51] *Ibid.*, II, 43, 79 (tr. 788, 850–1). *TFS*, 81.
[52] *TN*, II, 166 (tr. 1136–42).
[53] *JH*, BL ms. Or. 4392, fol. 127b, *muqaddima-yi Ya'jūj-u Ma'jūj*.
[54] *TN*, II, 92–4, 98 (omitted in Raverty's tr.).
[55] *Ibid.*, I, 422, 450, 462, and II, 189.
[56] See also *ibid.*, I, 440, and II, 48 (tr. 597, 800).
[57] *Ibid.*, II, 40 (tr. 786). For a useful analysis of Jūzjānī's view of the Mongols, see D. O.

It comes as something of a surprise, therefore, to find the Mongols in turn adopting a more conciliatory stance, in the last contacts recorded by Jūzjānī. In response to an indirect approach from Nāṣir al-Dīn Muḥammad b. Ḥasan Qarluq, who ruled Binbān as a Mongol satellite, Ulugh Khān Balaban had sent a chamberlain (*ḥājib*) with his consent to a marriage alliance between their two families. The envoy's mission became known to Küshlü Khān, who alerted the Mongols, and Nāṣir al-Dīn Muḥammad had to pass him on to Hülegü's court in Persia; but he did so, allegedly, with additional letters drafted by himself but purporting to come from Ulugh Khān. Hülegü welcomed the *ḥājib* and sent him back with his own emissaries, who were received by the sultan and Ulugh Khān in Rabīʿ II 658/March 1260. Jūzjānī makes great play of the review outside Delhi in which the Mongol envoys were treated to an impressive demonstration of the Sultanate's military strength. Hülegü allegedly instructed Sali Noyan that if a Mongol horse entered Maḥmūd Shāh's dominions its hooves were to be lopped off.[58]

From what Jūzjānī says, Nāṣir al-Dīn Muḥammad aimed to pass off Ulugh Khān's response as a gesture of submission to the Mongols and thereby acquire credit with them as the intermediary. But the chronology of the Mongol embassy may have a significance which was not apparent to Jūzjānī. Hülegü's representatives had already reached the vicinity of Delhi when Ulugh Khān Balaban left for a brief campaign against the Mēōs (Mīwāt) in Ṣafar 658/February 1260.[59] By the time of their despatch (towards the end of 657/1259) Hülegü would already have heard of the death of his brother the qaghan. Anticipating a disputed succession, he may have patched up peace with the Sultanate in order to leave his hands free while he completed the conquest of Iraq and Syria. Alternatively, the fact that Berke too was in diplomatic contact with Delhi in this same year has prompted the suggestion that both rulers were actuated by their rivalry, the one seeking the support of a fellow-Muslim in order to encircle the Ilkhanate, the other the sultan's neutrality.[60] It is equally possible, of course, that Jūzjānī's story masks a genuine offer of submission by Ulugh Khān, designed to buy time for the Sultanate. Such a scenario would better explain the emphatic manner in which Sali was forbidden to encroach on Delhi territory, reminiscent of the privilege of inviolability accorded, for instance, to Lesser Armenia when its king became a Mongol client in 1254.[61] But that the Mongols did not crown their spectacular advance of the

Morgan, 'Persian historians and the Mongols', in Morgan (ed.), *Medieval historical writing*, 111–13.

58 *TN*, II, 83–8 (tr. 856–63). 59 *Ibid.*, II, 79 (tr. 851).

60 Aziz Aḥmad, 'Mongol pressure in an alien land', *CAJ* 6 (1961), 183–4, 185. Aubin, 'L'ethnogénèse', 81. See *TN*, II, 218 (tr. 1292), for Berke's embassy to Delhi.

61 Kirakos Ganjakeçi, *Patmutʿyun Hayoç*, tr. Robert Bedrosian, *Kirakos Ganjakets'i's History of the Armenians* (New York, 1986), 304; see also J. A. Boyle, 'The journey of Hetʿum I, king of Little Armenia, to the court of the Great Khan Möngke', *CAJ* 9 (1964), 181.

past decade with the conquest of further Delhi territory was due primarily to the outbreak of strife within the imperial dynasty in 1260.

The advent of the Negüderis

In the Indian borderlands, special circumstances robbed Hülegü of his ability to direct military operations against the Delhi Sultanate. Some of the Jochid troops in Persia escaped massacre at the hands of Hülegü's forces and took refuge in Syria and Egypt with the Mamlūk Sultan.[62] Others fled into present-day Afghanistan to join Negüder, who commanded the Jochid contingent there. But Hülegü's forces in turn defeated Negüder's army, which moved eastwards and, according to Rashīd al-Dīn, overran the territory 'from the mountains of Ghazna and Bīnī-yi Gāw to Multān and Lahore'.[63] This is the first mention of Bīnī-yi Gāw, a locality which is closely associated with the Negüderis and which is known to have lain not far from Shāl (the modern Quetta).[64]

Iranian sources, regrettably, have no more to say about the arrival of the Negüderis, or Qara'unas as they were also known (appendix III), but a garbled story picked up in Kirmān by Marco Polo a few years later may throw some light upon it. He makes Negüder's band pass through Badakhshān, the Pashāī and Kashmir until they reached 'the city Dilivar', which they wrested from its ruler, 'Asidin Soldan', and which allegedly became Negüder's base.[65] The Polo account is here highly confused, and has attracted the attention of successive commentators.[66] There can be little doubt that his 'Asidin' is 'Izz al-Dīn Küshlü Khān,[67] though in this case 'Dilivar', which has been identified plausibly with Lahore ('città di Livar'), presents some difficulty,[68] since Küshlü Khān, who ruled in Sind, is not

[62] Jackson, 'Dissolution', 232–3. Ayalon, 'Wafidiya'.

[63] Sayfī, 270–2, with the date 660/1262, though in view of Rashīd al-Dīn's chronology 661/1263 is more likely. *JT*, II, 139 (tr. Boyle, 123/tr. Verkhovskii, 82); and cf. Aubin, 'L'ethnogénèse', 80–1, for an elucidation of the text.

[64] Sayfī, 270. For Shāl as the alternative name of Quetta, see *IG*, XXI, 13, 20. The identification of Bīnī-yi Gāw with Shashgāw (15 m. N.E. of Ghazna on the road to Kābul), cited in Boyle, 'Mongol commanders', 247 n.74, is therefore to be discarded.

[65] Marco Polo, *Le divisament dou monde*, tr. A. C. Moule and Paul Pelliot, *The description of the world* (London, 1938, 2 vols.), I, 121; tr. Sir Henry Yule, *The book of Ser Marco Polo the Venetian*, new edn. H. Cordier (London, 1903–20, 3 vols.), I, 98.

[66] Yule, *ibid.*, I, 103 n., rightly observed that Polo conflates two quite distinct episodes, one involving the Jochid general and the other, which occurred several years later, a Chaghadayid prince (actually named Tegüder) who was active in the Caucasus region. See also Pelliot, *Notes on Marco Polo*, 190–6. The confusion between Negüder and Tegüder is repeated in Spuler, *Mongolen in Iran*, 62, and Wink, *Al-Hind*, II, 206, 208. Sir Aurel Stein, 'Marco Polo's account of a Mongol inroad into Kashmir', *Geographical Journal* 54 (1919), 92–103, stands in need of revision.

[67] Pelliot, *Notes on Marco Polo*, 52, while agreeing with 'the general opinion that this must be Balaban' (Asidin > Ghiyāth al-Dīn), still had doubts and observed that the name 'looks more like ᶜIzz al-Dīn'.

[68] Yule, I, 104–5 n. Pelliot, *Notes on Marco Polo*, 626, on the other hand, was still prepared to

known ever to have held that city; the history of the Lahore region between its abandonment by Jalāl al-Dīn Masʿūd and its restoration by Balaban in *c.* 666/1268 is a blank. The only other author to speak of Küshlü Khān's fate is ʿIṣāmī, who alleges that Küshlü Khān lost Multān to Balaban and was obliged to take up residence in Binbān, though he brought the Mongols into Sind on two subsequent occasions.[69] On the other hand, contemporary poets praise Küshlü Khān's son, Nāṣir al-Dīn Muḥammad, who was clearly no hapless exile but a prince of some standing who ruled Uchch and Multān for a few years.[70] The whole question of Küshlü Khān and his dynasty is doubtless destined to remain unresolved.

Simultaneously with these upheavals, two other figures who had played a leading role in events on the frontier over the previous decade were likewise eliminated. Alughu's forces, at the point when that prince was still aligned with Arigh Böke, arrested Sali and took him as a prisoner to Transoxiana.[71] The downfall of Nāṣir al-Dīn Muḥammad b. Ḥasan Qarluq is attributed in the Ilkhanid sources to the intrigues of Shams al-Dīn Muḥammad Kart of Herat and an otherwise unknown 'Khudāwandzāda Barghundī'; he was summoned to Hülegü's court, along with certain other local rulers, and executed on a charge of disloyalty. A consequence of his removal was the flight to India of the Khalaj leader and future Delhi Sultan, Jalāl al-Dīn, who had been in his service.[72]

The Mongols and India after 664/1266

Given what we know of the era of Nāṣir al-Dīn Maḥmūd Shāh, it is surprising that some decades later, in the sketch of the Sultanate's history with which he prefaces his *Diwal Rānī*, Amīr Khusraw dated the onset of Mongol inroads from Balaban's reign.[73] But if Baranī is to be believed, these years did witness a revival of Mongol pressure on the Panjāb. He blames it on the fact that the successors of Shīr Khān, who had held the iqtaʿs in the path of the Mongol advance and had been poisoned on

envisage Delhi; though *ibid.*, 195–6, both 'Deli' and 'Malabar' of Ramusio's version are regarded with suspicion.

69 *FS*, 154–5 (tr. 278–80).

70 Siddiqi, 'Historical information', 66. ʿAmīd Sunnāmī, cited by Badā'ūnī, *Muntakhab al-Tawārīkh*, ed. M. A. ʿAli (Calcutta, 1864–9, 3 vols.), I, 110, 121. See also the laconic mention in *TFS*, 66.

71 Waṣṣāf, 12. Rashīd al-Dīn mentions only that Alughu sent troops to Samarqand, Bukhārā and other parts of Transoxiana, though adding, confusingly, that he attacked the possessions of Berke (like Alughu, a supporter of Arigh Böke): *JT*, II, 403–4 (tr. Boyle, 257–8/tr. Verkhovskii, 163). See Barthold, *Turkestan*, 488.

72 Waṣṣāf, 311. *JT*, ed. Jahn, *Indiengeschichte*, Ar. text Taf. 57, Pers. text Taf. 23 (German tr. 48–9 has 'Mamluken' in error for *mulūk*). Qāshānī, 186. Cf. also Siddiqui, 'Qarlūgh kingdom', 85–6.

73 *DR*, 50.

Balaban's orders, did not share his capacity.[74] Even if this is true, the Mongol inroads may simply reflect the fact that the Negüderis were now launching raids from bases closer at hand than those occupied by Sali Noyan's army. They almost certainly mounted the attack on Uchch and Multān which a later tradition placed in the year of the death of the Chishtī shaykh Farīd al-Dīn Ganj-shikar (664/1265–6).[75] At any rate, annual attacks once more became the pattern.[76] Later, Baranī asserts that the Mongols regularly advanced as far as Rūpar on the upper Sutlej.[77] The restoration of Lahore was the only recovery Balaban was able to make in the north; but there is, significantly, no mention of its being granted as iqta' again prior to the fourteenth century.

Sultan Balaban entrusted the task of guarding the western frontier to his sons: the elder, Muḥammad, was granted Sind, and the younger, Bughra Khān Maḥmūd, was stationed at Sāmāna. The two princes shared responsibility for defence against the Mongols with the *bārbeg*, Ikhtiyār al-Dīn Begbars, and Baranī pays tribute to the effectiveness of these arrangements.[78] Around 680/1281–2, however, Bughra Khān was transferred permanently to Lakhnawtī. It is possible that this weakened the frontier defences in the last years of Balaban's reign, since 'Iṣāmī records an invasion by two bands of Mongols in which the force sent to repel them by Muḥammad suffered a reverse.[79] A heavier blow was to fall in the winter of 683/1284–5, when Muḥammad himself was defeated and killed in battle with the Mongol commander Temür.[80] According to the most circumstantial account of the engagement, given in a *marthiya* by Amīr Ḥasan Dihlawī which is preserved by Sirhindī, it took place at Bāgh-i *Nīr, close to the junction of the Rāvī and the Greater Dhandh, on 29 Dhu'l-Ḥijja 683/8 March 1285. Amīr Ḥasan's friend and fellow-poet, Amīr Khusraw, who was briefly taken prisoner by the Mongols, commemorated the disaster in his *Wasaṭ al-Ḥayāt*.[81]

Temür again invaded India and ravaged the territory between Lahore

[74] *TFS*, 65–6. Baranī's analysis contradicts what we know about the disposition of iqta's at the time Jūzjānī wrote, when Shīr Khān had been moved from Tabarhindh to Bhayāna (see above, p. 112).

[75] Amīr Ḥasan Dihlawī, *Fawā'id al-Fu'ād*, ed. M. Laṭīf Malik (Lahore, 1386/1966), 373–4.

[76] *WH*, IOL Persian ms. 412, fols. 90a, 134b. *TFS*, 82; and see also 50–1, where a speech put into Balaban's mouth refers to annual invasions.

[77] *Ibid.*, 82, with the corrupt reading 'ZWBR: text restored by Hodivala, *Studies*, II, 85–6. On Rūpar, 'a town of considerable antiquity' situated at 30° 58′ N., 76° 32′ E., see *IG*, XXI, 339.

[78] *TFS*, 80, 81: for the *bārbeg*'s name, see above, p. 78.

[79] *FS*, 171–3 (tr. 299–300).

[80] The description of Temür as 'one of the great Chingīzī amirs, to whom belonged Herat, Qandahār, Balkh, Badakhshān, Ghaznayn, Ghūr and Bāmiyān' is not found in any source earlier than Firishta (I, 143) and is consequently suspect; it is nevertheless accepted by Aziz Aḥmad, *Political history*, 285.

[81] Quoted at length by Badā'ūnī, I, 138–55 (extensive citations in Mirza, *Life and works*, 56–9). See also *TFS*, 109 (with the year 684); *FS*, 175–81 (tr. 304–11). The date is supplied by Amīr Ḥasan (quoted in *TMS*, 45) and by Khusraw in *WH*, IOL ms. 412, fols. 133a, 134b

and Sāmāna early in 686/1287, when the new sultan, Balaban's grandson Muʿizz al-Dīn Kayqubād, had begun to move east in preparation for the confrontation with his father Bughra Khān in Awadh. On the approach of the *bārbeg* Khān Jahān Shāhik, the Mongols retreated without offering battle and, according to Sirhindī, were pursued as far as the foothills of Jammū.[82] But with the decay of the sultan's authority, and the concentration of power in the hands of Niẓām al-Dīn (above, pp. 53, 81), many nobles were eliminated, among them Shāhik (now Azhdar Khān and amir of Multān).[83] Responsibility for frontier defence appears thereafter to have fallen principally to the Khalaj amir Jalāl al-Dīn Fīrūz, whom Balaban had made muqtaʿ of Kaithal and na'ib of Sāmāna.[84] But although Jalāl al-Dīn is portrayed as a veteran of the Mongol front by the time he ascended the throne in 689/1290, we know virtually nothing of his exploits. Amīr Khusraw simply puts into the new sultan's mouth references to campaigns against the Mongols of 'Ghaznayn, Kurramān and *Birjand', and later alludes to his intention of advancing from Multān towards Ghazna; Baranī is even less specific.[85]

Soon after his accession, the sultan, who had entrusted the iqtaʿ of Multān to his second son, Erkli Khān, found time, amid the victories of a twelve-month period commemorated in Amīr Khusraw's *Miftāḥ al-Futūḥ*, to march against the Mongols. This campaign, from which he returned to Delhi at the onset of 690/1291 after an absence of one month, was directed against a region that cannot be identified.[86] It apparently provoked the next Mongol assault, in 691/1292, headed by the prince ʿAbd-Allāh. The sultan made camp in a locality called by both Baranī and ʿIṣāmī 'Bar Rām', where a river (the Sutlej?) separated the two armies. After some skirmishing between the two vanguards, however, a truce was declared. Jalāl al-Dīn and ʿAbd-Allāh exchanged friendly messages and gifts, and the Mongol prince withdrew, leaving behind under a commander named Alughu a group of his followers who accepted Islam and who were settled by the sultan in the neighbourhood of Delhi.[87] Thereafter we hear of no further invasions during Jalāl al-Dīn's reign. Following the old sultan's murder in 695/1296 by his nephew 'Alā' al-Dīn, his sons, having held out for a time in Multān, were forced to surrender and were later put to death. This crisis may well

(cited by Badā'ūnī, I, 147). The location given in *WH* varies: on the borders of Multān (fol. 78a), or in the vicinity of Lahore (fol. 132b).

82 *QS*, 62–5. *TMS*, 54. 83 *TFS*, 134. 84 *Ibid.*, 170, 194, 195.

85 *MF*, 8. *DR*, 51. *TFS*, 196. Birjand may be identical with 'Barghund' (above, p. 116), an alternative name of Naghar: Hodivala, *Studies*, I, 168; A. D. H. Bivar, 'Naghar and Īryāb: two little-known Islamic sites of the north-west frontier of Afghanistan and Pakistan', *Iran* 24 (1986), 131–8.

86 *MF*, 22, 23. The region is named as BALAGHTRK: the same reading is found in IOL Persian mss. 51, fol. 490a (margin), and 412, fol. 788b (margin).

87 *TFS*, 218–19. A different account of this episode is furnished in *FS*, 209–14 (tr. 372–9), where the Mongols retreat after an indecisive battle with Jalāl al-Dīn's brother, Malik Khāmush.

have weakened the defences of Sind, a situation of which, as we shall see in chapter 11, the Mongols were not slow to take advantage.

The Negüderis and their Mongol neighbours

The collapse of Mongol unity after Möngke's death had deposited in the Indian borderlands a body of Mongol troops with no allegiance to either the Ilkhans or the Chaghadayids; the region was now the camping-grounds of a smaller, independent grouping without access to the resources of the whole Mongol empire. The strength of the Negüderis was sufficiently modest not to jeopardize the survival of the Sultanate, but still powerful enough to form yet another barrier in India's defence, obstructing any expansionist tendencies on the part of the Mongols of Persia or of Transoxiana. Marco Polo heard tell of Negüder that he 'makes war on all the Tartars who dwell round about his kingdom'; and certainly the Negüderis acquired a name for brigandage and highway robbery and were notoriously unready to submit to any ruler.[88]

Their arrival in the Indian borderlands drove a wedge between India and Hülegü's dominions.[89] Ilkhanid sources speak of Negüderi raids on Fārs and Kirmān and assert that the people of Fārs lived in fear of such raids down until the end of the reign of the Ilkhan Arghun (d. 690/1291).[90] When the Chaghadayid khan Baraq invaded Khurāsān in 668/1269–70, Hülegü's son and successor, Abaqa, sought to deflect him with the offer of Ghazna and 'Kurramān-i Binbān'[91] – regions that were currently not in his gift. The Ilkhans may not have been primarily interested in this tract, and may at this stage have envisaged leaving its reduction to the Chaghadayids. This is not to say that they made no effort to exert indirect influence over the Negüderis or to mount punitive expeditions against them. Both Hülegü and Abaqa despatched a series of commanders against Negüder and his forces.[92] During Baraq's attack on Khurāsān, various Chaghadayid princes deserted to the Ilkhan, and Abaqa sent one of them, Mubārak Shāh, to head 'the army of Negüder in the confines of Ghaznayn'.[93] But Mubārak Shāh's death in 674/1275–6 while leading an attack on the province of Kirmān suggests that his allegiance to the Ilkhan was superficial.[94] Abaqa had also

[88] Marco Polo, tr. Moule and Pelliot, I, 122/tr. Yule and Cordier, I, 99. Sayfī, 432.

[89] Jahn's view ('Zum Problem', 618) that it was the constant need to defend their other frontiers which prevented Hülegü's successors from making good their claims to present-day Afghanistan fails to take account of the situation that had emerged there.

[90] *JT*, III, 151–2 (tr. Arends, 94). Ibn Zarkūb, *Shīrāz-Nāma* (*c.* 1344), ed. Bahman Karīmī (Tehran, 1310 Sh./1932), 66/ed. Ismāᶜīl Wāᶜiẓ Jawādī (Tehran, 1350 Sh./1971), 91–2. Waṣṣāf, 199–203.

[91] *JT*, III, 122 (tr. Arends, 78); and cf. Sayfī, 308.

[92] Aubin, 'L'ethnogénèse', 80 n.3, for textual references.

[93] *JT*, II, 193 (tr. Boyle, 153–4/tr. Verkhovskii, 100).

[94] Aubin, 'L'ethnogénèse', 83. Anonymous, *Ta'rīkh-i Shāhī-yi Qarakhitā'iyyān* (late thirteenth century), ed. Muḥammad Bāstānī-Pārīzī (Tehran, 2535 Shāhanshāhī/1976), 248–50.

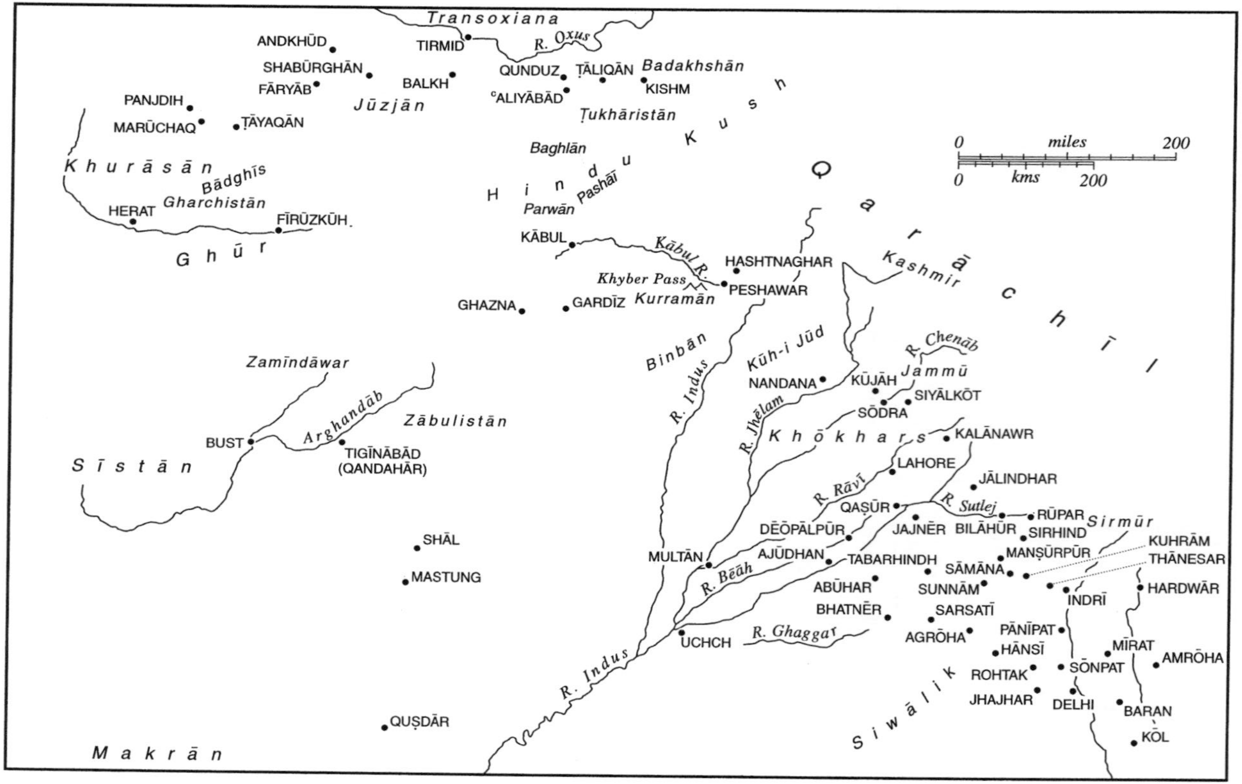

Map 2: The frontier with the Mongols

entrusted another Chaghadayid, Böjei, with a command among the Negüderis, and Böjei's son ʿAbd-Allāh, who would later invade India (above, p. 118), appears to have succeeded him by this juncture.[95] In 678/1279, in reprisal for a Negüderi raid on Kirmān and Fārs, Abaqa himself led an army as far as Herat, receiving the submission of Mubārak Shāh's sons, while his son Arghun was sent on ahead into Ghūr and Gharchistān. A number of Negüderi amirs and their dependants were subsequently employed in the Ilkhans' service in western Persia.[96]

These Ilkhanid campaigns, it seems, had strictly limited aims. The hypothesis advanced by Professor U. N. Day, that the sudden spate of Mongol incursions into India from *c.* 1285 reflects the disorders in Persia after Abaqa's death in 680/1282,[97] is difficult to sustain. The Mongols of Persia were cut off from India not only by the Negüderis but also by the sometimes recalcitrant Kartid kingdom of Herat and by the virtually autonomous kingdom of Sīstān. Abaqa's successor Aḥmad included Tigīnābād in a grant to the malik of Sīstān in 683/1284, and indeed Sīstān is described as still not subject (*īl*) to the Ilkhan in the reign of Ghazan (694–703/1295–1304).[98] The most we can say is that the Ilkhans' operations in eastern Khurāsān may have encouraged the Negüderis to devote more attention to the Panjāb. But there were certainly other, more local stimuli at work. The seizure of Qandahār in 680/1281 by the Kartid malik of Herat, Shams al-Dīn Muḥammad II,[99] would surely have menaced the Negüderis, and may therefore help to explain an apparent increase in Mongol pressure on the Delhi Sultanate in Balaban's last years.

As for the Chaghadayids, Alughu's advance into the Indian border

[95] Kirmānī, *Simṭ*, 49. *JT*, II, 177, *ḥākim-i charīk-i Qarā'ūna būd dar ḥudūd-i Ghaznayn* (tr. Boyle, 144; not in text used for Verkhovskii's tr.). Anonymous (fifteenth-century) Chinggisid genealogy, *Muʿizz al-Ansāb*, BN ms. Ancien fonds persan 67, fol. 29b, for Böjei's flight to Abaqa. In *JT* (but not in his genealogical work, *SP*, TSM ms. III Ahmet 2937, fol. 117b), Rashīd al-Dīn seems to list this branch of the Chaghadayids twice, and we need not assume, with Aubin ('L'ethnogénèse', 84 n.1), that there were two princes called Böjei. Baranī calls ʿAbd-Allāh 'grandson of Hulū [i.e. Hülegü]' (*TFS*, 218), an error which misled Lal, *History of the Khaljis*, 30; but it possibly reflects awareness at Delhi that ʿAbd-Allāh had been an Ilkhanid appointee.

[96] *JT*, III, 152–3, 252 (tr. Arends, 94, 143); cf. also *JT*, II, tr. Verkhovskii, 100 (sentence omitted from Blochet's text; see Boyle tr., 154 n.40). On this campaign, see Aubin, 'L'ethnogénèse', 85–6; and for the subsequent history of the Negüderi contingents transported westwards, *ibid.*, 87–90.

[97] U. N. Day, 'The north-west frontier of the Sultanate', in his *Some aspects of medieval Indian history* (New Delhi, 1971), 43–4; and cf. also his 'The north-west frontier under the Khalji Sultans of Delhi', *IC* 39 (1963), 99.

[98] Jaʿfar b. Muḥammad b. Ḥasan Jaʿfarī, *Ta'rīkh-i Yazd*, ed. Īraj Afshār (Tehran, 1338 Sh./1959), 27; for the grant, see Bosworth, *History of the Saffarids*, 435. On the kingdom of Herat, see T. W. Haig and B. Spuler, 'Kart', *Enc.Isl.*^{2}; also Spuler, *Mongolen in Iran*, 129–33, and his 'Das heutige afghanische Gebiet und sein Ringen um Selbständigkeit gegenüber die Mongolen im 13./14. JH.', in G. L. Ulmen (ed.), *Society and history. Essays in honor of Karl August Wittfogel* (The Hague, 1978), 403–9.

[99] Sayfī, 369–73: the date, of course, is not above question (above, p. 111, n.39).

regions – instanced in the overthrow of Sali Noyan – appears to have been a temporary phenomenon. Despite Aubin's assertion that 'the impossibility of maintaining contact with the Golden Horde soon condemned the Negüderis to a change of masters which was already complete around 1270', we may well question whether the Chaghadayids did effectively assert their authority here at this time.[100] Still less could they have retained it in the troubled years that followed. What links, if any, the renegade Chaghadayid princes whom the Ilkhans installed in the Ghazna region retained with the Chaghadayid ulus is not clear. In his account of Chaghadai's line, Rashīd al-Dīn, writing at the very beginning of the fourteenth century, speaks of 'the province of Ghazna and the Qara'una army, which has long had connections with them'.[101] But perhaps we should not read too much into this. The political organization of the Negüderis was doubtless a loose one, and the influence of the head of Chaghadai's ulus – like that of his enemy, the Ilkhan – varied at different times and from one contingent to another.[102] Not until the last decade or so of the thirteenth century was a successful effort made from Transoxiana to bring the Negüderis under control and to dominate the marches of India (see chapter 11); and then the impact on the Delhi Sultanate would be felt more keenly than at any previous time.

[100] Cf. Aubin, 'L'ethnogénèse', 82: 'L'impossibilité de maintenir le contact avec la Horde d'Or condamna bientôt les Negüderi à un transfert de sujétion qui était déjà chose faite vers 1270. Les Čaġataides en furent les bénéficiaires, et non les Ilkhans.'

[101] *JT*, II, 174, *lashgar-i Qarā'ūnā ki az qadīm bāz ba-īshān taᶜalluq dāshta and* (tr. Boyle, 142/tr. Verkhovskii, 92–3).

[102] See the remarks in Aubin, 'L'ethnogénèse', 87.

CHAPTER 7

Raid, conquest and settlement

To chart the progress of Muslim arms during the thirteenth century is by no means an easy task. There are no contemporary Hindu narrative sources, properly speaking; even the epic *Hammīramāhakāvya*, for example, dates from the end of the fifteenth century. From the Hindu side, inscriptions – whether on stone or in the form of copper-plate grants issued by rulers to their subordinates – are the best evidence we possess, although the references there to *Mlecchas* ('unclean ones'), *Turushkas* ('Turks') and *Yavanas* ('Westerners') are frequently vague. Muslim writers, less than forthright about reverses, provide fragmentary data. To notice, moreover, that Jūzjānī's accounts of military operations are largely confined to those on which Nāṣir al-Dīn Maḥmūd Shāh or Ulugh Khān Balaban were present is to recognize the extent of our ignorance. There must have been numerous military operations conducted at a local level by amirs and muqtaʿs which won fresh territory for the revenue-collector and the settler, but of which we know nothing. Although the distribution of iqtaʿs may serve as a pointer to Muslim conquest, the information available for any given time is hardly exhaustive. Here and there an inscription dating the construction of a mosque confirms the presence of a Muslim community; but even so we cannot tell whether this was the earliest mosque to be built in the town concerned.

It is important not to be misled by the terminology of holy war (*jihād*, *ghazw*) employed by Jūzjānī and others. The primary aims of the Islamic holy war are the defence of the *Dār al-Islām* and the extension of Muslim rule over pagan territory. In the circumstances of the early Sultanate period, the latter aim could only be realized in certain regions for perhaps a limited time; it might not be realizable at all. A case in point is the great fortress of Ranthanbōr in Rajasthan, which was taken twice, and repeatedly attacked, before its final capture by ʿAlāʾ al-Dīn Khaljī in 700/1301. During the thirteenth century the pious Muslim monarch might have to be content with swashbuckling raids. In the more spectacular cases, the capital of a Hindu kingdom was taken, looted and then abandoned so that its ruler was able to reoccupy it in the wake of the Muslim army's departure. Assaults of this kind rallied the faithful, weakened an infidel prince by depriving him of treasure, horses and elephants and diminished his standing in the eyes of his peers and his subjects. But many expeditions would have been designed simply to replenish stocks of cattle and slaves. For much of the period after 633/1236 Muslim domination either remained static or receded as the Sultanate proved unable even to hold on to the acquisitions made by Muʿizz al-Dīn and Aybeg or by Iltutmish.

Predatory incursions into Hindu territory might also have other mainsprings than conventional religious fervour. Ulugh Khān Balaban is said to have recommended military activity against the Hindu powers to Nāṣir al-Dīn Maḥmūd Shāh in order that plunder wrested from the Hindus might be used to pay the troops that resisted the Mongols.[1] Such campaigns also often served the interests of the individual commander. Balaban's own lucrative expedition to Ranthanbōr in 652/1254, which immediately preceded his return to power at court; Toghril's profitable raid on eastern Bengal just prior to his insurrection in *c.* 678/1279–80; and still more the booty obtained from the Deccan by ʿAlāʾ al-Dīn Khaljī in 695/1296 which greased his path to the throne, suffice to remind us of that.

Strongholds and refuges

Earlier we saw how the Ghurid conquests established a basis for Muslim rule in the north Gangetic plain, while leaving certain Hindu rulers on their thrones in return for the payment of tribute. At a local level, power remained in the hands of a host of lesser chieftains who frequently defied the sultan's government. When he wanted to conjure up a vivid image of the peace and order that prevailed under ʿAlāʾ al-Dīn Khaljī, it was enough for Baranī to depict these chiefs (*muqaddams*) and headmen (*khūts*/*khōts*) as standing guard on the highways and keeping watch over travellers and caravans.[2] Ibn Baṭṭūṭa, who visited the Sultanate during Muḥammad b. Tughluq's reign, was careful to distinguish Hindus who lived in villages subject to a Muslim officer (*ḥākim*) from those he terms 'rebels and warriors who maintain themselves in the fastnesses of the mountains and plunder travellers'.[3] And he returns to the theme at a later juncture:

> The infidels in the land of India inhabit a territory which is not geographically separated from that of the Muslims, and their lands are contiguous, but though the Muslims have the upper hand over them yet the infidels maintain themselves in inaccessible mountains and rugged places, and they have forests of reeds ... The infidels live in these forests, which for them are as good as city walls, and inside them they have their cattle and grain and supplies of water collected from the rains, so

[1] *TN*, II, 57 (tr. 816).

[2] *TFS*, 324; and see also 340. For the term *khōt*, see Yule and Burnell, *Hobson-Jobson*, 480–1; S. H. Hodivala, 'Notes on Hobson-Jobson', *IA* 58 (1929), 173; *idem*, *Studies*, I, 277–8.

[3] IB, III, 133 (tr. Gibb, 612).

that they cannot be overcome except by strong armies of men who go into these forests and cut down those reeds . . .[4]

These are the *mawāsāt* (sing. *mawās*, 'shelter', 'refuge') that figure so frequently in our Indian Muslim sources. The word applied to any of the countless regions of broken terrain, arduous defiles and jungles where the Muslim heavy cavalry could barely penetrate and the enemy could hold out with relative impunity.[5] One such region was surely the *tarai* beyond the river Sārū (Sarju) – 'the abundant jungles of Hindūstān, the narrow passes and the torrents, and the dense foliage of numerous trees', as Jūzjānī puts it – where Balaban advanced in 654/1256 in the fruitless pursuit of his Muslim enemies.[6] The *mawās*, of course, served as a refuge also for Muslim rebels like Qutlugh Khān, who passed through such territory on his way to seek asylum in Santūr in 654/1256;[7] although sometimes their hopes were cheated, as when Malik Chhajjū in 689/1290 and the adherents of ʿAyn al-Mulk Ibn Māhrū in *c.* 740/1339–40 were handed over to the sultan after seeking asylum in a *mawās*.[8] The term grew to be synonymous with defiance. 'All Gawr and Tirhut became *mawās*', says ʿIṣāmī when referring to the Muslim-led secession of Bengal and Bihār in Muḥammad b. Tughluq's reign.[9]

Hindu warriors were often ready to side with Muslim rebels against the government. Toghril's insurrection in *c.* 678/1279–80 drew in large numbers of foot from the landed gentry of Bengal – those 'renowned paiks', as Baranī calls them, who subsequently paid a heavy price when the victorious sultan Balaban had them all beheaded.[10] No more successful were the *rāwats* and paiks – termed merely 'some infidel troops from Hindūstān' (*az Hindūstān sipāhī-yi chand bī-dīn*) by Amīr Khusraw – who gathered around Balaban's nephew Malik Chhajjū at Kara in 689/1290 in an attempt to overthrow the Khaljī regime. They paraded before Chhajjū, taking up the betel-leaf (*tanbūl*) in their familiar ceremony of pledging allegiance, and boasted how they would fall upon Sultan Jalāl al-Dīn's canopy (*chatr*) in the heat of battle; but instead they were rounded up and taken prisoner when Chhajjū lost his nerve and fled.[11] Kara appears to have been a veritable nursery of such auxiliaries for Muslim rebels. Not only did ʿAlāʾ al-Dīn recruit two thousand paiks here only a few years later, but we find 'drug-quaffing paiks' allegedly behind a rising in *c.* 1338 in the same locality.[12]

[4] *Ibid.*, III, 389 (tr. Gibb, 741–2).

[5] Hodivala, *Studies*, I, 226–9. Examples are found in *TN*, I, 491, and II, 17–18, 19, 26, 27, 29, 47, 52, 53, 57, 61, 72, 76–7.

[6] *Ibid.*, II, 71, *jangalhā-yi Hindūstān-i gashn wa-maḍāʾiq-i lūrhā wa-iltifāf-i ashjār-i bisyār* (Raverty's tr., 837–8, modified).

[7] *Ibid.*, II, 72 (tr. 839); cf. also I, 491 (tr. 704–5 inaccurate).

[8] *TFS*, 182, 490–1.

[9] *FS*, 606 (tr. 902).

[10] *TFS*, 83, 91.

[11] *Ibid.*, 182–3. For Amīr Khusraw's dismissive phrase, see *MF*, 8.

[12] *TFS*, 222, 487. For the reservoir of armed men on which the Mughals later drew, see Dirk

In describing the Muslim and Hindu territories as geographically unseparated, Ibn Baṭṭūṭa was pointing to a feature of the Sultanate that marked it out from other Muslim polities. Elsewhere in the Islamic world it made sense to talk of the Dār al-Islām and the Dār al-Ḥarb; but not in India. A series of dots would indicate the extent of the sultans' rule with greater realism than does the uniform shading favoured in historical atlases. Obeisance (*pāībūs*, *zamīnbūs*), like tribute, was intermittent. Baranī makes Niẓām al-Dīn advise Sultan Kayqubād to advance to meet his father in 686/1287 at the head of an imposing army, in order that the rais and ranas might be induced to wait upon him en route.[13] The open countryside, the forests, the hills – these were the domain of the infidel. The Muslim population of the Sultanate largely resided in its fortified towns and cities, and even there they were not unusually a minority. Ibn Baṭṭūṭa observes of the great fortress of Gwāliyōr that it was 'an isolated and inaccessible castle, in the midst of the infidel Hindus', and that the generality of its inhabitants were infidels; so too were the majority of the people of the neighbouring town of ʿAlāpūr.[14] Not long afterwards we find ʿAyn al-Mulk Ibn Māhrū, as governor of Sind for the Tughluqid Fīrūz Shāh, commenting acidly on 'peasants (*dahāqīn*) and landholders (*zamīndārs*) who are only ostensibly subjects (*raʿāyā-yi ṣūrī*) and pay tax out of fear of the army or the blow of the sword'.[15] From each strongpoint the authority of the Muslim governor and tax-collector radiated outwards for a distance that waxed and waned with the conduct of local military operations or the proximity of a large field army sent from Delhi. In India the 'war zone', peopled by *ḥarbīs*, was never far away.

The heartlands

We are told very little of the relations of the sultan's governors in Sind with local Hindu powers. Sultan Balaban's son Muḥammad, when governor of Multān, was married to the daughter of a Hindu rai, who ransomed his son-in-law's body from the Mongols in 684/1285.[16] When not intent on repelling Mongol attacks, Muḥammad seems to have been engaged principally in asserting his authority over the partially Islamized Sūmra princes of the Indus delta. Having been tributary to Qubacha, they had submitted to Iltutmish, and Dīwal (Daybul) and Damrīla are said to have been subject to

H. A. Kolff, *Naukar, Rajput and Sepoy: the ethnohistory of the military labour market in Hindustan, 1450–1850* (Cambridge, 1990), chap. 1, esp. 3–17.

[13] *TFS*, 141; cf. also 108, where the chiefs come to wait upon Balaban after the Bengal campaign.

[14] IB, III, 188, 195, and IV, 29 (tr. Gibb, 642, 645, 785).

[15] *IM*, 75. For the varied groups who made up the class loosely termed *zamīndārs*, see I. Habib, 'Agrarian economy', 58–9.

[16] *FS*, 180–1 (tr. 311).

Raḍiyya.[17] But their allegiance could not be taken for granted, and it must have fallen to the sultan's representatives at Sīwistān to keep watch on them. Muḥammad's iqtaʿ is said to have extended as far as Janānī, a town some 120 miles upstream from Thatta and known to have been held by the Sūmras; but we know that in *c.* 680/1281–2 he reduced the Sūmra stronghold at Damrīla.[18] At some point early in the fourteenth century, says ʿAfīf, ʿAlā' al-Dīn Khaljī mounted an unsuccessful campaign in the region, although we also know that his muqtaʿ at Dēōpālpūr, Ghāzī Malik Tughluq, constructed in lower Sind a new fortress, which he named Ghāzīpūr.[19] Thereafter, no more is heard of this territory until the reign of Muḥammad b. Tughluq.

The Panjāb was home to a number of imperfectly subdued tribes, notably the Khōkhars, whose original territory lay between the Jhēlam and the Chenāb but who were by now encroaching on the regions east of the Bēāh.[20] They chiefly threatened Lahore. In 639/1241 Qaraqush Khān, the muqtaʿ of Lahore, massacred a band of Khōkhars whom he found scavenging in the stricken city for anything the Mongols might have left behind.[21] According to Baranī, Balaban's cousin Shīr Khān subdued the Khōkhars and other tribes, a feat which proved beyond the capacity of his successors; and Amīr Khusraw credits Jalāl al-Dīn Khaljī too with harrying them.[22] But in the following century we learn from one of Ibn Māhrū's letters that the road from Multān to Ajūdhan (now Pakpattan) was regularly harassed by marauding Khōkhars.[23]

Further east, and closer to the heart of the Sultanate, Muslim governors based at fortresses like Tabarhindh, Sunnām and Sāmāna had to contend with other turbulent peoples – the Bhattīs and Māins of the Abūhar region, the Mandāhars of Kaithal, and the Jats. They were for the most part hardy pastoralists who nomadized in the riverine tracts, and Baranī, while a prisoner in Bhatnēr, saw their *talwandīs*, laagers formed out of wagons within which they gathered their livestock close to a source of water.[24] Tōdars and Jats, as well as Khōkhars, are found among the troops with

17 *TN*, I, 459 (omitting Damrīla, but cf. Raverty's tr. 640). Damrīla is Danbharlo, 150 m. E. of Karachi: J. A. Boyle, 'Jalal al-Din Khwarazm-Shah in the Indus valley', in Khuhro (ed.), *Sind through the centuries*, 129 n.13.

18 *FS*, 175 (tr. 304): immediately prior to his overthrow by the Mongols (683/1285). *DGK*, 69. *WH*, IOL Persian ms. 412, fol. 140b; hence Badā'ūnī, I, 154 (WMRBLH in error). *TMS*, 43, for the southern boundary of Muḥammad's iqtaᶜ. For Janānī, see IB, III, 101 (tr. Gibb, 596–7).

19 Ghāzīpūr: *SFS*, 91. ᶜAlā' al-Dīn: ᶜAfīf, 251; the late and contradictory testimony on this is reviewed by Hodivala, *Studies*, II, 133–4.

20 Abdus Subhan, 'Khokar', *Enc.Isl.*². For their original territory, see *Tāj*, fol. 190a.

21 *TN*, II, 165–6 (tr. 1136). 22 *TFS*, 65. *DR*, 52. 23 *IM*, 168.

24 *TFS*, 568: and cf. Hodivala, *Studies*, I, 305, for a translation of this passage. On these tribes, see generally H. A. Rose, *A glossary of the tribes and castes of the Punjab and North-West Frontier province* (Lahore, 1911–19, 3 vols.), II, 101–6 (Bhattīs), 357–77 (Jats), and III, 65 (Mandāhars), 102–4 (Mīnīs or Māins); also Hodivala, *Studies*, I, 295–6. The Jats were abandoning their pastoralism for agriculture: Irfan Habib, 'Jatts of Punjāb and Sind', in

which Raḍiyya and *Altunapa opposed Bahrām Shāh in 638/1240.[25] The fortress at Bhatnēr was built by Shīr Khān as muqtaʿ of Dēōpālpūr, and he, according to Baranī, reduced these peoples to obedience.[26] But the future sultan Jalāl al-Dīn Khaljī fought against the Bhattīs and the Khōkhars and, when conducting a raid on Mandāhar territory as muqtaʿ of Kaithal (i.e. in the late 1280s), sustained two wounds in the face that left him scarred ever afterwards.[27] And periodic resistance continued into the fourteenth century, for Muḥammad b. Tughluq was to head a punitive campaign against the Mains, the Bhattīs and the Mandāhars in *c.* 1337. It would have been some such group which had attacked Ibn Baṭṭūṭa's party in 734/1334 in the plain between Ajūdhan and Abūhar.[28]

Immediately south of Delhi lay Alwar, a hilly region pitted with defiles and ravines and in the thirteenth century heavily forested. This, to the Muslims, was the *kūhpāya*, 'the highlands'. An alternative name was 'Mīwāt', after its inhabitants, the Mēōs, who appear to have been loosely subject to the Chawhān (Chāhamāna) kings of Ranthanbōr,[29] and whose depredations reached across Hariyāna in the north and to Bhayāna in the east. Muslim outposts had been created in this tract at Rēwārī, Nārnawl, Palwal and Kāma, which appear as iqtaʿs under Iltutmish and his immediate successors: Rēwārī was for a time the assignment of Balaban, who early in his career is said to have reduced to obedience 'the *mawāsāt* of the *kūhpāya*'.[30] In 658/1260, when his dependants on the outskirts of Hānsī had suffered from Mēō raids, Balaban led two devastating campaigns deep into their territory, bringing back 250 of their leading men for execution in Delhi and putting thousands of Mēōs to the sword.[31] Jūzjānī's fulsome narrative might easily persuade us that the Mēōs had been suppressed for all time, but for Baranī's claim that during the reigns of Iltutmish's offspring the Mēōs had continued unchecked, so that they were robbing the mansions (*sarāīhā*) in the neighbourhood of Delhi itself and harassing the water-carriers at the Ḥawḍ-i Shamsī. Balaban gave priority to crushing them, and spent the first year of his reign clearing the jungles in the environs of the capital and slaughtering the Mēōs. He constructed a fortress at Gōpālgīr and established various redoubts (*thānahā*). After this, alleges Baranī, the citizens of Delhi were spared the

Harbans Singh and N. Gerald Barrier (eds.), *Panjab past and present. Essays in honour of Dr. Ganda Singh* (Patiala, 1976), 92–103.

25 *FS*, 139 (tr. 259). 26 *TFS*, 65. 27 *Ibid.*, 195. *DR*, 52.

28 IB, III, 133–5 (tr. Gibb, 612–13). For Muḥammad's campaign, see *TFS*, 483.

29 See generally J. Burton-Page, 'Mē'ō', *Enc.Isl.*², and 'Mēwāt', *ibid.* For the link with Ranthanbōr, *TN*, II, 58–9 (tr. 818); Habibullah, *Foundation*, 152, 153.

30 *TN*, II, 6, 8, 41 (tr. 726, 730, 790); and for Balaban, II, 52 (tr. 806–7). For Kāma, in the Bharatpur territory, 39 m. N.W. of Mathura, at 27° 40′ N., 77° 20′ E., see Raverty, 790 n.9; for Palwal, see also Shuʿaib, 'Inscriptions from Palwal', 2–3; *RCEA*, X, 56, 72–3 (nos. 3678, 3703).

31 *TN*, II, 78–83, 89 (tr. 850–6, 864); also a brief reference to the first campaign at I, 496 (tr. 715).

threat of the Mēōs.[32] The mosque constructed at Nārnawl in 671/1272 may indicate the success of Balaban's policy.[33] Under Jalāl al-Dīn Khaljī, Nārnawl again appears under Muslim rule, and the fact that on his outward march against Ranthanbōr in 690/1291 the sultan was able to move by way of Rēwārī and Nārnawl suggests that he anticipated no trouble from the Mēōs.[34] But a chance remark by Ibn Baṭṭūṭa reveals that Muḥammad b. Tughluq had been obliged to send troops into the hilly regions near Delhi not long before the Moroccan traveller's arrival.[35] Nothing throws into sharper relief the limitations of Muslim governmental authority than these recurrent crises in a territory so close to the capital.

The north and west

Beyond the Khōkhars lay the people of the Salt Range (Kūh-i Jūd). Their suppression by Muʿizz al-Dīn in 601/1204 had not cowed them for long, and their conversion to Islam had been merely temporary. In 643/1245 the raja of the Salt Range, 'Jaspāl Sihrā', acted as guide to the invading Mongol army, for which he incurred a punitive attack by the Delhi forces under the *amīr-ḥājib* Balaban in the following year.[36] Soon after his accession as sultan in 664/1266, Balaban led another expedition to the Salt Range, bringing back the raja's two sons as hostages:[37] they appear to have accepted Islam, and are later found enrolled among the nobility (above, p. 79).

During the thirteenth century the sultans seem to have had little contact with the Hindu princes of the mountains to the north, for which the term Qarāchīl is employed by Jūzjānī and by Ibn Baṭṭūṭa;[38] Muḥammad b. Tughluq is the first sultan known to have launched a campaign to these distant regions. Our sources barely mention Kashmir and Jammū, each under its own dynasty of rajas, and there is no evidence that they ever acknowledged the overlordship of Delhi. But even in Jūzjānī's time expeditions were sent into the territories lying due north of Delhi. When the raja of Santūr, 'Ranpāl, paramount among the Hindus', gave asylum to

[32] *TFS*, 55–7. For Gōpālgīr, see also *FS*, 164 (tr. 291).

[33] S. S. Hussain, 'A new inscription of Sulṭān Balban from the State Museum, Patiālā', *EIAPS* (1972), 1–3; *ARIE* (1973–4), 13, 181 (no. D250).

[34] *MF*, 25; *ibid.*, 28, for an amir of Nārnawl. For this place, at 28° 3′ N., 76° 10′ E., see *IG*, XVIII, 380–1.

[35] IB, III, 293 (tr. Gibb, 696–7).

[36] *TN*, II, 56–7 (tr. 815); cf. also I, 479 (tr. 678–9).

[37] *TMS*, 40. *TFS*, 59–60, mentions the campaign only briefly.

[38] *TN*, II, 126 (tr. 1046); the form is given in *scriptio plena* by IB, III, 325. The name is Turkish and appears to mean 'opening in the snow', from *qar*, 'snow', and *achil-*, 'to open': Clauson, *Etymological dictionary*, 26, 641; Pelliot, *Notes sur l'histoire de la Horde d'Or*, 64 ('*qaračïl* ... endroit qui ne gèle pas dans une surface gelée'). The suggested link with Sanskrit *achala*, 'mountain', and hence with the location 'Kulārchak' (*recte* Kulārchal), near Kashmir, mentioned in the eleventh century by al-Bīrūnī, is therefore groundless.

Balaban's enemy Qutlugh Khān, Balaban sacked his residence at Silmūr (Sirmūr) in 655/1257.[39]

Rajasthan and the Siwālik

The northern part of the Aravalli range formed the backbone of the territory called by the Muslims 'Siwālik' (not to be confused with the modern usage, which refers to a section of the sub-Himalaya). This was a vast area, stretching from Hānsī and Sarsatī as far south as Nāgawr, Ajmēr, Sambhar Namak and Mandōr; and indeed a phrase of Baranī's suggests that it was deemed to include Jālōr also.[40] Early in his reign, Iltutmish led an expedition to Jālōr, ruled by a branch of the Chawhān dynasty. Its king, Udāyasimha ('Udaysa'), was reduced to submission and undertook to pay tribute.[41] The arrangement does not seem to have been long respected, since Iltutmish in 624/1227 attacked and captured Mandōr, which is known to have belonged to Udāyasimha, and indeed an inscription of his son Chachigadēva proclaims that Udāyasimha had 'curbed the pride of the Turushka'.[42] Perhaps this is an allusion to the recovery of Mandōr, which figures as part of an iqtaʿ only once, in 639/1242, and was clearly lost by the Muslims at some later date, since it had to be retaken by Jalāl al-Dīn Khaljī in 691/1292.[43] Of Jālōr, nothing more is heard until the following century.

Ajmēr, the former capital of the main branch of the Chawhān dynasty, had been seized by Aybeg following its occupation by Harīrāja, brother of Prthvīrāja III. During the reign of Iltutmish it was the centre of an iqtaʿ which comprised also Lāwa, Kāsilī and Sambhar Namak, and was held for a time by Naṣīr al-Dīn Aytemür al-Bahā'ī. But these latter districts do not appear again as Muslim territory in the thirteenth century, and when we next find Ajmēr granted as iqtaʿ it is in conjunction with Mandōr and Nāgawr, as part of the large assignment entrusted to Küshlü Khān in 639/1242.[44] By this time the southernmost regions of the Siwālik would have been under heavy pressure from the Chawhāns at Ranthanbōr, and the grant perhaps indicates that an amalgamation of local resources was deemed necessary. It must also be significant that thereafter Muslim authors do not refer to Ajmēr until the fourteenth century. A Sanskrit epic claims that the Chawhān king of Ranthanbōr, Hammīradēva (1283–1301), passed

[39] *TN*, II, 72–3 (tr. 839–40); see also I, 491 (tr. 704–6).

[40] *TFS*, 289. The narrower usage is found in *TN*, I, 284, 400–1 (tr. 200, 468). See generally Yule and Burnell, *Hobson-Jobson*, 843–4.

[41] *Tāj*, fols. 228a–232b. For Jālōr among Iltutmish's conquests, see *TN*, BL ms., fol. 179b.

[42] D. R. Bhandarkar, 'The Chahamanas of Mārwār', *EI* 11 (1911–12), 74 ff. For Udāyasimha's possession of Mandōr, see Ray, *Dynastic history*, 1128–31; and for Iltutmish's campaign, *TN*, I, 446 (tr. 611).

[43] *TFS*, 220. *FS*, 215 (tr. 379–80). *TMS*, 64, 65. For the kingdom of Jālōr, see generally Sharma, *Early Chauhān dynasties*, 167–79.

[44] *TN*, I, 468, and II, 8 (tr. 661–2, 728).

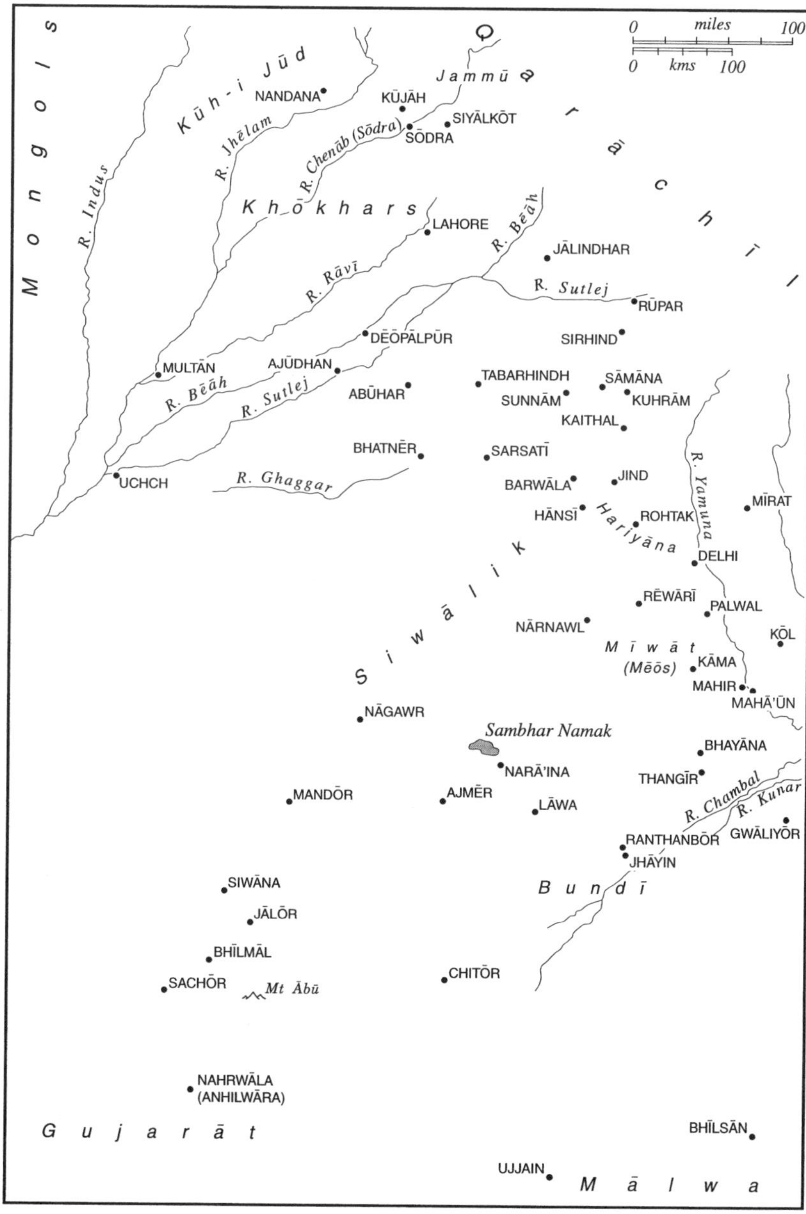

Map 3a: The war against the Hindu powers in northern India

through Ajmēr (Ajayameru) in the course of a victorious progress from Ābū back to his capital.[45] If reliable, this tradition suggests that the fortress no longer formed part of the Sultanate.

Ranthanbōr itself, reputed by Jūzjānī so impregnable as to have defied the attacks of some seventy Hindu kings down the ages,[46] had become tributary in 587/1191. The city was apparently still subordinate to Iltutmish in 1215, for an inscription at Manglānā, on the northern fringes of the Chawhān kingdom, mentions not only Prthvīrāja's grandson Vālhanadēva but also 'Samasadāna' (Shams al-Dīn) as the sovereign at Yoginī (Delhi). But Ranthanbōr had evidently defied the sultan by 623/1226, when his army captured the fortress after a long siege. Following Iltutmish's death, however, it was invested by the Hindus, and in *c.* 635/1237–8 Raḍiyya sent to its relief the Ghūrī malik Quṭb al-Dīn Ḥasan b. ʿAlī: he seems to have judged it impossible to hold, since he withdrew the Muslim garrison, dismantled the fortifications and abandoned the place.[47]

For several decades the war effort against the Chawhān kingdom did not prosper. At some time towards the end of Iltutmish's reign, Aytemür al-Bahā'ī met his death in an expedition from Ajmēr into the Bundī region,[48] which almost certainly belonged to Prthvīrāja's descendants. After its recovery by the Hindus, Ranthanbōr was attacked by the Delhi forces on a number of occasions. In 646/1248–9 Ulugh Khān Balaban led an army towards 'the highlands (*kūhpāya*) and Ranthanbōr' to chastise 'Bāhar Dēō', described by Jūzjānī as 'the greatest of the rais of Hindūstān' and identified by modern historians with the Chawhān king Vāgbhata, Vālhanadēva's successor. Balaban returned to the attack in 652/1254, during his exile at Nāgawr, and advanced in the direction of 'Ranthanbōr, Bundī and Chitōr'. On both occasions 'Bāhar Dēō' was routed, and the Muslim army obtained a considerable plunder.[49] A further campaign was launched against Ranthanbōr early in 657/1259, though the fact that we are told nothing of the outcome is probably an indication of failure.[50]

We do not hear of Ranthanbōr again in the Muslim sources until Jalāl al-Dīn Khaljī's attack in 690/1291, which is described in Amīr Khusraw's *Miftāḥ al-Futūḥ*. The sultan defeated an army sent against him by the Chawhān king, who then abandoned his capital at Jhāyin and fled into the hills. Jalāl al-Dīn occupied Jhāyin, and its idols were smashed to pieces to be taken back to Delhi; detachments were sent on plundering forays to the

45 Nilkantha Janârdan Kirtane, 'The Hammîra Mahâkâvya of Nayachandra Sûri', *IA* 8 (1879), 64–5.

46 *TN*, I, 445 (tr. 610–11).

47 Pandit Rama Karna, 'Manglana stone inscription of Jayatrasimha; (Vikrama-) Samvat 1272', *IA* 41 (1912), 85–8. *TN*, I, 445–6, 459–60 (tr. 611, 642).

48 *Ibid.*, II, 8 (tr. 728).

49 *Ibid.*, I, 482–3, and II, 58–9, 65 (tr. 684–5, 818–19, 828); Raverty adopted the reading 'Nāhar', but cf. Ray, *Dynastic history*, 1095–6.

50 *TN*, I, 495 (tr. 713).

south and east.[51] Writing at some remove from these events, Baranī gives the impression of a rather more limited achievement. According to him, Jalāl al-Dīn took Jhāyin, demolished its idols and plundered the territory, but spent less than a day inspecting his army's siege operations at Ranthanbōr before raising the investment to avoid further expenditure in Muslim lives. A second campaign against Jhāyin, towards the end of 691/1292, accomplished nothing more than the acquisition of booty.[52] Apart from this invasion, the Chawhān kings do not appear to have been seriously troubled by Muslim armies for the rest of the century, and were free to engage in conflict with their Hindu neighbours, notably the Paramāra kings of Mālwa.[53] The overthrow of the Chawhāns of Ranthanbōr was deferred until the reign of ʿAlā' al-Dīn Khaljī, and was to herald the Muslim advance on Chitōr, Mālwa and the lands beyond the Vindhyas. Not for nothing did Amīr Khusraw call Ranthanbōr 'the key to the south'.[54]

Muslim sources barely mention conflict in the thirteenth century with the Guhila kings who dominated Mēwār from their capital at Chitōr (now Chittaurgarh), and we are dependent on scattered references to Muslims in the epigraphy of the region. Of Jaitrasimha (d. just before 1260), the Chirwa inscription of his grandson Samarasimha claims that the Muslims, among others, failed to humble him. From the same source we learn that during his reign the troops of the *suratrāna* (sultan) attacked Nāgadraha (Nāgadā). Since Jaitrasimha's resistance to the Muslims elicits high praise in Samarasimha's Mount Ābū inscription also, it is possible that he was able to avenge this outrage. No further clashes with the Muslims are reported until the reign of Samarasimha himself (*c.* 1273–1301), who, in the florid language of that inscription, 'like unto the primaeval boar ... in a moment lifted the deeply sunk Gurjara land out of the Turushka sea'.[55] Whatever episode is in question here, the statement suggests at least that at some date prior to 1285 the Guhila monarch had profited from the relative passivity of the Sultanate under Balaban.

51 *MF*, 28–35. There is a briefer account in *FS*, 223–4 (tr. 388–9). Jhāyin has been identified by Satya Prakash Gupta, 'Jhain of the Delhi Sultanate', *MIM* 3 (1975), 209–15, with Chhain or Chhan, 7 m. S. of Ranthanbōr, at 25° 55′ N., 76° 27′ E.

52 *TFS*, 213–14, 220.

53 R. R. Halder, 'Inscription of the time of Hammir of Ranthambor, dated (V.S.) 1345', *EI* 19 (1927–8), 46. On the thirteenth-century Ranthanbōr kingdom, see Sharma, *Early Chauhān dynasties*, 118–25.

54 *KF*, 54.

55 Bernhard Geiger, 'Chîrwâ-Inschrift aus der Zeit des Guhila-Fürsten Samarasimha [Vikrama-]Saṁvat 1330 [A.D. 1273]', *WZKM* 21 (1907), 150. F. Kielhorn, 'Mount Abu stone inscription of Samarasimha [Vikrama-]samvat 1342', *IA* 16 (1887), 354. See generally Ray, *Dynastic history*, 1186–90, 1195; but his reference, *ibid.*, 1190, to an appearance in Mēwār by Jalāl al-Dīn Masʿūd, brother of Sultan Nāṣir al-Dīn Maḥmūd, is based on a misreading of ČTWR for SNTWR, i.e. Santūr (above, p. 73).

The Doab and Awadh

In the middle of the thirteenth century the Doab was still largely enemy territory, and Muslim control in all probability barely extended beyond the walls of the principal towns in the north: Mīrat (Meerut), Kōl (close to modern Aligarh) and Baran (now Bulandshahr), all of which had been occupied by the Muslims since the time of Aybeg. The extent of the problem confronting the government at Delhi is strikingly revealed by the fact that in 647/1249–50 Nāṣir al-Dīn Maḥmūd Shāh's forces, on their way to campaign in the Qinnawj region, were pinned down in warfare with an unidentified Hindu opponent immediately after crossing the Yamuna.[56] The iqtaʿ of Mīrat, which was conferred on Balaban's brother Kishli Khān in 653/1255, is said to have extended 'as far as the foothills of Bandiyārān', and the new muqtaʿ spent the next few years reducing 'the hills of Bandiyārān as far as Rurkī and Mayāpūr'.[57] Early in his reign Balaban constructed a fortress at Rurkī,[58] but the place is not mentioned again in the Sultanate period. Nor is Jhinjhāna, which appears as an iqtaʿ during Iltutmish's reign[59] and at that time was seemingly the most northerly Muslim outpost in the region. Nevertheless, the erection of mosques in the 1280s at Manglawr and Garhmuktesar testifies to the growth of a Muslim presence in the northern Doab.[60]

The advance of Muslim arms in the southern part of the Doab is better documented. Here certain towns were clearly under the sultan's rule by the middle of the thirteenth century and are mentioned in iqtaʿ grants. Mahā'ūn was joined with Mahir (Mathura), Bhayāna and Gwāliyōr to form extensive assignments both for Nuṣrat al-Dīn *Tāïsī in Iltutmish's day and for Shīr Khān in 657/1259. Jalēsar and Balārām, the latter an iqtaʿ already in Raḍiyya's time, also formed part of Shīr Khān's iqtaʿ.[61] On the other hand, the very size of these two extraordinary grants again alerts us to the fact that the Muslims' military resources had to be stretched over a vast area. Mahir and Mahā'ūn are not heard of again prior to the fourteenth century. It is possible that the reduction of these tracts had followed upon an obscure victory gained by Iltutmish at Chandawār in Etāwa (scene of the overthrow of the Gāhaḍavāla king Jāyachandra by the Ghurid forces in 590/1194), to which Jūzjānī makes one fleeting reference.[62] The enemy here

[56] *TN*, I, 483, and II, 60–1 (tr. 686–7, 821).
[57] *Ibid.*, II, 47 (tr. 799).
[58] *FS*, 164 (reading ZRKY, but cf. Husain's tr., 291).
[59] *TN*, II, 29 (tr. 759). For Jhinjhāna, see *DGUP*, III. *Muzaffarnagar*, 263–4.
[60] Yazdani, 'Inscriptions of the Turk Sulṭāns', 28–30; *ARIE* (1975–6), 178 (no. D254); *RCEA*, XIII (Cairo, 1944), 21–2 (no. 4832).
[61] *TN*, II, 11, 34, 44, 62, 78 (tr. 733, 767, 794, 824, 849). Balārām is possibly Bilram, 19 m. N. of Etah, at 27° 49′ N., 78° 38′ E.: *DGUP*, XII. *Etah*, 159–61.
[62] *TN*, II, 17 (tr. 742–3). For Chandawār, 'an ancient village of considerable historical importance', at 27° 7′ N., 78° 23′ E., see *DGUP*, VIII. *Agra*, 238–9; Irfan Habib, *An atlas of the Mughal Empire* (Oxford and Delhi, 1982), 27 and map 8A.

may have been Jāyachandra's nephew Ajāyasimha, who seems to have usurped control over the Etāwa region at least when the rest of the Gāhaḍavāla kingdom passed to the late king's son.[63] Whatever the case, local opposition was by no means at an end, and may have revived after Iltutmish's death. In 642/1244 Balaban inflicted severe devastation on the districts of Jarālī and Dēōlī 'and other *mawāsāt*' on the northern borders of Etāwa.[64] After his accession to the throne, he was obliged to conduct a lengthier campaign in the Doab, building fortresses at Kampīl, Patiyālī, Bhōjpūr and Jalālī. Of these, Patiyālī, at least, had been in Muslim hands for some time, having been the birthplace of Amīr Khusraw in *c.* 651/1253, and by Balaban's death had been renamed Mu'minpūr ('Town of the Faithful').[65] Baranī mentions that mosques were erected in these towns, and the date 665 (1267) found on the mosque at Jalālī enables us to date the sultan's operations with some accuracy.[66] Such military activity would have made possible the occupation of places like Sakīt (Sekit), where a mosque was raised in 684/1285.[67] But Muslim pressure on Etāwa was sporadic, and the assertion of Delhi's authority was a slow process. On its western borders Rāprī, lower down the Yamuna, is not referred to as a Muslim base prior to the reign of ʿAlā' al-Dīn Khaljī.[68]

The result of Balaban's operations in the Doab, says Baranī, was to 'open the road to Hindūstān' (i.e. Awadh and the regions to the east).[69] One aim had possibly been to safeguard communications with the isolated stronghold of Qinnawj, on the right bank of the Ganges. Within a short time of its capture by Aybeg in 595/1199 Qinnawj seems to have been recovered by the Hindus, since Iltutmish is credited with its conquest and issued coins inscribed 'from the tribute (*kharāj*) of Qinnawj'.[70] Thereafter it served as an important base of operations against the Hindu princes, its muqtaʿs not only conducting local raids on their own account[71] but also contributing troops, as we shall see, for warfare in 'Mālwa' to the south. The four-month

63 P. Prasad, *Sanskrit inscriptions*, xviii and 92–4.

64 *TN*, II, 53–4 (tr. 809). Raverty's identification of the former with 'Jurowli', at 28° 17′ N., 78° 17′ E. (809 n.7), is unconvincing. See Hodivala, *Studies*, I, 230, who suggests either 'Julowlee', 35 m. S. of Fatehgarh, or 'Joolee', 14 m. S. of Sekit; here and at I, 402, he equates Dēōlī with Thornton's 'Duhlee' in Etāwa, at 27° 2′ N., 78° 53′ E.: cf. *DGUP*, X. *Mainpuri*, 204 ('Dihuli').

65 *DGK*, 70. Mirzā, *Life and works*, 16–17.

66 *TFS*, 57–8. For the mosque at Jalālī, see Yazdani, 'Inscriptions of the Turk Sulṭāns', 25–6; *RCEA*, XII, 122 (no. 4585); for this 'ancient town', 13 m. E. of Aligarh, at 27° 52′ N., 28° 15′ E., see *DGUP*, VI. *Aligarh*, 261–3. Bhōjpūr lies at 27° 17′ N., 79° 41′ E., 6 m. S. of Fatehgarh: *DGUP*, IX. *Farrukhabad*, 184–5; for Kampīl, at 27° 39′ N., 79° 20′ E., see *ibid.*, 215–16; and for Patiyālī, at 27° 42′ N., 72° 5′ E., *DGUP*, XII. *Etah*, 201–3.

67 Yazdani, 'Inscriptions of the Turk Sulṭāns', 31–2; *RCEA*, XIII, 47–8 (no. 4870).

68 *TFS*, 328, 333; and see Hodivala, *Studies*, I, 281. G. H. Yazdani, 'Inscriptions of the Khaljī Sulṭāns of Delhi and their contemporaries in Bengal', *EIM* (1917–18), 30.

69 *TFS*, 58.

70 *CCIM*, I, part 2, 21 (no. 39). *CMSD*, 71–2 (no. 52). *Tāj*, in ED, II, 241. *TN*, I, 452 (tr. 627).

71 *Ibid.*, I, 470 (tr. 665).

campaign of 647/1249–50 by the army of Nāṣir al-Dīn Maḥmūd Shāh appears to have been directed at the Qinnawj region, for an inscription from Bilram records the martyrdom of a Muslim commander at this time at a village near Qinnawj.[72] It may similarly have taken some considerable time to wrest the region between Qinnawj and the distant outpost of Kara from the infidel. *Barīhūn (Barhamūn?), which is known to have lain in the vicinity of Qinnawj and which was twice granted as iqtaʿ by Iltutmish, is not mentioned again.[73] The walls of Tilsanda, which Jūzjānī likens to Alexander's Gates, succumbed only in 645/1248 to an attack by Maḥmūd Shāh's forces.[74] And there were in all likelihood reverses, which claimed the lives of the Muslims commemorated in various epitaphs from Bilram dated 658/1260, 683/1284 and 703/1303, the last of them in the fortress of Chandawār.[75]

East of the Ganges, the important stronghold of Badā'ūn, in Muslim hands since 594/1198, faced towards Katēhr (corresponding roughly to present-day Rohilkhand), which surfaces repeatedly in our sources as the territory of the most refractory of infidel peoples. The reduction of this tract by Iltutmish, to which Jūzjānī alludes, may have occurred in 1227.[76] But it was a shortlived affair, since Sanjar-i Qabaqulaq, as muqtaʿ of Badā'ūn under Masʿūd Shāh, is said to have overthrown 'the *mawāsāt* of Katēhr and Badā'ūn', conducted numerous expeditions and founded mosques.[77] Around the middle of the thirteenth century we hear of other Muslim-held centres in these parts, like Sambhal and Kasrak, which first appear as iqtaʿs in Maḥmūd Shāh's reign, and Amrōha, which became an iqtaʿ only under Balaban.[78] In 652/1254, during a campaign that had taken him through Bardār (Hardwār) and Bijnōr as far as the banks of the Rahab (Ramganga), Maḥmūd Shāh retaliated for the loss of one of his lieutenants by inflicting, in Jūzjānī's words, 'a reverse on the infidels of Katēhr that [the people of] that territory will remember for the rest of their lives'.[79] But memory, it

[72] *ARIE* (1966–7), 82 (no. D249). For the expedition, see *TN*, I, 483, and II, 60–1 (tr. 686–7, 821).

[73] *Ibid.*, II, 20, 36 (tr. 746, 779). This place is mentioned by tenth-century geographers: al-Muqaddasī, *Descriptio imperii Moslemici*, ed. M. J. De Goeje (Leiden, 1877), 478 (variant reading: BRHYN); *Ḥudūd al-ʿĀlam*, facs. edn V. V. Bartol'd (Leningrad, 1930), fol. 15b (tr. Minorsky, 90), placing it near Qinnawj.

[74] *TN*, I, 480, 481 (tr. 679–80, 681). See Raverty, 679–80 n. 6, and Hodivala, *Studies*, I, 222: the village of Tilsanda near Cawnpore (Kānpūr), mentioned by the latter, seems most likely.

[75] *ARIE* (1966–7), 83 (nos. D252, D253, D255).

[76] When Iltutmish is known to have been at Badā'ūn: P. Prasad, *Sanskrit inscriptions*, 80–9. Katēhr is omitted in the printed edition of *TN*, but cf. BL ms., fol. 180a (corrupted to 'LYHR). The varying significance of the term 'Katēhr' is discussed in Hodivala, *Studies*, I, 259.

[77] *TN*, II, 26 (tr. 755).

[78] Sambhal: *ibid.*, I, 482 (tr. 684). Amrōha: *TFS*, 36–7, and Habibullah, *Foundation*, 156. Kasrak: *TN*, II, 42 (KRK; but cf. BL ms., fol. 211a, KNRK, and Raverty's tr., 791); the place is identified by P. Prasad, *Sanskrit inscriptions*, 81–2, with a village in Tilhar tahsil in Shahjahanpur district.

[79] *TN*, I, 487–8 (tr. 696–8).

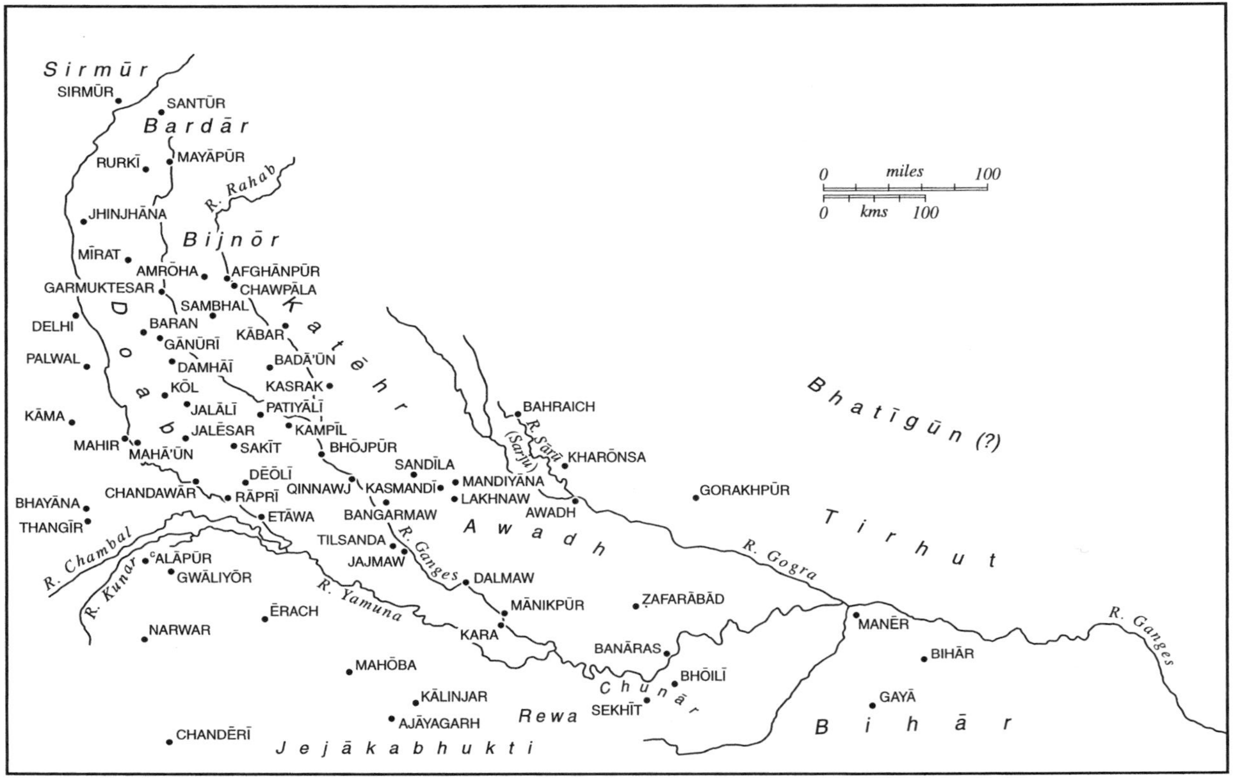

Map 3b: The war against the Hindu powers in northern India

seems, was brief. The disorders of *c.* 665/1266–7, in which Badā'ūn, Sambhal, Amrōha and Gānūrī were subject to further depredations by the infidel, brought down upon Katēhr the wrath of Balaban, who razed the town of that name and despatched five thousand archers to ravage the rest of the territory. As a result, claims Baranī, there was no further trouble from Katēhr until the end of the reign of Jalāl al-Dīn Khaljī.[80] During his time Gānūrī was joined with Chawpāla (present-day Moradabad) on the Rahab to form a sizeable iqtaʿ, indicating perhaps that resources here were thinly spread.[81] Yet Jalāl al-Dīn mounted plundering operations in the Kābar district, and under ʿAlā' al-Dīn the government's grip was sufficiently secure for it to be incorporated into the khalisa.[82]

South of Badā'ūn lay the extensive territory of Awadh. The Muslims had at some unspecified point occupied the city of this name, the ancient Ayōdhya, which in the 1190s was the iqtaʿ of Ḥusām al-Dīn Oghulbeg. Early in the thirteenth century we hear of other towns in the area which served as iqtaʿ headquarters, like Kasmandī and Mandiyāna (Mandiaon), both in the neighbourhood of the later city of Lakhnaw (Lucknow).[83] The muqtaʿs of Awadh played a prominent role in the interminable war against the infidel. It was while he was based in Awadh that not long after 623/1226 Iltutmish's eldest son, Nāṣir al-Dīn Maḥmūd, crushed a ruler 'Hardū Dal', called by Jūzjānī 'Bartū' (possibly a subordinate of the Gāhaḍavālas), who had been a thorn in the flesh of the Muslim settlers in the region. But the prince's victory, commemorated in verses of the poet Sirājī,[84] did not effect the pacification of Awadh, and in the following decades Tāj al-Dīn Sanjar *Kirit Khān and Tāj al-Dīn *Teniz Khān are each in turn credited with uprooting the *mawāsāt* of the region.[85] Thereafter, although we learn at intervals the names of Awadh's muqtaʿs, including for a short time the future sultan ʿAlā' al-Dīn, there is a gap in our knowledge of developments here until the Tughluqid period.

Banāras had been taken from the Gāhaḍavālas in 590/1194, and Muḥammad b. Bakhtiyār had profited from their troubles to establish a base in the districts of *Sekhit and Bhōilī, in the Chunār region on the opposite bank of the Ganges, from where he mounted operations against

80 *TFS*, 59. Gānūrī is identified by Hodivala, *Studies*, I, 259–60, with Thornton's 'Genori' or 'Genouri', in Bulandshahr, at 28° 20′ N., 78° 4′ E.

81 *TFS*, 204 (KANWD, to be corrected from BL ms., fol. 110b). For Chawpāla, see *MF*, 13; Hodivala, *Studies*, I, 366; *DGUP*, XVI. *Moradabad*, 232.

82 *MF*, 21–2. *TFS*, 323–4. For Kābar, later renamed Shergarh and 'an ancient town', at 28° 39′ N., 79° 22′ E., see *DGUP*, XIII. *Bareilly*, 268–9.

83 *TN*, II, 29, 72 (tr. 759, 838). For Kasmandī, see Hodivala, *Studies*, I, 233, and *DGUP*, XXXVII. *Lucknow*, 195–6. For Mandiaon, at 26° 56′ N., 80° 58′ E., see *ibid.*, 245–7; Habib, *Atlas*, map 8A.

84 Siddiqi, 'Historical information', 55–6. *TN*, I, 453 (tr. 628–9). For a different identification, see Habibullah, *Foundation*, 111 n.99. Hodivala, *Studies*, I, 218, was surely wrong to link 'Bartū' with a raja in the Bhitargarh district of eastern Bengal.

85 *TN*, II, 27, 29 (tr. 757, 760).

Manēr and Bihār.[86] But the Muslim foothold here may have been transient. The Gāhaḍavālas continued to hold out in the more inaccessible parts of the Banāras and Chunār regions;[87] and although Jūzjānī mentions Banāras among the strongpoints taken by Iltutmish from defeated Muslim rebels (p. 29 above), it is not mentioned as an iqtaʿ again and disappears from sight. The first inscription attesting Muslim rule belongs to the reign of Quṭb al-Dīn Mubārak Shāh Khaljī (716–20/1316–20).[88]

The road to Bengal

In the early thirteenth century the furthest Muslim base beyond Awadh in the direction of the infidel territories of Nepal and Tirhut was the old town of Bahraich, which housed the shrine of Sālār Masʿūd, a Muslim warrior of uncertain background, and had become a major focus of pilgrimage.[89] Bahraich was held by the Muslims in Iltutmish's reign; and here, as Jūzjānī proudly announces, his sovereign Nāṣir al-Dīn Maḥmūd Shāh waged holy war against unspecified Hindus prior to his accession.[90] It may have been the same regions that in 690/1291 were ravaged by Jalāl al-Dīn Khaljī following his victory over the rebel Malik Chhajjū, for Amīr Khusraw says that in cutting down the jungles he was seeking to open a road to Lakhnawtī: *mawās* after *mawās* yielded tribute to the sultan, but regrettably none of the places Khusraw mentions can be identified.[91] Baranī asserts that the rai of Gorakhpūr had paid tribute to the administrative district (*shiqq*) of Awadh prior to the upheavals of Muḥammad b. Tughluq's reign;[92] but it is doubtful if the relationship went back into the thirteenth century.

During the early Sultanate period Muslim armies were raiding both Tirhut (north Bihār) and the neighbouring region of Nepal known in Jūzjānī's time as 'Bhatīgūn'. Tirhut had paid tribute to Ghiyāth al-Dīn ʿIwaḍ, which is doubtless why Jūzjānī lists it among Iltutmish's conquests,[93]

86 *Ibid.*, I, 423 (readings corrupt; Raverty's tr., 549–50, has 'Bhagwat' for the first, but cf. BL ms., fol. 170a, SKHYT): see Hodivala, *Studies*, I, 206, on the identification of these places, of which the second, Thornton's 'Bhoelee', lies at 25° 6′ N., 83° 3′ E.; also *DGUP*, XXVII. *Mirzapur*, 278–84.

87 P. Prasad, *Sanskrit inscriptions*, 56–70 (nos. II:5–6). See more generally Niyogi, *History of the Gāhaḍavāla dynasty*, 113–19.

88 *ARIE* (1971–2), 91 (no. D170).

89 I. H. Siddiqui, 'A note on the Dargah of Salar Masᶜud in Bahraich in the light of the standard historical sources', in Christian W. Troll (ed.), *Muslim shrines in India* (Delhi, 1989), 44–7.

90 Iltutmish: ᶜAwfī, *Lubāb al-Albāb*, I, 115. Maḥmūd Shāh: *TN*, I, 470, 478 (tr. 665, 676).

91 *MF*, 22–3 (reading KSHWN for KYTHWN, i.e. *Kaithūn). *FS*, 224 (tr. 390–1), with 'BRY and KYTHWN. *TMS*, 64, includes a faint echo of this campaign ('NHRY KYTHWR) in an obviously corrupt sentence.

92 *TFS*, 587–8. *SFS*, 33, likewise claims that 'Karōsa' and Gorakhpūr were dependencies of Awadh.

93 *TN*, I, 437 (tr. 587–8); omitted in the list of Iltutmish's conquests at I, 452, but see BL ms., fol. 180a.

and in Raḍiyya's time Toghril Toghan Khān, as muqtaʿ of Bihār and Lakhnawtī, conducted a lucrative raid on Tirhut.[94] But Tirhut was also vulnerable to attacks from the opposite direction. Raḍiyya's muqtaʿ of Awadh, Temür Khān, penetrated 'as far as the limits of Tirhut' and exacted tribute from Bhatīgūn;[95] and at the beginning of 654/1256 Balaban, on the heels of his enemy Qutlugh Khān, led an army as far as 'Bhatīgūn and the limits of Tirhut', returning with a vast plunder.[96] In 702–3/1302–3, the muqtaʿ of Kara is found commanding the troops of 'the east, Bengal and Tirhut',[97] which is a mystery, given that Bengal did not then form part of the sultan's dominions. Otherwise we hear no more of Muslim attacks on Tirhut until Ghiyāth al-Dīn Tughluq's expedition of 724/1324.

The subjugation of Bihār, of which Jūzjānī gives no details apart from an account of the capture of the city itself (identical, in all probability, with Uddandapuri),[98] was clearly a piecemeal process. Gayā (Vajrasana), which was under Muslim rule in 1219,[99] was no longer in Muslim hands when the Buddhist monk Dharmasvāmīn passed through Bihār in 1234; although he bears eloquent testimony to continued Muslim military activity in both Bihār and Tirhut.[100] Following Balaban's recovery of the eastern provinces soon after *c*. 665/1267, Gayā may still have been unsubdued, since a local ruler boasts in an inscription of 1268 that he has preserved his territory from the sultan.[101]

Much of the credit for the implantation of Islam in west Bengal belongs to the Khalaj rulers, who are praised for building mosques, colleges (*madāris*) and hospices (*khānaqāhāt*), and for munificence towards Muslim scholars and sayyids.[102] A paucity of sources, however, renders the progress of Muslim settlement here even more obscure than it is elsewhere. After Jūzjānī's time, inscriptions show that one of the Muslim strongpoints he

94 *TN*, II, 14 (tr. 737).

95 *Ibid*., II, 17–18 (tr. 743). Here (n.3) Raverty, who had earlier identified this region correctly (*ibid*., 639 n.8; cf. also 567 n.1), defined it as 'the tract lying on the left bank of the Son, east of Banaras'. Cf. also Habibullah, *Foundation*, 150, who, following Cunningham, defines it as the Tons valley ('Bhath-gora'). But this is to ignore the link with Tirhut which Jūzjānī makes on both occasions. The name is perhaps connected with the town of Bhatgaon, on which see *IG*, VIII, 89.

96 *TN*, II, 71–2 (Raverty's tr., 838, reads 'Badīkōt', but the place is evidently identical with that mentioned in Temür Khān's biography).

97 *TFS*[1], Digby Coll. ms., fol. 113a; *TFS*, 300.

98 *TN*, I, 423 (tr. 551–2); a brief reference to the conquest of the territory of Bihār at I, 425 (tr. 556). For Uddandapuri, see Shri Ḥasan Nishat Ansari, 'Historical geography of Bihar on the eve of the early Turkish invasion', *JBRS* 49 (1963), 257 n.3.

99 *ARIE* (1962–3), 24, 80 (no. B261).

100 G. Roerich, *The biography of Dharmasvamin (Chag lo-tsa-ba Chos-rje-dpal)* (Patna, 1959), 61–4. For the date, see the introduction by A. S. Altekar, v-vi; and for Muslim pressure on Bihār, *ibid*., xix.

101 Ḥasan Nishat Ansari, 'Gaya epigraph of V.s. 1325 noticing Balban as *Biruban*', *JBRS* 53 (1967), 170–81: the editor is sceptical and suggests that this security was purchased with tribute.

102 *TN*, I, 427, 436 (tr. 559–60, 583).

mentions – Dēōkōt, which was the capital until ʿIwaḍ's accession – was still a centre of Muslim power at the end of the thirteenth century, under the independent Ghiyathid sultans; but others – like Narangūī, Gangūrī, or Basankōt (the last-named founded by ʿIwaḍ) – do not surface again.[103] Jūzjānī distinguishes the region of Rāl (Rārh), with its centre at Lakhnōr, west of the Ganges, from Bārind (Varendra), the tract to the east of the river, which included Dēōkōt.[104] After its capture by the Hindus in 642/1244 (below), we simply do not know when Lakhnōr was recovered.

ʿIwaḍ extorted tribute from the Sena kings in eastern Bengal (Bang), and after the conquest of Lakhnawtī by Iltutmish this pressure was maintained by his representatives. The second of these, Sayf al-Dīn Aybeg, owed his sobriquet *Yaghantut* to the great number of elephants he obtained by way of plunder from Bang and despatched to the sultan.[105] Toghril Khān Ikhtiyār al-Dīn Yüzbeg is found in 653/1255 striking coins from 'the revenue (*kharāj*) of the territory (*ʿarḍ*) of *Badar and Nūdiya';[106] the mention of the latter city demonstrates that the Senas had at some point reoccupied their old capital. They survived into the second half of the century, when they were apparently supplanted by a rival power which had arisen in Tipperah. This region, which Baranī calls 'Jājnagar', may have been the object of a lucrative expedition by Balaban's lieutenant Toghril, as governor of Lakhnawtī, immediately prior to his rebellion against the sultan and his assumption of the imperial title.[107] One of the two known kings of the Tipperah dynasty was the 'Danūj Rāī' of Sunārgā'ūn (Sonargaon) who sought his revenge by cooperating with Balaban and undertaking to obstruct the rebel's flight.[108]

Bang was only one of the territories that offered rich pickings to the Muslim rulers of Lakhnawtī. Nobody sought to emulate Muḥammad b. Bakhtiyār, who had returned a broken man from a disastrous campaign through the upper Brahmaputra region, possibly into the region of Assam the Muslims called Kāmrūp or Kāmrūd;[109] but his successors at Lakhnawtī

103 Basankōt: *ibid.*, I, 436 (tr. 581–2). Narangūī: I, 432, 434 (tr. 572, 574, 577). Gangūrī: I, 433 (tr. 575). Dēōkōt: I, 431–4 (tr. 572, 574, 576, 578); Abdul Karim (ed.), *Corpus of the Arabic and Persian inscriptions of Bengal* (Dacca, 1992), 48–53. On the possible location of some of these places, see Monmohan Chakravarti, 'Notes on Gaur and other old places in Bengal', *JASB* ns 5 (1909), 199–235.

104 *TN*, I, 436–7, and II, 13 (tr. 584–5, 737).

105 *Ibid.*, II, 9–10 (tr. 732). For Tu. *yaghantut*, 'seize elephants', see Clauson, *Etymological dictionary*, 904, in conjunction with Rásonyi, 'Noms de personnes', 241–2.

106 *CCIM*, II, 146 (no. 6). *CMSD*, 55 (no. 225D).

107 *TFS*, 82, 83. For Baranī's usage (*Jahājnagar*, 'city of boats or ships'), see Chakravarti, 'Notes on Gaur', 217.

108 *TFS*, 87. *TMS*, 42–3. He has been identified with Arirāja Danūjamadhava Daśarathadēva, who issued a copper-plate grant around this time: Habibullah, *Foundation*, 183 n.32; Ray, *Dynastic history*, 383 n.1; and for a survey of the later Senas, *ibid.*, 379ff.

109 *TN*, I, 427–32 (tr. 560–72). On this expedition, see the evidence reviewed in Digby, *War-horse and elephant*, 45–6; cf. the dubious hypothesis in Z. V. Togan, 'About the campaign of the Indian Khalach-Turks against the Keraits of Mongolia in Northern Tibet in the

conducted operations over a vast area. ʿIwaḍ levied tribute not merely on Kāmrūp but also on the Eastern Ganga kingdom of Orissa, usually designated in the Muslim sources as Jājnagar.[110] On balance the Delhi Sultan's governors were less successful. Toghan Khān was in 641/1244 worsted in continual warfare with the king of Jājnagar, with the result that a Hindu army took Lakhnōr, where Toghan Khān's lieutenant fell in the fighting, and menaced Lakhnawtī itself: it was saved only by the timely appearance of troops sent by the Delhi Sultan (above, p. 91).[111] The reverse at the hands of Jājnagar appears to be celebrated in an inscription of King Narasimha II of Orissa, referring to his father's victory over the 'Yavanas of Rāḍhā (Rārh) and Varendra'.[112] Toghan Khān's humiliation was avenged some ten years later by Yüzbeg, who sacked the Jājnagar king's capital at an unidentified place named '*Ūmardan'.[113] But Yüzbeg himself met his death in *c.* 655/1257 while engaged in an ambitious and heedless invasion of Kāmrūp.[114] From a *fatḥ-nāma* in Amīr Khusraw's *Rasāʾil al-Iʿjāz*, it appears that in 680/1282 Balaban himself led a campaign into Orissa which reduced King 'Māl Dēō' to submission.[115]

The era of the independent Ghiyathid sultans and of their successors of the line of Fīrūz-i Aytegin was marked by significant advances at the expense of the independent Hindu powers within Bengal proper. From a coin issued by Balaban's grandson Kaykāʾūs and struck 'from the *kharāj* of Bang', it is clear that part of the eastern delta was now once again tributary to the Muslims.[116] Under Shams al-Dīn Fīrūz Shāh, Sunārgāʾūn appears as a Muslim mint-town. Satgāʾūn (Satgaon) too appears to have been annexed in his reign, and a mosque was built at Tribeni, on the Hooghly, in 698/1298–9. Epigraphical evidence reveals that Sirihat (Sylhet), lying immediately east of the Brahmaputra, was reduced in 703/1303–4.[117] All these places would pass briefly under the rule of the Delhi Sultan as a result of Ghiyāth al-Dīn Tughluq's expedition of 724/1324 (below, pp. 200–1).

years 1205–1206', *JPHS* 12 (1964), 187–94, and in *Proceedings of the 36th International Congress of Orientalists* (Delhi, 1968), 174–8.

110 *TN*, I, 437 (tr. 587–8). 111 *Ibid.*, II, 15 (tr. 739–40).

112 N. Vasu, 'Copper-plate inscription of Nṛsiṁha-dēva II of Orissa, dated 1217 Çaka', *JASB* 65, part 1 (1896), 232–4, 267 (verse 84).

113 *TN*, II, 31 (tr. 762–3). Habibullah, *Foundation*, 144, was sceptical that '*Ūmardan' was actually deep within Orissa.

114 *TN*, II, 32–3 (tr. 764–6).

115 *RI*, V, 5–13: see 8–11 for 'Māl Dēō'; 13 for the date; ʾWDH must be an error for ʾWRSH. Khusraw's heading for the *fatḥ-nāma* refers only to Lakhnawtī, which misled Mirza, *Life and works*, 219.

116 H. E. Stapleton, 'Contributions to the history and ethnology of north-eastern India – IV. Bengal chronology during the period of independent Muslim rule. Part I, 686–735 A.H. (1286–1334 A.D.)', *JASB* ns 18 (1922), 410.

117 Abdul Karim, *Corpus*, 53–6. Stapleton, 411–12. For the Sylhet inscription, see Aḥmad Ḥasan Dani, *Muslim inscriptions of Bengal* (Dacca, 1957), 7 (no. 9). See generally Majumdar, *History of medieval Bengal*, 17–19.

Bundelkhand and Mālwa

The town of Bhayāna originated with the settlement of Sulṭānkōt, founded by Bahā' al-Dīn Toghril as part of his strategy to take Gwāliyōr.[118] Gwāliyōr, which had submitted to Aybeg in 597/1200–1, was retaken by the Hindus, doubtless after Aybeg's death, but in 630/1233 the city fell to Iltutmish after an eleven-month investment; the last Pratihāra (Parihar) king, 'Mangal Dēō', fled to Narwar.[119] Nuṣrat al-Dīn *Tāīsī, whom Iltutmish in 631/1234 appointed as muqtaʿ of Bhayāna and Sulṭānkōt and prefect (*shiḥna*) of Gwāliyōr, was in addition entrusted with overall command of the troops of Qinnawj, Mahir and Mahā'ūn, perhaps an indication of the importance attached by the sultan to this particular front.[120] From these bases Muslim commanders waged war on the Chandella kingdom of Jejākabhukti (modern Bundelkhand). Its capital, Kālinjar, had fallen to Quṭb al-Dīn Aybeg in 599/1203, following the death of King Paramardīdēva, and had briefly been an iqtaʿ.[121] But Trailokyavarman, Paramardīdēva's son and heir, had evidently recovered it by Iltutmish's last years.[122] *Tāīsī defeated Trailokyavarman, capturing the rai's ceremonial parasol and standards during the pursuit.[123] Yet Muslim military activity had little impact on the Chandella kingdom. Although Kālinjar itself was not re-established as the capital following its recovery, and the kings normally resided at Ajāyagarh, some twenty miles to the south-west, this seems to have been the sole concession made to the proximity of Muslim power by the Chandella ruler, who continued to style himself 'king of Kālinjar'. In an inscription of his son Vīravarman, Trailokyavarman is credited with 'lifting up the earth immersed in the ocean formed by the streams of the Turushkas'.[124] Vīravarman himself issued a copper-plate grant in 1280 to a nobleman who had vanquished the 'Turushkas' among others.[125] Nor were these monarchs deflected from the duty of warring against their Hindu neighbours, notably the Kalachuri kings of Chēdi and the Jajapellas of Narwar.[126]

118 *TN*, I, 421 (tr. 545); cf. also II, 34 (tr. 767).

119 *Ibid.*, I, 448 (tr. 619). The form adopted by Raverty is 'Mangal-dēv', though BL ms. reads MYKL DYW; another variant reading, MLKDYW, suggests something like 'Melugidēva' (cf. Hodivala, *Studies*, I, 216). For the last Pratihāra kings, see Ray, *Dynastic history*, 829 n.1, 834 n.1.

120 *TN*, II, 10–11 (tr. 732–3).

121 *Tāj*, fols. 182a–185a.

122 *TN*, II, 10–11, 12 (tr. 733, 734–5). K. N. Dikshit, 'Garra plates of the Chandella Trailokyavarman: [Vikrama-]samvat 1261', *EI* 16 (1921–2), 272–7. R. K. Dikshit, *Candellas*, 157–8, following Ray, *Dynastic history*, 725, suggests that Trailokyavarman recovered Kālinjar as early as 1205.

123 *TN*, II, 10–11, 12, 62–3 (tr. 733, 734–5, 834–5).

124 P. Prasad, *Sanskrit inscriptions*, 100–5 (verse 7).

125 Sir Alexander Cunningham, 'Report of a tour in Bundelkhand and Rewa in 1883–84', *ASIR* 21 (1885), 75. The grant is no longer extant: Ray, *Dynastic history*, 732, where the date cited, Vikrama samvat 1237, is an error for 1337.

126 For the attack on Narwar, see D. C. Sircar, 'Inscriptions of the time of Yajvapala Gopala',

During the return march from his invasion of the Chandella kingdom in 632/1235, *Tāīsī had been ambushed by a ruler whom Jūzjānī calls 'Chāhar-i Ajarī'. This was the earliest recorded Muslim clash with Chāhaḍadēva, the second of the Jajapella (Yajvapala) kings, who around this time wrested the stronghold of Narwar from the Pratihāras and made it their residence. Jūzjānī, who was then qadi of Gwāliyōr, heard an account of the engagement from the veteran amir's own mouth, and it is clear that *Tāīsī had extricated his army with considerable difficulty.[127] He died soon after Raḍiyya's accession, and in 635/1238 her troops evacuated the Muslim population of Gwāliyōr.[128] Jūzjānī retained the office of qadi, and this was confirmed in 643/1245, but on each occasion he simultaneously received an important post in Delhi, suggesting that the Gwāliyōr appointment was simply one *in partibus infidelium*.[129] That the great fortress was now in enemy territory emerges from the campaign launched at some point in Raḍiyya's reign by Temür Khān Qiran from Awadh towards 'Gwāliyōr and Mālwa' in which he is said to have done signal service.[130]

The enemy was undoubtedly the Jajapella king. Jūzjānī, describing Ulugh Khān Balaban's campaign against him in 649–50/1251–2, says that it headed towards 'Gwāliyōr, Chandērī, Nurwul (Narwar) and Mālwa' and speaks of him as 'the greatest of all the rais of that country'. Balaban succeeded in taking Narwar and putting it to the sack.[131] Gwāliyōr seems to have been recovered at this juncture, for in 657/1259 the governorship of the fortress, together with a large iqtaʿ comprising Kōl, Bhayāna, Balārām, Mahir, Mahā'ūn and other territories, was conferred on Balaban's cousin Shīr Khān.[132] Once again, the amalgamation of widely dispersed resources may indicate both the fragility of Muslim rule and the magnitude of the Hindu threat. Gwāliyōr, which Jūzjānī could call 'one of the celebrated strongholds of Islam', was apparently in Hindu hands once more by the last years of Balaban's reign, for among those overcome by the noble who received the above-mentioned grant from the Chandella monarch Vīra-varman in 1280 was Harīrāja of Gopagiri, i.e. Gwāliyōr.[133] Unless Harīrāja

EI 31 (1955–6), 326–7; and for relations with the Jajapellas generally, see R. K. Dikshit, *Candellas*, 168–70.

127 *TN*, II, 11–12, 62–3 (tr. 733–4, 824–5). For the correct identification of 'Chāhar', see M. B. Garde, 'A note on the Yajvapâlas or Jajapellas of Narwar', *IA* 47 (1918), 241–4, refuting the suggestion that he belonged to a branch of the Chawhāns; though the older view is reiterated by Ray, *Dynastic history*, 1103–4. The surname 'Ajarī' is discussed by Hodivala, *Studies*, I, 224–5, who connects it with the locality Arjar, some 40 m. S.E. of Narwar.

128 *TN*, II, 25–6 (tr. 754–5). Mongol envoys incarcerated at Gwāliyōr were transferred to Qinnawj: *ibid.*, II, 214 (tr. 1285). For *Tāīsī's death, see *ibid.*, I, 458, and II, 13 (tr. 639–40, 735–6).

129 *Ibid.*, I, 460, 470 (tr. 644, 667).

130 *Ibid.*, II, 17 (tr. 743).

131 *Ibid.*, I, 485–6, and II, 62, 63 (tr. 690–2, 824–5).

132 *Ibid.*, II, 44 (tr. 794); and for the date, cf. I, 495 (tr. 712–13).

133 Cunningham, 'Report of a tour in Bundelkhand and Rewa', 74–6. For the phrase from Jūzjānī, see *TN*, II, 44 (tr. 794).

was a client ruler under the sultan's overlordship, which is unlikely, then the grant shows that the fortress had once more slipped out of Muslim control. This possibility is borne out by the fact that Jalāl al-Dīn Khaljī is found conducting a plundering expedition to Gwāliyōr shortly before his murder in 695/1296.[134]

As for Chāhaḍadēva, little reliance can be placed on Jūzjānī's assertion that he had been totally overthrown and rooted out of his kingdom. The coins and inscriptions of the Jajapella dynasty dictate a more sober assessment, demonstrating as they do that Chāhaḍadēva and his successors maintained their hold on Narwar into the fourteenth century. The ultimate fate of the Jajapellas is obscure, and it is usually assumed that they fell victim to an unrecorded invasion by the forces of ʿAlā' al-Dīn Khaljī.[135] It would have been some such campaign that resulted in the Muslim occupation of Chandērī, which is known to have occurred prior to 711/1312.[136]

To the north-east of the Jajapella and Chandella kingdoms lay the Muslim outposts of Kara and Mānikpūr, which are frequently linked in the sources. Kara acknowledged Muslim authority as early as Aybeg's reign, and was the seat of an amir in the time of Iltutmish.[137] When muqtaʿ of Kara during Raḍiyya's reign, Temür Khān Qiran is said to have conducted numerous forays against the infidel, but no details are given.[138] In 645/1248 we find the army of Nāṣir al-Dīn Maḥmūd Shāh based at Kara, while Balaban led a detachment against a Hindu potentate called by Jūzjānī 'Dalakīmalakī' (?). The dynastic affiliations of this prince, said to have occupied the regions along the Yamuna between Kara and Kālinjar, are uncertain; but he was not, apparently, a Chandella, for we are told that 'the rais of the marches (*aṭrāf*) of Kālinjar and Mālwa' were unable to subdue him. His stronghold was looted by the Muslims, and his family and dependants were captured.[139] This was the victory which Jūzjānī tells us he commemorated in his lost *Nāṣirī-Nāma*; but for all the chronicler's bombast it is difficult to withstand the impression that the campaign was on a relatively trifling scale.[140] We do not hear of operations from Kara again

134 *TFS*, 223, 228. *TMS*, 67; for Sirhindī's claim that Gwāliyōr was in Muslim hands again by the first year of ᶜAlā' al-Dīn's reign, see *ibid.*, 72 (the text reads KALPWR).

135 Sircar, 'Inscriptions of the time of Yajvapala Gopala', 323–36; also his 'Yajvapāla Gopāla', *IHQ* 32 (1956), 399–405.

136 Z. A. Desai, 'The Chanderi inscription of ᶜAlau'd-din Khalji', *EIAPS* (1968), 4–10. Cf. also *TFS*, 323.

137 *ARIE* (1969–70), 11, 98 (no. D214). *TN*, I, 452 (reading KWH for KRH; but cf. Raverty's tr., 627). On Kara, see generally Laiq Aḥmad, 'Kara'.

138 *TN*, II, 17 (tr. 743).

139 *Ibid.*, I, 481–2, and II, 57–8 (tr. 681–3, 816–18). Ray, *Dynastic history*, 729–30, and Hodivala, *Studies*, I, 222–3, thought 'Dalakīmalakī' might be the Chandella king Trailokyavarman; but Jūzjānī's account suggests a less powerful chief.

140 Laiq Aḥmad, 'Kara', 84, assumes that Kishli Khān was appointed as muqtaᶜ of Kara in 653/1255 (*recte* 651/1253) and that for a few years prior to this it was in Hindu hands.

until ʿAlāʾ al-Dīn Khaljī became muqtaʿ of the region in 689/1290 and 'trampled underfoot numerous *mawāsāt*'.[141]

According to Jūzjānī, Aybeg had conquered the territory as far as the frontiers of Ujjain.[142] The Sultanate's first war against the Paramāra dynasty of Mālwa was deferred until the end of the reign of Iltutmish, who in 632/1235 invaded the kingdom and successively plundered the cities of Bhīlsān (Bhilsa) and Ujjain, destroying the temple at the former place and removing the idol of Māhakāla to Delhi.[143] Like so many other exploits of the period, however, this campaign had no permanent results; and we have no record of any subsequent Muslim attack on the Paramāras before the Khaljī era, when in *c.* 692/1293 the future sultan ʿAlāʾ al-Dīn, as muqtaʿ of Kara, plundered Bhīlsān and carried off its great bronze idol.[144] Jūzjānī speaks of campaigns towards Mālwa on a number of occasions, but he is not employing the term in its narrow sense, to refer to the Paramāra kingdom, which in his day was beyond the reach of the sultan's lieutenants. In the same vein Amīr Khusraw describes the troops of Jalāl al-Dīn Khaljī as advancing as far as the borders of Mālwa in 690/1291, when they crossed the Chambal and the Kunwārī (Kunar).[145] For these writers, 'Mālwa' appears to function as a general label for the entire region lying south and south-west of modern Bundelkhand.

The prospect of dominion

The idea of paramountcy over the entire subcontinent had a long pedigree,[146] and had possibly communicated itself to Delhi's sovereigns. A Sanskrit inscription of Balaban's reign might have appeared to give them every encouragement, since it depicts the sultan's authority as radiating over 'the Dravida country and Rameshvaram'.[147] Court poets, too, flattered Muslim rulers regarding their putative conquests. In the *Qirān al-Saʿdayn*, Muʿizz al-Dīn Kayqubād is made to boast: 'Sometimes I give my troops gold from Gujarāt; at others I write drafts [for them] on Dēōgīr . . . I make Mālwa the repository of my riches; Jājnagar I cause to meet the obligations of my treasury . . .'[148] At the time, however, this was mere fantasy. Prior to

141 *KF*, 8; see also *FS*, 227–8 (tr. 393–4), for his severity towards recalcitrant Hindus while at Kara.

142 *TN*, I, 417 (tr. 516–17); and see above, p. 19, n.62.

143 *TN*, I, 449 (with the year 631), 452 (cf. BL ms., fol. 180a; tr. 621–3, 628). Ray, *Dynastic history*, 907, places this invasion in the reign of Dēvapāla (*c.* 1218–36).

144 *TFS*, 220. 145 *MF*, 34.

146 André Wink, *Land and sovereignty in India* (Cambridge, 1986), sect. I, esp. 15–21.

147 Pālam Baoli inscription, V.s. 1333/1276, in P. Prasad, *Sanskrit inscriptions*, 5–6, 12 (no. I:4). See the comments of Peter Hardy, 'The authority of Muslim kings in mediaeval South Asia', in Marc Gaborieau (ed.), *Islam et société en Asie du Sud*, Collection Puruṣārthe 9 (Paris, 1986), 39.

148 *QS*, 63, *gah ba-ḥasham zar diham az Gūjarāt * gāh ba-Dīwgīr nawīsam barāt * . . . Mālwa-rā waqf-i dafāʾin kunam * Jāj* [printed text has *jām* in error] *nagar wajh-i khazāʾin kunam* (tr. in ED, III, 526).

'Alā' al-Dīn's audacious raid of 695/1296, the people of Dēōgīr had never even seen a Muslim army from the north.[149] For the Muslims of the thirteenth-century Sultanate, most of central and peninsular India was *terra incognita*. In this direction the Hindu territories seemed to stretch away indefinitely. The bounds of Mālwa, wrote Amīr Khusraw later – again fully availing himself of poetic licence – exceeded the ability of skilled surveyors (*muhandisān*) to measure them.[150] It is a striking testimony to the vigour of 'Alā' al-Dīn's regime that, as we shall see in chapter 10, events had already overtaken this observation some years before Khusraw died.

[149] *TFS*, 222–3. For Hindu poetry and epigraphy of the Yadava kingdom which seems to contradict Baranī, see P. M. Joshi and A. Mahdi Husain, 'Khaljis and Tughluqs in the Deccan', in H. K. Sherwani and P. M. Joshi (eds.), *History of medieval Deccan (1295–1724)* (Hyderabad, A. P., 1973, 2 vols.), I, 34–5, who suggest, however, that these refer to some clash with Muslims in the coastal region.

[150] *KF*, 56.

PART II
The zenith of the Sultanate

CHAPTER 8

Sultans, saints and sources

Sources for the period down to 752/1351

For the whole period from ʿAlāʾ al-Dīn's reign (695–715/1296–1316) through to the early 1350s, we continue to be dependent largely on three authors writing within India, namely Baranī, ʿIṣāmī and Sirhindī, together with – for Muḥammad b. Tughluq's reign (724–52/1324–51) – the memoirs of the Moroccan visitor Ibn Baṭṭūṭa. Authors writing in the Mughal era – notably Niẓām al-Dīn Aḥmad Harawī (d. 1003/1594), ʿAbd al-Qādir Badāʾūnī (late sixteenth century), and the seventeenth-century compilators Ulughkhānī (Ḥājjī al-Dabīr) and Muḥammad Qāsim Hindū Shāh Astarābādī (Firishta) – generally rely upon Baranī or Sirhindī and have no value as primary sources; but they occasionally preserve for us details gleaned from earlier works that are no longer extant. It should be noticed that there exists an earlier version of Baranī's *Taʾrīkh-i Fīrūz-Shāhī* (utilized by the fifteenth-century writer Bihāmadkhānī), of which there have survived three manuscripts[1] and which from ʿAlāʾ al-Dīn onwards begins to diverge from the revised text; while for his reign, at least, the manuscripts of this first recension differ even from each other. A reading of the standard version suggests, in fact, that Baranī may have drafted an account of ʿAlāʾ al-Dīn's reign as a separate work and subsequently incorporated it in a larger history, but without amending his treatment of the first few months.[2]

Chronology is no less a problem for this period than for the previous century. Baranī's very attention to analysis at the expense of chronology raises difficulties for the student of Muḥammad's reign in particular. Like ʿIṣāmī, he furnishes few dates, although there are more in his first recension than in the revised text; and in the latter Baranī expressly denies that he is presenting the crises of Muḥammad's reign in strict chronological order.[3] It is with some difficulty that a narrative framework can be reconstructed by

[1] Here I have relied primarily on Bodleian ms. Elliot 353 and a ms. in the private collection of Mr Simon Digby; but certain readings have been checked against RRL Persian ms. 2053.

[2] The events from late 695 to the autumn of 696 are thus covered twice: *TFS*, 239, 242–6.

[3] *Ibid.*, 468, 478.

means of these accounts with some assistance from Ibn Baṭṭūṭa, although he too is sparing of dates and many episodes to which he alludes preceded his arrival in 734/1333.[4]

How much is lost, we cannot be sure. Baranī tells us that ʿAlāʾ al-Dīn Khaljī's reign was distinguished by a number of prominent historians (*muʾarrikhān*). Kabīr al-Dīn, the sultan's *amīr-i dād-i lashgar*, is said to have excelled in the skills of a secretary (*dabīrī*) and in composition (*inshāʾ*). He allegedly completed volumes of *fatḥ-nāmas* and also wrote a *Taʾrīkh-i ʿAlāʾī*. Amīr Arslan *Kalāhī, too, had such a prodigious memory for the deeds of past sultans that he was able to answer ʿAlāʾ al-Dīn's questions without recourse to books. Baranī, claiming merely that his own *Taʾrīkh-i Fīrūz-Shāhī* was based simply on abridgement of past histories, does not say explicitly that these included anything written by Kabīr al-Dīn or Amīr Arslan.[5] In any event, no work by either man has survived, and what we are told of Amīr Arslan does not suggest that he wrote a history of his own.

Of the written sources known definitely to have existed, some would have been invaluable: Bījāpūrī's *Mulḥaqāt*, for instance, the 'long' *qaṣīda* on Fīrūz Shāh's exploits composed by Muṭahhar, and the *Shāh-Nāma* composed by Muḥammad b. Tughluq's court poet, Badr-i Chāch, and described by Badāʾūnī as a 'treasure'.[6] ʿAfīf, who dubs himself the author of 'the histories of sultans',[7] claims to have written biographies (*manāqib*) of ʿAlāʾ al-Dīn, of Ghiyāth al-Dīn Tughluq, of Muḥammad b. Tughluq and of Muḥammad b. Fīrūz, and an account of Temür's sack of Delhi in 801/1398 (*dhikr-i kharābī-yi Dihlī*);[8] but no trace of these works exists today. Similarly lost is another *Taʾrīkh-i Fīrūz-Shāhī*, to which a certain ʿAbd al-ʿAzīz[-i?] Shams *Bhanawrī lays claim in the preface to his translation of the *Kitāb-i Barāhī*.[9] In the 1540s a certain Ḥusām Khān composed in Gujarāt a *Ṭabaqāt* (or *Taʾrīkh*)-*i Bahādur-Shāhī* which is no longer extant but was

[4] The difficulties are compounded by later writers, beginning with *TMS*, where the sultan's campaign to Nagarkōt in 738/1337 is wrongly identified with an earlier expedition sent to the Qarāchīl region; this misled Ishwari Prasad, *A history of the Qaraunah Turks in India* (Allahabad, 1936), 126ff. The older schema based on this false chronology from 739 onwards is thereby skewed: see Sir Wolseley Haig, 'Five questions in the history of the Tughluq dynasty of Dihli', *JRAS* (1922), 336–65; and for some of the problems, N. Venkata Ramanayya, 'The date of the rebellions of Tilang and Kampila against Sultan Muḥammad bin Tughlaq', *Indian Culture* 5 (1938–9), 135–46, 261–9 (though his date for Fakhr al-Dīn's revolt in Bengal, *ibid.*, 138, 140, is surely too late).

[5] *TFS*, 14, 361. For Tāj al-Dīn ᶜIrāqī, see *ibid.*, 358.

[6] Muṭahhar: Bihāmadkhānī, fols. 407a, 413a–414b (tr. Zaki, 4, 15). Badr: Badāʾūnī, I, 241; P. Jackson, 'Badr-i Čāčī', *Enc.Isl.*², *Supplement*; the date of completion of the *Shāh-Nāma* is given in a chronogram in Badr's *Qaṣāʾid*, ed. M. Ḥādī ᶜAlī (Kānpūr, n.d.), 85 (see also ED, III, 572–3).

[7] ᶜAfīf, 256.

[8] ᶜAlāʾ al-Dīn: *ibid.*, 478. Ghiyāth al-Dīn: *ibid.*, 27, 36. Muḥammad b. Tughluq: *ibid.*, 42, 51, 92, 274, 394, 451. Muḥammad b. Fīrūz: *ibid.*, 148–9, 273, 428, 440. Sack of Delhi: *ibid.*, 182, 185.

[9] IOL Persian ms. 1262, fol. 2b; Ethé, *Catalogue*, col. 1112 (no. 1997), assumes that the author is to be identified with ᶜAfīf.

utilized by Ulughkhānī and is cited by Firishta.[10] From the excerpts we have, it is clear that Ḥusām Khān had access to sources other than Sirhindī or Bihāmadkhānī; his chronology, however, bears marked similarities to Sirhindī's.

The one chronicle contemporary with ʿAlā' al-Dīn that has come down to us is Amīr Khusraw's prose work, *Khazā'in al-Futūḥ*, which was completed in 711/1311–12 and provides a florid and bombastic account of the sultan's victories over various Mongol attacks and of Kāfūr's campaigns in the south; the poet himself calls it a '*fatḥ-nāma*'.[11] Khusraw's last historical works are the *Nuh Sipihr*, written in 718/1318 under Quṭb al-Dīn Mubārak Shāh and incorporating an account of the sultan's expedition to the Deccan; the *Diwal Rānī*, which was completed just after the end of the Khaljī period, in 720/1320, and contains details not found elsewhere; and the *Tughluq-Nāma*, commemorating the overthrow of the usurper Nāṣir al-Dīn Khusraw Shāh and the accession of Ghiyāth al-Dīn Tughluq (720–724/1320–1324).[12] In addition, although the treatise on prose composition, *Rasā'il al-Iʿjāz*, which Khusraw produced in 719/1319–20, is rather suspect, some of the documents it contains appear to be based in part on genuine originals.[13]

For the Tughluqid era, although it seems that we must discount the fragment of the alleged memoirs of Muḥammad b. Tughluq, which the majority of scholars no longer regard as authentic,[14] we have access to richer and more varied material than for any of the previous dynasties. There are a few works composed in order to commemorate specific events, like the *Basātīn al-Uns* (726/1325–6) in which Tāj al-Dīn Muḥammad-i Ṣadr-i Aʿlā Aḥmad-i Ḥasan ʿAydawsī, known as Ikhtisān-i Dabīr, describes Tughluq's Lakhnawtī campaign of 724/1324,[15] and some of the verses of Muḥammad's court poet Badr-i Chāch. The extensive correspondence (*inshā'*) of ʿAyn al-Mulk Ibn Māhrū, who served both Muḥammad and Fīrūz Shāh as governor of Multān and who died at some point before

[10] On Ḥusām Khān, see the introduction to *AHG*, Ross's edition of the *Ẓafar al-Wālih*, II, xxvii–xxix. He is cited by Firishta, I, 3, and II, 512.

[11] *KF*, 170; see *ibid.*, 26, for the current year.

[12] Useful summary of contents in Syed Hashimi, 'The Tughluq-namah', *IC* 8 (1934), 301–12, 413–24.

[13] For an analysis, see S. H. Askari, 'Risail [*sic*]-ul-Ijaz of Amir Khusrau: an appraisal', in *Dr. Zakir Husain presentation volume* (Delhi, 1968), 116–37; *idem*, 'Material of historical interest in Iᶜjaz-i-Khusravi', *MIM* 1 (1969), 1–20.

[14] BL ms. Add. 25785 (of *TN*), fols. 316ff.; tr. in A. M. Husain, *Tughluq dynasty* (Calcutta, 1963), 265–76, and facsimile of text at end. See *ibid.*, 567–72, for an analysis of the document, which Husain believed to be authentic; for the contrary (and now widely accepted) view, Nizami, *Studies in medieval Indian history*, 76–85, and his *On history and historians*, 198–205; the arguments are reviewed in Stephan Conermann, *Die Beschreibung Indiens in der 'Riḥla' des Ibn Baṭṭūṭa*, IU, 165 (Berlin, 1993), 47–9.

[15] S. H. Askari, 'Historical value of Basatin-al-Uns', *JBORS* 48, part 2 (1962), 1–29. Ikhtisān, *Basātīn*, BL ms. Add. 7717, fol. 19b, gives the current year as 726.

772/1370,[16] contains a good deal of material on fiscal and military affairs, mostly relating to Fīrūz Shāh's era, although some letters date from the time of Muḥammad. In the *Dastūr al-Albāb* which Ḥājjī ʿAbd al-Ḥamīd Ghaznawī began in 734/1333–4 and completed in 766/1364–5, we have a treatise on the administration of the Sultanate from the pen of a clerk (*muḥarrir*), of particular value on the subject of taxation.[17] For the fourteenth century, lastly, we also possess material relating to the *ṣūfī* orders (*silsilas*, *ṭarīqas*), in which reference is sometimes made to contemporary political events. Chief among these, for our purposes, are the collected biographies of sufi *shaykhs*, the *Siyar al-Awliyā'*, of Muḥammad b. Mubārak Kirmānī (Amīr Khwurd; d. 770/1368–9); Amīr Ḥasan Dihlawī's *Fawā'id al-Fu'ād*, comprising the discourses (*malfūẓāt*) of the influential Chishtī Shaykh Niẓām al-Dīn Awliyā' (d. 725/1325); and Ḥamīd Qalandar's *Khayr al-Majālis* (*c.* 755/1354), which contains those of Shaykh Naṣīr al-Dīn Maḥmūd *Chirāgh-i Dihlī* ('the Lamp of Delhi').[18]

Turning to sources from outside India, the so-called correspondence (*mukātibāt*) of the Ilkhanid statesman Rashīd al-Dīn must be discounted as a contemporary source for Indian affairs: many of the letters undeniably reflect a considerable familiarity with the administrative machinery in Persia and with the nature of the India trade, but it seems difficult to avoid the conclusion of Reuben Levy that they emanate from India itself in the fifteenth century.[19] With the onset of the Tughluqid era, data from external sources become more plentiful. Waṣṣāf's latest information on the Sultanate relates to the accession of Muḥammad b. Tughluq;[20] but the opening up of Muslim India during Muḥammad's reign to diplomatic contact with distant parts of the Islamic world, especially Mamlūk Egypt, is reflected in the encyclopaedia *Masālik al-Abṣār* of al-ʿUmarī (d. 749/1349), who was able to amass a veritable dossier of information about India; in notices on Muḥammad and his empire in the biographical dictionaries - *al-Wāfī bi'l-Wafayāt* and *A'yān al-'Aṣr* – of al-Ṣafadī (d. 764/1363), the chronicles of Ibn

[16] His death is mentioned in *SFS*, 154.

[17] The author states that he was forty-four in 734 and that he was 917 months old, i.e. in his seventy-seventh year, on completing the book. This is said to have occurred in 760: *DA*, fols. 3a, 4b, cited without question by Rashid, 'Dastur-ul-Albab', 59. But the details contradict one another, and the correct year must be 766.

[18] For these and other (often spurious) works, see Mohammad Habib, 'Chishti mystic records of the Sultanate period', *MIQ*, 1 (1950), no. 2, 1–42; Nizami, *On history and historians*, 163–80.

[19] R. Levy, 'The letters of Rashīd al-Dīn Faḍl-Allāh', *JRAS* (1946), 74–8. See now A. H. Morton, 'The letters of Rashīd al-Dīn: Ilkhanid fact or Timurid fantasy?', in Amitai-Preiss and Morgan, *The Mongol empire and its legacy* (forthcoming). K. A. Nizami, 'Rashid-u'd-Din Fazlullah as an Ilkhanid envoy to the court of Ala-u'd-Din Khalji', *PIHC* 29 *(Patiala 1967)* (Patna, 1968, 2 vols.), I, 139–43, and in *On history and historians*, 99–104, acknowledges some of the problems, but is inclined to accept the authenticity of the letters.

[20] Incorrectly placed in 723/1323. But the current year at one point appears as 727 (Waṣṣāf, 607). The date 718 (*ibid.*, 608) is manifestly an error for 728: Barthold, *Turkestan*, 49 n.2.

Abi'l-Faḍā'il (fl. 1340) and Shabānkāra'ī (738/1337–8),[21] and the travel narrative of Ibn Baṭṭūṭa. Of these, the *Tuḥfat al-Nuẓẓār* (often called simply the *Riḥla*) of Ibn Baṭṭūṭa, who spent several years in the Sultanate, furnishes a picture of life at Muḥammad's court and in his dominions between 734/1333 and *c.* 748/1347 that in its vividness is unmatched elsewhere. The archive of the shaykhs of Jām in Khurāsān, found in the fifteenth-century *Farā'id-i Ghiyāthī* of Yūsuf b. Muḥammad b. Shihāb al-Jāmī (Yūsuf-i Ahl), contains correspondence with the Delhi government during the reigns of both Muḥammad and his successor.[22]

Sources from 752/1351 onwards

The earlier recension of Baranī's *Ta'rīkh-i Fīrūz-Shāhī* embraced only the first four years of Fīrūz Shāh's reign, and the revised text was completed two years after that. We are told that when the sultan desired a history of his reign to be written, and invited applications from would-be chroniclers following Baranī's death in *c.* 762/1360–1, none came forward, and he was reduced to composing his own account, which he caused to be carved on the dome of the Jāmiᶜ Masjid at his new capital, Fīrūzābād.[23] Fortunately, however, this dearth of historiographical enterprise did not last, and for Fīrūz Shāh's reign (752–90/1351–88) we have access to a crop of literary sources. What might be called 'official' history is represented by the copy of Fīrūz Shāh's lengthy inscription that has come down to us as *Futūḥāt-i Fīrūz-Shāhī*,[24] and by the panegyrical *Sīrat-i Fīrūz-Shāhī*, produced for the sultan soon after *c.* 772/1370 by an anonymous author who may have been the poet Muṭahhar.[25] It was not, however, until the early fifteenth century that ᶜAfīf wrote his *Ta'rīkh-i Fīrūz-Shāhī*, which is the fullest source for the reign. ᶜAfīf, who belonged to a bureaucratic family that had served the Tughluqids and himself worked in the *dīwān-i wizārat* in the middle of the 1380s,[26] intended his biography of the sultan to be a sequel to Baranī's work, comprising the ninety *muqaddimas* which the older historian had

21 D. P. Little, 'Al-Ṣafadī as a biographer of his contemporaries', in Little (ed.), *Essays on Islamic civilization presented to Niyazi Berkes* (Leiden, 1976), 190–210. C. E. Bosworth and P. Jackson, 'Shabānkāra'ī', *Enc.Isl.*².

22 On this work, see Jean Aubin, 'Le khanat de Čaġatai et le Khorassan (1334–1380)', *Turcica* 8 (1976), 20 n.19; *PL*, III, part 2, 251–2 (no. 428).

23 ᶜAfīf, 176–7: around the time of the sultan's return from his Jājnagar campaign, which occurred in Shaᶜbān 762/June-July 1361 according to *SFS*, 74, and in Rajab/May-June according to *TMS*, 130. Hodivala, *Studies*, I, 129, warns against taking this as a precise indication of the date of Baranī's death.

24 K. A. Nizami, 'The Futuhat-i-Firuz Shahi as a medieval inscription', in *PSMI*, 28–33, and in his *On history and historians*, 205–10.

25 As suggested by K. A. Nizami, *Supplement to Elliot and Dowson's History of India*, III (Delhi, 1981), 63.

26 ᶜAfīf, 487–8: the context is the disgrace of Shams al-Dīn Abū-Rijā, which occurred in 785/1383–4 (*ibid.*, 497–8). For ᶜAfīf's forebears in the Tughluqids' service, see *ibid.*, 37, 127, 130–1, 138, 145, 196, 197, 339.

announced his intention of writing but had not lived to complete.[27] Regrettably, the text we have is defective at the end, to judge from the list of contents supplied by ʿAfīf himself. Both Sirhindī (838/1434) and Bihāmad-khānī (842/1438) supply information on Fīrūz Shāh's reign which is not found in ʿAfīf's *Taʾrīkh*; and they continue to be our principal sources from the 1380s onwards. Bihāmadkhānī's general chronicle, the *Taʾrīkh-i Muḥammadī*,[28] which down to 755/1354 relies on Baranī's earlier recension, becomes at that juncture an original source; and though less detailed than Sirhindī's work it has the particular merit that it was composed not at Delhi but in the newly autonomous principality of Kālpī and hence provides us with a different vantage-point from that of earlier chroniclers.

Temür's invasion of India is of course covered in some detail by the Timurid chronicles. The most immediately contemporary of these was the lost *Rūz-Nāma-yi Futūḥāt-i Hindūstān* of Qadi Naṣīr al-Dīn ʿUmar, who accompanied the conqueror. This was abridged both by Ghiyāth al-Dīn ʿAlī Yazdī, whose *Rūz-Nāma-yi Ghazawāt-i Hindūstān* has survived, and by Niẓām-i Shāmī, who incorporated it into his *Ẓafar-Nāma*, an account of Temür's career completed in 806/1404. Both works (and possibly also Qadi Naṣīr al-Dīn's original text) were in turn utilized by Sharaf al-Dīn ʿAlī Yazdī when he came to produce his own *Ẓafar-Nāma* in 828/1424–5.[29]

The Khaljī Sultans

Baranī depicts ʿAlāʾ al-Dīn Khaljī as an unlettered soldier with little time for the ʿulamaʾ, but a man of boundless ambition who had to be dissuaded from founding his own religion; he was amazed that such a sultan, who set *realpolitik* above the injunctions of the Sharīʿa, could have prospered to the extent that he did.[30] Yet for ʿIṣāmī the contrast could not have been stronger between ʿAlāʾ al-Dīn, who had done so much to implant Islam in India, and the contemporary sultan, Muḥammad b. Tughluq, who had presided over its collapse;[31] and at the time of Ibn Baṭṭūṭa's visit to Delhi a few years before, the citizens evidently looked back on ʿAlāʾ al-Dīn's era as a golden age.[32] It is true that the reign was marked both by the repulse of formidable Mongol invasions and by spectacular advances at the expense of independent Hindu powers in Rajasthan and the south. The capacity of the Sultanate to raise large and effective military forces was placed on a new footing by means of economic reforms which kept prices low in the capital.

27 *Ibid.*, 29–30; cf. *TFS*, 529–30, 602.

28 On which see Peter Hardy, 'The Tarikh-i-Muḥammadi by Muḥammad Bihamad Khani', in Gupta (ed.), *Essays presented to Sir Jadunath Sarkar*, 181–90.

29 For the relationship between these works, see John E. Woods, 'The rise of Tīmūrid historiography', *Journal of Near Eastern Studies* 46, part 2 (1987), 93–5.

30 *TFS*, 261–6, 289. For Baranī's view of the sultan, see generally Hardy, *Historians*, 32–4.

31 *FS*, 604, 605–6 (tr. 898, 900–1).

32 IB, III, 184 (tr. Gibb, 640).

Baranī describes such achievements in terms of the miraculous.[33] But he also cites the opinion of the mystic Shaykh Bashīr that ʿAlāʾ al-Dīn's regime, founded as it was on his uncle's murder, was inherently unstable;[34] and in the chronicler's own eyes the fate of ʿAlāʾ al-Dīn's sons was retribution for Jalāl al-Dīn's murder.[35]

During ʿAlāʾ al-Dīn's final illness, which Baranī calls dropsy (*istisqāʾ*), his heir, Khiḍr Khān, was imprisoned in Gwāliyōr at the instigation of the sultan's na'ib, the slave Kāfūr, and shortly blinded following his father's death on 7 Shawwāl 715/4 January 1316;[36] his brother Shādī Khān suffered the same fate. Kāfūr, whose aim, if Baranī is to be trusted, was to destroy the entire Khaljī dynasty,[37] ruled through an infant son of ʿAlāʾ al-Dīn, Shihāb al-Dīn ʿUmar; but he enjoyed power for a mere thirty-five days before being murdered by ʿAlāʾ al-Dīn's paiks. Another son then assumed the regency, but soon displaced the child ruler, on the pretext that the boy's mother had tried to poison him, and himself reigned as Quṭb al-Dīn Mubārak Shāh (716–20/1316–20). In 718/1318, on the return march from a campaign in the Deccan, Quṭb al-Dīn's cousins, the descendants of Jalāl al-Dīn's brother Khāmush (Yughrush Khān), were executed on suspicion of complicity in a plot to assassinate the sultan;[38] Khiḍr Khān, Shādī Khān and ʿUmar were put to death; and their remaining brothers were despatched to Gwāliyōr. In Jumādā II 720/July 1320 the sultan's favourite, the Indian slave Ḥasan, entitled Khusraw Khān, had him murdered and ascended the throne as Nāṣir al-Dīn Khusraw Shāh – the only Delhi monarch, in fact, who was an Indian convert to Islam. All ʿAlāʾ al-Dīn's surviving sons were now massacred.[39] The Khaljī dynasty appears to have been completely exterminated. When one of ʿAlāʾ al-Dīn's senior lieutenants, Ghāzī Malik Tughluq, the muqtaʿ of Dēōpālpūr, posing as the avenger of his master's heirs, marched on Delhi and overthrew Khusraw Shāh, no member of the dynasty could be found to take the throne.[40] Ghāzī Malik himself was accordingly proclaimed as Sultan Ghiyāth al-Dīn Tughluq Shāh (720–724/1320–1324).[41]

For some, says Baranī, the parallel between the reigns of Muʿizz al-Dīn Kayqubād and Quṭb al-Dīn Mubārak Shāh Khaljī was striking.[42] In both cases a young and profligate ruler succeeded a harsh and despotic one,

33 *TFS*, 339. 34 *Ibid.*, 377–8. 35 *Ibid.*, 237.

36 The date for ʿAlāʾ al-Dīn's death supplied in *DR*, 259. *TMS*, 81, gives 6 Shawwāl, and *TFS*, 369, the evening of that day; *FS*, 344 (tr. 524), has 11 Shawwāl.

37 *TFS*, 375. 38 *Ibid.*, 393. *FS*, 363–4 (tr. 562–3).

39 *DR*, 273–85; *Tughluq-Nāma*, 23–4, 31–2, 47; *TFS*[1], Bodleian ms., fol. 172a/Digby Coll. ms., fol. 146b (not in *TFS*, 408). For a relatively detailed version of their fate, as current in Delhi some years later, see IB, III, 189–90, 191–4 (tr. Gibb, 643, 644–5), who believed, however, that all Quṭb al-Dīn's brothers were put to death during his reign.

40 *TFS*, 421–2; and see also 237. *Tughluq-Nāma*, 140–1, does not actually confirm that the Khaljī dynasty was extinct.

41 For the date of Tughluq's death, usually given as 725/1325, see appendix V.

42 *TFS*, 383, 387–8.

leading to a general relaxation of state authority and public morals. Yet Quṭb al-Dīn manifested greater military energy than his precursor, heading a campaign which reasserted imperial rule over the Deccan in 718/1318. For a time at least the young sultan won great popularity through the abrogation of his father's repressive measures. Many matters are unexplained, however, and Baranī is guilty of his customary inconsistency. Even allowing for hyperbole, it is not clear, for instance, why, if the sultan could not bear to be parted even for one hour from Khusraw Khān,[43] he was prepared to send him on a lengthy expedition to the far south. Nor do the chroniclers indicate why amirs who threatened to report the favourite's treasonable plans to the sultan during that campaign ranged themselves under his banner against Tughluq a few years later (pp. 177, 179 below) – especially since the latter's revolt is portrayed by both Amīr Khusraw and Baranī as a Holy War (*ghazā'*).[44]

One answer to this second problem may well be that Nāṣir al-Dīn Khusraw Shāh's rule was less repugnant than our sources would have us believe. Baranī is conceivably right when he alleges that idolatry was practised within the royal palace, presumably by those of Khusraw Shāh's adherents who were not converts. But his story, on the other hand, that Khusraw Shāh and his lieutenants treated Qur'āns with blatant disrespect and set up idols in mosques is hardly worthy of credence; it is noteworthy that the *Tughluq-Nāma* talks of idolatry in less specific terms and that the version of events heard by Ibn Baṭṭūṭa, who singles out for mention only a prohibition on slaughtering cows, is rather less extreme.[45] Yet even if Khusraw Shāh's regime cannot be regarded as anti-Muslim, it is still necessary, on the other hand, to explain the widespread acquiescence in the murder of Quṭb al-Dīn Mubārak Shāh. Possibly Quṭb al-Dīn's assumption of the caliphal title, which is not mentioned in the literary sources but which can be dated to 717/1317–18,[46] had scandalized many Muslims. Some hint may be found, too, in Baranī's claim that Quṭb al-Dīn had been on bad terms with the Chishtī shaykh Niẓām al-Dīn Awliyā' as a result of the murder of Khiḍr Khān.[47] Given the sultan's poor relations with the Chishtī khanaqah, it is conceivable that in the eyes of the shaykh and his

43 *Ibid.*, 382.

44 *Ibid.*, 399–400, for the amirs' threats. *Tughluq-Nāma*, 62, 100, and *TFS*, 415–16, for holy war.

45 *Ibid.*, 410–11. *Tughluq-Nāma*, 44. IB, III, 200 (tr. Gibb, 648). For a balanced assessment of Khusraw Shāh's reign, see Lal, *History of the Khaljis*, 313–16; also Hardy, 'Force and violence', 172.

46 He is called merely *Qasīm Amīr al-Mu'minīn* in an inscription of 5 Muḥarram 718/9 March 1318: Z. A. Desai, 'The Jālor ᶜĪdgāh inscription of Quṭbu'd-Dīn Mubārak Shāh Khaljī', *EIAPS* (1972), 12–19. The title of caliph is found in inscriptions later in that year: Yazdani, 'Inscriptions of the Khaljī Sulṭāns of Delhi', 38–40; Z. A. Desai, 'Khaljī and Tughluq inscriptions from Gujarat', *EIAPS* (1962), 4–5. But it appears on coins of 717: *CMSD*, 96–101. Quṭb al-Dīn is frequently addressed as *khalīfa* in *NS*.

47 *TFS*, 394.

sympathizers the Indian upstart was preferable to the Khaljī. Quṭb al-Dīn may thus have alienated support and played into the hands of Khusraw Khān and his party.

Shaykhs and chroniclers

All monarchs and their kingdoms, wrote ʿIṣāmī, lay under the protection of a saint; and the first step of Providence when it wished to destroy a country was to effect the saint's departure.[48] Thus for him the death of Niẓām al-Dīn ushered in the horrors endured by Delhi in the era of Muḥammad b. Tughluq,[49] and the prosperity of Dawlatābād, prior to the revolt against Muḥammad from 745/1344 onwards, could be attributed to the presence of two shaykhs, Burhān al-Dīn and Zayn al-Dīn.[50] Sufis from Khurāsān had been present in India since the Ghurid era, and two orders had grown up – the Suhrawardiyya, with their principal base at Multān, and the Chishtiyya, whose headquarters were in Delhi. The orders differed in their attitudes towards the state: for the Suhrawardiyya, association with the powerful was permitted; the Chishtī shaykhs, by contrast, eschewed contact with the court and the nobility and rejected revenues and government service (*shughl*). Relations between the two groups were nevertheless harmonious and based on mutual respect.[51]

The view expressed by ʿIṣāmī is especially common, of course, among those who recorded the discourse of shaykhs and the hagiographers like Kirmānī (Amīr Khwurd), who saw the very presence of Muslims in India as a miracle (*karāmat*) on the part of the Chishtī Shaykh Muʿīn al-Dīn;[52] Amīr Ḥasan Dihlawī thought that Multān had been saved from the Mongols in Qubacha's time through the intervention of Shaykh Quṭb al-Dīn Bakhtiyār Kākī.[53] But such convictions were shared by other writers whose lifestyles and fortunes were less closely bound up with the orders. ʿAfīf believed it was the shrine of Quṭb al-Dīn Munawwar that preserved Hānsī during Temür's invasion.[54] Recalling to mind the tyranny of ʿAlāʾ al-Dīn Khaljī, Baranī could conceive of no reason for the continued success of the sultan's regime other than the fact that Niẓām al-Dīn Awliyāʾ graced his capital.[55]

The numinous power or spiritual charisma (*baraka*) of a shaykh could be seen as territorial and as constituting a rival locus of authority (*wilāyat*) to

48 *FS*, 455–6 (tr. 687–8).
49 *Ibid.*, 456–7 (tr. 688–9).
50 *Ibid.*, 458–9, 461–2 (tr. 691–2, 696–7).
51 K. A. Nizami, 'Early Indo-Muslim mystics and their attitude towards the state', *IC* 22 (1948), 388–92, 395–8, and 23 (1949), 13–21. Aziz Aḥmad, 'The sufi and the sultan in pre-Mughal Muslim India', *Der Islam* 38 (1962), 142–7. S. Digby, 'The sufi shaikh as a source of authority in mediaeval India', in Gaborieau (ed.), *Islam et société*, 63–5.
52 *Siyar*, 47, cited in Digby, 'The sufi shaikh as a source of authority', 72.
53 Amīr Ḥasan Dihlawī, *Fawāʾid al-Fuʾād*, 185.
54 ʿAfīf, 82; and cf. also 133, where it is attributed to the *baraka* of Munawwar's successor.
55 *TFS*, 324–5.

that of the sultan.[56] Several anecdotes show shaykhs conferring the sovereignty on a prince. Stories were current in Jūzjānī's day that kingship had been bestowed by *faqīrs* both on Ḥusām al-Dīn ʿIwaḍ and on Iltutmish; similar tales are told regarding Balaban and ʿAlāʾ al-Dīn Khaljī; and ʿAfīf reports no less than four anecdotes in which Fīrūz Shāh is promised the crown by shaykhs, among them Niẓām al-Dīn Awliyāʾ.[57] That the shaykh's khanaqah might also serve as a rallying-point for disaffected elements had been thrown into relief by the Sīdī Muwallih affair in the time of Jalāl al-Dīn Khaljī (above, p. 83).

In these circumstances, relations between court and khanaqah might not always be harmonious,[58] and for our chroniclers one of the most important criteria in evaluating a sultan's reign was his treatment of holy men. Here, for all his faults, ʿAlāʾ al-Dīn, who demonstrated a growing attachment to Shaykh Niẓām al-Dīn Awliyāʾ during his last years, proved relatively sound.[59] The reign of his son Quṭb al-Dīn Mubārak Shāh, however, was vitiated by his relations with Niẓām al-Dīn. When the saint condemned the murder of Khiḍr Khān, who had been his disciple (*murīd*), the sultan responded with slights and threats and attempted to set up the immigrant Shaykhzāda Shihāb al-Dīn Jāmī and the Suhrawardī Rukn al-Dīn of Multān as his rivals in Delhi.[60] Niẓām al-Dīn was extremely influential: we are told of several notables who were among his disciples.[61] During the brief reign of Nāṣir al-Dīn Khusraw Shāh, Niẓām al-Dīn accepted gifts of money from the usurper, and spent them on charitable causes. He thus made a new enemy of Ghiyāth al-Dīn Tughluq Shāh when that monarch sought to retrieve the sums disbursed by his predecessor.[62] Hostility between the two men persisted: Tughluq is said to have been contemplating further action against Niẓām al-Dīn during the return march from Bengal just before his death; though the shaykh's ironic comment, *Dillī az tū dūr ast* ('Delhi is some way off for you'), is not reported by any author prior to Sirhindī.[63]

Niẓām al-Dīn survived only a few months into the reign of Muḥammad b. Tughluq, with whom his relations had been cordial: Ibn Baṭṭūṭa was told

[56] Digby, 'The sufi shaikh as a source of authority', 62–3; *idem*, 'The sufi *shaykh* and the sultan: a conflict of claims to authority in medieval India', *Iran* 28 (1990), 71–81.
[57] *Ibid.*, 75–8. See further Eaton, *Rise of Islam*, 82–6.
[58] Nizami, 'Early Indo-Muslim mystics', *IC* 23 (1949), 312–21; for good relations, *ibid.*, 165–70.
[59] *TFS*, 332.
[60] *Ibid.*, 394, 396. For Quṭb al-Dīn's close relations with Shaykhzāda Jāmī, see IB, III, 294 (tr. Gibb, 697); also Digby, 'The sufi *shaykh* and the sultan', 79 n.20. Rukn al-Dīn's own relations with Niẓām al-Dīn remained harmonious: *idem*, 'The sufi shaikh as a source of authority', 64.
[61] ʿAfīf, 69, 445; and cf. also *TFS*, 396.
[62] For the cancellation of grants made from the treasury by Khusraw Shāh, see *ibid.*, 439.
[63] *TMS*, 96–7: the remark is embellished in later sources. For more details, see Digby, 'The sufi *shaykh* and the sultan', 72–4.

that Muḥammad carried the shaykh's bier.[64] Their contacts seem to have contributed to the strain between Tughluq and his heir-apparent. Yet the new sultan's own relations with shaykhs proved problematic when he sought to recruit the talents of sufi shaykhs for service to the state.[65] This created no difficulty for the Suhrawardī order, which had never objected to involvement in the world's affairs: Muʿizz al-Dīn, son of the Suhrawardī Shaykh ʿAlāʾ al-Dīn Ajūdhanī, seems to have accepted the governorship of Gujarāt without demur.[66] The sultan's relations with the descendants of the Chishtī shaykh Ḥamīd al-Dīn at Nāgawr were also cordial.[67] But for most of the Chishtiyya, his policy constituted a major crisis. Ibn Baṭṭūṭa retails numerous anecdotes demonstrating the shaykhs' resistance and the harsh punishments they suffered in consequence. It was Amīr Khwurd's opinion that Muḥammad's dismal end far from the capital was due to his treatment of holy men, chiefly Niẓām al-Dīn's successor (*khalīfa*), Naṣīr al-Dīn Maḥmūd *Chirāgh-i Dihlī*.[68]

From Ghiyāth al-Dīn to Fīrūz Shāh

The Tughluqids (720–815/1320–1412) proved to be the longest-lived of the dynasties that ruled over the Sultanate. During Tughluq Shāh's brief reign, Bengal was again subjected to the sultan's overlordship, the Kakatiya kingdom of Arangal (Tilang; Telingāna) was annexed, and Muslim authority was established over much of the Pāndya kingdom of Maʿbar. Baranī's view of Ghiyāth al-Dīn Tughluq is somewhat one-sided. He chooses to ignore the sultan's strained relations with Niẓām al-Dīn, and praises Tughluq for being in many respects a model Muslim ruler. He was like a father to his troops; his dominions enjoyed justice and security; his piety and personal morality were above criticism. Tughluq is said to have accomplished what ʿAlāʾ al-Dīn had done, but without bloodshed.[69] But when he comes to describe the punishment in Delhi in 721/1321–2 of those who had mutinied during the campaign in Tilang, Baranī lets his guard drop, revealing that the wives and children of the ringleaders were put to death.[70] Yet there is no hint of condemnation here for a practice which had begun under ʿAlāʾ al-Dīn and which Baranī clearly deplored.[71]

Tughluq perished when a newly constructed building at Afghānpūr collapsed on him. Although Baranī makes no such accusation, the suspicion

64 IB, III, 211 (tr. Gibb, 653–4); and see also *MA*, ed. Spies, 20 (German tr. 46)/ed. Fāriq, 38 (tr. Siddiqi and Aḥmad, 45).
65 IB, III, 294 (tr. Gibb, 697).
66 *TFS*, 507, 512. *SFS*, 20–1 (tr. Basu, in *JBORS* 23 [1937], 98). *Siyar*, 196.
67 K. A. Nizami, 'Some documents of Sultan Muḥammad bin Tughluq', *MIM* 1 (1969), 305–6, 307, 309–13.
68 *Siyar*, 245–6, cited in Digby, 'The sufi *shaykh* and the sultan', 74. For Muḥammad and the Chishtiyya, see generally Nizami, 'Early Indo-Muslim mystics', *IC* 24 (1950), 60–5.
69 *TFS*, 445. 70 *Ibid.*, 449. 71 *Ibid.*, 253.

that his eldest son and designated heir, Muḥammad (Ulugh Khān), had contrived his death was shared by ʿIṣāmī and by al-Ṣafadī's informants, while Ibn Baṭṭūṭa attributes it to the skill of the intendant of buildings (*shiḥna-yi ʿimārat*) Aḥmad b. Ayaz, whom Muḥammad rewarded with the post of wazir.[72] The smooth transition that followed Tughluq's death might have seemed to reinforce the impression that a new era of stability had dawned, for Muḥammad was apparently the first sultan to enjoy a peaceful succession. The image of the sultan conveyed by foreign writers and fostered by his own propaganda is one of a mighty warrior for the cause of Islam, whose triumphs are unprecedented and who unlike his predecessors has cowed the Mongols.[73] But in the event the reign of Muḥammad b. Tughluq (724–52/1324–51) was characterized by rebellion and disaster. Although a number of revolts in the years 727–8/1326–8 were suppressed, the sultan embarked on various ambitious projects which entailed considerable expenditure. The effects of their failure were accentuated by plague and famine. A further wave of rebellions from 734/1334 onwards absorbed the attention of Muḥammad and his lieutenants, and led to the definitive loss of Maʿbar, Tilang and Bengal; while a new Hindu power emerged from *c.* 1336 at Vijāyanagara. Although he secured a temporary respite after 741/1340, and successfully applied to the ʿAbbasid Caliph at Cairo for a diploma of investiture in 744/1343, his last years witnessed a widespread revolt by members of the military class, the *amīrān-i ṣada* ('amirs of a hundred') in Deccan and Gujarāt. The rebels in Gujarāt were defeated; but at Dēōgīr (Dawlatābād) in 748/1347 the rebel leader Ḥasan Gangū, the founder of the Bahmanid dynasty, established an independent sultanate. When Muḥammad died near Thatta on 21 Muḥarram 752/20 March 1351 he wielded no authority south of the Vindhyas.

Muḥammad b. Tughluq posed a problem for the historians: even the unimaginative Sirhindī interrupted his annalistic catalogue of events to try to explain the causes of the sultan's failure.[74] Yet we simply cannot take at face value all the charges levelled at the sultan by our principal sources. On certain heads, their testimony overlaps; to a degree they paint a similar picture of Muḥammad's character. Baranī, ʿIṣāmī and Ibn Baṭṭūṭa all comment, for instance, on the sultan's interest in philosophy;[75] but that is

[72] *FS*, 420 (tr. 633). al-Ṣafadī, *Wāfī*, III, 172, partial tr. M. S. Khān, 'An undiscovered Arabic source of the history of Sulṭān Muḥammad bin Tughlaq', *IC* 53 (1979), 187. IB, III, 212–15 (tr. Gibb, 654–6).

[73] Conquests and spread of Islam: Shabānkāra'ī, 87–8, 287; *MA*, ed. Spies, 29 (German tr. 55)/ ed. Fāriq, 53 (tr. Siddiqi and Aḥmad, 54). Mongols: *MA*, ed. Lech, 40 (German tr. 118). See Muḥammad's own appeal to the notables of Transoxiana in *FG*, SK ms. Fatıh 4012, fol. 456b.

[74] *TMS*, 113–15.

[75] *TFS*, 464–5. *FS*, 510 (tr. 759). IB, IV, 343 (tr. Gibb and Beckingham, 929). For Baranī's hostility towards philosophy, see *FJ*, 16, 168–9; tr. in W. T. de Bary, *Sources of Indian tradition* (New York, 1958), 481–2.

not to say that they comprehended it. Professor Nizami has argued persuasively that Muḥammad was greatly influenced by the Syrian scholar and jurist Ibn Taymiyya (d. 728/1327), whose pupil ʿAbd al-ʿAzīz Ardabīlī received a warm welcome at Muḥammad's court.[76] Ibn Taymiyya's aim was to reinvigorate what he saw as decadent Islamic society. To this end, he sought to promote both *ijtihād* (fresh interpretation of religious law) and *jihād* (holy war), and rejected the separation between state and religion as advocated by the Chishtiyya among others. According to Nizami, Muḥammad's attested view that 'Religion and the State are twins',[77] his concern to enforce orthodox Islamic observance and practice, his attempts to press sufis into the service of the state, and his adoption of the style *al-Mujāhid fī sabīli'llāh* ('The Warrior in the Path of God') were all symptomatic of his attachment to the ideology of Ibn Taymiyya; but his attitudes were misunderstood by those, like Baranī and ʿIṣāmī, who were unacquainted with currents of thought in the wider Islamic world.[78]

Baranī, ʿIṣāmī and Ibn Baṭṭūṭa speak with one voice regarding Muḥammad's penchant for inflicting harsh punishments.[79] But whereas Baranī and Ibn Baṭṭūṭa, like al-ʿUmarī's informants, are also impressed by his generosity and by his concern for orthodoxy,[80] ʿIṣāmī – a hostile witness writing for a rival monarch in the breakaway Bahmanid Sultanate of the Deccan – has nothing good to say of him following an alleged change in Muḥammad's temperament two years into the reign.[81] For ʿIṣāmī, Muḥammad is above all an apostate who consorts with Hindus and has thereby rendered it lawful for orthodox Muslims to repudiate his authority and to take his life. His suspension of the Friday khutba pending the arrival of a diploma from the caliph (the context supplied by Baranī) is distorted as the abrogation of the requirements of Islamic worship.[82] ʿIṣāmī, of course, makes no mention whatever of the caliphal diploma. In his account of the first check administered to the rebel forces of Nāṣir al-Dīn Ismāʿīl *Mukh in the Deccan, the insurgents are depicted as the 'faithful' (*mu'minān*) and Muḥammad's army as the forces of chaos (*fitna*).[83]

76 IB, II, 75–6, and III, 252–3 (tr. Gibb, 312–13, 676).

77 *Siyar*, 196.

78 K. A. Nizami, 'The impact of Ibn Taimiyya on South Asia', *JIS* 1 (1990), 120–34.

79 *TFS*, 459, 460. *FS*, 446, 468, 472 (tr. 675, 704, 708–9). IB, III, 216, 295–316 (tr. Gibb, 657, 695–708), provides numerous examples.

80 Muḥammad's generosity: *TFS*, 460–2; IB, III, 216, 217, 243ff. (tr. Gibb, 657, 658, 671ff.); *MA*, ed. Spies, 21–5 (German tr. 47–51)/ed. Fāriq, 41–7 (tr. Siddiqi and Aḥmad, 46–50). His attention to orthodoxy: *TFS*, 459, 460; IB, III, 216, 286–8 (tr. Gibb, 657, 693–4); *MA*, ed. Spies, 21, 25–6 (tr. 46–7, 51–2)/ed. Fāriq, 38–41, 47–8 (tr. Siddiqi and Aḥmad, 45–6, 50–1).

81 *FS*, 424 (tr. 650).

82 *Ibid.*, 515 (tr. 764–5); cf. also 450–1 (tr. 681–2), where Muḥammad is compared unfavourably with the epic tyrant Ḍaḥḥāk. For the suspension of the prayers, see *TFS*, 492.

83 *FS*, 535 (tr. 790); see also 538 (tr. 793), and 520 (tr. 771) for a description of some of Muḥammad's supporters as 'enemies of the Prophet's faith'. For a contrast between the two authors, see Nizami, *On history and historians*, 133–4; Conermann, *Beschreibung Indiens*, 112–23.

Baranī's attitude is more complex. Muḥammad was 'the wonder of the age', who represented a truly bewildering combination of the opposing qualities required in a sovereign (above, p. 54): in particular, he (Muḥammad) failed to distinguish between the duties of sultan and prophet.[84] The differences between the two recensions of his work are at their most glaring in their treatment of this reign, and Dr Hardy, in a comparison of the two versions, has drawn attention to the fact that the second is more moralistic in tone and attributes a greater degree of responsibility to the sultan.[85] Dedicating his work to Muḥammad's successor, a trusted servant of the late monarch whose own reign nevertheless witnessed a reaction against Muḥammad's excesses, Baranī is evidently anxious to distance himself from the previous regime. It seems that his need to do so grew between the two versions of the *Ta'rīkh*.[86] For Baranī, the most heinous feature of Muḥammad's government had been the slaughter of Muslims, and in particular the harsh punishments meted out to the 'ulama', shaykhs, sayyids, sufis, qalandars and members of the clerical and military classes.[87] But having been in attendance on Muḥammad for over seventeen years as a boon companion (*nadīm*),[88] Baranī was himself implicated in these crimes. Thus he is at pains to express remorse at his own fear of speaking out against his late master's policies or of offering Muḥammad salutary advice.[89] It is, however, difficult to assess what use Baranī made of his *Fatāwā-yi Jahāndārī* as a vehicle for criticism of the late sultan. The picture he draws of the tyrant Yazdagird, for instance, is in some (though by no means all) respects reminiscent of Muḥammad.[90]

For all its defects, Baranī's *Ta'rīkh* (particularly the later recension) operates on a far higher plane than 'Iṣāmī's work. The gulf between the two men emerges clearly in their handling of the creation of a second capital at Dawlatābād in the Deccan and of other enterprises such as the adoption of the so-called token currency and the ill-fated Qarāchīl expedition. 'Iṣāmī, whose aged grandfather had died soon after leaving Delhi for the south in the original emigration, devotes considerable space to the enormity of the

84 *TFS*, 457–60. See the comments of Hardy, *Historians*, 37, and 'Didactic historical writing', 49–51.

85 *Ibid.*, 51–7.

86 Iqtidar Husain Siddiqui, 'Fresh light on Ḍiyā' al-Dīn Baranī: the doyen of the Indo-Persian historians of medieval India', *IC* 63 (1989), 71–7.

87 *TFS*, 460, 472, 497, for Muslims in general; 459, 465–6 for the ᶜulama' etc.

88 In *TFS*[1], Bodleian ms., fol. 196a/Digby Coll. ms., fol. 163b, he describes himself as *dar miyān-i nudamā'*. *TFS*, 504, for the number of years; cf. also 466, 497, where he calls himself a *muqarrab*.

89 *Ibid.*, 466–7, 497, 517, for his silence; see also the comments of I. Habib, 'Barani's theory', 102.

90 *FJ*, 264–6. Yazdagird bribes an invader to retire, rather as Muḥammad, in one tradition, is said to have bought off the Chaghadayid khan Tarmashirin (see p. 232, n.101); and thereafter, like Muḥammad, raises the land tax (*kharāj*) by one-fifth and one-tenth (*yakī ba-panj-u yakī ba-dah*) in order to recruit a fresh army: see below, p. 262. But his fate (being torn to pieces by his resentful subjects) does not resemble Muḥammad's.

Dawlatābād project.[91] He sees Muḥammad's tyranny as a divine punishment for the readiness of Delhi's citizens to tolerate heresy and religious innovation (*bid'at*); the death of the saint Niẓām al-Dīn Awliyā' (725/1325) leaves the city bereft of the protection of his spiritual power; and the token currency and the Qarāchīl campaign become yet further means of victimizing the capital when Muḥammad perceives that the exodus of its leading families has not sufficiently crippled its prosperity.[92] We have here an echo of stories about the sultan's antipathy towards the people of the capital that were current when Ibn Baṭṭūṭa visited Delhi a few years later.[93] The idea that Muḥammad b. Tughluq, like certain of his predecessors (above, p. 59), regarded the citizens of Delhi with suspicion and hostility is not as outlandish as it might first seem; though precisely why he may have done so is obscure. As the chief impulse behind the establishment of the second capital, however, this is quite unconvincing. Baranī is doubtless more realistic in pointing to the geographical location of Dawlatābād, which made it ideally suited to be the centre of a considerably expanded Sultanate. This is a perspective found also in external sources; although as Roy observed, another reason for the sultan's choice of Dawlatābād was the desire to implant Islam more securely in the Deccan.[94]

In outline the analysis of Muḥammad b. Tughluq's reign given in Baranī's revised *Ta'rīkh* is the best thing we have, and it does provide a reasonably serviceable framework. An air of brilliance conceivably hung over the early years of the reign, and deluded Muḥammad, who enjoyed the strong position of being the first designated heir to succeed his father as sultan of Delhi, into believing that nothing lay beyond his capacities. Almost from the moment of his accession, the extensive tracts that now owed obedience to him were subjected to a control of greater intensity than in the time of any of his predecessors.[95] Baranī claims that had he reduced the whole world he would not have tolerated the least island or closet being exempt from his authority (a view faintly echoed by one of al-'Umarī's informants, who believed that only the islands and a mere span of coastline lay outside Muḥammad's empire);[96] and it certainly seems that he was determined to impose uniformity upon his dominions. Unfortunately, his vision proved impossible to realize, and his efforts to implement it led to the loss of a significant proportion of his empire. But although Baranī's insights

91 *FS*, 447–8 (tr. 677–8).
92 *Ibid.*, 424, 446, 454–6, 459–60, 466, 468 (tr. 650–1, 675–6, 686–9, 693, 702, 704). On ᶜIṣāmī's perspective, see also HN, 507.
93 IB, III, 314–15 (tr. Gibb, 707–8).
94 *TFS*, 473–4; also *TFS*[1], Bodleian ms., fols. 190b-191a/Digby Coll. ms., fols. 159b–160a. al-Ṣafadī, *Wāfī*, III, 174 (tr. Khān, 188); see also al-Ṣafadī, *Aᶜyān al-ᶜAṣr*, SK ms. Aşir Efendi 588, fol. 2a. N. B. Roy, 'The transfer of capital from Delhi to Daulatabad', *JIH* 20 (1941), 159–80 (esp. 160–8).
95 *TFS*, 468, 469. *TMS*, 97–8.
96 *TFS*, 458. *MA*, ed. Spies, 5 (German tr. 23)/ed. Fāriq, 11 (tr. Siddiqi and Aḥmad, 29).

are not therefore to be dismissed out of hand, the emphasis laid in the second recension on the illusory character of Muḥammad's enterprises is in fact highly tendentious, in that it plays down the connections between them (see chapter 13).

On Muḥammad's death in 752/1351, the army commanders and other leading figures present in Sind prevailed upon the late sultan's cousin and *amīr-ḥājib*, Fīrūz b. Rajab, to accept the throne; and after expressing a reluctance that may not have been totally assumed, he did so. The accession of Fīrūz Shāh did not go unchallenged. The claims of the the late monarch's nephew, Dāwar Malik, were advanced by his mother, Tughluq's daughter Khudāwandzāda, who was dissuaded by the amirs on the grounds of her son's inexperience.[97] In the capital the wazir Khwāja Jahān Aḥmad b. Ayaz had set up as sultan an alleged child of Muḥammad's as Ghiyāth al-Dīn Maḥmūd Shāh.[98] As Fīrūz Shāh moved on Delhi, he was joined by a great many notables who had deserted Khwāja Jahān. Eventually the wazir himself appeared in an attitude of humble submission. Fīrūz Shāh was disposed to be merciful, but yielded to pressure from his amirs, who were out for the old wazir's blood. Khwāja Jahān, despatched to his new iqtaʿ of Sāmāna, was overtaken and executed by Shīr Khān, its current muqtaʿ. A few of his associates were likewise put to death;[99] but the fate of the child sultan he had enthroned is a mystery.

Regarding this affair the sources differ. The *Sīrat-i Fīrūz-Shāhī*, which refers to several later plots against Fīrūz Shāh in the vaguest of terms, is even less forthcoming about the reaction at Delhi to the news of Muḥammad's death, making no mention of the child sultan and merely condemning the treachery of the wazir.[100] The most plausible account is given by ʿAfīf. The wazir, who was now the sole member present in Delhi of the triumvirate set up by Muḥammad to head the government during his absence, heard reports not simply of Muḥammad's death but also of upheavals in which Fīrūz and Tatar Khān had disappeared. After performing the mourning ceremonies both for the late sultan and for Fīrūz, to whom he was sincerely attached, the wazir enthroned a child of Muḥammad and distributed largesse in order to buttress the infant ruler's position. Only when it was too late to draw back did he learn that the troops in Sind had raised up Fīrūz

[97] She and her husband Khusraw Malik were later foiled in a bid to assassinate the sultan and were punished: ᶜAfīf, 45, 100–4. For the parentage of Dāwar Malik and the confusion in the sources between him and Khusraw Malik (who was actually his stepfather), see Hodivala, *Studies*, I, 309–10.

[98] *TMS*, 120, is the only literary source to give the style of the infant monarch, for whose coins see *CMSD*, 154 (nos 648–648B); J. G. Delmerick, 'Note on a new gold coin of Mahmúd Sháh bin Muḥammad Sháh bin Tughluq Sháh of Dihlí', *JASB*, 43 (1874), 97–8.

[99] *TFS*, 534–47. ᶜAfīf, 57–78.

[100] *SFS*, 12–13 (tr. Basu, *JBORS*, 22 [1936], 265ff.). For the plots, see *ibid.*, 7–12 (tr. Basu, 101–7); also *TFS*, 552, for an attempt to poison Fīrūz Shāh.

Shāh as sultan.[101] ʿAfīf appears to accept the boy as genuine;[102] and he expressly challenges the story that was current in his day – and retailed, for instance, by Baranī – in which the wazir set up some 'bastard child' (*walad al-zanāʾī*) after learning of the accession of Fīrūz Shāh, and scattered gifts with a view to the imminent struggle for the throne.[103] It is noteworthy that Baranī is the sole author to claim that Muḥammad had designated Fīrūz Shāh as his heir (*walī-ʿahd*).[104]

It is not easy to explain these discrepancies. The grounds for Baranī's stance are especially problematic. He is known to have suffered a loss of favour under the new sultan and been imprisoned for some time in the stronghold of Bhatnēr.[105] The earlier recension of his work is more outspoken regarding the dismissal and execution of Muḥammad's servitors by Fīrūz Shāh; the revised version, on the other hand, strikes a more positive note, contrasting that ruler's leniency with the bloodshed that had been required to ensure the triumph of previous Delhi Sultans.[106] It therefore looks as if one of the purposes behind the redrafting of the *Taʾrīkh-i Fīrūz-Shāhī* was to curry favour with the new monarch. ʿAfīf, writing well after Fīrūz Shāh's death, was perhaps under less pressure to lend legitimacy to his accession; although even he retails stories in which saints as eminent as the sufi shaykhs Niẓām al-Dīn Awliyāʾ and ʿAlāʾ al-Dīn Ajūdhanī predicted Fīrūz Shāh's sovereignty, and stresses that the caliphal patents that reached Fīrūz Shāh came unsolicited, in contrast with the recognition that Muḥammad had obtained only on request.[107]

Completing the revised version of his *Taʾrīkh-i Fīrūz-Shāhī* in 758/1357, Baranī was in a position only to assess Fīrūz Shāh's policies during his first few years. Yet he had little doubt what those policies were. There had been no milder sovereign than Fīrūz Shāh since the capture of Delhi; and no previous sultan had avoided shedding blood to the extent that Fīrūz Shāh had done with regard to Khwāja Jahān's supporters;[108] the harsh punishments of previous reigns were now discarded; spies and informers were a

[101] ᶜAfīf, 50–3. *TMS*, 119–20, gives a similar but briefer version.
[102] ᶜAfīf, 50, 60, 68, 396; cf. also 54, where the view of the army commanders in Sind, that Muḥammad had no son, is reported without comment.
[103] *TFS*, 539; *TFS*¹, Bodleian ms., fol. 212a, calls the child also *ghulāmzāda*. *TMS*, 120, describes him as 'of unknown ancestry and non-existent lineage' (*majhūl al-nasab-u mafqūd al-ḥasab*). al-Ṣafadī, *Wāfī*, III, 172–3 (tr. Khān, 187), heard that Muḥammad was incapable of fathering children. The boy is accepted as a genuine son of Muḥammad by Haig, 'Five questions', 365–72, and by Jamini Mohan Banerjee, *History of Firuz Shah Tughluq* (Delhi, 1967), 15–16. Husain, *Tughluq dynasty*, 387–8, and B. P. Saksena, in HN, 569–71, are noncommittal.
[104] *TFS*, 532; cf. also 539.
[105] Baranī, *Naᶜt-i Muḥammadī*, cited in M. Habib, 'Life and thought of Ziyauddin Barani', in M. Habib and A. U. S. Khan, *The political theory of the Delhi Sultanate* (Delhi, 1960), 162 (repr. in Nizami, *Politics and society*, II, 348–9). See also *TFS*, 125, 554, 557, and other references in *PL*, I, 506. I. Habib, 'Baranī's theory', 102.
[106] *TFS*¹, Bodleian ms., fol. 217a; *TFS*, 547–52. Siddiqui, 'Fresh light', 78–9.
[107] ᶜAfīf, 27–9, 273–4, 276. [108] *TFS*, 548, 551–2.

thing of the past.[109] The soldiery enjoyed unprecedented ease: they were able to benefit from the revenues of their villages without even having to serve in the field.[110] The new sultan's concern also for the welfare of the 'religious class', to which Baranī devotes a whole section of his work,[111] had been demonstrated at the very outset, in the course of his long journey from Thatta to Delhi. At Sīwistān he had restored to the 'ulama', the shaykhs and other notables the pensions, stipends and estates that Muḥammad had confiscated (presumably at the time of Qayṣar's rebellion: below, p. 271) and bestowed alms on the *faqīrs* and wayfarers. At Uchch he rebuilt the dilapidated khanaqah of Shaykh Jamāl al-Dīn and returned to the shaykh's grandsons their estates and orchards which his predecessor had resumed to the khalisa. The petitions of the people of Multān were granted, and gifts were made to the impoverished family of Shaykh Farīd al-Dīn at Ajūdhan.[112]

In some measure, these can be viewed as the policies of a new monarch with an insecure title and a consequent need to buy support. For this same reason – to avoid a recurrence of the troubles that had afflicted his predecessor – the sultan made concessions to the nobility and the military class. It was especially necessary for Fīrūz Shāh to promote an image that contrasted with Muḥammad's; and indeed the policies he followed tell us a good deal about those of Muḥammad which had aroused such resentment. In his *Futūḥāt* the sultan himself reveals clearly the orthodox Islamic credentials for which he wished to be remembered: the abandonment of draconian punishments; the abolition of uncanonical taxes; the suppression of deviant forms of Islamic practice; the destruction of newly built Hindu temples; the promotion of conversion to Islam among the Hindu populace; the foundation of new mosques and madrasas; the repair of structures erected by past Muslim sovereigns; and humble attentiveness to Muslim saints. Similar preoccupations – though with the addition of holy warfare against the infidel – are reflected in the *Sīrat*.[113]

Such attitudes might not necessarily have sprung from devotion alone. 'Afīf's *Ta'rīkh-i Fīrūz-Shāhī* reveals that it was Fīrūz Shāh's practice to visit and pray at the shrines of saints and past sultans on the eve of all his campaigns, as he did for instance before marching against Thatta;[114] and his halts at shrines in Sind had doubtless been designed to ensure victory over the faction of Khwāja Jahān. In any case we are told later that the sultan made a point of visiting shrines whenever he was out riding.[115] 'Afīf strongly suggests, in fact, that Fīrūz Shāh continued to identify himself with orthodox piety and with the interests of the religious élite throughout his

[109] *Ibid.*, 557, 572–4. [110] *Ibid.*, 553. [111] *Ibid.*, 558–61.
[112] *Ibid.*, 537–9, 543.
[113] For an interesting assessment of the sultan, see Khurram Qadir, 'Firoz Shah (Tughlaq): a personality study', *JCA* 9 (1986), no. 2, 17–39.
[114] ʿAfīf, 194–6; and see also 230–1, 250. [115] *Ibid.*, 371.

reign, even to the extent of having his head shaved like that of a sufi disciple (*murshid*) after the death of his heir Fatḥ Khān in 778/1376; it was immediately after this that he prohibited all practices in his dominions that were contrary to the Sharīʿa.[116]

In military terms Fīrūz Shāh's reign was undistinguished. He was obliged to acquiesce in the loss of the Deccan and the far south, and his few campaigns to the east – against Bengal in 754/1353 and 760/1359 and Jājnagar in *c.* 761/1360 – achieved little. His sole successes were the subjection of the Hindu ruler of Nagarkōt (Kāngra) in 766/1364–5 and the submission, after two invasions, of the Jāms of Thatta (767/1365–6). A whole section of ʿAfīf's *Ta'rīkh* is devoted to the sultan's abandonment of distant campaigns (there were still forays to regions nearer at hand, such as the Sirmūr hills, Katēhr and Etāwa)[117] and his concentration on settling the affairs of state.[118] But the reasons given vary. First ʿAfīf tells us that when the wazir Khān Jahān (I) deflected him from invading the Deccan Fīrūz Shāh promised not to lead an army against his co-religionists again,[119] a sentiment that recalls the inhibitions of Jalāl al-Dīn Khaljī. Elsewhere ʿAfīf provides what seems like an alternative explanation for the abandonment of military exploits: during the blockade of Thatta, Fīrūz Shāh allegedly vowed that if he reduced the place he would turn to other affairs.[120] At yet later points in the biography, the sultan is said to have given up campaigning after the death of the highly efficient and trusted Khān Jahān in 770/1368–9 (which would in fact have occurred soon after the end of the Thatta enterprise).[121] These various attempts to account for the sultan's military inactivity in his later years suggest, in fact, that his biographer may have found the matter a source of embarrassment. In the assertion that Fīrūz Shāh's victories caused the people to forget war and to neglect weaponry, there is just a hint that his government undermined the Sultanate's military capacity.[122]

ʿAfīf and the two authors who cover the entire reign, Sirhindī and Bihāmadkhānī, claim that the era was characterized by prosperity, justice, clemency and security. Old men assured Sirhindī that there had been no ruler more just, more merciful or more God-fearing since Nāṣir al-Dīn Maḥmūd Shāh.[123] The cheapness and plenty of the reign, according to

116 *Ibid.*, 372–3. The date is given as 777/1376: *ibid.*, 379. But Fatḥ Khān's death is later dated Ṣafar 778/June-July 1376, *ibid.*, 493–4, although *TMS*, 131–2, supplies the date 12 Ṣafar 776/23 July 1374.

117 *Ibid.*, 134–5. ʿAfīf, 493, 497. The dates given are inconsistent.

118 *Ibid.*, 261–7. 119 *Ibid.*, 266. 120 *Ibid.*, 216.

121 *Ibid.*, 399, 424. For the year of Khān Jahān's death, which is variously given as 770 (*ibid.*, 345) and 772 (*ibid.*, 422; *TMS*, 131), see Hodivala, *Studies*, I, 339, who opts for the earlier date.

122 ʿAfīf, 23. See further the comments of Hardy, 'Force and violence', 178.

123 *TMS*, 140–1. ʿAfīf, 94, 99–100, 178–80, 193, 456, 512. Bihāmadkhānī, fol. 407b (tr. Zaki, 4). See also the remarks in *TFS*, 553–4.

ʿAfīf, made Fīrūz Shāh's subjects forget the prosperity even of ʿAlāʾ al-Dīn's time; and whereas ʿAlāʾ al-Dīn had brought about low prices by decree, under Fīrūz Shāh they materialized without any effort on the part of the government.[124] Yet Bihāmadkhānī and Sirhindī wrote at a time when the Sultanate was a mere shadow of its former self; ʿAfīf, for his part, completed his biography in the wake of years of internecine strife among Fīrūz Shāh's descendants which had already erupted before he died, on 18 Ramaḍān 790/20 September 1388, and after the major cataclysm that was Temür's sack of Delhi in 801/1398.[125] Thus Fīrūz Shāh could be apostrophized, in terms evocative of the Prophet himself, as 'the seal (*khatm*) of the sovereigns of Delhi'. More strikingly, perhaps, ʿAfīf presents the sultan as a holy man; and the remark that the fall of Delhi ensued upon his death, with its hint that only his existence there had kept the city from destruction, forcefully echoes the idea of spiritual power (*baraka*), found in sufi literature, that we noticed earlier.[126] If Baranī measured the opening years of the reign against the background of Muḥammad's regime, for these later authors Fīrūz Shāh's day took on the colours of a golden age by comparison with what followed.[127]

124 ᶜAfīf, 293–4.

125 *Ibid.*, 133, where the sack is described as recent. But the fact that at 314–15 Temür is referred to, not in opprobrious terms, but by the appellation 'Ṣāḥib-Qirān' ('Lord of the Fortunate Conjunction') favoured in the Timurid sources, suggests that ᶜAfīf wrote under the Sayyids (i.e. after 1414), who acknowledged Timurid overlordship (below, pp. 318–19, 322).

126 ᶜAfīf, 21–2, 28. Digby, 'The sufi *shaykh* and the sultan', 77 and n.69. For an overview of ᶜAfīf's treatment of the sultan, see Hardy, *Historians*, 41–51.

127 ᶜAfīf, 292–3. For the importance to ᶜAfīf of Temür's attack, see Hardy, *Historians*, 41 (and cf. also 55).

CHAPTER 9

The Khaljī and Tughluqid nobility

The emergence of a new élite

We saw earlier (pp. 83–5) how at 'Alā' al-Dīn Khaljī's accession the nobility was little changed from that of the Ghiyathids. Only after a year or two did the new sultan move against the older aristocracy which he had inherited from his uncle and a noble class emerge which differed substantially from that of Balaban and Kayqubād. Baranī divides 'Alā' al-Dīn's reign into three periods, of which the first was the era of men who were closely linked with his seizure of the throne; the important figures of the second period appear to have been largely bureaucrats; and the third, lasting for four or five years, was dominated by the malign influence of the slave commander Kāfūr, by now the sultan's viceroy and hence generally called in the sources 'Malik Nā'ib'.[1]

The obscurity surrounding the origins of many of 'Alā' al-Dīn's nobles is perhaps only to be expected. Some of the new élite would have been of Khalaj stock, and like his predecessor the new sultan at first promoted close kinsmen, like his brother Almās Beg, now Ulugh Khān, who was made *bārbeg* (*amīr-ḥājib*) and given the iqta' of Bhayāna; subsequently, in 700/1301, he was granted the newly reduced territory of Ranthanbōr and Jhāyin as his iqta'.[2] Sanjar, entitled Alp Khān, who served 'Alā' al-Dīn as *amīr-i majlis*, was his wife's brother: at one point 'Iṣāmī says that 'Alā' al-Dīn had reared him since his childhood. He held Multān for a time and was later transferred to the iqta' of Gujarāt in *c.* 1310.[3] Of 'Alā' al-Dīn's brother's sons one, Sulaymān Shāh, became *wakīl-i dar* and received the style of Ikit Khān, while another was granted the title of Qutlugh Khān.[4] A maternal nephew, Hizabr al-Dīn Yūsuf, became Ẓafar Khān and *'āriḍ*.[5]

Apart from his kinsmen, the two principal amirs in the early years of the

[1] *TFS*, 336–7. [2] *Ibid.*, 242, 272, 283.

[3] *FS*, 287, 288 (tr. 461, 463), for his iqta'^c^s; *ibid.*, 338 (tr. 519), for his upbringing. The reading ḤRBWN found alongside Alp Khān's name in *TMS*, 71, is an error for *khusurpūra* ('father-in-law's son'), the reading of one of the mss.; this term is also used of him in *TFS*, 242.

[4] *Ibid.*, 273. *FS*, 259, 279 (tr. 431, 453). [5] *TFS*, 240, 242, 248. *TMS*, 71.

reign were both men who had formed part of ʿAlāʾ al-Dīn's entourage in Kara and Awadh prior to his accession. ʿAlāʾ al-Mulk, Baranī's uncle, first acted as the new sultan's lieutenant in Kara and Awadh and was then summoned to Delhi to become kotwal in succession to the former Malik al-Umarāʾ Fakhr al-Dīn.[6] The other, Malik Nuṣrat Jalēsarī, obtained at ʿAlāʾ al-Dīn's accession the title of Nuṣrat Khān; he may well have been of relatively humble origin, as doubtless were many of these old associates.[7] Nuṣrat Khān, who was instrumental in securing enormous sums for the treasury from the elimination of the Jalālī nobles, was one of the new sultan's most trusted amirs, and it is significant that ʿAlāʾ al-Dīn departed from the practice of his predecessors in making Nuṣrat Khān simultaneously his na'ib and kotwal of Delhi. In the following year he became wazir and surrendered the office of kotwal to ʿAlāʾ al-Mulk, after which he obtained the iqtaʿ of Kara.[8]

It was a source of grim satisfaction to Baranī that those of ʿAlāʾ al-Dīn's henchmen who participated in his uncle's murder all perished within a few years.[9] Ẓafar Khān, who had played a distinguished role against the invading Mongols, fell in battle with them in *c.* 1300.[10] If we are to believe the chronicler, who employs his uncle as a vehicle for advice to the sultan, ʿAlāʾ al-Mulk was still alive at the time of Qutlugh Qocha's attack; but he presumably died not long afterwards. Nuṣrat Khān perished during the siege of Ranthanbōr in 700/1300–1.[11] To what further heights this powerful officer might have risen, had he survived, can only be guessed. Members of his family also attained prominence: a brother, Malik ʿIzz al-Dīn, *amīr-ḥājib* to Ulugh Khān, had been killed by the neo-Muslim Mongols who mutinied on the Gujarāt expedition, and a nephew, Malik Fakhr al-Dīn *Qochu, is subsequently found in possession of the iqtaʿ of Kara (probably in succession to his uncle) and in command of the troops of 'the east, Bengal and Tirhut' in 702–3/1302–3, when he accompanied the *dādbeg* Fakhr al-Dīn ʿAlī Jawna on the abortive campaign against Arangal.[12] But the subsequent history of this emerging aristocratic dynasty is unknown.

Certain of the sultan's kinsmen may well have proved a disappointment to him. Baranī heard that Ulugh Khān died suddenly while planning an ambitious campaign to the far south: ʿIṣāmī transmits a rumour that he had been poisoned for reacting too swiftly to a false rumour of the sultan's

[6] *TFS*, 250 (reading, with BL ms., fol. 130b, *az maḥlūl-i malik al-umarā-yi qadīm*), 257.
[7] Iqtidar Husain Siddiqi, 'The nobility under the Khalji Sultans', *IC* 37 (1963), 59–60.
[8] *TFS*, 248, 249, 250, 272.
[9] *Ibid.*, 236–7. They included also Malik Aṣgharī the *sar-i dawātdār* and Malik Jawna the *dādbeg*, of whom little is known, apart from their offices.
[10] *Ibid.*, 253–4, 260–1. *FS*, 259, 262–7 (tr. 431, 434–40).
[11] *TFS*, 255–7, 266–72, for ʿAlāʾ al-Mulk; 272 for Nuṣrat Khān.
[12] ʿIzz al-Dīn: *ibid.*, 252. Fakhr al-Dīn: *TFS*[1], Digby Coll. ms., fol. 113a; *TFS*, 300 (reading QJW, with BL ms., fol. 149a, for the JHJW of the text).

death.[13] Ikit Khān aspired to emulate his uncle's success in seizing the throne. During a hunting excursion at Tilpat on the march towards Ranthanbōr (*c.* 1301), his men fired at ʿAlāʾ al-Dīn, who was, however, merely wounded. Duped by the sultan's paik guards into believing that ʿAlāʾ al-Dīn was really dead, Ikit Khān had himself proclaimed sovereign. But when ʿAlāʾ al-Dīn appeared on the scene, the troops rallied to him, and Ikit Khān was killed as he fled; his brother Qutlugh Khān was also put to death.[14] Not long afterwards, two of ʿAlāʾ al-Dīn's sister's sons, ʿUmar Khān and Mengü Khān, who held the iqtaʿs of Badāʾūn and Awadh respectively, were executed for treasonable designs.[15]

Our information regarding the amirs on whom ʿAlāʾ al-Dīn relied during the central part of his reign is relatively meagre; but the list given by Baranī suggests that they belonged in the main to the bureaucracy. They included Malik Ḥamīd al-Dīn, the son of ʿUmdat al-Mulk Khwāja ʿAlā-yi Dabīr, who became *nāʾib-i wakīl-i dar*, and his brother Malik ʿIzz al-Dīn, who was made chief secretary of the empire (*dabīr-i mamālik*): the brothers' rise seems to date from around the time of Ikit Khān's conspiracy and the Ranthanbōr campaign. Other major figures were Sharaf Qāʾinī, the *nāʾib-wazīr*, who is credited with imposing a uniform system of tax assessment on an unprecedented number of provinces (see chapter 12); ʿAyn al-Mulk Multānī, who had began his career as secretary (*dabīr*) to Ulugh Khān; and Khwāja Naṣīr al-Mulk Sirāj al-Dīn Ḥājjī, the *nāʾib-i ʿarḍ-i mamālik*, who later accompanied Kāfūr on his southern campaigns.[16] Although the ascendancy of these men may have stemmed from an increasing reluctance on ʿAlāʾ al-Dīn's part to depend on his relatives, it is also clearly linked with his administrative and military reforms, which enabled him to maintain the armies that both repelled the formidable Mongol threat, conquered a number of Hindu states in Rajasthan and the Yadava kingdom of Dēōgīr, and plundered the far south.

Appropriately enough for a sovereign whose reign was marked by numerous battles with invading Mongols, ʿAlāʾ al-Dīn's relations with Mongol amirs within India did not run smoothly. Baranī suggests that many or all of them forfeited their stipends.[17] Certain of these 'neo-Muslim' commanders accompanied the Gujarāt expedition in 698–9/1299–1300 and mutinied when the sultan's generals tried to deprive them of part of their plunder. The outbreak collapsed, and some fled to Karnadēva, the Vāghela

[13] *TFS*, 283. *FS*, 281–2 (tr. 456–7).
[14] *TFS*, 273–6. *FS*, 279–81 (tr. 453–5). A briefer account is given in IB, III, 185–6 (tr. Gibb, 641). For a distorted account that reached Mongol Persia, see Qāshānī, 190–2.
[15] *TFS*, 277–8.
[16] For Baranī's list, see *ibid.*, 337. On Ḥamīd al-Dīn and his brother, see also *ibid.*, 274–5, 282. For Sharaf Qāʾinī's activities, *ibid.*, 288–9 (the correct reading QAYNY is found in BL ms., fols. 143, 167a); see also Hodivala, *Studies*, I, 278. Khwāja Ḥājjī: *KF*, 82, 85, where his full style is given; *RI*, II, 56–60; *TFS*, 326, 328, 333.
[17] *Ibid.*, 334.

king of Gujarāt, while others sought refuge at Ranthanbōr. ʿAlāʾ al-Dīn took a terrible vengeance on their families in Delhi.[18] In the following year, Ikit Khān in his bid for the throne drew support from some neo-Muslim Mongol horsemen in his service; their subsequent fate is unknown.[19] Still later, during Kāfūr's Maʿbar campaign, a Mongol commander named Abachi planned to betray the Delhi forces to the enemy and to kill Kāfūr. The plot failed, and the sultan had Abachi executed in Delhi. In reaction, the Mongols in the capital, who allegedly numbered more than 10,000, conspired to kill ʿAlāʾ al-Dīn and to replace him with their own nominee, whereupon the sultan issued orders to his muqtaʿs to arrest all the Mongols in the empire and put them to death.[20] The victims may have included ʿAlī Beg and *Tartaq, who had commanded the Mongol invading forces in 705/1305 (below, p. 227) and had been recruited into the sultan's service.[21]

It seems that Turkish slaves now played a more restricted role than under the Shamsid and Ghiyathid monarchs. Only a few amirs – notably Ikhtiyār al-Dīn Temür, who appears as muqtaʿ of Chandērī and Ērach in an inscription of 711/1312 with the sobriquet 'Sulṭānī' (i.e. a slave of the reigning sultan), and Ikhtiyār al-Dīn Tegin, muqtaʿ of Awadh – are known from their names to have been Turks.[22] The apparent decline in the number of Turkish slave nobles may have been a matter of policy – a reluctance on ʿAlāʾ al-Dīn's part to allow Turkish ghulams the stranglehold on the administration that they had enjoyed in the thirteenth century. It could also have been a reflection of the rising cost of such slaves, since Baranī complains that their price had risen prohibitively by his day;[23] though this did not prevent the future sultan Muḥammad b. Tughluq from accumulating large numbers of Turkish slaves in the early 1320s (see below, pp. 183–4).

The partial eclipse of Turkish slave amirs could well be connected with the rise of two new groups of whom we first hear during this middle phase of ʿAlāʾ al-Dīn's reign. Afghans had served Balaban and Kayqubād (above, p. 62), and appear to have regularly formed part of the garrison troops of the Multān province, where they are found both under Muḥammad the 'Martyr Prince' and under Küshlü Khān in the early Tughluqid era.[24] But it is now that they first seem to have provided officers of high rank like Malik Ikhtiyār al-Dīn *Mall, listed by Baranī among the sultan's nobles and later described as one of his great maliks.[25] The other category is ʿAlāʾ al-Dīn's

[18] *Ibid.*, 252–3. *FS*, 253–5 (tr. 424–5). [19] *TFS*, 273.
[20] *FS*, 296–7, 298–9 (tr. 470–1, 473–4). *TFS*, 334–6, setting the total number slain at 20 or 30,000. *TMS*, 75, dates this episode in 697 and evidently confuses it with the mutiny on the Gujarāt campaign.
[21] *KF*, 41. *FS*, 305 (tr. 481–2).
[22] The readings in *TFS* (241, NKYN, JBAR; 323, BKTN), should be corrected from BL ms., fols. 125b–126a, 160b. For Temür, see also Desai, 'Chanderi inscription'.
[23] *TFS*, 314. [24] *TS*, IOL Persian ms. 412, fol. 52. IB, III, 322 (tr. Gibb, 712).
[25] *TFS*, 240–1, 448. See I. H. Siddiqui, 'The Afghāns and their emergence in India as ruling elite during the Delhi Sultanate period', *CAJ* 26 (1982), 252 and n.45.

Indian slave officers. A later source alleges that ʿAlā' al-Dīn possessed 50,000 slaves,[26] of whom the majority would have been Indians. The victorious campaigns by his forces against a number of major independent Hindu kingdoms afforded greater opportunities for the acquisition of choice Indian slaves, and it is in ʿAlā' al-Dīn's reign that we first encounter their promotion to high office. The earliest to be mentioned is Shāhīn, an obscure figure whom ʿIṣāmī calls the sultan's adopted son and Kāfūr's predecessor as na'ib. Put in command of Chitōr on its capture in 703/1303, he later took fright following Ulugh Khān's death and joined the exiled ruler of Gujarāt.[27] Malik Dīnār, who served ʿAlā' al-Dīn as *shiḥna-yi pīl*, was also an Indian slave.[28] Malik Nānak, another slave, helped to save ʿAlā' al-Dīn's life when his nephew Ikit Khān made a bid for the throne in *c.* 1301, and was *ākhūrbeg* and muqtaʿ of Sāmāna and Sunnām by 705/1305, when he defeated an invading Mongol army.[29] Indian slave officers were not necessarily converts to Islam: Amīr Khusraw expressly refers to this engagement as the victory of an infidel over other infidels.[30]

The most celebrated of ʿAlā' al-Dīn's slave lieutenants, of course, is Kāfūr, an Indian captured from his owner in Kanbhāya (Cambay) during the first invasion of Gujarāt in 698/1299. Kāfūr, a eunuch, acquired the nickname *Hazārdīnārī* ('of the thousand dinars') from the price the sultan paid for him.[31] His early career in ʿAlā' al-Dīn's service is nowhere described, but he fought against the invading Mongols and held the rank of *bārbeg* by 706/1306–7, when he enjoyed the sultan's confidence sufficiently to be given command of the army that reimposed tribute on the Yadava kingdom of Dēōgīr.[32] Kāfūr's first known base was Rāprī, on the Yamuna, which was his iqtaʿ by 709/1309–10;[33] but towards the end of the reign he was in command at Dēōgīr, which had by then been annexed to the Sultanate (p. 202 below); the date of his appointment as na'ib is unknown.

During the final phase of the reign, ʿAlā' al-Dīn was losing his grip: Baranī regards as symptomatic his appointment of Ḥamīd al-Dīn Multānī, a royal chamberlain and door-keeper (*kalīd-dār*), as chief qadi of the empire.[34] Baranī's scattered observations elsewhere suggest that the sultan had ceased to trust the majority of his higher servitors. He proved increas-

[26] ʿAfīf, 272. [27] *FS*, 281–3 (tr. 456–7). [28] *TFS*, 388–9.

[29] *Ibid.*, 273, 320, 323 (reading MANK, NAYK and TATK respectively, but cf. BL ms., fols. 142a, 158b; Hodivala, *Studies*, I, 243–4, 372, and II, 96, takes the name as 'Nāyak'). *KF*, 38–9, confirming that he was a personal slave (*banda-yi khāṣṣ*). *FS*, 302–5 (tr. 479–81).

[30] *DR*, 61. *KF*, 38. Siddiqi, 'Nobility under the Khalji Sultans', 60 n.47. See also Amīr Khusraw, *Baqiyya Naqiyya*, IOL Persian ms. 412, fols. 357b–358a.

[31] *TFS*, 251–2. IB, III, 187 (tr. Gibb, 642), refers to him as *al-Alfī*, again in reference to the price paid for him. That he was a eunuch (*majbūb*) emerges from *DR*, 257, and *TFS*, 368. See generally S. Digby 'Kāfūr, Malik', *Enc.Isl.*[2].

[32] *KF*, 65; for other references to him as *amīr-ḥājib*, see *ibid.*, 89, 114.

[33] *TFS*, 328, 333. Yazdani, 'Inscriptions of the Khaljī Sulṭāns', 30.

[34] *TFS*, 352; cf. also 298.

ingly unwilling to take advice, trying to supervise the conduct of all state business in person and to this end, it appears, dispensing with the office of wazir, whose duties he fulfilled himself. Certain senior officers, such as Malik Qiran the *amīr-i shikār* and Malik Qirabeg, still enjoyed ʿAlāʾ al-Dīn's favour; but they had no power and were little more than courtiers. Experienced and skilled administrators were removed, and in their place the sultan relied on those whom Baranī terms lazy slaves (*ghulāmbachagān*) and indiscreet eunuchs. The sultan also sought to concentrate power in the hands of his own family and his slaves: as a result, he promoted his pleasure-loving heir Khiḍr Khān prematurely and became too dependent on Kāfūr.[35] From the fact that the brothers Ḥamīd al-Dīn and ʿIzz al-Dīn were dismissed from office, and Sharaf Qāʾinī was put to death,[36] it looks as if Kāfūr perceived these officers as a threat and prevailed upon ʿAlāʾ al-Dīn to carry out a purge.

ʿAlāʾ al-Dīn's final months, already marred by illness, were clouded by a bitter rivalry between Malik Nāʾib Kāfūr and Alp Khān which in Baranī's view destroyed his regime.[37] As maternal uncle to the sultan's heir Khiḍr Khān, Alp Khān had retained some power and influence almost to the very end of the reign, since in what was clearly a bid to secure the succession the sultan married one of Alp Khān's daughters to Khiḍr Khān and another to a younger son, Shādī Khān.[38] But Alp Khān and his two sons-in-law alike fell victim to the machinations of Kāfūr. The naʾib observed that the sultan was tiring of his chief wife, Alp Khān's sister and Khiḍr Khān's mother, and set to work to undermine the influence of this family group. ʿAlāʾ al-Dīn was brought to sanction the murder of Alp Khān in the royal palace, and Khiḍr Khān was first banished from court to Amrōha and then imprisoned in Gwāliyōr. The story that reached Persia was that Khiḍr Khān, his mother and Alp Khān had poisoned ʿAlāʾ al-Dīn, who was able, however, to execute them all before he died; and to some extent this is corroborated by Ibn Baṭṭūṭa, who heard that they had conspired to replace the sultan with his son.[39] The story may, of course, be nothing more than propaganda circulated by Kāfūr.

The ailing sultan altered the succession in favour of a younger son, Shihāb al-Dīn ʿUmar, whose mother was the daughter of Rāmadēva, the Yadava king of Dēōgīr, and who was duly enthroned by Kāfūr when ʿAlāʾ al-Dīn died in 715/1316.[40] It is tempting to see behind Kāfūr's coup d'état an Indian faction, comprising slaves fronted by a puppet sultan who was

[35] *Ibid.*, 334, 337–8, 367–8. *TFS*[1], Digby Coll. ms., fol. 138a, says that Kāfūr was made wazir.
[36] *TFS*, 337.
[37] *Ibid.*, 368. For what follows, see generally Lal, *History of the Khaljis*, 265ff. Apart from *TFS*, 368–9, the main sources are *FS*, 337–44 (tr. 517–24), and *TMS*, 79–81.
[38] *TFS*, 368. *FS*, 336 (tr. 516).
[39] Qāshānī, 193–4. IB, III, 187 (tr. Gibb, 641–2).
[40] *TFS*, 374, reading RAMDYW for ZAYDH, as proposed by Hodivala, *Studies*, II, 106, and found in BL ms., fol. 185b. The relationship is confirmed by *FS*, 343 (tr. 524).

himself half Indian; but the evidence does not permit us to do so. Kāfūr seems to have enjoyed the cooperation of Kamāl al-Dīn *Gurg* ('the wolf'), whose family originated from Kābul.[41] It was this officer whom he sent to subjugate Gujarāt when the province revolted on the news of Alp Khān's death; and Sirhindī even has Kamāl al-Dīn participating with Kāfūr in Alp Khān's murder.[42] More probably, therefore, the two groups we are dealing with represent merely the old 'establishment', perhaps centred on persons of Khalaj origin, and a faction composed of relative newcomers, from widely differing backgrounds, which looked to the na'ib for preferment.

Despite Kāfūr's activities, a sufficient number of ʿAlā'ī maliks survived to provide some kind of continuity. They included not only Temür and Tegin but also two important figures associated with the middle period – Khwāja Ḥājjī and ʿAyn al-Mulk Multānī, who remained respectively *ʿāriḍ* and governor of Mālwa.[43] Hūshang, the son of Kamāl al-Dīn 'Gurg' who had been killed at the time of ʿAlā' al-Dīn's death while trying to put down a revolt in Gujarāt, succeeded to his father's iqtaʿ of Jālōr.[44] Quṭb al-Dīn Mubārak Shāh gave Malik Dīnār the style of Ẓafar Khān and sent him to govern Gujarāt.[45] It was also to the young sultan's credit that he subsequently appointed as governor of Gujarāt the able and well-born Waḥīd al-Dīn Qurayshī. Little is known regarding the background of the sultan's maternal kin, of whom Muḥammad *Mūlāī became Shīr Khān.[46]

Kāfūr's removal did not bring to an end the influence of Indian slave elements. Quite the contrary, for during his brief reign of four years (716–20/1316–20) the new monarch came to rely inordinately on an Indian slave Ḥasan, captured during the Mālwa campaign of 705/1305. Ḥasan, whom the sultan had acquired from his *nā'ib-i khāṣṣ-ḥājib*, Malik Shādī, and who initially served as a member of the watch (*pāsbān*), obtained the dignity of wazir and the style of Khusraw Khān.[47] Like Kāfūr, he aimed high, and attempted to revolt while heading a campaign to the south; but when his colleagues reported his designs, the infatuated sultan refused to believe them and had them punished.[48] Khusraw Khān shortly murdered his master (720/1320) and himself became sultan. What enabled him to do so was the fact that Quṭb al-Dīn had allowed him to accumulate a personal retinue of Parwārī warriors from his homeland in the region of Bhīlmāl and Gujarāt, whom he then introduced into the Hazār Sutūn palace.[49]

41 See Desai, 'Jālor ᶜĪdgāh inscription', where he appears as Maḥmūd b. Muḥammad b. ᶜUmar Kābulī.

42 *TFS*, 369. *TMS*, 80. *FS*, 340–1 (tr. 520–2), has Kāfūr also sending Malik Dīnār against the Gujarāt rebels.

43 *NS*, 100, 112. *TFS*, 379, 388.

44 Kamāl al-Dīn: *ibid.*, 369, 388. Hūshang: *ibid.*, 379–80 (with ŠWSMK in error for HWŠNG); *Tughluq-Nāma*, 57, 65.

45 *TFS*, 381, 388–9; and cf. also 379. *FS*, 360 (tr. 558).

46 *TFS*, 381.

47 *Ibid. TMS*, 82–3, for Khusraw Khān as *pāsbān*; also 86.

48 *TFS*, 399–400.

49 *Ibid.*, 402; and see Hodivala, *Studies*, I, 288. Khusraw Khān's brother Ḥasan had already

The Tughluqid coup and its beneficiaries

The origins of Tughluq, who had served ʿAlāʾ al-Dīn for many years as muqtaʿ of Dēōpālpūr, are a matter of controversy.[50] No other source corroborates the assertion by certain near-contemporary authors writing in the Mamlūk empire that he was a slave.[51] We can also, I suggest, discount the details obtained at Lahore over three centuries later by Firishta, namely that Tughluq's father, also named Tughluq, was a slave of Balaban who had married a Jat woman. Ibn Baṭṭūṭa, who arrived in Delhi within ten years of Tughluq's death, learned that the late sultan was one of the Turks known as Qara'unas who inhabited the territories between Sind and Turkestan (i.e. the Negüderis), and had reached India during the reign of ʿAlāʾ al-Dīn. ʿAfīf appears to have heard the same story some decades later, since he likewise describes Tughluq and his two brothers as coming from Khurāsān in ʿAlāʾ al-Dīn's time. But the earliest statement we have – and the most deserving of credence – is that found in Amīr Khusraw's *Tughluq-Nāma*, composed in honour of Tughluq's accession in 720/1320. Khusraw has Tughluq declare to the assembled grandees, following the overthrow of Nāṣir al-Dīn Khusraw Shāh, that he was 'a nomad' (*āwāra mardī*) and had arrived in Jalāl al-Dīn Khaljī's reign. This suggests that Tughluq was indeed of Mongol or Turco-Mongol stock, as Ibn Baṭṭūṭa's informant claimed; he may have been a follower of the Mongol chief Alughu who entered Jalāl al-Dīn's service in 691/1292 and settled near Delhi (above, p. 118).

The support for Tughluq's rising must have disappointed him. ʿIṣāmī, who claims that during his march on Delhi he was joined by many ʿAlāʾī and Quṭbī maliks,[52] supplies no names. Apart from Bahrām-i Ayba, muqtaʿ of Uchch, whose father may have been one of Sultan ʿAlāʾ al-Dīn's boon-companions (*nadīmān*),[53] not a single governor is known to have rallied to his side. Of the amirs who were his neighbours, Yaklakhī at Sāmāna, an Indian, actually moved against Tughluq, but was repulsed and was subsequently killed by his own people. The same fate met Mughaltai, the amir of Multān, who had declared for Khusraw Shāh. Muḥammad Shah Lur at Sīwistān was forced by elements within the town to support Tughluq, but in

attempted to gather Parwārīs during a short visit to Gujarāt as its governor: *TFS*, 396–7. *TFS*[1], Bodleian ms., fol. 173b/ Digby Coll. ms., fol. 147b, suggests that the Parwārīs came from Jālōr as well as Gujarāt. See S. R. Sharma, 'Nasir-ud-din Khusru Shah', in *Mahāmahōpādhyāya: Professor D. V. Potdar ... commemoration volume* (Poona, 1950), 70–81, for this warrior group.

50 For what follows, see R. C. Jauhri, 'Ghiyāthu'd-Dīn Tughluq – his original name and descent', in Horst Krüger (ed.), *Kunwar Mohammad Ashraf: an Indian scholar and revolutionary 1905–1962* (Berlin, 1966), 62–6.

51 Ibn Abi'l-Faḍā'il, ed. Kortantamer, 27 (German tr. 104). al-Ṣafadī, *Wāfī*, III, 172 (tr. Khān, 187).

52 *FS*, 381 (tr. 584).

53 Rukn al-Dīn Ayba: *TFS*, 358 (reading DABYR to be corrected from BL ms., fol. 177b: 'YBH). That Ayba was the name of Bahrām's father is clear from *FS*, 388 (tr. 593).

the event arrived too late to help him. Further afield, Malik Hūshang at Jālōr was unwilling to commit himself, and ʿAyn al-Mulk Multānī joined Khusraw Shāh only to desert him on the eve of battle and retire to his iqtaʿs of Dhār and Ujjain in Mālwa.[54] Tughluq's adherents were kinsmen like his son Malik Jawna (the future Sultan Muḥammad), a son-in-law Malik Shādī, and two nephews, Asad al-Dīn Arslan and Bahā' al-Dīn Garshāsp; or subordinates like Yūsuf, Tughluq's na'ib at Dēōpālpūr, and ʿAlī-yi Ḥaydar.[55] Otherwise his army was made up of outsiders. Amīr Khusraw's characterization of them – 'mostly from the Upper Country (*iqlīm-i bālā*), neither Indian nor Indian chiefs (*Hindū-wālā*): Ghuzz, Turks, and Mongols of Rūm and Rūs ... Tājīks from Khurāsān of pure stock'[56] – is more than a trifle disingenuous. It ignores the Khōkhars under their chiefs *Samaj Rāī and Gul Chand, to whom ʿIṣāmī attributes much of the credit for the victory at Sarsatī,[57] but whose presence on Tughluq's side was difficult to reconcile with the rhetoric of Holy War. Tughluq's affinity, in other words, was markedly regional; his lieutenants were commanders who had fought alongside him on the Mongol frontier, sometimes themselves Mongol renegades, or Hindu warlords who were his close neighbours in the western Panjāb.

Tughluq's following is decidedly less impressive than that of his antagonist. The nucleus, of course, comprised Parwārīs, headed by Khusraw Shāh's maternal uncle *Randhaval. But among the commanders whom Khusraw Shāh sent to check the rebels at Sarsatī were Temür, the muqtaʿ of Chandērī, Qutlugh the *amīr-i shikār*, and *Tulabugha Bughda.[58] When Tughluq pushed through to Delhi, Khusraw Shāh met him at the head of forces that included *Tulabugha Bughda, *Tulabugha Nāgawrī, Tegin the muqtaʿ of Awadh, Ikhtiyār al-Dīn Sunbul the *amīr-ḥājib*, Kāfūr the keeper of the seal (*muhrdār*), and Qabūl the supervisor of the market (*shiḥna-yi manda*).[59] None of these nobles was an upstart promoted by the usurper: all had held office under Quṭb al-Dīn Mubārak Shāh, and several – Temür, Tegin, Qutlugh and Qabūl – had served his father ʿAlā' al-Dīn before him. Support of this calibre belies the traditional view of Khusraw Shāh as a widely hated infidel and of his rival as the avenger of the Khaljī dynasty and the saviour of Islam.

Conscious, perhaps, of the relatively narrow support he had enjoyed, Ghiyāth al-Dīn Tughluq after his accession took care to draw in ʿAlā'ī

54 See Husain, *Tughluq dynasty*, 38–41. Muḥammad Shāh Lur appears among the nobles of ʿAlā' al-Dīn's reign: *TFS*, 240 (omitting 'Lur', but cf. BL ms., fol. 125b). For Yaklakhī's Indian extraction, see *Tughluq-Nāma*, 68.

55 *Ibid.*, 95. *FS*, 380, 382, 383 (tr. 582, 585, 586).

56 *Tughluq-Nāma*, 84.

57 *FS*, 378, 379–80, 382, 384, 385 (tr. 580, 582–3, 585, 588–9). For the SHJ of the printed edition, IOL Persian ms. 3089, fol. 208b, has SMJRAY.

58 *Tughluq-Nāma*, 101–2. *FS*, 379–80 (tr. 582–3).

59 *Tughluq-Nāma*, 118 (reading BKYN in error for TGYN). *FS*, 382, 383, 386 (tr. 585, 586, 589–90). *TFS*, 420.

maliks and to secure their good will with offices and iqtaʿs.[60] Khwāja Ḥājjī was retained as *ʿāriḍ*,[61] and ʿAyn al-Mulk Multānī remained governor of Mālwa, though neither seems to have survived Tughluq (this ʿAyn al-Mulk is to be distinguished from Ibn Māhrū, who later bore the same title: see appendix IV). But the alliance with many of the sultan's erstwhile colleagues seems to have been an uneasy one. Tensions emerged in 721/1321–2, when Tughluq deputed a number of amirs from the old regime, along with those of his own creation, to accompany his son and heir, now styled Ulugh Khān, to Arangal. As the result of an intrigue which involved principally a poet in Ulugh Khān's service, named ʿUbayd, and which the sources do little to elucidate, Temür, Tegin and Kāfūr (who had exchanged his office of *muhrdār* for that of *wakīl-i dar*) were easily brought to believe that Ulugh Khān planned to do away with them, and deserted with their contingents, thus jeopardizing the entire campaign. Ulugh Khān extricated himself, and troops were sent against the disaffected amirs. Temür and Tegin were both killed while seeking refuge in Hindu territory; Kāfūr was taken prisoner and executed in Delhi; their families were all put to death.[62] All the amirs in question had served ʿAlā' al-Dīn; it may be significant that even ʿUbayd had done so if, as is likely, we can identify him with the ʿUbayd-i Ḥakīm mentioned by Baranī among that sultan's boon-companions.[63] More importantly, some of these amirs, as we noticed earlier, had supported Khusraw Shāh in 720/1320. It is hard to resist the suspicion that the episode afforded the sultan a convenient pretext for eliminating powerful noble households in which he felt unable to repose complete trust. With their removal a significant number of the leading figures of ʿAlā' al-Dīn's era left the stage.

As might be expected of a monarch who had come to power with the aid of elements from the north-west, Tughluq favoured officers from those parts. Burhān al-Dīn, who obtained the post of kotwal and the style of ʿĀlim Malik, was the founder of an important noble family which had settled at Hānsī but originated from Ghazna.[64] Of his sons, Kamāl al-Dīn became chief qadi and Ṣadr-i Jahān under Muḥammad, and his high standing in the empire is attested both by Ibn Baṭṭūṭa and by al-ʿUmarī's

[60] *Ibid.*, 426. *TMS*, 92.

[61] For Khwāja Ḥājjī, see *TFS*, 438; *FS*, 395 (with ČAČY in error).

[62] Prasad, *Qaraunah Turks*, 29–33, and Husain, *Tughluq dynasty*, 65–9, summarize the data in the various sources. *TFS*, 448, 449, lists among the deserters the Afghan malik Ikhtiyār al-Dīn Mall (printed text has MX, but cf. *TFS*[1], Bodleian ms., fol. 183b/Digby Coll. ms., fol. 155a, with ML); but *FS*, 395–6 (tr. 603), says that he remained loyal. For Kāfūr's rank, see *ibid.*, 394, 400 (tr. 599, 606).

[63] *TFS*, 360.

[64] *Ibid.*, 424, for Burhān al-Dīn. For the family's origins, see IB, III, 143, 161 (tr. Gibb, 617, 628). Burhān al-Dīn's wife, the mother of Kamāl al-Dīn, was the sister of Mawlānā Fakhr al-Dīn Hānsawī: *Siyar*, 274.

informants.[65] Another was Qiwām al-Dīn, who served as *nā'ib-wazīr* at Dēōgīr and then, under Muḥammad b. Tughluq, was entitled Qutlugh Khān and promoted to *wakīl-i dar*. At the time of the sultan's abortive Maʿbar campaign in *c*. 1335, he was once more sent to Dēōgīr (by then renamed Dawlatābād), where he remained in authority for ten years. His recall in 745/1344–5 appears greatly to have undermined Muḥammad's authority in the Deccan province and contributed to its secession three years later.[66] Qutlugh Khān's son Muḥammad had received from his namesake the titles of Alp Khān and Niẓām al-Mulk, together with the iqtaʿ of Gujarāt. He did not, apparently, hold this position for long, and in the late 1330s is found deputizing for his father in Dawlatābād during the operations against the rebel Nuṣrat Khān.[67] A third son of Burhān al-Dīn, Niẓām al-Dīn, appears as one of Tughluq's maliks and subsequently, under Muḥammad, as ʿĀlim al-Mulk and governor of Bharūch (Broach).[68] From there he was transferred to Dawlatābād to replace his brother Qutlugh Khān temporarily, but was taken prisoner by rebels and later released and sent to Delhi.[69]

The clan Abū Rijā, another new lineage which seems to have attained prominence under the Tughluqids, is again expressly said to have originated from the 'upper country' (*mulk-i bālā*), i.e. the north-west. One of its members, Mujīr al-Dīn, had already been made *nā'ib-wazīr* at Dēōgīr by Quṭb al-Dīn Mubārak Shāh Khaljī.[70] He was still to be found in the region at the time of the Arangal campaign, when he furnished Ulugh Khān with valuable aid in overthrowing the mutinous nobles. This may have earned him the future sultan's trust, for Ibn Baṭṭūṭa refers to him as one of 'the great amirs' of Muḥammad b. Tughluq's reign and Baranī lists him among the evil influences on that monarch. He served Muḥammad loyally, participating with his forces in the campaigns against the rebel Bahā' al-Dīn Garshāsp and against ʿAyn al-Mulk Ibn Māhrū ten years or so later, when he was governor of Bhayāna.[71] Ḥusām al-Dīn Abū Rijā and Shihāb al-Dīn Abū Rijā were probably his brothers. The latter obtained the rank of 'king of the merchants' (*malik al-tujjār*) and the iqtaʿ of Nawsarī on Muḥammad's

[65] *TFS*, 454. *TMS*, 98. IB, III, 161, 215, 229 (tr. Gibb, 628, 657, 664). *MA*, ed. Spies, 16 (German tr. 41)/ed. Fāriq, 30 (tr. Siddiqi and Aḥmad, 41).

[66] *TMS*, 98. *TFS*, 454, 481, 501–2. *FS*, 422, 426 (tr. 648, 653), shows that he had remained at Dēōgīr in the early years of Muḥammad's reign.

[67] *TMS*, 98. *FS*, 477 (tr. 717). He does not appear among Muḥammad's maliks in the printed text of *TFS*, but cf. BL ms., fol. 225b.

[68] *TMS*, 98. *TFS*, 502. *FS*, 495, 503 (tr. 739, 749).

[69] *Ibid.*, 519 (tr. 770). *TMS*, 111.

[70] *FS*, 369 (tr. 569). *TFS*, 398, elucidated by Hodivala, *Studies*, I, 287–8; in the list of Quṭb al-Dīn's maliks in *TFS*, 379, he appears as 'Fakhr al-Dīn', but cf. BL ms., fol. 188b. See ʿAfīf, 454, for the provenance of this family.

[71] *TFS*, 472. *FS*, 397–9, 427, 473 (tr. 603–5, 653, 711). *TMS*, 101. IB, III, 230, 318, and IV, 5 (tr. Gibb, 665, 710, 775), commenting also on his cruelty. For a brief biography, see Hodivala, *Studies*, I, 287.

accession.[72] Ḥusām al-Dīn was *mustawfī* under Ghiyāth al-Dīn Tughluq and was detailed to secure Malik Tegin's household in the aftermath of the mutiny at Arangal. He retained his office into the reign of Muḥammad, who conferred on him the style of Niẓām al-Mulk: sent to Lakhnawtī as *nā'ib-wazīr*, he helped to put down the first revolt of Fakhr al-Dīn ('Fakhrā') at Sunārgā'ūn (*c.* 1335–6).[73] A nephew of Mujīr al-Dīn, Shams al-Dīn, who was to acquire notoriety by his activities as *mustawfī* under Fīrūz Shāh, was Ḥusām al-Dīn's son.[74] Another member of the family corresponded with Ibn Māhrū, and some of the Abū Rijā clan went on to serve the independent Gujarāt sultans in the early fifteenth century.[75]

The aristocracy under Muḥammad b. Tughluq

Little is known of the fate of Tughluq's sons, none of whom appears to have survived Muḥammad's reign. One, Mubārak Khān, acted in a judicial capacity during the new reign; but Ibn Baṭṭūṭa heard that another, Masᶜūd Khān, was put to death, perhaps because his mother was a daughter of ʿAlā' al-Dīn Khaljī.[76] Fīrūz (the future sultan), the son of the late monarch's brother Rajab, served Muḥammad as *bārbeg*.[77] Two adopted sons of Tughluq certainly enjoyed considerable favour: Tatar Malik (actually the son of a Mongol prince who had invaded India during Tughluq's lieutenancy at Dēōpālpūr) attained some prominence, despite temporary banishment following a quarrel with the sultan, while Bahrām Khān was entrusted with the government of Sunārgā'ūn.[78]

Virtually half of the appointments made by Muḥammad on his enthronement went to men who are known to have originated from the north-west, and included the amirs he had inherited from his father and who had played a leading role in Tughluq's revolt against Khusraw Shāh.[79] But within a few years Muḥammad was confronted with insurrections by two of these men, Bahā' al-Dīn Garshāsp and Küshlü Khān, which seem to have been provoked by his attempts to intensify his authority in the provinces

[72] *TMS*, 98. [73] *TFS*, 455 (cf. BL ms., fol. 226a). *TMS*, 94, 98, 104.

[74] ᶜAfīf, 451, 454. Anonymous, *Ghunyat al-Munya*, ed. Shahab Sarmadee (Delhi, 1978), 6–7, gives his full name, Shams al-Dawla wa'l-Dīn Ibrāhīm-i Ḥasan: Ḥusām al-Dīn is known to have been called Ḥasan.

[75] *IM*, 157–9 (Malik Bahā' al-Dīn Naṣr-Allāh, *nā'ib-i khāṣṣ-ḥājib*). Z. A. Desai, 'Inscriptions of the sultans of Gujarat from Saurashtra', *EIAPS* (1953–4), 51.

[76] Masᶜūd Khān: IB, III, 292 (tr. Gibb, 696). Mubārak Khān: *ibid.*, III, 230, 287–8 (tr. 664, 694); mentioned in *TFS*, 454.

[77] *Ibid.* ᶜAfīf, 42. *TMS*, 98.

[78] Biography of Tatar Malik in ᶜAfīf, 388–94. He had held the iqtaᶜ of Ẓafarābād under Tughluq (*TFS*, 428, 451), and was subsequently styled Tatar Khān by Muḥammad's successor (*TMS*, 124). Later the author of various legal works, he spoke fluent Arabic: IB, III, 281 (tr. Gibb, 690). On Bahrām Khān, see *FS*, 422, 444, 472 (tr. 648, 673, 709); *TFS*, 480; IB, III, 230, 317 (tr. Gibb, 665, 709), wrongly calling him Muḥammad's brother's son (Gibb's tr., 665 n.36, confuses Bahrām Khān with Tatar Khān).

[79] This emerges from the list given in *TMS*, 98.

(pp. 256–7 below). This may have provided the impetus to recruit a new body of servitors. He seems to have reposed great confidence in Aḥmad b. Ayaz, whom he made wazir in 732/1331–2 with the style of Khwāja Jahān and who is found on a number of occasions leading military forces against rebels.[80] Khwāja Jahān served Muḥammad loyally for the next twenty years, only to fall from power by becoming the focus of resistance to Fīrūz Shāh's accession. When Muḥammad left Delhi for the last time, he delegated authority in the capital to Khwāja Jahān, his cousin Fīrūz and Malik Qabūl 'Khalīfatī' (also known as 'Malik Kabīr').[81]

As undisputed heir-apparent throughout his father's reign, Muḥammad seems to have built up a power-base of his own. Nigam's assertion that the slave system did not receive much encouragement during Muḥammad's reign[82] is simply at variance with the testimony of our sources. Among his most trusted amirs was Malik Qabūl, his slave and probably an Indian; and we know that the sultan also recruited black slaves (Ḥabashīs), one of whom, presumably, was Badr al-Ḥabashī, his governor at ʿAlāpūr.[83] Turks may now have attained some prominence once more. Ibn Baṭṭūṭa heard that Muḥammad had alarmed his father by amassing a body of Turkish mamluks. Since the Moroccan traveller found 4,000 of them stationed at Amrōha alone, the total figure of 20,000 for Muḥammad's Turkish slaves transmitted by al-ʿUmarī is probably too low.[84] Ibn Baṭṭūṭa's vivid description of Muḥammad's processions suggests that many of his amirs may have been mamluks.[85] We know the names of only a few of these Turks who rose to high office. ʿImād al-Mulk Sartīz, who became *ʿāriḍ* and governor of Multān and was later transferred to the Deccan, where he fell fighting against the *amīrān-i ṣada*, was a slave and probably a Turk.[86] To judge from

[80] Date of his appointment: *Siyar*, 218. As a military commander: *TFS*, 481; *FS*, 425–31, 471 (tr. 651–8, 707–8); IB, III, 318, 324, 332–3, 348–9 (tr. Gibb, 710, 713, 716–17, 723–4). For his ancestry, see p. 189 below.

[81] *TFS*, 509, 522. ʿAfīf, 50, 452.

[82] Nigam, *Nobility*, 85.

[83] Qabūl: *TFS*, 493; IB, I, 365, and III, 230 (tr. Gibb, 226, 665), and *passim*. Ḥabashīs: *ibid.*, IV, 31 (tr. Gibb and Beckingham, 786); later, IV, 59–60 (tr. 800), he refers to a guard of fifty Ḥabashī men-at-arms who embarked with him at Gandhār.

[84] *Ibid.*, III, 211 (tr. Gibb, 654); and see III, 439 (tr. Gibb, 763), for Amrōha. *MA*, ed. Spies, 13 (German tr. 38)/ed. Fāriq, 25 (tr. Siddiqi and Aḥmad, 37); for another reference, to 12,000 mamluks accompanying the sultan, *ibid.*, ed. Spies, 19 (tr. 45)/ed. Fāriq, 37 (tr. Siddiqi and Aḥmad, 44). IB, III, 334 (tr. Gibb, 717), says that mamluks accompanied Muḥammad on his Maʿbar campaign in *c.* 1335. But we cannot be certain that these were Turks, since the same author employs the term for slaves whom we know from other sources to have been Indians: see, e.g., *ibid.*, III, 190, 191 (tr. Gibb, 643).

[85] *Ibid.*, III, 231 (tr. Gibb, 665).

[86] *Ibid.*, III, 44, 94 (tr. Gibb, 562–3, 593): at the latter place Gibb read *ʿāriḍ-i mamālīk*, 'inspector-general of the mamluks', for *ʿāriḍ-i mamālik*; but see the French editors' note at IB, III, 458–9. Although described both here and at III, 107–9 (tr. Gibb, 600), as governor of Sind, he was not appointed to this post until after Shāhū Lodī's revolt in *c.* 1337: see *TMS*, 107 (with the impossible year 744). Ibn Baṭṭūṭa may thus have confused two visits to the province: see C. F. Beckingham, 'Ibn Battuta in Sind', in Khuhro (ed.), *Sind through the centuries*, 140–1. Firishta, I, 522, calls Sartīz a 'Türkmen'.

his name, Malik Qiran Ṣafdar Malik Sulṭānī certainly was.[87] Another Turk, lastly, was Taghai, who passed from Malik Qiran into the possession of Sultan Muḥammad and was promoted to be *shiḥna-yi bārgāh*;[88] his revolt in Gujarāt towards the end of the reign proved the most intractable that the sultan had to face.

At this time the Sultanate still served as a magnet for dispossessed princes, adventurers and opportunists from the west. Küshlü Khān's rebellion in Sind had drawn on 'Turks, Afghans and the men of Khurāsān'.[89] Al-ʿUmarī speaks of Turks, natives of 'Khitā' (literally 'northern China', but doubtless Mongolia) and Persians in the sultan's own army, and Ibn Baṭṭūṭa refers more than once to the 'amirs of Khurāsān' (see below, p. 263) among Muḥammad's officers.[90] What particularly attracted great numbers of immigrant notables was Muḥammad's proverbial munificence;[91] the story of his generosity to Sayyid ʿAḍud al-Dīn of Yazd, an envoy from Mongol Persia, for example, gained wide currency.[92] Ibn Baṭṭūṭa, himself a beneficiary of this policy, describes how foreigners were promoted to governorships and to high office, and were treated with the greatest distinction, being addressed, on Muḥammad's express instructions, by the special title of *ʿazīz* ('honourable one').[93] In *c.* 733/1332–3, Niẓām al-Dīn, a scion of the former ruling dynasty of Qays in the Persian Gulf, arrived at Muḥammad's court, where he spent two years in a vain effort to secure the sultan's aid in recovering his patrimony.[94] A few years later, Ibn Baṭṭūṭa found Ḥājjī Ke'ün, a brother of the Ilkhan Mūsā, as the sultan's guest: he returned to south-western Persia in 743/1342 and was killed while endeavouring to occupy Shabānkāra.[95] Muḥammad is known to have sent agents

87 See Hodivala, *Studies*, I, 300–1. For Tu. *qiran*, 'one who slaughters', see above, p. 63, n.16.

88 The fullest account of his career is to be found in *SFS*, 19–28 (tr. Basu, *JBORS* 23 [1937], 97–106). For his office, see IB, III, 235 (tr. Gibb, 667). His name is Tu. *taghai*, 'maternal uncle': Clauson, *Etymological dictionary*, 474.

89 IB, III, 322 (tr. Gibb, 712).

90 *MA*, ed. Spies, 13 (German tr. 38)/ed. Fāriq, 24 (tr. Siddiqi and Aḥmad, 37). IB, III, 344, 348 (tr. Gibb, 721, 723); cf. also III, 332 (tr. 716), for 'Khurāsānīs'.

91 *Ibid.*, II, 72–7, and III, 97–9, 243–66 *passim*, 270, 279, 284 (tr. Gibb, 311–13, 595–6, 671–83 *passim*, 685, 689, 692). *MA*, ed. Spies, 22–5, 38 (German tr. 48–51, 65–6)/ed. Fāriq, 41–6, 70 (tr. Siddiqi and Aḥmad, 48–50, omitting, 48, a sentence about foreigners; 63–4).

92 Shabānkāra'ī, 288–9. *MA*, ed. Spies, 22 (German tr. 48–9)/ed. Fāriq, 42–3 (tr. Siddiqi and Aḥmad, 47–8). al-Ṣafadī, *Wāfī*, Biblioteca dell'Accademia dei Lincei, Rome, ms. Fondo Caetani 21, 435–6. A brief allusion in *TFS*, 461.

93 IB, III, 97–8, 243 (tr. Gibb, 595, 671).

94 Jean Aubin, 'Les princes d'Ormuz du XIIIe au XVe siècle', *JA* 241 (1953), 105; Shabānkāra'ī, 219. This was the dynasty to which Sirāj-i Taqī belonged (below, p. 208).

95 IB, III, 256–8 (tr. Gibb, 677–9). Jean Aubin, 'La question de Sīrğān au XIIIe siècle', *Studia Iranica* 6 (1977), 289, citing a passage found only in the Tabriz ms. of the third redaction of Shabānkāra'ī's *Majmaʿ*, which was used by the anonymous author of a general chronicle in Leiden University ms. Or. 1612, fol. 357a, and by Naṭanzī, *Muntakhab al-Tawārīkh* (816/1413–14), partial edn by J. Aubin, *Extraits du Muntakhab al-tawarikh-i Muʿini* (Tehran, 1957), 9–10.

to the Persian Gulf to recruit Arab amirs and their followers into his service.[96] In part this lavish patronage was linked to his expansionist designs in what is now Afghanistan (see chapter 13), and the many notables from Mongol territory who arrived with Ibn Baṭṭūṭa included Khudāwand-zāda Qiwām al-Dīn, qadi of Tirmid, his cousin Ghiyāth al-Dīn, two grandees from Transoxiana, and Bahrām, malik of Ghazna; later there arrived two Mongol amirs, *Qabtagha and Aḥmad-i Iqbāl, of whom the first was reputedly descended from the Mongol commander Temür who had overthrown Balaban's son in 683/1285.[97]

Despite Ibn Baṭṭūṭa's testimony that Muḥammad preferred foreigners to the indigenous aristocracy, and that the 'Indians' in turn hated the immigrant 'Khurāsānī' nobles,[98] there is clear evidence that the position was more complex; the sultan's favour extended to a much wider *clientela* and native Indians, like the future rebel ʿAyn al-Mulk Ibn Māhrū (see appendix IV), also benefited from his generosity and trust. The Moroccan himself was on friendly terms with the *muhrdār* 'Abū Muslim', one of the many sons of the rai of Kampila whom Muḥammad had maintained at his court since the conquest of that territory.[99] More notable was *Kannū, a Brahman taken prisoner to Delhi on the conquest of Tilang in *c.* 1322, who entered his service and embraced Islam, receiving the name Maqbūl and subsequently the style of Qiwām al-Mulk. Appointed governor of Multān by Muḥammad on the suppression of Küshlü Khān's rising in 728/1327–8, he briefly governed Tilang until its revolt in *c.* 1336, and later became deputy to the wazir Khwāja Jahān Aḥmad b. Ayaz. Following Fīrūz Shāh's accession, he obtained the style of Khān Jahān and succeeded Khwāja Jahān as wazir, an office he retained until his death and transmitted to his son.[100]

In general, however, Baranī stigmatizes Muḥammad's Indian servitors as lowborn.[101] They included the notorious ʿAzīz Khammār ('the Vintner'), on whom the sultan conferred the government of Mālwa.[102] A number of them were non-Muslims and – for all the chronicler's jaundiced remarks elsewhere about drapers (*bazzāzān*), goldsmiths and the like[103] – were probably

96 IB, IV, 104 (tr. Gibb and Beckingham, 818–19).

97 Notables from Transoxiana: *ibid.*, III, 374–5, 394–5 (tr. Gibb, 735, 743–4). Bahrām: *ibid.*, III, 264–5 (tr. Gibb, 682). Aḥmad and *Qabtagha: *TFS*, 520, 584–5; for the second name, probably Mo. *qabtagha*, 'purse', 'bag', see Lessing, *Mongolian–English Dictionary*, 899. P. Jackson, 'The Mongols and the Delhi Sultanate in the reign of Muḥammad Tughluq (1325–1351)', *CAJ* 19 (1975), 147–8.

98 IB, III, 344, 349 (tr. Gibb, 721–2, 724).

99 *Ibid.*, III, 320–1 (tr. Gibb, 711).

100 Multān: *TMS*, 98, 101. Tilang: *TFS*, 481 (reading QBWL to be amended as in BL ms., fol. 238a), 484. *Nā'ib-wazīr*: *ibid.*, 454, 512. Biography in ʿAfīf, 394–424. He is to be distinguished from two of Muḥammad's other maliks, Qabūl (p. 183 above) and Muqbil: see Hodivala, *Studies*, II, 112, 115–16.

101 List in *TFS*, 504–5 (to be corrected from BL ms., fol. 249b). *FJ*, 167–8.

102 *TFS*, 501–2, 503, 504.

103 *FJ*, 180–1; see also 295–302 (at 298 the reader is warned not to be taken in by their administrative skills).

kayasthas, members of an administrative class, like Ratan, described as 'a person skilled in calculation and writing', who was entrusted with the fiscal administration of Sind; Bhiran, auditor (*mutaṣarrif*) at Gulbarga; Samara Singh, who became governor of Tilang; and Dhārā, whom Muḥammad sent to Dawlatābād as deputy wazir in 745/1344–5, just a matter of months before his authority there disintegrated and the province seceded under the Bahmanid dynasty.[104]

The era of Fīrūz Shāh

In his first recension Baranī speaks of the number of maliks from the previous regime who were brought low at Fīrūz Shāh's accession.[105] In fact, however, Maqbūl was simply the most highly favoured among a significant number of men who came over to the new monarch from Khwāja Jahān during the early weeks and were retained in positions of trust. Ḥusām al-Dīn, son of Malik Nuwā, became na'ib of Awadh and received the style of Ḥusām al-Mulk.[106] Malik Mubārak, the son of Muḥammad's leading amir Malik Qabūl Khalīfatī, served as *ṣilāḥdār-i khāṣṣ* and later *wakīl-i dar*, surviving Fīrūz Shāh himself.[107] Even Aʿẓam Malik Shaykhzāda Bisṭāmī, who as one of the associates of Khwāja Jahān had been banished from Fīrūz Shāh's territories, was later pardoned when he reappeared with a caliphal robe, and was restored to favour with the style of Aʿẓam Khān.[108] And although Baranī mentions – with ill-disguised relish – how the new sultan dismissed the foreigners who had flocked to Muḥammad's court from Herat, Sīstān, Aden and Quṣdār in expectation of rewards,[109] Fīrūz Shāh's nobles included also some of the most distinguished immigrants of the previous reign. Khudāwandzāda Qiwām al-Dīn Tirmidī, Muḥammad's *nā'ib-i wakīl-i dar*, became Khudāwand Khān and *wakīl-i dar*, while his nephew was entitled Sayf al-Mulk and made *amīr-i shikār-i maymana*.[110] The Mongol amirs *Qabtagha and Aḥmad-i Iqbāl, too, enjoyed Fīrūz Shāh's favour, and Aḥmad's son Ḥusayn in turn served the sultan and married his daughter.[111]

104 Ratan: IB, III, 105–6 (tr. Gibb, 599). Bhiran: *FS*, 485 (tr. 726–7). Samara Singh: K. H. Kamdar, in *Proceedings of the 7th all India oriental conference (Baroda, 1933)* (Baroda, 1935), 629–33. Dhārā: *TFS*, 501. Others are named *ibid.*, 504–5. On this class, see generally Yusuf Husain, 'Les Kâyasthâs ou "scribes", caste hindoue iranisée, et la culture musulmane dans l'Inde', *REI* 1 (1927), 455–8.

105 *TFS*[1], Bodleian ms., fol. 217a. Siddiqui, 'Fresh light', 78.

106 *TFS*, 528 (to be completed by the still slightly corrupt reading in BL ms., fol. 261a). *TMS*, 133. Bihāmadkhānī, fol. 417a (tr. Zaki, 22).

107 *Ibid.*, fols. 416b-417a (tr. Zaki, 21). ʿAfīf, 287, 338, calling him ambiguously Mubārak-i Kabīr.

108 *TMS*, 127–8; cf. also ʿAfīf, 281; and for his partisanship of Khwāja Jahān, *TMS*, 120, 123, and *TFS*, 543, 545.

109 *TFS*, 538.

110 *Ibid.*, 454, 580. *TMS*, 124.

111 *TFS*, 527, 544, 584–5. ʿAfīf, 280. *TMS*, 140, for the marriage.

Like his predecessors Fīrūz Shāh built up a corps of amirs of his own creation. One of the most significant long-term developments of the reign was the accumulation of offices and iqtaʿs in the hands of his slaves. They are referred to by different authors, under the events of the following reigns, as 'Turkish' slaves and amirs (*bandagān-i turk*, *umarā-yi atrāk*) and as 'Hindūstānīs'. The apparent contradiction may be resolved if it is assumed that many of them were of eastern Indian provenance: thus Jūzjānī, over a century earlier, had written of the natives of Tibet and Arakan as 'Turks'.[112] According to ʿAfīf, Fīrūz Shāh made greater efforts to acquire slaves than any of his predecessors: provincial governors were under orders to forward the choicest slaves to court as part of their annual gift to the sultan, and the total number of royal slaves rose to 180,000. Of these, 40,000 were in attendance at court or formed part of Fīrūz Shāh's retinue; the remainder were occupied in a variety of tasks, some of them being taught a skilled craft.[113] The royal ghulams became such an important element in the state that responsibility for their affairs was transferred from the wazir's department (*dīwān-i aʿlā-yi wizārat*) to a completely new department, the *dīwān-i bandagān*, with its own officials and headed by the *ʿāriḍ-i bandagān-i khāṣṣ*.[114]

Some of his slaves had been in Fīrūz Shāh's service prior to his accession, like Malik Bashīr, who became *ʿāriḍ-i mamālik* with the style of ʿImād al-Mulk;[115] or Malik *Dīlān, who served the new sultan as *amīr-i shikār*, an office of increasing importance under a monarch who was so devoted to the chase;[116] or Malik Qabūl, nicknamed Tōrāband, who became amir of Badā'ūn[117] and is to be distinguished from a namesake and fellow slave, Malik Qabūl Qur'ān-khwān, the *amīr-i majlis* and muqtaʿ of Sāmāna.[118] Subsequent purchases would have included Malik Ikhtiyār al-Dīn Mufarrij Sulṭānī, the *dawādār*, who became na'ib of the iqtaʿ of Gujarāt and later acquired the style of Farḥat al-Mulk.[119] By Fīrūz Shāh's death, his slaves and their offspring constituted a major element in the aristocracy; we should be justified in speaking of the creation of a new élite. The activities

[112] Bihāmadkhānī, fols. 420a, 421a, 423, 424b, 425b, 432b (tr. Zaki, 27, 29, 32, 33, 34, 47). *TMS*, 150. Cf. Digby, 'Iletmish or Iltutmish?', 57 n.1. For Jūzjānī's usage, see *TN*, I, 429 and n.3 (tr. 566, 567).

[113] ᶜAfīf, 267–8, 269–70, 272: the figures are given at 270.

[114] *Ibid.*, 271.

[115] *TFS*, 581. ᶜAfīf, 285, 436–7. *TMS*, 119.

[116] *TFS*, 582. ᶜAfīf, 115, 318. Shokoohy, *Rajasthan I*, 62. On the importance of his office, see *TFS*, 600.

[117] *Ibid.*, 528. See also ᶜAfīf, 159–61. Bihāmadkhānī, fol. 417a: the text is slightly corrupt, reading NWRABAD, and Zaki's tr. (23 and n.5) confuses him with Qabūl Qur'ān-khwān, as does *TMS*, 135, when mentioning his appointment to Badā'ūn.

[118] ᶜAfīf, 454–5. Bihāmadkhānī, fol. 417a (tr. Zaki, 23). *TMS*, 134. He was sent against the invading Mongols in 759/1358: *ibid.*, 127.

[119] *Ibid.*, 133. He appears in epigraphs from 762 onwards: Desai, 'Khaljī and Tughluq inscriptions from Gujarat', 9–13, 19–21, 26–7, etc. (for a reconstruction of his career, see *ibid.*, 13–14); *idem*, 'A fourteenth-century epitaph from Konkan', *EIAPS* (1965), 9–10.

of these slaves under his successors would gravely undermine the stability of the empire.

Even discounting the amirs whom Fīrūz Shāh had inherited from his cousin, however, there were still several nobles of free stock. Ẓafar Khān (II), the muqtaʿ of Gujarāt, was the son and successor of Ẓafar Khān (I), whose full name, Tāj al-Dīn Muḥammad Lur Fārsī, indicates that his family probably came from south-west Persia.[120] Malikzāda Fīrūz (ancestor of the dynasty that ruled at Kālpī in the fifteenth century), who held the extensive new *shiqq* of Fīrūzpūr, was the son of Tāj al-Dīn Turk, who had served Ghiyāth al-Dīn Tughluq Shāh.[121] The free maliks also comprised a group of Afghan amirs: Malik Bayyū, muqtaʿ of Bihār; Malik Khaṭṭāb, appointed to the *shiqq* of Sambhal in 782/1380; and Malik Muḥammad Shāh, muqtaʿ of Tughluqpūr in Etāwa.[122] Indian converts related to the sultan by marriage, too, found a place in the ranks of the aristocracy. If we can believe a seventeenth-century historian of Gujarāt, Sadhāran, entitled Wajīh al-Mulk, the ancestor of the independent sultans, was the brother of one of Fīrūz Shāh's wives; he had accompanied the sultan to Delhi and adopted Islam.[123] By this time, lastly, leading figures among the local princes enjoyed a place at court. After his campaign against Damrīla, the sultan took its princes, the Jām and his brother Banbhīna, back to Delhi.[124] By his death Uddharān, brother of the Tomara rai of Gwāliyōr, and *Sumēr, the Chawhān rai of Etāwa, were also both in attendance.[125]

Lineage and continuity

We would wish to know more about the ancestry of most of the great nobles of the Khaljī and Tughluqid periods mentioned in our sources. ʿIṣāmī tells us, for example, that Alp Khān, one of ʿAlāʾ al-Dīn's early associates and subsequently governor of Gujarāt, was of royal descent, and later alludes to the illustrious ancestry of Bahāʾ al-Dīn Garshāsp, whose

120 *TMS*, 126; cf. also *SFS*, 91. Desai, 'Khaljī and Tughluq inscriptions from Gujarat', 15–17.

121 Bihāmadkhānī, fol. 412b (tr. Zaki, 13–14); for the date, see *TMS*, 134, and on his background, ᶜAfīf, 480. For Tāj al-Dīn Turk, see *TFS*, 424.

122 Bayyū: Bihāmadkhānī, fol. 417a (tr. Zaki, 22, reading 'Babbu [?]'); *TMS*, 133 (BYR in error for BYW); cf. also Z. A. Desai, 'Arabic and Persian inscriptions from the Indian Museum, Calcutta', *EIAPS* (1955–6), 6–8, for his epitaph of 753/1353 (here called Ibrāhīm Bayyū); Q. Aḥmad, *Corpus*, 34–7 (nos. 11–13). Khaṭṭāb: *TMS*, 135. Muḥammad Shāh: Bihāmad-khānī, fols. 412a, 417a (tr. Zaki, 13, 23).

123 Sikandar b. Muḥammad, alias (*ᶜurf*) Manjhū, *Mir'āt-i Sikandarī*, ed. S. C. Misra and Muḥammad Luṭf al-Raḥmān (Baroda, 1961), 4–10; tr. in Sir E. C. Bayley, *The local Muḥammadan dynasties. Gujarat* (London, 1886), 67–70.

124 *SFS*, 93–4. ᶜAfīf, 247–8, 252–4. Riazul Islam, 'The rise of the Sammas in Sind', *IC* 22 (1948), 377–9.

125 ᶜAfīf, 281. *TMS*, 134. Bihāmadkhānī, fol. 414b (tr. Zaki, 17). For the identification of these princes, see Hodivala, *Studies*, I, 394–5; K. S. Lal, *Twilight of the Sultanate*, revised edn. (New Delhi, 1980), 6–7, n.35.

mother was Tughluq's sister.[126] But in neither case does he inform us who were the forebears of the amir in question. On balance, our ignorance of lineage probably means that the aristocracy contained fewer *parvenus* than might seem to have been the case, and we should not be unduly influenced by Baranī's evident obsession with birth as a qualification for office. Baranī is in any case glaringly inconsistent, in that he ignores the fact that the great noble families of Balaban's reign were descended from that sultan's fellow-slaves, who could hardly be described as of good birth; and when impugning the birth of those who rose to high office in ʿAlā' al-Dīn's last years, he neglects to level the same charge at the upstart nobles of the early part of the reign.[127]

Given the sudden and arbitrary manner in which amirs could be deprived of life and property and their families disinherited, it is easy to ignore continuity. There were always grandees whose period of service spanned different dynasties. Khwāja Jahān Aḥmad b. Ayaz, wazir to Muḥammad b. Tughluq, was the son of ʿAlā' al-Dīn Ayaz, kotwal of the Ḥiṣār-i Naw at Delhi (i.e. the new fortress of Sīrī) under ʿAlā' al-Dīn Khaljī and kotwal of the capital in 720/1320, when he sent his son out with the keys to welcome Ghiyāth al-Dīn Tughluq; Ibn Baṭṭūṭa was told that the family was of Rūmī origin.[128] Malik Bashīr Muʿizzī, *nā'ib-i khāṣṣ-ḥājib* to Quṭb al-Dīn Mubārak Shāh, may well be identical with the Malik Bashīr Sulṭānī who appears among the nobles of Muʿizz al-Dīn Kayqubād thirty years before.[129] One of Quṭb al-Dīn Mubārak Shāh's amirs was Ārām Shāh, the son of Malik Khurram Kūhijūdī, who had served the Ghiyathids.[130] The father of Aḥmad-i *Chhītam, ʿAlā' al-Dīn's *qirabeg*, who with his sons held office under Quṭb al-Dīn and Ghiyāth al-Dīn Tughluq, was Balaban's slave, Malik *Buqubuq (above, p. 101).[131] Malik Ḥusām al-Dīn Pindār Khaljī, who served Quṭb al-Dīn, received from Ghiyāth al-Dīn the style of Qadr Khān, was sent at the accession of Muḥammad b. Tughluq to govern Lakhnawtī, and was assassinated there on the outbreak of insurrection in

[126] Alp Khān: *FS*, 250, *ki aṣlash bud az nuṭfa-yi shahryār* (tr. 420). Bahā' al-Dīn: *ibid.*, 384, *ān sipahdār-i wālā-nasab* (tr. 588).

[127] I. Habib, 'Baranī's theory', 107. Siddiqi, 'Nobility under the Khalji Sultans', 64–5.

[128] IB, III, 144 (tr. Gibb, 617–18). For Ayaz, see *TFS*, 278; *FS*, 386–7 (tr. 590). The source cited by A. M. Husain, *The Rehla of Ibn Baṭṭūṭa* (Baroda, 1953), 54 n.3 (and in turn in Gibb's tr., 655 n.131), which makes Aḥmad b. Ayaz out to be of Indian origin, must be regarded as less trustworthy. HN, 447, 457, mistakenly calls the father Aḥmad and the son Muḥammad.

[129] *TFS*, 126 (reading BŠYR, with BL ms., fol. 67b, for the YŠR of the text). *TMS*, 83.

[130] *Ibid.*, 84.

[131] Buqubuq: *TFS*, 40. *Qirabeg*: *ibid.*, 331–2, 337, 379, 396, 424. *FS*, 287 (tr. 461), gives his name. His sons: *TFS*, 409, 410. For the youngest, Badr al-Dīn Abū Bakr b. Aḥmad, also named in an inscription of 723/1323, see *TFS*, 379; G. H. Yazdani, 'Inscriptions in the tomb of Baba Arjun Shah, Petlad (Baroda State)', *EIM* (1915–16), 16–18; *ARIE* (1975–6), 145 (no. D114).

c. 1336.[132] His father, Jamāl al-Dīn Khaljī, *nā'ib-i amīr-i dād* under both Balaban and Jalāl al-Dīn, had supported Jalāl al-Dīn's sons in 695/1296 but was one of the very few maliks spared by 'Alā' al-Dīn in his purge of the Jalālī nobles shortly afterwards.[133] As we saw (p. 80), he may possibly be the Khalaj chamberlain Jamāl al-Dīn ʿAlī who had acted as Balaban's agent on a mission to the Mongols.

The service of some noble families straddled three generations or more, though not always in a strictly office-holding capacity. Baranī, whose father, uncle and maternal grandfather all held office in the latter half of the thirteenth century, seems never to have been more than a boon-companion (*nadīm*) to Muḥammad b. Tughluq. From what he says of the descendants of the thirteenth-century wazirs Junaydī and Muhadhdhab al-Dīn, it appears that they were living as private citizens until the reign of Ghiyāth al-Dīn Tughluq, who restored them to favour, so that we find Ḥusām al-Dīn Junaydī master-minding the assessment of the total revenue demand of the empire in Fīrūz Shāh's reign, and his son Rukn al-Dīn Junaydī ('Junda') briefly serving as wazir to Abū Bakr Shāh in 791/1389.[134] The *sayyid al-ḥujjāb* Maʿrūf, boon-companion to Fīrūz Shāh, had been merely a military officer (*pīshwā*) under Muḥammad's amir Sartīz; but his father was no less a figure than Waḥīd al-Dīn Qurayshī, *nā'ib-wazīr* and governor of Gujarāt for Quṭb al-Dīn Mubārak Shāh.[135] Malik Maḥmūd Beg, who held Sunnām and Sāmāna under Muḥammad b. Tughluq and Fīrūz Shāh successively, and on whom the latter conferred the title of Shīr Khān, belonged to a family from Bilāhūr that produced a series of office-holders proper. In view of Shīr Khān's advanced age (somewhat implausibly set at ninety by Baranī), his father Rustam-i Yaḥyā, muqtaʿ of Bidar, must have been promoted at some time during the Khaljī era.[136] Shīr Khān's own sons, Malik Abū Muslim and Malik Shāhīn Beg, are later mentioned as officers of Fīrūz Shāh.[137] Perhaps the most striking instance of continuity is provided by the genealogy of Dāwar Malik, son of a sister, and also son-in-law, of Muḥammad b. Tughluq: through his father Ṣadr al-Dīn ʿĀrif, deputy chief

[132] *TFS*, 379, 424 (with BYDAR in error; cf. BL ms., fols. 188b, 211a), 450, 454, 480. *FS*, 396 (tr. 601). *TMS*, 98.

[133] *TFS*[1], Bodleian ms., fol. 132a, calling him 'Jamāl al-Dīn Khaljī, *nā'ib-i amīr-i dād*'; the corresponding passage in *TFS*, 251, specifies that he was Qadr Khān's father, but calls him simply 'Amīr Jamāl Khaljī' (the printed text reads JMALY in error).

[134] Ghiyāth al-Dīn Tughluq: *ibid.*, 427. Ḥusām al-Dīn: ᶜAfīf, 94, 460, 469–70, 481. Rukn al-Dīn: *ibid.*, 482; *TMS*, 143–4; and see also Hodivala, *Studies*, I, 391–2.

[135] Sayyid al-Ḥujjāb: ᶜAfīf, 445–6. Qurayshī: *TFS*, 397–8.

[136] *Ibid.*, 545, 583. *TMS*, 119, 120–1. Malik Rustam-i Yaḥyā is found among Muḥammad b. Tughluq's maliks only in the BN ms. of *TFS*, Suppl. persan 251, fol. 282b. For the *nisba* Bilāhūrī, see *IM*, 106 (BLAHWDY in error); for Bilāhūr (modern Phillaur), on the right bank of the Sutlej, at 31° 1′ N., 75° 48′ E., *Punjab district gazetteers, XIVA. Jullundur* (Lahore, 1904), 301. Shīr Khān was dead by 765/1364, when 'Malik Fakhr al-Dawla wa'l-Dīn, son of Shīr Khān Maḥmūd Beg', built a mosque at Patan: Desai, 'Khaljī and Tughluq inscriptions from Gujarat', 14–15.

[137] *TMS*, 122. One of these may have been the builder of the above-mentioned mosque.

qadi to ʿAlāʾ al-Dīn Khaljī, he was a great-grandson of the chronicler Jūzjānī, chief qadi to two of Iltutmish's sons and under Ghiyāth al-Dīn Balaban.[138]

The survival of aristocratic families from one reign or dynasty to another was simply not newsworthy in the way that the downfall of established amirs or the promotion of 'new men' always was; it demanded less attention on the part of the chroniclers. Baranī says in a few words that Ghiyāth al-Dīn Tughluq maintained in position the nobles of ʿAlāʾ al-Dīn Khaljī's reign; he devotes rather more space to the predilection of Muḥammad b. Tughluq for lowborn servitors. Yet Ghiyāth al-Dīn, as we have seen, did not simply nurture the aristocrats who represented the Khaljī era: he also brought with him from Dēōpālpūr, and installed in office, members of his own retinue, men whose ability, courage and loyalty had been proven in his service over the past twenty years or so on the Mongol frontier. And in Muḥammad's reign, conversely, a good deal of evidence is to be found that old established families were still represented among the office-holders.

We have little information about local aristocracies. The sources afford the occasional glance at a local power-base – ʿAlāʾ al-Dīn Khaljī's at Kara, for instance, where his capacity for intrigue was exacerbated by the influence of former associates of the Ghiyathid Malik Chhajjū;[139] or Malik Kāfūr's at Rāprī on the middle Yamuna and later at Dēōgīr.[140] But it is not until the last decades of the fourteenth century that Bihāmadkhānī's *Ta'rīkh-i Muḥammadī* enables us to trace what may truly be called 'local history', in this case of the region around Kālpī; and even then the ruling dynasty was an importation from Delhi – the progeny of Malik Tāj al-Dīn Turk.

Otherwise the material that could have told us about Muslim notables in the provinces is meagre indeed. Baranī devotes some space to the families of sayyids resident in various towns of the Sultanate in ʿAlāʾ al-Dīn's time, giving especial prominence to those of Badāʾūn, who served as qadis there. Two members of the family, Sayyid Tāj al-Dīn and his nephew Sayyid Rukn al-Dīn, attained the dignity of qadi at Awadh and Kara respectively, and Baranī says that he was privileged to meet them. He himself was descended through his paternal grandmother from another distinguished clan, the sayyids of Kaithal. Sayyids from Gardīz (presumably now dispersed around the empire) and those of Jajnēr and of Bhayāna are also mentioned.[141] Members of these prestigious families emerge occasionally in the higher ranks of the aristocracy. Malik Tāj al-Dīn Jaʿfar, of the line of sayyids of Jajnēr, is listed among the maliks of ʿAlāʾ al-Dīn and Quṭb al-Dīn and subsequently became *nāʾib-i ʿarḍ* and governor of Gujarāt under

138 *TFS*, 351. *TMS*, 98. See also Hodivala, *Studies*, I, 309–10.
139 *TFS*, 224.
140 *Ibid.*, 328, 333. Yazdani, 'Inscriptions of the Khaljī Sulṭāns of Delhi', 30.
141 Badāʾūn: *TFS*, 348–9. Kaithal: *ibid.*, 349–50. Gardīz and Jajnēr: *ibid.*, 350. Bhayāna: *ibid.*, 351.

Ghiyāth al-Dīn Tughluq.[142] And on occasions these local lineages might find their fortunes disrupted by royal violence. The sayyids of Kaithal paid dearly when one of their number, Sayyid Ḥasan, kotwal of Madura, successfully revolted against Muḥammad b. Tughluq in 734/1334 and (as Sultan Jalāl al-Dīn Aḥsan Shāh) founded the independent sultanate of Maʿbar: they were all massacred on the sultan's return from an abortive attempt to recover the province.[143] Sayyid Ḥasan's son Ibrāhim, keeper of the purse (*kharīṭadār*) to Muḥammad and governor of Hānsī and Sarsatī, was executed later on a charge of conspiracy to revolt.[144]

In the provinces a rare shaft of light illuminates the resilience of distinguished local families even over a stretch of a few centuries. We might think it highly improbable that any Indian locality in the reign of Fīrūz Shāh could preserve some connection with the Ghaznawid era. Yet an inscription from the Nāgawr region enshrines precisely that when it commemorates five brothers who fell in battle with the Hindus near Bari Khatu in 761/1360.[145] They bore the surname 'Bāhalīm', and hence must have belonged to the clan of the powerful amir and founder of Nāgawr, Muḥammad Bāhalīm, who had rebelled against the Ghaznawid Sultan Bahrām Shāh in 513/1119.[146] It is a tantalizing thought that many more such venerable Muslim aristocracies in the regions, beyond the horizons of our literary sources, may have survived every upheaval at Delhi.

142 *Ibid.*, 240, 379, 424, 428; see 350 for his ancestry.

143 *TMS*, 106 (with incorrect date 742); and see 107 for the massacre of the sayyids. *FS*, 469 (tr. 705), for Sayyid Ḥasan's rank: N. Venkataramanyya, *The early Muslim expansion in South India* (Madras, 1942), 123–4 n.50 and 160, therefore argues that he did not govern the entire province, *pace* IB, III, 328–9 (tr. Gibb, 715). He is earlier found acting as na'ib to the governor of the Damōh region in 725/1325: B. D. Verma, 'Inscriptions from the Central Museum, Nagpur', *EIAPS* (1955–6), 109–12; *ARIE* (1969–70), 84 (no. D66).

144 IB, III, 337–9 (tr. Gibb, 718–19).

145 N. M. Ganam, 'An epitaph of six martyrs from Baṛi Khāṭu in Rājasthān', *EIAPS* (1973), 10–13.

146 *TN*, I, 242 (tr. 110); and see also *AH*, 378–81. Bosworth, *Later Ghaznavids*, 102–3.

CHAPTER 10

An age of conquest

In chapter 7 an attempt was made to depict the constraints to which Muslim expansion was subject in the thirteenth century. This is not to say that territories outside the control of the Delhi Sultan at that time were untouched by Islam. Muslim traders had been active in the maritime cities of the peninsula and in Ceylon since the ninth century,[1] and these regions retained close links with the Gulf: in the early thirteenth, the khutba in different parts of 'Hind' was made in the name of the ruler of Fārs.[2] Kanbhāya (Cambay) in Gujarāt had its population of Muslim traders, scholars and lawyers for several decades before ʿAlā' al-Dīn Khaljī's forces first entered the country in 698–9/1299–1300. The presence of a flourishing Muslim community in the twelfth and thirteenth centuries is demonstrated by the number of epitaphs that have come to light.[3] These Muslims had their own prefect (*ḥākim*) on the eve of the Khaljī invasion, and ʿAwfī had been qadi there for a time in the early 1220s.[4] It was the same in the far south. Ibn Baṭṭūṭa's description of the Mulaybār (Malabar) coast demonstrates that communities of Muslims had settled in its ports and constructed mosques and hospices.[5] At the time of his visit, there were 20,000 Muslims in the army of the Hoysala king of Dvārasamudra; and a generation earlier ʿAlā' al-Dīn's invading army had encountered Muslims among the forces of

[1] Geneviève Bouchon, 'Quelques aspects de l'islamisation des régions maritimes de l'Inde à l'époque médiévale (XIIe-XVIe s.)', in Gaborieau, *Islam et société en Asie du sud*, 29–36. Wink, *Al-Hind*, I, 67–83.

[2] Ibn Zarkūb, ed. Karīmī, 56/ed. Jawādī, 80.

[3] Z. A. Desai, 'Arabic inscriptions of the Rajput period from Gujarat', *EIAPS* (1961), 1–24; *idem*, 'Early Kufi epitaphs from Bhadreswar in Gujarat', *EIAPS* (1965), 1–8; *ARIE* (1961–2), 33, 179 (nos. D22–29).

[4] Desai, 'Khaljī and Tughluq inscriptions from Gujarat', 3–4. For ᶜAwfī's position at Kanbhāya, which was misunderstood by Nizámu'd-dín, *Introduction*, 14, see Hodivala, *Studies*, I, 171, and II, 44.

[5] IB, IV, 71–103 (tr. Gibb and Beckingham, 805–18). See generally G. F. Hourani, *Arab seafaring in the Indian Ocean* (Princeton, 1951); Stephen F. Dale, *Islamic society on the South Asian frontier: the Māppilas of Malabar 1498–1922* (Oxford, 1980), chapter 1; Wink, *Al-Hind*, II, 276–80.

the Pāndya kingdom of Maʿbar.[6] Muslim rule, then as now, has never kept pace with the Muslim *diaspora*.

The decisive forward thrust is associated with the era of ʿAlāʾ al-Dīn Khaljī (695–715/1296–1316). His seizure of the throne had been made possible by a raid of unprecedented audacity upon the distant Yadava kingdom of Dēōgir; and his reign as sultan was characterized by equally ambitious campaigns against independent Hindu powers in Rajasthan, in Mālwa and south of the Narbada. Yet for all that we may feel confronted at this juncture by some kind of quantum leap in the process of expansion, we should beware of identifying every triumph as a landmark. Some of ʿAlāʾ al-Dīn's campaigns were simply an extension of the activity of thirteenth-century sultans: his reduction of Ranthanbōr, for instance, representing the recovery of a stronghold that had twice previously been in Muslim hands.

Nor are we necessarily faced everywhere with a new stage of conquest and absorption. True, the military reach of the Sultanate had been dramatically extended; Hindu fortresses which had hitherto yielded merely spasmodic tribute now became the seat of a Muslim governor or muqtaʿ. But the push to the south often did no more than replicate the pattern discernible in the north over the previous hundred years or so. In Baranī's account of the first successful invasion of Tilang, ʿAlāʾ al-Dīn instructs his general, Malik Kāfūr, not to make any effort to take the fortress of Arangal or to overthrow its king: if treasure, jewels, elephants and horses were offered, and tribute guaranteed for future years, he was to reach a rapid settlement.[7] Frequently the submission of a prince was accepted by the sultan or his representatives with the characteristic reassuring gesture of the hand on the back, extended to the envoys of Rudradēva of Tilang by Kāfūr and to the rai of Nagarkōt by Fīrūz Shāh.[8] There is the same pronounced gap between the ideal – exercise of immediate administrative control over the entire territory of a defunct Hindu kingdom – and a reality that resided in inevitable compromise with local powers or confined direct Muslim rule to a handful of major strongpoints. As we shall see, the last years of the Khaljī era would witness the beginnings of a more forward policy.

[6] Hoysalas: IB, IV, 195–6 (tr. Gibb and Beckingham, 861). Pāndyas: *KF*, 149; *DR*, 72.

[7] *TFS*, 327: a line is omitted here which is found in BL ms., fol. 162a, *ki dar giriftan-i ḥiṣār-i Arankal wa-bar andākhtan-i rāī Laddar Dīw mubālighī makunī wa-agar Laddar Dīw rāī-yi Arankal khizāna* . . .

[8] *KF*, 104. ʿAfīf, 189, 244. For Nagarkōt, see also L. S. Chandel, 'References to Kangra and Sirmur in the early medieval Persian sources', in his *Early medieval state (a study of Delhi Sultanate)* (New Delhi, 1989), 104 and n.39; further references in Hodivala, *Studies*, I, 321.

The campaigns in northern India

Gujarāt

Maḥmūd of Ghazna had sacked the temple city of Sōmnāth on the coast and the wealthy entrepot of Nahrwāla (Anhilwāra; modern Patan); and in 593/1197 Nahrwāla had again been looted by Quṭb al-Dīn Aybeg. But no Muslim attacks on Gujarāt are recorded thereafter, either upon the Chaulukyas or upon their Vāghela kinsmen who succeeded them around 1242, until almost the end of the century. Then in 698/1299 ʿAlāʾ al-Dīn sent his brother Ulugh Khān and the wazir Nuṣrat Khān against the Vāghela kingdom. The principal goal of the expedition may have been to sack Sōmnāth, doubtless in conscious emulation of Maḥmūd of Ghazna. The Vāghela king Karnadēva seems to have disputed the passage of the Muslim army as it neared Gujarāt, and was defeated and fled south-east to Baglāna (in the Nasik region). Sōmnāth and Nahrwāla were plundered, and Nuṣrat Khān sacked Kanbhāya, probably in Dhu'l-Ḥijja/September 1299. A Jain inscription tells us that although Satyapura (Sachōr) was saved by a miracle the sultan's forces overran the Kathiawāḍ peninsula. After this, ʿAlāʾ al-Dīn's generals withdrew to Delhi with an enormous booty, their progress interrupted only by an abortive mutiny on the part of some neo-Muslim Mongol commanders.[9]

Contrary to the impression sometimes given, this campaign did not entail a Muslim conquest or the definitive overthrow of the Vāghelas. Baranī's account of the campaign includes the misleading statement that Karnadēva sought asylum at Dēōgīr with the Yadava king Rāmadēva. In fact, this occurred a few years later. A bilingual inscription of 704/1304 shows Karnadēva established at Vadodara (Barōda), on the eastern marches of his kingdom, and flanked, incidentally, by two of the neo-Muslim Mongol amirs who had deserted the Delhi army.[10] Moreover, ʿIṣāmī describes a second invasion of Gujarāt, effected by the *qirabeg* Aḥmad-i *Chhītam. It seems to

9 See generally S. C. Misra, *The rise of Muslim power in Gujarat*, 2nd edn (New Delhi, 1982), 61–4; Lal, *History of the Khaljis*, 67–73; HN, 334–6. The date of the *farmān* ordering the *ʿāriḍ* to prepare for the expedition is given as Wed. 20 Jumādā I 698 in a couplet in *KF*, 47 (Lal, *History of the Khaljis*, 68, mistakes this for the actual date of departure): since the 20th was in reality a Monday (23 February 1299), Hodivala (*Studies*, I, 248–9) assumed that the year intended was 697. But the correct date is in fact found in a chronogram a few lines earlier: 22 Jumādā I 698/25 Feb. 1299 (*KF*, 46–7). The month Dhu'l-Ḥijja given by Waṣṣāf, 447, probably refers to the attack on Kanbhāya. For the date of the sack of Sōmnāth (June 1299), see D. B. Diskalkar, 'Inscriptions of Kathiawad', *NIA* 1 (1938–9), 695. The campaign must have extended into the year V.s. 1356 (1299–1300) given in Jīnaprabha's *Tirthakalpa* almost thirty years later: G. Bühler, 'A Jaina account of the end of the Vaghelas of Gujarat', *IA* 26 (1897), 194–5.

10 *TFS*, 251. Z. A. Desai, 'A Persian-Sanskrit inscription of Karna Deva Vaghela of Gujarāt', *EIAPS* (1975), 13–20; *ARIE* (1980–1), 6–7, 123–4 (no. B98). See *FS*, 255 (tr. 425), for the flight of the two Mongol amirs to Karnadēva.

have been this expedition which sacked Sachōr in 1310; and it was only now that Karnadēva fled to the Deccan and hence to Tilang and that ʿAlāʾ al-Dīn appointed the first Muslim governor in the person of Alp Khān.[11]

Even after this second assault, however, Muslim domination of Gujarāt remained patchy: it may, in fact, have been undermined by the revolt of the provincial garrison troops that followed Alp Khān's execution (p. 177). In Gujarāt, as elsewhere, Ibn Baṭṭūṭa notices 'rebels who inhabit inaccessible retreats in the mountains'.[12] An early seventeenth-century author asserts that ʿAlāʾ al-Dīn established the light of Islam only in the territories lying east of a line drawn from Nahrwāla to Bharūch, and that the eradication of pagan practices in the outlying parts (*aṭrāf-u jawānib*) dated from the period of the independent sultans from the fifteenth century onwards.[13] This may not do justice to the Tughluqid era, but it is true that local political conditions varied widely. Epigraphical evidence of Muslim rule down to Muḥammad b. Tughluq's reign is concentrated in the east, in Petlāḍ, Patan, Bharūch and Kanbhāya.[14] Nawsarī is found as an iqtaʿ by 725/1325.[15] But in 745/1344–5 Nānadēva, the chief (*muqaddam*) of Sālher (Sālir) and Mulher (Mālir) in Baglāna, appears to have been virtually independent.[16] And much of the Kathiawāḍ peninsula lay outside the writ of the sultan's governors. Gandhār's ruler paid tribute to Delhi at the time of Ibn Baṭṭūṭa's visit in the early 1340s; yet the Hindu ruler of Gogha (Qūqa), he tells us, who had at one time professed allegiance to Delhi, did so no longer.[17] Members of the Vāghela dynasty continued to rule at Dandahideśa under the overlordship of Delhi and, later still, in subordination to the independent Gujarāt sultans.[18] At Vamanathali (Vanthali), whose rana Mamdalikka had been chastised by Ulugh Khān in the 1299 campaign, his dynasty, the Chudasamas, contrived to extend their power over much of the Girnār (Junagarh) region.[19] When he entered Gujarāt in

[11] Misra, *Muslim power*, 64–6, though dating this second invasion in 704/1304–5. *FS*, 286–8 (tr. 461–3). For the sack of Satyapura (Sachōr) in V.s. 1366/1310, see Bühler, 'Jaina account', 195. That Karnadēva was not welcomed in Dēōgir suggests that his flight postdated the Yadava king's submission to Delhi in 706/1307 (below).

[12] IB, III, 245 (tr. Gibb, 672).

[13] Sikandar 'Manjhū', *Mirʾāt-i Sikandarī*, 42 (tr. Bayley, 97).

[14] Petlāḍ: Misra, *Muslim power*, 67; *ARIE* (1975–6), 145 (no. D114, 723/1323; no. D115, 713/1313). Patan: Z. A. Desai, 'An early fourteenth century epigraph from Gujarat', *EIAPS* (1970), 13–15 (715/1315). Bharūch: M. Nāẓim, 'Inscriptions from the Bombay Presidency', *EIM* (1933–4), *Supplement*, 25–6 (721/1321–2), 27 (726/1326). Kanbhāya: A. M. Husain, 'Six inscriptions of Sulṭān Muḥammad bin Tughluq Shāh', *EIAPS* (1957–8), 29–34 (725/1325); *ARIE* (1973–4), 143 (no. D80, 734/1334).

[15] *TMS*, 98. Q. M. Moneer, 'Two unpublished inscriptions of the time of Sulṭān Muḥammad bin Tughluq', *EIM* (1939–40), 24–6.

[16] *TFS*, 512, calling him 'Mān Dīw'; for the identification, see Hodivala, *Studies*, I, 299.

[17] IB, IV, 58, 59, 61 (tr. Gibb and Beckingham, 799, 800, 801).

[18] Ray, *Dynastic history*, 1046 n.1.

[19] For Mamdalikka, see Bühler, 'Jaina account', 194; for the epigraphy of the dynasty, Diskalkar, 'Inscriptions of Kathiawad', 576–90, etc. (especially 578–9).

pursuit of the rebel Taghai in 1349, Muḥammad b. Tughluq arrested 'Kanhgār', rana of Girnār, and imposed his own revenue-collectors on the region.[20] It is indeed possible that his three-year stay in Gujarāt – the first visit by a reigning Delhi Sultan – brought about an intensification of control over the province.

Rajasthan and Mālwa

In the thirteenth century Ranthanbōr had been the objective of several campaigns from Delhi. Its raja, Hammīradēva, who is described by ʿIṣāmī as a friend of ʿAlāʾ al-Dīn, had nevertheless created a *casus belli* by giving shelter to certain of the Mongol amirs who mutinied during the first Gujarāt campaign;[21] and following the great Mongol invasion by Qutlugh Qocha in 1299–1300, the sultan sent Ulugh Khān, then muqtaʿ of Bhayāna, and Nuṣrat Khān, muqtaʿ of Kara, with the army of 'Hindūstān' to attack the fortress. The two generals took Jhāyin, but during their investment of Ranthanbōr Nuṣrat Khān was mortally wounded. The sultan therefore set out in person to take charge of the siege operations. According to Amīr Khusraw, who dates the beginning of the siege in Rajab 700/March 1301, Ranthanbōr was taken on 3 Dhu'l-Qaʿda/11 July.[22] Hammīradēva and his neo-Muslim guests fell in the fighting. Ranthanbōr and its dependencies were conferred on Ulugh Khān, who died, however, within a few months.[23] It is a measure of the firmness of the Muslim hold here that under his successor, Malik ʿIzz al-Dīn *Būra Khān, Jhāyin, renamed *Shahr-i Naw* ('New City'), could be subjected to the same system for collection of the land-tax (*kharāj*) that obtained in the heartlands of the Sultanate (see below, pp. 242–4).[24]

During the outward march of Ulugh Khān and Nuṣrat Khān towards Gujarāt in 698/1299, Samarasimha, raja of Chitōr, had protected his kingdom by paying tribute.[25] It seems that he subsequently reneged on his submission, for in Jumādā II 702/January 1303 ʿAlāʾ al-Dīn in person set out for Chitōr. Baranī makes only fleeting mention of this campaign, describing the siege as brief. But Khusraw says that the place capitulated on 11 Muḥarram 703/26 August, and that the raja surrendered to ʿAlāʾ al-Dīn.[26]

20 *TFS*, 521, 523; for the identification of 'Kanhgār', see Hodivala, *Studies*, I, 302–3.

21 *TFS*, 283. *FS*, 255, 271–3 (tr. 425, 446–7). *TMS*, 77.

22 *KF*, 51, 54, for these dates, on which see Hodivala, *Studies*, I, 249. On the Ranthanbōr campaign, see Lal, *History of the Khaljis*, 83–6, 89, 93–6.

23 *DR*, 66. *TFS*, 283; cf. also 299 for Ulugh Khān's death.

24 *Ibid.*, 288, 299, 306. For the renaming of Jhāyin, see *KF*, 54; more references in Gupta, 'Jhain of the Delhi Sultanate'.

25 Bühler, 'Jaina account', 194. The phrasing is ambiguous: see Lal, *History of the Khaljis*, 69.

26 *KF*, 60, 61–2, 63. *TFS*, 299. *FS*, 281 (tr. 456), calling the raja Samarasimha in error for the latter's son and successor Ratan Singh. The date is discussed by Hodivala, *Studies*, I, 250; for the siege, see Lal, *History of the Khaljis*, 99–102.

Chitōr was renamed Khiḍrābād in honour of the sultan's son and heir-presumptive, Khiḍr Khān, who became its nominal governor.[27] ʿIṣāmī makes it clear, however, that the administration was entrusted to ʿAlāʾ al-Dīn's slave Malik Shāhīn.[28] The story found in Sanskrit epic and purveyed also by Firishta, according to which after ʿAlāʾ al-Dīn's death the fortress was first occupied by a brother of the raja of Jālōr and then passed into the hands of the rajas of Sisodia for two centuries, is not borne out by epigraphical evidence, which shows that Chitōr was still ruled by governors sent from Delhi in the reigns of the first two Tughluqid sultans.[29]

According to Amīr Khusraw, the Delhi forces had been investing Siwāna (Sevana) for five or six years before it fell.[30] Be that as it may, after ʿAlāʾ al-Dīn took charge of the investment the fortress was taken in Rabīʿ I 708/August-September 1308 and the raja 'Satal Dēō' was killed. Siwāna, renamed Khayrābād, was conferred on Malik Kamāl al-Dīn 'Gurg',[31] who is also credited by Sirhindī with the capture of Jālōr and the overthrow of its raja, 'Kanhar Dēō' (Kānhaḍadēva, son and successor of Samantasimha) around the same time. Baranī makes only a passing allusion to the incorporation of both places within the sultan's dominions, mentioning neither campaign; but it seems that Jālōr fell in 1311 to the same army that had sacked Sachōr in the previous year.[32] It is clear from inscriptions of 1318 and 1323 that Jālōr remained under Muslim rule into the Tughluqid era.[33]

In the course of his Ranthanbōr campaign of 700/1301, the Delhi Sultan's forces had overrun 'the territory (*wilāyat*) of Jhāyin as far as the frontier of Dhār'.[34] But it was not until after the fall of Chitōr that ʿAlāʾ al-Dīn determined, in the words of Amīr Khusraw, to 'seize the kingdoms of the southern rais'. In 705/1305 his army duly advanced into the Paramāra kingdom of Mālwa. The Delhi forces first defeated a potentate named 'Kōkā Pradhān', whom Khusraw calls a 'wazir' more powerful even than the rai himself and who was at loggerheads with the king, 'Mahlak Dēō'.

[27] *KF*, 63–4. *DR*, 67. *TMS*, 77.

[28] *FS*, 281, 282 (tr. 456, 457). According to *TFS*, 323, the governor was Malik Abū Muḥammad, who is otherwise unknown.

[29] Z. A. Desai, 'Inscriptions from the Victoria Hall Museum, Udaipur', *EIAPS* (1955–6), 67–70. Cf. Lal, *History of the Khaljis*, 110–12; HN, 371.

[30] *DR*, 69.

[31] *KF*, 68–72. For another account of the campaign, where the raja is called 'Sital', see *FS*, 315–17 (tr. 492–4). For Kamāl al-Dīn's nickname, see Hodivala, *Studies*, I, 251.

[32] *TMS*, 78, but dating the fall of both Siwāna and Jālōr in 700, which must be too early and clashes with the testimony of Amīr Khusraw. *TFS*, 323. Bhandarkar, 'Chahamanas of Mārwār', 77–8, for the date and the identification of 'Kanhar' (KSTMR in the printed text of *TMS*, and KTHR in one ms.); also Lal, *History of the Khaljis*, 118–19.

[33] 1318: Desai, 'Jālor ʿĪdgāh inscription', correcting the earlier reading of G. H. Yazdani, 'Inscription of Mubārak Shāh Khaljī from Jalor, Jodhpur State', *EIM* (1935–6), 49–50. 1323: M. A. Chaghtai, 'Some inscriptions from Jodhpur State, Rajputana', *EIM* (1949–50), 32. Shokoohy, *Rajasthan I*, 45–7.

[34] *TFS*, 277.

Then ʿAyn al-Mulk Multānī was sent against Mandū, where he besieged the raja in person. The place was taken on 5 Jumādā I/23 November 1305, and ʿAyn al-Mulk, on whom the sultan had already conferred Mālwa, was rewarded with the further grant of Mandū.[35] Baranī says nothing about the conquest of Mālwa, but confirms that during ʿAlāʾ al-Dīn's reign Mandal-khūr, Dhār, Ujjain, Mandūgarh (Mandū), ʿAlāʾīpūr, Chandērī and Ērach were all allotted to governors (*wālīs*) and muqtaʿs.[36] Precisely when most of these places were taken is unknown. Ērach, renamed Sulṭānpūr, was in Muslim hands by 709/1309, when Malik Kāfūr halted there for five days en route for Arangal.[37] Chandērī first appears as an iqtaʿ in 711/1312 (p. 174 above). An inscription of 1310 at Udayapura (in the present-day Vidisha district) reveals that the Paramāra dynasty survived here in the north-eastern part of the country; but in 739/1338 the inscription on a new mosque testified to the sovereignty of Muḥammad b. Tughluq.[38]

The Chandellas of Jejākabhukti (Bundelkhand) were in all likelihood subdued at some point during the campaigns in Mālwa, since an inscription of 1309 in a village near Bamhni acknowledges ʿAlāʾ al-Dīn's sovereignty, where only five years before a feudatory of Hammīravarman had been named. At any rate, an epigraph of 1315 accords the obscure king Vīravarman II only a shadow of the titles borne by his predecessors.[39] A consequence of this, presumably, was the capture of Mahōba, although we have no evidence of Muslim occupation prior to the construction of a mosque there in 722/1322, during the reign of Ghiyāth al-Dīn Tughluq.[40] Further south, the Pratihāras appear finally to have been subjugated either by Tughluq or by his successor, to judge from inscriptions of 1325–42 found in the Damōh and Jabalpur districts.[41] Beyond this region lay Gondhiyāna (Gondwana), which Muḥammad b. Tughluq penetrated in *c.* 1326, on his way back from the Deccan: Nāg Nāyak, 'chief of the Kōlīs', yielded after a lengthy siege of his stronghold, but we do not know for how long he remained submissive and the history of this immense tract is obscure.[42]

35 *DR*, 67–8. Hodivala, *Studies*, I, 249–50. For the grants to ʿAyn al-Mulk, see *KF*, 56, 59, with the date of the fall of Mandū (wrongly given in *TMS*, 77, as 700); *DR*, 69.

36 *TFS*, 323; for Chandērī, see also *ibid.*, 328. ʿAlāʾīpūr must be ʿAlāpūr, near Gwāliyōr: IB, IV, 31 (tr. Gibb and Beckingham, 786).

37 *KF*, 75. On Ērach/Sulṭānpūr, on the S. bank of the Betwa, at 25° 47′ N., 79° 9′ E., see Hodivala, *Studies*, I, 252–3, and *DGUP*, XXIV. *Jhansi*, 254–6.

38 *ARIE* (1961–2), 169 (no. C1637); also Ray, *Dynastic history*, 905–6, 908. For the mosque, see *ARIE* (1964–5), 23, 145 (nos. D77–78).

39 P. Prasad (ed.), *Sanskrit inscriptions*, xviii-xix and 156–8. R. K. Dikshit, *Candellas*, 177–8, citing Rai Bahadur Hiralal, 'Mahoba plates of Paramardi-deva: (Vikrama-) samvat 1230', *EI* 16 (1921–2), 9–15.

40 Z. A. Desai, 'Two inscriptions of Ghiyāthu'd-Dīn Tughluq from Uttar Pradesh', *EIAPS* (1966), 23–6.

41 Verma, 'Inscriptions from the Central Museum, Nagpur'. *ARIE* (1962–3), 96 (no. B430). *ARIE* (1967–8), 6, 27 (no. B108). *ARIE* (1969–70), 84 (no. D66).

42 *FS*, 432–3 (tr. 659–61): following the suppression of Garshāsp's revolt.

The Doab, Awadh and beyond

ʿAlāʾ al-Dīn appears also to have tightened his grip on the regions east of Delhi, though we are ill informed about both the details and the chronology. In the southern Doab, Jajmaw was under Muslim occupation by 706/1307.[43] The appearance of Rāprī, on the Yamuna, as an iqtaʿ by 709/1309; an inscription of ʿAlāʾ al-Dīn's time at Mathura, dating from soon after the first invasion of Gujarāt; and the emergence of Gwāliyōr by the end of the reign as a place of confinement for important prisoners of state – all this throws a faint light on the steady growth of the sultan's authority in regions where the government's hold in the thirteenth century had been tenuous.[44] More arresting are Baranī's claims that under ʿAlāʾ al-Dīn Katēhr was subjected, like traditionally less recalcitrant districts in the heartlands of the Sultanate, to the land-tax on the basis of measurement (see below, p. 243), and that an advance base like Kābar could be incorporated in the crown lands (khalisa).[45]

The early Tughluqid period is notable in particular for an intensification of Muslim settlement in the fertile region of Awadh. Iqtaʿs appeared here – Dalmaw, Bangarmaw, Lakhnaw (Lucknow) and Sandīla – which as far as we know had not existed in the Khaljī era.[46] From the beginning of Ghiyāth al-Dīn Tughluq's reign new strongpoints too were being constructed. The fortress at Ẓafarābād (later renamed Jawnpūr), for instance, which was conferred as iqtaʿ on the sultan's adopted son Tatar Khān, had been completed in Rabīʿ I 721/April 1321 by Malik Mall, who also left an inscription dated Muḥarram of that year/January 1321 in the Allahabad district.[47] Possibly this burst of activity was designed as a prelude to the sultan's intervention in the independent sultanate of Bengal in 724/1324, when he reinstated one of the two sons of Shams al-Dīn Fīrūz (above, p. 95), Nāṣir al-Dīn, at Lakhnawtī as his subordinate and replaced the other, Ghiyāth al-Dīn Bahādur 'Būra', at Sunārgā'ūn, with his own

[43] W. H. Siddiqi and Z. A. Desai, 'Khaljī and Tughluq inscriptions from Uttar Pradesh', *EIAPS* (1964), 3–4.

[44] Rāprī: *TFS*, 328; and see Yazdani, 'Inscriptions of the Khaljī Sulṭāns of Delhi', 30, and Hodivala, *Studies*, I, 281. Mathura: Khan Bahadur Zafar Ḥasan, 'An inscription of ᶜAlāu'd-Dīn Khaljī recently discovered at Muttra', *EIM* (1937–8), 59–61. Gwāliyōr: *TFS*, 368; *TMS*, 72 (claiming that Aḥmad-i Chap and Alughu were incarcerated there at the very beginning of ᶜAlāʾ al-Dīn's reign, although this is at variance with *TFS* and could well be an error); IB, III, 188, 333 (tr. Gibb, 642, 717).

[45] *TFS*, 288; for Kābar, see *ibid.*, 323–4.

[46] IB, III, 342, 349 (tr. Gibb, 721, 724). *TMS*, 93. Troops from the iqtaᶜ of Bangarmaw participated in the Tilang campaign of 721/1321: *TFS*[1], Bodleian ms., fol. 183a/Digby Coll. ms., fol. 154b.

[47] Desai, 'Two inscriptions of Ghiyāthu'd-Dīn Tughluq from Uttar Pradesh', 19–23. G. H. Yazdani, 'Inscription of Ghiyāthu'd-Dīn Tughluq from Asrawa Khurd near Allahabad', *EIM* (1937–8), 6–7. For the grant of Ẓafarābād, see *TFS*, 428, 451.

officers.[48] This was the first time the authority of the Delhi monarch had been recognized in Bengal since the death of Balaban.

Nepal is said to have acknowledged ʿAlāʾ al-Dīn Khaljī's overlordship,[49] and the sixteenth-century writer Mullā Taqiya alleges that he imposed tribute on the raja of Tirhut. This seems to be corroborated by the earlier recension of Baranī's history, which suggests that Tirhut was already supplying troops in 702/1302–3 for that sultan's ill-starred expedition to Tilang.[50] But the raja must have asserted his autonomy following ʿAlāʾ al-Dīn's death, for Tirhut was raided during Quṭb al-Dīn's reign by Malik Kāfūr the *muhrdār* (not to be confused with the late Malik Nāʾib), who extorted tribute from him. Only a few years later, while returning from his Bengal campaign in 724/1324, Ghiyāth al-Dīn Tughluq headed an attack on Tirhut of which the fullest account is given by Ikhtisān-i Dabīr, an eye-witness. The raja, Harisimhadēva, fled to Nepal, and his capital fell to the Delhi forces. ʿIṣāmī tells us that Aḥmad b. *Tulabugha was left there when the sultan returned to Delhi.[51] Baranī counted Tirhut as a province subject to Muḥammad b. Tughluq a few years later, and coins were struck in his name at 'Tughluqpūr, alias (*ʿurf*) Tirhut' from at least 731/1330–1.[52]

Beyond the Narbada

The Deccan, Tilang (Telingāna) and Kampila

At the time of ʿAlāʾ al-Dīn's raid on Dēōgīr in 695/1296, the Yadava king Rāmadēva had undertaken to pay regular tribute. But at some point – perhaps in reaction to the Delhi forces' unsuccessful campaign against Tilang in 702/1302–3 – he neglected to do so, and in 706/1306–7 ʿAlāʾ al-Dīn sent his favourite, the Malik Nāʾib Kāfūr 'Hazārdīnārī', against Dēōgīr. On 19 Ramaḍān/25 March 1307 Rāmadēva's army was defeated and he himself captured. ʿAlāʾ al-Dīn detained him in Delhi for about six months, treating him kindly before sending him back to his capital as a subordinate ruler, with the title *rāī-yi rāyān* ('rai of rais') and a chatr. Baranī observes that Rāmadēva remained submissive for the rest of his life;[53] and when in

48 For this campaign, see Husain, *Tughluq dynasty*, 74–6. *TFS*^{1}, Bodleian ms., fols. 184b-185a/ Digby Coll. ms., fols. 155b-156a, furnishes a slightly fuller account than other sources.

49 Luciano Petech, *Mediaeval Nepal (c. 750–1480)*, Serie Orientale Roma, X (Rome, 1958), 103–4.

50 Ḥasan Nishat Ansari, 'Political history of Bihar under the Khaljis (A.D. 1290–1320/A.H. 690–720)', *JBRS* 54 (1968), 260–3. *TFS*^{1}, Digby Coll. ms., fol. 113a.

51 Ikhtisān, *Basātīn*, fols. 10a–11b (tr. Askari, 'Historical value', 11–12). *FS*, 365, 416–18 (tr. 564, 628–30): the editor, Usha, points out that some lines are omitted from the account of Tughluq's campaign here. For Harisimha's flight, see Petech, *Mediaeval Nepal*, 111–13.

52 *TFS*, 467. *CMSD*, 117 (no. 478), 140 (nos. 579–81).

53 *TFS*, 326. A more detailed account in *KF*, 64–8, with the date, on which see Hodivala, *Studies*, I, 250.

710/1310–11 Kāfūr arrived at Dēōgīr en route to attack Maʿbar, Rāmadēva was not only assiduous in furnishing provisions and reinforcements but ordered a subordinate rai to guide the Delhi army on to Dvārasamudra.[54] The route to Tilang through Dēōgīr was safer than that by way of Sirpūr as taken by Kāfūr in 709/1309, so that as ʿIṣāmī – himself an inhabitant of the Deccan – recognized, the possession of an advance base here was essential to campaigns elsewhere in the south.[55] For a time Rāmadēva's compliance furnished the Delhi armies with just such a base; only after his death, when hostile elements took control of the Yadava kingdom, was it necessary for ʿAlā' al-Dīn and, later, Quṭb al-Dīn Mubārak Shāh to annex Dēōgīr.

After Rāmadēva's death, towards the end of ʿAlā' al-Dīn's reign, his son Singhanadēva headed a reaction and had to be quelled by yet another expedition under Kāfūr, at whose approach he fled into the hills. Kāfūr, who was appointed as governor and who is duly said to have demanded the account-books (*jarā'id*) from the clerks (*ahl-i qalam*), was under instructions to levy taxes (*māl*) on the cultivators and to build mosques.[56] From 714/1314–15 coins were being struck in ʿAlā' al-Dīn's name at the Dēōgīr mint.[57] It is therefore clear that these operations by Kāfūr represent the first attempt at annexation of the Yadava kingdom, a development which has sometimes been placed in the reign of Quṭb al-Dīn Mubārak Shāh. But with ʿAlā' al-Dīn's final illness and death, the bonds between Dēōgīr and the capital slackened. The sultan recalled Kāfūr, who is subsequently said to have ordered his deputy ʿAyn al-Mulk to bring the Muslim inhabitants of Dēōgīr to Delhi.[58]

Quṭb al-Dīn's march south in 717/1317, according to Amīr Khusraw, brought him the submission of 'all the rais' except 'Rāghū', deputy and minister to the late Rāmadēva, who raised an army but was defeated by the sultan's favourite Khusraw Khān and fled. On his way to rejoin the sultan, Khusraw Khān also defeated and executed 'Harpāl Dēō', Rāmadēva's son-in-law and a member of the defunct Chālukya dynasty formerly ruling in

[54] *KF*, 122–4, 126. Rāmadēva was not dead by this time, as alleged in *TFS*, 333: Venkataramanyya, *Early Muslim expansion*, 50–1 n.88; Lal, *History of the Khaljis*, 245–6; later (*ibid.*, 255) Lal dates his death in 1312–13. Despite *TFS*, 328–9, Kāfūr advanced on Tilang in 1309, not by way of Dēōgīr, but via Basirāgarh (variant reading for the BYJAGRHH of the text: this is Wairagarh in the Chandrapur district) and Sarbar (i.e. Sirpūr): *KF*, 80; Hodivala, *Studies*, I, 254–5; also Joshi and Husain, 'Khaljis and Tughluqs in the Deccan', 45 (though stating that Rāmadēva placed troops at his disposal).

[55] *FS*, 360 (tr. 558). P. M. Joshi, 'Historical geography of medieval Deccan', in Sherwani and Joshi (eds.), *History of medieval Deccan*, I, 12.

[56] *FS*, 333–6 (tr. 513–16), is the sole source for this episode; see Lal, *History of the Khaljis*, 255–7. Work on one mosque, at Nāltawār in the Bījāpūr district, was completed in 715/1316: G. H. Yazdani, 'An inscription of ᶜAlā'-u-dīn Khaljī from Rakkasgi in the Bijapur district', *EIM* (1927–8), 16–17.

[57] *CMSD*, 89 (no. 305C), 91 (nos. 321–2).

[58] *TFS*, 368. *FS*, 336 (tr. 516), links Kāfūr's recall with the festivities for the marriage of the sultan's son Shādī Khān; see *ibid.*, 347–8 (tr. 528–9) for ᶜAyn al-Mulk.

Kalyānī, who had been entrusted with authority in the region but had risen in revolt.[59] Other sources make no mention of 'Rāghū' and speak as if 'Harpāl Dēō' was the principal antagonist. ʿIṣāmī's account suggests additional motives for the campaign, saying that Quṭb al-Dīn was able to lay hands on the wealth amassed in the region by Malik Kāfūr and making Harpāl out to be a former confederate of the late na'ib.[60] Dēōgīr, temporarily renamed Quṭbābād in the sultan's honour, again became a mint and was provided with an administration in the form of a wazir and revenue officials; the territory was apportioned among muqtaʿs.[61] Several years later, in 1333–4, a certain Mēlugidēva, son of Singhanadēva, built a temple in the Dhule region and named Muḥammad b. Tughluq as his sovereign: if this figure is indeed Rāmadēva's grandson, the Yadavas had lingered on as the sultan's subordinates.[62]

In the course of his last Deccan expedition, Malik Nā'ib Kāfūr had briefly raided the kingdom of Kampila, which had been founded in the latter part of the thirteenth century. Profiting from the collapse of the Yadavas in the second decade of the fourteenth, its rulers had extended their authority over the modern districts of Bellary, Chitaldrug, Raichur and Dharwāḍ and established Kūmta and Husdurg (Anegondi) as their two principal centres.[63] Kāfūr ravaged the furthest parts of the territory and advanced as far as Kūmta.[64] This same region may have been attacked by the future sultan Muḥammad b. Tughluq following his second Tilang expedition, since ʿIṣāmī refers obliquely to the reduction of Gūttī (embracing parts of the Anantapur and Bellary districts) and Kuntī (Kūmta?).[65] But the conquest of the kingdom was deferred until *c.* 1327, when the raja refused to surrender the rebel Bahā' al-Dīn Garshāsp to Muḥammad b. Tughluq's forces, which took Kūmta by storm. Husdurg, whither Garshāsp and his host fled, was taken in turn; Garshāsp escaped to Dvārasamudra, but the raja of Kampila was killed in the fighting.[66] Kampila was now subjected to the sultan's overlordship and Baranī includes it in his list of

59 *NS*, 62–73, 195–202; see *ibid.*, 196–7, for the earlier commission to Harpāl. Joshi and Husain, 'Khaljis and Tughluqs', 50. *TFS*[1], Bodleian ms., fol.167a/Digby Coll. ms., fol. 143a, dates this expedition in 718/1318–19.

60 *FS*, 360–1 (tr. 558–9). *TFS*, 389–90, likewise mentions only 'Harpāl'.

61 *Ibid.*, 390. For coins of Quṭb al-Dīn from 'Quṭbābād', see *CMSD*, 98 (no. 374A). See further HN, 434–5; Joshi and Husain, 'Khaljis and Tughluqs', 51.

62 *ARIE* (1962–3), 24–5, 132 (no. B744).

63 See M. H. Rama Sharma, 'The kingdom of Kampila', *Journal of the Bombay Historical Society* 2 (1929), 201–8; K. A. Nilakanta Sastri and N. Venkataramanyya (eds.), *Further sources of Vijayanagara history* (Madras, 1946, 3 vols.), I, 9–21; Venkataramanyya, *Early Muslim expansion*, 74–5.

64 *FS*, 335–6 (tr. 515–16).

65 *Ibid.*, 31 (omitted in Husain's tr., 70). Venkataramanyya, *Early Muslim expansion*, 120–1. On Gūttī (Gooty) town, at 15° 7′ N., 77° 39′ E., see *IG*, XII, 327–9.

66 *FS*, 427–30 (tr. 654–8). IB, III, 318–20 (tr. Gibb, 710–11). *TFS*[1], Bodleian ms., fol. 192b/Digby Coll. ms., fol. 161a.

provinces ruled by Muḥammad;[67] although within a few years it became part of the kingdom of Vijāyanagara (*c.* 1336).

About the extension of the sultan's influence to the coast of Maharashtra, little evidence is available. A European traveller tells us that Tāna had been forcibly incorporated into the Delhi Sultanate by *c.* 1321,[68] but Ibn Baṭṭūṭa suggests that the Hindu ruler of the uplands between Dawlatābād and the Konkan ('Kūkan Tāna', as he calls it) was independent at the time of Hūshang's revolt.[69] Judging by the same author's testimony, the rulers of the Malabar coast were independent, with the exception of the Muslim prince of Hinawr, who was then subordinate to the rising power of Vijāyanagara.[70] If Ibn Baṭṭūṭa's claim that the Muslim rulers of the Maldives feared the Delhi Sultan, despite the distance that separated them from his dominions,[71] is well grounded, it must have been *a fortiori* more true of the rulers of Malabar, whose territories lay on the fringes of the Delhi empire.

The extensive territories south and south-east of the Yadava dominions had begun to attract the attention of 'Alā' al-Dīn and his officers as early as *c.* 701/1301–2, when the sultan's brother Ulugh Khān had died while gathering troops at Ranthanbōr for an expedition to Tilang and Maʿbar.[72] Doubts have been expressed concerning the final destination of levies from Awadh and Kara which 'Alā' al-Dīn despatched in 702/1302–3 to attack Tilang; but epigraphical evidence reveals an engagement with the Muslims near Upparapalli (in the present-day Hyderabad State) not long before 1304.[73] Baranī tells us simply that the troops became bogged down in the monsoon rains and the campaign was a failure.[74] Then in 709/1309 Kāfūr was sent to Tilang. The Delhi forces invested Arangal (Warangal), capital of the Kakatiya king Rudradēva II (the 'Laddar Dēō' of Muslim authors), and had taken the outer, clay walls of the fortress when Rudradēva asked for terms. He was left in peace in return for a written agreement to provide an annual tribute.[75] In 711/1311–12 Rudradēva duly forwarded a number

67 *TFS*, 467.

68 Odoric of Pordenone, 'Relatio', vii, 5, in Van den Wyngaert, *Sinica Franciscana*, I, 423, and tr. in Sir Henry Yule, *Cathay and the way thither*, 2nd edn by H. Cordier, HS, 2nd series, 33, 37, 38, 41 (London, 1913–16, 4 vols.), II, 114–15.

69 IB, III, 335–6 (tr. Gibb, 718).

70 *Ibid.*, IV, 67–8 (tr. Gibb and Beckingham, 803–4): he calls the Vijāyanagara king (Harīhāra) 'Haryab'.

71 *Ibid.*, IV, 158 (tr. Gibb and Beckingham, 843).

72 *TFS*, 283.

73 Venkataramanyya, *Early Muslim expansion*, 24–5.

74 *TFS*, 300; slightly fuller in *TFS*[1], Digby Coll. ms., fol. 113. K. S. Lal, 'A note on Alauddin's expedition to Warangal (1302–3 A.D.)', *JUPHS* 16, part 1 (1943), 118–24, and *History of the Khaljis*, 78–80, develops an unconvincing line of argument that this expedition was actually sent against Bengal rather than to Tilang *by way of* Bengal and Orissa, as Baranī claims.

75 *TFS*, 329–30; see 326–7 for the date. Waṣṣāf, 527, briefly refers to this campaign, which he says was led by 'Malik Nabū', Ẓafar Khān and 'Nānak [the printed text reads BABK] the Hindī': the latter two commanders are not mentioned in other accounts of the expedition.

of elephants to Delhi as a gesture of submission.[76] After ʿAlāʾ al-Dīn's death, however, he evidently forgot his promises, for in 718/1318, towards the end of Quṭb al-Dīn's Dēōgīr campaign, Khusraw Khān was sent to extort tribute from Arangal. Once again Rudradēva yielded before the Delhi troops could breach the inner fort; once again he handed over treasure and elephants and entered into undertakings for the future, receiving in exchange a chatr, a durbash and a jewelled robe. Khusraw Khān had initially demanded the surrender of five districts, Bidar (Bidarkōt), Kailas, Bōdhan, Alūr and Kōyir (Koher), but at length agreed to be content with Bidar.[77] Yet the overthrow of the Khaljīs and the events leading to the accession of Ghiyāth al-Dīn Tughluq in 720/1320 evidently enabled Rudradēva to repudiate the overlordship of Delhi a third time and to reoccupy Bidar.[78] The new regime seems to have decided on his removal. In 721/1321–2 an army led by the sultan's son Ulugh Khān (the future sultan Muḥammad) invested Arangal. These operations were abandoned owing to a mutiny on the part of some leading amirs (above, p. 180), but on the arrival of reinforcements from Delhi the prince returned to Tilang, taking Bidar and threatening Bōdhan, whose rai yielded and accepted Islam. Then he again invested Arangal, rejecting Rudradēva's offer to resume payments of tribute. Arangal fell after a five-month investment, and Rudradēva was sent off to Delhi, only to die en route. Ulugh Khān, who remained in the south for some time, brought Tilang under subjection, appointing governors, muqtaʿs and revenue officers for the new province and taking one year's land-tax (*kharāj*). Arangal itself, which is found as a mint-town a few years later, was renamed Sulṭānpūr.[79]

The sultan's armies penetrated the eastern coastal regions only rarely. Khusraw Khān raided Motupalli (Marco Polo's 'Mutfili') on his way from Tilang to Maʿbar in 718/1318;[80] and in the wake of his second Tilang expedition Ulugh Khān invaded Jājnagar, routing the king's army and gaining a considerable plunder.[81] Al-ʿUmarī was told that he had conquered the country, and lists Jājnagar among the provinces of the Sultanate.[82] But

[76] *TFS*, 334.

[77] *NS*, 114–35, gives the most detailed account: see 128, 132 for the territorial stipulations; the printed text reads BDRKWB, BSWDN and KWBR. *FS*, 361–3 (tr. 560–2). Venkataramanyya, *Early Muslim expansion*, 83–6, discusses the conflicting testimony in *NS* and *FS* regarding this campaign.

[78] *Ibid.*, 97–8.

[79] *TFS*, 446–50. *TMS*, 95. *FS*, 392–6, 400–2 (tr. 597–603, 606–9; some lines omitted at 608), alone mentions Bōdhan. For Rudradēva's death, see ʿAfīf, 395; also Hodivala, *Studies*, I, 337–8, and Venkataramanyya, *Early Muslim expansion*, 119–20 and n.38. For coins from 'Sulṭānpūr' (729/1328–9 onwards), see *CMSD*, 118 (no. 482), 120 (no. 486), 142 (no. 593A).

[80] *TMS*, 85. For this territory, see Marco Polo, tr. Moule and Pelliot, I, 394–7/tr. Yule and Cordier, II, 359–61 and n.1 at 362; Pelliot, *Notes on Marco Polo*, 787–8. Motupalli lies at 15° 43′ N., 80° 20′ E.

[81] *FS*, 402–3 (tr. 609–11). *TFS*, 450, is laconic.

[82] *MA*, ed. Spies, 5, 6 (German tr. 24, 26)/ed. Fāriq, 11, 14 (tr. Siddiqi and Aḥmad, 29, 30).

an inscription of 724/1324 from Rajahmundrī, in the Godaviri delta and doubtless close to the Jājnagar kingdom's southern frontier, may well be the only memorial of Ulugh Khān's 'conquests' here.[83] The relationship was purely a tributary one. When Sultan Fīrūz Shāh invaded Jājnagar some decades later, the rai, Vīrabhanūdēva III of the Eastern Ganga dynasty, claimed that he and his father had both been servants of the court of Delhi.[84] But 'Afīf, whose father had accompanied the sultan, observes that the country contained no Muslims.[85]

The far south

The wealth of the Coromandel coast, known to the Muslims as Maʿbar, was proverbial, and had attracted comment from Marco Polo at the turn of the century.[86] In 710/1310–11 Malik Nā'ib Kāfūr advanced on Maʿbar by way of Dvārasamudra, whose Hoysala king, Ballāla III, was just about to exploit the civil war in Maʿbar (below): taken by surprise, he submitted and acted as guide to the sultan's forces.[87] This subservience persisted, for when Kāfūr withdrew north in the wake of the Maʿbar campaign he took with him to Delhi Ballāla III's son Vīra Ballāla, who did obeisance to 'Alā' al-Dīn and was rewarded with a robe (*khilʿat*), chatr and treasure before being sent back with honour to Dvārasamudra.[88] Thereafter we know little of Ballāla III's activities. Although he seems to have asserted his autonomy after the fall of the Khaljī dynasty, he was not disposed to defy Muslim armies. When Garshāsp took refuge with him from Kampila in *c.* 1327, he made no attempt to emulate the raja of Kampila but duly handed over the fugitive to the representatives of Muḥammad b. Tughluq.[89]

Kāfūr, who reached the borders of Maʿbar in Shawwāl 710/March 1311, was less successful here than in Dvārasamudra, despite the opportunities offered by the civil war within the kingdom. According to rumours that reached Persia, the king had been murdered in 709/1309–10 by his son Sundara Pāndya, who resented being supplanted in the succession by an illegitimate brother Vīra Pāndya, and a struggle then ensued between the brothers.[90] At Kāfūr's approach Vīra Pāndya fled from his capital at Vīradhāvelan (Amīr Khusraw's 'Bīrdhūl'), and Kāfūr abandoned the search

[83] G. H. Yazdani, 'Inscription of Ghiyāthu'd Dīn Tughluq from Rajahmundry', *EIM* (1923–4), 13–14.
[84] *SFS*, 67 (tr. Roy, 'Jajnagar expedition', 72); and see also ʿAfīf, 171.
[85] *Ibid.*, 165; for ʿAfīf's father, 163.
[86] Marco Polo, tr. Moule and Pelliot, I, 381–6/tr. Yule and Cordier, II, 338–40.
[87] *KF*, 127; date of Kāfūr's departure *ibid.*, 116. *FS*, 293–5, 297 (tr. 468–70, 471).
[88] *Ibid.*, 298 (tr. 473). Venkataramanyya, *Early Muslim expansion*, 67 and n.129.
[89] *FS*, 431 (tr. 658–9). IB, III, 321 (tr. Gibb, 711), does not mention Ballāla by name. J. Duncan M. Derrett, *The Hoysaḷas: a medieval Indian royal family* (Oxford, 1957), 162–4. Venkataramanyya, *Early Muslim expansion*, 143–4.
[90] Waṣṣāf, 530–1. *KF*, 127, briefly refers to the parricide and the conflict. For the date of Kāfūr's arrival, see *ibid.*, 143: five days after his departure from Dvārasamudra (*ibid.*, 142).

for him when it became clear that the king had taken refuge in the jungle. Sundara Pāndya in turn abandoned his residence at Mathura (Madura) prior to the arrival of the sultan's army. But in Dhu'l-Ḥijja 710/April 1311 Kāfūr withdrew from the country.[91] The Delhi forces had been impeded by the monsoon rains, and reports reached Persia that a large army had been mustered against them.[92] In the wake of Kāfūr's attack, the brothers continued their conflict, in which Maʿbar's neighbours, the sultans included, were only too happy to intervene. Sundara Pāndya was defeated and took refuge with ʿAlā' al-Dīn's forces (presumably at Dēōgīr), with whose help he had, by the beginning of 1314, re-established himself in the South Arcot district.[93] In *c.* 718/1318 Quṭb al-Dīn Mubārak Shāh, fresh from the suppression of a rebellious Muslim governor at Dēōgīr, sent Khusraw Khān against Maʿbar; the city of Pattan was taken and sacked, and the Delhi forces acquired an enormous plunder.[94]

The real advance of the sultan's armies in this region, however, dates from the reign of Ghiyāth al-Dīn Tughluq. Muslim sources tell us nothing of the conquest, although Sirhindī asserts that Ulugh Khān was sent against Maʿbar as well as Tilang in 721/1321. According to a Pandyan chronicle, however, the reduction of Maʿbar, along with the capture of a king called Parākramadēva, occurred in the Śaka year 1246 (1323);[95] although the temple at Śrīrangam may not have been destroyed until 1327.[96] King Sundara Pāndya and other members of his dynasty seem still to have been acknowledged in parts of the kingdom in the 1330s and even later, and it appears that the southernmost dominions of the Pāndyas were never absorbed into either the province of Maʿbar or the independent sultanate that replaced it after 1334.[97]

[91] *Ibid.*, 148, 150, 152–3, for Vīra Pāndya's flight; 154–5 for the abandonment of the search; 160 for Sundara Pāndya's flight from Madura; 166 for Kāfūr's withdrawal. 'Bīrdhūl' (Uyyakkonddān Tirumalai, a few miles from Uraiyūr) is identified by V. Venkatasubha Aiyar, 'Srirangam inscription of Kakatiya Prataparudra: Śaka 1239', *EI* 27 (1947–8), 311; Derrett, *Hoysaḷas*, 233. For the failure of the campaign, see Venkataramanyya, *Early Muslim expansion*, 65–7.

[92] *KF*, 150–1. Waṣṣāf, 528.

[93] *Ibid.*, 531: Waṣṣāf, the sole Muslim source to mention Sundara Pāndya's appeal to ʿAlā' al-Dīn's forces, gives the false impression that it occurred during Kāfūr's invasion of 1311. Venkataramanyya, *Early Muslim expansion*, 88–90 and n.16.

[94] *FS*, 369–71 (tr. 569–72). See Venkataramanyya, *Early Muslim expansion*, 93–4, for these operations: as he points out, *TMS*, 84–5, links up the two quite separate campaigns against Tilang and Maʿbar.

[95] *TMS*, 93. Venkataramanyya, *Early Muslim expansion*, 122–5; see also *ibid.*, 70 and n.136, for the date. HN, 472.

[96] G.W. Spencer, 'Crisis of authority in a Hindu temple under the impact of Islam: Śrīraṅgam in the fourteenth century', in Bardwell L. Smith (ed.), *Religion and the legitimation of power in South Asia* (Leiden, 1978), 20–3 and n.18.

[97] Venkataramanyya, *Early Muslim expansion*, 156 n.15. *ARIE* (1980–1), 5, 77 (no. B199). K. G. Krishnan, 'New light on Madurai Sultanate', in *PSMI*, 156–7.

War aims and achievements

The initial purpose of the campaigns into peninsular India was to obtain plunder and the guarantee of tribute. In the advice to ʿAlāʾ al-Dīn which Baranī puts into the mouth of his own uncle ʿAlāʾ al-Mulk, the sultan is urged to leave in the hands of the rais and ranas no elephants, horses or wealth and to require these things every year.[98] Vanquished Hindu rulers were regularly mulcted of their treasure. The enormous tribute which Khusraw Khān imposed on Rudradēva of Tilang, even when reduced, stood at 48 *laks* (4,800,000) of gold coins.[99] Temples, too, yielded up large quantities of gold, like that at Bīrdhūl or the golden temple at the place called both 'Barmatpurī' and 'Marhatpurī' by Amīr Khusraw, which Kāfūr left in ruins during his Maʿbar campaign.[100] Plunder on such a scale rapidly acquired a legendary character. Baranī claims that in his own day some of the riches disgorged by Rāmadēva in 695/1296 were still to be found in Muḥammad b. Tughluq's treasury, while the amount obtained from Dvārasamudra and Maʿbar in 710/1311 was indeed phenomenal, allegedly totalling 96,000 *manns* of gold as well as gems and pearls – a booty that evidently made a profound impression on Delhi's older residents.[101]

In Maʿbar Hindu princes and temples were not the only victims of predatory Muslim commanders. During the 718/1318 campaign Khusraw Khān is accused of despoiling a wealthy and respectable Muslim merchant who had not judged it necessary to flee before an army led by his co-religionists. This person, whom Baranī calls Khwāja Taqī and who appears in ʿIṣāmī's more detailed account as Sirāj-i Taqī, chargé d'affaires (*farmān-nuwā*) in Pattan,[102] belonged to the dynasty which controlled the island of Qays in the Persian Gulf. According to Waṣṣāf, his uncle Taqī al-Dīn ʿAbd al-Raḥmān (d. 702/1302–3), wazir and counsellor to the king of Maʿbar, had been responsible for the importation of war-horses from Qays and adjacent regions.[103] Waṣṣāf also tells us that Sirāj al-Dīn's property had been looted during an invasion of Maʿbar by Kāfūr in 715/1315 (possibly the one in support of Sundara Pāndya: see p. 207), just before the death of ʿAlāʾ al-Dīn Khaljī, but that it had been restored to him when he complained. Since Sirāj al-Dīn's father is here said to have enjoyed friendly relations with ʿAlāʾ al-Dīn,[104] it is possible that Khusraw Khān's actions a few years later reflect a change in policy; but no doubt the conqueror was simply greedy for Sirāj al-Dīn's wealth.

98 *TFS*, 270. 99 *NS*, 128, 132. 100 *KF*, 156–9, 160. *DR*, 72.

101 *TFS*, 223, 333–4. Hodivala, *Studies*, II, 103–5, discusses the large quantities of gold obtained in 1311. It is unlikely that we can base our calculations, as he did, on the Delhi *mann* of the thirteenth-fourteenth centuries, which ranges from 11.25 to 12.824 kg.: see Walther Hinz, *Islamische Masse und Gewichte* (Leiden, 1955), 22–3.

102 *TFS*, 398–9. *FS*, 369–70 (tr. 570–1).

103 Waṣṣāf, 302–3, 505. On the dynasty, see Aubin, 'Les princes d'Ormuz', 89–99.

104 Waṣṣāf, 646–7.

Elephants, horses and specie loom large as both plunder and tribute in the chroniclers' accounts. Precise figures for the horses obtained on these southern campaigns are sometimes given in the sources. ʿAlā' al-Dīn had obtained several thousand on his Dēōgīr campaign of 695/1296.[105] Kāfūr brought back 20,000 horses from Arangal in 709/1310 and 5000 Yamanī horses from Maʿbar two years later.[106] Rudradēva handed over 12,000 Arabian (*tāzī*) horses to Khusraw Khān and promised to send 1000 every year in future.[107] In comparison, the figures for elephants sometimes seem rather modest: from Gujarāt in 698/1299, 20; from Rāmadēva, thirty or so in 695/1296 and a further seventeen in 706/1307; forty from Jājnagar in 1324.[108] From Rudradēva of Tilang in 709/1309 Kāfūr extorted a hundred, while after he had crossed the Narbada during his Maʿbar expedition in 710/1311 the king sent him another twenty-three, which Kāfūr forwarded to ʿAlā' al-Dīn at Delhi.[109] In the course of Khusraw Khān's attack, Rudradēva offered 100 elephants, and the victor stipulated that 100 should be sent annually.[110] The acquisition of large numbers of high-quality elephants appears to have been a major aim of the invasion of Maʿbar in 710/1311. It is mentioned as such in Khusraw's *Diwal Rānī* and by ʿIṣāmī in his account of the sultan's instructions to Kāfūr. Certainly Kāfūr came to give priority to the seizure of elephants even over the capture of Vīra Pāndya, and Khusraw describes his fury at finding only two or three of the beasts in Madura.[111] Yet despite such disappointments the Maʿbar campaigns yielded significantly larger numbers of elephants than did raids further north. Amīr Khusraw says that Kāfūr brought back to Delhi 512 of them, although this may have made things more difficult for those who came after him, since Khusraw Khān in 718/1318 captured hardly more than a hundred.[112]

The transition from a policy of plunder and levying tribute to one of imposing direct rule, already made in the Deccan a few years previously, is visible during the attack on Arangal in 721/1321, when Ulugh Khān rejected Rudradēva's offer of submission and pressed ahead with the siege.[113] One may well ask, nevertheless, to what extent these far-flung provinces were

[105] *TFS*, 223.
[106] *KF*, 101, 163. *TFS*, 330, numbers 7000 horses among the booty from Arangal in 709/1310; *ibid.*, 333, for 20,000 from Maʿbar in 710/1311.
[107] *NS*, 120, 128, 132.
[108] Gujarāt: *TMS*, 76. Dēōgīr: *TFS*, 223, 326. Jājnagar: *ibid.*, 450; hence *TMS*, 96.
[109] *DR*, 70; *TFS*, 330. *FS*, 291 (tr. 466), specifies twenty-three on the former occasion, but these are clearly the elephants despatched in 1311: *KF*, 120; Venkataramanyya, *Early Muslim expansion*, 39–40 and n.56. *TFS*, 334, mentions their arrival at Delhi (though giving the total as twenty).
[110] *NS*, 120, 128, 132. See also *FS*, 362 (tr. 561), for the initial surrender of 100 elephants.
[111] *DR*, 70. *FS*, 293–4 (tr. 468). *KF*, 155, 160.
[112] 1311: *ibid.*, 161: the total of 612, of which thirty-six were taken from Dvārasamudra, found in *TFS*, 333, is probably an error; so too is the round figure of 700 in *FS*, 298 (tr. 472). 1318: *TFS*, 398, 400.
[113] *TFS*[1], Bodleian ms., fol. 183b/Digby Coll. ms., fol. 155a. *TFS*, 447.

ever truly annexed. Vast distances separated Delhi from its new provinces: Ibn Baṭṭūṭa believed, with pardonable exaggeration, that Tilang was three months' journey from the capital and Maʿbar six.[114] Such distances gave rise to the most alarming delays in the transmission of news. The fourteenth-century sultans extended the postal relay system to the outlying regions of their empire.[115] But sometimes it broke down; armies receded beyond the horizon of communications and appeared to have been swallowed up in some limbo zone. In 721/1321–2 the commanders outside Arangal mutinied because a delay of a few weeks, in which couriers failed to get through from Delhi, spawned rumours that Sultan Tughluq had been overthrown.[116] There is sometimes a starkly unreal quality about the links that bound such remote territories to their imperial master.

The Deccan recognized the Delhi Sultan for less than thirty years; eastern Tilang, Kampila and Maʿbar, for an even briefer interval. And yet the transient rule of the sultans bequeathed to the Deccan one legacy, of major importance. Because this region had a strategic value relative to the other southern kingdoms, the Khaljī and Tughluqid monarchs made positive efforts to bring about Muslim colonization of the former Yadava dominions. As a consequence, this territory alone – when barely more than a generation, astonishingly enough, had elapsed since its conquest – had received a solid engrafting of Islam. The other southern provinces swiftly repudiated the sultans' faith along with their sovereignty and reverted to the infidel. But the impress of some years' subjection to Delhi would remain, even so, in the culture and titulature of the Vijāyanagara court, where the fourteenth-century monarchs styled themselves 'sultans among Hindu kings'.[117]

Striking testimony to the government's authority in the Deccan emerges from an incident during the mutiny in Tilang in 721/1321–2, when Mujīr al-Dīn Abū Rijā, the *mushrif* of Dēōgīr, met the mutineers at Kalyānī at the head of a large number of landholders (*zamīndārs*) – presumably the Hindu landed gentry.[118] Muḥammad b. Tughluq's own efforts from 727/1326–7 to turn Dēōgīr, now renamed Dawlatābād, into the second capital of his empire (below, pp. 258–60), could perhaps be seen, at one level, as the most impressive witness to the strength of Muslim rule here. But even in the Deccan, where it became firmly established, Muslim rule was uneven and extended to only a limited number of strongpoints by the time the province seceded from Delhi.

The consolidation of Muslim rule and implantation of Islam are processes largely hidden from us. A significant role may have been played by warrior

114 IB, III, 192, 208, 328 (tr. Gibb, 644, 652, 715).
115 E.g., *TFS*, 330–1.
116 *Ibid.*, 447–8.
117 Phillip B. Waggoner, '"Sultan among Hindu kings": dress, titles, the Islamicization of Hindu culture at Vijayanagara', *Journal of Asian Studies* 55 (1996), 851–80.
118 *FS*, 398–9 (tr. 604–5).

sufis, whose activities are described in later hagiographical sources. An account has survived of the career of one such warrior saint, Maʿbarī Khandayat, in Bījāpūr in the wake of Kāfūr's Maʿbar campaign of 710/1311, and Professor Eaton has made out a good case for accepting the outline as authentic and for identifying Khandayat as one of the Muslims formerly in the service of the Pāndyas.[119] The militant sufi ʿAbd-Allāh Shāh Changāl, to judge from the mid fifteenth-century inscription on his tomb, seems to have entered Mālwa at the head of a military following and played much the same role in the conversion of that province; his activities too are in all probability to be assigned to the era of ʿAlā' al-Dīn.[120] But it should be borne in mind that not all sufis resorted to force, for Ibn Baṭṭūṭa learned that the infidels of Sylhet had been won for Islam by the peaceful agency of Shāh Jalāl.[121]

We seldom hear of specific territories being granted as iqtaʿs during the years immediately following the conquest, although Sāgar, south of Gulbarga, was conferred before 1326 on Bahā' al-Dīn Garshāsp, a cousin of Muḥammad b. Tughluq;[122] and the gradual build-up of Muslim authority in the Deccan can be determined only to a limited extent on the basis of epigraphical evidence. Inscriptions show, for instance, that Jālnā, only a few miles from Dēōgīr, was under Muslim occupation by 724/1324 and that Bhadgā'ūn (in eastern Khandesh) received a mosque in 728/1328;[123] Bījāpūr was already the seat of a Muslim governor by 1320, when a mosque was built in the town.[124] Otherwise, to form some idea of the number of centres under Muslim control we must rely on ʿIṣāmī's account of events in the Deccan in the 1340s. There we learn, for example, that Dāngirī and Chanchiwāl, in the north-west of the former Yadava realm, had to be taken from Hindu chiefs by Bahmanid troops in *c.* 1350.[125] But the strongpoints of which we hear tend mostly to be concentrated in the south and south-east of the province, in an arc between Dēōgīr and the erstwhile Kakatiya capital of Arangal. Here Gulbarga, Bidar, Kalyānī and Kōyir (Koher) appear as a compact group of Muslim-held fortresses.[126] Bidar – like Bōdhan to the north – had been taken from Rudradēva by Ulugh Khān in *c.* 1322, and in Kalyānī we find mosques being constructed in the 1320s.[127] On the other hand,

119 Richard M. Eaton, *Sufis of Bijapur 1300–1700* (Princeton, NJ, 1978), 27–30.

120 G. H. Yazdani, 'The inscription on the tomb of ʿAbdullāh Shāh Changāl at Dhār', *EIM* (1909–10), 1–5; and see *ARIE* (1971–2), 80 (no. D71). More generally, see David N. Lorenzen, 'Warrior ascetics in medieval Indian history', *JAOS* 98 (1978), 61–75.

121 IB, IV, 216–17 (tr. Gibb and Beckingham, 870). Eaton, *Rise of Islam*, 73–6.

122 *FS*, 424–5 (tr. 651).

123 Jālnā: *ARIE* (1964–5), 23, 153 (no. D161). Bhadgā'ūn: Moneer, 23–4.

124 M. Nāzim, *Inscriptions of Bijapur*, MASI 49 (Delhi, 1936), 25.

125 *FS*, 560 (tr. 834).

126 Gulbarga: *ibid.*, 485 (tr. 726). Bidar and Kōyir: *ibid.*, 476 (tr. 715).

127 723/1323: *ARIE* (1965–6), 155 (no. D246), correcting the earlier reading of G. Yazdani,

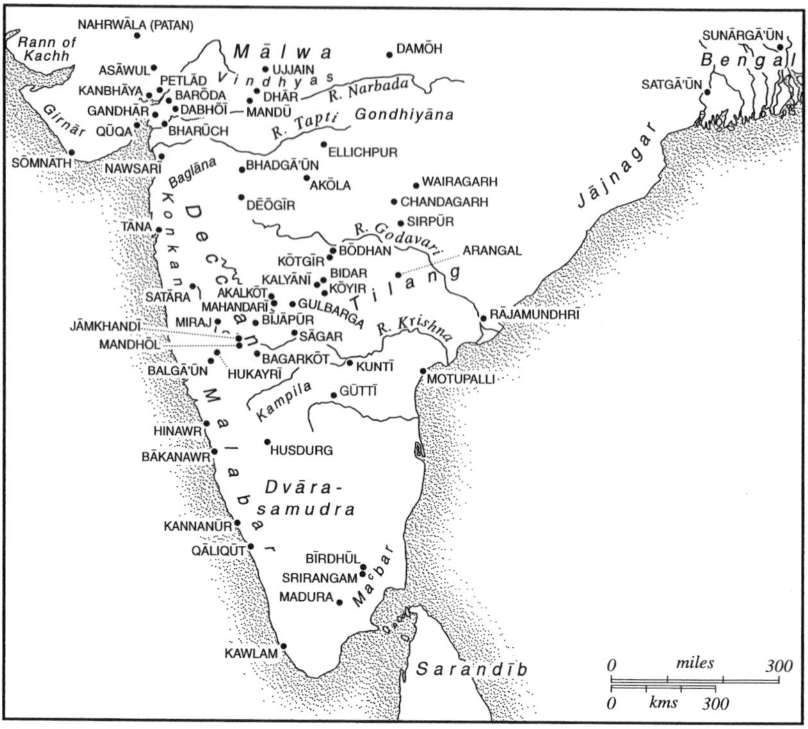

Map 4: The conquest of Gujarāt, Mālwa and the south

the neighbouring fortresses of Maram, Akalkōt and Mahandarī (Mahendri) were still in the possession of infidel rais at the onset of the Bahmanid era.[128] Towards the Western Ghats, Satāra and Miraj were in Muslim hands by the 1340s.[129] But just south of Miraj, Balgā'ūn (now Belgaum) and Hukayrī (Hakeri), at that time the iqtaʿ of the future Bahmanid Sultan, Ḥasan Gangū, are described repeatedly by ʿIṣāmī as a marcher lordship (*sarḥadd*).[130] Close by these tracts lay Mandhōl (present-day Mudhol), Jāmkhandī, Terdol and Bagarkōt (now Bagalkot), the territories of the independent Hindu prince Narāyan, who would prove a redoubtable antagonist for the infant Bahmanid regime.[131]

Baranī says that in 709/1309 the chiefs (*muqaddams*) of Tilang abandoned the strongholds along the route taken by the sultan's army; whether

'Inscriptions from Kalyāni', *EIM* (1935–6), 1–3. 726/1326: *ARIE* (1965–6), 14–15, 157 (no. D271).

128 *FS*, 562 (tr. 836). See H. K. Sherwani, *The Bahmanis of the Deccan* (Hyderabad, AP, 1953), 53.

129 Satāra: *FS*, 519–20 (tr. 770). Miraj: *ibid.*, 540–2 (tr. 811–12).

130 *Ibid.*, 521, 526, 532 (tr. 772, 778, 785). 131 *Ibid.*, 590–1 (tr. 871–2).

garrisons were immediately installed in such places we are not told.[132] But some fortresses put up resistance. Kāfūr had to halt at Sirpūr, which he took and entrusted to the brother of its chief.[133] Kōtgīr, which Mujīr al-Dīn Abū Rijā was besieging several years later, at the time of the mutiny against Ulugh Khān, seems nonetheless to have remained in enemy hands, for in the early 1340s Qutlugh Khān, who governed the Deccan on behalf of Muḥammad b. Tughluq, took Kōtgīr from a Hindu 'rebel' and stationed there one of his own lieutenants. The Chāndagarh (Chanda, i.e. Chandrapur) region, which he sent his son to plunder at around this time, was clearly independent under its own Hindu princes.[134]

Muslim military superiority

'The Hindu always falls prey to the Turk', wrote Amīr Khusraw in his *Nuh Sipihr*.[135] A little later, having likened the Turk to the lion and the Hindu to the gazelle, he claims that the Turks, whenever they bestir themselves, can vanquish the Hindus and may seize and buy and sell them.[136] 'A mere six or seven thousand Muslim horsemen,' Baranī makes Sultan Balaban tell his sons, 'could rout one *lak* of Hindu paiks and archers (*dhānuks*).'[137] Marco Polo, commenting that the men of Maʿbar – whose only defence in battle was shield and spear – made wretched warriors, was doubtless citing Muslim informants.[138] The superiority of the Muslim troops is almost a commonplace in our (Muslim) sources. Satisfactory explanations for it are less forthcoming. There is clearly a link between the assertion of Muslim paramountcy throughout the greater part of the subcontinent and ʿAlāʾ al-Dīn's administrative reforms, which enabled the sultan to raise larger numbers of troops on lower pay and which will be examined in a later chapter.[139] At times ʿAlāʾ al-Dīn's troops also profited from the fact that their Hindu adversaries were bitterly divided, as in Mālwa in 705/1305 or – at least after their first unsuccessful attempt – in Maʿbar.

Observers within the Sultanate, however, thought they could account for the sultans' victories over the Hindu on technical grounds also. The Hindus were not good marksmen, according to Khusraw;[140] there was no force in

132 *TFS*, 329. 133 *KF*, 80–2; for the identification, see p. 202, n.54 above.

134 *FS*, 397–8, 482–3, 500–1 (tr. 603–4, 723–5, 747–8). The identification of the last seems fairly certain, since the Muslim army is said to have gone by way of Akōla ('Ānkūla' in the text).

135 *NS*, 89, *Hindū buwad ṣayd-i Turkān hamīsha*. Cf. the view attributed to Ballāla III in *KF*, 131, *hargaz Hindū pīsh-i Turk . . . tāb nayārad*.

136 *NS*, 130, 131. 137 *TFS*, 52.

138 Marco Polo, tr. Moule and Pelliot, I, 389/tr. Yule and Cordier, II, 342. For other allusions to Muslim superiority in the sources, see Aziz Aḥmad, 'Epic and counter-epic in medieval India', *JAOS* 83 (1963), 470–1.

139 *TFS*, 303ff., 326.

140 *KF*, 135, *Hindūānrā kīsh-i durust nīst* (speech put into the mouths of Ballāla III's envoys). Cf. also the description of the envoys themselves, *ibid.*, 137, *kamān-wār-i kazh-nishīn*.

their arrows, remarked Ibn Baṭṭūṭa.[141] It has been proposed that the sultans' Indian opponents never adopted mounted archery.[142] This may perhaps have been true of certain Hindu armies. ʿIṣāmī, for instance, characterizes the troops of Dēōgīr led by Rāmadēva's son in 695/1296 and those of Jājnagar whom Ulugh Khān defeated in *c.* 1322 as 'all spear-wielders and swordsmen', though the phrase could owe more to style than to critical observation.[143] The Delhi forces conceivably enjoyed a superiority in terms of certain types of weaponry. ʿIṣāmī's account of Kāfūr's Arangal campaign gives some prominence to the crossbow (*nāwak*; see p. 16 above), and when Ulugh Khān attacked Arangal for the second time he is said to have taken both the outer and inner defences by dint of firing *nāwaks* and stones from catapults.[144] The *nāwak* certainly figures prominently in the catalogue of weaponry employed by the sultan's troops.[145] An anecdote of ʿIṣāmī's, in which a *gurūha* fired by a 'Turk' not only penetrated the wheel of a wagon but embedded itself in the earth beyond right up to the feather, suggests that this particular weapon (expressly called an arrow, and hence presumably a crossbow-bolt) was calculated to strike terror into the enemy.[146]

It is fair to say, on the evidence of the narrative sources, that the sultan's forces were seldom granted the opportunity of a pitched battle. On the few occasions when it did happen, the Delhi army is portrayed as having won an almost effortless victory – as when the army of Mālwa challenged ʿAyn al-Mulk in 705/1305, or when Rāmadēva's son marched out to challenge Kāfūr in 706/1307 or when Vīra Pāndya's *rāwats* met Kāfūr outside Bīrdhūl four years later.[147] But Rudradēva is expressly said to have avoided a pitched battle in 721/1321–2.[148] The reason for this apparent Muslim advantage may have been a chronic inability on the part of many Hindu rulers to match the sultan's armies in terms of horses; and the eagerness of the monarchs of peninsular India to obtain horses in large numbers from Arabia and the Persian Gulf was notorious.[149] There are already indications in the middle of the thirteenth century of an imbalance in this respect

141 IB, III, 134 (tr. Gibb, 613).
142 P. K. Gode, 'The mounted bowman on Indian battle-fields – from the invasion of Alexander (B.C. 326) to the battle of Panipat (A.D. 1761)', in his *Studies in Indian cultural history* (Hoshiarpur and Poona, 1960–9, 3 vols.), II, 57–70. Wink, *Al-Hind*, II, 82–3. For mounted combat, see Digby, *War-horse*, 12 and n.5.
143 *FS*, 234, 402 (tr. 403, 609).
144 Kāfūr: *ibid.*, 290–1 (Husain's tr., 465, does not bring out the sense). Ulugh Khān: *TFS*, 449; *TMS*, 95.
145 E.g. *KF*, 55, 56, 57, 58–9, 80–1, 93, 128, 136, 150. Perhaps this is the arrow that pierces seven plates of iron: *ibid.*, 96.
146 *FS*, 230 (tr. 397–8); see *ibid.*, 54 (tr. 108), for a *gurha* [*sic*] which transfixed a deer during one of Maḥmūd of Ghazna's campaigns. By contrast, the *gurūha-yi maghribī* mentioned in *KF*, 90, was clearly fired from a mangonel.
147 *KF*, 65–6, for Dēōgīr; 151–2 for Bīrdhūl.
148 *TFS*, 446.
149 Digby, *War-horse*, 29–32. Wink, *Al-Hind*, II, 83–7.

between the Muslims and Hindu rulers, as when Jūzjānī alleges that the Jajapella king Chāhaḍadēva possessed a mere 5000 horse as against 200,000 foot or when he mentions only paiks and elephants in the army that the king of Orissa brought into Muslim Bengal in 642/1244.[150] Similarly, at the very end of the century Hammīradēva of Ranthanbōr is credited with 'countless infantry' but just 12,000 horse.[151] Yet, while such figures suggest that the Delhi forces enjoyed a greater striking power than their Hindu opponents, in other cases the proportion of cavalry to infantry would seem to have been roughly similar on both sides. Karnadēva of Gujarāt, for instance, had 30,000 horse as against 80,000 foot in his army, and Kōka in Mālwa had 40,000 horse and one *lak* of foot.[152]

Whatever the case, the *leitmotiv* of the Khaljī and Tughluqid campaigns both north and south of the Vindhyas is one of sieges. An inscription of 1261 at Ajāyagarh calls the Chandella king Trailokyavarman 'a very creator in providing strong places', and it has been suggested that this provides a genuine hint as to the tactics followed in resisting Muslim incursions.[153] It may be that Muslim siege warfare of the early fourteenth century represents an advance on that of the Shamsid and Ghiyathid eras, but unfortunately neither the thirteenth-century sources nor those for ʿAlā' al-Dīn's reign furnish enough information to warrant firm conclusions, and Professor Lal's case that the Muslims enjoyed a definite superiority in this respect must be regarded as unproven.[154] Amīr Khusraw says that the walls of Ranthanbōr were demolished by *maghribīs* (mangonels); but we know, on the other hand, that Chitōr surrendered and that Mandū was taken through the treachery of a Hindu deserter, who showed ʿAyn al-Mulk a way into the fortress. At the investment of Siwāna the sultan's troops constructed a *pāshīb*, a gradated platform made out of earth, mounting to the level of the walls, and this was clearly important in their success.[155] So too the *pāshīb* raised by Khusraw Khān for the investment of the inner fortress at Arangal in 718/1318 was instrumental in bringing Rudradēva to ask for terms.[156] At other times, however, the role of the *pāshīb* is difficult to assess, since it is also clear that such a device had earlier been employed at Ranthanbōr and had suffered considerable damage from the enemy cata-

[150] Jajapellas: *TN*, I, 485 (tr. 691): for this and other relevant evidence, see Digby, *War-horse*, 49. Orissa: *TN*, II, 15 (tr. 739).

[151] *TMS*, 77. [152] The figures are from *ibid*., 76.

[153] P. Prasad, *Sanskrit inscriptions*, 100–5 (verse 7). Ray, *Dynastic history*, 727.

[154] K. S. Lal, 'The striking power of the army of the Sultanate', *JIH* 55 (1977), part 3, 100–1.

[155] Ranthanbōr: *DR*, 65–6. Chitōr: *KF*, 62; *FS*, 281 (tr. 456). Mandū: *KF*, 58; *DR*, 68, mentions a 'breach'. Siwāna: *KF*, 50–1, 70; *TMS*, 78, indicates that the fortress was stormed. Hodivala, *Studies*, I, 112, renders *pāshīb*, somewhat loosely, as 'earthworks'; for this and other devices, see Athar Ali, 'Siegecraft techniques of the Delhi Sultans during 13th and 14th century [*sic*]', *PIHC* 51. *Calcutta 1990* (Delhi, 1991), 217–26, and his 'Military technology', 171–3.

[156] *NS*, 111–14.

pults.[157] At Arangal in 709/1309 the besiegers did not wait for the completion of the *pāshīb* before launching their assault on the outer, mud wall.[158]

In the current state of our knowledge, questions about the capacity of the sultans' armies to vanquish their Hindu opponents are unanswerable. But if the inferiority of such antagonists was more often than not taken for granted, developments elsewhere had put it in a new perspective. 'Where should the army that defeats the Mongol host be afraid of fighting the Hindu?' asked ʿIṣāmī sardonically.[159] Long before the time at which he wrote, the sultans had been given greater reason to hate and fear the other infidel enemy, to the north-west.

[157] *KF*, 50–1. *TFS*, 277.

[158] *KF*, 91.

[159] *FS*, 284 (cf. tr. 459).

CHAPTER 11

The Chaghadayid invasions

The southward advance of the Central Asian Mongols

Chapter 6 surveyed the disintegration of the unitary Mongol empire, culminating in the creation of a confederacy of princes under Ögödei's grandson Qaidu in Central Asia in opposition to the qaghan Qubilai. Although Qaidu's own campaigns seem always to have been directed against Qubilai's lieutenants and supporters in Mongolia, he also pursued, if less directly, an expansionist policy south of the Oxus. The rulers of Chaghadai's ulus, whom he nominated, appear to have acted as his subordinates: the last and most important of them was Du'a, Baraq's son, who became khan in *c.* 681/1282.[1] Under Qaidu's aegis Du'a, in Rashīd al-Dīn's words, 'gradually gathered together the armies of Chaghadai';[2] and their forces collaborated both in eastern Persia and in Afghanistan. Qaidu's son Sarban and one of Du'a's chief noyans, Yasa'ur, were stationed south of the Oxus by 690/1291.[3] That the allies were already seeking, at this early date, to assert their influence among the Negüderis is clear from Qaidu's dealings with the renegade Ilkhanid general, Nawrūz, who operated on his behalf in Afghanistan from 690/1291 until he rejoined the Ilkhan in 694/1294.[4] Waṣṣāf, whose account of these events is geographically more specific than Rashīd al-Dīn's, has Nawrūz taking up his quarters in 'Sīstān' (i.e. Ghūr and Gharchistān), where he won over the Negüderi forces, and says that he particularly relied on them; at another juncture Nawrūz is referred to as their chief (*ḥākim*).[5] It looks very much as if Qaidu relied on Nawrūz

1 Jamāl al-Qarshī, 138–9. *JT*, II, 192–3 (tr. Boyle, 154/tr. Verkhovskii, 100). Biran, *Qaidu*, 32–3.

2 *JT*, II, 172 (tr. Boyle, 141/tr. Verkhovskii, 92).

3 Sarban: *JT*, ed. Karl Jahn, *Geschichte Ġāzān Ḫān's*, GMS, ns, XIV (London, 1940), 26 (fuller than *JT*, III, ed. Alizade). Yasa'ur near Balkh: *JT*, I, part 2, ed. I. N. Berezin, 'Sbornik letopisei', *TVOIRAO* 15 (1888), 217; tr. O. I. Smirnova, *Sbornik letopisei*, I, part 2 (Moscow and Leningrad, 1952), 275.

4 *JT*, ed. Jahn, *Geschichte Ġāzān Ḫān's*, 24–6, 29, here fuller than *JT*, III, 268–72 (tr. Arends, 150–2). On Nawrūz, see generally Biran, *Qaidu*, 57–9.

5 Waṣṣāf, 253, 314; for this sense of the term 'Sīstān', see Aubin, 'L'ethnogénèse', 91.

as his agent in maintaining a fragile control over parts of Afghanistan. Towards the end of the thirteenth century, however, that control markedly intensified.

It may have been in response to Nawrūz's defection that Qaidu instituted the military dispositions outlined by Waṣṣāf. Sarban was put in overall command of forces totalling five tümens (50,000), three of them from Qaidu's own armies and two belonging to Du'a. His lieutenants included the Ögödeyid prince Küresbe; Temür, son of Ebügen, a descendant of one of Chinggis Khan's brothers; and Du'a's son Qutlugh Qocha.[6] Of Sarban's colleagues, the last-named, for our purposes, is the most important. According to Rashīd al-Dīn, Du'a recalled the Chaghadayid prince ʿAbd-Allāh and set Qutlugh Qocha over the Negüderis in his place.[7] The Negüderi commander Abachi, who in the early 1290s had obeyed Nawrūz, now appears as Qutlugh Qocha's subordinate.[8] Rashīd al-Dīn says that Qutlugh Qocha spent the summer in the confines of Ghūr and Gharchistān and wintered in 'the territory of Ghaznayn and that direction'; Qāshānī says that he resided in Bīnī-yi Gāw, which the sources, as we have seen, traditionally link with the Negüderis; while Waṣṣāf describes his headquarters as the valley of the 'Arghantūā' (Arghandāb).[9] He came to rule a vast principality, which extended from the Oxus down to the hot regions around the latitude of Qandahār.[10] He struck coins at Ghazna in his own name,[11] and his exalted status emerges from Rashīd al-Dīn's allusion to him in terms that suggest he was practically joint ruler of Chaghadai's ulus with his father Du'a, an impression also in evidence in the Indian chronicle tradition.[12] He appears to have had at his disposal considerable reserves of manpower, since Waṣṣāf sets his forces at five tümens; though ʿIṣāmī exaggerates in claiming that at the time of his invasion of India in 699/1299–1300 (below) there were 200,000 men on his muster-roll.[13]

[6] Waṣṣāf, 509–10. For Küresbe, see *JT*, II, 14 = II, part 1, ed. Alizade, 38–9 (tr. Boyle, 28/tr. Verkhovskii, 17). For Temür, see *SP*, fols. 103b–104a; *Muʿizz al-Ansāb*, fols. 9b, 10b, 11b: this branch of the dynasty is omitted in *JT*, I, part 2, ed. Berezin, in *TVOIRAO* 13 (1868), 86–95 (tr. Smirnova, 51–4). Both princes accompanied Sarban's army in 1302–3 (below): Qāshānī, 18.

[7] *JT*, III, 152 (tr. Arends, 94), with the date 698/1299, which is probably too late; at II, 177 (tr. Boyle, 144), the text is corrupt, and for the correct reading see Aubin, 'L'ethnogénèse', 84 n.2.

[8] Sayfī, 379–82. Waṣṣāf, 368. Kirmānī, *Simṭ al-ʿUlā'*, 89. Aubin, 'L'ethnogénèse', 88. He was probably the unnamed Negüderi chief (*shāh*) killed by the Ilkhan's troops in 1301: Waṣṣāf, 417–18.

[9] *JT*, II, 173 (tr. Boyle, 142/tr. Verkhovskii, 93). Qāshānī, 201. Waṣṣāf, 367.

[10] *Ibid.*, 368, listing 'Balkh and its dependencies (*maḍāfāt*), Shabūrghān, Jūzjān, Badakhshān, Kishm, Ṭāyaqān, Dara-yi Sūf, Dara-yi Gaz, Fīrūzkūh, ʿAliyābād, Malikābād, Marw (Merv) and its appendages (*lawāḥiq*), Andkhūī, Fāryāb, Ṭāliqān, Marūchaq and Panjdih'. For the localization of some of these places, see map 2; also Aubin, 'L'ethnogénèse', 92 n.4.

[11] Thomas, 175–6. E. Blochet, 'Les monnaies mongoles de la collection Decourdemanche', *Revue de l'Orient Chrétien* 11 (1906), 119–20.

[12] *JT*, I, part 2, ed. Berezin, in *TVOIRAO* 13 (1868), 125 (tr. Smirnova, 69). *AHG*, II, 796.

[13] Waṣṣāf, 367. *FS*, 256 (tr. 427).

From these forward bases, both Sarban and Qutlugh Qocha, according to Rashīd al-Dīn, mounted repeated attacks on the Ilkhan's eastern provinces.[14] Waṣṣāf describes the Herat region as a bone of contention between the Ilkhan's forces and Qutlugh Qocha's Mongols.[15] But the latter's raids, like those of the Negüderis earlier, penetrated much more deeply into Persia, as when in 700/1301 (actually after Qutlugh Qocha's death) one tümen of his forces ravaged Fārs and Kirmān and even rode as far as Hurmuz.[16] Both on that occasion and in 702/1302–3, when Sarban attempted to link up with Qutlugh Qocha's troops in a joint attack on Khurāsān,[17] the Central Asian Mongols, who sought to profit from the absence of the Ilkhan Ghazan in Syria, were worsted by his brother, the viceroy Kharbanda.[18]

At what stage responsibility for assaults on the Sultanate passed from the Negüderi bands to the armies of Qaidu and Du'a, it is difficult to say. When Balaban's grandson Kaykhusraw sought assistance from the Mongols at Ghazna following the enthronement of his cousin Kayqubād in 685/1287, says ʿIṣāmī, he was unsuccessful because the Mongols were preoccupied with internal disputes.[19] This could conceivably refer to the early stages of Qaidu's intervention in Afghanistan; but the evidence at our disposal is inadequate. Even after the definite appearance of Qaidu's commanders on the scene, there were still small-scale initiatives by what were presumably Negüderi contingents acting independently. In *c.* 698/1298–9 ʿAlāʾ al-Dīn sent his general Ẓafar Khān against a body of Mongols who had occupied Sīwistān in lower Sind, perhaps seeking to take advantage of the recent overthrow of Jalāl al-Dīn Khaljī's sons and their supporters at Multān. The invaders were dislodged, and their chief *Sögedei was captured with his brother and brought to Delhi.[20] ʿIṣāmī describes him as a 'Turk' and one of his companions as a 'Balūch',[21] suggesting that the episode represents a

14 *JT*, II, 11 (= II, part 1, ed. Alizade, 28), 173 (tr. Boyle, 25, 142/tr. Verkhovskii, 14, 93).

15 Waṣṣāf, 368.

16 The date in *JT*, III, 152 (tr. 94), and supported by the lost chronicle of Hurmuz: W. F. Sinclair, *The travels of Pedro Teixeira*, HS, 2nd series, 9 (London, 1902), 160–1 (but at 161 n.1, Sinclair mistakes the marauders for the Ilkhan's forces). Fuller account in Waṣṣāf, 368–71, with confused dating.

17 *JT*, II, 11–12 = *JT*, II, part 1, ed. Alizade, 28–30 (tr. Boyle, 25–6/tr. Verkhovskii, 14–15). Qāshānī, 18.

18 Waṣṣāf, 368. Qāshānī, 19.

19 *FS*, 196–7, *Mughalrā dar ān waqt bā ahl-i khwīsh * magar būd dīgar muhimmī ba-pīsh* (tr. 329).

20 *TFS*, 253–4, placing the invasion in the same year as the sultan's Gujarāt campaign, i.e. the third year of the reign (*ibid.*, 251), 697–8/1298–9; on the chronology of that expedition, see above, p. 195 and n.9. *AHG*, II, 787, 790, dates the occupation of Sīwistān in 697 and its recovery in 698.

21 *FS*, 251 (tr. 421–2). The name of the invading chief, usually given as 'Saldi', appears in *TFS*[1], Bodleian ms., fol. 133a, as SKNY, probably an error for SKTY, i.e. Sögetei. In the critical apparatus to his edition of *FS*, Usha in fact proposes SGDY. On the etymology of Sögetei/Sögedei, see Pelliot and Hambis, *Histoire des campagnes de Gengis Khan*, 129–30, 255–6.

local foray from the southern parts of what is now Afghanistan. We know that Naṣīr al-Dīn, the malik of Sīstān, had sent an expedition in 695/1295–6 to 'the hot country (*garmsīr*) and the environs of Bust and Tigīnābād' and had cleared the region of 'brigands' (*duzdān-u runūd*).[22] Sögedei's forces were possibly fugitives from the more southerly camping-grounds of the Negüderis, which were in a state of ferment prior to the advent of Qutlugh Qocha and had become a prey to neighbouring dynasts. Incursions from this area may have continued into the early years of the fourteenth century. We learn of a second Mongol assault on Sīwistān in 703/1303, coinciding with Taraghai's investment of Delhi (below, p. 223), and a later one still, which was repulsed in the Tharī (Thar) region by Alp Khān, the governor of Gujarāt, acting in concert with Tughluq, the muqtaʿ of Dēōpālpūr and future sultan.[23]

Qaidu died in present-day Kazakhstan in 702/1303 and was succeeded by his eldest son Chapar. The new sovereign, whose accession did not pass unchallenged, was prepared to be guided by his sponsor Du'a, who proposed that the Central Asian Mongols recognize Qubilai's successor, the qaghan Temür, and inaugurate a general peace throughout the Mongol world. The initiative met with a willing response, too, from his father's enemies. When in 704/1304 Temür Qa'an's ambassadors arrived at the Ilkhan's court along with those of Chapar and Du'a to announce the good news, they were welcomed by Kharbanda, who had recently succeeded Ghazan and now reigned as Öljeitü Sulṭān.[24] As a result of this mission, in which were represented also the Mongols of Qutlugh Qocha and other subordinate princes,[25] the Ilkhan's dominions were incorporated in the peace established among the rulers of the various Mongol khanates. It was to this general reconciliation that Khurāsān owed the respite from Chaghadayid aggression which it now secured for almost a decade.

Crisis: the invasions of Qutlugh Qocha and Taraghai

Not so the Delhi Sultanate. In his letter to the qaghan Temür, Chapar had advocated a settlement in order that the energies of Chinggis Khan's descendants might be released for conflict with their external enemies, and had mentioned as the specific target of the Central Asian Mongols the

22 Anonymous, *Ta'rīkh-i Sīstān*, 408 (tr. Smirnova, 379).

23 *TFS*[1], Digby Coll. ms., fol. 113b. *FS*, 288–9 (tr. 463–4). Since Gujarāt had just undergone a second invasion by the Delhi forces (above, pp. 195–6), the Mongol attack occurred no earlier than 1309–10.

24 See generally Biran, *Qaidu*, 69–74. I prefer the date given for Qaidu's death by Qāshānī, 32, which is supported by Rashīd al-Dīn's statement that the news reached Ghazan in Iraq early in Shaʿbān 702/late in March 1303: *JT*, III, 356 (tr. Arends, 199).

25 Waṣṣāf, 475: the date given here, Jumādā I 705/November–December 1305, is too late and, unless simply an error, must refer to a later embassy than the one which prompted Öljeitü's letter to Philip IV (Biran, *Qaidu*, 71–2).

territories of Sind and Hindūstān.[26] For on the frontiers of these regions, no less than of Khurāsān, the forces of Qaidu and Du'a had assumed the direction of military operations, with the result that Mongol pressure on India had considerably increased. Rashīd al-Dīn says of Qutlugh Qocha's forces that 'they must forever be doing battle with the sultan of Delhi, and the army of Delhi has many times defeated them'.[27] The reign of ʿAlā' al-Dīn Khaljī (695–715/1296–1316) witnessed several Mongol invasions, two of them on a scale far surpassing those of previous decades and threatening the capital itself. The Mongols appear to have been kept well informed of circumstances within the Sultanate, and it seems that, just as in their dealings with the Ilkhan, Qaidu and Du'a profited from distractions on ʿAlā' al-Dīn's other frontiers in order to mount heavy assaults on his empire. Indeed, the sultan's policy of aggrandizement at the expense of Hindu powers (see chapter 10) afforded them considerable opportunity.

The earliest unequivocal evidence of operations in India by the Central Asian Mongols belongs to 697/1297–8, when Qaidu's noyan Keder[28] invaded the Panjāb, ravaging the territory as far as the neighbourhood of Qaṣūr. But Sultan ʿAlā' al-Dīn's brother Ulugh Khān crushed the invaders at a locality named Jāran Manjūr near the banks of the Sutlej on 22 Rabīʿ II/6 February 1298. The Mongol dead numbered 20,000, and the prisoners were taken to Delhi to be executed.[29] A greater threat was posed by Qutlugh Qocha's forces. Their first major strike occurred in 699/1299–1300, during the absence of the Delhi army on the first Gujarāt campaign, with which Egyptian sources expressly link it.[30] Qutlugh Qocha, accompanied by

[26] Waṣṣāf, 454.

[27] *JT*, II, 173 (tr. Boyle, 142/tr. Verkhovskii, 93).

[28] He served under Sarban in Khurāsān in 702/1302–3 (Qāshānī, 18), and is listed by Waṣṣāf, 511, among those of Qaidu's noyans who crossed the Oxus with Sarban in 706/1306 to submit to the Ilkhan. The name is almost certainly Mo. *keder*, 'obstinate', 'quarrelsome': Lessing, *Mongolian–English dictionary*, 441. *KF*, 36, calls his forces 'Qaidu's carrion-eaters' (*murdār-khwār*).

[29] *Ibid.*, 33–6, for the fullest account; a briefer notice in *DR*, 59–60. *TFS*, 250, which places the invasion in 696/1296–7 and does not name the Mongol leader, gives the sultan's commanders as Ulugh Khān and Ẓafar Khān. Jāran and Manjūr, named in all these sources (though arbitrarily changed to 'Jālindhar' by the editors of *TFS*), appear from a later reference in *TMS*, 218, to have lain in the Jālindhar region: Hodivala, *Studies*, I, 407; *ibid.*, 246–7, he identifies the two elements as Jagraon and Macchiwara, respectively S.W. and S.E. of Ludhiana. For Qaṣūr, on the old north bank of the Bēāh, at 31° 8′ N., 74° 28′ E., see *IG*, XV, 149–50.

[30] Ibn al-Dawādārī, IX, 57; hence Ibn Abi'l-Faḍā'il, ed. Blochet, 556–7. The link between the sultan's own plundering campaigns and Qutlugh Qocha's attack is also implicit at Qāshānī, 189. The Egyptian sources suggest that it fell in 699. *TFS*, 254, places it 'at the end of the aforementioned year', i.e. of the third year of the reign (697–8), which would suggest the late summer of 1298; but the Mongols surely arrived in the cold season. Bihāmadkhānī, fol. 386b, erroneously makes the invasion coincide with the Ranthanbōr campaign. Waṣṣāf, 312, gives 694 in error; Rashīd al-Dīn, *JT*, ed. Jahn, *Indiengeschichte*, Ar. text Taf. 59, Pers. text Taf. 25 (German tr. 50), is vague.

his brother Temür Buqa,[31] advanced directly on Delhi. ʿAlāʾ al-Dīn met the Mongols at Kīlī, a place whose location is now unknown but which apparently lay some fifteen miles north of the capital.[32] His right wing, led by Ẓafar Khān, crushed the Mongol left but on the way back from the pursuit was ambushed by the enemy rearguard under the noyan Taraghai and annihilated. Yet the Mongol army then retired.[33] Baranī's explanation – that their appetite for further conflict had been reduced by the strenuous resistance of Ẓafar Khān, whose name was to become a byword among them – is hardly satisfactory.[34] The real reason appears to be that, as we learn from contemporary sources, Qutlugh Qocha had been mortally wounded: he died during the long return journey to his base.[35]

Over the next few years Mongol bands numbering 10,000 or 15,000 horse continued to make plundering raids on the Panjāb, but caused no general alarm and retired on each occasion without a pitched battle.[36] But when in 702/1302–3 ʿAlāʾ al-Dīn's forces were again scattered on distant campaigns, Taraghai, now in command of Qutlugh Qocha's army,[37] felt strong enough to threaten Delhi a second time. This invasion appears to have posed an even greater danger than that of Qutlugh Qocha. ʿAlāʾ al-Dīn was reduced to following the defensive tactics he had eschewed during the earlier attack, barricading himself and his army in the Sīrī plain. The Mongols' position extended from the Yamuna as far as the plain of Lohrāwat; but although they launched raids into the suburbs of the old city, where they penetrated as far as the Ḥawḍ-i Khāṣṣ, they were unable to move there in force for fear of exposing their flank. This stalemate situation lasted for about two months; then Taraghai suddenly withdrew to his own territory.[38]

31 So called in *FS*, 260 (tr. 431). This is correct: although he does not appear in *JT* or in *Muʿizz al-Ansāb*, he is listed among Du'a's sons in *SP*, fol. 120a.

32 Hodivala, *Studies*, I, 271, for a discussion. Of the sources he does not cite, *FS*, 259 (tr. 430), says merely that Kīlī was in the Doab; but *TFS*[1], Bodleian ms., fol. 145a, and RRL ms., 219, makes the sultan march seven *kurōhs* (1 *kurōh* = approx. 2 miles) from Delhi to the battlefield. On the strength of the word-play in *DR*, 60, the spelling 'Kailī' is advocated in ED, III, 548 n.4; but this is hardly conclusive, as Khusraw's puns are often just visual.

33 *TFS*, 260–1. *FS*, 262–5 (tr. 430–41); *ibid.*, 265–9 (tr. 441–3), ʿIṣāmī speaks of a further confrontation the next day between the Mongols and the sultan's main force. The spelling 'Targhi' usually found in secondary literature is incorrect: this is Tu. *taraqai*, 'bald' (Pelliot, *Notes on Marco Polo*, 69, 568), and the meaning is confirmed by Khusraw's pun in *KF*, 37, *sar-i aṣlaʿ*.

34 *TFS*, 261.

35 Qāshānī, 193, 201. *DR*, 61, *agarchi ḥālī az shamshīr jān burd* * *wa-līk az sahm-i ḥarba raftanā murd*: this detail, which is omitted in ED, III, 548, is reproduced in Bihāmadkhānī, fol. 387b (with the verse), *TMS*, 72–3, and Badā'ūnī, I, 185. For the meaning of *raftanā*[*n*], see Hodivala, *Studies*, I, 268.

36 *TFS*[1], Bodleian ms., fol. 145b/RRL ms., 220.

37 Waṣṣāf, 510 (describing the events of 705/1305–6), *lashgar-i Qutlugh Khwājarā mīdānist*. Qāshānī, 36, calls Taraghai the amir of Qutlugh Qocha's *ordo* (camp).

38 *TFS*, 301–2; *TFS*[1], Digby Coll. ms., fols. 113b–114a, but Bodleian ms., fols. 145b–146a, omits the duration of the siege. *FS*, 285–6, 291–2 (tr. 460–1, 466–7), recounts two invasions by Taraghai, the first lasting forty days and the second one month. He accompanied a later raid, in 1305 (below), when he certainly did not reach the capital.

The invasions of Qutlugh Qocha and Taraghai represented crises of the first magnitude. The size of their armies varies considerably in Baranī's accounts, but the lowest figure he gives for Qutlugh Qocha's force is ten tümens or one *lak* (100,000); he supplies no statistics for ʿAlāʾ al-Dīn's army, which may have been outnumbered, since reports reaching Egypt put it at a mere 30,000.[39] In 703/1303 Taraghai may have brought with him as many as 120,000 men, whereas in one manuscript of Baranī's first recension the sultan is said to have withstood the siege with only 10,000 horsemen and 50,000 foot.[40] Although Qutlugh Qocha's Mongols did not penetrate as far as the outskirts of the city, Delhi felt the impact of the invasion, since refugees from the surrounding countryside drove up the price of foodstuffs when wary traders were unwilling to venture near the city.[41] At the time of Taraghai's attack, Delhi suffered all the rigours of a blockade. ʿAlāʾ al-Dīn, himself busy with the reduction of Chitōr, had only belatedly realised the magnitude of the crisis.[42] There was no hope of reinforcements: not only were the garrisons at Multān, Dēōpālpūr and Sāmāna distracted by a Mongol inroad into Sīwistān (p. 220 above), but Taraghai had secured all the Yamuna crossings, so that the divisions of ʿAlāʾ al-Dīn's forces returning from Tilang were obliged to halt at Kōl and Baran.[43]

Taraghai's retreat was widely regarded as one of the miracles of the age;[44] and certainly the sources offer no explanation. It may well be that, on the basis of his previous experience of the sultan's military tactics, he had anticipated a pitched battle and had come unprepared for an investment;[45] more probably, his attention was demanded by events beyond the Oxus, which we shall examine below. His invasion roused ʿAlāʾ al-Dīn to repair various fortresses lying in the path of the Mongol advance: Kaithal was refortified, and an inscription on the Barsī Gate at Hānsī enables us to date

39 Ibn al-Dawādārī, IX, 57, and Ibn Abi'l-Faḍā'il, ed. Blochet, 557, for the Delhi army. For the Mongols, see *TFS*, 256, although earlier, 254, the figure is twenty tümens; the mss. of *TFS*[1] differ, Digby Coll. ms. agreeing here with the printed text, while Bodleian ms., fol. 145a, and RRL ms., 219, give the number of tümens respectively as 'ten or fifteen' and 'ten or twelve'.

40 *Ibid.*, Digby Coll. ms., fol. 114a, for the sultan's forces. For Taraghai's army, see *ibid.*, fol. 113, with first 'ten or twelve tümens' and then 'twelve'; RRL ms., 220, gives 'one *lak* and 20,000' (the phrase employed later in *TMS*, 73); Bodleian ms., fol. 145b, has 20 or 30,000, suggesting that a phrase has dropped out. *TFS*, 300, has at one point twelve tümens (but cf. BL ms., with 'two or three tümens') and at another '30 or 40,000' (BL ms. again differs, with '20 or 30,000'). *FS*, 285 (tr. 460), has the ludicrously high figure of 200,000 for the Mongols.

41 *TFS*, 254–5.

42 *TFS*[1], Digby Coll. ms., fol. 113/Bodleian ms., fol. 145b/RRL ms., 220. Less than a month elapsed before the Mongol army reached the Yamuna about 10 m. N. of the capital.

43 *TFS*, 300–1.

44 *Ibid.*, 302. *TFS*[1], Digby Coll. ms., fol. 114a/Bodleian ms., fol. 146a/RRL ms., 221.

45 Biran, *Qaidu*, 89–90, proposes that Chaghadayid armies were 'relatively unskilled in siege tactics'. I am not convinced by the argument of Iqtidar Alam Khan, 'Coming of gunpowder to the Islamic world and North India: spotlight on the role of the Mongols', *JAH* 30 (1996), 27–45, on the strength of a single reference in *KF*, that the Mongols were using gunpowder in siege warfare in India by 1300.

the restoration here in Rabīʿ II 703/November 1303.[46] The sultan also enacted various fiscal and administrative measures, designed to increase the armed forces and to avert any repetition of the crisis (see chapter 12); but however salutary these proved, the people of Delhi had good reason to be thankful also for the internecine strife which erupted around this time in Central Asia.

The collapse of Qaidu's confederacy and the rise of the Chaghadayids

It was ironic that Chapar, alone of all the Mongol rulers, failed to reap any benefit from the general peace that he had promoted. His submission to the qaghan placed him on an equal footing with his erstwhile subordinate, Du'a, who further undermined his position by encouraging the disaffection of various princes in Chapar's ulus.[47] In the war that broke out in 705/1305 Du'a was supported not only by many Ögödeyid princes, notably Küresbe and his brothers, but also by the frontier forces of the qaghan in the east: Chapar was compelled to submit to Du'a and received a much smaller appanage.[48] We are concerned less with these wars as a whole than with their ramifications in Afghanistan and along the upper Oxus, where the first blow appears to have been struck in the summer of 705/1305 by Taraghai, acting on secret orders from Du'a. Repulsed by Sarban's forces, he made for India.[49] But following an attack by Du'a's son Esen Buqa, whom his father had sent out to rule Qutlugh Qocha's ulus, Sarban abandoned his bases in Baghlān and in 706/1306, accompanied by Temür, son of Ebügen, and Keder, moved into Khurāsān to seek the protection of the Ilkhan Öljeitü.[50] Scattered details in our sources confirm the impression that Afghanistan was in turmoil. Taraghai's attempt to flee to India in 705/1305, says Waṣṣāf, had been obstructed by Qutlugh Qocha's wives, who would not let him pass on account of his hostility to Sarban, and he therefore joined the Negüderis.[51] Not long afterwards he was killed when Esen Buqa was obliged to go to 'Hindūstān' – presumably the Indian borderlands – to quell dissension (*mukhālafāt*) within Qutlugh Qocha's army.[52]

Conflict continued in Central Asia following the death of Du'a in 1306 and during the brief reign of his son Könchek, who died in 1308, and peace was restored only in 709/1309 when Esen Buqa was summoned from Bīnī-yi Gāw to be khan of an ulus that now comprised not only his father's

46 Wahid Mirza, 'Some Arabic and Persian inscriptions from the East Punjab', *EIAPS* (1953–4), 8–9. Mehrdad Shokoohy (ed.), *Haryana I* (London, 1988), 31–3.
47 Qāshānī, 33–5. 48 See generally Biran, *Qaidu*, 73–7.
49 Waṣṣāf, 510. Qāshānī, 36, having begun to describe this struggle, then abruptly breaks off.
50 Waṣṣāf, 510–11. Qāshānī, 54, reports the arrival of Sarban and Temür at Öljeitü's court in Rajab 706/Jan. 1307, but according to Waṣṣāf, 512, Sarban remained in Khurāsān and died soon afterwards.
51 *Ibid.*, 510, *ba-Qarā'ūnās mulḥaq shud.* 52 *Ibid.*, 517.

territories but most of Qaidu's also.[53] Within a few years, however, this calm was dissipated by events that had their roots, once more, in the frontier zone of Afghanistan. After the brief rule of Esen Buqa's younger brother It Qul over the Negüderis,[54] we find the region under the control of Dā'ūd Qocha, the son or nephew of Qutlugh Qocha. Like Qutlugh Qocha himself, Dā'ūd Qocha moved between the banks of the Oxus and 'the furthest parts of Shabūrghān', on the one hand, and the hot regions (*garmsīr*) of Ghazna, Bīnī-yi Gāw, Bust, Tigīnābād and the Indus valley on the other. He proved an energetic ruler, nourishing designs on Herat and attempting to bring to heel two chiefs, Abachi's sons Temür and *Lakchir. Since they are described as leading 'the remnants (*baqāyā*) of the Negüderis', it may be that part of the Negüderi forces had profited from the recent upheavals to escape from the Chaghadayid orbit. At any rate, Temür and *Lakchir sought help from the Ilkhan Öljeitü, whose forces in 712/1312 fell on Dā'ūd Qocha and sacked his headquarters at Tigīnābād.[55]

Öljeitü's response to the Negüderi appeal was consistent with the pronounced interest he had displayed from the outset in his eastern frontier, replacing the local dynasty in Kirmān by an Ilkhanid appointee, reasserting control over Quhistān, and in 706/1307 taking Herat, which for some years had defied his overlordship. According to reports that reached Egypt the main object of the Ilkhan's ill-starred campaign of that year to subdue Gīlān was to facilitate communications with Khurāsān.[56] It is tempting to link this burst of military activity with the embassy which Öljeitü sent to Delhi in 710/1310–11, demanding the submission of ʿAlā' al-Dīn and the hand of a Khaljī princess in marriage. This seems to have been an isolated contact, however, and it certainly bore no fruit, since the envoys were detained and eighteen members of their suite were crushed beneath the feet of elephants.[57]

53 *Ibid.*, 513–14, 518–20. Qāshānī, 147–50. Barthold, *Four studies*, I, 131–3.

54 Qāshānī, 150. *SP*, fol. 120a ('YTQWLY), and *Muʿizz al-Ansāb*, fol. 32b, list him among Du'a's sons. The name is Tu. *it*, 'dog', + *qul*, 'slave': Clauson, *Etymological dictionary*, 34, 615.

55 Qāshānī, 152–3, 201–2, describing these events twice. Sayfī, 595–8, *sub anno* 713 and calling Dā'ūd Qocha Du'a's son in error: he alone mentions the sack of Tigīnābād. Dā'ūd Qocha is not mentioned in *SP*, but appears in *Muʿizz al-Ansāb*, fol. 32b, as the son of a brother of Qutlugh Qocha named Qutlugh. Negüderi chiefs: Qāshānī, 152; also 201, *baqāyā-yi Qarā'unās-i Nikūdarī*. For the second brother's name (LKMYR in the printed text), Istanbul ms. Ayasofya 3019, fols. 67a, 89a, reads LKḤYR.

56 Kirmān: Qāshānī, 43; Qazwīnī, *Ta'rīkh-i Guzīda*, 536. Quhistān: Qāshānī, 54. Herat: Sayfī, 461–97, 503–43; Spuler, *Mongolen in Iran*, 93–4. Gīlān: Ibn al-Dawādārī, IX, 149; Ibn Abi'l-Faḍā'il, ed. Blochet, 641; Boyle, 'Dynastic and political history', 400–1. Cf. Spuler's view of his foreign policy: *Mongolen in Iran*, 89–90.

57 Waṣṣāf, 528; this is misrepresented as a friendly embassy in Aziz Aḥmad, 'Mongol pressure', 187–8, and his *Studies*, 16. Akbar's minister Abu'l-Faḍl ʿAllāmī mentions an embassy sent by Öljeitü to Quṭb al-Dīn Mubārak Shāh Khaljī and headed by no less a figure than Rashīd al-Dīn: *Ā'īn-i Akbarī*, ed. H. Blochmann, BI (Calcutta, 1872–7, 2 vols.), II, 206; tr. H. S. Jarrett, BI (Calcutta, 1891–4, 3 vols.), III, 348. But it is unlikely that the Ilkhan would have employed such a high-ranking minister for such a mission. On Rashīd al-Dīn's own correspondence, see p. 154 above.

Dā'ūd Qocha's flight across the Oxus and his appeal to Esen Buqa unleashed a war between Chaghadai's ulus and the Ilkhanate which lasted for some years. The forces of the qaghan, whose frontier had advanced considerably westwards since the collapse of Qaidu's empire, also engaged in hostilities with Esen Buqa, and the number of embassies between Persia and China suggests that Toluid solidarity had re-emerged as a factor in the politics of the Mongol world. At one point the Golden Horde too became embroiled with Chaghadai's ulus.[58] The Central Asian Mongols temporarily forfeited control of the strategic regions of Afghanistan which gave them access to India. We do not even know whether Dā'ūd Qocha was reinstated in his old camping grounds.[59]

When Öljeitü died, his youthful successor Abū Saʿīd (716–36/1316–35) was confronted by a revolt on the part of a renegade Chaghadayid prince, Yasa'ur, who had quarrelled with Esen Buqa and had been allowed by the Ilkhan to settle south of the Oxus. Yasa'ur threatened Herat and invaded Sīstān, where in 717/1317–18 he killed the Ilkhan's adherent, the Negüderi amir Temür. But in 720/1320, before Abū Saʿīd's advancing forces had located him, Yasa'ur perished in an attack by Kebek, Esen Buqa's brother and deputy in Transoxiana. His ambitions had been sufficiently dangerous to induce his Chaghadayid kinsmen and the Ilkhans temporarily to collaborate in his removal.[60]

For a time, it had appeared as if the Ilkhans might exercise authority in eastern Khurāsān and Afghanistan, whether via compliant Negüderi leaders such as Abachi's son Temür or mediated in the treaty arrangements with refugee princes from Central Asia like Yasa'ur.[61] Öljeitü's death, however, followed by the elimination first of Temür and then of Yasa'ur, facilitated the revival of Chaghadayid power here. This fresh advance may date from an invasion of eastern Persia in 722/1322 by Kebek, who had now followed Esen Buqa as khan of Chaghadai's ulus (*c.* 718–726/1318–1326).[62] His

58 Spuler, *Mongolen in Iran*, 97–8. Barthold, *Four studies*, I, 133. T. T. Allsen, 'The Yüan dynasty and the Uighurs of Turfan in the 13th century', in Morris Rossabi (ed.), *China among equals: the Middle Kingdom and its neighbours, 10th–14th centuries* (Berkeley and Los Angeles, 1983), 259–60. For the participation of the Golden Horde, see *MA*, ed. Lech, 79 (German tr. 144–5).

59 The anonymous continuation (*dhayl*) of *JT*, Istanbul ms. Nuruosmaniye Kütüphanesi 2799 (old numbering: 3271), fol. 25b, claims that he was, but is not supported by Qāshānī or by Sayfī.

60 Russell G. Kempiners, Jr, 'Vaṣṣāf's *Tajziyat al-Amṣār wa Tazjiyat al-Aʿṣār* as a source for the history of the Chaghadayid khanate', *JAH* 22 (1988), 178, 185–6. Katō Kazuhide, 'Kebek and Yasawr – the establishment of the Chaghatai Khanate', *Memoirs of the Research Department of the Toyo Bunko* 49 (1991), 97–118. Spuler, *Mongolen in Iran*, 98–101. For Temür, see Sayfī, 677.

61 Kempiners, '*Tajziyat al-Amṣār*', 184–5.

62 al-ʿAynī (d. 855/1451), *Ta'rīkh al-Badr fī Awṣāf Ahli'l-ʿAṣr*, BL ms. Ar. 985 (Add. 22360), fol. 13a; also in V. G. Frhr. von Tiesenhausen, *Sbornik materialov otnosiashchikhsia k istorii Zolotoi Ordy*, I (St Petersburg, 1884), Ar. text 494, tr. 524–5. Cf. the anonymous *dhayl* of *JT*, fol. 57a.

successor Tarmashirin (726–35/1326–34), yet another of Du'a's sons, was attacked by the Ilkhan's forces and defeated in the region of Kābul and Zābul in *c.* 726/1326; Ghazna was sacked.[63] But the reverse did not, it seems, bring about a change of masters. Ibn Baṭṭūṭa, passing through Chaghadai's ulus on his way to India in 733/1332–3, refers to Ghazna as part of Tarmashirin's dominions, although it was largely in ruins. It was subject to the khan's chief amir Boroldai, who was based at Parwān in the Hindu Kush but had his officers (*nuwwāb*) in Ghazna.[64] The indications are that the Ghazna region remained within the Chaghadayid sphere of influence until the rise of Temür-i Lang.

The later incursions

Inroads into the subcontinent by the armies of Du'a and Qaidu did not cease during the upheavals that followed the latter's death. Early in 705/in the autumn of 1305 Du'a's forces under ʿAlī Beg[65] and *Tartaq entered India. Undeterred by the desertion of Taraghai, who turned back after crossing the Jhēlam,[66] they pushed deep into the Panjāb, ravaging the Siwālik foothills, and then overran Badā'ūn and Awadh. The *ākhūrbeg* Malik Nānak, who held the iqtaʿs of Sunnām and Sāmāna and who was accompanied by a number of other amirs, including Tughluq, routed the invaders on 12 Jumādā II/30 December in the neighbourhood of Amrōha. ʿAlī Beg and *Tartaq were taken to Delhi, but their lives were spared and they were kept for a time in honourable captivity.[67]

The details of the last Mongol attacks of ʿAlā' al-Dīn's reign are somewhat blurred. It seems that Amīr Khusraw, writing only a few years afterwards, describes one invasion by an army comprising three main divisions, and that subsequent authors, beginning with Baranī, misinterpreted him and assumed that there were a number of separate incursions, each falling in a different year. The Mongols were apparently under the

63 Qazwīnī, *Ta'rīkh-i Guzīda*, 617.

64 IB, III, 42, 82–3, 87 (tr. Gibb, 561, 585–6, 589). Aubin, 'Khanat de Čaġatai', 17–18. For Ghazna's ruined state, see IB, III, 88 (tr. 590).

65 ʿAlī Beg, called a descendant of Chinggis Khan in *TFS*, 320, belonged in fact to the Qonqurat tribe and was married to a Chinggisid princess: hence the style *küregen*, 'son-in-law', given him by Waṣṣāf, 526. His wife was a great-grand-daughter of Ögödei: *SP*, fol. 127a, adding *aknūn dar Dillī ast*; hence *Muʿizz al-Ansāb*, fol. 42b, *ba-Dillī raft*. Waṣṣāf confirms that his troops were Du'a's (*tūā'ī*).

66 *KF*, 37–8, *sahm-i baylak-zanān-i ghuzzā' dar dil gudharānīd wa-ham az ʿaqab khala kard* ('he let the ... arrows of the *ghāzīs* pierce his resolve, and turned about'). This figurative phrase has been misinterpreted to mean that he was killed, e.g. by ED, III, 72, and Lal, *History of the Khaljis*, 144.

67 Waṣṣāf, 527 (with the year 708 in error). *KF*, 38–9, supplies the date. Only *TFS*, 320, specifies the locality. See also *FS*, 303–5 (tr. 479–82); Waṣṣāf, 526–7. One ms. of *KF* reads NAYB in error for NANK, and later authors duly name the sultan's general on this occasion as Malik Nā'ib (Kāfūr): thus *TMS*, 73, and Badā'ūnī, I, 185, who wrongly equates Malik 'Mānak' (above, p. 175) with Malik Nā'ib.

overall leadership of Köpek, who commanded Du'a's forces south of the Oxus,[68] and his two colleagues are named as Iqbāl and Taibu. Entering the Sultanate in the vicinity of Multān and plundering along the banks of the Rāvī, the Mongols moved on Kuhrām and Sāmāna, but then turned south towards Nāgawr.[69] Malik Kāfūr 'Hazārdīnārī', Tughluq, and other amirs were sent against the invaders, who were surprised near a river which Khusraw calls the "ʿAlī-Wāhan' but which figures in Baranī's account as the Ghaggar. The Mongol vanguard was completely routed, and Köpek taken prisoner. Kāfūr then crushed the forces which were following at some distance, and Iqbāl and Taibu fled back across the Indus.[70]

Baranī then furnishes details of two other incursions. First, three or four tümen-commanders invaded the Siwālik region, but the Delhi army occupied the river-crossings and cut off their retreat. Having extended their lines of communication deep into a waste country, the Mongols were easily overcome. On the sultan's orders, the survivors were massacred in the fortress of Narā'ina. Lastly Iqbāl, whom Baranī calls Iqbālmanda, invaded India, but was defeated and killed in the vicinity of the ʿAlī-Wāhan.[71] The term 'Siwālik', which in its broadest sense embraces the territory from the foothills down to Nāgawr; the reference to Narā'ina, not far east of Nāgawr; and the recurrence of ʿAlī-Wāhan – all these details suggest that the three episodes noticed in the *Ta'rīkh-i Fīrūz-Shāhī* were in reality part of the same invasion as recounted by Amīr Khusraw.[72]

Although they penetrated more deeply into the sultan's territories, and in 1305, at least, beyond the Ganges, these later attacks posed less of a menace than those of Qutlugh Qocha and Taraghai. In each case the Mongol army appears to have been smaller. ʿAlī Beg and *Tartaq brought 50,000 horse, according to Khusraw, though other sources supply lower numbers.[73] The figure of 100,000 given by ʿIṣāmī for the army of Köpek and his colleagues

[68] *JT*, II, 570 (tr. Boyle, 313/tr. Verkhovskii, 202). *FS*, 318, calls him *sar-āhang-i ān kishwar* ('the vanguard of that country'). He was with Sarban in Khurāsān in 1302–3: Qāshānī, 18.

[69] *KF*, 42. *DR*, 61.

[70] They are listed with Köpek in the brief account *ibid.*, 61–2. Fuller narrative in *KF*, 43–4. The correct form of Taibu's name, which appears as TABW or TYHW in *DR* and as TAYBW in *KF*, is discussed by Hodivala, *Studies*, I, 248, 372. It could represent either *tabu*, 'five', or *tayibu*, 'quiet', 'calm': Lessing, 761, 767. The river ᶜAlī-Wāhan is mentioned also in *FS*, 319 (tr. 496); see *TFS*, 321, for the Ghaggar.

[71] *Ibid.*, 321–2. The word before ᶜAlī-Wāhan, which in the printed text reads TNBDH, proves, on comparison with the mss., to be a corruption of DHNDH. This was assumed to be the Dhandh: see Hodivala, *Studies*, I, 397. But the word occurs in *TFS*[1], in a quite different context (Bodleian ms., fol. 137b/Digby Coll. ms., fol. 103b), as a synonym for *dih*, 'village'. Baranī also inserts *amīr* before ᶜAlī-Wāhan, and *AHG*, II, 816–17, explains that Amīr ᶜAlī commanded at Dhandh as a subordinate of Tughluq. We cannot rely on this, given *AHG*'s frequent errors regarding earlier invasions.

[72] The verdict of Lal, *History of the Khaljis*, 147–9.

[73] *KF*, 38. Waṣṣaf, 526, has three tümens, though this is difficult to reconcile with the figure of 60,000 for the heads of slain Mongols. *TFS*, 320, has 30 or 40,000: of the mss. of *TFS*[1], Digby Coll. ms., fol. 121b, gives the same figure, while Bodleian ms., fol. 146b, and RRL ms., 221, have simply 'several thousand'.

is clearly exaggerated, in view of the fact that they turned south from Sāmāna because they lacked the strength to proceed further.[74] Baranī's reference to 'three or four tümen-commanders',[75] although it occurs in a passage which is probably confused, gives a more realistic idea of the size of these invading armies. By this time the Mongol heartlands on the upper Oxus and in Transoxiana were torn by civil war. To some extent organized expeditions may have been superseded by the inroads of fugitives seeking to settle on a more permanent basis, as was happening both in Khurāsān and on the Chinese frontier.

As a result of 'Alā' al-Dīn's victories, says Khusraw, the Mongols withdrew into 'the mountains of Ghazna' and were unable to pass through Sind.[76] During these years the Delhi forces may have moved over to the offensive. According to Baranī, Ghāzī Malik Tughluq, who had at some point received the additional iqta' of Lahore, not only kept the Mongols at bay but took the offensive against them, heading an expedition every winter into their territory. Later he credits Tughluq with twenty victories over them.[77] No details are supplied, and his assertions might be questioned were it not for other testimony regarding Tughluq's exploits. Amīr Khusraw, in his *Tughluq-Nāma*, written to commemorate Tughluq's enthronement in 720/1320, alludes to eighteen victories, mostly over the Mongols; while Ibn Baṭṭūṭa saw an inscription in the mosque at Multān in which Tughluq himself laid claim to twenty-nine victories over the Mongols alone.[78] Whether these campaigns were responsible for the devastation of an extensive tract between Ghazna and India, which al-'Umarī's informants attributed to the strife between the 'king of India' and the 'king of Turkestan and Mā warā' al-Nahr',[79] is uncertain.

That the Sultanate now enjoyed immunity from major Mongol attacks for some years was due in large measure to conditions in Afghanistan, which are momentarily but vividly illuminated for us by a remarkable document preserved in Amīr Khusraw's *Rasā'il al-I'jāz*.[80] It purports to be a memorial (*'arḍ-dāsht*) from the chamberlain (*ḥājib*) Badr to Sultan 'Alā' al-Dīn's son Khiḍr Khān, narrating a winter campaign against the Mongols of Ghazna. The Delhi forces, led by an unnamed grandee who is designated simply as the *khān-i a'ẓam*, had allegedly occupied the city of Ghazna,

[74] *KF*, 42. *FS*, 318 (tr. 495), for the alleged 100,000.
[75] *TFS*, 321. [76] *KF*, 113.
[77] *TFS*, 322–3; and see 416 for the twenty victories. Later, 490, Baranī ascribes these twenty victories to Tughluq and his brother (Rajab) – doubtless in an effort to curry favour with Rajab's son Fīrūz Shāh.
[78] *Tughluq-Nāma*, 138. IB, III, 202 (tr. Gibb, 649).
[79] *MA*, ed. Spies, 8 (German tr. 30)/ed. Fāriq, 16 (tr. Siddiqi and Aḥmad, 32).
[80] *RI*, IV, 144–56; for a brief abstract, see ED, III, 566–7. The document has been studied by Askari, 'Material', 18–20, and by M. Y. Z. Siddiqi, 'Arzdasht of Badr Hajib', *MIM* 2 (1972), 291–7.

where the khutba was read in ʿAlā' al-Dīn's name.[81] Badr's memorial has justifiably aroused considerable suspicion among scholars.[82] Such a major triumph as the capture of Ghazna – uncorroborated in any other source – is improbable. The document nevertheless contains enough circumstantial detail to suggest that it is based on a genuine intelligence report from the north-west frontier to the sultan's government.[83] Badr refers to the fratricidal war that was raging between Du'a and Qaidu's people,[84] and describes how it had spread to the Mongol army based at Hashtnaghar and Peshawar, with the result that chaos reigned between Ghazna and the Indus.[85] He goes on to say that Esen Buqa had moved north in response to a message from Könchek: before his departure, he had presented Badr with several gifts for his master Khiḍr Khān, by way of a conciliatory gesture. The memorial may safely be dated, therefore, to the years 706–7/1306–8, when Könchek was head of Chaghadai's ulus.[86] For all the problems attached to it, the document does at least furnish first-hand evidence that the principality built up by Qutlugh Qocha south of the Oxus had begun to disintegrate.

Defeat meant for many Mongol warriors an unpleasant form of execution. The crushing of Mongol captives beneath the feet of elephants has made ʿAlā' al-Dīn notorious, although these tactics are first encountered in the reign of Muʿizz al-Dīn Kayqubād.[87] Following the incursion by ʿAlī Beg and *Tartaq a durbar was held in which captured Mongols were executed in this fashion as a spectacle for the citizens of Delhi; and nemesis took the same form subsequently both for Köpek and for Iqbāl's officers.[88] An unsavoury practice which does date from around this time was the construction of towers at Delhi with the heads of the slain. According to Baranī, such a tower could still be seen in front of the Badā'ūn Gate in his own day;

[81] *RI*, IV, 148, 150–1.

[82] See, e.g., Day, 'North-west frontier', 106–7 n.20, and in his *Some aspects*, 55 n.22. Askari, 'Risail [*sic*]-ul-Ijaz', 122, appears to believe the report is Khusraw's own invention.

[83] See Khusraw's own comment on the document: *RI*, IV, 18.

[84] *Ibid.*, IV, 151–2. The printed text reads: DWAYR *laʿīn* TBR QYD W MYAN *gardunān-i kāfir tīgh uftāda ast*. But for the first word, IOL Persian ms. 570 (Ethé, no. 1219), fol. 223b, and BL ms. Add. 16842, fol. 404b, read DW, and the subject can only be Du'a 'the Accursed' (*laʿīn*). The next few words are problematic: a line is possibly omitted not only in the mss. but – since Khusraw was himself transcribing a document – in the original. QYD W MYAN can only be *Qaydū'iyyān*, 'Qaidu's people'.

[85] *Ibid.*, IV, 153–4 (HYBT NḌYR to be corrected to HŠTNГR from IOL ms., fol. 224a, and BL ms. Add. 26841, fol. 382b); for Hashtnaghar, 16 m. N.W. of Peshawar, see IB, tr. Gibb, 591 n.212.

[86] *RI*, IV, 154, 155. The Mongol leader's name appears both here and *ibid.*, 147, as 'YS BГA, a form which prevented Askari ('Material', 18 n.50) from identifying him; but the best mss. have clearly 'YSN BГA. His name is Tu. *esen*, 'healthy', + *buqa*, 'bull': Clauson, *Etymological dictionary*, 248, 312. Könchek's name appears as QPČK. The margin of 1307–14 allowed by Siddiqi, 'Arzdasht', 292, is unnecessarily wide.

[87] *QS*, 96–8: on this occasion it was only one among several kinds of grisly death on offer.

[88] *TFS*, 321, 322. *FS*, 322, on the other hand, says that Köpek was initially spared and was later beheaded (verses omitted in Husain's tr., 500).

although the sources differ as to whether it was built from the skulls of Köpek's soldiers or those of ʿAlī Beg.[89] No doubt successive invasions permitted the tower to be completed in two stages. If we are to believe Khusraw, who dwells on the marauders' fate with particular pleasure, similar towers arose in other cities of the Sultanate and Mongol prisoners' remains were also incorporated in the new fortifications at Delhi.[90] Whether such exercises were as effective in deterring the Mongols from future inroads as they were in entertaining the populace of the capital, we cannot tell.

Baranī asserts that the respite from Mongol attacks lasted until the end of the reign of Quṭb al-Dīn Mubārak Shāh (720/1320);[91] and Khusraw claims that Quṭb al-Dīn contemplated the conquest of Ghazna but was dissuaded by his amirs.[92] But Baranī's statement that the Mongols had been so cowed by Tughluq as not to dare to invade India during his reign[93] is contradicted by his own evidence, for he tells us of one raid which occurred shortly after the Deccan campaign of 721/1321–2. A fuller account of this attack is provided by ʿIṣāmī, who says that the sultan sent reinforcements to his nephew and lieutenant at Sāmāna, Bahā' al-Dīn Garshāsp. Garshāsp attacked the Mongol rearguard, which had remained behind at a base camp in the foothills, and routed them, slaying their commander, *Shir (Shira). Thereupon he ambushed and destroyed the rest of the invading army, under three commanders named Hindu, Zakariyya and Orus, close to the left bank of the Bēāh as they returned from plundering the Doab. Among the prisoners was Zakariyya, who was taken to Delhi in triumph.[94]

Muḥammad b. Tughluq and the Mongols

Soon after his accession (724/1324), Muḥammad b. Tughluq headed an expedition to the north-west. While the sultan halted at Lahore, his troops took Kalānawr and Peshawar and had the khutba read there in his name. Within a few weeks, Muḥammad's generals were obliged to retreat owing to lack of grain and fodder, and rejoined the sultan, who remained at Lahore for two or three months in order to pacify the region before returning to Delhi. It may have been at this time that the sultan set in motion the repair of the fortress of Kalānawr, which appears in al-ʿUmarī's incomplete list of his territories.[95] Another consequence of this campaign seems to have been

89 Köpek's troops: *TFS*, 321; *KF*, 45–6. ʿAlī Beg's: *FS*, 305 (tr. 481); Waṣṣāf, 527. Towers had been built earlier from the heads of slaughtered Hindus: *Tāj*, fol. 137b.

90 *KF*, 28. *RI*, I, 17, *dar aqāṣī-yi mamālik nīz burjhā-yi dīgar ham bar īn nahj sarāsar ba-rās-i falak rasānīdand.*

91 *TFS*, 322, 323; cf. also 387. 92 *NS*, 54–5. 93 *TFS*, 441.

94 *FS*, 405–9 (tr. 611–18). The brief account in *TFS*, 450, says that two Mongol leaders were captured.

95 *FS*, 423–4 (tr. 649–50). *TMS*, 101, for Kalānawr, though dating its restoration in the wake of Tarmashirin's invasion. *MA*, ed. Spies, 6 (German tr. 26)/ed. Fāriq, 14 (tr. Siddiqi and Aḥmad, 30).

the incorporation of the Peshawar region into Muḥammad's dominions, since Ibn Baṭṭūṭa describes Hashtnaghar as 'the last inhabited place on the confines of the land of the Turks [i.e. the Mongols]' and elsewhere indicates that it was a frontier post where the sultan's customs officals levied duty on imported horses.[96]

Yet a third effect of Muḥammad's expedition was to bring down upon the Sultanate an invasion by the khan Tarmashirin, who resided in the western half of Chaghadai's ulus, possibly at Tirmid on the middle Oxus. The authenticity of this invasion was long doubted, on the grounds that it is not mentioned in the standard text of Baranī's *Ta'rīkh-i Fīrūz-Shāhī*, and it was suggested that Tarmashirin paid a friendly visit to India to seek Muḥammad's assistance. The unearthing of an earlier recension, however, in which the invasion is in fact described, has undermined this hypothesis.[97] Tarmashirin clearly profited from the poor state of frontier defence in the wake of Küshlü Khān's revolt at Multān (below, p. 257).[98] At a date which Baranī places within the two or three years after Delhi's citizens had been transferred to Dawlatābād, and which Sirhindī gives as 729/1328–9,[99] the Chaghadayid forces overran a considerable area, capturing several fortresses and taking prisoners throughout the regions of Lahore, Sāmāna and Indrī. They then advanced into the Doab. The sultan mustered a large force, which he stationed north of Delhi, setting up his headquarters at Indrapat, close to the Yamuna,[100] so that unlike 'Alā' al-Dīn in 703/1303 he controlled at least one of the crossings. A division of his forces under Yūsuf-i Bughra, who had been sent to relieve Mīrat, routed part of Tarmashirin's army and captured his nephew. The Mongols shortly withdrew, followed by Muḥammad and his army: 'Iṣāmī says that the sultan halted at Thānesar and sent troops in pursuit; Sirhindī, that he advanced as far as Kalānawr.[101] This was the last major Chaghadayid invasion prior to Temür's conquest of Delhi at the end of the century.

96 IB, II, 373, and III, 90 (tr. Gibb, 478, 'Shashnaqār', 591, 'Shāshnagār').

97 Jackson, 'The Mongols and the Delhi Sultanate', 119–26, surveys the evidence. For the older view, see especially A. M. Husain, *The rise and fall of Muḥammad bin Tughluq* (London, 1938), 100–8, and *Tughluq dynasty*, 119–43.

98 *TFS*, 479.

99 *TFS*[1], Digby Coll. ms., fol. 160b/Bodleian ms., fol. 192a. *TMS*, 101.

100 Best text in *TFS*[1], RRL ms., 287; cf. Bodleian ms., fol. 192a/Digby Coll. ms., fols. 160b–161a. Bihāmadkhānī, fol. 400a, specifies Indrapat. This attempt to control the crossing seems more plausible than the statement in *FS*, 463 (tr. 698), that Muḥammad's army stretched from Sīrī to the Bāgh-i Jūd.

101 *Ibid.*, 463–5 (tr. 699–701). *TMS*, 101. A less reliable account of the episode is furnished by a Timurid chronicler, who alleges that Tarmashirin was bought off by the sultan and that he ravaged Gujarāt as he withdrew: Yazdī, *ZN*, ed. A. Urunbaev (Tashkent, 1972), fols. 80b–81a. For his failure at Mīrat, see Ghiyāth al-Dīn ᶜAlī Yazdī, *Rūz-Nāma-yi Ghazawāt-i Hindūstān*, tr. A. A. Semenov, *Dnevnik pokhoda Tīmūra v Indiiu* (Moscow, 1958), 129, 131; Shāmī, *ZN*, I, 194; Yazdī, *ZN*, ed. M. M. Ilahdād, BI (Calcutta, 1885–8), II, 129, 132/ed. Urunbaev, fols. 328a–329a.

Muḥammad endeavoured to form a coalition against the Chaghadayids with the Ilkhan Abū Saʿīd. A local historian writing in southern Persia a few years later has transmitted an account of a friendly embassy from the sultan to the Ilkhan in 728/1327–8, and the letter it conveyed, in which Muḥammad sought military collaboration against Tarmashirin, has also survived.[102] Nothing came of these negotiations, as far as we are aware, apart from an equally cordial reply from the Ilkhan, but Muḥammad allegedly continued to send annual embassies down to Abū Saʿīd's death.[103] Subsequently, according to Ibn Baṭṭūṭa, Muḥammad and Tarmashirin too were on friendly terms and exchanged letters and gifts. Professor Siddiqui ascribes this to the khan's conversion to Islam, which seems to have occurred after 729/1328–9.[104] But the reconciliation may be connected with his conflict in the eastern half of the khanate with his brother Döre Temür, who was overthrown late in 1331.[105] Within a few years, Tarmashirin himself was overthrown and killed, ushering in a period of instability within the Chaghadayid khanate. The new khan, Döre Temür's son Buzun, though described by Ibn Baṭṭūṭa as a Muslim, apparently preferred the Mongol customary law, the Yasa, to the Sharīʿa, and was in any case unable to establish his authority before he in turn was displaced in 1335 by a pagan cousin, Changshi, who was hostile to Islam.[106] These upheavals, al-ʿUmarī was informed, provided the Sultanate with a respite from Mongol attacks.[107]

His co-religionists' plight furnished Muḥammad with an alternative means of extending his influence beyond the Indus. The *manshūr* drafted on his behalf in 734/1333–4 and sent to Transoxiana to invite sayyids, shaykhs, ʿulama', bureaucrats and soldiers to come to India and enter the sultan's service is preserved in the early fifteenth-century *inshā'* collection, *Farā'id-i*

[102] Shabānkāra'ī, 287–8, naming Ikhtisān (above, p. 153) among the party; brief mention in Faṣīḥ-i Khwāfī, *Mujmal-i Faṣīḥī* (845/1441–2), ed. Maḥmūd Farrukh (Tehran, 1339 Sh./1960, 3 vols.), III, 39. *Bayāḍ-i Tāj al-Dīn Aḥmad Wazīr*, ed. Īraj Afshār and Murtaḍā Taymūrī (Isfahan, 1353 Sh./1974), 404–8, for the letter; also I. H. Siddiqui, 'Sultan Muḥammad bin Tughluq's foreign policy: a reappraisal', *IC* 62 (1988), part 4, 10–12. The details of another embassy by Ikhtisān to Abū Saʿīd (dating his return at the time of Muḥammad's death!) in Bihāmadkhānī, fol. 405b, are chronologically dubious.

[103] Shabānkāra'ī, 88, 288 (naming the ambassador as ʿAḍud al-Dīn of Yazd: see above, p. 184). For the Ilkhan's reply, see *Bayāḍ*, 408–9.

[104] IB, III, 43 (tr. Gibb, 562). Siddiqui, 'Sultan Muḥammad bin Tughluq's foreign policy', 14. *MA*, ed. Lech, Ar. text 38, simply dates his conversion as 'since 725' (tr. 117 has 'seit 750' in error).

[105] *Yüan Shih*, cap. 35, cited in *MA*, ed. Lech, 241 n.167.

[106] Barthold, *Four studies*, I, 135–6. al-Ṣafadī, *Wāfī*, X, 383, dates Tarmashirin's death in 735. For Buzun, see Yazdī, *ZN*, ed. Urunbaev, fol. 81a. *MA*, ed. Lech, Ar. text 22 (German tr. 105), describes the Chaghadayid khanate as in a state of upheaval (*mutakhabbat*[an]) until Changshi's accession, for the date of which see Aubin, 'Khanat de Čaġatai', 24–5 n.34.

[107] *MA*, ed. Lech, Ar. text 40 (tr. 118 renders *wa-ikhtalafat kalimat ahl hādhihi'l-bilād ʿalā mulūkihā* as 'Die Inder waren mit ihren Fürsten uneins'; but the subject is the people of Chaghadai's ulus).

Ghiyāthī.[108] That it was effective is clear from the number of notables from Transoxiana who arrived in the Sultanate at approximately the same time as Ibn Baṭṭūṭa (above, p. 185). It is in this context too that we must place the fresh influx of Mongols into the Sultanate. Soon after Buzun's seizure of power, Muḥammad had welcomed Tarmashirin's son *Pashaitai, his daughter and her husband Nawrūz Küregen; and within a short time the number of Mongols from Tarmashirin's dominions in the Sultanate is set by Ibn Baṭṭūṭa at 40,000.[109] In the 1340s refugees were arriving in great numbers. Every winter, according to Baranī, Mongol commanders of tümens and hundreds, their wives (*khātūnān*) and sons (*ughliyān*) arrived in India and received presents of money, jewels and horses.[110] Elsewhere the same author says that Muḥammad caused any amirs from Khurāsān and Mughalistān who entered his service to take an oath of allegiance with the caliphal diploma prior to the conferment of gifts.[111] Since the ʿAbbasid embassy did not reach Delhi until 744/1343–4 at the earliest (see below, p. 272), this indicates that immigrants from the Mongol world were still arriving several years after Tarmashirin's death. But the greater significance of Baranī's information is that these immigrants were Muslims; otherwise oaths involving the caliphal diploma would have been meaningless. Their flight from Transoxiana may have been connected with the overthrow, in *c.* 743/1342, of the ephemeral Muslim khan Khalīl, allegedly a son of Yasa'ur (above, p. 226), an obscure episode for which the somewhat dubious account furnished by Ibn Baṭṭūṭa is regrettably our sole evidence.[112]

Muḥammad profited from the disturbances within Chaghadai's ulus and used the enormous patronage at his disposal in order to cement harmonious relations with Mongol chiefs and other rulers in Khurāsān. In his first recension, Baranī goes so far as to claim that 'the whole of Mongol territory (*Mughalistān*) on this side of Transoxiana became Sultan Muḥammad's obedient client (*banda-yi parwarda*)'.[113] If Ibn Baṭṭūṭa is to be believed, even Muʿizz al-Dīn Ḥusayn, the Kartid malik of Herat, at some point became

[108] *FG*, SK ms. Fatıh 4012, fols. 456a–457b; at fol. 457a he refers to their tribulations. Aubin, 'Khanat de Čaġatai', 22.

[109] IB, III, 43, 46 (tr. Gibb, 562, 564). For Nawrūz, see also *TFS*, 533; *SFS*, 4 (tr. Basu, *JBORS* 22 [1936], 96). The name of Tarmashirin's son appears as 'Bashāī' in the mss. of IB, but the form in *Muʿizz al-Ansāb*, fol. 32a, suggests Bashaitai, 'man of the Pashai', a people and region of the Hindu Kush and situated roughly N. of Kabul: see Pelliot, *Notes on Marco Polo*, 799–800.

[110] *TFS*, 499; and cf. also *TFS*[1], Bodleian ms., fol. 199/Digby Coll. ms., fols. 165b–166a.

[111] *TFS*, 494–5.

[112] IB, III, 48–51 (tr. Gibb, 565–7). On this, see W. Barthold, *Zwölf Vorlesungen über die Türken Mittelasiens*, tr. Th. Menzel (Hildesheim, 1935; repr. 1962), 206–7; Jürgen Paul, 'Scheiche und Herrscher im Khanat Čaġatay', *Der Islam* 67 (1990), 284–91.

[113] *TFS*[1], Digby Coll. ms., fol. 166a; the text in Bodleian ms., fol. 199b, is corrupt here and reads WBRDH for *parwarda*. *TFS*, 505, speaks more vaguely of the homage of the rulers (*ḍābiṭān*) of Mughalistān.

Muḥammad's client: the malik was evidently concerned that his adoption of the style of sultan in 750/1349 should not prejudice his relations with Delhi.[114] Possibly Ḥusayn's usefulness lay partly in his recently acquired control over the Mongols of the puppet Ilkhan Togha Temür, who from their bases in the Herat region were in the habit of raiding India.[115] By the end of his life, Muḥammad had entered into amicable relations with the noyan Qazaghan, who since 747/1346–7 had been the real power in the western half of Chaghadai's ulus. Qazaghan, a Muslim of Qara'unas stock (as the Tughluqids themselves may have been: above, p. 178), furnished him with 4–5000 Mongol troops for his final campaign against rebels in Sind.[116]

Plunder or conquest?

Regarding the war-aims of the Mongols, the sources are ambivalent. It is significant that Amīr Khusraw neglects to mention the invasions of Qutlugh Qocha and Taraghai in his *Khazā'in al-Futūḥ*, presumably because neither episode redounded to ʿAlā' al-Dīn's credit. On both occasions the Mongols appeared in large numbers; on both occasions they advanced by forced marches and caught the sultan perilously off guard. Qutlugh Qocha's forces are expressly said to have abandoned their usual practice of plundering the territory on their route.[117] One or two contemporary references indicate that Qutlugh Qocha and Taraghai actually aimed to conquer the Sultanate,[118] and the idea has been taken up in turn by historians writing in this century.[119] A policy of long-term conquest might well have been explained by Aziz Aḥmad's proposal that the Chaghadayids sought an outlet in India because they were restive under Qaidu's tutelage and were caught, moreover, between the armies of the qaghan in the east and of the Ilkhans.[120] It is true that the late thirteenth-century Chaghadayid khanate presents an appearance of being largely hemmed in by other Mongol states, and that Rashīd al-Dīn makes the khan Baraq, for instance, complain at the quriltai of 667/1269 that his ulus, in contrast with those of his kinsmen, had no

114 IB, III, 74 (tr. Gibb, 580). *FG*, I, 146–9, 182–5, and SK ms. Fatıh 4012, fols. 196b–197b. Aubin, 'Khanat de Čaġatai', 32–3. Siddiqui, 'Sultan Muḥammad bin Tughluq's foreign policy', 19.

115 IB, III, 70, 71 (tr. Gibb, 578); on him, see P. Jackson, 'Togha Temür', *Enc.Isl.*^{2}.

116 *TFS*, 524. For Qazaghan, see Beatrice Forbes Manz, *The rise and rule of Tamerlane* (Cambridge, 1989), 33–4, 43–4. Bihāmadkhānī, fol. 328b, speaks of their friendship.

117 *TFS*, 254, *gīrāgīr*; cf. *TFS*^{1}, Digby Coll. ms., fol. 94a, *kūch ba-kūch-i mutawātir*. But the later *SFS*, 187 (tr. Page, 34), refers to Qutlugh Qocha's forces entering the Tōpra region, near the Sirmūr hills.

118 Qutlugh Qocha: Waṣṣāf, 312; *JT*, ed. Jahn, *Indiengeschichte*, Ar. text Taf. 59, Pers. text Taf. 25 (German tr. 50); Qāshānī, 189. Taraghai: *FS*, 292 (tr. 467). See also *AHG*, II, 796; Badā'ūnī, I, 184.

119 Haig, in *Cambridge history of India*, III, 102. Dharam Pal, "ᶜAla'-ud-Din Khilji's Mongol policy', *IC* 21 (1947), 258. Lal, *History of the Khaljis*, 134. HN, 338.

120 Aziz Aḥmad, 'Mongol pressure', 186, and in his *Studies*, 15. Cf. also Pal, "ᶜAla'-ud-Din Khilji's Mongol policy', 257.

room for manoeuvre.[121] Yet the idea that such constriction explains the expansionism of later decades runs counter to the evidence in three respects. Firstly, Du'a and Qaidu appear to have acted in close cooperation right down to the latter's death. In the second place, the Ilkhan's eastern provinces offered as fruitful an opportunity for expansion as did the Indian borderlands; the Ilkhans were, if anything, on the defensive and Ghazan at least evinced a far greater interest in the frontier with the Mamlūks. Nor, thirdly, is there reason at this stage to posit pressure from the Far East. Qubilai had jettisoned his policy of expansion in Central Asia during the 1280s – that is, before Qaidu and his allies began to assert their control over the borderlands of India – and Uighuristān was abandoned to the Chaghadayids by *c*. 1300.[122]

The Mongol invasions of India in 699/1300 and 703/1303, therefore, were probably no more than plundering expeditions on the scale necessary for such a formidable objective as Delhi; though even then the purpose may have been to 'soften up' the region as a preparation for campaigns of conquest in future years. The evidence, regrettably, does not permit us to go further. We need not be influenced, incidentally, by the presence, on a number of occasions, of women and children in the Mongol armies. Thus women are said to have ridden with Qutlugh Qocha during his march on Delhi; *Sögedei's troops were taken prisoner with their wives and offspring; and of the 18,000 prisoners who fell into the hands of Alp Khān at Tharī, some 3000 were women. Not long afterwards, more women and children were spared and sent to Delhi to be sold in the slave markets when their menfolk were massacred at Narā'ina.[123] None of this need surprise us. Thirteenth-century European and Chinese sources show Mongol women riding to war alongside their menfolk.[124] In any case, if the Mongol attacks were essentially seasonal migrations between summer pastures in the uplands of Ghūr and Ghazna and winter quarters in the Panjāb and beyond, then we should expect the entire 'horde' to be on the move rather than just the male warriors.

It is already clear in the thirteenth century that the Mongol campaigns in India were designed to amass great numbers of slaves.[125] Sali Noyan's

121 *JT*, III, 110–11 (tr. Arends, 72).

122 Dardess, 'Mongol empire to Yüan dynasty', 142–3. Allsen, 'Yüan dynasty and the Uighurs of Turfan', 255, 258–9.

123 Qutlugh Qocha: *FS*, 256 (tr. 427). Sögedei: *TFS*, 254. Tharī: *FS*, 289 (tr. 464). Narā'ina: *TFS*, 321–2. Note also women and children with ᶜAbd-Allāh's invading army in 691/1292: *ibid.*, 219.

124 Paul Ratchnevsky, 'La condition de la femme mongole au 12ᵉ/13ᵉ siècle', in Walther Heissig *et al.* (eds.), *Tractata Altaica Denis Sinor sexagenario ... dedicata* (Wiesbaden, 1976), 511. Thomas Spalatensis, 'Historia pontificum Salonitarum', in A. F. Gombos (ed.), *Catalogus fontium historiae Hungaricae* (Budapest, 1937–43, 4 vols. with continuous pagination), 2236–7.

125 Lahore (639/1241): *TN*, II, 165 (tr. 1135). Numerous captives, both Muslim and Hindu, left behind in 643/1245–6: *ibid.*, II, 55–6 (tr. 813).

campaigns in Kashmir and India yielded Hülegü a great booty in Indian slaves, according to Rashīd al-Dīn, who says that their descendants were still to be found in his own day on the royal estates (*injü*) in Persia.[126] We owe the unflattering descriptions of the Mongols by Amīr Khusraw to the circumstance of his being taken prisoner in 684/1285 on the defeat and death of his master Muḥammad b. Balaban.[127] That the seizure of slaves continued to be an important aim cannot be in doubt. ʿIṣāmī's account of the Mongol raid on the Tharī region suggests that the invaders fell prey to Alp Khān's forces because they were unduly encumbered with booty and prisoners.[128] Regarding other forms of plunder, the sources have less to say. We know that the Mongols ravaged not only Muslim territories but those of the Khōkhars, whose *talwāras* (or *talwandīs*) were looted and burned in 697/1298 during Keder's attack.[129] Here one item of booty may have been horses, since the Khōkhar territory was among those parts of the Panjāb that produced choice mounts.[130] We can also presumably take it for granted that the Mongols came in the hope of acquiring gold and silver, and in this connection we may have an explanation for India's enhanced attractiveness. With the ambitious raids on independent Hindu kingdoms in the south from 695/1296 onwards, Delhi's rulers were known to be amassing great quantities of specie, of which the Mongols, consequently, must have been tempted to relieve them.

126 *JT*, I, part 1, 189 (tr. Khetagurov, 110). For prisoners taken in the Kashmir campaign, see also *JT*, III, 22 (tr. Arends, 21), and ed. Jahn, *Indiengeschichte*, Ar. text Taf. 61 (German tr. 56).

127 The fullest account is in *DR*, 36–7. See also *WH*, IOL ms. 412, fol. 78 (cited in Badā'ūnī, I, 153); and the brief allusion in *DGK*, 70. Mirza, *Life and works*, 60–2.

128 *FS*, 289 (tr. 464). For other references to Hindu captives, see Zafarul Islam, 'The *Fatāwā Fīrūz Shāhī* as a source for the socio-economic history of the Sultanate period', *IC* 60, part 2 (1986), 104 n.27.

129 *KF*, 33. Cf. also the statement put in Balaban's mouth in *TFS*, 51.

130 *Ibid.*, 53; and see Digby, *War-horse*, 27–8 and n.63.

CHAPTER 12

The military, the economy and administrative reform

The army

In 656/1258, when an expedition was being prepared to dislodge the Mongol army of Sali Noyan from Sind, the muqtaʿs of Kara and Awadh failed to bring their contingents.[1] On other occasions, too, it is significant that Jūzjānī depicts the Delhi Sultan mustering troops from 'Hindūstān' or 'from the regions' (*az aṭrāf*) in order to repel Mongol attacks.[2] At this stage, in other words, the forces of the Sultanate still appear to have been undifferentiated in terms of their respective fields of operation. Sultan Balaban is credited with the establishment of a separate army designed specifically to combat the Mongols. It comprised divisions under his two sons, Muḥammad in Sind and Bughra Khān at Sāmāna, of whom the latter at least had been given the task of recruiting fresh troops, and additional forces headed by the *bārbeg* Begbars from Delhi: the combined total, we are told, was less than 17 or 18,000 horsemen.[3] Even so, there are indications in the sources that the troops with which Jalāl al-Dīn and ʿAlāʾ al-Dīn met the invading Mongols in the 1290s had no experience of an opponent other than the Hindus.[4] This is presumably why ʿAlāʾ al-Dīn is credited with efforts to recruit fresh troops with which to oppose the Mongols. The expeditions into peninsular India were another matter, and it fell to ʿAlāʾ al-Dīn, again, to raise and organize for this purpose another force, distinct from the troops he maintained in the face of the Mongol threat.[5]

The evidence, slight as it is, presupposes a substantial increase in the total size of the Sultanate's army.[6] Figures for the number of troops on the sultan's muster-roll surface with regrettable infrequency in the sources, and

[1] *TN*, II, 76–7 (tr. 846–7).
[2] *Ibid.*, I, 471, 486, and II, 171 (tr. 667, 692–3, 1156).
[3] *TFS*, 81; for Bughra Khān, see also 80.
[4] *FS*, 213 (tr. 376). *TFS*, 257, *ḥasham-i Hindūstān*. [5] *Ibid.*, 302, 326.
[6] Much of what follows is to be found in P. Jackson, 'Delhi: the problem of a vast military encampment', in R. E. Frykenberg (ed.), *Delhi through the ages: essays in urban history, culture and society* (Oxford and Delhi, 1986), 20–22.

may not be very reliable when they do.[7] When Hülegü's envoys visited Delhi in 658/1260, Balaban intimidated them by staging a review of some 200,000 foot and 50,000 horse. How many of these were the centre forces stationed in and around Delhi, and to what extent Balaban had drawn on levies from the iqtaʿs, we cannot say: Jūzjānī describes the troops as being brought both 'from the provinces and from about the regions of the capital' (*az aṭrāf-u ḥawālī-yi ḥaḍrat-i aʿlā*).[8] Subsequently, Balaban as sultan was able to review an army of 200,000 men at Awadh, on his way to crush Toghril's revolt in Bengal. Not all of these were fighting men, however. Baranī's characterization of them – as 'cavalry, foot, paiks, archers [*dhānuk*], pavilion-bearers [*kaywānī*], irregulars [*khwudaspa*; literally 'with own horse'], archers, ghulams, servants [*chākir*], traders and bazaar people'[9] – does not inspire confidence. One is reminded of Bernier's slightly contemptuous observation, apropos of Awrangzīb's empire, that the numbers of the army of the 'Mogol' were inflated by the inclusion of 'servants, sutlers ... and all those individuals belonging to *bazars*, or markets, who accompany the troops'.[10] Nevertheless, the idea that the Sultanate was militarily strong enjoyed a wide currency. The late thirteenth-century Maghribī geographer Ibn Saʿīd thought that the Mongols were unable to conquer India because of the numbers of men and elephants at the sultan's disposal.[11]

The following reigns appear to have witnessed a steady expansion of the sultans' military establishment. Word reached Mamlūk Egypt of a build-up of military forces under ʿAlā' al-Dīn Khaljī.[12] We can probably discount the figure of six or seven *laks* (600,000 or 700,000) of horse furnished in Baranī's first recension for the total numbers available to ʿAlā' al-Dīn (as also to his enemy, the Mongol prince Qutlugh Qocha) at the time of the battle of Kīlī, which definitely smacks of hyperbole; according to the revised version, the sultan could raise 200,000 or 300,000 horsemen.[13] Other figures come from Mongol Persia. Waṣṣāf and Rashīd al-Dīn believed that the Delhi forces stood at over 300,000;[14] and in his final volume, completed some twenty or more years later, Waṣṣāf cites 475,000 as the current size of

7 See Kolff, *Naukar*, 2–4, regarding the problematic figures given for Mughal armies.
8 *TN*, II, 83 (tr., 856, modified).
9 *TFS*, 86. For *kaywānīs*, see IB, III, 415 (tr. Gibb, 753); also *TFS*, 400; ᶜAfīf, 322.
10 François Bernier, *Travels in the Mogul empire, 1656–68*, ed. Archibald Constable (London, 1891), 219–20.
11 Ibn Saᶜīd, *Kitāb al-Jughrāfiyya*, 163–4.
12 Ibn Abi'l-Faḍā'il, ed. Kortantamer, Ar. text 29, *jannada'l-junūd wa'l-ᶜasākir* (German tr. 109).
13 *TFS*[1], Digby Coll. ms., fol. 96a. *TFS*, 267. But it should be noted that Khusraw makes Ghiyāth al-Dīn Tughluq say that there were 200,000 men on the muster-rolls: *Tughluq-Nāma*, 71.
14 Waṣṣāf, 309; *JT*, ed. Jahn, *Indiengeschichte*, Ar. text Taf. 54, Pers. text Taf. 18 (German tr. 43); Qāshānī, 183.

the sultan's army.[15] The figure of 400,000 horse gleaned by the cosmographer Dimishqī (d. 727/1327), fits neatly in between.[16] Under Muḥammad b. Tughluq, who is said to have built up an unprecedentedly large force within a relatively short space of time, the figures transmitted westwards, as we shall see (pp. 260–1), are still more impressive.

The priority given to the maintenance of such vast armies entailed certain problems. In the first place, the troops had to be kept occupied and in training. Baranī describes how Balaban instituted annual winter hunting expeditions for this purpose. They are said to have aroused Hülegü's admiration; and the Mongol hunt, in which the game was enclosed within a vast but contracting circle (*nerge*), and of which Juwaynī furnishes the classic account, was indeed designed as a form of annual winter manoeuvres.[17] But it should be noted that hunts very similar to those of the Mongols – even incorporating the *nerge* – had been organized by the Delhi Sultans' Ghurid precursors;[18] Mongol influence is therefore hardly incontestable. Be that as it may, we occasionally glimpse Balaban's successors on large-scale hunting expeditions;[19] and under Fīrūz Shāh, who was especially addicted to hunting, a considerable tract in Katēhr was reserved for the chase.[20] The most effective means of keeping the troops in training, however, was undoubtedly regular campaigning against the Hindus. One of Baranī's complaints about the vast host raised by Muḥammad b. Tughluq for the conquest of 'Khurāsān' is that it was not found possible to occupy it with holy war during the first of the two years before it was disbanded.[21] In all probability, Baranī is guilty of inconsistency here, since as we shall see part of the army was sent to Qarāchīl; but the remark does indicate the importance attached to the problem of a large inactive standing army.[22]

Two further problems posed by the maintenance of large armies related to pay and provisions. ʿAlā' al-Dīn determined both to maintain a standing (*mustaqīm*) army and to do so on low pay.[23] The salaries cited – 234 *tangas* for a *murattab*, and seventy-eight *tangas* for a *dūaspa* – mean little to us, since we have no data on the level of remuneration previously available to the Sultanate's troops; and indeed the ranks themselves are not defined. The

[15] Waṣṣāf, 528. The figure is ultimately reproduced by Firishta (I, 199–200) in connection with ʿAlā' al-Dīn's reforms: the intermediate source is not clear, and does not appear to be Khwānd-Amīr.

[16] *Nukhbat al-Dahr fī ʿAjā'ibi'l-Barr wa'l-Baḥr*, ed. A. F. Mehren, *Cosmographie de Chems ed-din Abou Abdallah Mohammed ed-Dimichqui* (St Petersburg, 1866), 180.

[17] *TFS*, 55. Hülegü in fact died before Balaban's accession. For the Mongol hunt, see *TJG*, I, 19–21 (tr. Boyle, 27–9); Morgan, *The Mongols*, 84–5.

[18] *TN*, I, 364–5 (tr. 385–7). Baranī employs the term *nerge* in connection with one of ʿAlā' al-Dīn's hunts: *TFS*, 272–3.

[19] E.g. Quṭb al-Dīn Mubārak Shāh: *FS*, 364–5 (tr. 563–4). Muḥammad b. Tughluq, sometimes accompanied by 'not more than 100,000 horsemen': *MA*, ed. Spies, 19 (German tr. 44)/ed. Fāriq, 36 (tr. Siddiqi and Aḥmad, 44).

[20] ʿAfīf, 321; and cf. 455. [21] *TFS*, 477. [22] See also *FJ*, 107.

[23] *TFS*, 303–4.

obscurity of Baranī's account is further accentuated by the vagaries of the printed edition of the *Ta'rīkh*. S.H. Hodivala came nearest to elucidating what ʿAlā' al-Dīn is actually supposed to have said, which is: 'I shall require two horses and the corresponding equipment from a *murattab*, and one horse and the equipment appropriate for one horse from a *dūaspa*.'[24] In his first recension, Baranī expressly equates the *murattab* with a heavy-armoured (*bar-gustuwānī*) horseman and the *dūaspa* with one who is not equipped with horse-armour.[25] The *murattab* thus emerges as a trooper who was expected to provide two mounts, and the *dūaspa*, paradoxically, as one whose second horse was supplied by the state. In the circumstances, the seventy-eight *tangas* paid to the *dūaspa* must reflect the lower investment in essential war-gear which was required of him. That the *murattab* was the better equipped of the two emerges also from Baranī's rhetorical observation elsewhere, in the context of successful defence against the Mongols, that one *dūaspa* would bring in ten Mongols yoked together, while a single Muslim cavalryman (clearly the *murattab* is intended here) drove a hundred before him.[26]

In the time of Iltutmish and Balaban troopers in the centre (*qalb*) were paid by assignments on villages in the districts around Delhi and in the Doab (see p. 95). ʿAlā' al-Dīn discarded this system. Indeed, if a later author is to be believed, the sultan disapproved of the practice of assigning villages to ordinary cavalrymen on the grounds that it nurtured local attachments and gave rise to regional rebellion.[27] Whether this was really the impulse behind his reform, we cannot be certain, but it would be in keeping with his known concerns about conspiracy and revolt. At any rate, apart from a brief period under Muḥammad b. Tughluq (below, p. 262) the troops were henceforward paid in cash until the reign of Fīrūz Shāh.

The final problem was how ʿAlā' al-Dīn was to pay his troops. Very early in his reign he had confiscated the property of the vast majority of his uncle's amirs and resumed their iqtaʿs into the khalisa. At some later point, probably in the wake of Ḥājjī Mawla's rising in Delhi, the sultan further resumed all private property (*milk*) and all existing grants, including *wuqūf* (those to religious or charitable establishments) and *inʿām* grants (which were exempt from any obligation of service). Baranī says that the only people left with money were the maliks, amirs, office-holders, Multānīs and *sāhs* (Hindu bankers and moneylenders).[28] Although by these means the sultan would have considerably augmented the resources at his disposal, we

[24] Cf. with *TFS*, 303, the BL ms., fol. 150b: *dū asp-u istiʿdād-i andāza-yi ān az* [here both the ms. and the printed text insert a redundant *w*] *murattab ṭalbam wa-yak asp-u istiʿdād-i* [printed text inserts *bar*] *andāza-yi yak asp az dūaspa* [ms. has *dū asp* in error; printed text has simply *ū*] *ṭalbam*. See further Hodivala, *Studies*, I, xv and 280. The wages of each rank are again specified at *TFS*, 319.

[25] *TFS*[1], Digby Coll. ms., fol. 115a. The term *murattab* is also encountered in *TN*, II, 26.

[26] *TFS*, 320. [27] ʿAfīf, 95. [28] *TFS*, 283–4.

have to assume, therefore, that much of this wealth would have had to be granted out again to those in favour. In the interests of expanding his forces and of maintaining them on low pay, therefore, ʿAlāʾ al-Dīn had recourse to other expedients. These involved (1) major changes in the taxation system and in the collection of grain, and (2) measures designed to ensure low prices.

Taxation and the grain supply

We do not know what proportion of the crop the cultivator surrendered to the ruler prior to the Muslim conquest of northern India: the terms employed for taxation in cash and in kind are as vague as they are numerous.[29] During the early Sultanate period, the *rānas* and *rāutas* were left to collect revenue from their headmen (*khūts*, *muqaddams*) in order to raise the tribute to be paid to the sultan's representatives (see pp. 99–100). The *kharāj* of which our sources speak was not in this period, therefore, the Islamic land tax which it usually denotes. That tax, it has been suggested, was probably levied in the former Ghaznawid territories in the western Panjāb, and may have been extended to the immediate vicinity of Delhi by the end of the thirteenth century; if so, our sources do not record such a development.[30] ʿAlāʾ al-Dīn, however, imposed the Islamic *kharāj* over a considerable area of northern India, setting it at 50 per cent.[31] This was the maximum allowed by the Ḥanafī school which was dominant in the Sultanate;[32] but ʿAlāʾ al-Dīn's rigour lay not so much in the percentage at which the *kharāj* was set, but in the manner in which it was levied and in the additional taxes imposed on the cultivators.

Baranī is our principal source for ʿAlāʾ al-Dīn's fiscal measures, although other writers provide odd details and Professor Irfan Habib has argued convincingly that their combined testimony on price control, at least, affords Baranī an impressive degree of support.[33] One difficulty is that Baranī refers to these reforms twice, in two quite distinct contexts: first as part of a deliberate policy of reducing the power of Hindu chiefs and headmen, and then several pages later, when he links the changes to the sultan's need to make fullest use of his resources in order to maintain his unprecedentedly large army. Yet clearly the same measures are involved. Under the new system, the revenue due was determined by means of measurement (*misāḥat*) on the basis of the *biswa* (i.e. one-twentieth of a

[29] For an examination of such terms, see Gopal, *Economic life*, chapter 2.

[30] I. Habib, 'Agrarian economy', 60–1. [31] *TFS*, 287.

[32] Nicolas P. Aghnides, *Mohammedan theories of finance* (New York, 1916; repr. 1969), 379–80. Similarly, IB, IV, 223 (tr. Gibb and Beckingham, 872), says that the infidels of 'Habanq' (near Sylhet) paid half their produce to their Muslim rulers.

[33] Irfan Habib, 'The price regulations of ʿAlāʾuddīn Khaljī – a defence of Ẓiāʾ Baranī', *IESHR* 21 (1984), 394–7.

bīgha): that is to say, the yield (*wafā'*) per *biswa* was estimated, and the amount due from the cultivator was arrived at by multiplying this figure by the number of *biswas* he held; of this total, half was required. For the most part, the *kharāj* was to be paid not as a share of the crop but in cash, and Baranī alleges that the collectors demanded the tax so insistently that the peasants were compelled to sell their crop to the grain merchants (*kārwāniyān*) as it stood in the field (*bar sar-i kisht*).[34] One consequence of the new system of assessment was that the contribution of the individual became all the more important. As a letter of Ibn Māhrū reveals in the middle of the fourteenth century, the peasant, though technically free (*ḥurr aṣl*), was now effectively bound to the soil, since were he to abscond the total *kharāj* due from the village would suffer a reduction.[35]

In addition to a *kharāj* assessed on a new basis, 'Alā' al-Dīn imposed two further taxes: the *charā'ī*, or grazing-tax, and a *sukūnat-gharī* (or *-garhī*), a tax on dwellings.[36] We are told little about either impost in the standard version of the *Ta'rīkh-i Fīrūz-Shāhī*, but learn more about the *charā'ī* in the first recension, where the quantity of livestock yielded (per village?) is said to comprise four oxen (*sutūr*), two buffaloes (*gāw-i mīsh*), two cows (*mādagāw*) and twelve sheep.[37] Whether the *charā'ī* was levied on – among others – the transhumant peoples of the eastern Panjāb, whose lifestyle was predominantly pastoral, is uncertain. We have to assume that the dwelling-tax fell on the urban population as well as on peasants. It should be noted that unlike the *kharāj* such taxes enjoyed no sanction in Islamic law.

The two recensions of Baranī's work differ when they come to name the official who was given responsibility for implementing the reforms. In the first, it is Malik Yaklakhī; in the second, Sharaf al-Dīn Qā'inī. Both are entitled *nā'ib-wazīr*.[38] Over a period of some years (six, according to Baranī's first version), the *nā'ib-wazīr* saw to it that the *kharāj* on the basis of measurement, together with the grazing- and dwelling-taxes, were applied uniformly to a vast area, as if it were a single village. The tract in question is defined as 'all the villages in the regions of the capital, the townships (*qaṣabāt*) of the Doab country, the land from Bhayāna to Jhāyin, from Pālam to Dēōpālpūr and Lahore, all the territory of Sunnām and Sāmāna, and from Rēwārī to Nāgawr, from Khōr to Gānūrī, and from Amrōha, Afghānpūr and Kābar, from Damhāī to Badā'ūn, Kasrak and *Kōtla, and the whole of Katēhr'. Qā'inī is further credited with strenuous measures to eliminate bribery and embezzlement among local

[34] *TFS*, 287, 288, 305, 307. For the phrase *wafā-yi biswa*, see Hodivala, *Studies*, II, 97–8; Habib, 'Agrarian economy', 61. The *bīgha* later adopted in British India approximated to five-eighths of an acre: Yule and Burnell, *Hobson-Jobson*, 79 (*s.v.* 'beegah').

[35] *IM*, 61–3. I. Habib, 'Economic history of the Delhi Sultanate', 297–8, and 'Agrarian economy', 54.

[36] *TFS*, 287, 288.

[37] *TFS*[1], Digby Coll. ms., fol. 112a.

[38] *Ibid. TFS*, 288. For the latter's *nisba*, see above, p. 173, n.16.

functionaries, to the extent of inspecting the records (*bahī*) of the village accountant (*patwārī*).[39]

A significant proportion of this region was incorporated into the khalisa, as the territories of Kōl, Baran, Mīrat, Amrōha, Afghānpūr and Kābar and the whole of the Doab were resumed from the existing muqtaʿs and brought under the sultan's revenue ministry.[40] Within the Doab khalisa specifically, the *kharāj* was to be paid entirely in grain, which was to be conveyed to the sultan's grain reserves in the capital; in the Jhāyin region, on the other hand, the tax was to be paid half in cash and half in grain, and the grain to be stored in Jhāyin and its townships.[41] The enormous stores of grain kept in Delhi made a strong impression on Ibn Baṭṭūṭa some decades later.[42] These reserves of grain were designed for periods of famine, which afflicted the capital from time to time, notably in Jalāl al-Dīn Khaljī's reign, when the reserves had been exhausted;[43] though the sultan will also have had in mind the more recent crisis provoked by the Mongol attack of 703/1303 led by Taraghai (above, pp. 222–3). We cannot dismiss the possibility, too, that 'Alā' al-Dīn's vigorous campaign against the manufacture and consumption of wine and drugs, which if effective would have entailed a loss of revenue to the state, did not spring simply from religious and moral impulses. He may have aimed simultaneously at encouraging concentration within the agrarian sector on cereal production.[44]

39 *TFS*, 287–9; *TFS*[1], Digby Coll. ms., fol. 112a, adds 'and the whole of Hindūstān as far as Bengal'. Khōr (BL ms. KHR) appears in error as KRH (Kara) in the printed text, which also has JHABN for JHAYN and DBHAY for DHMHAY. Khōr, an old town mentioned also at *TFS*, 485 (text has KHWD in error), stands at 27° 39′ N., 79° 28′ E.: Hodivala, *Studies*, I, 296; *IG*, XXII, 229. For Damhāī, on the route from Badā'ūn to Delhi, at 28° 12′ N., 78° 16′ E., see Hodivala, *Studies*, I, 269. From the context, *Kōtla (thus *TFS*[1]; mss. of the later recension read KWYLH) must be the Kōpila of Timurid sources, which Lal, *Twilight*, 34, identifies as Hardwār.

40 *TFS*, 323–4. For Afghānpūr, see I. Habib, *Atlas*, 27 and map 8A.

41 *TFS*, 305–6. For this interpretation of seemingly conflicting statements by Baranī, see I. Habib, 'Agrarian economy', 61–2.

42 IB, III, 148 (tr. Gibb, 621): he was under the impression, however, that the stores dated from Balaban's day.

43 *FS*, 217–19 (tr. 383–4). *TFS*, 212. For the opening of the granaries during times of dearth under ᶜAlā' al-Dīn himself, see *KF*, 21.

44 *TFS*, 284–6. Baranī alleges, however, that the aim was to reduce the incidence of convivial gatherings of the nobles which might lead to conspiracy. According to Sir George Watt, *A dictionary of the economic products of India* (London and Calcutta, 1889–93, 6 vols. in 9), VI, part 4, 273–4, the grapes of the N.W. provinces and Awadh are hardly suitable for the manufacture of wine; and IB, III, 129 (tr. Gibb, 610), confirms that the grape was rare in India, being found in the Delhi region and one other province whose name is blank in all the mss. Nevertheless, other sources suggest that wine production was prominent in Awadh and in Kōl and Mīrat, all of them regions which were the object of ᶜAlā' al-Dīn's economic reforms: *TFS*, 157; Mirza, *Life and works*, 72. It is noteworthy that at least one intoxicating drink, *bagnī*, was made from grain: Hodivala, *Studies*, I, 276.

Price control

The accumulation of stocks of grain was only partly designed as an insurance against dearth; it was also an essential component of ʿAlā' al-Dīn's policy of price control.[45] In order to maintain a large standing army on relatively low pay, it was necessary to secure low prices of essential items. The government therefore fixed maximum prices for a number of commodities. These comprised basic foodstuffs – wheat (*ḥinṭa*), barley (*jaw*), rice (*shālī*), pulse (*māsh*, *nukhūd*) and *mōth*; cloth, sugar, sugar-cane (*nabāt*), fruit, animal fat (*rawghan-i sutūr*) and wax (*rawghan-i chirāgh*); and slaves, horses and livestock.[46] To oversee the maintenance of low grain prices, Malik Qabūl Ulughkhānī was appointed as intendant of the market (*shiḥna-yi manda*), assisted by an intelligence officer (*barīd*), and all the merchants (*kārwāniyān*) were subject to his jurisdiction. The leading merchants, according to Ḥamīd Qalandar, were advanced money from the treasury and were paid their expenses. On the other hand, Baranī says that they had to give sureties and were obliged, together with their wives and families, to take up residence in the villages along the banks of the Yamuna. Their operations, too, were closely supervised. Hoarding and regrating of grain – whether by cultivator, merchant or broker (*baqqāl*) – were forbidden, under strict penalties which included confiscation of the grain in question. In order to ensure that cultivators sold the requisite quantities of grain to the merchants in the fields (*bar sar-i kisht*) and that the merchants brought it promptly to the sultan's markets, certificates were issued by the local officials confirming that the transaction had taken place.[47] The marketing of commodities other than grain was centred on a new institution called the *Sarāī-yi ʿAdl*, which was established in a vacant area inside the Badā'ūn Gate and for which a group of prosperous Multānīs were made responsible. Orders were issued that no goods were to be sold anywhere but in the Sarāī-yi ʿAdl, on pain of confiscation.[48]

Overall responsibility for the maintenance of low prices was entrusted to a certain Yaʿqūb, who combined the office of chief inspector of revenue

[45] See generally Dharam Pal, 'ʿAlā'-ud-Dīn's price control system', *IC* 18 (1944), 45–52; P. Saran, 'The economic policy and price control of Alauddin Khalji', *Bhāratiya Vidyā* 11 (1950), 195–215 (repr. in his *Studies*); Shaikh Abdur Rashid, 'Price control under Alauddin Khilji', in *Proceedings of the All-Pakistan History Conference. First Session, held at Karachi . . . 1951* (Karachi, [n.d.]), 203–10; I. Habib, 'Non-agricultural production and urban economy', in Raychaudhuri and Habib, *Cambridge economic history*, 83, 86–7.

[46] Basic foodstuffs: *TFS*, 305. Cloth etc.: *ibid.*, 309, 310. Horses: *ibid.*, 312–13. Slaves: *ibid.*, 314. Livestock: *ibid.*, 315. Habib, 'Non-agricultural production', 87, points out that the price of wheat quoted by Baranī is confirmed by Ḥamīd Qalandar, *Khayr al-Majālis*, ed. K. A. Nizami (Aligarh, [1959]), 185 (cf. also 241).

[47] *TFS*, 305, 306–8. Ḥamīd Qalandar, *Khayr al-Majālis*, 241, cited in I. Habib, 'Non-agricultural production', 83. On Malik Qabūl, see Hodivala, *Studies*, II, 100: he had presumably been a slave of the sultan's brother Ulugh Khān.

[48] *TFS*, 309–10. See also *KF*, 21–2.

(*nāẓir*) with those of *ra'īs* of the capital and *muḥtasib* of the whole empire.[49] He in turn appointed for each market an overseer (*shiḥna*) whose task was to keep prices under surveillance.[50] The *ra'īs*'s department (*dīwān-i riyāsat*) was to keep a register (*daftar*, *tadhkira*) of the names of all traders, both those of the capital and those of the provinces. Written undertakings were required from them that they would convey agreed amounts of certain commodities annually to be sold in the Sarāī-yi ʿAdl.[51] Twenty *laks* (2,000,000) of *tangas* were advanced by the government to Multānīs who were to convey goods from the provinces in order to ensure cheap prices if the merchants delayed to bring their wares to the Sarāī-yi ʿAdl.[52] For the purchase of luxury items, it was necessary to obtain a certificate (*parwāna*) from the *ra'īs*, in order that traders or wealthy citizens might not buy up goods cheaply in the capital and sell them elsewhere at a high profit.[53] The entire system rested on a network of spies, who reported abuses to the sultan.[54]

ʿAlā' al-Dīn's policies were reinforced by harsh penalties. To some extent the victims were middlemen: horse-traders and horse-brokers, for instance, whose operations tended to inflate prices, were in many cases fined or expelled from the capital and imprisoned in distant forts.[55] For his part, the uncompromising stance of the *ra'īs* Yaʿqūb made him an object of terror to those who infringed the market regulations. Lashings and imprisonment were common. Flesh was cut from the faces of some offenders, notably dealers who attempted to offset their low profits by selling short weight; they were additionally ejected from the bazaar.[56] Despite these draconian punishments, however, the government failed to eradicate fraudulent trading.[57]

Purpose and effect of ʿAlā' al-Dīn's policies

Baranī is emphatic that ʿAlā' al-Dīn's control of prices was a source of wonder to his contemporaries;[58] and indeed the policy – involving the enforcement of maximum prices for a wide range of commodities and in some cases the elimination of middlemen – appears to have been a remarkable piece of government interventionism, all the more impressive in the conditions that obtained during the early fourteenth century. We should therefore be inclined to approach Baranī's testimony warily, if other witnesses did not confirm that the effectiveness of ʿAlā' al-Dīn's price control was a byword among later generations. Ibn Baṭṭūṭa, visiting the Sultanate in the 1330s and early 1340s, heard ʿAlā' al-Dīn praised in this connection as one of the best of previous sultans, and mentions in particular

[49] *TFS*, 317. [50] *Ibid.*, 317–18. [51] *Ibid.*, 309, 310–11.
[52] *Ibid.*, 309, 311. [53] *Ibid.*, 311–12.
[54] *Ibid.*, 315, 319; see also 308 for spies in the *manda*. [55] *Ibid.*, 313–14.
[56] *Ibid.*, 316, 319. [57] *Ibid.*, 317. [58] *Ibid.*, 305, 308, 312, 339, 340–1.

the prices of meat, woven cloth and grain. Ḥamīd Qalandar, writing in *c.* 755/1354, likewise pays tribute to the sultan's achievement in reducing the cost of grain and to the low wages paid in his reign.[59]

The overall effect of ʿAlāʾ al-Dīn's measures was to transfer a significantly larger share of the agricultural surplus from the countryside to the towns and from the Hindu chiefs to the Muslim governing class. But the essentially militaristic thrust of his economic policy is made explicit by Baranī, who specifies that the entire revenue demand (*maḥṣūl*) of certain khalisa territories was set aside for the pay (*wajh*) of the army (*ḥasham*) and the expenses of the imperial manufactories (*kārkhānas*).[60] He also links the control of prices (in the first recension, the price of horses in particular) with the need to recruit soldiers on low pay.[61] That the needs of the army were uppermost in the sultan's mind is also clear from the categorization of horses into four classes, of which the lowest comprised those which would not pass muster.[62] Modern scholarly opinion has posited in addition other stimuli, though the weight ascribed to each varies. The hypothesis advanced by Dharam Pal, who viewed the sultan's policy as also a reaction to inflationary forces generated by the influx of gold from the south, lacks plausibility, given that the reforms seem to have been instituted within two or three years of ʿAlāʾ al-Dīn's accession and therefore to have predated Kāfūr's exploits beyond the Vindhyas.[63] Shaikh Abdur Rashid believed that ʿAlāʾ al-Dīn's measures were intended to benefit not merely the state but 'the consumer at large'; and for what it is worth Ḥamīd Qalandar does impute humanitarian motives to the sultan, who allegedly sought to confer benefits on his people at large.[64]

The most convincing analysis, however, is that of Kehrer. The drafting of peasants for the army and for ʿAlāʾ al-Dīn's construction projects served to diminish the production of food and cloth; while the recruitment of a certain number of foreign mercenaries would have occasioned an absolute increase in consumption. Furthermore, in addition to the fall in supplies, there was a growing problem of distribution: the concentration of great numbers of non-producing consumers – the troops – in the capital and its environs accentuated difficulties in transportation from the provinces. To remedy these problems, the government had two alternatives: controlling prices artificially and increasing the supply of money.[65] Where ʿAlāʾ al-Dīn

59 IB, III, 184–5 (tr. Gibb, 640–1). Ḥamīd Qalandar, *Khayr al-Majālis*, 240–1.
60 *TFS*, 323–4. On the significance of *maḥṣūl* as 'revenue demand' rather than 'produce', at least from the time of ᶜAfīf, see Moreland, *Agrarian system*, 232 n.1, 249.
61 *TFS*, 304; cf. also 340. For horses, see *TFS*[1], Digby Coll. ms., fol. 115a.
62 *TFS*, 313, *ānchi dar dīwān nagudharad*.
63 Pal, 'ᶜAlāʾ-ud-Din's price control system', 46. Cf. Saran, 'The economic policy', 202. Chronological indications: *TFS*[1], Digby Coll. ms., fol. 109a.
64 Ḥamīd Qalandar, *Khayr al-Majālis*, 241. Abdur Rashid, 'Price control'.
65 Kenneth C. Kehrer, 'The economic policies of Ala-ud-Din Khalji', *Journal of the Panjab University Historical Society* 16 (1963), 55–66.

had recourse to the first of these expedients, Muḥammad b. Tughluq, as we shall see, would resort to the second.

ʿAlāʾ al-Dīn's tax reforms subjected the *khūts* and *muqaddams* to the same assessment as the peasants within their localities. The revenue was to be levied 'without discrimination' (*bī tafāwutī*), so that for this purpose the headman (*khūt*) was treated in exactly the same way as the inhabitants of his village: Baranī says explicitly that there was to be no difference 'between the *khūt* and the *balāhar*' (the sweeper).[66] Moreover, the chiefs' perquisites (*ḥuqūq*) were abolished, including their exemption from the *charāʾī* and *gharī* taxes, and it was no longer possible for them to pass their own tax burden on to those who were less well off than themselves.[67] They thus suffered a twofold loss. Baranī claims approvingly that the 'Hindus' (by which he means the rural Hindu aristocracy) forfeited their surplus wealth and that their wives found it necessary to earn wages by taking work in Muslim households. Steps were taken to reduce the potential for rebellion. The *chawdhurīs*, *khūts* and *muqaddams* were compelled to give up riding and bearing arms and could no longer 'eat the betel-leaf' (*tanbūl*) – a reference to the ceremony whereby *rāwats* (*rāutas*) rallied to the support of some leader, whether a Hindu prince or a rebel Muslim amir like Malik Chhajjū in 689/1290 (p. 125 above). A single official of the local revenue collectorate (*sarhang-i dīwān-i qaṣabāt*), we are told, might now rope together twenty or so of them and extract the tax from them by means of blows and kicks. In his first recension, Baranī adds that any Hindu's house in which arms were discovered became the sultan's property.[68] At a later juncture he endeavours to express the subjection of this rural aristocracy in equally vivid terms when he depicts them guarding the highways on the sultan's behalf and keeping watch on caravans and travellers.[69]

Whether humiliation of the Hindu chiefs was the main impulse behind the reforms, however, as Baranī claims, is to be doubted: it was more probably a by-product of the government's efforts to increase its revenue and to leave no pockets of immunity. But lest we incline to doubt the truth behind Baranī's vivid statements, ʿAfīf's account of the birth of the future sultan Fīrūz Shāh corroborates the earlier historian's testimony regarding conditions under ʿAlāʾ al-Dīn. Ghāzī Malik Tughluq, at that time (*c.* 706/1306–7) muqtaʿ of Dēōpālpūr, approached the local chief, Rāna Mal Bhattī, and sought his daughter in marriage for his brother Rajab. Meeting with a proud refusal, Tughluq – allegedly on the advice of ʿAfīf's

66 *TFS*, 287. For *khūt*, see above, p. 124 n.2; for the meaning of *balāhar* ('village menial'), I. Habib, 'Agrarian economy', 48.

67 *TFS*, 287, 291. I. Habib, 'Agrarian economy', 55.

68 *TFS*[1], Digby Coll. ms., fol. 112a. *TFS*, 288; for the ceremony of taking up the betel-leaf, see *ibid.*, 182, and Hodivala, *Studies*, I, 265.

69 *TFS*, 324; cf. also 340.

great-grandfather, who was his representative in the Abūhar district – entered Rāna Mal's territory (*talwandī*) and proceeded to extort the whole year's tax (*māl*) in cash at once, rather than in instalments (*ba-martaba*) as was the usual practice. All the *muqaddams* and *chawdhurīs* of the territory were beaten, and Rāna Mal's people were in great straits. When she discovered from her weeping grandmother that she was the cause of this affliction, Rāna Mal's daughter told her father to surrender her to the Muslim amir and to imagine that she had been carried off by the Mongols (why this should have afforded him any consolation is not readily apparent). She thus became the wife of Rajab and subsequently the mother of Fīrūz Shāh. ʿAfīf assures his readers that Rāna Mal had no choice, for 'this was the era of ʿAlāʾ al-Dīn and they were in no position to make any murmur or outcry'.[70]

It is clear from this anecdote that Ghāzī Malik extorted the tax direct from the headmen. Professor Irfan Habib sees this as part of a process whereby the older rural aristocracy of ranas and rautas was subverted. Yet at the same time a new superior rural class was emerging, and he has proposed that at its apex stood the *chawdhurī*, defined by Ibn Baṭṭūṭa as 'the chief of the infidels' in each *ṣadī*; the *ṣadī* was a unit of a hundred villages and doubtless corresponded to the *pargana*, a term first employed by ʿIṣāmī and Ibn Māhrū in the middle of the fourteenth century and more commonly used by ʿAfīf.[71]

Parallel with a reduction in the perquisites of Hindu intermediaries went a growing encroachment by the sultan's bureaucracy on the position of the Muslim muqtaʿs. ʿAlāʾ al-Dīn's expansion of the khalisa had curtailed the area to be granted out as iqtaʿs; though to a large extent this was compensated for by the availability of iqtaʿs in newly conquered territories like Gujarāt, Mālwa and the Deccan. But the application of the new method of *kharāj* assessment to territory which, like Awadh, was still held as iqtaʿ would certainly have brought about a closer supervision of the local finances by the sultan's own functionaries.[72]

ʿAlāʾ al-Dīn's successors

According to Baranī, of all ʿAlāʾ al-Dīn's measures Quṭb al-Dīn Mubārak Shāh retained only that concerning the consumption of wine (although even

70 ᶜAfīf, 37–8. That Fīrūz Shāh was born not in 709/1309–10 (as ᶜAfīf, 36, claims) but in 707/1307–8 is clear from ᶜAfīf's other statements that he became sultan at the age of forty-five (*ibid.*, 20) and that he was fourteen at Ghiyāth al-Dīn Tughluq's accession and eighteen at that of Muḥammad b. Tughluq (*ibid.*, 41–2); see also Hodivala, *Studies*, I, 390–1.

71 I. Habib, 'Agrarian economy', 56–9. For the *chawdhurī*, see IB, III, 388 (tr. Gibb, 741); and for the *pargana*, *FS*, 450, 597 (tr. 680, 881); *IM*, 23, 146; ᶜAfīf, 99, 236, 288, 295, 297, 339, 432, 437, 479, 483, 500; also 272 for *parganadārs*.

72 I. Habib, 'Agrarian economy', 70.

this was flouted).[73] Price control was abandoned. Quṭb al-Dīn proved unable to enforce it, and his reign thus witnessed a substantial rise in the prices of grain and other foodstuffs; vendors set their own rates for fabrics; the regulations surrounding the Sarāī-yi ʿAdl were discontinued, and the Multānīs became absorbed in their own commercial interests.[74] The spy network fell into abeyance, and the *Dīwān-i Riyāsat* no longer had any authority.[75] Even the *kharāj* did not remain at the level ʿAlāʾ al-Dīn had decreed, although the extent of the reduction is uncertain. Baranī asserts merely that Quṭb al-Dīn abolished 'the heavy land taxes (*kharājhā*) and burdensome requisitions from the people' and that as a consequence of the reduction of the *kharāj* the 'Hindus' (again meaning, presumably, the headmen and chiefs) enjoyed ease and affluence.[76] Two other pillars in the edifice constructed by ʿAlāʾ al-Dīn were removed when much of the land recently taken into the khalisa was granted out once more and the soldiers' pay, along with other charges on the government's resources, like the stipends of the ʿulama', were increased, doubtless in response to the rise in prices.[77]

Like ʿAlāʾ al-Dīn, Ghiyāth al-Dīn Tughluq began his reign by boosting the contents of his treasury. Although ʿAlāʾ al-Dīn's grants were confirmed, the new sultan cancelled all those made by his predecessor Khusraw Shāh, and instituted, as it were, *quo warranto* proceedings into the rest. ʿIṣāmī, whose ancestors thereby forfeited two villages in the Delhi region that they held by tax-free grant (*inʿām*) from earlier sovereigns, does not conceal his outrage at this conduct – for which, in his view, the sultan soon paid the penalty with his life.[78] Yet by Baranī Tughluq's reign is depicted as one of moderation towards both the peasantry and the amirs. The sultan demonstrated his concern for the livelihood of ordinary peasants and for the extension of cultivation.[79] The *kharāj* was no longer to be assessed in terms of estimated yields, but was to be based on the actual yield (*ḥāṣil*): the cultivators, says Baranī, were thereby relieved of the difference between the real produce and the non-existent (*būd-u nābūd*). The amount taken as *kharāj* was not to be raised by more than one-tenth or one-eleventh annually. It is accordingly clear that an increase in the rate of the *kharāj* was seen as desirable; but it was to be achieved in stages.[80]

Ghiyāth al-Dīn Tughluq permitted the muqtaʿs to supplement their stipends (*mawājib*) by retaining up to one-fifteenth or one-twentieth of the *kharāj* levied within their territory, as a perquisite of their office.[81] But on

[73] *TFS*, 384: slightly later (385) he contradicts himself with the statement that not a single ʿAlāʾī measure was retained.
[74] *Ibid.*, 319, 384–5. [75] *Ibid.*, 385.
[76] *Ibid.*, 383, 385. *FS*, 355 (tr. 552), might suggest that Quṭb al-Dīn merely remitted the *kharāj* for the first year of his reign.
[77] *TFS*, 382–3. [78] *Ibid.*, 438–9. *FS*, 390–1 (tr. 594–6). [79] *TFS*, 442.
[80] *Ibid.*, 429–30. [81] *Ibid.*, 431, 432.

the other hand we find the sultan warning his amirs not to encroach on the pay of their soldiers: this shows both that a part of the revenues of the iqtaʿ was set aside for the maintenance of the troops and that the muqtaʿ at this date still had access to the portion of the revenues which was earmarked for his men.[82] This was to change under Muḥammad b. Tughluq, whose policy further undermined the powers of the muqtaʿ and may well have underlain many of the rebellions of his reign.

The economy and the expansion of the Sultanate

The idea that the establishment of the Delhi Sultanate accelerated the process of urbanization over much of northern India, as well as fostering the development of a money economy and an expansion in craft production, is now widely accepted. Under ʿAlāʾ al-Dīn, whose mint output seems to have outstripped that of his predecessors, the increase in the *kharāj* and its realization in cash further contributed to the monetization of the economy.[83] We have no figures for the tax yield from the empire as a whole prior to the reign of the Tughluqid Sultan Fīrūz Shāh. In the Shamsid and Ghiyathid eras the Sultanate already included flourishing ports like Lāharī on the lower Indus, which Ibn Baṭṭūṭa was informed was worth sixty *laks* (i.e. 6,000,000 silver *tangas*) per annum to Muḥammad b. Tughluq;[84] there is no reason to believe that it would have yielded, say, less than half this amount in the latter half of the thirteenth century. Although, of course, the sultans forfeited the extensive revenue of Bengal from its secession in 685/1287 until its recovery by Ghiyāth al-Dīn Tughluq in 724/1324, this would have been more than offset by the conquests of ʿAlāʾ al-Dīn Khaljī and his successors, which greatly increased the material and fiscal resources of the Sultanate. The fertility of Awadh and Ẓafarābād, over which, as we have seen (p. 200), the sultan's hold seems to have intensified in the early fourteenth century, would be a byword at a time when the regions west of the Yamuna were in the grip of famine during Muḥammad b. Tughluq's reign.[85] Ibn Baṭṭūṭa comments, too, on the density of cultivation around Dhār and the prosperity of Ujjain, and on the great value of the land revenue of the Dawlatābād province to the sultan's treasury; and indeed Muḥammad fixed the revenue of the 'Marhat' territory at six or seven *krōrs* (i.e. sixty or seventy million *tangas*).[86]

[82] *Ibid.*, 431. Irfan Habib, 'The social distribution of landed property in pre-British India', *Enquiry* 2, part 3 (Winter 1965), 48; see also his 'Agrarian economy', 70.

[83] I. Habib, 'Economic history of the Delhi Sultanate', 289–98. H. C. Verma, *Dynamics of urban life in pre-Mughal India* (New Delhi, 1986), chaps. 2, 4 and 5. Shireen Moosvi, 'Numismatic evidence and the economic history of the Delhi Sultanate', *PIHC* 50. *Gorakhpur 1989* (Delhi, 1990), 207–18.

[84] IB, III, 112 (tr Gibb, 602)

[85] *Ibid.*, III, 342 (tr. Gibb, 720–1). *TFS*, 485, 486.

[86] IB, IV, 42, 45, 49 (tr. Gibb and Beckingham, 791, 793, 795). Muḥammad b. Tughluq: *TFS*, 501. For the *krōr* (= 100 *laks*), see Yule and Burnell, *Hobson-Jobson*, 276 (*s.v.* 'crore').

India had long been portrayed as insatiably consuming the wealth of lands further west.[87] Acquisition of the ports of Gujarāt, especially, enabled the Delhi government to tap the flourishing commerce of the Arabian Sea and the Persian Gulf; and it is perhaps no accident that in ʿAlāʾ al-Dīn's time we first encounter the *malik al-tujjār*, 'king of the merchants', who was responsible to the sultan for overseeing commercial activity, or that one of al-ʿUmarī's informants was a Kārimī merchant – i.e. a member of an important corporation of traders based in Egypt – who had twice visited Quṭb al-Dīn Mubārak Shāh.[88] To the anonymous author of the *Sīrat-i Fīrūz-Shāhī*, Kanbhāya was 'the rendezvous of merchants, the haven of travellers by land and by sea';[89] and the affluence of its mercantile class was vividly demonstrated in the magnificence of their mansions.[90] At the beginning of the century Gujarāt had attracted praise in Rashīd al-Dīn's history of India, and Marco Polo had earlier heard impressive tales of its manufactures.[91] We know that the province produced fine cotton cloths (exported to China); was a place of transhipment for diamonds and other precious stones; and imported black slaves from East Africa. A *farmān* of 709/1309–10 reproduced in Amīr Khusraw's *Rasāʾil al-Iʿjāz* lists numerous high-value commodities found at Kanbhāya.[92] The revenue-demand (*maḥṣūl*) of Gujarāt in the late 1360s is set at two *krōrs* (twenty million *tangas*) by ʿAfīf; it is worth comparing this sum with that given for the Doab (eighty *laks*, i.e. eight million *tangas*) at approximately the same time.[93] And yet the Sultanate did not benefit merely from the possession of outlets onto the Arabian Sea. By Muḥammad b. Tughluq's reign there is fragmentary evidence that his dominions were attracting traders from as far afield as Western Europe, who profited from the encouragement of Mongol rulers to travel by the

[87] Waṣṣāf, 300. See also *JT*, III, 493 (tr. Arends, 281).

[88] *TFS*, 352. *MA*, ed. Spies, Ar. text 35 (German tr. 62)/ed. Fāriq, 64 (tr. Siddiqi and Aḥmad, 60). The *malik al-tujjār* of Iltutmish's day mentioned in *TN*, II, 41 (tr. 790), of course, was not the Delhi Sultan's own agent, but represented merchants from Persia, Iraq, Khwārazm and other territories outside the empire. On the Kārimīs, see Gaston Wiet, 'Les marchands d'épices sous les sultans mamlouks', *Cahiers d'Histoire Egyptienne* 7 (1955), 81–147; S. D. Goitein, 'The beginnings of the Kārim merchants and the character of their organization', in his *Studies in Islamic history and institutions* (Leiden, 1966), 351–60; M. S. Labib, 'Les marchands Kārimīs en Orient et sur l'Océan Indien', in M. Mollat du Jourdain (ed.), *Sociétés et compagnies de commerce en Orient et dans l'Océan Indien* (Paris, 1970), 209–14.

[89] *SFS*, 21, *marjaʿ-i tujjār-u maʾman-i suffār* (tr. Basu, in *JBORS* 23 [1937], 99). See also the author's reaction to Kanbhāya in *IM*, 133.

[90] IB, IV, 53, 55 (tr. Gibb and Beckingham, 797, 798).

[91] *JT*, ed. Jahn, *Indiengeschichte*, Pers. text Taf. 13, Ar. text Taf. 51 (German tr. 36). Marco Polo, tr. Moule and Pelliot, I, 420–1, 422–3/tr. Yule and Cordier, II, 393–4, 398–9.

[92] *RI*, IV, 141–3. See generally Simon Digby, 'The maritime trade of India', in Raychaudhuri and Habib, *Cambridge economic history*, 139–40, 142, 149; V. K. Jain, *Trade and traders in Western India (AD 1000–1300)* (New Delhi, 1990), 98–105.

[93] ʿAfīf, 221, 296.

overland route through Ürgench and Ghazna, for a group of Venetians is known to have visited Delhi in 1338.[94]

Changing priorities

Alongside the marked increase in the revenue from conquered territory, however, the sultans' government relied on the fruits of predatory campaigns against the Hindu powers of the subcontinent. The Mongol threat appears to have modified the order of priorities within the framework of military policy, for as early as 645/1247 Jūzjānī has Ulugh Khān Balaban advocate the looting of Hindu territory not merely in order to chastise the infidel but to amass booty which could then be used to maintain a defensive army in the face of Mongol invasions.[95] The fact that Jūzjānī wrote as a contemporary, and still more his proximity to Ulugh Khān, make it very likely that these sentiments illustrate the adoption of a conscious policy by Delhi's rulers following the intensification of Mongol pressure after 1241. They contrast sharply with the more simplistic analysis of Baranī, who depicts Balaban (now sultan) as refusing to launch campaigns against the Hindus as long as the Mongol menace persisted.[96] This statement is in any case rendered suspect by the passage that follows: a ringing denunciation of the expansionist policy, leading as it does to the overtaxing of resources and possibly rebellion, with the ultimate consequences of bloodshed and harsh punishments.[97] Clearly what Baranī had in mind here was not Balaban's reign at all, but the recent chaos caused by the expansionist designs of Muḥammad b. Tughluq.

A certain degree of military activity against the Hindus was vital both to keep the armed forces in proper training and also to harvest the resources with which to reward them; otherwise it would have been far more difficult to maintain a large army to repel the Mongols. Hence we have good reason to distrust Baranī again when he describes how Taraghai's invasion prompted 'Alā' al-Dīn Khaljī to give up 'campaigning and taking fortresses' (*lashgarkashī-u ḥiṣārgīrī*).[98] We know in any case that this was simply not so: even were we to disregard the expeditions which 'Alā' al-Dīn personally headed against Siwāna and Jālōr, and which Baranī fails to mention, the notice he gives of Malik Nā'ib Kāfūr's campaigns in the south would alone indicate that the above statement is worthless. It might have been interpreted to mean that in the face of Mongol pressure 'Alā' al-Dīn confined himself to plundering raids and abandoned the policy of outright annexation instanced in the fate of Ranthanbōr and Chitōr; but this inference is precluded, again, by the annexation of Mālwa from 705/1305 onwards and

94 R. S. Lopez, 'European merchants in the medieval Indies: the evidence of commercial documents', *Journal of Economic History* 3 (1943), 174–80.

95 *TN*, II, 57 (tr. 816).

96 *TFS*, 50–1.

97 *Ibid.*, 51–2, 53.

98 *Ibid.*, 302.

of Dēōgīr in *c.* 1314. Nevertheless, under ʿAlāʾ al-Dīn the two arms of military policy – plundering operations and the imposition of direct rule – appear at least to have been kept in tension. The succeeding reigns, by contrast, witnessed a steady move towards the absorption of vast tracts of territory into the empire.

CHAPTER 13

Stupor mundi: the reign of Muḥammad b. Tughluq

The reign of Muḥammad b. Tughluq throws up perhaps more problems than any other in the history of the Sultanate. At the sultan's accession the authority of Delhi was acknowledged over a larger area of the subcontinent than under any previous monarch. It is to this process of expansion that Baranī refers when he describes the unprecedented scope and efficiency of the revenue department in Muḥammad's early years.[1] And yet the reign appears to be dominated by an extraordinary number of revolts. By the sultan's death in 752/1351 Bengal and every tract south of the Vindhyas had declared their independence, and none of these provinces was ever recovered.

In the revised version of his *Ta'rīkh*, Baranī blames the disasters of the reign on the sultan's chimerical designs.[2] But it needs to be borne in mind that by the accession of Muḥammad b. Tughluq, a policy of direct rule was progressively replacing that of plundering and levying tribute on Hindu kingdoms. The absorption of such vast areas of territory brought its own problems in its wake; and they were very probably a major factor underlying the acute economic difficulties which overwhelmed the Sultanate in the 1330s. Launching regular attacks on enemy territory in order largely to finance a sizeable standing army for other purposes was one matter; it was quite another to maintain garrisons and a civil administration in a conquered province, with all the expense involved in annual accounting and transportation of revenues.[3] Newly acquired provinces, moreover, could not be treated in the same rapacious manner that characterizes warfare in enemy country. The Delhi Sultans therefore suffered a twofold loss. It would have been most keenly felt, perhaps, in respect of gold bullion, which had loomed so large in the looting campaigns of ʿAlāʾ al-Dīn and Kāfūr. The problems were exacerbated by Muḥammad b. Tughluq's extraordinary expenditure and proverbial generosity.[4]

Wider economic trends, too, about which we are imperfectly informed,

[1] *TFS*, 468–9. [2] *Ibid.*, 471. [3] As Baranī in fact realized: *ibid.*, 51–2.
[4] Firishta, I, 239, says that he was spending the treasure amassed by ᶜAlāʾ al-Dīn Khaljī.

may have contributed to the problems during Muḥammad's reign. It is easily forgotten that two great Mongol powers – the Ilkhanate and the Chaghadayid polity in Central Asia – also underwent considerable upheavals during the second quarter of the fourteenth century, as did the Golden Horde slightly later,[5] and that the Mamlūk Sultanate was a prey to monetary crises during the third reign of Sultan al-Nāṣir Muḥammad b. Qalā'ūn (709–741/1310–1341).[6] This suggests that the Delhi Sultanate and its neighbours and major trading-partners may have been enveloped in a common economic turbulence; but firm conclusions must await further research.

Opposition from Tughluq's old adherents

The sultan's initial attempts to intensify his authority in the provinces seem to have lain behind three insurrections during the years 727–8/1326–8. On the face of it, the revolts of his cousin Bahā' al-Dīn Garshāsp, at Sāgar in the Deccan, and of Küshlü Khān in Sind are puzzling. Both men had played a central role in the revolt of Tughluq against Nāṣir al-Dīn Khusraw Shāh in 720/1320 and were among the many adherents of the Tughluqid regime who were confirmed in office at Muḥammad's accession. It looks as if Muḥammad's own policies may have alienated these leading amirs whom he had inherited from his father. Tughluq had banned informers (*munhiyān*) from the iqtaʿs, but Ibn Baṭṭūṭa tells us that Muḥammad employed a network of spies who reported his amirs' actions to the sultan;[7] at what stage the practice had been reintroduced, however, we cannot be certain. More importantly, Baranī's statements that during the first few years of the reign the accounts even of far distant provinces were audited on just the same basis as were those of the Doab, and that a hundred or two hundred orders arrived daily in the office of the *kharīṭadār* for transmission to the walis and muqtaʿs,[8] are a sign that the new sultan was from the outset exercising a far closer supervision over the affairs of the provinces than his predecessors had done. The great provincial governors, for whom Ghiyāth al-Dīn Tughluq had been *primus inter pares*, must have received the distinct impression that his son aimed to preside over a centralized despotism.

More particularly, the creation of a second capital at Dawlatābād (formerly Dēōgīr) in the Deccan may have played its own part in prompting

5 Boyle, 'Dynastic and political history', 413–16. Barthold, *Zwölf Vorlesungen*, 205–9, and *Four studies*, I, 134–8. P. Jackson, 'Chaghatayid dynasty', *Enc.Ir.*, V, 346. Berthold Spuler, *Die Goldene Horde: die Mongolen in Rußland 1223–1502*, 2nd edn (Wiesbaden, 1965), 109ff.

6 Hassanein Rabie, *The financial system of Egypt A.H. 564–741/A.D. 1169–1341* (Oxford and London, 1972), 189–97. Jere Bacharach, 'Monetary movements in medieval Egypt, 1171–1517', in J. F. Richards (ed.), *Precious metals in the later medieval and early modern worlds* (Durham, NC, 1984), 167.

7 *TFS*, 429, for Tughluq. IB, III, 343–4 (tr. Gibb, 721), for Muḥammad's spies.

8 *TFS*, 470.

these two insurrections. About the affair at Sāgar we are told very little; but in view of its proximity to Dawlatābād, Garshāsp conceivably felt threatened by the establishment there of a new bastion of central power. We know more about Küshlü Khān's rising. According to Sirhindī, the sultan sent an officer to superintend the removal of Küshlü Khān's family and household to court (i.e. to Dawlatābād), and the officer's arrogant behaviour stung the amir's son-in-law into murdering him.[9] Both insurrections were crushed. Garshāsp was defeated by Aḥmad b. Ayaz, taking refuge first with the Hindu ruler of Kampila and then with the Hoysala king Vīra Ballāla III, who handed him over to the sultan's forces for execution. Muḥammad personally moved against Küshlü Khān, who was defeated and killed.[10]

The third rising, that of Ghiyāth al-Dīn Bahādur Būra in Bengal, seems to represent nothing more than a bid by the previously sovereign dynasty to throw off Tughluqid overlordship. At his accession, Muḥammad had released Būra from prison, conferred a chatr on him, and sent him to Sunārgā'ūn, where he was to enjoy the status of joint ruler with Muḥammad under the watchful eye of the sultan's adopted brother Bahrām Khān, from Lakhnawtī. Būra revolted – probably in or after 728/1327–8, when his coins still carry Muḥammad's name – but was overthrown by Bahrām Khān with the aid of reinforcements from Delhi.[11] The fate of Būra's brother Nāṣir al-Dīn is unknown: there may be some connection with an attempt by 'the amirs and grandees of Lakhnawtī' who were with the sultan in Delhi at the time of Tarmashirin's invasion (*c.* 729/1328–9) to return to their own country and stir up rebellion.[12] But in any event it appears that for the next few years Bengal was administered by officers appointed by the Delhi Sultan.

[9] *TMS*, 99–100.

[10] Garshāsp: *TFS*[1], Digby Coll. ms., fol. 161a (Bodleian ms., fol. 192b, has KYTHL in error for KNPL); *FS*, 424–31 (tr. 651–9); IB, III, 318–21 (tr. Gibb, 710–11). Küshlü Khān: *TFS*, 478–9; *FS*, 435–43 (tr. 663–72); IB, III, 321–4 (tr. Gibb, 711–12), ascribing the rift with the sultan to Küshlü Khān's refusal to exhibit the skins of Garshāsp and Bahādur Būra; but see below. The date of Garshāsp's rebellion is known from an inscription of Nov. 1326: P. B. Desai, 'Kalyana inscription of Sultan Muḥammad, Śaka 1248', *EI* 32 (1957–8), 165–70. Küshlü Khān's revolt is dated in 'the latter part of that year' [727] in *TFS*[1], Bodleian ms., fol. 191b/Digby Coll. ms., fol. 160a. The Lahore campaign in Jumādā II 728/April 1328 (*Siyar*, 215) must have been part of Muḥammad's operations against Küshlü Khān.

[11] IB, III, 316–17 (tr. Gibb, 709–10); also IV, 213 (tr. Gibb and Beckingham, 869). He erroneously makes it out to be anterior to Küshlü Khān's revolt, however, since he has the skins of Garshāsp and Būra circulated round the empire at the same time. *FS*, 422, 444 (tr. 648, 673), is brief. For coins of Bahādur Būra, see *CMSD*, 130 (no. 505C). I. Prasad (*Qaraunah Turks*, 150), Husain (*Tughluq dynasty*, 223) and Nizami (in HN, 506) all date his revolt in 730/1329–30.

[12] Only in *TFS*[1], Bodleian ms., fol. 192a/Digby Coll. ms., fol. 161a.

The creation of a second capital at Dawlatābād and military build-up at Delhi

In the first recension of his work, Baranī, who in the standard version supplies no date for the so-called transfer of the capital to Dawlatābād, places it in 727/1326–7.[13] The abandonment of the project can be dated to the time of Muḥammad's visit to Dawlatābād in *c.* 736/1335–6, on his way back from the abortive expedition to suppress the rebellion in Maʿbar, when we are told that he granted permission to those who wished to return to Delhi.[14] Although the element of compulsion cannot be denied and conditions on the journey to Dawlatābād were surely difficult, even ʿIṣāmī alludes in passing to the fact that those citizens of Delhi who cooperated received gold from the treasury. Baranī amplifies this by stating that the shaykhs, ʿulamaʾ and notables of the capital were allotted cash and villages in the Dēōgīr territory, and that the government purchased from the ordinary citizens their houses in Delhi.[15] Arbitrary the project may have been; but its enforcement was not conducted in a totally unfeeling manner.

Who was required to move south, however, and to what extent Delhi was left deserted, have been a matter of dispute. In his first recension Baranī depicts two stages, of which the former comprised the transfer of the sultan's mother, Makhdūma-yi Jahān, and her household, together with those of the grandees; the latter exodus, following on Küshlü Khān's revolt (and therefore to be placed in or after 728/1327–8), involved the people of the townships (*qaṣabāt*) around the capital as well as those of Delhi.[16] But claims in the sources that the city was completely emptied of its inhabitants are deeply suspect. Husain cites the testimony of Sanskrit inscriptions of 1327–8 indicating that Hindus continued to live in the vicinity of the old capital;[17] and Sirhindī refers to the 'vulgar and riff-raff' (*mardum-i ʿawāmm-u awbāsh*) left behind to plunder the goods of the citizens.[18] In his first recension, Baranī says that the sultan had the ʿulamaʾ and shaykhs of the 'districts and townships' (*khiṭaṭ-u qaṣabāt*) brought to live in the city and given pensions and stipends.[19]

In order to understand Muḥammad's so-called transfer of capital, it is necessary to recognize that for our sources 'the people' (*khalq*) denoted the

13 *Ibid.*, Bodleian ms., fol. 190b/Digby Coll. ms., fol. 159b.

14 *TFS*, 481. For the date of Muḥammad's departure on the Maʿbar campaign (9 Jumādā I 735/5 Jan. 1335), see IB, III, 427, in conjunction with Venkata Ramanayya, 'Date of the rebellions', 141 and n.1 (correcting the year 1341 given in Gibb's tr., 758).

15 *FS*, 446 (tr. 676). *TFS*[1], Bodleian ms., fols. 191b, 192a/Digby Coll. ms., fol. 160. Cf. also *TMS*, 102.

16 *TFS*[1], Bodleian ms., fols. 191, 192a/Digby Coll. ms., fol. 160. *TMS*, 102, speaks of the inhabitants of Delhi and the *qaṣabāt*.

17 Husain, *Tughluq dynasty*, 146–8: these epigraphs are now most readily accessible in P. Prasad, *Sanskrit inscriptions*, 22–31 (nos. I:10 and I:11). Roy, 'Transfer of capital', 170–1, however, dismissed the inscriptions as irrelevant.

18 *TMS*, 102.

19 *TFS*[1], Bodleian ms., fol. 192a/Digby Coll. ms., fol. 160b.

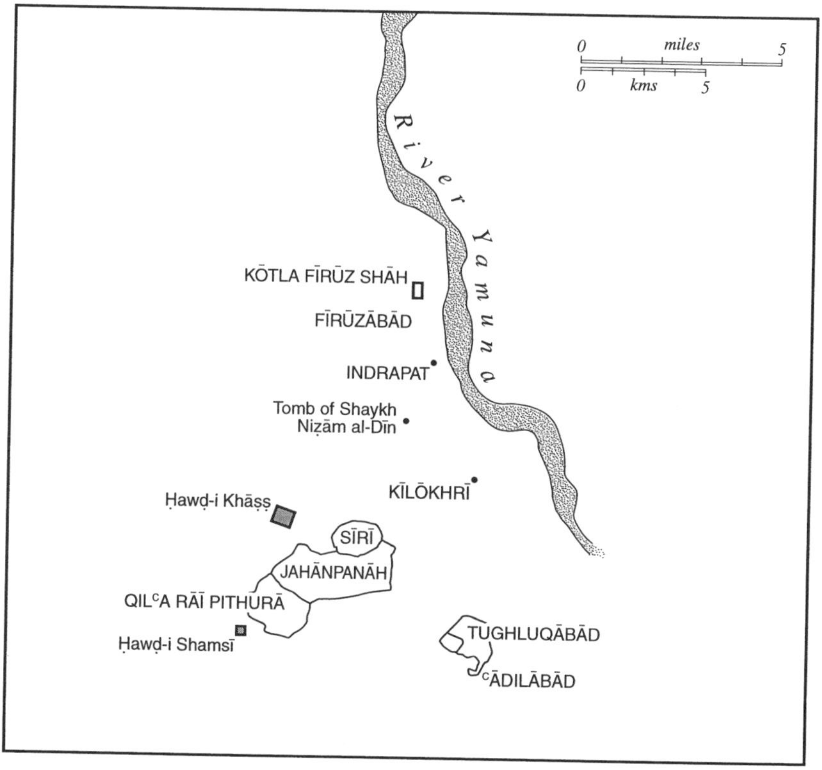

Map 5: The cities of Delhi

more illustrious Muslim families of the capital.[20] And even the term *shahr*, 'the city', when employed in the context of Delhi, is susceptible of two meanings. When Baranī talks of 'the city', he sometimes means simply the old city of Delhi – Qilʿa Rāī Pithūrā, the city of Aybeg and Iltutmish – as opposed to the entire complex of settlements and royal residences – Kīlōkhrī, Sīrī, Hazār Sutūn and Tughluqābād – that had grown up in the intervening decades.[21] During the very time that he is known to have been transferring personnel from Delhi to the Deccan, Muḥammad was engaged in ambitious new construction projects within the Delhi region. He built in 727/1326–7 a new fortress, ʿĀdilābād, not far from Tughluqābād, and linked the old city of Delhi to Sīrī with walls that enclosed an area henceforth known as Jahānpanāh.[22] It is evident from Ibn Baṭṭūṭa's

[20] As observed by Husain, *Tughluq dynasty*, 149, 152 n.2. [21] E.g., *TFS*, 449–50.

[22] Hilary Waddington, "ᶜĀdilābād: a part of the "fourth" Delhi', *Ancient India* 1 (1946), 60–76. Anthony Welch and Howard Crane, 'The Tughluqs: master builders of the Delhi Sultanate', *Muqarnas* 1 (1983), 128–9. For the date 727, see Husain, *Tughluq dynasty*, 167 and n.2, citing Badr-i Chāch.

account that Muḥammad, like his Khaljī predecessors, resided in the palace of Hazār Sutūn, which had been built by ʿAlāʾ al-Dīn outside Sīrī and lay within Jahānpanāh. According to the same author, the sultan had intended at one point to surround all four 'cities' (old Delhi, Sīrī, Jahānpanāh and Tughluqābād) with a single wall, but relinquished the idea in view of the expense involved.[23]

It is hard to reconcile this extensive programme with the notion that Muḥammad envisaged the abandonment of the entire Delhi conurbation. What really seems to have occurred is that the principal Muslim residents of the *old* city, with their large households, were despatched to Dawlatābād.[24] Excepted were the military. The exodus is known to have included the households of the grandees and provincial governors; but during the two years in which the sultan remained in Delhi following the suppression of Küshlü Khān's insurrection, says Baranī, 'the amirs, maliks and troops' were with him, while their families were in Dawlatābād.[25] The old city was not deserted, precisely because it was being turned into a military encampment, a development closely connected with the recruitment of an enormous army for Muḥammad's so-called 'Khurāsān project' which will be discussed later. This is surely what ʿIṣāmī is referring to when he asserts that the city was repopulated with those whom he scornfully terms 'rustics' from the surrounding territory (*parganāt*) and who were clearly Hindus.[26] The two projects – the invasion of Khurāsān and the partial emigration to Dawlatābād – had to coincide, as one source indicates they did,[27] in order to minimize the increase in consumption in Delhi and the setting of impossible targets for the grain producers. Nor does it appear that the sultan had miscalculated here, since Baranī ascribes the disbandment of the Khurāsān force after one year not to a shortage of supplies but to a dearth of funds to pay the troops.[28]

Regarding the size of the Khurāsān force, Baranī supplies conflicting details. In his first recension, he cites a figure of 470,000 on the testimony of the *nāʾib-i ʿāriḍ* himself, Ẓahīr al-Juyūsh; the later version tones this down to 370,000 and does not mention his informant.[29] This has been taken as the total number of men in the sultan's army, which recalls the comparable figures for ʿAlāʾ al-Dīn's reign and thus renders Muḥammad's Khurāsān force much less remarkable.[30] But whichever number we choose to accept, these figures clearly apply, rather, to a specially raised force, over and above the usual total for the military establishment.[31] Al-ʿUmarī was told that

[23] For Hazār Sutūn, see IB, III, 220, 399 (tr. Gibb, 660, 746); for the wall, *ibid.*, III, 147 (tr. Gibb, 619, 621).

[24] *TFS*, 473, *khawāṣṣ-i khalq ... mardum-i guzīda wa-chīda*. See also Husain, *Rise and fall*, 110ff.; *Tughluq dynasty*, 146ff.

[25] *TFS*, 479. [26] *FS*, 450, 453 (tr. 680–1, 684–5). [27] *Siyar*, 271.

[28] *TFS*[1], Bodleian ms., fol. 201b/Digby Coll. ms., fol. 167a. *TFS*, 477.

[29] *TFS*[1], Bodleian ms., fol. 201b/Digby Coll. ms., fol. 167. *TFS*, 477.

[30] Digby, *War-horse*, 24 and n.41a. [31] This is the testimony at least of Firishta, I, 240.

Muḥammad's troops in the capital and in the provinces totalled 900,000. Al-Ṣafadī, however, who reproduces this figure on the authority of an official envoy from Delhi to the Egyptian Sultan al-Nāṣir Muḥammad, ʿAbd-Allāh 'Daftar-khwān', is sceptical, adding that the true number is reputed to be nearer 600,000.[32]

That the mustering of such a vast army posed difficulties for the government was due particularly, it seems, to a change in the system of remuneration. As al-ʿUmarī was told, all the troops now received pay from the sultan's (revenue) ministry (*dīwān*).[33] It was also during these years that Muḥammad introduced the token currency – actually a low-denomination bronze (*muhr-i mis*) coinage – which Baranī again links implicitly with the recruitment of large numbers of troops and Sirhindī with the need for cash advances to Delhi's new inhabitants.[34] The plan has also to be viewed against the background of the quickening pace of commerce (pp. 252–3 above) and of pressure on the gold–silver parity of 10:1 that underpinned the monetary system. The dethesaurization of large quantities of gold seems to have upset this ratio, accentuating the problem of a shortage of silver that had grown more acute by Muḥammad's reign. Indications are seen in his earlier issues of debased silver *tangas* since 727/1326–7 and in the urgency with which Qadr Khān, his governor in Bengal (a region which through commerce enjoyed access to plentiful supplies of silver in Yün-nan and Burma), would amass large quantities of coined silver for despatch to Delhi prior to his assassination and the rebellion of the province in *c.* 736/1335–6.[35] The Qarāchīl expedition and Muḥammad's attack on Nagarkōt in 738/1337 were doubtless also actuated by a need for silver. That the gold–silver ratio had temporarily worsened is shown by the remark, in a geographical work composed in Persia in *c.* 740/1339, that Muḥammad had terminated the practice of hoarding treasure and was spending his gold reserves. His heavy expenditure had caused a fall in the price of gold, so

32 *MA*, ed. Spies, 12–13 (tr. 37)/ed. Fāriq, 24 (tr. Siddiqi and Aḥmad, 37). Al-Ṣafadī, *Wāfī*, III, 173 (tr. Khān, 187); but cf. his *Aʿyān al-ʿAṣr*, fol. 3a, which reads 700,000 for 900,000: his informant may have been the *ḥājib* ʿAbd-Allāh who arrived in Persia as Muḥammad's ambassador in 1327–8: Shabānkāra'ī, 288. Ibn Ḥajar al-ʿAsqalānī (d. 852/1449), *al-Durar al-Kāmina fī Aʿyāni'l-Mi'ati'l-Thāmina* (Hyderabad, Deccan, 1348–50/1929–32, 4 vols.), III, 461, follows *Wāfī* but cites only the lower number of 600,000. The figure of forty *laks* (four million) given for the infantry, lastly, by Ibn Abi'l-Faḍā'il, ed. Kortantamer, Ar. text 27 (German tr. 104), is doubtless due to a confusion of units and should perhaps stand at 400,000; his figure for cavalry is 300,000.

33 *MA*, ed. Spies, 13 (German tr. 37, 38)/ed. Fāriq, 24, 25 (tr. Siddiqi and Aḥmad, 37–8).

34 *TFS*, 475; also *TFS*[1], Bodleian ms., fol. 201b/Digby Coll. ms., fol. 167b, where it is linked with the sultan's generous gifts as well as the raising of troops. *TMS*, 102.

35 Simon Digby, 'The currency system', in Raychaudhuri and Habib (eds.), *Cambridge economic history*, 97–8, especially the quotation from *TMS*, 104–5. Moosvi, 'Numismatic evidence,' 215–16. *CMSD*, 162–6. For sources of silver, see John Deyell, 'The China connection: problems of silver supply in medieval Bengal', in Richards (ed.), *Precious metals*, 207–27.

that it was no longer economical to export it to India and the direction of this traffic was now reversed.[36]

We have to ignore most of the somewhat jejune account given by ʿIṣāmī, who refers to coins made of iron and leather as well as bronze; though his assertion that the coins were current over a period of three years is corroborated by those relatively numerous pieces that have survived, which bear dates from 730 to 732.[37] Baranī's fuller narrative suggests that the scheme failed owing to widespread forgery of the coins in the countryside by Hindu chiefs and their agents, who accordingly used them to pay the land-tax. In this fashion great quantities of bronze coins reached the treasury, giving rise to a loss of confidence and a depreciation of their value; the government was obliged to recall the coins and to issue gold and silver *tangas* in exchange.[38] But Baranī's frequent claims that the treasury was emptied as a result of the project (or indeed Muḥammad's other policies) must be treated with caution. Had this been so, Muḥammad would have been in no position to redeem the bronze coins; still less would he have been able to advance huge sums to the peasantry for the purpose of restoring cultivation (see below).

It is nevertheless a measure of the strain placed on the sultan's finances by the Khurāsān project that ʿAlā' al-Dīn's system was abandoned, the army being paid partly in cash and partly in iqtaʿs,[39] and that in order to pay his considerably increased army Muḥammad imposed on his subjects in the Doab a heavier burden of taxation than even ʿAlā' al-Dīn had done. Any increase in taxation, following so swiftly on Tarmashirin's devastation of the province (see above, p. 232),[40] would have provoked severe discontent; but the precise nature of the measure is unclear. Baranī's claim in the standard version of his *Ta'rīkh* that the *kharāj* underwent a ten- or twentyfold (*yakī ba-dah wa-yakī ba-bīst*) increase was rightly dismissed by Moreland as a mere rhetorical device.[41] The *kharāj*, as far as we know, already stood at the fifty per cent established by ʿAlā' al-Dīn, the legal maximum according to the Ḥanafī school. But there are further hints. Firstly, Baranī suggests in his earlier recension (which is even vaguer regarding the proportion of the increase) that what the peasants found so intolerable was that they were now being required to pay at least a part of the assessment in cash (*zar*, 'gold'); and in the second place he refers to other numerous and heavy exactions (*abwāb*).[42] The uncanonical taxes

[36] Ḥamd-Allāh Mustawfī Qazwīnī, *Nuzhat al-Qulūb*, ed. and tr. Guy Le Strange, *The geographical part of the Nuzhat al-Qulub*, GMS, XXIII (Leiden and London, 1915–19, 2 vols.), I (text), 230, *ān zarhārā ṣarf mīkunad*, and II (tr.), 222.

[37] *FS*, 459–61 (tr. 693–5). *CMSD*, 139–46 (nos. 574–616).

[38] *TFS*, 475–6; *TFS*[1], Bodleian ms., fols. 201b–202b/Digby Coll. ms., fols. 167b–168a.

[39] *TFS*, 476–7.

[40] Referred to explicitly in this context by *TMS*, 113.

[41] *TFS*, 473. Moreland, 48 n.1; also I. Prasad, *Qaraunah Turks*, 71–3. *TMS*, 101–2, has *yakī ba-bīst*, but later (113) says one in ten or one in twenty.

[42] *TFS*, 479, *shadā'id-i muṭālaba wa-bisyārī-yi abwāb*; see also 473. *TFS*[1], Bodleian ms., fol. 192b/Digby Coll. ms., fol. 161a.

abolished by Muḥammad's successor included a whole range of imposts, over and above the house tax (*gharī*) and grazing tax (*charā'ī*) which had been instituted by 'Alā' al-Dīn (above, p. 243).[43] It is accordingly possible that many of these imposts were innovations dating from Muḥammad's reign and that the phrasing in Baranī's later recension is meant to signify a considerable increase in the total number of taxes levied rather than in the percentage of income taken by the state. Lastly, Sirhindī speaks of all three taxes being levied with much greater rigour: the yield assessed was a standard one rather than the actual harvest, and the value was calculated according to decreed prices and not those current in the market.[44]

The Khurāsān project and relations with the Mongols

The object of Muḥammad's heavy expenditure on the military in the years from 1329 onwards was the taking of the offensive against the Mongols. There had long been a tendency for the sultans to look over their shoulder at the prospect of expansion beyond the Indus, inclinations which were doubtless encouraged by the numerous refugees from these regions at their court. The spectacular success of the Delhi Sultanate in reducing and governing an unprecedentedly large proportion of peninsular India may well have furnished a fresh inducement for Muḥammad in particular to turn his attention to the north-west. We have seen (p. 231) how at the very beginning of his reign he headed an expedition to the Mongol frontiers; although Tarmashirin's invasion seems to have been the immediate impulse behind the 'Khurāsān project'.

Baranī's misleading use, at one point in the standard recension, of the phrase 'Khurāsān and 'Irāq' for the territories that were the object of Muḥammad's designs[45] has needlessly confused the issue. The term 'Khurāsān' is itself ambiguous. For the inhabitants of India during the Sultanate period, and even as late as Bābur's era, it denoted loosely the territories west of the Indus.[46] Ishwari Prasad and Agha Mahdi Husain therefore concluded that Muḥammad planned to attack the Ilkhanate.[47] But 'Khurāsān' also designated the regions that today comprise northern Afghanistan and were at this time subject to the Chaghadayid khans. In his first recension Baranī is more specific, referring to the object of Muḥammad's ambitions as the 'upper country' (*aqālīm-i bālā* or *bālā-dast*); and at one point in the later version he, in common with other sources, speaks of

[43] *FFS*, 5 (tr. Roy, 453).
[44] *TMS*, 101–2: he was under the false impression that the *charā'ī* and the *gharī* had been introduced by Muḥammad. I. Habib, 'Agrarian economy', 63.
[45] *TFS*, 476.
[46] IB, III, 229 (tr. Gibb, 664). *Bābur-Nāma*, I, 202.
[47] I. Prasad, *Qaraunah Turks*, 118–24; Husain, *Tughluq dynasty*, 138–43. But cf. Aziz Aḥmad, 'Mongol pressure', 189, though he erroneously dates the Khurāsān project after Tarmashirin's death.

the sultan's plan to conquer 'Khurāsān and Transoxiana (Mā warā' al-Nahr)'.[48] From this we can be certain that Muḥammad intended to attack the old enemy, the Chaghadayids; with the Ilkhanate his relations were in fact amicable (above, p. 233). Professor Siddiqui has suggested that one reason for the abandonment of Muḥammad's plans was the onset of friendly relations between the sultan and Tarmashirin, although Baranī, intent on surveying the sultan's internal policies, makes no mention of this.

Baranī says that part of the Khurāsān force was sent to Qarāchīl.[49] Like 'Khurāsān', this is a highly unspecific term, which in its broadest sense denotes the entire Himalayan range.[50] But it is clear that in the particular context of Muḥammad's ambitions the sources are referring to a major Hindu principality. In an article published some years ago, I proposed that the objective of the sultan's army was Kashmir, which is known from indigenous sources to have undergone at least two invasions during the second quarter of the fourteenth century.[51] There are admittedly difficulties with this identification, but Muḥammad allegedly envisaged sending a Muslim divine to Kashmir around this very time,[52] and some tract in the north-west must be in question, given the connection with the Khurāsān project which Baranī makes so emphatically:

It occurred to Sultan Muḥammad that since the preliminaries (*pīsh-nihādhā*) for the conquest of Khurāsān and Transoxiana had been effected (*dar kār shuda ast*), the Qarāchīl mountains, which lay on the direct route (*dar rāh-i nazdīk*), as a boundary and a screen between the empire of India and the empire of China, should be subjected to the banner of Islam, so that the path of the army's advance and the entry of horses should be made easy.[53]

It is to be noted that the mention of China, which misled the seventeenth-century compilator Firishta into believing that Muḥammad planned the conquest of that country,[54] is purely incidental. From Baranī's phrasing, it looks as if one purpose was to protect the route by which *bālā-dastī* war-horses entered the Sultanate. It is thus hard to see how the sultan would have been interested, for example, in sending part of the Khurāsān force into the Kumaon-Gahrwal region.[55] Whatever the case, the Delhi forces were lured into the mountains and there annihilated by the enemy; only a fraction of the army returned. Sirhindī sets the total strength of the force at 80,000 horse, excluding servants (*chākir*) and slaves; 'Iṣāmī gives one *lak*

48 *TFS*, 477. *TFS*[1], Bodleian ms., fol. 200a/Digby Coll., fol. 166b, reads 'Khurāsān, ᶜIrāq and Mā warā' al-Nahr', but cf. fol. 201b/fol. 167a, *aqālīm-i bālā-dast*. *Siyar*, 271 ('Khurāsān and Turkistān'). Siddiqui, 'Sultan Muḥammad bin Tughluq's foreign policy', 9–10.

49 *TFS*, 477.

50 E.g. IB, III, 325, 438–9 (tr. Gibb, 713, 763).

51 Jackson, 'The Mongols and the Delhi Sultanate', 135–42; but cf. Siddiqui, 'Sultan Muḥammad bin Tughluq's foreign policy', 15 and n.45.

52 *Siyar*, 228.

53 *TFS*, 477 (to be corrected from BL ms., fol. 236b).

54 Firishta, I, 240. I. Prasad, *Qaraunah Turks*, 126–8, 134–6, was rightly sceptical.

55 As proposed by Prasad, *ibid.*, 128–31, and by Nizami (HN, 522), who (misquoting Baranī) dismisses any connection between the Khurāsān project and the Qarāchīl enterprise.

(100,000) of horse, of whom 5–6000 returned.[56] The figure given by Baranī in the course of a very brief account in his first recension is significantly lower, at 30,000 or 40,000; his assertion in the revised text that the survivors totalled a mere ten horsemen is an obvious hyperbole.[57] Subsequently, alleges Ibn Baṭṭūṭa, Muḥammad was able to come to terms with the inhabitants of Qarāchīl, who undertook to pay him tribute: that they had become tributary to Delhi is further confirmed by al-ʿUmarī, though he does not mention the sultan's failure to overcome them by military means.[58]

Peasant revolt and economic dislocation

Muḥammad's enhanced revenue demands provoked a widespread revolt among the cultivators in the Doab, who burned their crops, drove off their cattle and took refuge in the jungles. Having first ordered his revenue officers (*shiqqdārān*) and military commanders (*fawjdārān*) to plunder the recalcitrant territories, the sultan subsequently took the field in person and mounted punitive attacks on Baran and Kōl. The uprising probably occurred in *c.* 1332–3, but it appears that Muḥammad headed two expeditions into 'Hindūstān' and that his operations in the vicinity of Qinnawj and Dalmaw (where he was absent at the time of Ibn Baṭṭūṭa's arrival in Delhi in 734/1334) likewise formed part of his attempt to suppress the Doab rebellion.[59] The failure of grain to reach Delhi from the Doab gave rise to famine, and the situation was exacerbated by the onset of a lengthy period of drought following the sultan's return from his Maʿbar expedition.[60] Baranī speaks of its impact on Delhi, many of whose inhabitants either perished or fled into the countryside; and it is surely to this date (*sc.* 735–6/1335–6) that we must ascribe the comment by Ibn Baṭṭūṭa that he found the capital relatively deserted.[61] It appears, however, that a far wider area came to be affected by famine, for when Muḥammad had passed through Mālwa en route for Maʿbar, he had found the network of runners (the *dhāwa*) along the route abandoned, and similarly we read of famine in the town-

56 *TMS*, 114. *FS*, 467 (tr. 703).
57 *TFS*[1], Bodleian ms., fol. 193a/Digby Coll. ms., fol. 161b. *TFS*, 477–8.
58 IB, III, 327–8 (tr. Gibb, 714). *MA*, ed. Spies, 5 (German tr. 23)/ed. Fāriq, 11 (tr. Siddiqi and Aḥmad, 29).
59 This is clearer in *TFS*[1], Bodleian ms., fols. 192b–193b/Digby Coll. ms., fol. 161b, than in *TFS*, 479, 480; for the Qinnawj campaign, see IB, III, 144 (tr. Gibb, 617).
60 *TFS*, 473; a clearer chronological indication at 482. I cannot agree with Nizami (in HN, 524), who sees high taxation in the Doab as a response to famine in Delhi rather than as its ultimate cause.
61 *TFS*, 482. IB, III, 316 (tr. Gibb, 708): the remark, made in the context of the transfer of capital, seems to apply to his initial entry into Delhi, rather than to a subsequent visit, which is why Husain, *Rise and fall*, 121–3, and *Tughluq dynasty*, 171–3, dismissed it as based on hearsay.

ships of the eastern Panjāb, where the sultan was obliged to campaign against refractory peasants later, in *c*. 738/1337–8.[62]

The sultan's efforts to encourage cultivation, after his return from the south, by having wells dug in the vicinity of Delhi and by advancing seed and loans (*sōndhār*) to peasants were unavailing.[63] Campaigns into Katēhr to plunder the grain for the use of his troops and of the people of Delhi were merely short-term palliatives.[64] Two years after his return to Delhi from the south, Muḥammad was obliged to permit a large-scale emigration from the capital to the fertile Awadh region, and himself set up a temporary residence on the Ganges, at a locality named Sargadwārī.[65] His stay here of some two and a half years seems to have alleviated the problems to some extent; and if Sirhindī is correct in claiming that the drought lasted for seven years,[66] the sultan's return to Delhi would have coincided with its end, i.e. *c*. 741/1340–1. Measures to restore cultivation were still deemed necessary during the last years of the reign, although the enormous cash advances to potential cultivators were not put to proper use and Baranī believed that had Muḥammad returned alive from Sind the guilty parties would have been executed.[67]

We know that Muḥammad's devaluation of the currency gave rise to a considerable degree of inflation, entailing something like a fivefold rise in prices.[68] The Sultanate's economic problems were doubtless accentuated by the policy of the Chaghadayid khanate, since following his conversion Tarmashirin had abolished those commercial duties not sanctioned by the Sharīʿa (*mukūs*) and thus attracted to Transoxiana merchants from Egypt and Syria in great numbers.[69] This may have diverted a certain proportion of the Egyptian trade north of the Hindu Kush, and might explain Muḥammad's abolition of the *mukūs* within his own dominions (below, p. 272). The incentive could equally have been a general decline in foreign trade as a result of the debasement; but it is significant that the Chaghadayid *dīnār* enjoyed a high reputation on account of its fineness.[70] Possibly Muḥammad's monetary policy had affected the balance of trade between India and Central Asia.

62 Mālwa: *TFS*, 481–2. E. Panjāb: *TFS*[1], Bodleian ms., fol. 194b/Digby Coll. ms., fol. 162b; *TFS*, 483–4, refers only to the peasants' refusal to pay the *kharāj*, but does not link it with famine; IB, III, 372–3 (tr. Gibb, 734), for famine at Agrōha.

63 *TFS*, 482, 484. IB, III, 299 (tr. Gibb, 700).

64 *TFS*[1], Bodleian ms., fol. 195a/Digby Coll. ms., fol. 163a; *TFS*, 484–5, speaks merely of pasturage (*charākhūr*).

65 *Ibid.*, 485–6. 66 *TMS*, 113.

67 *TFS*, 498–9. ʿAfīf, 92. I. Habib, 'Agrarian economy', 65–6.

68 Digby, *War-horse*, 39–40.

69 *MA*, ed. Lech, Ar. text 41 (German tr. 119). Al-Ṣafadī, *Wāfī*, X, 383, alone mentions the abolition. For *mukūs*, in origin customs duties, see generally W. Björkman, 'Maks', *Enc.Isl.*[2]; P. G. Forand, 'Notes on *ʿušr* and *maks*', *Arabica* 13 (1966), 137–41.

70 *MA*, ed. Lech, Ar. text 47 (German tr. 123).

Military weakness and endemic rebellion

From Baranī's testimony, it appears that prolonged unrest in the Doab acted as a spur to the next wave of revolts in more distant provinces from *c.* 1334 onwards, notably those in Maʿbar, Bengal and Tilang.[71] The revolt of Sayyid Jalāl al-Dīn Ḥasan, apparently kotwal of Madura, who assumed the title of Sultan Jalāl al-Dīn Aḥsan Shāh, was probably the first and is believed to have occurred in 734/1333–4. Muḥammad's representatives were killed, and the troops supposedly garrisoning the province did nothing.[72] This crisis was closely followed by the loss of Bengal. Fakhr al-Dīn (also known as 'Fakhrā') was the former armour-bearer (*ṣilāḥdār*) of the sultan's adopted brother Bahrām Khān, and had already made an unsuccessful bid to seize power at Sunārgā'ūn on his master's death. The rising was checked by Qadr Khān, Muḥammad's representative at Lakhnawtī; but not long afterwards a prolonged struggle broke out for control of the province. First Qadr Khān's troops mutinied, slew him and went over to the rebel Fakhr al-Dīn, who established his residence at Sunārgā'ūn. Then Fakhr al-Dīn's lieutenant at Lakhnawtī was killed by Qadr Khān's former *ʿāriḍ*, ʿAlī Mubārak, at the head of loyalist troops. When the sultan proved unable to comply with his request that a new governor be dispatched from Delhi, ʿAlī Mubārak found himself obliged to assume the royal title himself as Sultan ʿAlā' al-Dīn ʿAlī Shāh in order to rally support against the hostile activities of Fakhr al-Dīn. Both ʿAlī Shāh in the middle of the 1340s and Fakhr al-Dīn's son and successor, Ikhtiyār al-Dīn Ghāzī Shāh, in the early 1350s would be overthrown by a third candidate for the sovereignty, a former retainer (*chākir*) of ʿAlī Mubārak named Ilyās Ḥājjī, who reigned as Sultan Shams al-Dīn.[73] Like ʿAlī Shāh, Ilyās seems to have recognized the authority of Delhi, since a *farmān* of Muḥammad's successor Fīrūz Shāh

[71] The link is explicit in the first recension: *TFS*[1], Bodleian ms., fol. 193/Digby Coll. ms., fols. 161b–162a.

[72] Meagre details in *TFS*, 480, except that Muḥammad is said to have been campaigning around Qinnawj when the news arrived. *FS*, 469 (tr. 705). IB, III, 144 (tr. Gibb, 617). For the date, see S. A. Q. Husaini, 'The chronology of the first two sultans of Madura', *Proceedings of the Pakistan History Conference, 5th session, Khairpur 1955* (Karachi, n.d. [1958]), 193–7, and 'The history of the Madura Sultanate', *JASP* 2 (1957), 91–5, citing a coin of Aḥsan Shāh dated 734. J. Burton-Page, 'Djalāl al-Dīn Aḥsan', *Enc.Isl.*[2], is therefore in need of updating.

[73] *TMS*, 104–5, provides the fullest account, though with incorrect dates. *TFS*, 480, and *FS*, 472 (tr. 709), are laconic. IB, IV, 213–14 (tr. Gibb and Beckingham, 869), garbles the details and does not mention Ilyās, on whom see *SFS*, 47 (tr. Basu, *JBORS* 27 [1941], 92); this last source calls ʿAlī Shāh the armour-bearer of Dīnār, one of Qadr Khān's eunuchs. For a survey of events, see Abdul Karim, 'Circumstances that led to the independence of Bengal (1338 A.D.)', *Proceedings of the Pakistan History Conference, 5th session*, 209–22. Coins of ʿAlī Shāh go down to 744: *CCIM*, II, 150 (nos. 22–3). Ghāzī Shāh struck coins in 751: *ibid.*, II, 149 (no. 21). Ilyās had begun to reign by 743/1342: Dani, 'Shamsuddīn Ilyās Shāh', 55; Eaton, *Rise of Islam*, 86.

would later claim that he had remained submissive until after Muḥammad's death.[74]

It may have been the presence of actively loyal troops in Bengal that induced Muḥammad to give priority to the suppression of Aḥsan Shāh in Maʿbar. At the head of a sizeable force, he moved south in 735/1334–5 and passed through the Deccan. But on its arrival in Tilang, the army was struck by some kind of epidemic (*wubāʾ*), and the sultan was obliged to retreat; he himself fell gravely sick when he reached Dawlatābād, recovering only after his return to Delhi. That the campaign had been a major disaster was apparent to Ibn Baṭṭūṭa, who dates from this juncture the falling-away of outlying provinces.[75] The failure to recover Maʿbar gave the signal to other would-be dissidents, and encouraging rumours of Muḥammad's death circulated widely. Already, as the sultan marched southwards, one of his officers, Tāj al-Dīn Hūshang (the son of Kamāl al-Dīn 'Gurg'), muqtaʿ of Hānsī, fled to the Vindhyas and thence into the Konkan; Qutlugh Khān, Muḥammad's old tutor and governor of the Deccan, moved against him and eventually induced him to yield with a promise of safe-conduct.[76] Around the same time a Mongol commander named Hülechü occupied Lahore in alliance with the Khōkhar chief Gul Chand, the one-time ally of Muḥammad's father; the rebels were defeated and the city retaken by the wazir Khwāja Jahān.[77] The seizure of Multān by the Afghan chief Shāhū, which ʿIṣāmī makes part of this insurrection in the western Panjāb, is treated by other sources as a separate episode. Muḥammad, who had now returned to Delhi, viewed this revolt as sufficiently threatening to warrant dealing with it himself; but Shāhū made off on his approach and sent a message of submission.[78] More serious were the loss of Kampila, which now became the nucleus of the kingdom of Vijāyanagara, and a rising in Tilang, whence the governor, Malik Maqbūl, was expelled by Kapaya Nāyak and fled to Delhi, arriving a matter of days after the sultan himself.[79]

The loss of Tilang, the province whose reduction during the previous reign had been his personal achievement, dealt Muḥammad an especially severe blow. He is said to have wanted to mount an expedition to recover it, but to have been prevented from doing so because of the famine.[80] If ʿIṣāmī is to be trusted, half the army commanders and a third of the troops had perished in the epidemic;[81] while the view both of Baranī and of Ibn

[74] *IM*, 16. [75] IB, III, 334–5 (tr. Gibb, 717).

[76] *FS*, 469–70 (tr. 706–7). *TMS*, 106. IB, III, 335–6 (tr. Gibb, 717–18).

[77] *FS*, 471 (tr. 707–8), erroneously making this part of the same episode as Shāhū's revolt (below). IB, III, 331–3 (tr. Gibb, 716–17).

[78] *TFS*, 482–3. IB, III, 362 (tr. Gibb, 729).

[79] Brief reference to both revolts in *FS*, 606 (tr. 902). Tilang: *TFS*, 484. For the limited material on the emergence of Vijāyanagara, see Husain, *Tughluq dynasty*, 248–9.

[80] *TFS*[1], Bodleian ms., fol. 195a/Digby Coll. ms., fol. 163a, says that he was inwardly (*dar bāṭin*) afflicted. *TFS*, 484, is briefer.

[81] *FS*, 469, 471 (tr. 706, 708). IB, III, 334 (tr. Gibb, 717), says merely that the greater part of

Baṭṭūṭa's informants was that the Qarāchīl campaign had gravely weakened the army of the Sultanate.[82] We have here the two circumstances that bedevilled Muḥammad's government for several years to come: a heavy reduction in the number of troops at his disposal, combined with a considerable loss of revenue owing to a decline in cultivation, so that the sultan was unable to rebuild his forces.

The revolts of the middle period of the reign that we have considered so far smack of opportunistic responses to a prolonged crisis, whether on the part of disaffected amirs or by Hindu elements on the periphery of the Sultanate. But are there any signs of a deeper malaise affecting the ruling class itself? In contrast with the system that obtained in the Mamlūk empire, there was now a direct link between the imperial treasury and the ordinary trooper, and the amirs had lost the capacity to bind troops to their own interests with iqtaʿ grants from their assignments, which were intended exclusively for their personal maintenance.[83] In addition, Ibn Baṭṭūṭa reveals that the military command had become completely separated from the fiscal administration of the iqtaʿ, so that within the territory of Amrōha, for instance, a *wālī al-kharāj*, responsible directly to the sultan, is found alongside the amir.[84] This assault on the position of provincial commanders, it has been plausibly suggested, was one factor underlying the revolts in Gujarāt and the Deccan that plagued the sultan's last years.[85]

Loss of revenue accompanying the secession of a number of major provinces also had the insidious effect of increasing pressure on Muḥammad to demand larger sums from the regions that remained loyal. Officers who had entered into contracts for the farming of revenue seem to have undertaken to transmit unrealistically high sums to the sultan. Ibn Baṭṭūṭa was told of a Hindu who contracted to farm the revenues of the entire Deccan province for seventeen *krōrs* (170,000,000 *tangas*), but was unable to meet his obligations and was flayed alive on Muḥammad's orders.[86] The story cannot be tied in with any episode recounted elsewhere, but it illustrates the impact that such arrangements made on contemporaries. The impossibility of supplying the government's needs in this fashion could at times engender rebellion by hitherto loyal servitors. Two risings which occurred during Muḥammad's stay at Sargadwārī fall into this category. Niẓām Mā'in, who farmed the revenues of Kara, and Shihāb Sulṭānī, styled Nuṣrat Khān, who had undertaken to extract one *krōr* (10,000,000 *tangas*) from Bidar and its iqtaʿs over three years, were both

the army that had accompanied the sultan perished. Cf. also *FS*, 472 (tr. 709), where the loss of provinces is put down to Muḥammad's lack of troops, and 510–11 (tr. 759).

82 IB, III, 327 (tr. Gibb, 714). *TFS*, 477, 478.

83 *MA*, ed. Spies, 13 (German tr. 37, 38)/ed. Fāriq, 24, 25 (tr. Siddiqi and Aḥmad, 37–8). For conditions in Ayyubid and Mamlūk Egypt, see Rabie, *Financial system*, 32–8.

84 IB, III, 436, 439 (tr. Gibb, 762, 763). Conermann, *Beschreibung Indiens*, 146, 147–8.

85 Habib, 'Agrarian economy', 71–3.

86 IB, IV, 49 (tr. Gibb and Beckingham, 795).

pushed into rebellion by their failure to raise the sums promised; Nuṣrat Khān is said to have been unable to recover even a third or a quarter of the farm. Niẓām Mā'in's feeble bid for independence was snuffed out by the sultan's governor of Awadh, ʿAyn al-Mulk Ibn Māhrū, and his brothers. Nuṣrat Khān was dealt with by the ubiquitous Qutlugh Khān, who gathered troops from Dawlatābād but eventually persuaded him to surrender under guarantee of safe-conduct.[87]

There are other signs that Muḥammad's regime was becoming the prisoner of its own reputation for harshness. Baranī asserts more than once that the uncompromising punishments inflicted at Delhi occasioned fear and disaffection elsewhere in the empire, which played their own part in fomenting revolt.[88] The rising of ʿAyn al-Mulk Ibn Māhrū in Awadh provides an illustration. Suspecting that Qutlugh Khān's officials were embezzling some of the tax revenues in the Deccan, the sultan contemplated recalling his old tutor and transferring to Dawlatābād Ibn Māhrū, who had recently demonstrated his loyalty and efficiency by shipping large quantities of grain and other goods from Awadh to Sargadwārī and Delhi at the height of the famine. In his first recension, Baranī has Muḥammad eagerly anticipating the increased sums that an administrator of Ibn Māhrū's calibre might obtain from the much wealthier Deccan.[89] Unfortunately, the sultan also learned that large numbers of Delhi's residents had fled from the capital to Awadh, attracted by its prosperity and by Ibn Māhrū's mild government, and demanded that they be sent back. Ibn Māhrū, who was warned of Muḥammad's anger over this, inferred that the planned transfer to the Deccan was simply a ruse to dispose of him, and he and his brothers decided to pre-empt their execution by rebellion. Muḥammad defeated them on the Ganges, not far from Qinnawj. Ibn Māhrū's brothers were killed in the fighting or disappeared, and he himself was taken prisoner; but it is a measure of his stature, and of the sultan's understanding of the reasons for his revolt, that he was not long afterwards restored to favour.[90] He was later appointed governor of Multān at the time of Muḥammad's final campaign against the rebel Taghai and his Sūmra allies in Sind.[91]

87 *TFS*, 487, 488. 88 *Ibid.*, 472, 484, 499–500, 517.

89 *TFS*[1], Bodleian ms., fol. 196a/Digby Coll. ms., fol. 163b.

90 IB, III, 341–54, 357 (tr. Gibb, 720–6, 727), provides a detailed account of the campaign, in which he participated, but is unaware of the impulses behind the revolt. So too is *FS*, 472–5 (tr. 709–14). *TFS*[1], Bodleian ms., fols. 195b–196a/Digby Coll. ms., fol. 163, and *TFS*, 486–7, 489–91, analyse Ibn Māhrū's motives. The suspicions about revenue from the Deccan are mentioned only in *TFS*, 500–1: Hardy, 'Didactic historical writing', 53–5, compares the two recensions at this point. There is a brief account of the revolt in *TMS*, 109–10. ʿAfīf, 406–8, for Ibn Māhrū's restoration to favour.

91 *IM*, 106, 107. Despite the doubts expressed by Abdur Rashid in his introduction (27), Ibn Māhrū's reference to the sultan's having spared him makes it certain that these two letters date from Muḥammad's reign rather than that of Fīrūz Shāh. He also says that at the time of his appointment he has been ordered to supply troops and ships, which places the date of the letters around the time that Muḥammad crossed the Indus not long before his death:

Describing how Muḥammad's forces took up position near Qinnawj for the encounter with Ibn Māhrū, Ibn Baṭṭūṭa alludes to the antipathy between the rebel, who was of Indian extraction, and the 'amirs of Khurāsān and foreigners' accompanying the sultan.[92] From *c.* 734/1333–4, as we have seen, Muḥammad was intent on making clients of local rulers in Khurāsān and neighbouring regions and thus achieving by means of patronage what he had been unable to accomplish through the Khurāsān project. This was in turn part of a wider policy of favouring foreigners over the indigenous aristocracy (above, pp. 184–5). Whether this in itself was enough to incite members of the Indian Muslim aristocracy to revolt, we cannot know; but it may well have played a role in the unrest of the sultan's later years. We are perhaps on surer ground in identifying resentment towards Muḥammad's pagan Hindu agents as one of the mainsprings of disaffection. In *c.* 1341 there was a rising in Sīwistān, in which the local Sūmra ruler Unār (Ibn Baṭṭūṭa's 'Wūnār') and a military officer named Qayṣar-i Rūmī slew the Hindu bureaucrat 'Ratan' whom the sultan had appointed as muqtaʿ of the province. Unār soon deserted his associates, and Qayṣar and his followers were put down without difficulty by the governor of Multān, 'Imād al-Mulk Sartīz.[93] Similarly, as we shall see, Bhiran, the pagan muqtaʿ of Gulbarga, would be the first victim of the rising of ʿAlī Shāh Kar in the Deccan.[94] Yet until the middle of the 1340s Muḥammad seems to have retained the support of the military class as a whole. Baranī describes Nuṣrat Khān as a grain-dealer (*baqqāl*), and scornfully contrasts Ibn Māhrū and his adherents, who were 'clerks and grain-dealers' (*nawīsandagān-u baqqālān*), with the sultan and the seasoned troops who had served both him and his father Tughluq and who could hardly have been expected to desert him.[95] The implication is that Muḥammad was a military man's sovereign.

Muḥammad took various steps during the early 1340s that were undoubtedly designed to rally support behind his regime. Although Baranī gives the impression that the sultan entered into relations with the puppet ʿAbbasid Caliphate at Cairo during his stay at Sargadwārī,[96] we know from Egyptian sources that he had already been in contact with the Caliph al-Mustakfī bi'llāh as early as 731/1330–1, and that at least three embassies had been

TFS, 523. The date 9 Shawwāl, when Ibn Māhrū was despatched to Multān, must therefore belong to 751 (10 December 1350). Nevertheless ʿAfīf makes out that Fīrūz Shāh appointed Ibn Māhrū to the province (below, p. 303).

92 IB, III, 344, 349 (tr. Gibb, 721–2, 724).

93 Described only *ibid.*, III, 105–8 (tr. Gibb, 599–600). This episode must have fallen not just prior to IB's arrival in India, as its place in the narrative suggests, but before the visit to Sīwistān in 742/1341 mentioned later, III, 447 (tr. Gibb, 766–7). One reason for dating the Sīwistān revolt this late is that Sartīz was not appointed to Multān until after Shāhū's rising, i.e. *c.* 1337 (above, p. 183, n.86).

94 *TFS*, 488. Cf. also *FS*, 485–6, 487–8 (tr. 726–8, 730–1). Nizami (in HN, 565) reaches similar conclusions about the role of hostility towards the sultan's Hindu servitors.

95 *TFS*, 488, 490.

96 *Ibid.*, 491–2.

sent from Delhi.[97] In 741/1340–1 Muḥammad substituted the name of al-Mustakfī (who had in fact died in the previous year) for his own on the coinage and in the khutba.[98] It was in this same year, according to Ibn Baṭṭūṭa, that he abolished all uncanonical taxation (*mukūs*);[99] and perhaps also that he took to presiding in person over the *maẓālim* tribunal for the redress of his subjects' grievances.[100]

Not until 746/1345–6 did Muḥammad's envoy, Ḥājjī Rajab Burquʿī, return to Delhi with the personal robe of the Caliph al-Ḥākim bi-amri'llāh, al-Mustakfī's son and successor, and a diploma conferring on the sultan the rank of the caliph's lieutenant; he was accompanied by the Egyptian grand qadi, the *shaykh al-shuyūkh* Rukn al-Dīn al-Malaṭī, head of the convent of Siryāqūs. In the meantime, in 744/1343, an unofficial envoy from Cairo, Ḥājjī Saʿīd Ṣarṣarī, had brought Muḥammad a diploma, a banner and a robe. The ceremonial surrounding these occasions, when the sultan adopted a stance of extreme humility, clearly made a powerful impression on Baranī.[101] By such propagandistic gestures the sultan hoped, perhaps, to recover the support of the 'ulama' and others of the 'religious class' and hence, presumably, to legitimize his position in the face of would-be rebellious amirs.

Confrontation with the *amīrān-i ṣada*

Within the next year or two, however, the situation once again deteriorated. Muḥammad had come to believe that the local commanders in Gujarāt and the Deccan, the amirs of a hundred (*amīrān-i ṣada*), were responsible for the fiscal problems of his government, and decided to supersede them by bringing the revenues of the two provinces under closer control by the centre. According to Baranī, the sultan in 745/1345 believed that large sums

97 Jackson, 'The Mongols and the Delhi Sultanate', 131–2 n.74.

98 *CMSD*, 122–4 (nos. 491–491H), 147–8 (nos. 617–622A).

99 IB, III, 288 (tr. Gibb, 694), for the abolition of *mukūs*; at III, 117 (tr. Gibb, 605), this is said to have coincided with Muḥammad's recognition of the caliph, but is dated two years after IB's arrival in India, i.e. *c.* 736/1335–6. A list of taxes abolished in Muḥammad's reign – *mandūh*, **tarka*, *māl-i mawjūd*, *chahār bāzār*, *ḍarā'ib*, *gudharhā* and *kharāj-i muhtarifa-yi muslim* – is given in *IM*, 79; for those abolished by Fīrūz Shāh, see *SFS*, 124; *FFS*, 5 (tr. Roy, 453); I. H. Qureshi, *The administration of the Sultanate of Dehli*, 4th edn (Karachi, 1958), 244–7 (appendix H).

100 IB, III, 288–9 (tr. Gibb, 694–5).

101 *TFS*, 492–6; and cf. also 460. There is a fuller and clearer account in *SFS*, 280–2; tr. in Shaikh Abdur Rashid, 'Firuz Shah's investiture by the Caliph', *MIQ* 1 (1950), 69. See also IB, I, 363–70, and III, 248–9 (tr. Gibb, 225–8, 674), who distinguishes the status of the two envoys Ḥājjī Saʿīd and Ḥājjī Rajab. For the arrival of Rajab's party in Cairo in 744 and for Rukn al-Dīn, see al-Shujāʿī, *Ta'rīkh al-Nāṣir Muḥammad ibn Qalā'ūni'l-Ṣāliḥī wa-Awlādihi*, ed. and tr. Barbara Schäfer, *Die Chronik aš-Šuǧāʿī's*, QGIA, II (Wiesbaden, 1977–85, 2 vols.), I (text), 257–8, and II (tr.), 290–1; the date Rabīʿ I 743 for Rukn al-Dīn's departure from Cairo given by al-Maqrīzī (d. 845/1442), *al-Sulūk li-Maʿrifat Duwali'l-Mulūk*, ed. M.M. Ziada *et al.* (Cairo, 1934– in progress), II, part 3, 887, must be an error.

had been held back for years by the officials in Bharūch;[102] and in his account of the revolt of ʿAlī Shāh *Kar* ('the Deaf') at Bidar, ʿIṣāmī, who is particularly well informed about the Deccan and accordingly furnishes much greater detail than other writers, suggests that the rebellion was sparked off by new revenue-raising arrangements.

ʿAlī Shāh, a Khalaj officer and a nephew of Sultan ʿAlāʾ al-Dīn's general Ẓafar Khān, is described as an *amīr-i ṣada* of Qutlugh Khān[103] who had rendered signal service by fighting against Nuṣrat Khān and by reducing the district of Kōyir. He continued to serve faithfully and transmitted the stipulated monies, until a Hindu named Bhiran, who held the iqtaʿ of Gulbarga, grew aware of the sums being retained from Kōyir and prevailed upon Qutlugh Khān to let him farm the revenues, undertaking to increase them by 50 per cent. ʿAlī Shāh reacted by seizing Bidar and Gulbarga and killing Bhiran, and assumed the royal title as Sultan ʿAlāʾ al-Dīn. After some time Qutlugh Khān, aided by reinforcements from the sultan, was able to induce him to surrender.[104] His uprising, which occurred in a region whose officers Muḥammad viewed with suspicion, looks like a localized rehearsal for the wider insurrection against the sultan during his last years.

At some point early in 745/in the spring–summer of 1344 the sultan took the decision to separate the enormous Deccan province currently supervised by Qutlugh Khān into four divisions (*shiqqs*). Qutlugh Khān was to be recalled and replaced as wazir at Dawlatābād by ʿImād al-Mulk Sartīz, hitherto governor of Multān; in the interval the command at Dawlatābād was to be exercised by Qutlugh Khān's brother ʿĀlim al-Mulk Niẓām al-Dīn, the governor of Bharūch. According to Baranī, the men chosen to command the *shiqqs* all had a reputation for shedding blood, and both he and ʿIṣāmī allege that the people of the Deccan, who had come to regard Qutlugh Khān's regime as a safeguard against the ordeals experienced in Muḥammad's other territories, were dismayed at the amir's departure.[105]

The principal target of the new administration, however, was the *amīrān-i ṣada*. Baranī says that the men sent from Delhi were under instructions from the sultan to regard these officers as the chief instigators of unrest. We might be tempted to discount reports of Sartīz's previous exactions in the

102 *TFS*, 513.

103 Thus only *ibid.*, 488, where he is described as the son of Ẓafar Khān's sister (as also in *TMS*, 108); though *TFS*, 508, calls him the son of a brother.

104 By far the most detailed account in *FS*, 483–500 (tr. 725–47); see 479 (tr. 718–20) for his service against Nuṣrat Khān. The information in *TFS*, 488–9, and IB, III, 357–8 (tr. Gibb, 727–8), is limited. Baranī dates the revolt during Muḥammad's stay at Sargadwārī, whereas IB places it after his return to Delhi.

105 *TFS*, 501–2. *FS*, 503 (tr. 749–50); and see also 462 (tr. 696–7), where the security of the people of the Deccan, however, is attributed ultimately to the presence there of the saint Shaykh Zayn al-Dīn. IB, III, 336–7 (tr. Gibb, 718), comments on the confidence inspired by Qutlugh Khān and on his liberality. The date of the order recalling Qutlugh Khān to Delhi is given as 1 Shaʿbān 745/8 Dec. 1344 by Badr-i Chāch, *Qaṣāʾid*, ed. Ḥādī ʿAlī, 64/ lithograph ed. M. ʿUthmān Khān (Rāmpūr, 1872–3, 2 vols.), II, 407.

Multān province, which according to the correspondence of his successor there, Ibn Māhrū, had still not recovered a few years later.[106] But it is surely no accident that ʿAzīz Khammār, the sultan's newly appointed governor of Dhār and one of the four *shiqq*-commanders, had made a name for himself as an oppressive revenue-collector in the Amrōha district, in which capacity he had clashed with the local military commander.[107] Now, soon after his arrival at Dhār, ʿAzīz summarily executed some eighty *amīrān-i ṣada*. When this news reached their counterparts in Gujarāt and the Deccan, they rose in revolt.[108] Ibn Baṭṭūṭa likewise mentions instructions for the killing of military commanders, but he makes the revolt start in Gujarāt, where Malik Muqbil allegedly received orders to put them to death. We should not necessarily accept the testimony of Ibn Baṭṭūṭa (who does not employ the term 'amirs of a hundred') that the victims were all Afghans: he seems to have been misled by the fact that the leaders of the ensuing revolt – Qāḍī Jalāl in Gujarāt and Ismāʿīl *Mukh in the Deccan – both belonged to that race. He is certainly in error, moreover, in linking Muḥammad's orders to massacre 'Afghans' with his campaign against the Afghan Shāhū in Sind, which had occurred some eight years or so prior to these developments (see above, p. 268).[109]

The atrocity perpetrated by ʿAzīz Khammār turned the explosive situation in the south into one of open rebellion. Whereas hitherto Muḥammad had been confronted by the recalcitrance of individual grandees and their retinues, he now faced a widespread insurrection embracing the officer class in two major provinces. When the news reached the *amīrān-i ṣada* in Dabhōī and Barōda, they attacked and routed Malik Muqbil, the *nā'ib-wazīr* of Gujarāt, and plundered a convoy of treasure he was escorting on its way to Delhi. Kanbhāya was surrendered to them, and they were able to take Asāwul.[110] ʿAzīz Khammār, who moved against them from Dhār and was joined by Muqbil, was defeated and captured by the insurgents and put to death. Returning to Kanbhāya, Qāḍī Jalāl and his adherents settled

106 *IM*, 78–9, 88.

107 IB, III, 436–40 (tr. Gibb, 762–3): this seems to have transpired at the time of Muḥammad's absence on the Maʿbar campaign.

108 *TFS*[1], Bodleian ms., fols. 202b–203a/Digby Coll. ms., fol. 168a, is more explicit here than *TFS*, 503–4, 507. IB, III, 364 (tr. Gibb, 730–1), also links the revolts in Gujarāt and the Deccan. For these revolts, see generally I. Prasad, *Qaraunah Turks*, 208–53; Husain, *Tughluq dynasty*, 283–97; HN, 540–55.

109 *FS*, 504 (tr. 750), for royal orders. IB, III, 362, 364–6 (tr. Gibb, 729, 730–1). *TFS*, 514, at one point appears to support the equation, by speaking of the rebels at Dawlatābād as 'these Afghans'; but BL ms., fol. 254a, reads not *īn afghānān* but *īn afghān*, i.e. the singular, denoting the leader Ismāʿīl *Mukh. *SFS*, 20, calls the rebel officers in Gujarāt simply 'army chiefs' (*sarān-i gurūh*). For other Afghan officers in the Gujarāt and Deccan revolts, see Siddiqui, 'The Afghāns and their emergence', 255–6.

110 *FS*, 503–6 (tr. 750–3), provides the fullest account; and see also *TFS*, 507. *TMS*, 111, gives a brief notice (*sub anno* 748 in error). IB does not mention the plundering of the convoy.

down to besiege the city.[111] Muḥammad, who had been preparing to head an army against the rebels since learning of the attack on Muqbil in the latter half of Ramaḍān 745/late January 1345, halted at Bharūch. Here he instituted oppressive measures for the extraction of the arrears of revenue, ordering Malik Maqbūl, the *nā'ib-wazīr* of the empire, who had pursued the enemy as far as the banks of the Narbada, to kill the *amīrān-i ṣada* of Bharūch under his command. The back of the Gujarāt revolt appeared to be completely broken. Qāḍī Jalāl and his lieutenants narrowly escaped being handed over to the sultan by Nānadeva ('Mān Dēō'), the Hindu raja of Baglāna, Salher and Mulher, and fled to Dawlatābād, where the *amīrān-i ṣada* were by now similarly in arms against the sultan.[112]

In the Deccan Muḥammad's policies had provoked a major crisis. Two of the sultan's principal agents were known to be already on their way to Dawlatābād to conduct an inquiry into the loyalties of the province; and in addition the sultan sent two other amirs to ʿĀlim al-Mulk Niẓām al-Dīn with instructions to have the more important *amīrān-i ṣada* of that region brought under guard to Bharūch. The proposed victims of the purge set off from Dawlatābād, but realized Muḥammad's intentions and turned back. ʿĀlim al-Mulk was arrested, and the two royal agents were put to death. The province fell under the control of the *amīrān-i ṣada*; Ismāʿīl *Mukh, a brother of the Afghan Malik Mall who had held a command in Tughluq's reign, was proclaimed sultan as Nāṣir al-Dīn.[113]

On receipt of this news, Muḥammad advanced by forced marches to the Deccan and inflicted a heavy defeat upon the rebels. He took up his quarters in the royal palace at Dawlatābād, and his troops invested the fortress of Dhārāgīr, where Ismāʿīl *Mukh and his chief adherents had taken refuge.[114] But as the sultan busied himself with setting the affairs of the region in order, he received reports of a fresh rising in Gujarāt, led by a Turkish slave named Taghai. Taghai, formerly Muḥammad's *shiḥna-yi bārgāh*, had been banished by the sultan to the Yemen as a punishment for some misdemeanour, but had been caught up in the fighting at Kanbhāya while awaiting embarkation. Having played a crucial role in the city's defence against Qāḍī Jalāl, he was restored to favour. In the sultan's absence, however, he fell out with Muḥammad's lieutenant at Asāwul, Tatar Malik, and made common cause with the *amīrān-i ṣada* of Gujarāt. The rebels entered Nahrwāla, slew its governor, sacked Kanbhāya, and laid siege to Bharūch. When

[111] *FS*, 506–10 (tr. 753–9). *TFS*, 509, reports the sultan's receipt of the news of ʿAzīz's defeat and death. IB, III, 364 (tr. Gibb, 730), is very brief.

[112] *FS*, 512–14, 522 (tr. 760–4, 773–4). *TFS*, 511–13, has the rebels being defeated by Malik Maqbūl near Dabhōī and Barōda; Baranī alone describes Muḥammad's conduct at Bharūch. For the identity of 'Mān Dēō', see Hodivala, *Studies*, I, 299.

[113] *TFS*, 512, 513–14. A fuller account in *FS*, 516–21 (tr. 766–73). IB, III, 365–6 (tr. Gibb, 731), is relatively brief and calls the rebel leader Malik Mall's son in error.

[114] *FS*, 530–6 (tr. 783–91). *TFS*, 514–15. IB, III, 368–9 (tr. Gibb, 732–3): this is his latest information on the revolt.

Muḥammad advanced on Bharūch, Taghai fled to Kanbhāya, where he defeated a force that the sultan had sent in pursuit and killed its commander, Yūsuf-i Bughra, before taking flight again when Muḥammad hurried after him.[115]

While receiving the submission of various local ranas and chiefs in Girnār (Junagadh; the modern Kathiawāḍ), Muḥammad was recalled to the Deccan by the news that his amir ʿImād al-Mulk Sartīz, whom he had deputed to reduce Gulbarga following the victory over Ismāʿīl *Mukh, had been defeated and killed by another group of *amīrān-i ṣada* under one of Ismāʿīl's lieutenants, Ḥasan Gangū, styled Ẓafar Khān. The troops the sultan had left at Dhārāgīr had fallen back on Dhār, and Ḥasan Gangū had made a triumphal entry into Dawlatābād. Ismāʿīl *Mukh renounced the royal title in favour of his deliverer: Ḥasan Gangū, who was enthroned on 24 Rabīʿ II 748/3 August 1347 as ʿAlāʾ al-Dīn Bahman Shāh, thereby became the first sovereign of the independent Bahmanid dynasty that ruled in the Deccan until the sixteenth century. According to Baranī, Muḥammad summoned various commanders from Delhi and planned to send them to regain the Deccan, but abandoned the idea when he heard reports of the great numbers rallying to Ḥasan Gangū's standard. It seemed advisable to deal first with Taghai and to postpone turning his attention to the south until later.[116]

Muḥammad spent the next three monsoons in ineffectual pursuit of Taghai, moving from Nahrwāla to Kathiawāḍ and back again, before making an abortive attempt to assault Thatta, with whose Sūmra princes the rebel had taken shelter. The sultan was preparing for a second attack on Thatta when he fell ill and died on the banks of the Indus on 21 Muḥarram 752/20 March 1351.[117] His achievements during these last years should not be underestimated. By concentrating on the overthrow of Taghai, a task which was not in fact completed in his lifetime, he had at least accomplished the subjugation of Gujarāt – including regions that do not seem to have acknowledged his predecessors – and ensured that the province remained part of the Sultanate for another two generations. But any larger enterprise was beyond the depleted resources at his disposal. An alleged conversation between the sultan and Baranī, in which Muḥammad complained that a new revolt erupted in one direction every time he turned towards another,

115 There is valuable information on the origins of Taghai's revolt in *SFS*, 19–21, 23–4 (tr. Basu, *JBORS* 23 [1937], 97–102). *TFS*, 515–16, 517–20, gives a narrative. *FS*, 538–9 (tr. 793–4), is brief.

116 *TFS*, 520–1, 522, but giving only a short notice of events in the Deccan; see also 515 for the despatch of Sartīz towards Gulbarga. *FS*, 540–54 (tr. 811–28), provides a full account of Ḥasan Gangū's operations, with the date of his accession.

117 His movements have now been elucidated, on the basis of material in *TFS*[1], by Simon Digby, 'Muḥammad bin Tughluq's last years in Kathiavad and his invasions of Thattha', in Khuhro (ed.), *Sind through the centuries*, 130–8.

conveys his exasperation.[118] The disaffection of the *amīrān-i ṣada*, which Muḥammad himself had done so much to foster, was too intense and geographically too widespread to be overcome, given the sultan's fiscal problems and the decline in the impressive military establishment he had presided over in the early years of his reign.

[118] *TFS*, 521. *FS*, 538 (tr. 794), similarly catches the dilemma confronting Muḥammad at Dawlatābād when he first heard news of Taghai's rebellion.

CHAPTER 14

The sultans and their Hindu subjects

The Delhi Sultans were first and foremost Islamic rulers. Fakhr-i Mudabbir calls Iltutmish 'the sovereign of Islam' (*pādishāh-i Islām*).[1] Jūzjānī saw Nāṣir al-Dīn Maḥmūd Shāh as the 'Sultan' (or 'Sultan of the Sultans') 'of Islam', or as 'Emperor of the Peoples of Islam'.[2] Alternatively, the monarch could be hailed as 'Sultan of the Turks and Persians (*ʿAjam*)'[3] – ruler, in other words, over the war-lords, soldiers and scholars who made up the immigrant Muslim population. In the eyes of the Sultanate's chroniclers, the Muslims constituted what in more recent times would be termed a *Staatsvolk*. The monarch was emphatically not sultan of the Hindus or of, say, the people of Hariyāna; it has been observed that in our Muslim sources Hindus 'are never interesting in themselves, but only as converts, as capitation tax-payers, or as corpses'.[4] All the sultans with one exception proclaimed the spirit in which they approached their task by assuming on their coins and in their inscriptions the style (*kunya*) of *Abu'l-Muẓaffar* ('Father of the Victorious One'); the exception, Muḥammad b. Tughluq, styled himself *al-Mujāhid fī Sabīli'llāh* ('The Warrior in the Path of God'). For many Muslim observers, the ultimate justification for any ruler within the Islamic world was the protection and advancement of the faith. For the sultans, as for their Ghaznawid and Ghurid predecessors, this entailed the suppression of heterodox Muslims, and Fīrūz Shāh attached some importance to the fact that he had acted against the *aṣḥāb-i Ilḥād-u Ibāḥat* ('deviators and latitudinarians').[5] It also involved plundering, and extorting

[1] *AH*, 15.

[2] *TN*, I, 273, and II, 91, 166, 185 and n.3; cf. also II, 91, *pādishāh-i ahl-i aymān*, 205, *pādishāh-i Musulmānān*.

[3] *Tāj*, fol. 217b. *TN*, I, 297 (tr. 231); cf. also I, 275, 366 (tr. 183, 388). Shuᶜaib, 'Inscriptions from Palwal', 2, 3; Yazdani, 'Inscriptions of the Turk Sulṭāns', 15; *RCEA*, X, 72–3 (no. 3703).

[4] Hardy, *Historians*, 114.

[5] *FFS*, 6–8 (tr. Roy, 454–6). *SFS*, 129 ff. See also *KF*, 20, and *TFS*, 336, for ᶜAlā' al-Dīn's treatment of *aṣḥāb-i Ibāḥat*. *Qarāmiṭa* – probably Ismāᶜīlīs – had attempted a coup in Delhi during Raḍiyya's reign: *TN*, I, 461–2 (tr. 646–7); *FS*, 122 (tr. 236–7), seems to date this to Iltutmish's era.

tribute from, independent Hindu principalities. That the Muslim ruler had a further duty to eradicate infidelity and humiliate his Hindu subjects was a view expressed with particular frequency and stridency by Baranī, both in the *Ta'rīkh-i Fīrūz-Shāhī* and in his *Fatāwā-yi Jahāndārī*, a mirror for princes composed a few years later.[6] To what extent these policies were actually implemented within the Sultanate is the question to which we now turn.

Hindus in the service of Islam

It comes as no surprise to find Hindus carrying on their normal avocations in the service, and for the benefit, of their Muslim rulers. The Turko-Persian nobility in the thirteenth-century Sultanate accumulated enormous debts to Hindu bankers and brokers, the 'Multānīs' and *sāhs*, who could still be numbered among the sultan's wealthiest and most important subjects in the wake of 'Alā' al-Dīn Khaljī's economic reforms.[7] A Hindu chieftain, Sādhārana, is said to have served as 'Alā' al-Dīn's treasurer.[8] Moving down the social scale, the sultans depended, for their ambitious construction projects, on a host of Hindu labourers (70,000 of them in the service of 'Alā' al-Dīn, if we can believe Baranī),[9] who were doubtless usually slaves. But these projects also relied on the expertise of a lesser number of master craftsmen, like 'Mokha Mehta, son of Keta Mehta the Indian' who is commemorated in an inscription dated 740/1340 in the mosque at Barōda,[10] and the masons recruited to repair the Quṭb Minār.[11] Such skilled artisans seem to have been rewarded with immunities, as was the Hindu carpenter to whom the sultan's governor of Bījāpūr in 1320 granted an estate free of taxes and other incidents for his services in the construction of the great mosque.[12] Members of the Hindu clerical class, too, were needed to staff the administration, even if under the supervision of Muslim ministers and officials: a Hindu clerk in the service of Quṭb al-Dīn Khaljī wrote a treatise on the operation of the mint in 1318,[13] and another, Gujar Sāh, was responsible for overseeing the introduction of a new coin, the *shashgānī*,

6 See especially *FJ*, 165.
7 *TFS*, 120, 284. For the Multānīs, see further *ibid.*, 311, 385; and for the *sāhs* of Dēōgīr, IB, IV, 49 (tr. Gibb and Beckingham, 794–5).
8 Pandit Ram Karna, 'Ladnu inscription of Sadharana of Vikrama samvat 1373', *EI* 12 (1913–14), 19 (verse 13).
9 *TFS*, 341.
10 *ARIE* (1963–4), 125 (no. 85); for the Sanskrit portion of this epigraph, see *ARIE* (1961–2), 143 (no. 1311).
11 P. Prasad, *Sanskrit inscriptions*, 21–2, 32–5 (nos. I:9 and I:14).
12 Nāẓim, *Inscriptions of Bijapur*, 25.
13 V. S. Agarwala, 'A unique treatise on medieval Indian coins', in H. K. Sherwani (ed.), *Dr. Ghulam Yazdani commemoration volume* (Hyderabad, AP, 1966), 87–101. G. H. Khare, 'Dravyaparīkshā of Thakkura Pherū – a study', *JNSI* 28 (1966), 25–37.

under the Tughluqid Fīrūz Shāh.[14] The sultans relied, lastly, on members of the Hindu menial class for the execution of Muslim and Hindu rebels alike.[15]

It was the same in the military sphere, where the sultans, like their Ghaznawid predecessors, maintained bodies of Hindu as well as Turkish troops. The slave infantry-guards and paiks in the sultan's entourage may well have come to enjoy the kind of privileged status that had belonged to Turkish ghulams for much of the thirteenth century. Prior to the Khaljī era the evidence is sketchy: we know, for instance, only that Balaban, prior to his accession, was attended by a body of a thousand paiks.[16] ʿAlāʾ al-Dīn Khaljī is known to have recruited some two thousand paiks at Kara for his expedition to Dēōgīr in 695/1296,[17] and they presumably remained in his service when he became sultan later that year. In the face of a bid by his nephew Ikit Khān to kill him and seize the throne, ʿAlāʾ al-Dīn was defended by an Indian slave, Nānak (subsequently raised to the rank of malik), and by his paiks.[18] When after his death his minister Malik Kāfūr, himself a converted Hindu slave, set aside the late sultan's adult sons and tried to rule through one of the younger princes, it was ʿAlāʾ al-Dīn's old paiks again who in 715/1316 killed Kāfūr and secured the throne for Quṭb al-Dīn; although as a result, says Baranī, they started to give themselves intolerable airs and had to be suppressed.[19] Quṭb al-Dīn himself, however, like his father, may have maintained a body of paiks.[20] Even the sternly Muslim Fīrūz Shāh, whose mother was the daughter of a Bhattī chieftain from the Panjāb, employed members of his maternal kin: on one occasion, when his life was threatened by a conspiracy, he was attended by his uncle, Rāī Pheru ('Bhirū') Bhattī, who lent him his sword.[21] In only a few instances – that of Khusraw Khān, for example, in sharp contrast with his Parwārī followers – do we know that these Indian servitors converted to Islam.

Patronage of Hindus is associated particularly with the reign of Muḥammad b. Tughluq. Jain sources repeatedly mention the sultan's favour towards Jain scholars.[22] Of the lowborn officers listed by Baranī whom Muḥammad appointed to administrative positions, some were Hindus (above, pp. 185–6). It is very probable that by Muḥammad's death the position of the capital's Brahmans, at least, as representatives of the Hindu population had been in some way regularized, since we are told that on Fīrūz Shāh's entry into Delhi Brahmans were among those admitted to perform obeisance to the new sovereign;[23] this is not mentioned in connection with any earlier accession.

14 ᶜAfīf, 344–9.
15 E.g. *TN*, II, 82 (tr. 855); IB, III, 298, 339–40 (tr. Gibb, 700, 719–20).
16 *TFS*, 55. 17 *Ibid.*, 222. 18 *Ibid.*, 273. For Nānak, see above, p. 175.
19 *TFS*, 376–7. 20 *Ibid.*, 392. 21 ᶜAfīf, 103–4.
22 Husain, *Tughluq dynasty*, chapter 11, with full references.
23 *TFS*, 546. ᶜAfīf, 88.

We have only meagre evidence for the attitudes of the Sultanate's Hindu subjects towards their Muslim rulers. The significance of inscriptions in which the victorious (and sometimes fictitious) exploits of the 'Śaka' kings are extolled is open to question.[24] An anecdote related by Ibn Baṭṭūṭa may carry greater weight. He tells how a Hindu chief brought a charge against Muḥammad b. Tughluq himself that he had killed his (the chief's) brother without cause, and cited him to appear before the qadi. The sultan duly went, unarmed and on foot, having in advance forbidden the qadi to show him any of the deference due to his rank, and remained standing while the qadi gave judgement against him and ordered him to make reparation to his accuser.[25] This is an isolated instance, and the purpose of the story is to highlight the sultan's humility and sense of equity; but it harmonizes with the general picture of Muḥammad as a ruler who, in the first half of his reign, took care to cultivate the Hindu. And if it embodies authentic fact, it demonstrates that one Hindu, of some standing, recognized the authority of the Muslim qadi.[26]

As early as Iltutmish's reign, the sultans are soon found adopting practices that were distinctively Indian, as for example riding elephants on ceremonial occasions, consulting astrologers and taking horoscopes in advance of important occasions like an enthronement, and so on. Cultural borrowings of this kind by Muslim rulers cannot be taken, of course, as a sign of accommodation with the infidel; they represent merely an adaptation to Indian conditions (in much the same way as the first-generation immigrants Fakhr-i Mudabbir and Jūzjānī employ the name of the Hindu month Ahār).[27] Nevertheless, the fact that in some degree they conducted their public lives in an Indian idiom may have facilitated the acceptance of Muslim monarchs by Hindu chiefs.[28]

The problem of 'protection' and the *jizya*

Generally speaking, then, Hindus of diverse categories seem to have shown themselves indispensable to the exercise of Islamic government and to the maintenance of Islamic institutions. But what was their status under Islamic rule? According to the Sharī'a, the 'people of the Book' (*ahl al-kitāb*) – those possessing scriptures which were seen as an inadequate expression of the truth contained in the Qur'ān – were to be treated as 'protected peoples' (*ahl al-dhimma* or *dhimmīs*), once they had capitulated and accepted Muslim

24 Pālam *baoli* inscription of V.s. 1333/1276, in P. Prasad, *Sanskrit inscriptions*, 3–15 (no. I:4).
25 IB, III, 285 (tr. Gibb, 692–3).
26 Hardy, 'Growth of authority', 194.
27 Horoscopes etc.: *TN*, I, 449 (tr. 623); *TFS*, 142, 456; *FS*, 393–4 (tr. 598–9); *TMS*, 79. Ahār: *SA*, 31 (text reads 'HA in error); *TN*, II, 21 (tr. 748).
28 Hardy, 'Growth of authority', 201, and 'Authority of Muslim kings', 49.

government.[29] The term 'people of the Book' was originally meant to apply to the monotheistic Christians and Jews, but the mention in the Qur'ān of a third, somewhat obscure people, the Sabians, enabled the Muslim authorities to extend the category of dhimmis to the Zoroastrians in Iran. Dhimmis had the right to practise their own faith, but they were not allowed to proselytize or to construct new places of worship. They were also subject to the *jizya*, a capitation-tax in lieu of the military service performed by adult male Muslims. In addition, at different times in different parts of the Islamic world rulers had introduced discriminatory laws regulating the dress of dhimmis, forbidding them to ride horses or to bear weapons, and so on. Muslim legal scholars differed over the rights dhimmis might enjoy: thus the Ḥanafī school, which was dominant in the Sultanate, is alone in setting the blood-money for a dhimmi at the same level as that for a Muslim.[30]

Whether the polytheists who confronted the Muslim conquerors within the Indian subcontinent could be classed as a 'people of the Book' might appear at first sight to be a moot question. But in fact Balādhurī's *Futūḥ al-Buldān*, one of the principal sources for the Muslim conquest of Sind in the early eighth century, tells us that the Arab general Muḥammad b. Qāsim treated the idol-houses (*budd*) on a par with Christian churches, Jewish synagogues, or Zoroastrian fire-temples.[31] The term dhimmi was extended to embrace Hindu princes and their peoples who submitted and offered tribute, so that we read of the acceptance of *dhimma* status by the inhabitants of Dvārasamudra in 711/1311–12, the ruler of Tilang in 718/1318, and the rai of Nagarkōt in *c*. 766/1364–5.[32] The list of those prepared to recognize the Sultanate's Hindu subjects as dhimmis includes not merely Ḥasan-i Niẓāmī, Jūzjānī, ʿAfīf, Ibn Māhrū, ʿAbd al-Ḥamīd Ghaznawī and the anonymous author of the *Sīrat*, but also Baranī, who as we shall see was by no means well disposed towards even the submissive infidel, and the supposedly uncompromising Tughluqid Sultan Fīrūz Shāh in his *Futūḥāt*, drafted originally as an inscription and hence for public consumption.[33] Even a legal text of Fīrūz Shāh's reign includes several references to dhimmis, by which it clearly means Hindus.[34]

[29] For what follows, see Cl. Cahen, 'Dhimma', *Enc.Isl.*^{2}; Bernard Lewis, *The Jews of Islam* (Princeton, 1984), chapter 1 (for *jizya*, see especially 14–16).

[30] E. Tyan, 'Diya', *Enc.Isl.*^{2}, III, 341. For a classic restatement of the disabilities to which dhimmis were subject according to the 'Covenant of ᶜUmar', see Sayyid ᶜAlī Hamadānī (d. 786/1385), *Dhakīrat al-Mulūk*, ed. Sayyid Maḥmūd Anwārī (Tabriz, 1358 Sh./1979), 285–7; tr. in De Bary, 489–90.

[31] Balādhurī, *Futūḥ al-Buldān*, ed. De Goeje, 439/ed. al-Munajjid, 538.

[32] Dvārasamudra: *KF*, 132, 135, 136. Tilang: *NS*, 116, 129. Nagarkōt: *SFS*, 82. Cf. also *DR*, 46.

[33] *Tāj*, fols. 149a, 155a. *TN*, II, 79. ᶜAfīf, 180, 264. *IM*, 63, 102. *DA*, fols. 32b, 33b-34a (tr. Rashid, 64, 65–6). *TFS*, 290, 586. *SFS*, 129, 167. *FFS*, 9, 10, 16 (tr. Roy, 456, 458, 462).

[34] *Fatāwā-yi Fīrūz-Shāhī*, IOL Persian ms. 2987 (Ethé, no. 2564), fols. 410a, 412a, 414, 416a, 418b, 419a.

That the Indian polytheists who submitted to Islamic rule qualified, therefore, as 'protected peoples' seems to have won acceptance among a fairly wide spectrum of the educated Muslim community within the subcontinent. But the precise nature of the disabilities to be imposed on the infidel was a more difficult matter. Early in the thirteenth century, Fakhr-i Mudabbir dedicated to Iltutmish his *Ādāb al-Ḥarb wa'l-Shajā'a* or *Ādāb al-Mulūk*, a manual of statecraft for kings which is largely concerned with military matters. In chapter 26 he reviews the principles and practice of Islamic governments regarding their non-Muslim subjects, and lists the restrictions under which such people should live: their adornment (*zayn*), dress (*jāma*) and deportment (*nishast*) are to be different from those of Muslims. He also lists the categories of people who should pay the jizya, which includes Jews, Christians, Sabians, Zoroastrians (*mugh*) and 'idolators' (*butparastān*).[35] This could be taken as evidence that Hindus were acceptable in the eyes of the Ghurid conquerors of India as payers of the poll-tax; though it has been pointed out that the *Ādāb al-Ḥarb* is not a legal text and that it contains no explicit statement that Hindus are to be classed as dhimmis.[36]

Given the political circumstances prevailing in Muslim-ruled India in Fakhr-i Mudabbir's time, how, where and upon whom was the jizya levied? We might expect some assistance in tackling the problem from the accounts that have come down to us of the Muslim conquest of Sind in the eighth century, and which could have served the thirteenth-century conquerors for precedent. Unfortunately, the conquest of Sind preceded the emergence of a clear differentiation between the jizya and the kharaj. The earliest chronicles therefore afford us no real assistance. Balādhurī's *Futūḥ al-Buldān* says, in the course of an otherwise full narrative, merely that Muḥammad b. Qāsim imposed the kharaj – either the land-tax or just tribute – on the vanquished city of Alōr.[37] Not until a century later, in the caliphate of al-Mu'taṣim (218–27/833–42), do we find the Muslim governor of Sind taking jizya, in this case from the Jats.[38] It is true that a later source, the *Chach-Nāma*, which purports to be a Persian translation, drawn up in Sind in 613/1216–17, of an Arabic history of the Islamic conquest of the region, shows jizya being levied at the very outset. Here Muḥammad b. Qāsim is alleged to have agreed that the inhabitants of Brahmanābād were to be regarded as dhimmis and imposed on them a graduated tax in accordance with the tradition (*sunan*) of the Prophet.[39] The reliability of the *Chach-Nāma* is admittedly open to question. Dismissed by S. H. Hodivala in 1939 as 'every whit as unhistorical as the similar lucubrations of Sanskrit poems and

[35] *AH*, 404–5. [36] Hardy, 'Growth of authority', 205–6.
[37] Balādhurī, *Futūḥ al-Buldān*, ed. De Goeje, 439/ed. al-Munajjid, 538.
[38] *Ibid.*, ed. De Goeje, 445–6/ed. al-Munajjid, 544.
[39] *CN*, 158–9. See also N. A. Baloch, 'Early advent and consolidation of Islam in the lands of Pakistan', *HI* 3 (1980), 66.

Rajput bards',[40] the work has more recently been rehabilitated, and it is now believed to incorporate material from a lost Arabic historical tradition, most probably the ninth-century chronicle of al-Madā'inī. Nevertheless, the data on the poll-tax are undoubtedly anachronistic; and Dr Peter Hardy has proposed that this kind of testimony in the *Chach-Nāma* was designed to justify what had become standard practice by the early thirteenth century. If he is right, this means at least that the jizya was being levied in Sind on the very eve of the creation of the Delhi Sultanate.[41]

It is some measure of the problems surrounding the jizya that one of our most important sources, Jūzjānī's *Ṭabaqāt*, neglects even to mention it. The term surfaces fitfully in the sources for the thirteenth- and early fourteenth-century Sultanate, but it evidently carries a variety of meanings.[42] At times the usage is bizarre, as when the jizya is allegedly taken from a rebel Muslim commander in the breakaway Deccan Sultanate or demanded from a Muslim mystic (*darwīsh*).[43] The phrase *kharāj-u jizya* has contributed to the confusion. Amīr Khusraw uses it in a general sense, to mean tribute payable, for instance, by the enemy's paiks, and such is clearly the sense also in Baranī's *Ta'rīkh-i Fīrūz-Shāhī*.[44] According to the *Fatāwā-yi Jahāndārī*, Hindu rais levy the jizya and the kharaj from their own people.[45] In none of these instances can we discern the lineaments of the Islamic poll-tax.

Fakhr-i Mudabbir distinguishes two kinds of jizya. One is the tribute (*gazīd*) agreed upon as the price for a cessation of hostilities. The other type of jizya is the sum levied by a Muslim sovereign upon the wealth – the houses, estates and moveables (*khāna-u ḍiyā'-u 'aqār*) – of individual infidels, and is gradated. The annual rates given in the *Ādāb al-Ḥarb* are precisely those specified in the *Chach-Nāma*, namely forty-eight silver *dirhams* for the richest, twenty-four for those of middling wealth, and twelve for the poorest.[46] Ghaznawī, who here evidently follows Fakhr-i Mudabbir and gives the same figures, equates the first type of jizya with the *kharāj-i muqāsima* (i.e. the land-tax proper). He also writes of two kinds of tribute: that rendered when a Muslim army has actually taken up its quarters in the infidel kingdom, which he classes merely as booty (*ghanīma*), and that offered prior to a Muslim invasion, which he calls *jizya*. At another point he is prepared to class as jizya even money and gifts despatched

[40] Hodivala, *Studies*, I, 83–4.

[41] See P. Hardy, 'Is the *Chach-nama* intelligible to the historian as political theory?', in Khuhro (ed.), *Sind through the centuries*, 116–17; *idem*, 'Djizya, iii. India', *Enc.Isl.*²; also Yohanan Friedmann, 'The origins and significance of the *Chach-nama*', in Friedmann (ed.), *Islam in Asia*, I, 23–37; Wink, *Al-Hind*, I, 192–6.

[42] For what follows, see especially Hardy, 'Djizya'; I. Habib, 'Agrarian economy', 67.

[43] *FS*, 602 (tr. 888). Amīr Ḥasan Dihlawī, *Fawā'id al-Fu'ād*, 233.

[44] *RI*, I, 33, and IV, 140. *TFS*, 291, 574. *TMS*, 147. This is what misled Lal (below, n.49).

[45] *FJ*, 166. [46] *AH*, 404. *CN*, 158.

intermittently by infidel princes.[47] It is clearly jizya in the sense of tribute – a share of the land-revenue, surrendered by a Hindu rai – that was imposed, for instance, on King Rudradēva of Arangal in the course of Malik Kāfūr's expedition in 710/1310–11 and again when Khusraw Khān invaded his dominions in 718/1318.[48]

Certain historians have assumed that the jizya was levied on the subject Hindu population throughout the era of the Delhi Sultanate.[49] This seems unlikely. One relevant consideration is that the jizya was a tax in lieu of military service and that – unlike Jews and (at least during this period) Christians in other Islamic polities – Hindus, as we have seen, frequently fought in the ranks of Muslim armies; this would have warranted the suspension of the tax in Muslim India.[50] More relevantly, it has been argued that the logistics of collection, involving enormous numbers of tax-payers and given the relatively unsophisticated administrative apparatus of even a medieval Islamic state, must have presented an insuperable obstacle.[51] On such grounds, it has seemed natural to conclude that the jizya did not exist as a distinct tax but was subsumed within the kharaj or land-tax.[52] Ghaznawī indeed envisaged that the two might be consolidated as a single tax; though he urged that the respective proportions should be clearly defined.[53]

Perhaps a distinction can be drawn between the Hindus of the rural areas and those living in the Muslim-held towns and fortresses. In the case of the former, the jizya may have been perceived as forming part of the land-tax or tribute rendered up by the chiefs;[54] and this would make sense of the perplexing remark cited above, from Baranī's *Fatāwā*, that Hindu kings (i.e. those tributary to the Muslim sovereign) exacted kharaj and jizya from their own subjects. On the other hand, Baranī attributes to Jalāl al-Dīn Khaljī a speech in which he refers to the paltry sums he accepts as *ṣadaqa* from the

47 *DA*, fols. 35a–36b (tr. Rashid, 67–8).

48 1311: *KF*, 111. 1318: *NS*, 84, 121. For *jizya* as tribute, see also *QS*, 35, 63; *NS*, 84, 121; *FS*, 275, 402 (tr. 450, 608–9); cf. also 35–7 (tr. 84–5), for a similar usage apropos of the Ghaznawid era, and 596 (tr. 879), where we are clearly dealing with the payment of two years' kharaj and the promise of future tribute (*sā-u bāj*). Likewise, IB, IV, 231 (tr. Gibb and Beckingham, 877), speaks of *jizya* being paid to the Muslim ruler of Sumatra by his infidel neighbours.

49 Lal, *History of the Khaljis*, 184–5 (context is ᶜAlā' al-Dīn's reign). U. N. Day, *Administrative system of Dehli Sultanat (1206–1413 A.D.)* (Allahabad, 1959), 106; in his *The government of the Sultanate* (New Delhi, 1972; 2nd edn 1993), 91–2, Day is more non-committal, though without implying that the tax was introduced at a late stage. Zafarul Islam, 'Fīrūz Shāh's attitude towards non-Muslims – a reappraisal', *IC* 64 (1990), part 4, 66, sees the jizya imposed in Fīrūz Shāh's era as 'a revived impost'.

50 Aziz Aḥmad, *Studies in Islamic culture*, 80–1: the context is the reign of the Mughal emperor Akbar.

51 Hardy, 'Djizya', and 'Authority of Muslim kings', 48.

52 Nizami, *Some aspects of religion and politics*, 314–15. See also Qureshi, *Administration of the Sultanate*, 119.

53 *DA*, fol. 34a (tr. Rashid, 66).

54 This suggestion was made by Habibullah, *Foundation*, 250.

Hindus of the capital. *Ṣadaqa* normally denotes the alms paid by Muslims, of course, and its use here is a piece of irony, to suggest that the Muslim sovereign is in receipt of the unbeliever's charity. The payment referred to may be the jizya.[55] Conceivably the urban Hindu populace – artisans, members of guilds, shopkeepers, and so on – who were in more direct contact with the Muslim fiscal authorities, had to pay on an individual basis, i.e. a true poll-tax. It is surely no accident that Fakhr-i Mudabbir, in the passage quoted earlier, speaks of the imposition of the canonical jizya in the context of the surrender of a town.[56] As far as I am aware, this solution to the problem has not been proposed before, but I offer it for what it is worth (which, in the absence of strong textual backing, is not much). Whatever the truth, however, we first meet with incontrovertible evidence of the jizya as a discriminatory tax on individual non-Muslims only in the reign of Fīrūz Shāh (752–90/1351–88).

Fīrūz Shāh's anonymous biographer assures us of that sultan's concern to impose no more than the canonical taxes, including 'the jizya of the Hindus' (*jizya-yi Hunūd*).[57] According to ʿAfīf, he was the first monarch to impose the jizya on the Brahmans, who had hitherto been exempt. (It is uncertain whether this means that the jizya had actually been levied on other Hindu groups prior to Fīrūz Shāh's time, or merely that the sultan had himself excepted the Brahmans on a previous occasion, when imposing the tax on the rest of Hindu society.) The Brahmans were scandalized and assembled outside his palace, threatening to burn themselves to death. The sultan told them that they had better get on with it, since this was the only way they would avoid payment – a somewhat cavalier response which gave no grounds for optimism. But a crisis was averted when the principal Hindu residents of the capital came forward with the offer to pay the tax on the Brahmans' behalf. Fīrūz Shāh in turn was ready to be more conciliatory, and taxed the Brahmans at the lowest point on the scale, though using a *tanga* of different value.[58] In his autobiography, Fīrūz Shāh mentions the jizya among the canonical sources of revenue permitted to a Muslim ruler, speaks of the Hindus as submitting to the tax in return for protection of their property, and claims to have won over countless Hindus to the true faith with an edict promising them release from the jizya if they would convert.[59]

ʿAfīf appears to specify that the rates he cites (ranging from twenty to forty *tangas*) applied in Delhi. There is also evidence, however, from at least one province for the imposition of the jizya during Fīrūz Shāh's reign. The tax is referred to twice in the correspondence of one of the sultan's officers, ʿAyn al-Mulk Ibn Māhrū, governor of Sind. In the first case ʿAyn al-Mulk

55 *TFS*, 217. Cf. the remark in *FJ*, 167, that the infidels pay 'a few *tangas* by way of *jizya*'.
56 *AH*, 404. 57 *SFS*, 125.
58 ʿAfīf, 382–4. For the significance of this passage, see Hodivala, *Studies*, I, 336–7.
59 *FFS*, 6, 9, 16–17 (tr. Roy, 453, 456, 462).

responds to protests at an increase in the jizya levied on Hindu shopkeepers.[60] Later he refers to the fact that the sultan had allocated to a military officer, as his stipend, the jizya paid by the peasants of a certain district. The terms used show (a) that the tax was related to the protection of the dhimmi and (b) that the owner (*mālik*) of the land (in this case the qadis of Thānesar) had no claim upon it.[61] This excludes any possibility that we are dealing with the ordinary land-tax. The balance of the evidence, consequently, is that in the latter half of the fourteenth century, if not before, the jizya was levied as a discriminatory tax on non-Muslims;[62] though even then it is difficult to see how such a measure could have been enforced outside the principal centres of Muslim authority.

Latitude towards Hindu religious practice

There is little information in the sources about the attitude of the sultans towards Hindu religious observance in general; and most of the evidence comes from the reign of Muḥammad b. Tughluq, who was hardly typical. Muḥammad was notoriously interested in Hindu practices. He is charged by ʿIṣāmī, admittedly no friend of the sultan, with attending the Hindu religious festival of Hōlī and (as Ibn Baṭṭūṭa confirms) with frequenting the company of jogis.[63] Ibn Baṭṭūṭa observes that the sultan's permission was required for the ceremony of *satī* ('suttee'), the burning of a widow on her husband's funeral-pyre.[64]

Otherwise, the limited material at our disposal is concerned with the construction or repair of Hindu temples. We saw earlier how in strict Islamic law it was not permissible for Hindus to build new idol-temples or to restore those that had been destroyed. That this was being disregarded, however, in ʿAlāʾ al-Dīn Khaljī's reign is clear from Jain works which praise Alp Khān, his governor in Gujarāt, for permitting the reconstruction of temples destroyed during the Muslim conquest.[65] Fuller testimony is provided by an inscription of 1326 from the Deccan. During the rebellion of Bahāʾ al-Dīn Garshāsp, the governor of Kalyānī, Aḥmad Jajnērī, was called away; and in the ensuing upheavals a Hindu temple at Kalyānī was damaged and the Śiva *liṅga* was broken. Local Hindu notables, headed by the person in charge of the management of the temple, therefore approached the governor on his return and sought his permission for the repair of the temple and the resumption of the worship of the god. Aḥmad Jajnērī consulted his secretary, whose name is certainly not a Muslim one, and granted permission, adding that since the worship of the god was a duty it

60 *IM*, 48. 61 *Ibid.*, 62–3.
62 See also Zakir Husain, 'Some original Tughluq documents and their significance', *PIHC* 50. *(Gorakhpur 1989)* (Delhi, 1990), 222.
63 *FS*, 515 (tr. 765). IB, IV, 36, 38–9 (tr. Gibb and Beckingham, 788, 789–90).
64 *Ibid.*, III, 137 (tr. Gibb, 614). 65 Misra, *Rise of Muslim power*, 68–9.

was right that the petitioners should pursue it. This testimony has been cited as indicating the existence of a striking degree of tolerance.[66] But it comes, of course, like the material relating to Alp Khān, from a region that had only recently come under direct Muslim rule, and one where the sultan's authority must have been highly precarious. It does not tell us what might have been the response had a similar situation arisen in a core territory like Hariyāna.

We have, in fact, other evidence for the latitude enjoyed by local Hindu religious authorities at this time. Ibn Baṭṭūṭa writes of an embassy from 'the king of China' (i.e. the Mongol Yüan emperor) to Muḥammad b. Tughluq, requesting permission for the reconstruction of a temple in the Sambhal region which had allegedly been sacked by a Muslim army. The envoys were told in reply that permission to restore such temples within Muslim territory could be given only to those who paid the jizya (and not, in other words, to infidels resident in the Dār al-Ḥarb).[67] The authenticity of this embassy is questionable, and it is in any case conceivable that Ibn Baṭṭūṭa, as an outsider, misconstrued the state of affairs. But the likelihood is that his testimony regarding the reconstruction of idol-temples is reliable. For indeed Fīrūz Shāh claims that prior to his accession *new* temples had been built in Delhi and its environs – contrary, of course, to the Sharīʿa.[68] Of this there survives, unfortunately, only meagre direct evidence. An inscription shows that a new temple was built at Revasa, in the Nāgawr region, in 1326;[69] a fragment of a bilingual inscription, in Sanskrit and Persian, of uncertain date but very probably from the Sultanate period, records the purchase of twelve *bīghas* of land near the Qilʿa Kuhna in Delhi itself and the erection of the temple of Śri Krishna Bhagwan.[70]

It is not beyond the bounds of possibility that such foundations received endowments from the Muslim authorities. Alp Khān is said to have made a donation towards the repair of Jain temples in Gujarāt;[71] but otherwise the large numbers of documents that attest the conferment of land and tax exemptions by Muslim kings on Brahmans, Jains, jogis and Parsis and on temples to Śiva and Viśnu tend to originate from the Mughal emperors and their contemporaries in the successor-states to the Delhi Sultanate. Although many of these confer new revenues, some are clearly renewals or extensions of grants made by Muslim rulers of an earlier era.[72] There are signs of donations of tax-free land (*madad-i maʿāsh*) to Brahmans during at

[66] P. B. Desai, 'Kalyana inscription of Sultan Muḥammad', 165–70. See HN, 503; also W. H. Siddiqi, 'Religious tolerance as gleaned from medieval inscriptions', in *PSMI*, 54, where the governor is mistakenly identified, however, as Aḥmad-i Ayaz, the sultan's future wazir.

[67] IB, IV, 1–2 (tr. Gibb and Beckingham, 773).

[68] *FFS*, 9–10 (tr. Roy, 456–8).

[69] *Progress Report of the ASI (Western Circle)* (1909–10), 52, cited in Welch and Crane, 'The Tughluqs: master-builders', 160 n.11.

[70] *ASIR* (1909–10), 131.

[71] Misra, *Rise of Muslim power*, 69.

[72] Ernst, *Eternal garden*, 48–9.

least the period of the Lodī sultans, and it may be that such grants were made by their predecessors also. Professor Siddiqui sees this as the sultans' response to the need to bring 'the countryside with its influential chiefs under effective control'.[73]

Generally speaking, Fīrūz Shāh's policies weighed more heavily upon the subject Hindu population than those of his predecessors. ʿAfīf tells how the sultan burned a Brahman at the palace gates.[74] Fīrūz Shāh himself, in describing the new temples that had arisen under his predecessors, claims to have set about destroying them and replacing them with mosques, and in one instance to have repopulated a township with Muslim settlers.[75] Two points must be emphasized here. Firstly, these were all new edifices: there was no question of destroying temples and shrines which had already existed before the Islamic conquest and whose devotees lived peacefully under Islamic government. And secondly, these events all transpired in the vicinity of Delhi. The sultan's writ would hardly have extended to enforcing such a policy over a wider radius. This is clear from his conduct in sparing the idol of Jawālamukhī at Nagarkōt, a step that was, in fact, perfectly in keeping with the policy of earlier Muslim rulers. But it was difficult to reconcile with his iconoclastic image, and gave rise to rumours spread by 'certain infidels' – and which ʿAfīf was at pains to refute – that the sultan had paid his respects to the idol and unfurled a chatr over its head.[76] Nevertheless, whatever qualifications are made as to scale, it cannot be denied that Fīrūz Shāh's reign witnessed a reaction against previous regimes. After his death, the Hindus' situation may have deteriorated further in certain regions: a temple at Ketlai, in the Gurgā'ūn district, was destroyed in 795/1392 and replaced by a mosque.[77]

Hindu–Muslim relations: an assessment

In relating military encounters with the Hindu, the narrative sources abound in unflattering, if conventional, allusions: one of the most frequent is the description of the enemy as 'crow-faced (*zāgh-chihra*)'.[78] But at times a more neutral tone is heard. Jūzjānī hoped that the qualities of King Lakśmanasena of Bengal, who had gained a reputation for justice and

[73] I. H. Siddiqui, 'Wajh-i Maᶜash grants under the Afghan kings (1451–1555)', *MIM* 2 (1972), 21, 36. For the Mughal era, see B. N. Goswamy and J. S. Grewal (eds.), *The Mughals and the Jogis of Jakhbar* (Simla, 1967): evidence from the regional sultanates in the pre-Mughal period is given *ibid.*, 20.

[74] ᶜAfīf, 379–81. [75] *FFS*, 9–10 (tr. Roy, 456–8).

[76] ᶜAfīf, 186–7. The sparing of the idol is mentioned briefly in *SFS*, 83.

[77] *ARIE* (1963–4), 146 (no. D286).

[78] Annemarie Schimmel, 'Turk and Hindu: a poetical image and its application to historical fact', in Speros Vryonis, Jr (ed.), *Islam and cultural change in the Middle Ages* (Wiesbaden, 1975), 107–26: see esp. 109–16.

generosity, would earn him alleviation of his torments in Hell.[79] When Toghril Khān Yüzbeg, the muqtaʿ of Lakhnawtī, repudiated the sovereignty of Sultan Nāṣir al-Dīn Maḥmūd (*c.* 652/1254), says the same author, his action incurred the disapproval of Hindus and Muslims alike within the Sultanate.[80] Amīr Khusraw has been singled out as one who in his *Nuh Sipihr* drew attention to the kinship between certain Hindu religious beliefs and those of Islam.[81] At the tragic death of Balaban's son Muḥammad in battle with the Mongols, wrote Khusraw, 'the Hindu lost his blackness and the Turk his whiteness'. Literary device this may be; but the implication is that Khusraw, like Jūzjānī, thought the Hindu's view could be taken on board. And it seems that the Hindu merited a place in the divine dispensation when compared with other pagans. The Mongols, who were viewed as harbingers of the last things (p. 113 above), were described in much more opprobrious terms than were the Hindus in Indo-Muslim writings. Khusraw derived some satisfaction from the fact that Providence had used ʿAlāʾ al-Dīn's infidel general Nānak to defeat the infidel Mongols.[82] Legal texts of the fourteenth century reveal a concern about the relations of ordinary Muslims with the Hindu population. The *Fatāwā-yi Fīrūz-Shāhī*, in particular, pronounces on the proper conduct of social intercourse with Hindus, the right treatment of Hindu parents by a Muslim son, the equal rights of Hindu and Muslim creditors, and so on.[83]

All this might seem to stand in sharp contrast with the tone adopted by Baranī. A theme that recurs frequently in Baranī's writings is that the infidels must on no account be allowed to live in ease and affluence. In the preface to his life of the Prophet, *Naʿt-i Muḥammadī*, he cites a dispute that allegedly took place at the court of Iltutmish a century and a quarter earlier. When the ʿulamaʾ declared that the Hindus had no right to be treated as 'Peoples of the Book' and should be given only the choice between death and Islam, the sultan's wazir Junaydī is said to have agreed with them. But, he continued, such a course would be highly impolitic, given that the Muslims were still few in number, and its implementation should be deferred until they were in a stronger position. The ʿulamaʾ thereupon insisted that the sultan should at least refrain from treating Hindus with honour or permitting idolatry in the capital. But it was because of this failure to slaughter the Hindus, says Baranī, that polytheism had taken root.[84] This is echoed in another hypothetical conversation from the same

[79] *TN*, I, 425 (tr. 555–6). [80] *Ibid.*, II, 32 (tr. 764).
[81] Yohanan Friedmann, 'Medieval Muslim views of Indian religions', *JAOS* 95 (1975), 216–17.
[82] *WH*, IOL Persian ms. 412, fol. 135a. *KF*, 38. *DR*, 61. The comparison with the treatment of the Mongols is made in Hardy, 'Growth of authority', 193.
[83] Z. Islam, '*Fatāwā Fīrūz Shāhī* as a source', 105–7.
[84] Baranī, *Naʿt-i Muḥammadī*, RRL Pers. ms. 1295, fols. 195b-196a; tr. in S. Nurul Ḥasan, 'Sahifa-i-Naʿt-i-Muḥammadi of Zia-ud-din Barani', *MIQ* 1 (1950), 101–3 (Pers. text at 104–5).

era which is found in Baranī's *Ta'rīkh*. The sign that a ruler protects the true faith, Sayyid Nūr al-Dīn Ghaznawī tells Iltutmish, is that when he espies a Hindu his face grows red and he wants to bury him alive. If the polytheists are so numerous that the Muslim ruler cannot possibly eradicate them, then at the very least he should strive to insult them and bring disgrace, dishonour and ignominy upon them.[85] And the same theme recurs in a speech attributed to one of ʿAlā' al-Dīn Khaljī's advisers, Qadi Mughīth al-Dīn of Bhayāna. In answer to a question from the sultan about the status of the Hindu in the Sharīʿa as regards taxation, the qadi asserts that when the tax-collector demands silver from the Hindu he should mildly, humbly and respectfully hand over gold; and if the tax-collector throws dirt in his mouth, he should open his mouth to receive it.[86]

Such views are commonly encountered in polemical writing against the infidel in different parts of the Islamic world at different times.[87] But there are other notions that are peculiar to Baranī himself. For Baranī, it is one of the primary duties of Muslim kings to redeem the inherently sinful and evil nature of kingship by rooting out paganism, polytheism and idolatry.[88] The Hindus are the worst enemies of God and his Prophet.[89] Indeed, the Prophet had commanded that they were to be looted and enslaved or killed.[90] The Brahmans in particular, who are the leaders and instigators of idolatry, should be massacred.[91] Only the Ḥanafī school of law allows that the Hindus qualify to pay the jizya; the founders of all the other schools insist that the sole choice to be offered to Hindus is Islam or death.[92] Much of this is blatantly unhistorical. In his *Fatāwā-yi Jahāndārī*, which masquerades as a political testament from Maḥmūd of Ghazna, Baranī makes further statements that are equally dubious. Had Maḥmūd invaded India just once more, he would have slaughtered all the Brahmans and beheaded 200,000 or 300,000 Hindu chiefs (an intriguing demographic statistic).[93] Maḥmūd is said to have confided to Qadir Khān, the Qarakhanid ruler of Kāshghar, his fear that on the Day of Judgement he would be asked why he had not killed the Brahmans[94] – and this when the real Maḥmūd had been condemned by contemporary Muslim chroniclers for employing infidel Hindu troops against fellow Muslims during his campaigns in Persia.[95]

Yet Baranī's antipathy towards the infidel Hindu can be overstated. For all his railings, he is evidently aware that the contradiction between the demands of orthodox Islam and the situation in India cannot be resolved.[96] Moreover, he does permit himself the occasional neutral reference to the

[85] *TFS*, 41–2. [86] *Ibid.*, 290.
[87] For examples, see Lewis, *Jews of Islam*, 32ff.
[88] *TFS*, 41. See generally Hardy, '*Oratio recta*', 319.
[89] *TFS*, 42, 290; *Na*ʿ*t-i Muḥammadī*, fols. 195b-196a, tr. Nurul Ḥasan, 102 (Pers. text 104, 105).
[90] *TFS*, 290–1. [91] *Ibid.*, 42. *FJ*, 165. [92] *TFS*, 291. Cf. also *FJ*, 18.
[93] *Ibid.* [94] *Ibid.*, 230. [95] Bosworth, *Ghaznavids*, 89, 110.
[96] I. Habib, 'Baranī's theory', 111–13.

Hindus. He thinks it worth mentioning that during the famine of 1291 in Delhi Hindus came in groups of twenty or thirty to throw themselves into the Yamuna.[97] And he observes that Hindus as well as Muslims prayed for Muḥammad b. Tughluq on his accession and rejoiced at the advent of Fīrūz Shāh in 752/1351 and at his safe return from his first Bengal expedition a few years later.[98] These remarks suggest that, although Baranī would not for one second have considered his *Ta'rīkh-i Fīrūz-Shāhī* as a history of the entire population of the Sultanate, he did not, even so, deem the non-Muslim section of that population to be totally beneath the historian's notice. Perhaps the most arresting indication of a different frame of mind from the polemics outlined above is his statement that he is now ready to contemplate the life of a Brahman.[99] In other words, he does not at this juncture, as one might expect, hold up as his goal the calling of a sufi. It is possible that in his old age, and confronted by a sharp decline in his material condition, Baranī found something to commend in the degree of self-abnegation attained by certain leading exponents of the rival faith.

Whatever the case, Baranī's fulminations against gentle treatment of the non-Muslim must be seen for what they are. Not merely were his writings drafted largely from memory by a man advanced in age; not merely do they exhibit at times a lamentable ignorance of history; they are also the product of a courtier who had fallen from favour after the death of Muḥammad b. Tughluq and who bitterly resented his change of fortune. Baranī wrote, moreover, as the representative of a family that had served Balaban's officers and ʿAlā' al-Dīn Khaljī. His paternal ancestors may have been Turkish; more probably they were of Persian stock. His father's mother was of the illustrious lineage of the sayyids of Kaithal.[100] Baranī accordingly prides himself on his high birth and has no time for those of lowly origin. Significantly, his list of Muḥammad b. Tughluq's lowborn servitors includes not only Hindus but also those who, to judge from their names, had embraced Islam. Professor Irfan Habib has in fact pointed out that, unlike ʿIṣāmī, Baranī did not attack the sultan for his favour towards Hindus and that his objection to the promotion of these men – Hindu and Muslim alike – was based above all on their humble origins.[101] In some measure, certainly, Baranī's assertions about the status of the infidel are part of his more general indictment that men of low birth had benefited (and more than he himself had done) from his late master's patronage. But in fact Baranī, in his denial that the essentials of Islam can be implanted in the minds of Indian converts, seems to share the prejudice of ʿIṣāmī, for whom 'a Hindu ghulam will flee in the end, though he attain the rank of chief *ṣadr*'.[102]

[97] *TFS*, 212. [98] *Ibid.*, 457, 547, 596. I. Habib, 'Baranī's theory', 113.
[99] *TFS*, 200. [100] *Ibid.*, 350.
[101] *Ibid.*, 504–5; and cf. *FS*, 486, 515 (tr. 728, 765). I. Habib, 'Baranī's theory', 110.
[102] *FS*, 552 (my translation); cf. also 370 (tr. 571). *FJ*, 105.

It may be possible to identify more general causes of antagonism towards the infidel on the part of Muslim writers and rulers. One may have been a fear of apostasy on the part of ordinary Muslims. Here a parallel offers itself with Western Christian attitudes towards Islam in the Middle Ages. A common theme in Christian polemical writings on Islam and the Muslims is the low standard of sexual morality encouraged by the rival faith, whether on the level of polygamy, concubinage, ease of divorce, and ideas about paradise on the one hand or, on the other, the charge of dark and unnatural practices which would have been harder to substantiate but was no less sinister for being left vague.[103] In harping on such matters, Christian authors unconsciously testified to the attractive force of a religion that in their eyes was calculated to appeal to the sensual and the self-indulgent. We can, I suggest, detect a parallel phenomenon within Muslim circles in India. Beneath the surface of the political events on which our narrative sources focus lay a substratum of everyday Muslim–Hindu intercourse. Both Muslim and Hindu musicians performed at the celebrations for the marriage of Prince Khiḍr Khān.[104] Hindus are said to have mingled with Muslims in the crowds that gathered to celebrate the festival of Barāt (14 Shaʿbān).[105] Hindus and Muslims sometimes rubbed shoulders at the entrance to the hospices (khanaqahs) of sufi shaykhs.[106] Conversely, many Muslims attached themselves to a group of jogis at Khajuraho (Kajarrā) in order to acquire their skills.[107] Muḥammad b. Tughluq was only the most eminent figure to share in Hindu festivities: Ibn Baṭṭūṭa saw Muslims in the throng accompanying a widow on her way to be burned, and both Fīrūz Shāh and his biographer accuse ordinary Muslims of participating in Hindu religious rites.[108] The Brahman executed on Fīrūz Shāh's orders was charged not merely with hosting idolatrous ceremonies in his house that were attended by Muslims, but also with inducing a Muslim woman to apostatize.[109]

Muslims had been known, moreover, to flee into infidel territory. Some were prominent nobles like those implicated in the conspiracy during the Tilang campaign of 721/1321–2; but there were always renegades like the Muslims Ibn Baṭṭūṭa claims to have met when captured by Hindus near Jalālī.[110] For just as Hindu troops fought under the banner of Muslim sultans, so did Muslim soldiers fight for infidel rulers – whether it was the Muslims in the army of the Pāndya king of Maʿbar in 710/1310–11 or, some three decades later, the 20,000 Muslims, 'rascals, criminals and runaway slaves', who are reported in the service of the Hoysala king Ballāla III, or

103 Norman Daniel, *Islam and the West: the making of an image* (Edinburgh, 1960), 135–61.
104 *TMS*, 79. 105 ᶜAfīf, 366. 106 Troll (ed.) *Muslim shrines*, 7, 14.
107 IB, IV, 40 (tr. Gibb and Beckingham, 790).
108 *Ibid.*, III, 137 (tr. Gibb, 614). ᶜAfīf, 380. *FFS*, 9–10 (tr. Roy, 457). See also Ernst, *Eternal garden*, 27 and 289 n.107.
109 ᶜAfīf, 379–81. 110 IB, IV, 10–11 (tr. Gibb and Beckingham, 777).

the 'worthless' (*nābakār*) Muslims under the banner of Narāyan when he marched against the founder of the Bahmanid dynasty.[111] In the circumstances, there was perhaps an uneasy sense that the Muslim minority in an overwhelmingly pagan land might be seduced into infidelity. Mihrābī's *Ḥujjat al-Hind*, a treatise that has survived from the end of the fourteenth century, aims at countering just such apostasy in the countryside.[112]

The sultans were undoubtedly also a prey to pressures of a different sort. Historians of the Islamic world, notably Professor Bernard Lewis, have demonstrated that Muslim rulers can never be treated as monolithic in their approach to their non-Muslim subjects. Their policies fluctuated according to circumstance: an external military threat posed by the co-religionists of the subject group in question; the need on the part of the ruler to reassure the Muslim population if it was felt that other confessional groups had benefited from excessive leniency or favour; or simply the desire of a new sultan to buttress an authority that was of doubtful legitimacy with the support of orthodox jurists and preachers.[113] Circumstances of this order cannot be ignored either in an analysis of Hindu–Muslim relations within the Delhi Sultanate. Take, for example, the patronage of Hindus by Muḥammad b. Tughluq. Muḥammad also made greater efforts than any other Delhi ruler to attract into his service Muslims from every part of the Islamic world (pp. 184–5, 233–4). The paradox here is more apparent than real. These were two arms of a policy which aimed at creating a counterweight to the Indian Muslim nobility, since the Tughluqid dynasty had come to power only a few years previously in the teeth of determined Indian Muslim opposition. We should also bear in mind that a dramatic extension of Muslim power had occurred. The wars of the past three decades had eliminated most of those major independent Hindu kingdoms which might have presented a competing focus of allegiance. It is instructive in this respect to compare the position of Christians in, say, Egypt or Anatolia, where the Muslims could not afford to forget their relations with interested foreign powers. The Delhi Sultan was able to promote Hindu servitors as he did, or patronize Hindu religious establishments when it suited him, precisely because India contained no rival *imperium* like Byzantium or the states of Catholic Europe.[114]

Fīrūz Shāh, in turn, may well have been a more orthodox and pious figure than his late cousin; but extraneous factors also surely underlay his policies. The sultan's accession had not gone unchallenged; and he was

111 *KF*, 149, and *DR*, 72, for the Pāndya army; IB, IV, 195–6 (tr. Gibb and Beckingham, 861), for that of Ballāla III; *FS*, 592 (tr. 873), for Narāyan. Other examples in Bouchon, 'Quelques aspects', 30.

112 Peter Hardy, 'Islam and Muslims in South Asia', in Raphael Israeli (ed.), *The crescent in the east: Islam in Asia Major* (London, 1982), 43.

113 Lewis, *Jews of Islam*, 32–61 *passim*.

114 A point well made by Ernst, *Eternal garden*, 50–1.

clearly conscious, moreover, of a need to distance himself from the extravagances of Muḥammad, who had clashed with the Islamic 'religious establishment' and executed not a few of its members. It is also important, in this connection, that policies towards dhimmis are not seen in isolation from other measures. They were often linked with attempts to suppress heterodox Muslims or with the abolition of uncanonical taxes, both actions for which Fīrūz Shāh took care to be known and for which he is lauded by his biographer 'Afīf.[115] A clampdown on the dhimmi, rather than being seen as an end in itself, has to be viewed as part of a broader policy.

I have tried, in examining the all too meagre evidence at our disposal, to offer a perspective on Hindu–Muslim relations which might indicate that conventional formulations will not do. It is impossible to tell how far Baranī typified, in his attitude towards the Hindus, the class of Muslim *literati*; and even his outlook was a curious amalgam. But his very stridency at times suggests, and the evidence of other sources confirms, that there was a wide gulf between Islamic law and the inclinations and practices of rulers and the military class. The sultans were faced with a situation which had not confronted Muslim rulers elsewhere for a few centuries. 'Do you not see,' Baranī makes Jalāl al-Dīn Khaljī ask,

> 'how every day the Hindus ... pass beneath my palace, beating their drums and blowing on their conches, and make their way to the Yamuna to practise their idolatry, and how they fulfil the requirements of polytheism and paganism before my eyes ... – I, who have myself called the ruler of the Muslims and sovereign of Islam? ... Shame on me and on my kingship ... that I permit my name to be recited from the pulpit every Friday and the preachers with their lying tongues to proclaim me as the defender of Islam, when under my rule the enemies of God and of the faith, in my sight and in my capital, live in affluence and ease and surrounded by a thousand luxuries ... and strut about among Muslims and openly practise idolatry ...'[116]

The speech is apocryphal like all the others, but the words Baranī has put into the sultan's mouth have an authentic ring: they describe not what ought to be, but what is. The decisions made by the sultans, of how to comport themselves towards the infidels who represented the majority of their subjects, were informed by more complex considerations than we have often supposed. We surely have to begin with the presumption that within their own dominions, for some of the time, they managed to approach the problem, not as iconoclastic holy warriors, but with a degree of delicacy. Perhaps for them the paramount distinction was not that between Muslim and Hindu (important as that may have been) but between peaceful subject and agent of government on the one hand and troublemaker and rebel on the other.

[115] *FFS*, 5–6 (tr. Roy, 453–4). ᶜAfīf, 373–9. See generally Z. Islam, 'Fīrūz Shāh's attitude'.
[116] *TFS*, 216–17.

CHAPTER 15

Stasis and decline: Fīrūz Shāh and his successors

The contracted Sultanate

To judge from the remarks of the 'official' chronicler, it was a matter of some pride at Fīrūz Shāh's court that Ilyās Shāh, the upstart sultan of Bengal, had begun his career as merely the servant of an officer of one of Muḥammad b. Tughluq's servitors (see above, p. 267).[1] He was, moreover, a tyrant, and Fīrūz Shāh could not be impervious to the appeals of his wretched subjects for deliverance.[2] So too, the patents which the new sultan received from the ʿAbbasid Caliph – judging, again, by the treatment they are accorded in the *Sīrat* – had an important share in buttressing the exclusive legitimacy of his government. The Egyptian *shaykh al-shuyūkh* Rukn al-Dīn al-Malaṭī, who had brought a diploma for Muḥammad from al-Ḥākim, left India early in Fīrūz Shāh's reign, arriving back in Cairo early in 754/1353 after an absence of nearly ten years.[3] But that same year an embassy arrived in Delhi from the Caliph al-Muʿtaḍid bi'llāh, bringing Fīrūz Shāh a mandate (*manshūr*) for the government of India and conferring on him the titles *Sayf al-Khilāfat* ('Sword of the Caliphate') and *Qasīm Amīr al-Mu'minīn* ('Partner of the Commander of the Faithful'). In 764/1362–3 the next caliph, al-Mutawakkil ilā'llāh, despatched another mission to Delhi with a mandate in which Fīrūz Shāh was addressed as *Sayyid al-Salāṭīn* ('Lord of Sultans') and declared to be the caliph's *wālī*. Similar embassies followed in 766/1364–5 and, according to the *Sīrat*, each year thereafter.[4]

Al-Mutawakkil was at pains to stress that to obey the sultan was to obey

[1] *SFS*, 47.

[2] *Farmān* of Fīrūz Shāh reproduced in *IM*, 16; tr. in Maulavī ᶜAbdu'l Walī, 'Life and letters of Malik ᶜAynu'l-Mulk Māhrū and side-lights on Fīrūz Shāh's expeditions to Lakhnautī and Jājnagar', *JASB* ns 19 (1923), 279. *SFS*, 34 (tr. Basu, *JBORS* 23 [1937], 111). ᶜAfīf, 137–40, 143.

[3] al-Maqrīzī, *Sulūk*, II, part 3, 887. His figure of ten years and nine months must be incorrect (above, p. 272).

[4] *SFS*, 282–5 (tr. Rashid, 'Firuz Shah's investiture', 70–1). ᶜAfīf, 274–6, mentions only one caliphal embassy to Fīrūz Shāh, from al-Muᶜtaḍid. *TMS*, 126, has the first one (but from al-Ḥākim) in 757/1356; see also 127.

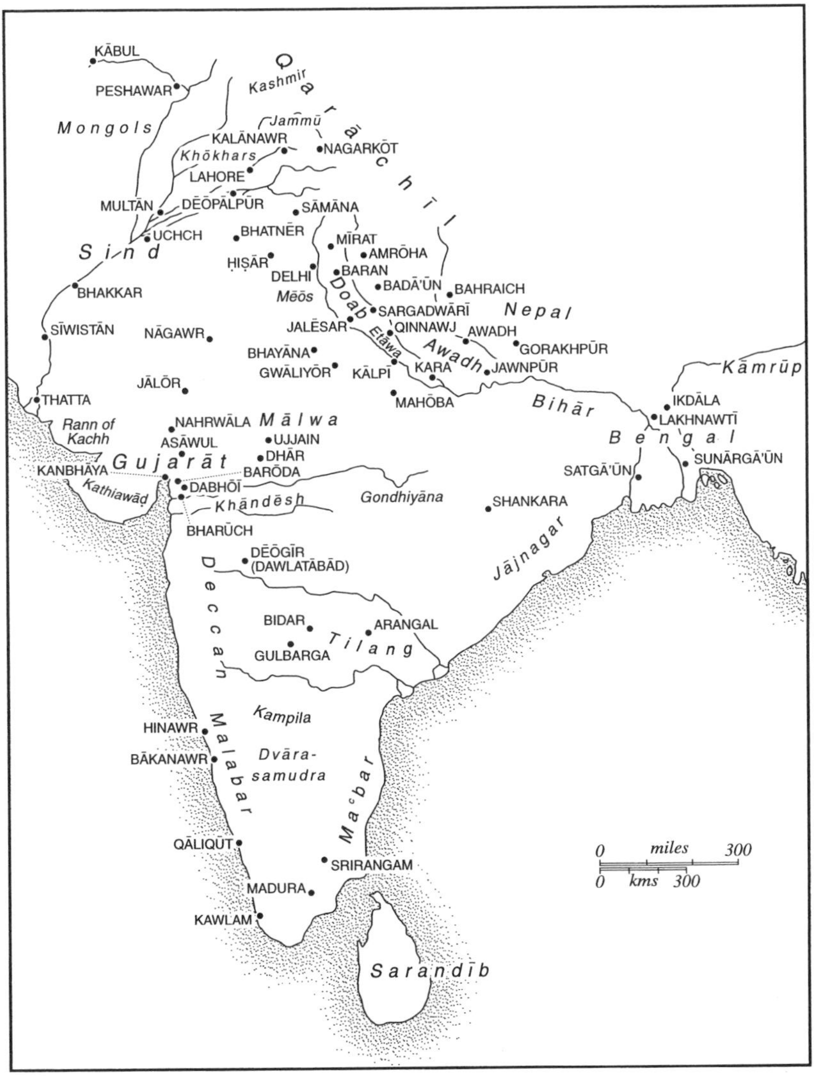

Map 6: The Sultanate under the Tughluqids

the caliph himself; that the sultan was empowered to wage *jihād* against rebels; and that neither he nor his two predecessors had issued a mandate to any Indian ruler other than the Delhi sovereign.[5] The caliph thus constituted Fīrūz Shāh his intermediary in dealing with other Muslim princes in the subcontinent. The territories listed in al-Muʿtaḍid's diploma included not merely Bengal, Maʿbar, Tilang, Dēōgīr, Kawlam (Quilon), Hinawr, Bākanawr and the rest of the coastal regions (*sawāḥil-i baḥr*), but also 'the island of Sarandīb' (Ceylon), 'the Jāwāt' (Greater and Lesser Java), the Qarāchīl mountains, 'the Afghan territory (*ḥudūd-i Afghāniyya*) and its mountains as far as Kashmīr, and Zāwulistān as far as the frontiers of the Turks and Mā warā' al-Nahr'.[6] This was, at best, a programme for future conquest (and reconquest).

In the early part of the reign, ʿAfīf learned from his parents, there had been a period of seven years in which Fīrūz Shāh spent a total of merely thirteen days in Delhi: each time he returned from some protracted campaign, he was off again almost as soon as he entered the capital.[7] This restlessness may have sprung from a consciousness of the grave territorial losses inflicted on the Sultanate in the time of Muḥammad b. Tughluq. The welcome news of Taghai's death at the hands of loyalist commanders in Gujarāt had reached Fīrūz Shāh on the day of Khwāja Jahān's submission.[8] But the rebel's Sūmra allies were still at large; and we are given the impression that the sultan was deeply sensitive to the humiliations suffered by his cousin in Sind and determined on vengeance.[9] Nor could he remain oblivious of the loss of provinces south of the Vindhyas.

The reality, of course, was that Fīrūz Shāh was in no position to retrieve the territories lost in his predecessor's reign. Maʿbar had to be consigned to oblivion. Envoys from Maʿbar who waited on the sultan following his return from the Thatta campaign claimed that their ruler had been defeated and put to death by Bukka, the king of Vijāyanagara, and that the Muslims were in desperate straits. Fīrūz Shāh temporized, observing petulantly that when he had sent them a *farmān* at his accession the people of Maʿbar had failed to acknowledge his authority and now implored his aid because they were hard pressed; he would march south once his troops were rested.[10] At another point, we are told, the sultan set off hunting in the direction of

[5] *SFS*, 283–4 (tr. Rashid, 70–1).

[6] *Ibid.*, 283 (tr. Rashid, 70, omits Dēōgīr *inter alia*). Bākanawr is the Fākanūr of IB, IV, 78–9 (tr. Gibb and Beckingham, 808). For the two Javas, i.e. Sumatra and Java proper (sometimes called Mul Jāwa in Islamic sources), see *ibid.*, IV, 228–47 (tr. Gibb and Beckingham, 876–84); Pelliot, *Notes on Marco Polo*, 755–8.

[7] ʿAfīf, 399. [8] *SFS*, 19, 27–8 (tr. Basu, *JBORS* 23 [1937], 105–6).

[9] ʿAfīf, 191–2.

[10] *Ibid.*, 261–3. Hodivala, *Studies*, I, 326–7, proposes that the dead ruler, called a kinsman of Ḥasan Gangū, was Fakhr al-Dīn Mubārak Shāh, the penultimate sultan of Maʿbar. For the rulers of Maʿbar during this period, see S. Abdul Qadir Husaini, 'The Sultanat of Madura', in HN, 1023–5.

Dawlatābād, but turned back at Bhayāna in view of 'the interests of the kingdom' and headed an expedition to Nagarkōt instead.[11] At the time of his second attack on Thatta, Bahrām Khān Māzandarānī, son-in-law of Ḥasan Gangū, in the course of a struggle with the latter's son, sent word inviting Fīrūz Shāh to come south and take over at Dawlatābād; but the sultan, who was currently refitting his army in Gujarāt, decided to give priority to Thatta and the opportunity was lost.[12] Subsequently, Fīrūz Shāh announced his intention of marching on Dawlatābād, i.e. to overthrow the Bahmanids, only to be dissuaded by the wazir Khān Jahān on the grounds that it was unacceptable to make war on Muslims.[13] Nevertheless, the Bahmanids may have continued to fear an invasion from the north, since according to ʿAfīf the effective administration of his governor Ẓafar Khān (II) in Gujarāt (in the late 1370s) caused trembling (*larza*) in Dawlatābād.[14]

Those military enterprises that Fīrūz Shāh did embark on have scarcely commended him to modern historians. Dr Banerjee characterizes him as 'not even a mediocre military leader'; for Professor Saksena he was 'not the stuff conquerors are made of'; and Professor Riazul Islam declares that 'as a general he was thoroughly incompetent'.[15] These views find ample support from the sultan's operations in Bengal.[16] Large armies were mustered in 754/1353 against Shams al-Dīn Ilyās Shāh, who had twice encroached upon the Delhi Sultan's territory, and in 760/1359 against his son and successor Sikandar. During both invasions, the Delhi forces holed up the enemy in the island fortress of Ikdāla,[17] only then to abandon the campaign. On the first occasion, Fīrūz Shāh managed to defeat Ilyās's forces in a pitched battle and to occupy the town of Ikdāla but, moved by the lamentations of Muslim women in the citadel, he rejected his generals' advice to storm it.[18] In the campaign against Sikandar, Fīrūz Shāh was bought off with gifts and made peace on condition that his client Ẓafar Khān was installed as ruler of Sunārgā'ūn; but the affair drifted into farce when Ẓafar Khān, conscious that he lacked any real power-base in Sunārgā'ūn, opted instead to return with the sultan to Delhi.[19] As the Delhi army retired via Jājnagar, it lost its way, and it was six months before the sultan rejoined his heavy baggage at Kara.[20] In the wake of each campaign, the Bengal ruler sent elephants and other gifts to Fīrūz Shāh, and ʿAfīf

[11] ʿAfīf, 185–6.

[12] *Ibid.*, 224–5. See Hodivala, *Studies*, I, 322, for the chronology.

[13] ʿAfīf, 263–6. [14] *Ibid.*, 499.

[15] Banerjee, *History of Firuz Shah*, 28; see also 26, 32–3. Saksena, in HN, 582. Riazul Islam, 'Fīrūz Shāh Tughluḳ', *Enc.Isl.*², II, 924.

[16] For Fīrūz Shāh's Bengal campaigns, see Banerjee, *History of Firuz Shah*, 28–36, and HN, 582–5, 589–91.

[17] For the location of Ikdāla, now a village in the Dinajpur district and situated about 23 m. N. of Pandūa and 42 m. N. of Lakhnawtī, see Hodivala, *Studies*, I, 311–12.

[18] ʿAfīf, 118–19. [19] *Ibid.*, 156–8, 162.

[20] *Ibid.*, 172–3. Saksena (in HN, 593) discounts this story, which is found in no other source.

claims that the sultan remained on friendly terms with Sikandar, exchanging presents annually with him until his own death.[21]

It was not until *c.* 767/1365–6 that the sultan moved against the Indus delta, now the domain of the two Samma princes, ʿAlā' al-Dīn Jawna, who bore the title of *jām*, and his nephew Banbhīna.[22] Their villainy (*fasād*), according to the *Sīrat*, had lasted for a generation.[23] Ibn Māhrū's correspondence shows that Banbhīna had raided Gujarāt and had attacked the Panjāb with Mongol assistance, probably during Fīrūz Shāh's second absence in Bengal. The government was endeavouring to bolster the position of the Sūmra prince, Hammīr Dūda, who was likewise under threat from the Sammas.[24] The *Sīrat*, composed only a few years later, would have us believe that the Jām and his nephew were forced to sue for peace and that Fīrūz Shāh generously granted them terms, but other authors are less sanguine. In ʿAfīf's version, the tone of which is echoed by Sirhindī, Fīrūz Shāh's operations had been a failure. An epidemic had carried off three-quarters of his horses, and rising grain prices caused a famine among the troops, so that after a few weeks of skirmishing he withdrew into Gujarāt to refit his army. During the retreat the entire fleet fell into the hands of the enemy, and en route for Gujarāt the guides led the Delhi army into the Rann of Kachh, a saline wilderness where the troops suffered dreadfully. When Fīrūz Shāh finally reached Gujarāt, its governor was dismissed for his failure to furnish provisions and fresh troops.[25] But at length the sultan was able to return to Sind, and timed his arrival so as to appropriate the harvest on which the Samma forces had relied. Nevertheless, they offered a desperate resistance, and a prolonged conflict was averted only by the intervention of the local saint Jalāl al-Dīn Bukhārī, which may have been as timely for the Delhi army as it was for the Sammas. The Jām and Banbhīna submitted and the sultan took them back with him to attend his court at Delhi, leaving the Jām's son and Banbhīna's brother Tamachi as joint rulers to represent his interests.[26] Trouble continued from this quarter, however, and Fīrūz Shāh later had to send the Jām to suppress a revolt by Tamachi.

[21] ʿAfīf, 161. *TMS*, 126, 128. *TFS*, 597, also refers briefly to gifts from Ilyās.

[22] For the operations in the Indus delta, see generally Banerjee, *History of Firuz Shah*, 36–40; HN, 595–9. The date is discussed in Hodivala, *Studies*, I, 322, on the basis of the statement in ʿAfīf, 191, that four full years had elapsed since Fīrūz Shāh's return from Jājnagar (dated 762/1361 in *TMS*, 130).

[23] *SFS*, 84.

[24] *IM*, 100–3, 230–5; tr. in Riazul Islam, 'Rise of the Sammas', 361–2, 368. N. B. Ray, 'Interesting side-light on Firuz Shah Tughlaq's expedition to Tatta', *JASB*, *Letters*, 3rd series, 4 (1936), 285–92, gives the first of these letters in full, but Hammīr Dūda's name is garbled so that the translation omits all mention of him: see *ibid.*, 286 n.2, for the date of this letter.

[25] *SFS*, 86–7. ʿAfīf, 200, 201, 207–8, for the epidemic and the famine; 203–5, 220, for the decision to refit the army in Gujarāt; 207 for the loss of the fleet; 208–19 for the Rann; 219–20 for the governor's dismissal. *TMS*, 131. Bihāmadkhānī, fol. 410b (tr. Zaki, 9).

[26] Riazul Islam, 'Rise of the Sammas', 377–9, citing two versions of the saint's table-talk, the *Malfūẓāt-i Makhdūm-i Jahāniyān* and the *Sirāj al-Hidāya*.

The Sammas appear eventually also to have vanquished the Sūmra prince Hammīr Dūda, who is found in exile in Gujarāt before the end of Fīrūz Shāh's reign.[27]

Nor were Fīrūz Shāh's military triumphs over Hindu powers on such a scale as to redeem his reputation. Every year, says ʿAfīf in one of his encomiastic passages, the people of the Dār al-Ḥarb were raided and plundered.[28] The purpose, as so often in the past, was to obtain overdue tribute. En route for Bengal in 754/1353, the sultan had taken the opportunity to assert his authority over the local Hindu chiefs when he reached Awadh and to exact arrears of tribute from the rais of Kharōnsa and Gorakhpūr, of whom the latter, Sirhindī tells us, handed over twenty *laks* (2,000,000) of silver *tangas*.[29] The limited nature of the sultan's aims emerges from his dealings with Jājnagar (Orissa). Having mounted a brief attack on the kingdom of Shankara (Sarangarh), whose ruler fled,[30] he advanced into Jājnagar, whose rai, Vīrabhanūdēva III, had ceased to send tribute.[31] When Fīrūz Shāh had uprooted the idol of Jagannāth and obtained a considerable booty, including a number of elephants, the Hindu king sent an offer of submission, and the two monarchs performed a diplomatic minuet in which the rai claimed to have been the sultan's obedient subject from the first and the sultan alleged that he had entered the country only for the purpose of hunting elephants.

Fīrūz Shāh's most successful campaign – though hardly a triumph[32] – seems to have been that against Nagarkōt. The Hindu prince who had submitted to Muḥammad b. Tughluq in 738/1337 had died, and his son and successor repudiated the overlordship of Delhi. The sultan moved against him in *c.* 766/1365, and subjected the fortress to an investment of several months. At length the rai yielded and undertook to resume tribute payments. Fīrūz Shāh treated the place with consideration, and notably refrained from destroying the idol of Jawālamukhī at the rai's express request.[33] The Nagarkōt region remained submissive thereafter, and would

[27] ᶜAfīf, 254. Riazul Islam, 'Rise of the Sammas', 380. Inscription dated 784/1382 at Fath Masjid, Paranrij, Sabarkantha district, in Desai, 'Khaljī and Tughluq inscriptions from Gujarat', 21–2.

[28] ᶜAfīf, 180.

[29] *TFS*, 587–8. *TMS*, 124–5. ᶜAfīf, 111, mentions merely that the sultan conferred a chatr on the rai of 'Chapāran': for the identification of this Hindu prince with Baranī's rai of Gorakhpūr, see Hodivala, *Studies*, I, 311.

[30] *TMS*, 129. Bihāmadkhānī, fols. 409b-410a (tr. Zaki, 8), describing Shankara as 'one of the great cities of Jājnagar'. The city was identified by Hodivala, *Studies*, I, 387, and II, 149, on the basis of *IM*, 30. Sarangarh lies 32 m. N.W. of Sambalpur, at 21° 36′ N., 83° 7′ E.

[31] Thus according to the *fatḥ-nāma* reproduced in *IM*, 28. Both *SFS*, 54ff. (tr. Roy, 'Jajnagar expedition', 62, 63–4), and ᶜAfīf, 163, comment on the prosperity of Jājnagar. For the identification of the rai, see Hodivala, *Studies*, I, 318. The campaign is discussed in Banerjee, *History of Firuz Shah*, 40–2, and in HN, 591–3.

[32] R. C. Jauhri, 'A medieval invasion of Nagarkot (1363 A.D.)', *JIH* 44 (1966), 571–6.

[33] *SFS*, 82–3. ᶜAfīf, 186–90. For the date, see Hodivala, *Studies*, I, 322.

serve as a valuable base for Fīrūz Shāh's son Muḥammad during the civil war of the early 1390s.

The acquisition of large numbers of elephants was clearly one of the desired objects of these expeditions. Forty-seven were captured from Ilyās, forty were presented by Sikandar, and thirty-three were taken in Jājnagar. According to Ibn Māhrū, the rai of Jājnagar had ceased to send elephants to the sultan, and the account of this campaign in the *Sīrat* reflects the high priority given to the capture of elephants.[34] In addition, Bengal was agriculturally wealthy – a Chinese visitor in the 1340s testifies that reclamation had brought under the plough vast new tracts in the delta[35] – and Ilyās had in 1346 made a lucrative raid on Nepal.[36] Fīrūz Shāh also brought back large quantities of silver, to which, as we saw (p. 261), Bengal had access in plenty and which was still in short supply within his own dominions.[37] Perhaps the sultan, who allegedly observed to Tatar Khān in 754/1353 that his predecessors had reduced Bengal but had proved unable to control it in view of the nature of the terrain,[38] aimed no higher than replenishing his treasury and the *pīlkhāna*.

The great majority of the operations against the Hindus of which ʿAfīf speaks did not involve the sultan's participation, being presumably conducted under the aegis of the local muqtaʿs; and Sirhindī praises the great amirs in the direction of 'Hindūstān' for chastizing 'rebellious infidels' and maintaining the authority of Delhi.[39] But conditions may have deteriorated during the sultan's last twelve years, when he is supposed to have abandoned military activity but we suddenly see him campaigning personally in Katēhr and Etāwa for the purpose of securing tribute; ʿAfīf, taking his cue from Fīrūz Shāh himself, dresses up these attacks as hunting expeditions.[40] In 787/1385–6 the sultan constructed the new fortress of Fīrūzpūr at Bīūlī (Beoli), some fifteen miles from Badā'ūn, as part of his defence measures in the region.[41] In Etāwa, during a campaign in 779/1377–8, the two *muqaddams*, Sumēr and Uddharān, were taken to Delhi, and fortresses were built at Akhal (renamed Tughluqpūr) and *Patlāhī. A new fortress at Fīrūzpūr (near Kanar) became the centre of a new *shiqq*, incorporating Tughluqpūr and Rāprī, which was entrusted to Malikzāda

[34] *IM*, 28. *SFS*, 54, 58, 63 (tr. Roy, 'Jajnagar expedition', 61–2, 65). ʿAfīf, 123, 161, 163, 167, 171; cf. also 172, 175, for the total of seventy-three elephants from Bengal and Jājnagar. *IM*, 32, gives fifty-three as the number of elephants surrendered by the rai of Jājnagar. *TFS*, 592, 594, gives the total number of elephants taken on the first Bengal expedition as forty-four.

[35] W. W. Rockhill, 'Notes on the relations and trade of China with the eastern archipelago and the coast of the Indian Ocean during the fourteenth century', *T'oung Pao* 16 (1915), 435–6, citing the *Tao-i chih-lüeh* of Wang Ta-yüan (1350).

[36] K. P. Jayaswal, 'An unrecorded Muḥammadan inscription of Nepal', *JBORS* 22 (1936), part 2, 93–5. Dani, *Muslim inscriptions of Bengal*, 129.

[37] *TFS*, 597. Simon Digby, 'The Broach coin-hoard as evidence of the import of valuta across the Arabian Sea during the 13th and 14th centuries', *JRAS* (1980), 129, 135–6 n.4.

[38] ʿAfīf, 119. [39] *TMS*, 133. [40] ʿAfīf, 493, 497.

[41] *TMS*, 135. For the location of Beoli, see Hodivala, *Studies*, I, 389.

Fīrūz (later wazir to Sultan Tughluq Shāh II), son of Tāj al-Dīn Turk: it was to become the nucleus of the principality of Kālpī.[42]

The sultan and the nobility

Both ʿAfīf and Sirhindī point to the fact that Fīrūz Shāh's era witnessed only one revolt (namely, by a Muslim noble), that of Shams al-Dīn Dāmghānī in 782/1380–1, and the former expressly draws a contrast with the turbulence of Muḥammad b. Tughluq's reign.[43] Dāmghānī, appointed na'ib of the iqtaʿ of Gujarāt in 778/1377, failed to realize the enormous sums for which he had contracted, omitted to despatch to court any of the revenue he had raised, and rose in open rebellion. His extortionate measures, however, had alienated those on whose support his revolt depended, the *amīrān-i ṣada* of Gujarāt, who remained loyal to the sultan; they attacked and killed him. Apart from this episode, which ʿAfīf dismisses as a farce,[44] the absence of revolt by Muslim nobles bears out the picture of the reign furnished by our sources, as an era of contentment among the aristocracy.[45]

Yet such remarkable quiescence was obtained at a price. Unlike his predecessor, Fīrūz Shāh was notoriously uninterested in the details of day-to-day fiscal administration,[46] and almost from the beginning left the conduct of affairs to the wazir Khān Jahān. The new wazir proved to be the main pillar of the regime. During Fīrūz Shāh's absences on campaign, he contrived to overawe the capital with demonstrations of military force, and skilfully concealed from the citizens the lack of news from the sultan when the Delhi army got lost on the way back from Jājnagar and again when Fīrūz Shāh found himself in the Rann of Kachh.[47] But as Baranī had pointedly observed, Khān Jahān enjoyed more extensive powers than had been vouchsafed to any previous wazir, and ʿAfīf quotes the sultan himself as saying that Khān Jahān was the real ruler of Delhi.[48] When the wazir clashed with ʿAyn al-Mulk Ibn Māhrū, who was then serving as accountant-general (*mushrif-i mamālik*), he got his own way by threatening to leave for Mecca. The sultan capitulated and gave Khān Jahān permission to employ and dismiss whomsoever he wished. Ibn Māhrū thus forfeited his post; though when shortly granted the iqtaʿs of Multān, Sīwistān and Bhakkar, he secured from Fīrūz Shāh the concession that the finances of these territories would lie outside the wazir's jurisdiction.[49]

Fīrūz Shāh seems to have assigned a significantly higher proportion of

[42] Bihāmadkhānī, fol. 412b (tr. Zaki, 13–14). *TMS*, 133–4.
[43] ʿAfīf, 492–3; 497 for the date of the revolt, which is discussed in Hodivala, *Studies*, I, 388–9. *TMS*, 132, gives 778, the year of Dāmghānī's appointment.
[44] ʿAfīf, 499–502. [45] *Ibid.*, 288, 297–8. [46] *Ibid.*, 341–2.
[47] *Ibid.*, 173, 211–14, 398–9. [48] *TFS*, 578–9. ʿAfīf, 400; cf. also 411.
[49] *Ibid.*, 408–14.

the Sultanate's territories as iqtaʿ, thus reducing the extent of the khalisa. The nobility as a whole, moreover, now enjoyed greater privileges than in the time of Muḥammad b. Tughluq. We may perhaps explain the fact that the salaries of khans and maliks were now considerably higher than in the previous reign as a measure designed to protect them against inflation (see below, p. 316).[50] But already, within the first six years of Fīrūz Shāh's era, Baranī could observe that the revenue from the iqtaʿs was not audited with the same rigour as before; and ʿAfīf tells us specifically that the sultan departed from previous practice in having the annual gifts presented by the provincial governors valued and offset against the revenue-demand from their territories. Certain of the amirs, notably the *ʿāriḍ* ʿImād al-Mulk Bashīr, accumulated enormous fortunes.[51]

It was the sultan's policy also to allow the heir of an amir, a muqtaʿ or an official to inherit his father's position, title, and iqtaʿs or other emoluments. In some measure this pattern of inheritance had obtained previously – certainly in the thirteenth century (pp. 101–2 above), even if it had perhaps been attenuated under ʿAlāʾ al-Dīn and discontinued by the first two Tughluqids. But under Fīrūz Shāh it undoubtedly became the norm. When Khān Jahān (I) died, for instance, his office of wazir and his title both passed to his son Jawnān, who was henceforth known as Khān Jahān (II); Ẓafar Khān, the refugee amir from Bengal, was succeeded in his iqtaʿ of Gujarāt by his son Daryā Khān, who was likewise given the title of Ẓafar Khān (II); and the rank and title of the *ʿāriḍ* ʿImād al-Mulk Bashīr passed on his death to his son Isḥāq.[52] Such examples could be multiplied, and they extended to all levels of the bureaucracy.[53] Even in an emergency, as when he transferred Malik Naṣīr al-Mulk Mardān Dawlat from the east to the Multān frontier to deal with the Mongol threat, Fīrūz Shāh did not disregard the hereditary principle: Naṣīr al-Mulk's iqtaʿs of Kara and Mahōba were simply assigned to his adopted son Sulaymān.[54] Naṣīr al-Mulk's son Malik Shaykh followed him for a short time in the command at Multān; and after his death, Sulaymān was transferred to Multān, where he in turn was soon succeeded by his own son Khiḍr Khān.[55]

The allusion to the system of hereditary offices in the *Futūḥāt-i Fīrūz-Shāhī* indicates that the sultan took some pride in it, and it is laid to his credit also by the author of the *Sīrat*.[56] But that such a policy was likely to

[50] *Ibid.*, 296–7. Habib, 'Agrarian economy', 73.

[51] *TFS*, 555–6. ᶜAfīf, 268–9. For Bashīr's wealth, see *ibid.*, 438, 439–40, 445.

[52] Khān Jahān: *ibid.*, 425–6. Ẓafar Khān: *ibid.*, 286, 499; *TMS*, 131. ᶜImād al-Mulk: ᶜAfīf, 445. *SFS*, 153–4, gives a list of such hereditary appointments, headed by Khān Jahān (I).

[53] For two instances from the *dīwān-i wizārat*, see ᶜAfīf, 482.

[54] *TMS*, 133.

[55] *Ibid.*, 182. HN, 632, may be wrong in emphasizing that the appointments of Mardān's successors dated from after Fīrūz Shāh's death; Khiḍr Khān, who received his title in 791/1389, had previously, as muqtaᶜ of Multān, himself borne the style of Naṣīr al-Mulk: *TMS*, 146, 147.

[56] *FFS*, 18 (tr. Roy, 463). *SFS*, 153–5.

implant in the *dīwān-i wizārat*, for example, officials who were unequal to their task was the complaint of Shams al-Dīn Abū-Rijā when auditor-general (*mustawfī-yi mamālik*).[57] When applied to provincial governorships, it would in time have the effect of creating entrenched regional interests and the autonomous principalities which emerged in the era of Fīrūz Shāh's grandsons.

The first civil war

Of the events of the crisis that began in the twilight years of Fīrūz Shāh's reign, we learn a good deal from two authors, Sirhindī and Bihāmadkhānī.[58] But the wherewithal to explain it is more elusive; and here ʿAfīf, through occasional references to the troubles in his *Ta'rīkh-i Fīrūz-Shāhī*, provides greater insight. It seems that the activities of Shams al-Dīn Abū Rijā, who had made enemies of all the amirs and whose disgrace in 786/1384 preceded the crisis, had already thrown the state into confusion,[59] perhaps because the nobility saw its fiscal autonomy as under threat. It needs also to be borne in mind that Fīrūz Shāh was by now relatively advanced in age (he was eighty-three lunar years old when he died in 790/1388) and had been ill since 786/1384, and according to ʿAfīf most or all of his contemporaries among the grandees had predeceased him.[60] The links that bound together the sultan and the new generation of amirs had presumably slackened. But what especially brought disaster on the empire was, in ʿAfīf's view, the rivalry between the wazir, Khān Jahān (II), and Fīrūz Shāh's son Muḥammad.[61]

During the sultan's last years, the wazir was able to exercise virtually untrammelled power and used the opportunity to remove various amirs and maliks who opposed him.[62] The death of Fīrūz Shāh's grandson Fatḥ Khān in 778/1376 had been a heavy blow to him,[63] and Bihāmadkhānī claims that he selected as his heir his great-grandson, Fatḥ Khān's son Tughluq Shāh (see appendix VI).[64] When in 789/1387 the wazir endeavoured to turn the subservient sultan against his only surviving son, Prince Muḥammad, a crisis arose; he was obliged to flee from Fīrūzābād and was subsequently killed in Mēō territory. Those of the wazir's adherents who were executed after his overthrow included Malik Bihzād-i Fatḥkhānī, presumably a former slave of Prince Fatḥ Khān,[65] and it may be that we are dealing

57 ᶜAfīf, 474–5.
58 For what follows, see generally HN, 618–22; Husain, *Tughluq dynasty*, 441–50.
59 ᶜAfīf, 455–6, 457, 459, 492, 498.
60 *Ibid.*, 444–5, 497 (where the majority are said to have died in 781/1379–80), 498. For a list of leading nobles who died before 772/1370–1, including Khudāwand Khān, Dā'ūd Khān b. Bayyū, Ibn Māhrū and Ikhtiyār al-Dīn-i Nuwā, see *SFS*, 154. For the year of Fīrūz Shāh's birth, see above, p. 249, n.70.
61 ᶜAfīf, 427.
62 *TMS*, 135–6.
63 ᶜAfīf, 494.
64 Bihāmadkhānī, fol. 414a (tr. Zaki, 16).
65 *TMS*, 137.

simply with two groups that had coalesced around Muḥammad and around the descendants of his eldest brother. Muḥammad was now made wazir and then enthroned as joint sultan in Shaʿbān 789/August 1387. At this stage, we are told, he enjoyed the sympathy of not only the amirs and the people of the capital but also Fīrūz Shāh's slaves.[66] This group may have joined him out of hatred for the wazir, since the principal slaves are said to have been alarmed at an earlier date by the growing power of Khān Jahān (I).[67] But after five months the slaves turned against Muḥammad, according to Sirhindī, out of antipathy towards his favourites, Samā' al-Dīn (now entitled Muʿīn al-Mulk) and Kamāl al-Dīn (Dastūr Khān), the two sons of Malik ʿUmar, the *ʿāriḍ-i bandagān-i khāṣṣ*; although ʿAfīf, obscurely, attributes the change of allegiance to the enormous sums left by the old sultan's *ʿāriḍ*, Malik Bashīr ʿImād al-Mulk.[68]

Muḥammad in turn was expelled from the capital and retired to Nagarkōt, and the old sultan now recognized as co-ruler Tughluq Shāh, who was enthroned as Sultan Ghiyāth al-Dīn when Fīrūz Shāh died on 18 Ramaḍān 790/20 September 1388. On 21 Ṣafar 791/20 February 1389, however, Tughluq Shāh and his wazir, Malikzāda Fīrūz (Fīrūz Khān) b. Tāj al-Dīn Turk (ancestor of the later rulers of Kālpī), were killed in a rising by the *nā'ib-wazīr* Rukn al-Dīn Junda (p. 190 above), who put Abū Bakr Shāh, a grandson of Fīrūz Shāh, on the throne. Junda was promoted to wazir, but shortly plotted to remove Abū Bakr in turn, perhaps proclaiming another of Fīrūz Shāh's grandsons, Fīrūz Shāh b. Ẓafar,[69] and was killed. Over the next two years Muḥammad, based first at Sāmāna and then at Jalēsar in the Doab, sent troops to ravage the territory surrounding Delhi and himself made three unsuccessful attempts on the capital.

The situation, as Sirhindī observed, was one of stalemate, for Abū Bakr could not be dislodged but when victorious was unable to leave the capital and pursue his enemy; with Muḥammad, on the other hand, were ranged 'all the amirs, maliks, troops (*ḥasham*), retainers (*khadam*) and subjects (*raʿāyā*) of the empire'.[70] Abū Bakr's strength lay in his possession of the capital and the elephantry and in the allegiance of his grandfather's slaves.[71] Muḥammad, who recognized them as the principal obstacle to his success, ordered his adherents in the provinces to arrest and kill all the old sultan's slaves on 19 Ramaḍān 791/11 September 1389.[72] This mass execution testifies to the widespread support for Muḥammad among the military class outside the Delhi complex. Tughluq Shāh had exiled Ghālib Khān, the son

[66] *Ibid.*, 136–7. [67] ᶜAfīf, 415. [68] *TMS*, 139. ᶜAfīf, 440.

[69] 'Note on a gold coin bearing the name of Prince Fírúz Sháh Zafar, son of Fírúz Sháh of Dihlí', *JASB* 40 (1871), 160. Thomas, 300. But both authors assume incorrectly that the prince named is the old sultan's son Ẓafar and that this issue of 791 was therefore posthumous. Cf. also *CMSD*, 191–4 (nos. 771–779A), 223–4.

[70] *TMS*, 148. [71] *Ibid.*, 146. Bihāmadkhānī, fols. 421b, 422a (tr. Zaki, 30, 31).

[72] *TMS*, 146; for the massacre, see 147.

and successor of Malik Qabūl 'Qur'ān-khwān', and deprived him of Sāmāna; but his own nominee as muqtaʿ was killed in Ṣafar 791/February 1389 by the *amīrān-i ṣada* of that territory, who invited in Muḥammad, and Ghālib Khān was restored.[73] The commanders who joined Muḥammad with their forces for his various attacks on Delhi included the muqtaʿs of Multān and Bihār, the sons of the governors of Qinnawj and Awadh, the Mā'in and Bhattī chiefs who held iqtaʿs in the eastern Panjāb, *muqaddams* from the hills (presumably the Qarāchīl foothills) and rais and ranas from Etāwa.[74] Support for Abū Bakr is found only in Alwar, where he could count on the Mēō chieftain Bahādur Nāhir.[75] In Gujarāt the na'ib, the Fīrūz Shāhī slave Malik Mufarrij Sulṭānī, had in 789/1387 killed Sikandar Khān, newly arrived as governor on Muḥammad's behalf, and had been recognized by Tughluq Shāh as governor with the style of Rāstī Khān; but whether he transferred his allegiance to Abū Bakr is unknown.[76]

It is unclear why in Ramaḍān 792/August 1390 a split emerged within the slaves' ranks, and a group of them, headed by Islām Khān Mubashshir-i Chap Sulṭānī, invited in Muḥammad. The fact that the prince's own party included Fīrūz Shāhī slaves – Malik Sarwar Sulṭānī, the *shiḥna* of Delhi, whom Muḥammad had made wazir with the style of Khwāja Jahān, appears throughout as his loyal adherent[77] – may help to explain the readiness of certain of the slaves in Abū Bakr's camp to give him possession of the capital. Bihāmadkhānī, moreover, says that Malik Shāhīn Sulṭānī, entitled ʿImād al-Mulk, the former commander of Fīrūz Shāh's *pīlkhāna*, had been driven from the city by the amirs responsible for the overtures to Muḥammad,[78] suggesting that the change of allegiance may have been connected with rivalry between Islām Khān and ʿImād al-Mulk. Once securely in possession of the elephantry, however, and possibly after offering a guarantee to his new ally Islām Khān, Muḥammad had all the slaves expelled from Delhi or put to death.[79] In 794/1392 Khwāja Jahān Sarwar, whom Islām Khān had replaced as wazir, trumped up charges against his rival; and despite his services in the final engagement with Abū Bakr, Islām Khān was executed.[80] We still hear occasionally of Fīrūz Shāhī

[73] *Ibid.*, 140, 145; for Ghālib Khān restored in Sāmāna, *ibid.*, 147, 156. His genealogy is given in Bihāmadkhānī, fol. 431b (tr. Zaki, 45).

[74] *TMS*, 145, 146–7.

[75] *Ibid.*, 146, 149, 151; he had supported Tughluq Shāh also (*ibid.*, 142). Bihāmadkhānī, fols. 423a, 426 (tr. Zaki, 32, 35).

[76] *TMS*, 138; also 142 for Tughluq Shāh's recognition.

[77] *Ibid.*, 146, 147, 152–3. Bihāmadkhānī, fol. 421b (tr. Zaki, 30). ᶜAfīf, 338, says that he was in charge of Fīrūz Shāh's jewel-house (*jawāhir-khāna*).

[78] *TMS*, 148, 149–50. Bihāmadkhānī, fols. 421a, 423a (tr. Zaki, 29, 32). For Shāhīn, see also ᶜAfīf, 338.

[79] *TMS*, 149–50. Bihāmadkhānī, fol. 425b, saying that the sultan *ᶜahd-u paymān ba-tajdīd dar āwurd* with Islām Khān (tr. Zaki, 34).

[80] *TMS*, 152–3. Bihāmadkhānī, fol. 430b (tr. Zaki, 44), gives a briefer account of the plot, but does not mention Khwāja Jahān's role.

slaves thereafter;[81] but Muḥammad's accession marks the destruction of this highly volatile element as a force capable of making and unmaking sultans.

According to Bihāmadkhānī, Muḥammad's triumph brought about peace and repose.[82] Abū Bakr, expelled from Delhi, fled to Alwar, where his uncle's forces defeated him in Muḥarram of the following year/December 1390; he shortly died as a prisoner at Amrōha. The sultan also acted quickly to restore his authority in Gujarāt, where in Ṣafar 794/January 1392 the hostile Mufarrij (Rāstī Khān) was defeated and killed by Muḥammad's appointee, Ẓafar Khān Wajīh al-Mulk.[83] But Bihāmadkhānī's encomium can only have applied to the capital and the more westerly provinces, since the sultan had to spend the rest of his reign fighting Hindu chieftains in Alwar and the Doab.

Loss of territory to the infidel

'Thanks to the contest among the Muslims for the sovereignty,' says Sirhindī, 'the infidels of Hindūstān gained in strength, refrained from paying the jizya and the kharaj and plundered the Muslim townships (*qaṣabāt*).'[84] As we have seen, the old sultan's last years had not been free of disturbances, but Hindu princes appear to have asserted themselves more vigorously in the wake of Muḥammad's expulsion from Delhi in 789/1387. There are signs of a struggle with the local Hindus around Nāgawr in that year and again in 791/1389, when the na'ib of the *shiqq* of Nāgawr and Jālōr was killed.[85] We are more fully informed about conditions in the southern Doab, as in Etāwa for instance, and the territories south of the Yamuna which would later form the independent principality of Kālpī. In Etāwa, Uddharān and Sumēr, who had supported Muḥammad, returned home and rose in revolt following Tughluq Shāh's accession, inflicting a heavy defeat on Malik Maḥmūd, who now governed the *shiqq* of Fīrūzpūr in succession to his father, the wazir Fīrūz Khān b. Tāj al-Dīn Turk. Tughluqpūr was surrendered to the enemy, and the towns of Chandāwar, Bhōngā'ūn and Rewa, among others, all fell into the hands of Hindu princes. For the moment, Malik Maḥmūd was able to do no more than occupy Kālpī, which he renamed Muḥammadābād, in 792/1390 and to make it his headquarters.[86]

In 794/1391–2 Sultan Muḥammad took the field against the enemy in

81 *TMS*, 160. Yazdī, *ZN*, ed. Ilahdād, II, 64/ed. Urunbaev, fol. 310a, however, seems to apply the term (wrongly) to Mallū Iqbāl Khān and his associates.

82 Bihāmadkhānī, fol. 424b (tr. Zaki, 33).

83 Harawī, III, 83, 84–5. Misra, 141–2, citing the *Ṭabaqāt-i Maḥmūd-Shāhī* and the *Mir'āt-i Sikandarī*, respectively fifteenth- and sixteenth-century chronicles of Gujarāt.

84 *TMS*, 147.

85 *ARIE* (1975–6), 163 (D188). *ARIE* (1969–70), 93 (D167).

86 These events are described only by Bihāmadkhānī, fols. 418b–419b (reading RYWH for RTWH), 436b–437a (tr. Zaki, 26–7, 54).

Etāwa, where Uddharān and Sumēr had sacked Balārām. Having razed Etāwa to the ground, the sultan moved back across the Ganges and chastised the Hindus of Qinnawj and Dalmaw, building a fortress at Jalēsar, which he renamed Muḥammadābād. In Alwar Bahādur Nāhir, who had consistently sided with Muḥammad Shāh's enemies, continued to defy him and had to be driven from Kōtla; in the west, the Khōkhar chief Shaikha rebelled and sacked Lahore in 796/1394, and a punitive expedition was in preparation under Muḥammad Shāh's son Humāyūn Khān when the sultan died.[87]

The second civil war

Muḥammad did not long enjoy the throne for which he had mounted such a determined struggle, dying on 17 Rabīʿ I 796/20 January 1394.[88] Humāyūn Khān, who succeeded him as 'Alā' al-Dīn Sikandar Shāh, followed him to the grave on 5 Jumādā I/8 March, and a younger son was thereupon proclaimed sultan as Nāṣir al-Dīn Maḥmūd Shāh. The new monarch was to prove little more than a cipher. There is a suggestion that his enthronement commanded scant support, for the wazir Khwāja Jahān Sarwar had to persuade the amirs whose territories lay to the west, like Ghālib Khān of Sāmāna and Rai Kamāl al-Dīn Mā'in, not to leave Delhi without pledging their allegiance.[89] But in Rajab 796/May 1394 Khwāja Jahān was sent east with an army, twenty elephants and the title of Sulṭān al-Sharq, and entrusted with the territories 'from Qinnawj to Bihār', so that he might clear the region of recalcitrant Hindu chieftains.[90] He set up his headquarters at Jawnpūr and never returned to Delhi. Power at court was disputed among a number of war-lords, notably Muḥammad (Tatar Khān), son of Wajīh al-Mulk Ẓafar Khān the governor of Gujarāt, and a group whom Bihāmadkhānī calls Muḥammad Shāh's more important slaves (*bandagān-i kibār*), notably Muqarrab al-Mulk (styled Muqarrab Khān), ʿAbd al-Rashīd Sulṭānī (entitled Saʿādat Khān) and Mallū (later Iqbāl Khān). Saʿādat Khān was ousted by a conspiracy in which Mallū was implicated, and took refuge with Tatar Khān. Having lost possession of the sultan, Tatar Khān's party in Muḥarram 797/October 1394 enthroned at Fīrūzābād a younger brother of Tughluq Shāh II as Nāṣir al-Dīn Nuṣrat Shāh.[91]

There were now once more two rival sultans, each with his own capital

[87] *TMS*, 154.

[88] For the second civil war, see generally HN, 623–5; Husain, *Tughluq dynasty*, 452–60; Lal, *Twilight*, 8–12.

[89] *TMS*, 156.

[90] *Ibid.*, 156–7. His career is traced in Mian Muḥammad Saeed, *The Sharqi Sultanate of Jaunpur* (Karachi, 1972), 20–35.

[91] *TMS*, 158–9. Bihāmadkhānī, fols. 432b–433a (tr. Zaki, 47–8), alone refers to Mallū and the others as slaves of Muḥammad Shāh; he does not mention the conspiracy against Saʿādat Khān, and gives greater prominence to Tatar Khān's role than does Sirhindī. Nuṣrat Shāh's

city and military establishment and each a puppet in the hands of powerful grandees. This situation persisted for three years, with fighting between the two sides an almost daily occurrence. According to Sirhindī, Maḥmūd Shāh's party controlled only Old Delhi and Sīrī. At Fīrūzābād, Nuṣrat Shāh and Tatar Khān commanded the allegiance of the Doab, together with Sōnpat, Pānīpat, Jhajhar and Rohtak.[92] The omission of any of the Sultanate's other territories demonstrates how little impact events at the centre now had on the governors of major provinces, although coins and inscriptions continued to indicate a nominal allegiance: thus Maḥmūd Shāh was recognized in the regions controlled by Khwāja Jahān, whereas Ẓafar Khān in Gujarāt acknowledged Nuṣrat Shāh.[93]

When recounting Temür's invasion a few years later, the Timurid chronicler Sharaf al-Dīn Yazdī was under the impression that Mallū and his brother Sārang Khān, since Maḥmūd Shāh's accession governor of Dēōpālpūr, were the real masters of his empire;[94] and Professor Hambly has shown how the partnership sought to dominate the Sultanate from two distinct bases, Sārang Khān in the Panjāb and Mallū Iqbāl Khān at Delhi.[95] From Dēōpālpūr Sārang Khān had embarked in 798/1395–6 on a sustained effort to bring the neighbouring territories under his own control (and hence, very indirectly, under that of Maḥmūd Shāh). Shaikha was defeated, and Lahore reoccupied.[96] For a time Sārang Khān also held Multān; the muqtaʿ, Khiḍr Khān, was taken prisoner but later escaped. But when Sārang Khān attacked Sāmāna, Ghālib Khān appealed to Tatar Khān, who in Muḥarram 800/October 1397 defeated Sārang Khān and drove him back to Multān, reinstating his protégé in Sāmāna.[97] In Dhu'l-Qaʿda/October–November 1398 Mallū, who had meanwhile briefly declared for Nuṣrat Shāh only to seize control of his elephants and had then put himself at the head of the rival group by the elimination of Muqarrab Khān, moved against Tatar Khān's base at Pānīpat, which he captured. Tatar Khān, weakened by the desertion of prominent supporters, retired to his father in Gujarāt.[98] Mallū Iqbāl Khān was thus left in undisputed control of both

laqab appears as Shams al-Dīn in an inscription of 797/1395: Desai, 'Khaljī and Tughluq inscriptions from Gujarat', 37–8.

92 *TMS*, 159–61. Bihāmadkhānī, fol. 433 (tr. Zaki, 48).

93 Desai, 'Khaljī and Tughluq inscriptions from Gujarat', 34–8. Sayyid Yūsuf Kamāl Bukhārī, 'Inscriptions from Manēr', *EIAPS* (1951–2), 15–16.

94 Yazdī, *ZN*, ed. Ilahdād, II, 14–15/ed. Urunbaev, fol. 296a (duplicated at 301a). For Sārang Khān's appointment, see *TMS*, 156.

95 Gavin R. G. Hambly, 'Twilight of Tughluqid Delhi', in Frykenberg (ed.), *Delhi through the ages*, 47–56.

96 *TMS*, 157–8.

97 *Ibid.*, 161–2. Khiḍr Khān's capture is mentioned only by Yazdī, *ZN*, ed. Ilahdād, II, 175 (omitted in Urunbaev edn, fol. 341a).

98 *TMS*, 163–5. Bihāmadkhānī, fols. 433b-434b (tr. Zaki, 49–50). Faḍl-Allāh Balkhī as Mallū's lieutenant in 801/1398: Ghiyāth al-Dīn Yazdī, tr. Semenov, 121; Shāmī, *ZN*, I, 191; Yazdī, *ZN*, ed. Ilahdād, II, 116/ed. Urunbaev, fol. 324b. *TMS*, 160, earlier lists him among Nuṣrat Shāh's adherents.

capitals, Delhi and Fīrūzābād, and of Sultan Maḥmūd Shāh. The chronology of his various acts of duplicity suggests that he was attempting to shore up his position in reaction to the elimination of his brother Sārang Khān at Multān by Temür's forces (p. 313 below). Only a few weeks later, however, Mallū in turn was effectively swept away by Temür.[99]

The north-west frontier and Temür's invasion

The sources depict Fīrūz Shāh's reign as relatively free of Mongol attacks.[100] Nevertheless, they appear still to have been a regular occurrence. Baranī mentions just two minor inroads in the period of six years before he ceased writing.[101] One took place in the neighbourhood of the Sōdra river (the Chenāb), while the other, into Gujarāt, which was checked partly by the sultan's troops and in part by the *muqaddams* of the region, may have been connected with the encouragement given to the Mongols by the Samma prince Banbhīna, about which Ibn Māhrū complains.[102] Sirhindī tells us briefly that towards the end of 759/1358 the Mongols invaded the Dēōpālpūr territory but withdrew on the advance of the sultan's forces under Malik Qabūl ('Qur'ān-khwān').[103] The *Sīrat*, lastly, claims that the Mongols were in the habit of advancing to the Bēāh and harassing the villages, but refers to a defeat inflicted on them by the army of Delhi in the year of Fīrūz Shāh's Nagarkōt campaign (i.e. *c.* 767/1365–6).[104] The sultan was sufficiently anxious about the Mongol frontier to transfer there from the east Naṣīr al-Mulk Malik Mardān Dawlat, because he allegedly had no one else of the calibre necessary to deal with the Mongol danger.[105]

More than this we are not told; nor are the attacks we know of easily linked up with events in the Chaghadayid territories. Here the death in 759/1358 of Muḥammad b. Tughluq's ally, the Qara'unas noyan Qazaghan, had inaugurated a lengthy period of strife among the clan leaders and provoked two brief interventions in Transoxiana by the eastern Chaghadayid khan, Tughluq Temür. Temür, a member of the Turco-Mongol clan of the Barlas, collaborated for a time against the invaders with Qazaghan's grandson Ḥusayn; but the allies shortly fell out, and in 771/1369–70 Temür vanquished Ḥusayn and replaced him as the real ruler of the western Chaghadayid ulus.[106] The effects of these upheavals were felt in the Indian

[99] Hambly, 'Twilight', 50–1, similarly proposes that the activities of Mallū and Sārang Khān were closely connected. But I am not convinced by his suggestion that Sārang Khān's move against Sāmāna was part of a plan to join forces with his brother in order better to resist the imminent invasion of Pīr Muḥammad. Sirhindī's chronology makes it clear that Sārang Khān was eliminated before Mallū embarked upon his complicated intrigues between the two rival sultans.

[100] ᶜAfīf, 321. [101] *TFS*, 601. [102] *IM*, 101; and see also 230.

[103] *TMS*, 127. Qur'ān-khwān subsequently became muqtaᶜ of Sāmāna (p. 187 above).

[104] *SFS*, 285–6. [105] *TMS*, 133: the context suggests the 1370s.

[106] Beatrice Forbes Manz, 'The ulus Chaghatay before and after Temür's rise to power: the

borderlands as well as in Transoxiana. In 763/1361–2 Tughluq Temür's army is said to have plundered the territory as far as the Hindu Kush.[107] Qazaghan's sons had fled to Kābul and Ghazna on their father's murder, and the region seems to have served as the power-base of Ḥusayn, who was active there in 761/1360 and later, with Temür's aid, recovered Kābul from his enemies.[108] We have seen (pp. 224, 228–9) how Mongol amirs sought refuge across the Indus during the early years of the century; and commanders who lost out in these fresh conflicts likewise turned towards India, as Ḥusayn at one point contemplated doing and as his sons did following his overthrow in 771/1369–70.[109] But our Indian sources supply too little detail to enable us to make any connections with the few Mongol inroads they record.

Once Temür had supplanted Ḥusayn as *de facto* ruler of the western half of Chaghadai's ulus, it was vital for him to absorb the energies of the tribes in external campaigns; and this was also a means of denying a refuge outside the ulus to dissident noyans.[110] But Temür, who was not of Chinggisid blood and who ruled the ulus through a puppet khan (actually chosen from the line of Ögödei), appears to have seen it as his task to reconstitute Chinggis Khan's empire, though largely in the form of protectorates under Chaghadayid overlordship.[111] With this in view, he launched attacks on the Kartid kingdom of Herat, whose 'Tājīk' ruler had displayed the effrontery to assume the style of sultan (p. 235 above); on the various other powers that had sprung up amid the ruins of the Ilkhanate; and on the Golden Horde.[112] Although the justification given for his invasion of India towards the end of the century was religious and couched in terms of the spread of Islam, it can only have been a façade: the most that can be said on this count is that the aim was perhaps to punish Muslim rulers for permitting such licence to their vast numbers of Hindu subjects and servitors.[113]

According to Bihāmadkhānī, Temür and Fīrūz Shāh had corresponded, and it may be for this reason that Muḥammad b. Fīrūz at one point thought

transformation from tribal confederation to army of conquest', *CAJ* 27 (1983), 86–95, and her *Rise and rule*, 41–57.

107 Shāmī, *ZN*, I, 18–19. Yazdī, *ZN*, ed. Ilahdād, I, 59/ed. Urunbaev, fol. 100a. P. Jackson, 'Tughluḳ Temür', *Enc.Isl.*^{2}.

108 Naṭanzī, 197. Shāmī, *ZN*, I, 51. Yazdī, *ZN*, ed. Ilahdād, I, 48, 175/ed. Urunbaev, fols. 97a, 130b.

109 Shāmī, *ZN*, I, 31. Yazdī, *ZN*, ed. Ilahdād, I, 71, 206/ed. Urunbaev, fols. 103a, 139a.

110 Manz, 'Ulus Chaghatay', 98.

111 Hans Robert Roemer, 'Tīmūr in Iran', in P. Jackson and L. Lockhart (eds.), *The Cambridge history of Iran*, VI. *The Timurid and Safavid periods* (Cambridge, 1986), 52, 57, 72.

112 For these campaigns, see *ibid.*, 46–73; Tilman Nagel, *Timur der Eroberer und die islamische Welt des späten Mittelalters* (Munich, 1993), 377–86; a brief survey in Manz, *Rise and rule*, 67–73.

113 See, e.g., Ghiyāth al-Dīn Yazdī, *Rūz-Nāma*, tr. Semenov, 60; Shāmī, *ZN*, I, 170; Yazdī, *ZN*, ed. Ilahdād, II, 15/ed. Urunbaev, fol. 296a.

of abandoning the struggle against Abū Bakr Shāh and seeking Temür's assistance; he had actually set out for Samarqand with a small group of followers when he was invited to come to Delhi and take the throne.[114] Although the journey to Transoxiana proved unnecessary, it is possible that some message had been despatched to Samarqand in advance. But in all likelihood Temür needed no invitation to intervene in the chaos within the Delhi Sultanate, which presented him with an ideal opportunity for plunder.[115]

Temür's grandson Pīr Muḥammad, who governed much of present-day Afghanistan from Kābul, crossed the Indus in Rabīʿ I 800/November–December 1397 and defeated the troops sent to relieve Uchch by Sārang Khān, who was then himself forced to surrender Multān in Ramaḍān/June 1398. Pīr Muḥammad established his headquarters in the city.[116] Temür arrived in the Multān region in mid Ṣafar 801/late in October. Sending his main force by way of Dēōpālpūr and Sāmāna, he marched via Bhatnēr and Sarsatī, putting both strongholds to the sack, before rejoining the rest of his troops on the banks of the Ghaggar. On 7 Rabīʿ II 801/16 December 1398 he did battle with Mallū Iqbāl Khān and Maḥmūd Shāh in the plain outside the capital. Although the Indian army put up a brave fight, it was routed. The sultan and Mallū withdrew into the city, and shortly fled, Mallū into the Doab and Maḥmūd Shāh to Gujarāt, while the khutba in Delhi was read in the name of Temür's nominal sovereign, the Ögödeyid Maḥmūd Khan.[117] The amnesty granted to the citizens of Delhi meant nothing once Temür's troops were inside the city and disorders broke out: the sack began on 9 Rabīʿ II/18 December and lasted for some days. After campaigning east of the Yamuna, where he stormed Mīrat (which had successfully withstood Tarmashirin seventy years previously) and launched an unsuccessful attack on the fortress of Hardwār, Temür finally withdrew westwards through the foothills, attacking Jammū en route (middle of Jumādā II/late February 1399).[118] For all his posturings, his invasion had enveloped Muslim amir and Hindu chief alike in a common destruction. According to Bihāmadkhānī, Sārang Khān had been put to death; Bahādur Nāhir, who had submitted to him after the sack of Delhi, may have been put in chains, and the Khōkhar chief Shaikha, who had acted as guide to the invaders, was arrested with his family during the conqueror's return march.[119]

It may well be asked what enabled Temür to succeed – to defeat the army of the Sultanate and to capture its capital – where his Chaghadayid

114 Bihāmadkhānī, fols. 422b–423a (tr. Zaki, 32); for Fīrūz Shāh and Temür, see fol. 442b (tr. Zaki, 59–60).

115 The view of Roemer, 'Tīmūr in Iran', 70. 116 *TMS*, 162–3.

117 Shāmī, *ZN*, I, 192; and see Woods, 'Rise of Tīmūrid historiography', 104–5.

118 For a detailed survey of the Indian campaign, see Lal, *Twilight*, 16–40.

119 Yazdī, *ZN*, ed. Ilahdād, II, 127–8/ed. Urunbaev, fols. 327b-328a. *TMS*, 166–7. Bihāmadkhānī, fol. 307a (tr. Zaki, 93).

predecessors had failed. The reasons are manifold. One was that the conqueror had at his disposal resources of revenue and manpower that had not been available to Chaghadayid princes like Qutlugh Qocha and Tarmashirin, since his campaigns in Persia and against the Golden Horde had won for him tribute and contingents of troops from areas that had lain outside Chaghadai's ulus earlier in the century; he had also welded the Chaghadayid tribal forces into a far more formidable war-machine.[120] But it is still more important to register the sharp decline that had occurred in the military establishment of the Delhi Sultanate under Fīrūz Shāh and his successors.

The decline in the Sultanate's resources

Timurid authors – by no means inclined, we can be sure, to minimize the opposition that their hero vanquished outside Delhi – set the army with which Maḥmūd Shāh and Mallū met him at 10,000 horsemen, 20,000 foot and 120 elephants.[121] These numbers constitute a pitiful force compared with those that had accompanied Fīrūz Shāh on campaign. For his two invasions of Bengal, that sultan had been able to raise armies of 80,000 or 90,000 horsemen and 450 elephants;[122] for his Thatta expedition, 90,000 horse and 480 elephants.[123] ʿAfīf, probably indebted for these figures to his father, who worked in the *dīwān-i wizārat*, tells us at another juncture that the sultan possessed a total of 80,000 horsemen excluding his slaves.[124] Yet even such statistics as these are a pale reflection of the numbers on the muster-roll under ʿAlāʾ al-Dīn Khaljī or in the early years of Muḥammad b. Tughluq.

Blame for the unimpressive military establishment by the time of Temür's invasion cannot all be heaped upon Fīrūz Shāh. The drop in the number of elephants in all probability reflects the fact that those animals formerly despatched to the Delhi Sultan as tribute from Bengal and Jājnagar were now being sent instead to Khwāja Jahān at Jawnpūr.[125] Even where decline can be traced to his era, it would be foolish to disregard circumstances over which Fīrūz Shāh had no control. Security from external attack brings its own penalty, as ʿAfīf recognized, in a deterioration in the quality of the military.[126] In this process the decline in the incidence of Mongol attacks

120 Manz, *Rise and rule*, chapters 4–5.
121 Ghiyāth al-Dīn Yazdī, *Rūz-Nāma*, tr. Semenov, 115. Shāmī, *ZN*, I, 189. Yazdī, *ZN*, ed. Ilahdād, II, 100/ed. Urunbaev, fol. 320b, gives 40,000 foot, and does not at this stage specify the number of elephants. But later we are told that 120 were captured: ed. Ilahdād, II, 118/ed. Urunbaev, fol. 325a.
122 ᶜAfīf, 144; but for the first expedition, cf. 115 (three divisions of 30,000 horse each), and Hodivala, *Studies*, II, 123–4.
123 ᶜAfīf, 197, 200.
124 *Ibid.*, 298. For ᶜAfīf's father, see *ibid.*, 197. Digby, *War-horse*, 24–5.
125 *TMS*, 157. Digby, *War-horse*, 64, 76–7.
126 ᶜAfīf, 23.

would no doubt have played a part. Nor should we discount extraneous factors operating on the supply of warhorses. At the time of Ibn Baṭṭūṭa's travels, the lands of the Golden Horde had exported fine mounts in droves of around 6000; but their availability would almost certainly have been considerably reduced by the struggles among numerous rival Jochid khans since 759/1358.[127] It is significant that no Sultanate coins later than Fīrūz Shāh's reign have been found in hoards from Russia.[128]

To what extent can the decline in military effectiveness be related to economic conditions? The reputation Fīrūz Shāh's reign acquired for widespread prosperity (above, pp. 169–70) seems to have been derived from two closely related circumstances: a restoration of agrarian productivity following the death of Muḥammad b. Tughluq, and a fall in the price of grain and many other commodities. As far as the first is concerned, Fīrūz Shāh's personal efforts to promote cultivation are well known. The several canals that he caused to be excavated transformed traditional areas of pasture into flourishing agricultural land.[129] ʿAfīf devotes space especially to the two canals that irrigated the territory of the sultan's new foundation of Ḥiṣār Fīrūza, making a spring crop possible for the first time in addition to the autumn crops that had traditionally been harvested in the region.[130] Steps were also taken to bring waste land under the plough and to restore the settlements that were attached to pious foundations like the tombs of shaykhs and past sultans.[131] A hundred thousand *bīghas* of waste land were made over to *faqīrs* and the needy.[132]

Yet the agrarian recovery does not seem to have brought in its wake a revival of the military strength that had characterized the first decade of Muḥammad b. Tughluq's reign; and two reasons appear to have been a reduction in the government's revenues, and an increase in expenditure on building works and for charitable purposes. There is some evidence that by this time the land-tax (*kharāj*) had been reduced to 20 – or even 10 – per cent.[133] In *c.* 759/1358, moreover, on the basis of a tour of the empire by Ḥusām al-Dīn Junaydī, the gross revenue-demand was fixed at six *krōrs* and seventy-five *laks* (67,500,000) of *tangas*, and it remained at that level throughout, with the result that the government failed to benefit from enhanced production in the provinces.[134] ʿAfīf was told, too, that the

[127] On the horse trade, see IB, II, 372–4 (tr. Gibb, 478–9); Digby, *War-horse*, 35–6.

[128] Digby, 'Currency system', 100; A. A. Bykov, 'Finds of Indian medieval coins in east Europe', *JNSI* 27 (1965), 151–5.

[129] *TFS*, 566, 567–71. *SFS*, 74–5, 161ff., 216–17.

[130] ᶜAfīf, 127–8.

[131] *Ibid.*, 130, 332–3.

[132] *Ibid.*, 179: for the correct reading of this sentence, see Hodivala, *Studies*, II, 129–30.

[133] Riazul Islam, 'Some aspects of the economy of northern South Asia during the fourteenth century', *JCA* 11, part 2 (1988), 9 and n.21 (citing Muṭahhar). But cf. ᶜAfīf, 484, *yakī ba-dah*.

[134] *Ibid.*, 94, saying that Junaydī toured the empire for six years; at 296 the figure given is six *krōrs* and eighty-five *laks*. Riazul Islam, 'Some aspects', 17–18.

abolition of uncanonical taxes in 777/1375–6 cost Fīrūz Shāh thirty *laks* (3,000,000) of *tangas*.[135] At the same time, the sultan is said to have set aside a total of 3,600,000 *tangas* for the 'ulama', shaykhs and holy men.[136] A letter of Ibn Māhrū provides some insight into conditions in the Multān province, probably within a few years of Fīrūz Shāh's accession. Answering the criticism, among others, that he had been assigning unproductive land by way of pensions and allowances, Ibn Māhrū draws attention to the fact that the abolition of *mukūs* under Muḥammad b. Tughluq, and Fīrūz Shāh's failure to reinstate them, has reduced the sultan's revenue; and points at the same time to Fīrūz Shāh's generosity in allocating an unprecedentedly high sum of 300,000 *tangas* to the payment of pensions and gifts.[137]

Ibn Māhrū's letter throws into sharp relief another problem confronting the government. The value of stipends and pensions that had been fixed in kind at a time of high grain prices had been severely reduced when those prices fell – from as much as eighty *jītals* to a mere eight *jītals* per *mann*, if Ibn Māhrū's figures are reliable. Even without the sultan's partiality for sayyids, shaykhs and other deserving causes, it would therefore have been deemed necessary to raise the grain-price equivalent of such grants in order to protect the recipients against hardship.[138] On the other hand, the sharp inflation of other prices consequent upon Muḥammad's debasement of the currency had not gone into reverse, so that the government was confronted with a much higher bill for the purchase of essential war-material. The price of horses, for instance, appears to have risen six- to eightfold since the time of 'Alā' al-Dīn Khaljī.[139]

Thus the sums available for expenditure on the military had undergone a reduction on several counts. It was perhaps for this reason that Fīrūz Shāh – at an early date, since it is mentioned by Baranī – had reverted to the policy of paying the regular troops in assignments of land; and 'Afīf may be referring to this when he claims that the sultan gave away his whole empire in iqta's.[140] The soldiers in question he terms *wajhdārs*, as opposed to those (*ghayr-wajhīs*) who received pay either in cash or in drafts (*barāt*) on provincial revenue. 'Afīf, commenting on 'Alā' al-Dīn Khaljī's refusal to follow such a practice on the grounds that it created entrenched local interests, gives it as his own opinion that nevertheless no ill effects could be detected during the forty years of Fīrūz Shāh's reign.[141] Yet short-term problems can certainly be discerned. One distinction between the two types of trooper was that the *wajhdārs* were expected to provide their own

135 'Afīf, 378–9.
136 *Ibid.*, 179. *TFS*, 559, refers simply to an increase in the sum disbursed on pensions.
137 *IM*, 79–80. 138 *Ibid.*, 74. 139 Digby, *War-horse*, 37–40.
140 'Afīf, 94–5, 279. *TFS*, 553.
141 'Afīf, 96. On the two different types of trooper, see also *ibid.*, 193–4, 296; Hodivala, *Studies*, I, 321–2.

mounts, which put them at a disadvantage as compared to the *ghayr-wajhīs* and caused no little hardship among them at the time of the sultan's retreat from Thatta to Gujarāt, when most of the horses had been lost: their assignments being far away, it was necessary to advance them loans from the treasury.[142] But there were also unwelcome longer-term effects. Troopers presenting their drafts in the iqta‘s, ‘Afīf tells us, received only half the sum to which they were entitled. In these circumstances, many of them were prepared to sell their drafts in Delhi for one-third of the total payment due, thus sparing themselves the effort and expense of travelling to the iqta‘. A brisk traffic thus developed in the drafts for soldiers' pay, and many persons became wealthy by buying drafts at one-third of the nominal value and receiving in the locality fifty per cent.[143]

At the same time as the introduction of pay through assignments, the sultan had also enacted another measure permitting the *wajhdār* to transmit his establishment (*istiqāmat*) to his son or son-in-law: failing them, it should pass to his slave or to some kinsman; and in the absence of these, lastly, to his womenfolk (*‘awrāt*).[144] The undesirable consequences of such a provision from the military vantage-point are obvious. The complaint made to the sultan by Malik Isḥāq, son of the *‘āriḍ* Bashīr ‘Imād al-Mulk, that many of the troops had grown too old for service, echoes Baranī's account of Balaban's attempt to change the state of affairs in the *ḥawālī* and the Doab soon after his accession (see p. 95). Fīrūz Shāh ordered that any soldier incapable of fulfilling his duties should provide a substitute (*wakīl*).[145] Nevertheless, the object of the sultan's system may well have been to encourage exploitation of the land by giving each family a permanent stake in the particular area allotted to it. The letter of Ibn Māhrū cited above advocates giving, as pay or pensions, a combination of cultivated and waste land.[146] This would certainly have been in keeping with the sultan's personal interest in extending cultivation.

But whatever the case, the number of Maḥmūd Shāh's troops in 1398 must also give some idea of the toll taken of the sultans' resources first by decades of mismanagement and then by some years of internal conflict. In the early years of Fīrūz Shāh's reign, Baranī had commented on the new sultan's indulgence towards the military.[147] ‘Afīf would be more outspoken, describing how Fīrūz Shāh turned a blind eye to the presentation of substandard horses and weapons at the annual review and retailing an anecdote about the sultan's own efforts to help a trooper who had neglected to appear on time.[148] Detailed evidence is regrettably meagre; but we are left with the impression that the Sultanate's military establishment had been run down. This trend can only have been accentuated by the internal strife and

[142] ‘Afīf, 220–1. [143] *Ibid.*, 296–7.
[144] *Ibid.*, 96. The mention of women precludes the rendering of *istiqāmat* as 'rank'.
[145] *Ibid.*, 302–3. [146] *IM*, 79–80. [147] *TFS*, 553.
[148] ‘Afīf, 298–302.

regional rebellion that characterized the years following the old sultan's death. ʿAfīf writes in lyrical terms about the flourishing condition of the Doab under Fīrūz Shāh;[149] but within a few years much of the province had been devastated by the campaigns of Hindu rais and rival Tughluqid princes.

The successor states

Sirhindī dates the emergence of autonomous provincial rulers from the time of the second civil war, when, he claims, 'the amirs and maliks of the empire were independent sovereigns and would appropriate the revenue and the produce themselves'.[150] The process had in fact begun well before this, in the reign of Fīrūz Shāh, with the creation of an independent principality in Khāndēsh in 782/1380 under Malik Rajā, of whom we know little.[151] It is a striking fact that apart from Malik Rajā and with the qualified exception of the creator of the Kālpī polity, Maḥmūd b. Fīrūz Khān, whose family had initially supported Tughluq Shāh II, the founders of the provincial dynasties[152] – Khiḍr Khān at Multān, Ẓafar Khān Wajīh al-Mulk in Gujarāt, ʿAmīd Shāh (Dilāwar Khān) in Mālwa, Shams Khān Awhadī at Bhayāna and Khwāja Jahān Sarwar at Jawnpūr – were all originally nominees or supporters of Sultan Muḥammad Shāh b. Fīrūz.[153] Even Maḥmūd b. Fīrūz Khān must have made his peace with Muḥammad Shāh, who at the time of his visit to the region in 794/1391–2 had conferred on him the iqtaʿ of Mahōba in addition to the entire *shiqq* of Fīrūzpūr which he already held.[154] Bihāmadkhānī goes so far as to equate the emergence of the new kingdoms with an act of administrative convenience by Muḥammad Shāh, a formal division of his territories into large administrative units following his triumph over Abū Bakr.[155] The chronology of Malik Maḥmūd's career alone suggests that we can take this story *cum grano salis*.

Khiḍr Khān at Multān is a special case. As we have seen, he had lost control of his province to Sārang Khān, and doubtless no longer felt any loyalty – if he ever had done – to Sultan Maḥmūd Shāh, who was a puppet of Sārang Khān's brother Mallū. Escaping from Sārang Khān's hands, he had fled to Bhayāna, and from there he made his way to Temür's encampment and offered his submission. Sirhindī's claim that Temür bestowed Delhi upon him is surely apocryphal, an attempt to bolster the legitimacy of

149 *Ibid.*, 295. 150 *TMS*, 160–1. 151 P. Hardy, 'Fārūḳids', *Enc.Isl.*².

152 They are mostly listed in *TMS*, 168–9.

153 All referred to by Bihāmadkhānī, fols. 416a, 421b–422a, 426b (tr. Zaki, 19, 30, 36), except Shams Khān, for whom see *TMS*, 147. Khiḍr Khān had also been an adherent of Muḥammad Shāh, *ibid.*, 146, 147.

154 *Ibid.*, 152. Bihāmadkhānī, fols. 429b–430a (tr. Zaki, 42–3).

155 *Ibid.*, fols. 426b, 429 (tr. Zaki, 36, 42). He may have been the source of the similar version in Harawī, III, 288.

the Sayyid dynasty, for whom he was writing and who acknowledged Timurid overlordship, by means of the conqueror's *imprimatur*. His statement that Temür confirmed Khiḍr Khān as governor of Multān and Dēōpālpūr, however, we have no reason to doubt.[156] In view of Khiḍr Khān's allegiance, these territories had ceased to form part of the Delhi Sultanate.

Otherwise, however, the new rulers did not represent men who had come to power by any formal act of rebellion. Khwāja Jahān Sarwar, wazir successively to Muḥammad Shāh and to Maḥmūd Shāh and viceroy to the latter throughout the eastern regions, is perhaps the most obvious case of a loyalist who found autonomy thrust upon him. It is noteworthy, too, how hesitant these provincial governors were to proclaim their own sovereignty and to repudiate the authority of the sultan in Delhi. At no time did Khwāja Jahān assume the style of sultan; it was not until his death in 802/1399 (and therefore after the sack of Delhi) that his adopted son and successor at Jawnpūr took the title of Sultan Mubārak Shāh, thereby provoking an abortive campaign by Mallū Iqbāl Khān from Delhi.[157] In Gujarāt Ẓafar Khān b. Wajīh al-Mulk, despite Bihāmadkhānī's statement to the contrary, displayed a reluctance to adopt the royal title which is all the more surprising in one who had acknowledged Nuṣrat Shāh and whose son Tatar Khān had been that sultan's wazir. This would presumably explain Ẓafar Khān's embarrassment when Nuṣrat Shāh's rival Maḥmūd Shāh appeared in Gujarāt a year or so later, following Temür's invasion; the fugitive sultan seems to have obtained no assistance and to have left for Mālwa.[158] In 806/1404 Ẓafar Khān, whom an inscription of that year styles merely 'wazir', was briefly displaced by his ambitious son Tatar Khān, who had designs on Delhi and adopted the title of Sultan Nāṣir al-Dīn Muḥammad Shāh. But even after Tatar Khān's death and his own restoration two months later, Ẓafar Khān still called himself muqtaʿ of Gujarāt; he did not take the title of sultan until 810/1407.[159] It has been claimed that Dilāwar Khān did so in 804/1401–2, after Maḥmūd Shāh's visit to Mālwa, but the only evidence for this appears to be an inscription of 807/1405; the

156 *TMS*, 166–7. Yazdī, *ZN*, ed. Ilahdād, II, 175 (abridged in Urunbaev edn, fol. 341a), refers only to the government of Multān.

157 *TMS*, 169. Harawī, III, 274. Saeed, *Sharqi Sultanate*, 32–3, says that around the time of Temür's invasion he assumed the style of *Atabeg al-Aʿẓam* and had the khutba read in his own name; but Bihāmadkhānī, the source cited, does not support him. Cf. also Nizami, in HN, 713.

158 Bihāmadkhānī, fol. 427b (tr. Zaki, 38). *TMS*, 166, 170. Harawī, III, 89. Sikandar 'Manjhū', 20 (tr. Bayley, 79–80). Lal, *Twilight*, 47.

159 G. H. Yazdani, 'Seven new inscriptions from Baroda State', *EIM* (1939–40), 2–3. Z. A. Desai, 'Inscriptions of the Gujarat Sultans', *EIAPS* (1963), 6–10; *idem*, 'Khaljī and Tughluq inscriptions from Gujarat', 32–3, 38–40. *TMS*, 172. Harawī, III, 90–3, implying he took the royal title after Tatar Khān's death. Sikandar 'Manjhū', 21–5 (tr. Bayley, 80, 81, 83–4). Misra, *Muslim power*, 152–6.

evidence for the assumption of the royal title by his successor Hūshang Shāh is much stronger.[160]

The eventual assumption of sovereign status by Maḥmūd b. Fīrūz Khān, the founder of the principality of Kālpī who reigned as Nāṣir al-Dīn Maḥmūd Shāh, is a matter concerning which the local chronicler, Bihāmadkhānī, is disarmingly confused. At one point he alleges that the Delhi Sultan Maḥmūd Shāh b. Muḥammad sent Maḥmūd b. Fīrūz Khān a chatr and a durbash, together with the title of sultan. Slightly later, Maḥmūd is said to have established himself at Kālpī following the death of Maḥmūd Shāh – an impossible feat, since he died in 813/1410–11 and the Delhi Sultan survived for another two years. With Bihāmadkhānī's statement immediately below, that Maḥmūd adopted the insignia of sovereignty in the wake of Temür's invasion, we are doubtless as near to the truth as we shall get.[161]

Temür's assault on Delhi had been decisive. The artisans and other skilled workers who had helped to beautify Fīrūz Shāh's residences had been carried off to adorn the invader's headquarters at Samarqand.[162] Many of the city's other inhabitants had fled elsewhere for safety and had not returned. Certainly, Bihāmadkhānī gives the impression that the security and prosperity of Kālpī were greatly enhanced by the influx of refugees from Delhi in the wake of its sack by the Chaghadayid Mongols.[163] The collapse of the Delhi Sultanate was as much a matter of the death-blow to the capital city and its region as of the secession of most of its remaining provinces.

[160] U. N. Day, *Medieval Malwa: a political and cultural history, 1401–1562* (Delhi, 1965), 21; HN, 898, 899. For the inscription, see *EIM* (1909–10), 11–12, summarized by Day, 435. For Hūshang, see *ibid.*, 25.

[161] Bihāmadkhānī, fol. 436 (tr. Zaki, 52, 53); and see also fol. 412b (tr. 15). For the death of Maḥmūd Shāh of Kālpī, see *ibid.*, fol. 445b (tr. 62).

[162] Ghiyāth al-Dīn Yazdī, *Rūz-Nāma*, tr. Semenov, 124–5. Yazdī, *ZN*, ed. Ilahdād, II, 124/ed. Urunbaev, fol. 326b. For other towns sacked, see Verma, *Dynamics of urban life*, 65–6.

[163] Bihāmadkhānī, fols. 436b, 442b–443a (tr. Zaki, 53, 59–60). On the Kālpī polity, see generally Iqtidar Husain Siddiqui, 'Kalpi in the 15th century', *IC* 61 (1987), part 3, 90–120.

Epilogue (*c.* 1400–1526)

The end of the Tughluqids

During the decade following Temür's attack, the Sultanate reverted to being simply one of a number of competing powers in the northern half of the subcontinent, as Fīrūz Shāh's empire split into several states. For three years after Temür's onslaught, there was not even a sultan in Delhi. Nuṣrat Shāh, who returned from the Doab to take up residence at Fīrūzābād in Rajab 801/March–April 1399, was defeated by Mallū Iqbāl Khān and obliged to flee into the Mēō territory, where he died. Mallū then established his headquarters at Sīrī, from where he is said to have brought back under control 'the *shiqq* of the Doab and the iqta's of the *ḥawālī*'.[1] But although he routed Sumēr and his allies near Patiyālī in 803/1401, he was unable to recover Gwāliyōr from the successor of the Tomara chief Vīrasinha, who had seized it during the chaos of Temür's onslaught.[2] For a time Mallū was able to rule through Maḥmūd Shāh, whom he persuaded to rejoin him; but the sultan grew suspicious of him during a campaign against Jawnpūr and established himself at Qinnawj. He returned to Delhi only after Mallū's death in battle with Khiḍr Khān in 808/1405, and maintained a shadowy authority there until his own death in 815/1412. After the short reign of the leading amir Dawlat Khān, Khiḍr Khān finally obtained possession of Delhi.

The Sayyid and Lodī dynasties

The rulers of the so-called Sayyid (817–855/1414–1451) and Lodī (855–932/1451–1526) dynasties[3] presided over an empire that was a mere shadow of its former self and which continued to fragment. The truncated Sultanate was surrounded, and sometimes threatened, by Muslim rivals like Jawnpūr,

[1] *TMS*, 167–8. [2] *Ibid.*, 169–70, 171–2.

[3] For these dynasties, see generally K. A. Nizami, 'Sayyids', *Enc.Isl.*²; *idem*, 'The Saiyids (1414–51)', in HN, 630–63; *idem*, 'The Lodis (1451–1526)', *ibid.*, 664–709; S. M. Imamuddin, 'Lōdīs', *Enc.Isl.*²; Lal, *Twilight*.

Gujarāt, Mālwa and Bengal, and by renascent Hindu principalities in Mēwār, Alwar and the Doab. On occasions Delhi itself was menaced by invaders from one of the rival Muslim kingdoms, as it was by the sultan of Mālwa in 844/1440 and by the sultan of Jawnpūr in 810/1407, in 856/1452, in *c*. 1466 and in 883/1479, just before the final overthrow of the Jawnpūr Sultanate by Bahlūl Lodī. Caliphal diplomas from Cairo were now despatched to other Muslim monarchs in the subcontinent.[4]

The title 'Sayyids' applied to the dynasty of Khiḍr Khān (817–24/1414–21) is based on the descent from the Prophet ascribed to them on inadequate grounds by Sirhindī. At no time did Khiḍr Khān assume sovereign status, preferring the title *Rāyat-i Aʿlā* ('exalted standard'). As befitted a ruler who owed his office to Temür, he paid tribute to the conqueror's youngest son Shāh Rukh, who now dominated the eastern Islamic world from his capital at Herat, and was sent in exchange a robe of honour and a banner. And although Sirhindī salutes Khiḍr Khān's son and successor Mubārak Shāh (824–837/1421–1434) as sultan,[5] we know that he too received from Herat a robe and a chatr.[6] Sirhindī is silent on these contacts, and the Sayyids' coinage did not bear Shāh Rukh's name, comprising simply updated Tughluqid issues. We should know nothing of the allegiance of the rulers of Delhi were it not for Bihāmadkhānī, who assures us that Shāh Rukh's orders had been received in Delhi for almost forty years and that the current ruler, Mubārak's nephew Muḥammad Shāh (837–849/1434–45), was still obedient to him at the time of writing.[7] The subservience of Khiḍr Khān and his successors did not guarantee the Delhi Sultanate freedom from Mongol attacks. Shaykh ʿAlī, who governed Kābul on behalf of Shāh Rukh's son, profited from the Sayyids' difficulties to invade India on a number of occasions, briefly occupying Lahore in 836/1432–3.

Shāh Rukh's influence in the subcontinent seems to have been extensive. Bihāmadkhānī, who includes verses in praise of that monarch's sovereignty (*salṭanat*) and refers to him as 'the seal of kings' (*khatam al-mulūk*),[8] claims that Sultan Hūshang Shāh of Mālwa appealed to him for assistance against an invasion from Gujarāt; while a Timurid source depicts the sultan of Bengal likewise seeking aid from Herat against Jawnpūr.[9] This overlordship in all likelihood lapsed with the onset of civil war following Shāh Rukh's death in 850/1447 and the emergence of the threat to the Timurids from the Türkmens in western Persia.[10] But when Temür's descendant Bābur

[4] Otto Spies, 'Ein Investiturschreiben des abbasidischen Kalifen in Kairo an einen indischen König', in S. M. Abdullah (ed.), *Professor Muḥammad Shafīʿ presentation volume* (Lahore, 1955), 241–53.

[5] *TMS*, 193.

[6] Bihāmadkhānī, fols. 311b-312a (tr. Zaki, 95).

[7] *Ibid*., fol. 312a (tr. Zaki, 95).

[8] *Ibid*., fols. 312b-313a (not in Zaki's tr.).

[9] *Ibid*., fol. 312b (tr. Zaki, 96). ʿAbd al-Razzāq Samarqandī, *Maṭlaʿ al-Saʿdayn*, ed. M. Shafīʿ (Lahore, 1941–9, 2 vols.), II, 782–3, cited in HN, 719.

[10] See H. R. Roemer, 'The successors of Tīmūr', in Jackson and Lockhart (eds.), *Cambridge history of Iran*, VI, 105ff.

launched his five invasions of India from Kābul early in the sixteenth century, he was reviving the claims of his forebears to sovereignty east of the Indus, although the conquest of Delhi itself became his objective only with time.[11]

The early fifteenth-century sultans were barely able to impose their authority either on their own muqtaʿs or on local Hindu princes. Multān, once Khiḍr Khān's power-base, seceded in 847/1443 under Shaykh Yūsuf Qurayshī, a descendant of Shaykh Bahā' al-Dīn Zakariyya, who was subsequently supplanted by the Afghan dynasty of the Langāhs. Sirhindī's survey of the first decades of the Sayyid dynasty amounts to little more than a tedious litany of campaigns against the Khōkhars, the Mēōs, the *muqaddams* of Katēhr, the Chawhāns of Etāwa and the Tomaras of Gwāliyōr, designed to raise 'revenue' in the form of tribute payments. The sultanate of Delhi consisted of little more than the territories immediately surrounding the capital itself, the *ḥawālī* as they had long been known. One contemporary wag immortalized by a sixteenth-century chronicler described the sway of the last Sayyid ruler, ʿAlā' al-Dīn ʿĀlam Shāh (*shāh-i ʿālam*, 'world-king'), as extending from Delhi to Pālam.[12]

In pursuit of his designs on Delhi, Khiḍr Khān had recruited considerable numbers of Afghan chiefs and their retinues. Already in his reign the Lodī chieftain Sulṭān Shāh (later styled Islām Khān), who had killed Mallū Iqbāl Khān, held Sirhind; he fell in 834/1431 fighting against a Timurid invading force. During the 1440s Afghan nobles became the real power in the Sultanate. Islām Khān's nephew and successor at Sirhind, Bahlūl Lodī, who had been granted Lahore and Dēōpālpūr in return for assistance against the invading Mālwa forces, went on to occupy most of the Panjāb and made two attempts on Delhi. ʿĀlam Shāh abandoned the capital for Badā'ūn in 852/1448, and three years later Bahlūl entered the city and was enthroned as sultan.

The Lodī era witnessed something of a revival. A protracted duel with Jawnpūr ended with its annexation (884/1479); the region was later conferred on Sultan Bahlūl's younger son Bārbak Shāh; the last Sharqī sultan fled into Bihār. Here he maintained himself until his expulsion and the annexation of that territory by Bahlūl's son Sikandar Shāh (894–923/1489–517), who had earlier removed his brother Bārbak from Jawnpūr. Under Sikandar significant gains were also made to the south. The Awhadīs, who had continued to rule Bhayāna under the overlordship of Delhi, were finally ousted in 898/1492, when the place was subjected to a nominee of the sultan. Narwar was wrested from the prince of Gwāliyōr in 914/1508 and Chandērī from the sultanate of Mālwa in 921/1515; and in

[11] *Bābur-Nāma*, tr. Beveridge, II, 377, 380, 382, 478.

[12] Aḥmad Yādgār, *Ta'rīkh-i Shāhī* or *Ta'rīkh-i Salāṭīn-i Afāghina*, ed. M. Hidayat Hosain, BI (Calcutta, 1939), 5, cited in Lal, *Twilight*, 124 n.64.

915/1509 Nāgawr became subordinate to Delhi. Sikandar's son and successor, Ibrāhīm (923–32/1517–26) succeeded in the conquest of Gwāliyōr, which had eluded his father, but lost Chandērī and Nāgawr to the Hindu princes of Mēwar and Marwar respectively. It is symptomatic of the sultans' preoccupation with the subjection of Alwar, Gwāliyōr and Bhayāna that Sikandar had in 911/1505 removed his residence from Delhi to Āgra. But the corollary of this forward policy in the south was neglect of the vulnerable frontier in the Panjāb.

The immigration of Afghan chiefs and their followers continued apace under the first two Lodīs, particularly when Bahlūl, confronted by the threat from Jawnpūr, sought to enhance his military strength by inviting in tribesmen from the Rōh clans.[13] The position of the Afghan chiefs, and one or two non-Afghan clans from the north-west with whom they shared power, was considerably stronger than that of their precursors during the fourteenth century: it is noteworthy that the sultan around this time lost his long-cherished monopoly of the elephantry.[14] Bahlūl ruled merely as *primus inter pares*. Sikandar, whose ambitions were more autocratic, consolidated his position gradually and with tact; but Ibrāhīm from the outset showed himself to be uncompromising in his designs to curb the power of the older nobility and to build up an élite upon which he could rely.[15] His arbitrary actions against leading figures eventually provoked the secession of Bihār under a rival, who seized the territory as far west as Qinnawj,[16] and an invitation from Dawlat Khān Lodī, governor of the Panjāb, to the Timurid prince Bābur to embark on his last two invasions of India. In the fourth expedition, Lahore was occupied (930/1524), and in the fifth Bābur conquered the Delhi Sultanate. On 8 Rajab 932/20 April 1526, at Pānīpat, Ibrāhīm's superior numbers were outclassed by Bābur's artillery, and he fell in the fighting. Although the expulsion of Bābur's son Humāyūn, and the temporary establishment of a new Afghan-ruled polity by Shīr Shāh in 947/1540, has some claim to be regarded as a recreation of the Delhi Sultanate, the engagement at Pānīpat marks the beginning of the Mughal empire.

Bābur is keen to contrast his own victory over the ruler of most of northern India with the triumphs of the earlier conquerors, Maḥmūd of Ghazna and Muʿizz al-Dīn Muḥammad of Ghūr, whose opponents had been smaller fry. In his opinion, Ibrāhīm's avarice was to blame for the fact that his army stood at not more than 100,000 troops when he might have mustered twice or three times as many.[17] But this may not do justice to the

[13] *Ta'rīkh-i Shīr-Shāhī*, cited in HN, 679–80.
[14] HN, 665. For the position of the Afghans in the Lodī Sultanate, see Iqtidar Husain Siddiqui, 'The composition of the nobility under the Lodi Sultans', *MIM* 4 (1977), 10–66.
[15] For the relations of the Lodī sultans with their nobles, see generally Iqtidar Husain Siddiqi, *Some aspects of Afghan despotism in India* (Aligarh, 1969), chapters 1–2.
[16] *Bābur-Nāma*, tr. Beveridge, 523.
[17] *Ibid.*, 470, 480; see also his comment on the wealth of India in gold and silver, *ibid.*, 518, 519.

absence of aid from the Lodī sultan's rebellious eastern provinces and a more widespread alienation on the part of his army which is mentioned by a later source.[18] It is also possible that Bābur over-estimated his enemy's wealth. The discontinuance of silver and gold coinage under the Sayyid and Lodī sultans and the employment of baser metals such as billon and copper testify to the economic weakness of the fifteenth- and early sixteenth-century Sultanate, which had forfeited control of much of its land revenue and no longer enjoyed access to the enormous sums gained in plunder or in tribute during the Khaljī and Tughluqid eras.

[18] Aḥmad Yādgār, *Ta'rīkh-i Shāhī*, 96.

APPENDIX I

Jūzjānī's use of the word 'Turk'

Sometimes Jūzjānī employs the word 'Turk' as a general ethnicon, as when we read of the khan (or khaqans) of 'the Turks': *TN*, I, 230, 231 (tr. 84, 85); cf. also I, 281 (tr. 194), for 'the cap of the Turks'. In its broadest sense, it could even embrace for Jūzjānī, as for other Muslim authors, the non-Turkish Qara-Khitan and Mongols, as *ibid.*, II, 94, 98 (tr. 900, 935). He also refers to the inhabitants of the regions lying to the north and north-east of Lakhnawtī, against whom Muḥammad b. Bakhtiyār headed his disastrous invasion, as 'Turks': *ibid.*, I, 429 and n.4 (tr. 566, 567). The reason seems to be that their facial features were thought to resemble those of the Turks: *ibid.*, I, 427 (tr. 560); IB, IV, 216 (tr. Gibb and Beckingham, 869).

But there is also evidence that for Jūzjānī the word 'Turk' denoted a Turkish ghulam. The clearest indication of this is that in his section on the last Ghaznawid Sultan he employs the phrase 'Turk and free' (*atrāk-u aḥrār*): *TN*, I, 243 (Raverty's tr., 114, does not quite bring out the sense). At other points the context usually suggests that the Turkish slave guards of, say, the Ghaznawids are in question: *ibid.*, I, 234 (tr. 95, 97); also I, 230, 235, 236, 250, 251, 258, 286, 314 (tr. 83–4, 98, 100, 129, 131, 149, 180, 204–5, 282). By contrast, the word 'Turk' is applied to nomadic Turkish groups far more sparingly. Jūzjānī employs the term 'Turk' for only one free Turkish chieftain, the founder of the dynasty of the Khwārazmshāhs (although in reality he too was a ghulam): *TN*, I, 297 (tr. 233). When the Turkish nomads of the steppe are not called specifically Seljüks or Ghuzz, they are referred to as 'Türkmen' (e.g., II, 94), a designation applied, for instance, to Seljük himself: *ibid.*, I, 213 (*turkān* to read *turkmānān*, as in BL ms., fol. 93a), 245 (tr. 45, 116). *Türkmen* seems to be used by the twelfth-century writer Marwazī to denote Turkish nomads who had accepted Islam: *Ṭabā'iʿ al-Ḥayawān*, partial edn and tr. V. Minorsky, *Sharaf al-Zamān Ṭāhir Marvazī on China, the Turks and India* (London, 1942), Ar. text 18, tr. 29 (and notes at 94–5). But cf. İ. Kafesoğlu, 'A propos du nom Türkmen', *Oriens* 11 (1958), 146–50.

APPENDIX II

Qilich Khān Mas'ūd b. 'Alā' al-Dīn Jānī

The widespread confusion regarding this important noble of the middle of the thirteenth century is due to the vagaries of the *Ṭabaqāt-i Nāṣirī* manuscript tradition and of the two printed editions by Nassau Lees and by Ḥabībī. Thus 'Qilich' sometimes occurs as 'Qutlugh', causing Nizami to identify him with Balaban's great enemy Qutlugh Khān (HN, 262, 271–2); Nigam, 41, 198–9, 203, similarly confuses the two men. The same form Qutlugh is also adopted by Aziz Aḥmad, *Political history*, 245, 246, 258, although he distinguishes Mas'ūd-i Jānī from Qutlugh Khān. Qilich Khān's full name can be determined from *TN*, I, 476 (tr. 673), where he is listed among the maliks of Nāṣir al-Dīn Maḥmūd Shāh as Malik Jalāl al-Dīn Qilich Khān-i Malik Jānī (text reads XLJ; BL ms., fol. 188b, here has 'Toghril' in error), and I, 495 (tr. 712), where he is called Malik Jalāl al-Dīn Mas'ūd Shāh-i Malik Jānī. At II, 35 (as in BL ms., fol. 208a), he is called 'Qutlugh Khān son of Malik Jānī' (see also Raverty's tr., 769). At II, 78 (as in BL ms., fol. 223), however, he appears as Qilich (QLJ) Khān (cf. Raverty's tentative 'Qutlugh [Qulij]' at 848–9). The title is from Tu. *qilich*, 'sword': Sauvaget, 'Noms et surnoms', no. 178.

APPENDIX III

Qara'unas and Negüderis

I have throughout accepted the identification of the Qara'unas with the Negüderis made by Aubin ('L'ethnogénèse', 84–5), and do not intend to devote further space to the origins of this grouping. Our Indian sources never refer to Negüderis, but they do occasionally employ the term Qara'unas. The following examples are from two authors writing in the fourteenth century. In his account of the death of Balaban's son Muḥammad in battle with the Mongols in 683/1285, 'Iṣāmī says that the prince was killed by a Qara'una horseman. The word is misread in Usha's edition, 179, 180, as *fuzūna* (defined in his glossary as 'a soldier not present at review and not entered on the muster-roll'), but the correct form is found in the otherwise inferior text edited by Husain (Agra, [1938], 174, 175). Amīr Khusraw too employs the term of the Mongol warrior who was briefly his captor following the overthrow of Muḥammad b. Balaban (*GK*, IOL ms. 412, fol. 78b, with HRWNH in error; correct spelling in Badā'ūnī, I, 153). And in describing the punishment meted out to Mongols captured during the invasion by Iqbāl, Köpek and Taibu in *c.* 1306, he says (*KF*, 46), 'And through the mingling of Qara'una and Mongol, there was seen in every fortress the junction of Saturn and Mars.'

There are several word-plays in this sentence, which hinges on the double meaning of *burj* as 'tower' and 'sign of the Zodiac'. 'Qara'una' could be read also as *qarūna*, 'soul', and 'Mughal' as *maghal*, 'sleep'. It is possible, lastly, that in 'Saturn', used by Indian Muslim writers to denote the infidel Hindu, we have an allusion to the mixed Mongol-Indian descent of the Qara'unas – assuming, of course, that Marco Polo's definition (*guasmil*, 'half-breeds') is reliable (Aubin, 'L'ethnogénèse', 66–9); but this is a matter of conjecture.

Together with the evidence of IB, III, 201 (tr. Gibb, 649), who heard from Shaykh Rukn al-Dīn of Multān that the Qara'unas were 'Turks' who 'dwelt in the mountains between Sind and the Turks [i.e. Transoxiana and Turkestan]', these examples suggest that the term Qara'unas was widely current in Muslim India and that the term Negüderis was used only by the Mongols themselves and by authors writing in Mongol Persia.

APPENDIX IV

ʿAyn al-Mulk Multānī and ʿAyn al-Mulk Ibn Māhrū

Some confusion has arisen between ʿAyn al-Mulk Multānī, who conquered Mālwa for ʿAlāʾ al-Dīn Khaljī, and ʿAyn al-Mulk Ibn Māhrū, who governed Multān under Muḥammad b. Tughluq and Fīrūz Shāh successively and whose correspondence has come down to us. For the equation of the two men, see ʿAbduʾl Walī, 254–5; ʿAbdur Rashid's introduction to *IM*, 1ff.; Lal, *History of the Khaljis*, 340; Husain, *Tughluq dynasty*, 80–1, 87, etc., and index; Nigam, 13, 18, 79, 82, 88, 158–9, 171, 173, 174, 179 (though distinguishing them in the index!); Nizami, *On history and historians*, 211–16, esp. 212 n.1, and in *Supplement to Elliot and Dowson's History of India*, III, 64–5; Conermann, *Beschreibung Indiens*, 163–4. By contrast, B. P. Saksena, in HN, 615 n.67, and I. H. Siddiqui, "ʿAyn al-Mulk Multānī', *Enc. Isl.*[2], *Supplement*, 104–5, make them two separate individuals.

ʿAyn al-Mulk Ibn Māhrū is known to have been an Indian: IB, III, 344 (tr. Gibb, 722). His patronymic, for which see *ibid.*, III, 342 (tr. 721), probably indicates that his father had been a convert to Islam. His name appears in fuller form twice in his correspondence. On the first occasion, the diploma appointing him to Multān calls him 'Malik al-Sharq waʾl-Wuzarāʾ ʿAyn al-Mulk ʿAyn al-Dawla waʾl-Dīn . . . ʿAbd-Allāh-i Māhrūʾ (*IM*, 12; cf. also *SFS*, 154, "ʿAyn al-Mulk ʿAyn al-Dīn-i Māhrūʾ). Later, the author refers to himself as "ʿAbd-Allāh-i Muḥammad Sharaf, known as (*al-madʿū ba-*) ʿAyn-i Māhrūʾ (*IM*, 176). This appears to preclude his identification with ʿAyn al-Mulk Multānī, whose full name is given as ʿAyn al-Mulk Shihāb-i Tāj Multānī in *TMS*, 77, 87, and who is not heard of after Tughluq Shāh's reign. In *Tughluq-Nāma*, 67, this earlier ʿAyn al-Mulk is made to claim Muslim ancestry as far back as ten generations (*ba-dah pusht*), which suggests that he belonged to an immigrant Muslim family. The 'Malik Nāṣir al-Dīn, son of ʿAyn al-Mulk', who according to IB, IV, 45 (tr. Gibb and Beckingham, 793), died when taking part in an attack on Sindāpūr (Goa), would have been his son, since we are told that he lived at Ujjain.

APPENDIX V

The date of Ghiyāth al-Dīn Tughluq Shāh's death

Ghiyāth al-Dīn Tughluq's death at Afghānpūr and the accession of Muḥammad have traditionally been placed by historians in 725, in accordance with the date given in *TFS*, 456, for the latter event and the month Rabīʿ I of that year (February–March 1325) supplied for the Afghānpūr episode by *TMS*, 96–7. But the sources are far from unanimous. ʿIṣāmī – like Baranī, a contemporary (though admittedly far from reliable as regards dates) – places Tughluq's death in 724 (*FS*, 421), and Ḥusām Khān specifies the last day (*salkh*) of that year (*AHG*, III, 862). Our data on the duration of Tughluq's reign are similarly vague. ʿAfīf, 41, puts it at four and a half years; Baranī at one point gives 'four or five years' (*TFS*, 438), but more often puts it at 'four years and some months' (*ibid.*, 22, 445); in this he is followed by Sirhindī, although in one ms. *chand* is amended to *hasht* (*TMS*, 97 and n.1). But Baranī's first recension, in this respect a hitherto untapped source, furnishes a more exact figure of 'four years and four months' (*TFS*[1], Bodleian ms., fol. 11a). Now Amīr Khusraw dates Tughluq's accession on 1 Shaʿbān 720/6 September 1320 (*Tughluq-Nāma*, 135), and the figure in *TFS*[1] would put his death somewhere in Dhu'l-Ḥijja 724 – in other words, at the very end of the year, as indicated by Ḥusām Khān. This conclusion is supported by a *farmān* of Muḥammad b. Tughluq, dated 14 Dhu'l-Ḥijja 724/2 Dec. 1324, in which he is clearly the ruling sultan and his father is not mentioned (Nizami, 'Some documents', 308–9). It is also very probable that an inscription on Fīrūz Shāh's column at Fatḥābād, in which Tughluq's death is dated Rajab 725 and Muḥammad's accession on 1 Shaʿbān is in error by a whole year, given that this same epigraph sets the sultan's reign at four years and two months (i.e. middle of 720–late 724): for the text, see Shokoohy, *Haryana I*, 21 and Pls. 28a, 29b-e; and cf. review by Jackson, *JRAS* (1990), 171–2.

We further possess an inscription of Muḥammad, as sultan, from Kanbhāya dated 18 Muḥarram 725/4 January 1325: this was edited by Husain ('Six inscriptions', 29–33), who goes to great lengths to prove that this date fell within Tughluq's reign and that it therefore applies to the commencement of the building, which must have been completed several months later. An inscription from Batihāgarh, north-west of Damōh, admittedly bears the date 725 and names Tughluq as the reigning sultan (Verma, 'Inscriptions from the Central Museum, Nagpur', 111–12). Nevertheless, since no month is given, it possibly belongs to the beginning of the year. The balance of the evidence seems to be that the sultan died at the very end of 724, and I have accordingly adopted this date.

APPENDIX VI

The ancestry of Tughluq Shāh II

Tughluq Shāh II is everywhere called the son of Fatḥ Khān. Although both Bihāmadkhānī, fol. 416a (tr. Zaki, 19), and *TMS*, 140, also call him Fīrūz Shāh's grandson, it seems that this is an error. He was in reality the old sultan's great-grandson, and the conventional genealogy of the later Tughluqids (e.g. in Haig, *Cambridge history of India*, III, 189, 692; Banerjee, *History of Firuz Shah*, 47; Lal, *Twilight*, 2) stands in need of emendation. Fīrūz Shāh had four sons, Fīrūz Khān (known as *shāhzāda-yi buzurg*, 'the great prince'), Ẓafar Khān, Muḥammad Khān (the future sultan) and Shādī Khān, as listed in *TFS*, BL ms., fol. 260b (the phrase that follows in the printed text, 527, is corrupt and omits the two lastnamed princes), and in Bihāmadkhānī, fol. 416b (tr. Zaki, 20). Fatḥ Khān is explicitly referred to as Fīrūz Khān's son both by Bihāmadkhānī (*ibid.*) and in *TFS*, 527 (the phrase *a'nī sulṭān muḥammad* is a later interpolation, applying to Muḥammad Khān, and has become displaced); cf. also 'Afīf, 65, where Fatḥ Khān is said to have been born in Fīrūz Khān's house. Since his birth occurred in 752/1351 (*TMS*, 122), Fatḥ Khān could easily have had a young son by the time of his death – the sources comment on Tughluq Shāh's youth: Bihāmadkhānī, fols. 418a, 419b (tr. Zaki, 25, 27); *TMS*, 142. It has helped to confuse matters that Fatḥ Khān was in fact virtually a year older than his uncle Muḥammad, for whose birth, on 3 Jumādā I 753/17 June 1352, see *TMS*, 123.

THE SHAMSIDS

- I. SHAMS AL-DĪN ILTUTMISH (607–33/1210–36)
  - Nāṣir al-Dīn Maḥmūd d. 626/1229
  - II. RUKN AL-DĪN FĪRŪZ SHĀH (633–4/1236)
    - V. ʿALĀʾ AL-DĪN MASʿŪD SHĀH (639–644/1242–1246)
  - III. RAḌIYYA (634–37/1236–40)
  - Ghiyāth al-Dīn Muḥammad
  - IV. MUʿIZZ AL-DĪN BAHRĀM SHĀH (637–9/1240–2)
  - VI. NĀṢIR AL-DĪN MAḤMŪD SHĀH (644–64/1246–66)
  - Jalāl al-Dīn Masʿūd

THE GHIYATHIDS

- I. GHIYĀTH AL-DĪN BALABAN (664–85/1266–87)
  - Muḥammad ʻKhān-i Shahīdʼ
    - Kaykhusraw
  - Nāṣir al-Dīn Maḥmūd Bughra Khān (*at Lakhnawtī*)
    - II. MUʿIZZ AL-DĪN KAYQUBĀD (685–9/1287–90)
      - III. SHAMS AL-DĪN KAYŪMARTH (689/1290)
    - Rukn al-Dīn Kaykāʾūs (*at Lakhnawtī*)

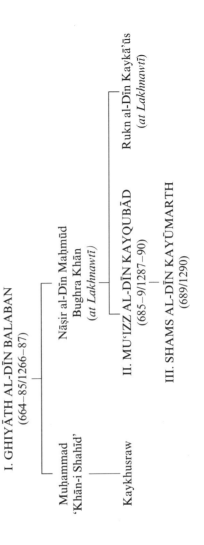

THE KHALJĪS

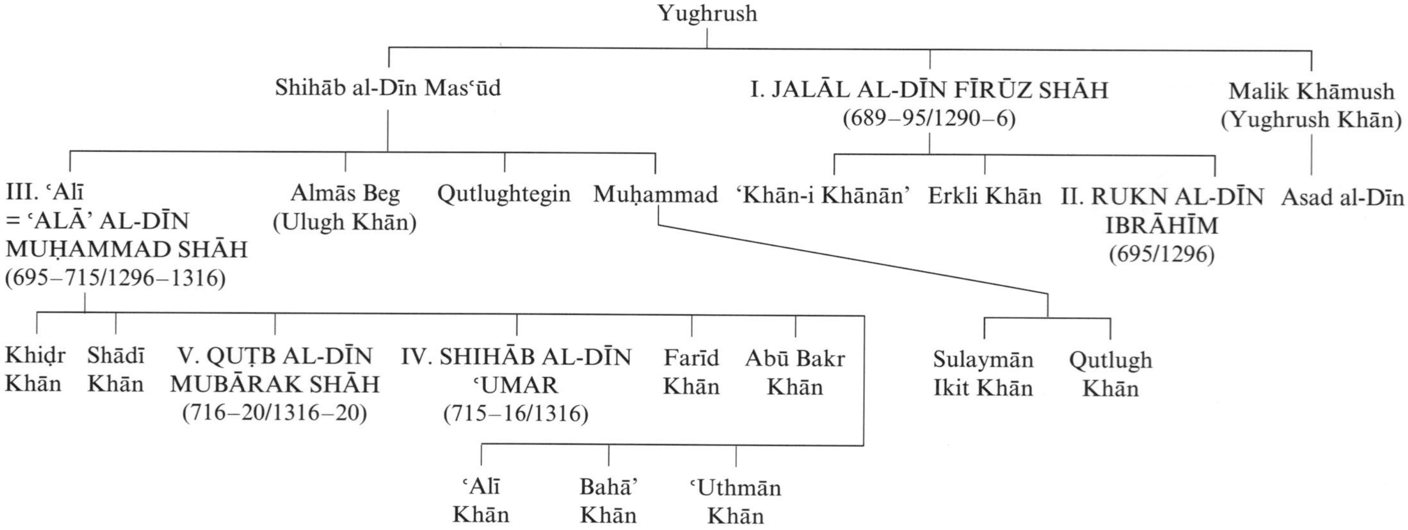
Yughrush
Shihāb al-Dīn Mas'ūd
I. JALĀL AL-DĪN FĪRŪZ SHĀH (689–95/1290–6)
Malik Khāmush (Yughrush Khān)
III. 'Alī = 'ALĀ' AL-DĪN MUḤAMMAD SHĀH (695–715/1296–1316)
Almās Beg (Ulugh Khān)
Qutlughtegin
Muḥammad
'Khān-i Khānān'
Erkli Khān
II. RUKN AL-DĪN IBRĀHĪM (695/1296)
Asad al-Dīn
Khiḍr Khān
Shādī Khān
V. QUṬB AL-DĪN MUBĀRAK SHĀH (716–20/1316–20)
IV. SHIHĀB AL-DĪN 'UMAR (715–16/1316)
Farīd Khān
Abū Bakr Khān
Sulaymān Ikit Khān
Qutlugh Khān
'Alī Khān
Bahā' Khān
'Uthmān Khān

THE TUGHLUQIDS

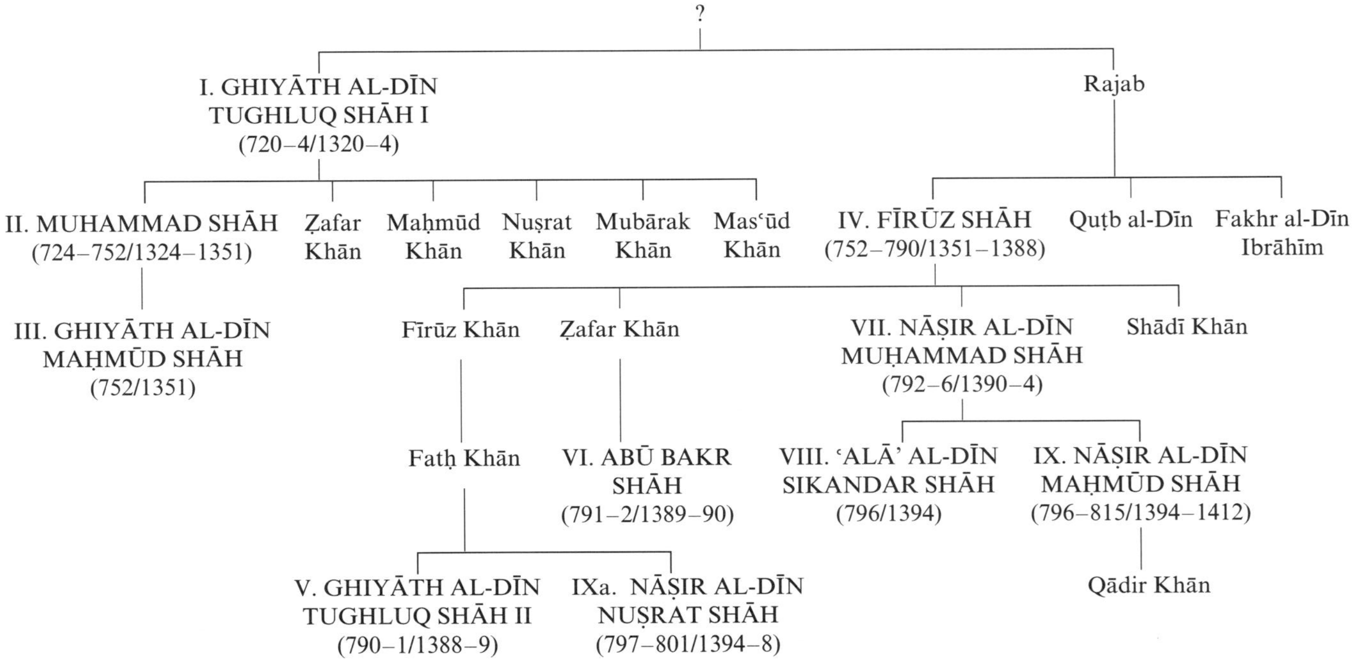

Glossary

ākhūrbeg/amīr-i ākhūr	intendant of the stables
amīr-ḥājib	military chamberlain
amīr-i dād	military justiciar
amīr-i majlis	intendant of the private assembly
amīr-i ṣada	commander of a unit of 100
amīr-i shikār	intendant of the hunt
ʿāriḍ	muster-master
bārbeg	= *amīr-ḥājib*
barīd	intelligence officer; spy
chāshnīgīr	cupbearer
chatr	ceremonial parasol
chawdhurī	Hindu chief/official in charge of a district
dādbeg	= *amīr-i dād*
dhimma	status of *dhimmī*
dhimmīs	'Protected peoples' living under Islamic rule
dīwān-i wizārat	imperial revenue ministry
dūrbāsh	ceremonial baton
farrāsh	palace attendant (literally 'carpet-spreader')
fatḥ-nāma	victory despatch
ghayr-wajhīs	troops paid other than by assignments of land (see pp. 316–17)
ghulām	slave
ḥājib	chamberlain
ḥawālī	territory in the environs of Delhi
inʿām	(revenue grant) exempt from service
inshā'	correspondence; the art of prose composition
iqṭāʿ	transferable revenue assignment in lieu of salary
jizya	capitation tax imposed on non-Muslims
kārkhāna	manufactory, workshop
khāliṣa	crown lands
khānaqāh	sufi hospice

kharāj	land-tax; tribute; (more generally) revenue
kharīṭadār	keeper of the purse
khāṣṣ-ḥājib	privy chamberlain
khūt/khōt	(Hindu) headman
kōtwāl	castellan
krōr	100 *laks*, i.e. 10 million
kurōh	approximately 2 miles
lak	100,000
mawās	(Hindu) territory inaccessible to Muslim attack (see p. 125)
mawlāzāda	son of a freed slave
muhrdār	keeper of the seal
muḥtasib	overseer of public morality; inspector of the markets
mukūs	taxes not sanctioned by the Sharīʿa
muqaddam	(Hindu) chief
muqṭaʿ	holder of an *iqṭāʿ*
mushrif-i mamālik	accountant-general of imperial revenue
mustawfī-yi mamālik	auditor-general
mutaṣarrif	(provincial) revenue-collector
nā'ib [-*i*]	viceroy; (deputy-)
nā'ib-i ʿarḍ	deputy muster-master
nawbat	band playing outside royal or noble residence as a mark of honour
noyan	(Mongol) commander
pāīk	(Hindu) infantryman
pīlkhāna	elephant-stable
qāḍī-yi lashgar	judge of the army
quriltai	(Mongol) assembly of princes and generals
ṣadī	hundred (administrative division)
sāh	Hindu banker/moneylender
sar-i chatrdār	chief parasol-bearer
sar-i dawātdār	chief inkwell-holder
sar-i jāndār	commander of the sultan's guards or executioners
sar-i ṣilāḥdār	chief armour-bearer
shiḥna	governor; (Mongol) resident at the court of a subject ruler
shiḥna-yi bārgāh	intendant of the audience-hall
shiḥna-yi manda	intendant of the markets
shiḥna-yi pīl	intendant of the elephantry
shiqq	administrative division
ṣilāḥdār	armour-bearer
talwāra/talwandī	(Hindu) territory or encampment

tümen	(Mongol) military unit of 10,000
ulus	complex of people, livestock and grazing grounds allotted to a prince of the Mongol imperial dynasty
wajhdārs	regular troops paid in assignments of land (see pp. 316–17)
wakīl-i dar	comptroller of the household
wālī	governor

Select bibliography

Primary sources

(a) Literary sources

Anonymous, *Bayāḍ-i Tāj al-Dīn Aḥmad Wazīr*, ed. Īraj Afshār and Murtaḍā Taymūrī (Isfahan, 1353 Sh./1974)
Anonymous, continuation of Rashīd al-Dīn, *Jāmiʿ al-Tawārīkh*, Istanbul ms. Nuruosmaniye Kütüphanesi 2799 (old numbering: 3271)
Anonymous, *al-Ḥawādith al-Jāmiʿa* (wrongly attributed to Ibn al-Fuwaṭī), ed. Muṣṭafā Jawād (Baghdad, 1351/1932)
Anonymous, *Ḥudūd al-ʿĀlam*, facsimile edn by V. V. Bartol'd (Leningrad, 1930); tr. V. Minorsky, 2nd edn, GMS, ns, XI (London, 1970)
Anonymous, *Muʿizz al-Ansāb*, BN ms. Ancien fonds persan 67
Anonymous, *Sīrat-i Fīrūz-Shāhī*, SOAS ms. 283116 (copy of ms. in Bankipore Library, Patna); extracts tr. K. K. Basu, 'An account of Firoz Shāh Tughluq', *JBORS* 22 (1936), 96–107, 265–74; 23 (1937), 97–112; K. K. Basu, 'Firoz Tughluq and his Bengal campaign', *JBORS* 27 (1941), 79–95; N. B. Roy, 'Jajnagar expedition of Sulṭān Fīrūz Shāh', *JRASB, Letters* 8 (1942), 57–98; J. A. Page, 'A memoir on Kotla Firuz Shah', *MASI* 52 (1937), 33–42; Sh. Abdur Rashid, 'Firoz Shah's investiture by the Caliph', *MIQ* 1 (1950), 66–71
Anonymous, tr. of Rāzī's *Sirr al-Makhtūma*, BN ms. Suppl. persan 384
Anonymous, *Ta'rīkh-i Sīstān*, ed. Malik al-Shuʿarā Bahār (Tehran, 1314 Sh./1935); tr. L. P. Smirnova (Moscow, 1974)
ʿAfīf, Shams-i Sirāj, *Ta'rīkh-i Fīrūz-Shāhī*, ed. Maulavi Vilayat Hosain, BI (Calcutta, 1888–91)
Aḥmad Yādgār, *Ta'rīkh-i Shāhī* or *Ta'rīkh-i Salāṭīn-i Afāghina*, ed. M. Hidayat Hosain, BI (Calcutta, 1939)
Amīr Ḥasan Dihlawī, *Fawā'id al-Fu'ād*, ed. M. Laṭīf Malik (Lahore, 1386/1966)
Amīr Khusraw Dihlawī, *Dībacha-yi Ghurrat al-Kamāl*, ed. Sayyid Wazīr al-Ḥasan ʿĀbidī (Lahore, 1975); IOL Persian ms. 51 (Ethé, no. 1186)
  Diwal Rānī-yi Khaḍir Khān, ed. Rashīd Aḥmad Sālim Anṣārī (Aligarh, 1336/1917)
  Ghurrat al-Kamāl, IOL Persian ms. 412 (Ethé, no. 1187)
  Khazā'in al-Futūḥ, ed. M. Wahid Mirza, BI (Calcutta, 1953)
  Miftāḥ al-Futūḥ, ed. Sh. Abdur Rashid (Aligarh, 1954)
  Nuh Sipihr, ed. M. Wahid Mirza (London, 1950)

Qirān al-Sa'dayn, ed. Maulavi Muḥammad Isma'īl and Sayyid Ḥasan Baranī (Aligarh, 1337/1918)

Rasā'il al-I'jāz, lithograph edn (Lucknow, 1876, 5 vols. in 2); IOL Persian ms. 570 (Ethé, no. 1219) and BL mss. Add. 16841, Add. 16842

Tughluq-Nāma, ed. Sayyid Hāshimī Farīdābādī (Aurangābād, 1352/1933)

Tuḥfat al-Ṣighār, IOL Persian ms. 412 (Ethé, no. 1187)

Wasaṭ al-Ḥayāt, IOL Persian ms. 412 (Ethé, no. 1187)

'Awfī, Sadīd al-Dīn Muḥammad b. Muḥammad Bukhārī, *Jawāmi' al-Ḥikāyāt*, I (preface), ed. Muḥammad Mu'īn, 2nd edn (Tehran, 1350 Sh./1971); BL mss. Or. 4392 and Or. 2676; BN ms. Anc. fonds persan 75

Lubāb al-Albāb, ed. E. G. Browne and M. M. Qazwīnī (Leiden and London, 1903–6, 2 vols.)

Bābur, Ẓahīr al-Dīn Muḥammad, *Bābur-Nāma*, tr. Annette S. Beveridge, *The Bābur-nāma in English* (London, 1921–2; repr. 1969)

Badā'ūnī, 'Abd al-Qādir, *Muntakhab al-Tawārīkh*, ed. Maulavi Aḥmad 'Ali, BI (Calcutta, 1864–9, 3 vols.)

Badr-i Chāch, *Qaṣā'id*, lithograph edn by M. Ḥādī 'Alī (Kānpūr, n.d.); lithograph edn by M. 'Uthmān Khān (Rampur, 1872–3, 2 vols.)

Balādhurī, *Futūḥ al-Buldān*, ed. M. J. De Goeje, *Liber expugnationis regionum* (Leiden, 1866); ed. S. al-Munajjid (Beirut, n.d.)

Baranī, Ḍiyā', *Fatāwā-yi Jahāndārī*, ed. Afsar Saleem Khan (Lahore, 1972)

Na't-i Muḥammadī, RRL Persian ms. 1895; extract tr. in S. Nurul Ḥasan, 'Sahifa-i-Na't-i-Muḥammadi of Zia-ud-din Barani', *MIQ* 1 (1950), 100–6

Ta'rīkh-i Fīrūz-Shāhī, ed. Saiyid Aḥmad Khán, BI (Calcutta, 1860–2); BL ms. Or. 2039

Ta'rīkh-i Fīrūz-Shāhī, first recension: Bodleian ms. Elliot 353; RRL Persian ms. 2053; ms. in private collection of Simon Digby

Bihāmadkhānī, Muḥammad, *Ta'rīkh-i Muḥammadī*, BL ms. Or. 137; partial tr. (from 755/1354) Muḥammad Zaki (Aligarh, 1972)

Fakhr-i Mudabbir (Muḥammad b. Manṣūr b. Sa'īd Qurashī), *Ādāb al-Ḥarb wa'l-Shajā'a* (or *Ādāb al-Mulūk*), ed. Aḥmad Suhaylī Khwānsārī (Tehran, 1346 Sh./ 1967)

Shajarat (or *Baḥr*) *al-Ansāb*, partial edn by Sir E. Denison Ross, *Ta'ríkh* [sic]-*i Fakhr al-Dín Mubárakshâh* (London, 1927)

Firishta (Muḥammad Qāsim Hindū Shāh Astarābādī), *Gulshan-i Ibrāhīmī*, lithograph edn (Bombay, 1247/1831–2, 2 vols.)

Fīrūz Shāh b. Rajab (Sultan), *Futūḥāt-i Fīrūz-Shāhī*, ed. Sh. Abdur Rashid (Aligarh, 1954); tr. N. B. Roy, 'The victories of Sulṭān Fīrūz Shāh of Tughluq dynasty', *IC* 15 (1941), 449–64

Ghaznawī, 'Abd al-Ḥamīd Muḥarrir, *Dastūr al-Albāb fī 'Ilmi'l-Ḥisāb*, RRL Persian ms. 1231; partial tr. Sh. Abdur Rashid, 'Dastur-ul-Albab fi 'Ilm-il-Hisab', *MIQ* 1 (1950), 59–99

Ḥamīd Qalandar, *Khayr al-Majālis*, ed. K. A. Nizami (Aligarh, [1959])

Harawī, Niẓam al-Dīn Aḥmad, *Ṭabaqāt-i Akbarī*, ed. B. De *et al.*, BI (Calcutta, 1931–5, 3 vols.)

Ḥasan-i Niẓāmī (Tāj al-Dīn Ḥasan b. Niẓāmī Nīshāpūrī), *Tāj al-Ma'āthir*, IOL Persian ms. 15 (Ethé, no. 210)

Ibn Abi'l-Faḍā'il, al-Mufaḍḍal, *al-Nahj al-Sadīd*, partial edn and tr. E. Blochet,

'Moufazzal Ibn Abil-Fazaïl. Histoire des Sultans Mamlouks', *Patrologia Orientalis* 12–20 (1919–29) (references are to the separatum); partial edn and tr. Samira Kortantamer, *Ägypten und Syrien zwischen 1317 und 1341*, IU 23 (Freiburg i. Br., 1973)

Ibn al-Athīr, ʿIzz al-Dīn, *al-Kāmil fi'l-Ta'rīkh*, ed. C. J. Tornberg, *Ibn-El-Athiri Chronicon quod perfectissimum inscribitur* (Leiden, 1851–76, 12 vols.); repr. (with different pagination) Dar al-Sader (Beirut, 1386/1966, 12 vols.) (references are to both editions, in that order)

Ibn al-Dawādārī, Abū Bakr b. ʿAlī b. Aybak, *Kanz al-Durar wa-Jāmiʿ al-Ghurar*, ed. Saʿīd ʿĀshūr *et al.*, *Die Chronik des Ibn ad-Dawādārī*, QGIA, I: VII (Cairo, 1392/1972); VIII (Cairo, 1391/1971); IX (Cairo, 1379/1960)

Ibn Baṭṭūṭa, Abū ʿAbd-Allāh Muḥammad b. ʿAbd-Allāh al-Lawātī al-Ṭanjī, *Tuḥfat al-Nuẓẓār fī Gharā'ibi'l-Amṣār*, ed. Ch. Defrémery and B. S. Sanguinetti (Paris, 1853–8, 4 vols.); tr. H. A. R. Gibb, *The travels of Ibn Baṭṭūṭa A.D. 1325–1354*, HS, 2nd series, 110, 117, 141, 178 (Cambridge and London, 1958–94, 4 vols. of 5 so far; vol. IV ed. by C. F. Beckingham)

Ibn Māhrū, ʿAyn al-Mulk ʿAbd-Allāh-i Muḥammad Sharaf, *Inshā-yi Māhrū*, ed. Sh. Abdur Rashid (Lahore, 1965)

Ibn Saʿīd al-Maghribī, *Kitāb al-Jughrāfiyya*, ed. Ismāʿīl al-ʿArabī (Beirut, 1970)

Ibn Zarkūb, Muʿīn al-Dīn Aḥmad b. Abi'l-Khayr Shīrāzī, *Shīrāz-Nāma*, ed. Bahman Karīmī (Tehran, 1310 Sh./1932); ed. Ismaʿīl Wāʿiẓ Jawādī (Tehran, 1350 Sh./1971)

Ikhtisān-i Dabīr (Tāj al-Dīn Muḥammad b. Aḥmad b. Ḥasan), *Basātīn al-Uns*, BL ms. Add. 7717

ʿIṣāmī, ʿAbd al-Malik, *Futūḥ al-Salāṭīn*, ed. A. S. Usha (Madras, 1948); tr. A. M. Husain (Aligarh, 1967–77, 3 vols. with continuous pagination)

Jaʿfar b. Muḥammad b. Ḥasan Jaʿfarī, *Ta'rīkh-i Yazd*, ed. Īraj Afshār (Tehran, 1338 Sh./1959)

Jājarmī, preface to his tr. of Ghazālī's *Iḥyā' ʿUlūmi'l-Dīn*, BL ms. Or. 8194

Jamāl al-Qarshī, *Mulḥaqāt al-Ṣurāḥ*, ed. in V. V. Bartol'd, *Turkestan v epokhu mongol'skogo nashestviia* (St Petersburg, 1898–1900, 2 vols.), I (texts)

Juwaynī, ʿAlā' al-Dīn Aṭā Malik, *Ta'rīkh-i Jahān-Gushā*, ed. Mīrzā Muḥammad Qazwīnī, GMS, XVI (Leiden and London, 1912–37, 3 vols.); tr. J. A. Boyle, *The history of the world-conqueror* (Manchester, 1958, 2 vols. with continuous pagination)

Jūzjānī, Minhāj al-Dīn Abū ʿUmar ʿUthmān b. Sirāj al-Dīn, *Ṭabaqāt-i Nāṣirī*, ed. ʿAbd al-Ḥayy Ḥabībī, 2nd edn (Kabul, 1342–3 Sh./1963–4, 2 vols.); tr. H. G. Raverty, *Ṭabaḳāt-i Nāṣirī: a general history of the Muḥammadan dynasties of Asia*, BI (London, 1872–81, 2 vols. with continuous pagination); BL ms. Add. 26189; IOL ms. 3745; Berlin ms. Petermann 386 (Pertsch, no. 367)

Kirmānī, Muḥammad b. Mubārak (Mīr-i Khwurd), *Siyar al-Awliyā' fī Maḥabbati'l-Ḥaqq jalla wa-ʿAlā'*, lithograph edn (Delhi, 1302/1885)

Kirmānī, Nāṣir al-Dīn, *Simṭ al-ʿUlā li'l-Ḥaḍrati'l-ʿUlyā'*, ed. ʿAbbās Iqbāl (Tehran, 1328 Sh./1949)

Kūfī, ʿAlī b. Ḥāmid b. Abī Bakr, *Chach-Nāma*, ed. N. A. Baloch, *Fathnāmah-i Sind* (Islamabad, 1403/1983)

Maqrīzī, Taqī' al-Dīn Aḥmad b. ʿAlī al-, *al-Sulūk li-Maʿrifat Duwali'l-Mulūk*, ed. M.M. Ziada *et al.* (Cairo, 1934– in progress)

Marco Polo, *Le divisament dou monde*, tr. A. C. Moule and Paul Pelliot, *The description of the world* (London, 1938, 2 vols.); tr. Sir Henry Yule, *The book of Ser Marco Polo the Venetian*, new edn by H. Cordier (London, 1920, 3 vols.)

Nasawī, Muḥammad b. Aḥmad b. ʿAlī, *Sīrat al-Sulṭān Jalāl al-Dīn*, ed. Octave Houdas (Paris, 1891); tr. Z. M. Buniiatov, *Zhizneopisanie Sultana Dzhalal ad-Dina Mankburny* (Baku, 1973)

Naṭanzī, Muʿīn al-Dīn, *Muntakhab al-Tawārīkh*, partial edn by Jean Aubin, *Extraits du Muntakhab al-tawarikh-i Mu'ini* (Tehran, 1957)

Nizami, K. A. (ed.), 'Some documents of Sultan Muḥammad bin Tughluq', *MIM* 1 (1969), 305–13

Qāshānī, Jamāl al-Dīn ʿAbd-Allāh b. ʿAlī, *Ta'rīkh-i Uljāītū Sulṭān*, ed. Mahin Hambly (Tehran, 1348 Sh./1969)

Qazwīnī, Ḥamd-Allāh Mustawfī, *Ta'rīkh-i Guzīda*, ed. ʿAbd al-Ḥusayn Nawā'ī (Tehran, 1339 Sh./1960)

Rashīd al-Dīn Faḍl-Allāh al-Hamadānī, *Jāmiʿ al-Tawārīkh*, divided as follows:

A. History of the Mongols:

I, part 1 [account of the Turkish and Mongol tribes], ed. A. A. Romaskevich *et al.* (Moscow, 1965); tr. A. A. Khetagurov, *Sbornik letopisei*, I, part 1 (Moscow and Leningrad, 1952); I, part 2 [history of Chinggis Khan], ed. I. N. Berezin, 'Sbornik letopisei', *TVOIRAO* 13 (1868), 1–239, and 15 (1888), 1–231; tr. O. I. Smirnova, *Sbornik letopisei*, I, part 2 (Moscow and Leningrad, 1952);

II [history of Chinggis Khan's successors], ed. E. Blochet, GMS, XVIII, part 1 (Leiden and London, 1911); tr. J. A. Boyle, *The successors of Genghis Khan* (New York, 1971); tr. Iu.P. Verkhovskii, *Sbornik letopisei*, II (Moscow and Leningrad, 1960); II, part 1 (only), ed. A. A. Alizade (Moscow, 1980);

III [history of the Ilkhans], ed. A. A. Alizade and tr. A. K. Arends (Baku, 1957); partial edn by Karl Jahn, *Geschichte Ġāzān Ḫān's*, GMS, ns, XIV (London, 1940);

B. History of India, ed. and tr. Karl Jahn, *Die Indiengeschichte des Rašīd ad-Dīn*, 2nd edn (Vienna, 1980)

Shuʿab-i Panjgāna, TSM ms. III Ahmet 2937

Ṣafadī, Khalīl b. Aybak al-, *Aʿyān al-ʿAṣr*, SK ms. Aşir Efendi 588

al-Wāfī bi'l-Wafayāt, ed. H. Ritter *et al.* (Damascus, 1931–in progress); extract tr. M. S. Khān, 'An undiscovered Arabic source of the history of Sulṭān Muḥammad bin Tughlaq', *IC* 53 (1979), 187–205, with addenda (comprising Arabic text), *IC* 54 (1980), 47–8

Sayfī (Sayf b. Muḥammad b. Yaʿqūb al-Harawī), *Ta'rīkh-Nāma-yi Harāt*, ed. M. Z. as-Siddíquí (Calcutta, 1944)

Sayyid Ashraf Jahāngīr Simnānī, *Maktūbāt-i Ashrafī*, BL ms. Or. 267

Shabānkāra'ī, Muḥammad b. ʿAlī, *Majmaʿ al-Ansāb*, ed. Mīr Hāshim Muḥaddith (Tehran, 1363 Sh./1984)

Shāmī, Niẓām-i, *Ẓafar-Nāma*, ed. Felix Tauer, *Histoire des conquêtes de Tamerlan intitulée Ẓafarnāma*, Monografie Archivu Orientálního, V (Prague, 1937–56, 2 vols.)

Sikandar b. Muḥammad, alias Manjhū, *Mir'āt-i Sikandarī*, ed. S. C. Misra and Muḥammad Luṭf al-Raḥmān (Baroda, 1961); tr. in Sir E. C. Bayley, *The local Muḥammadan dynasties. Gujarat* (London, 1886)

Sirhindī, Yaḥyā b. Aḥmad, *Ta'rīkh-i Mubārak-Shāhī*, ed. S.M. Hidayat Husain, BI (Calcutta, 1931)

Ulughkhānī, 'Abd-Allāh Muḥammad al-Makkī, *Ẓafar al-Wālih bi-Muẓaffar wa-Ālih*, ed. Sir E. Denison Ross, *An Arabic history of Gujarat* (London, 1910–28, 3 vols.)

'Umarī, Shihāb al-Dīn Abu'l-'Abbās Aḥmad b. Yaḥyā ibn Faḍl-Allāh al-, *Masālik al-Abṣār fī Mamālikiʾl-Amṣār*, (section on India), ed. and tr. Otto Spies, *Ibn Faḍlallāh al-'Omarī's Bericht über Indien in seinem Werke*..., Sammlung Orientalischer Arbeiten, XIV (Leipzig, 1943); ed. Khurshīd Aḥmad Fāriq (Delhi, [1961]); tr. Iqtidar Husain Siddiqi and Qazi Muḥammad Aḥmad, *A fourteenth century Arab account of India under Sulṭān Muḥammad bin Tughlaq* (Aligarh, [1975]); (section on the Mongol empire) ed. and tr. Klaus Lech, *Das mongolische Weltreich: al-'Umarī's Darstellung der mongolischen Reiche in seinem Werk*..., AF, XXII (Wiesbaden, 1968)

Van den Wyngaert, Anastasius (ed.), *Sinica Franciscana*, I. *Itinera et relationes Fratrum Minorum saeculi XIII et XIV* (Quaracchi-Firenze, 1929)

Waṣṣāf (Shihāb al-Dīn 'Abd-Allāh b. 'Izz al-Dīn Faḍl-Allāh Shīrāzī), *Tajziyat al-Amṣār wa-Tazjiyat al-A'ṣār*, lithograph edn (Bombay, 1269/1853)

Yazdī, Ghiyāth al-Dīn 'Alī, *Rūz-Nāma-yi Ghazawāt-i Hindūstān*, tr. A. A. Semenov, *Dnevnik pokhoda Tīmūra v Indiiu* (Moscow, 1958)

Yazdī, Sharaf al-Dīn 'Alī, *Ẓafar-Nāma*, ed. M. M. Ilahdād, BI (Calcutta, 1885–8, 2 vols.); facsimile (including *muqaddima*) edn by A. Urunbaev (Tashkent, 1972)

Yūnīnī, Quṭb al-Dīn Mūsā b. Muḥammad al-, *al-Dhayl 'alā' Mir'ātiʾl-Zamān* (Hyderabad, AP, 1374–80/1954–61, 4 vols. so far); TSM ms. III Ahmet 2907/e.3

Yūsuf-i Ahl, Jalāl al-Dīn, *Farā'id-i Ghiyāthī*, ed. Hishmat Mu'ayyad (Tehran, 2536 Shāhanshāhī/1977 and 1358 Sh./1979, 2 vols. so far); SK ms. Fatıh 4012

(b) Epigraphy and numismatics

Abdul Karim (ed.), *Corpus of the Arabic and Persian inscriptions of Bengal* (Dacca, 1992)

Aḥmad, Q. (ed.), *Corpus of Arabic and Persian inscriptions of Bihar (AH 640–1200)* (Patna, 1973)

Bühler, G., 'A Jaina account of the end of the Vaghelas of Gujarat', *IA* 26 (1897), 194–5

Dani, Aḥmad Ḥasan, *Muslim inscriptions of Bengal*, Appendix to *JASP* 2 (Dacca, 1957)

Desai, P. B., 'Kalyana inscription of Sultan Muḥammad, Śaka 1248', *EI* 32 (1957–8), 165–70

Desai, Z. A., 'Inscriptions of the Mamlūk Sulṭāns of Delhi', *EIAPS* (1966), 4–18

'Khaljī and Tughluq inscriptions from Gujarat', *EIAPS* (1962), 1–40

'The Chanderi inscription of 'Alau'd-din Khalji', *EIAPS* (1968), 4–10

'The Jālor 'Īdgāh inscription of Quṭbu'd-Dīn Mubārak Shāh Khaljī', *EIAPS* (1972), 12–19

'Two inscriptions of Ghiyāthu'd-Dīn Tughluq from Uttar Pradesh', *EIAPS* (1966), 19–26

Diskalkar, D. B., 'Inscriptions of Kathiawad', *NIA* 1 (1938–9), 686–96

Husain, A. M., 'Six inscriptions of Sulṭān Muḥammad bin Tughluq Shāh', *EIAPS* (1957–8), 29–42

Moneer, Q. M., 'Two unpublished inscriptions of the time of Sulṭān Muḥammad bin Tughluq', *EIM* (1939–40), 23–6

Nāẓim, M., *Inscriptions of Bijapur*, MASI 49 (Delhi, 1936)

Prasad, Pushpa (ed.), *Sanskrit inscriptions of Delhi Sultanate 1191–1526* (Delhi, 1992)

Shokoohy, Mehrdad (ed.), *Haryana I*, Corpus inscriptionum Iranicarum, part IV: Persian inscriptions down to the early Safavid period, XLVII (London, 1988)

Rajasthan I, Corpus inscriptionum Iranicarum, part IV: Persian inscriptions down to the early Safavid period, XLIX (London, 1986)

Shu'aib, M. M., 'Inscriptions from Palwal', *EIM* (1911–12), 1–5

Sircar, D.C., 'Inscriptions of the time of Yajvapala Gopala', *EI* 31 (1955–6), 323–36

Thomas, Edward, *Chronicles of the Pathan kings of Delhi* (Delhi, 1871)

Verma, B. D., 'Inscriptions from the Central Museum, Nagpur', *EIAPS* (1955–6), 109–18

Wright, H. Nelson, *Catalogue of the coins of the Indian Museum, Calcutta*, II (Oxford, 1907)

The coinage and metrology of the Sulṭāns of Dehlī (Delhi, 1936)

Yazdani, Ghulam Husain, 'Inscriptions of the Khaljī Sulṭāns of Delhi and their contemporaries in Bengal', *EIM* (1917–18), 8–42

'The inscriptions of the Turk Sulṭāns of Delhi – Mu'izzu-d-dīn Bahrām, 'Alā'u-d-dīn Mas'ūd, Nāṣiru-d-dīn Maḥmūd, Ghiyāthu-d-dīn Balban and Mu'izzu-d-dīn Kaiqubād', *EIM* (1913–14), 13–46

Secondary sources

'Abdu'l Walī, Maulavī, 'Life and letters of Malik 'Aynu'l-Mulk Māhrū, and side-lights on Fīrūz Shāh's expeditions to Lakhnautī and Jājnagar', *JASB* ns 19 (1923), 253–90

Aḥmad, Aziz, 'Mongol pressure in an alien land', *CAJ* 6 (1961), 182–93

Studies in Islamic culture in the Indian environment (Oxford, 1964)

'The early Turkish nucleus in India', *Turcica* 9 (1977), 99–109

'The sufi and the sultan in pre-Mughal Muslim India', *Der Islam* 38 (1962), 142–53

Aḥmad, Laiq, 'Kara, a medieval Indian city', *IC* 55 (1981), 83–92

Aḥmad, Muḥammad 'Azīz, *Political history and institutions of the early Turkish empire of Delhi (1206–1290AD)* (Lahore, 1949)

Ali, Athar, 'Military technology of the Delhi Sultanate (13–14th C.)', in *PIHC* 50 *(Gorakhpur 1989)* (Delhi, 1990), 166–82

Allsen, T. T., *Mongol imperialism: the policies of the Grand Qan Möngke in China, Russia, and the Islamic lands, 1251–1259* (Berkeley and Los Angeles, 1987)

'The Yüan dynasty and the Uighurs of Turfan in the 13th century', in Morris Rossabi (ed.), *China among equals: the Middle Kingdom and its neighbours, 10th–14th centuries* (Berkeley and Los Angeles, 1983), 243–80

Askari, S. H., 'Material of historical interest in I'jaz-i-Khusravi', *MIM* 1 (1969), 1–20

'Risail (*sic*)-ul-Ijaz of Amir Khusrau: an appraisal', in *Dr. Zakir Husain presentation volume* (Delhi, 1968), 116–37
Aubin, Jean, 'L'ethnogénèse des Qaraunas', *Turcica* 1 (1969), 65–94
'Le khanat de Čaġatai et le Khorassan (1334–1380)', *Turcica* 8 (1976), 16–60
'Les princes d'Ormuz du XIIIe au XVe siècle', *JA* 241 (1953), 77–138
Ayalon, David, 'Aspects of the Mamlūk phenomenon, I. The importance of the Mamlūk institution', *Der Islam* 53 (1976), 196–225; repr. in his *The Mamlūk military society* (London, 1979)
Studies on the Mamlūks of Egypt (1250–1517) (London, 1977)
'Studies on the structure of the Mamluk army – II', *BSOAS* 15 (1953), 448–76; repr. in his *Studies*
'The Wafidiya in the Mamluk kingdom', *IC* 25 (1951), 81–104; repr. in his *Studies*
Banerjee, Jamini Mohan, *History of Firuz Shah Tughluq* (Delhi, 1967)
Barthold, W., *Four studies on the history of Central Asia* (Leiden, 1956–62, 4 parts in 3 vols.)
Turkestan down to the Mongol invasion, 3rd edn by C. E. Bosworth, GMS, ns, V (London, 1968)
Zwölf Vorlesungen über die Türken Mittelasiens, tr. Th. Menzel (Hildesheim, 1935; repr. 1962)
Bhandarkar, D. R., 'The Chahamanas of Mārwār', *EI* 11 (1911–12), 26–79
Biran, Michal, *Qaidu and the rise of the independent Mongol state in Central Asia* (Richmond, Surrey, 1997)
Bosworth, C. E., *The Ghaznavids. Their empire in Afghanistan and eastern Iran 994:1040*, 2nd edn (Beirut, 1973)
The history of the Saffarids of Sistan and the maliks of Nimruz (247/861 to 949/1542–3) (Costa Mesa, California, 1994)
The later Ghaznavids, splendour and decay: the dynasty in Afghanistan and northern India 1040–1186 (Edinburgh, 1977)
The medieval history of Iran, Afghanistan and Central Asia (London, 1977)
'The political and dynastic history of the Iranian world (A.D. 1000–1217)', in Boyle (ed.), *Cambridge history of Iran*, V, 1–202
Bouchon, Geneviève, 'Quelques aspects de l'islamisation des régions maritimes de l'Inde à l'époque médiévale (XIIe–XVIe s.)', in Gaborieau (ed.), *Islam et société*, 29–36
Boyle, J. A., 'Dynastic and political history of the Īl-khāns', in Boyle (ed.), *Cambridge history of Iran*, V, 303–421
'The Mongol commanders in Afghanistan and India according to the *Ṭabaqāt-i Nāṣirī* of Jūzjānī', *IS* 2 (1963), 235–47
Boyle, J. A. (ed.) *The Cambridge history of Iran*, V. *The Saljuq and Mongol periods* (Cambridge, 1968)
Chakravarti, Monmohan, 'Notes on Gaur and other old places in Bengal', *JASB* ns 5 (1909), 199–235
Clauson, Sir Gerard, *An etymological dictionary of pre-thirteenth-century Turkish* (Oxford, 1972)
Conermann, Stephan, *Die Beschreibung Indiens in der 'Riḥla' des Ibn Baṭṭūṭa: Aspekte einer herrschaftssoziologischen Einordnung des Delhi-Sultanates unter Muḥammad Ibn Tuġluq*, IU, 165 (Berlin, 1993)

Cunningham, Sir Alexander, 'Report of a tour in Bundelkhand and Rewa in 1883–84', *ASIR* 21 (1885), 1–137
Dani, Aḥmad Ḥasan, 'Shamsuddīn Ilyās Shāh, Shāh-i Bangālah', in Gupta *et al.* (eds.), 50–8
Dardess, John W., 'From Mongol empire to Yüan dynasty: changing forms of imperial rule in Mongolia and Central Asia', *Monumenta Serica* 30 (1972–3), 117–65
Day, U. N., *The government of the Sultanate*, 2nd edn (New Delhi, 1993)
'The north-west frontier of the Sultanate', in his *Some aspects of medieval Indian history* (New Delhi, 1971), 29–57
'The north-west frontier under the Khalji Sultans of Delhi', *IC* 39 (1963), 98–108
De Bary, W. T. (ed.), *Sources of Indian tradition* (New York, 1958)
Derrett, J. Duncan M., *The Hoysaḷas: a medieval Indian royal family* (Oxford, 1957)
Deyell, John S., *Living without silver: the monetary history of early medieval North India* (Oxford and Delhi, 1990)
Digby, Simon, 'Iletmish or Iltutmish? A reconsideration of the name of the Dehli Sultan', *Iran* 8 (1970), 57–64
'The currency system', in Raychaudhuri and Habib, (eds.), *Cambridge economic history*, 93–101
'The sufi *shaykh* and the sultan: a conflict of claims to authority in medieval India', *Iran* 28 (1990), 71–81
'The sufi shaikh as a source of authority in mediaeval India', in Gaborieau (ed.), *Islam et société*, 55–77
War-horse and elephant in the Delhi Sultanate: a problem of military supplies (Oxford and Karachi, 1971)
Dikshit, R. K., *The Candellas of Jejākabhukti* (New Delhi, 1977)
Doerfer, Gerhard, *Türkische und mongolische Elemente im Neupersischen* (Wiesbaden, 1963–75, 4 vols.)
Eaton, Richard M., *The rise of Islam and the Bengal frontier, 1204–1760* (Berkeley and Los Angeles, 1993)
Ernst, Carl W., *Eternal garden. Mysticism, history, and politics at a South Asian sufi center* (Albany, New York, 1992)
Friedmann, Yohanan, 'A contribution to the early history of Islam in India', in M. Rosen-Ayalon (ed.), *Studies in memory of Gaston Wiet* (Jerusalem, 1977), 309–33
Friedmann, Yohanan (ed.), *Islam in Asia*, I. *South Asia* (Jerusalem, 1984)
Gaborieau, Marc (ed.), *Islam et société en Asie du Sud*, Collection Puruṣārthe 9 (Paris, 1986)
Golden, P. B., 'Cumanica II. The Ölberli (Ölperli): the fortunes and misfortunes of an Inner Asian nomadic clan', *AEMA* 6 (1986 [1988]), 5–29
Gopal, Lallanji, *The economic life of northern India, c. A.D. 700–1200*, 2nd edn (Delhi, 1989)
Gupta, Hari Ram, *et al.* (eds.), *Essays presented to Sir Jadunath Sarkar*, Sir Jadunath Sarkar commemoration volume, II (Hoshiarpur, 1958)
Gupta, Satya Prakash, 'Jhain of the Delhi Sultanate', *MIM* 3 (1975), 209–15
Habib, Irfan, 'Agrarian economy', in Raychaudhuri and Habib (eds.), *Cambridge economic history*, 48–76
An atlas of the Mughal empire (Delhi, 1982; repr. 1986)

'Baranī's theory of the history of the Delhi Sultanate', *IHR* 7 (1980–1), 99–115

'Economic history of the Delhi Sultanate – an essay in interpretation', *IHR* 4 (1977), 287–303

'Formation of the Sultanate ruling class of the thirteenth century', in I. Habib (ed.), *Medieval India 1*, 1–21

'Non-agricultural production and urban economy', in Raychaudhuri and Habib (eds.), *Cambridge economic history*, 76–93

'The price regulations of 'Alā'uddīn Khaljī – a defence of Ẓiā' Baranī', *IESHR* 21 (1984), 393–414

Habib, Irfan (ed.), *Medieval India 1. Researches in the history of India 1200–1750* (Oxford and Delhi, 1992)

Habib, Moḥammad, and Nizami, Khaliq Aḥmad (eds.), *The Delhi Sultanat (A.D. 1206–1526)*, A comprehensive history of India, V (Delhi, 1970)

Habibullah, A. B. M., *The foundation of Muslim rule in India*, 2nd edn (Allahabad, 1961)

Haig, Sir Wolseley, 'Five questions in the history of the Tughluq dynasty of Dihli', *JRAS* (1922), 319–72

Haig, Sir Wolseley (ed.), *The Cambridge history of India*, III. *Turks and Afghans* (Cambridge, 1928)

Hambly, Gavin R. G., 'Twilight of Tughluqid Delhi', in R. E. Frykenberg (ed.), *Delhi through the ages: essays in urban history, culture and society* (Oxford and Delhi, 1986), 47–56

'Who were the Chihilgānī, the Forty Slaves of Sultan Shams al-Dīn Iltutmish of Delhi?', *Iran* 10 (1972), 57–62

Hardy, Peter, 'Didactic historical writing in Indian Islam: Żiyā al-Dīn Baranī's treatment of the reign of Sultan Muḥammad Tughluq (1324–1351)', in Friedmann (ed.), *Islam in Asia*, I, 38–59

'Dihlī Sultanate', *Enc.Isl.*[2]

'Djizya, iii. India', *Enc.Isl.*[2]

'Force and violence in Indo-Persian writing on history and government in medieval South Asia', in Milton Israel and N. K. Wagle (eds.), *Islamic society and culture. Essays in honour of Professor Aziz Aḥmad* (Delhi, 1983), 165–208

Historians of medieval India (London, 1960)

'The authority of Muslim kings in mediaeval South Asia', in Gaborieau (ed.), *Islam et société*, 37–55

'The growth of authority over a conquered political elite: the early Delhi Sultanate as a possible case study', in John S. Richards (ed.), *Kingship and authority in South Asia* (Madison, Wisconsin, 1978), 192–214

'The *oratio recta* of Baranī's *Ta'rīkh-i Fīrūz Shāhī* – fact or fiction?', *BSOAS* 20 (1957), 315–21

Hodivala, S. H., *Studies in Indo-Muslim history* (Bombay, 1939–57, 2 vols.)

Husain, A. Mahdi, *The rise and fall of Muḥammad bin Tughluq* (London, 1938)

Tughluq dynasty (Calcutta, 1963)

Irwin, Robert, *The Middle East in the middle ages: the early Mamluk Sultanate 1250–1382* (London and Sydney, 1986)

Islam, Riazul, 'Some aspects of the economy of northern South Asia during the fourteenth century', *JCA* 11 (1988), no. 2, 5–39.

'The rise of the Sammas in Sind', *IC* 22 (1948), 359–82
Islam, Ẓafarul, 'Fīrūz Shāh's attitude towards non-Muslims – a reappraisal', *IC* 64 (1990), part 4, 65–79
'The *Fatāwā Fīrūz Shāhī* as a source for the socio-economic history of the Sultanate period', *IC* 60 (1986), part 2, 97–117
Jackson, Peter, 'Jalāl al-Dīn, the Mongols and the Khwarazmian conquest of the Panjāb and Sind', *Iran* 28 (1990), 45–54
'Ḳuṭb al-Dīn Aybak', *Enc.Isl.*^{2}
'The dissolution of the Mongol empire', *CAJ* 22 (1978), 186–244
'The fall of the Ghurid dynasty', in Carole Hillenbrand (ed.), *Festschrift for Professor Edmund Bosworth* (Edinburgh; forthcoming)
'The *Mamlūk* institution in early Muslim India', *JRAS* (1990), 340–58
'The Mongols and India, 1221–1351', unpublished PhD thesis, Cambridge, 1977
'The Mongols and the Delhi Sultanate in the reign of Muḥammad Tughluq (1325–1351)', *CAJ* 19 (1975), 118–57
Jackson, Peter, and Lockhart, Laurence (eds.), *The Cambridge history of Iran*, VI. *The Timurid and Safavid periods* (Cambridge, 1986)
Jahn, Karl, 'Zum Problem der mongolischen Eroberungen in Indien (13.–14. Jahrhundert)', in *Akten des XXIV. internationalen Orientalisten-Kongresses München . . . 1957* (Wiesbaden, 1959), 617–19
Joshi, P. M., and Husain, A. Mahdi, 'Khaljis and Tughluqs in the Deccan', in Sherwani and Joshi, *History of medieval Deccan*, I, 29–55
Kehrer, Kenneth C., 'The economic policies of Ala-ud-Din Khalji', *Journal of the Panjab University Historical Society* 16 (1963), 55–66
Kempiners, Russell G., Jr, 'Vaṣṣāf's *Tajziyat al-Amṣār wa Tazjiyat al-A'ṣār* as a source for the history of the Chaghadayid khanate', *JAH* 22 (1988), 160–87
Khuhro, Hamida (ed.), *Sind through the centuries* (Oxford and Karachi, 1981)
Kolff, Dirk H. A., *Naukar, Rajput and Sepoy: the ethnohistory of the military labour market in Hindustan, 1450–1850* (Cambridge, 1990)
Lal, Kishori Saran, *History of the Khaljis A.D. 1290–1320*, 3rd edn (Delhi, 1980)
Twilight of the Sultanate, revised edn (New Delhi, 1980)
Lessing, F. D., *A Mongolian–English dictionary* (Berkeley and Los Angeles, 1960)
Lewis, Bernard, *The Jews of Islam* (Princeton, 1984)
Majumdar, R. C., *Chaulukyas of Gujarat* (Bombay, 1956)
History of medieval Bengal (Calcutta, 1973)
Manz, Beatrice Forbes, *The rise and rule of Tamerlane* (Cambridge, 1989)
'The ulus Chaghatay before and after Temür's rise to power: the transformation from tribal confederation to army of conquest', *CAJ* 27 (1983), 79–100
Mirza, M. Wahid, *The life and works of Amir Khusrau* (Calcutta, 1935)
Misra, S. C., *The rise of Muslim power in Gujarat*, 2nd edn (New Delhi, 1982)
Moosvi, Shireen, 'Numismatic evidence and the economic history of the Delhi Sultanate', in *PIHC* 50. *Gorakhpur 1989* (Delhi, 1990), 207–18
Moreland, W. H., *The agrarian system of Moslem India* (Cambridge, 1929)
Morgan, D. O., *The Mongols* (Oxford, 1986)
Morgan, D. O. (ed.), *Medieval historical writing in the Christian and Islamic worlds* (London, 1982)
Nigam, S. B. P., *Nobility under the Sultans of Delhi A.D. 1206–1398* (Delhi, 1968)
Niyogi, Roma, *The history of the Gāhaḍavāla dynasty* (Calcutta, 1959)

Nizami, K. A., 'Early Indo-Muslim mystics and their attitude towards the state', *IC* 22 (1948), 387–98; 23 (1949), 13–21, 162–70, 312–21; 24 (1950), 60–71

On history and historians in medieval India (New Delhi, 1983)

Some aspects of religion and politics in India in the thirteenth century (Aligarh, 1961)

Studies in medieval Indian history (Aligarh, 1956)

Supplement to Elliot and Dowson's History of India, II–III (Delhi, 1981)

'The impact of Ibn Taimiyya on South Asia', *JIS* 1 (1990), 120–49

Nizami, K. A. (ed.), *Politics and society during the early medieval period. Collected works of Professor Mohammad Habib* (New Delhi, 1974, 2 vols.)

Niẓámu'd-Dín, M., *Introduction to the Jawámi'u'l-ḥikáyát*, GMS, ns, VIII (London, 1929)

Pal, Dharam, ''Alā'-ud-Dīn Khiljī's Mongol policy', *IC* 21 (1947), 255–63

''Alā'-ud-Dīn's price control system', *IC* 18 (1944), 45–52

Parry, V. J., and Yapp, M. E. (eds.), *War, technology and society in the Middle East* (Oxford and London, 1975)

Pelliot, Paul, *Notes on Marco Polo* (Paris, 1959–73, 3 vols. with continuous pagination)

Notes sur l'histoire de la Horde d'Or (Paris, 1950)

Pelliot, P., and Hambis, L. (eds.), *Histoire des campagnes de Gengis Khan. Cheng-wou Ts'in tcheng-lou* (Leiden, 1951, vol. I only)

Petech, Luciano, *Mediaeval Nepal (c. 750–1480)*, Serie Orientale Roma, X (Rome, 1958)

Prasad, Ishwari, *A history of the Qaraunah Turks in India* (Allahabad, 1936, vol. I only)

Qureshi, I. H., *The administration of the Sultanate of Dehli*, 4th edn (Karachi, 1958)

Rabie, Hassanein, *The financial system of Egypt A.H. 564–741/A.D. 1169–1341* (Oxford and London, 1972)

Rashid, Shaikh Abdur, 'Price control under Alauddin Khilji', in *Proceedings of the All-Pakistan History Conference. First Session, held at Karachi ... 1951* (Karachi, [n.d.]), 203–10

Rásonyi, L., 'Les noms de personnes impératifs chez les peuples turques', *AOH* 15 (1962), 233–43

Ray, H. C., *The dynastic history of northern India* (Calcutta, 1931–5, 2 vols. with continuous pagination)

Raychaudhuri, T., and Habib, I. (eds.), *The Cambridge economic history of India*, I. *c. 1200– c. 1750* (Cambridge, 1982)

Richards, J. F. (ed.), *Precious metals in the later medieval and early modern worlds* (Durham, North Carolina, 1984)

Roemer, Hans Robert, 'Tīmūr in Iran', in Jackson and Lockhart, 42–97

Roy, N. B., 'The transfer of capital from Delhi to Daulatabad', *JIH* 20 (1941), 159–80

Saeed, Mian Muḥammad, *The Sharqi Sultanate of Jaunpur* (Karachi, 1972)

Saran, P., 'Politics and personalities in the reign of Nasir-ud-din Mahmud the Slave [*sic*]', in his *Studies in medieval Indian history* (Delhi, 1952), 223–48

'The economic policy and price control of Alauddin Khalji', *Bhāratiya Vidyā* 11 (1950), 195–215; repr. in his *Studies* (above)

Sauvaget, Jean, 'Noms et surnoms de Mamelouks', *JA* 238 (1950), 31–58

Sharma, Dasharatha, *Early Chauhān dynasties*, 2nd edn (Delhi, 1975)
Sherwani, H. K., and Joshi, P.M. (eds.), *History of medieval Deccan (1295–1724)* (Hyderabad, AP, 1973, 2 vols.)
Siddiqi, M. Y. Z., 'Arzdasht of Badr Hajib', *MIM* 2 (1972), 291–7
Siddiq[u]i, Iqtidar Husain, 'Historical information in the thirteenth century collections of Persian poems', *Studies in Islam* 19 (1982), 47–76
'The nobility under the Khalji Sultans', *IC* 37 (1963), 52–66
'Fresh light on Ḍiyā' al-Dīn Baranī: the doyen of the Indo-Persian historians of medieval India', *IC* 63 (1989), 69–84
'Social mobility in the Delhi Sultanate', in I. Habib (ed.), *Medieval India 1*, 22–48
'Sultan Muḥammad bin Tughluq's foreign policy: a reappraisal', *IC* 62 (1988), part 4, 1–22
'The Afghāns and their emergence in India as ruling elite during the Delhi Sultanate period', *CAJ* 26 (1982), 241–61
'The Qarlūgh kingdom in north-western India during the thirteenth century', *IC* 54 (1980), 75–91
Smail, R. C., *Crusading warfare 1097–1193* (Cambridge, 1956; 2nd edn, 1995)
Spuler, Berthold, *Die Goldene Horde: die Mongolen in Rußland 1223–1502*, 2nd edn (Wiesbaden, 1965)
Die Mongolen in Iran: Politik, Verwaltung und Kultur der Ilchanzeit 1220–1350, 4th edn (Leiden, 1985)
Stapleton, H. E., 'Contributions to the history and ethnology of north-eastern India – IV. Bengal chronology during the period of independent Muslim rule. Part I, 686–735 A.H. (1286–1334 A.D.)', *JASB* ns 18 (1922), 407–30
Troll, Christian W. (ed.) *Muslim shrines in India* (Oxford and Delhi, 1989)
Venkata Ramanayya (Venkataramanyya), N., 'The date of the rebellions of Tilang and Kampila against Sultan Muḥammad bin Tughlaq', *Indian Culture* 5 (1938–9), 135–46, 261–9
The early Muslim expansion in South India (Madras, 1942)
Verma, H. C., *Dynamics of urban life in pre-Mughal India* (New Delhi, 1986)
Welch, Anthony, and Crane, Howard, 'The Tughluqs: master-builders of the Delhi Sultanate', *Muqarnas* 1 (1983), 123–66
Wink, André, *Al-Hind: the making of the Indo-Islamic world*, I. *Early medieval India and the expansion of Islam, 7th–11th centuries* (Leiden, 1990)
Al-Hind: the making of the Indo-Islamic world, II. *The Slave Kings and the Islamic conquest, 11th–13th centuries* (Leiden, 1997)
Woods, John E., 'The rise of Tīmūrid historiography', *Journal of Near Eastern Studies* 46, part 2 (1987), 81–108
Yule, Sir Henry, and Burnell, A. C., *Hobson-Jobson: a glossary of colloquial Anglo-Indian words and phrases*, new edn by W. Crooke (London, 1903)

Index

The Delhi Sultanate was the first Islamic state to be established in India. In a broad-ranging and accessible narrative, Peter Jackson traces the history of the Sultanate from its foundation in 1210 to its demise in around 1400 following the sack of Delhi by the Central Asian conqueror, Temür (Tamerlane). During the thirteenth and fourteenth centuries, the Sultanate was the principal bastion of Islam in the subcontinent. While the book focuses on military and political affairs, tracing the Sultanate's expansion, its resistance to formidable Mongol invasions from the north-west and the administrative developments that underpinned these exploits, it also explores the Sultans' relations with their non-Muslim subjects. As a comprehensive treatment of the political history of this period, the book will make a significant contribution to the literature on medieval Indo-Muslim history. Students of Islamic and South Asian history, and those with a general interest in the region, will find it a valuable resource.